W9-AAH-099

THE WHOLE POP CATALOG

THE WHOLE POP CATALOG

the Berkeley Pop Culture Project

AVON BOOKS ◆ NEW YORK

THE WHOLE POP CATALOG is an original publication of Avon Books. This work has never before appeared in book form.

AVON BOOKS
A division of
The Hearst Corporation
1350 Avenue of the Americas
New York, New York 10019

Copyright © 1991 by Jack Mingo and John Javna
Cover art/design by Tom Nikosey
Published by arrangement with The Berkeley Pop Culture Project
Library of Congress Catalog Card Number: 91-27547
ISBN: 0-380-76094-0

The Library of Congress Cataloging in Publication Data:

The whole pop catalog / the Berkeley Pop Culture Project.
    p.   cm.
        1. United States—Popular culture—Collectors and collecting—
Directories. 2. Americana—Collectors and collecting—Directories.
3. Americana—Catalogs.   I. Berkeley Pop Culture Project.
E169.12.W484   1991   91-27547
973'.075—dc20   CIP

First Avon Books Trade Printing: November 1991

Introduction

It has been about 20 years since the *Whole Earth Catalog* first appeared with a revolutionary idea—that a catalog could be more than just a source of products.

Sure, it gave us access to scores of practical "tools for living." But it also gave us information—history, advice, even the occasional weird side-trip. Most important, it gave a sense that somehow they all fit together in our lives.

That's the spirit behind the *Whole Pop Catalog*.

Pop culture has an increasingly important function. It is the means by which contemporary Americans stamp our collective identity on the world, sort of like an animal marking off familiar territory by leaving its scent. Pop reassures us that we belong here.

Pop is our true culture. It—not highbrow culture—embodies the shared experiences, thoughts, and values of modern Americans. "Institutions" like McDonald's, Barbie, and the Beatles are the building blocks with which we're constructing contemporary society.

We've tried to give you access to the products, people, clubs, dealers, books—even "pilgrimage" sites—to help you chronicle, understand and even own the pieces of it.

You won't find everything here. That would be an impossible task, and each of these subjects could fill a book of its own. We tried to stuff the book as full as possible, which explains why each page looks as cluttered as our attics and closets. We hope you find the *Whole Pop Catalog* as fascinating and mind-boggling to use as it was for us to compile.

—the Berkeley Pop Culture Project

Special Thanks

Philip "Fred the Bubblesmith" Abrams
Academy of Model Aeronautics
American Breweriana Association
American Kitefliers Association
American Yo-Yo Association
Animation Magazine
Apex Novelties
ASIFA/San Francisco Chapter
Astronomical Society of the Pacific
Bill Baker
The Barbie Hall of Fame
Bartender Magazine
Bears & Baubles
The Beer Institute
Bogue Kansas Doll Museum
Bob Boni
Stefano Boni
Don Bostick
John Boswell
Mark Boxer
Patty Brown
Evelyn Burkhalter
Jeff Busby Magic
Jim Callahan
Georgia Carlson
Kurt Carlson
Cartoon Art Museum
Richard Chen
Church of the Sub-Genius
Cathy Colvin
Clowns of America International
Comics Buyer's Guide
Stuart F. Crump
Jane Davies
Don Donahue
Paul A. Dunn
Earthworks Press
East Bay Vivarium
Marilyn Edwards
Fantaco
Bruce Fife
Fifth Street Computers
Jeff Fink
Ray Foley
For Amusement Only
Jim Forcier
The Funny Papers
Stan and Chris Galloway
Alana Gentry
Barbara Giffen
Golden Gate Model Railroad Club
David Gomberg
Valerie Govig
Ross Gualco
Walter J. Gydesen

Don Herron
Scott Hildreth
Elizabeth M. Hlinko
Sandy Holder
Indian Rock Imagesetting
International Brotherhood of Magicians
International Home & Private
  Poker Players' Association
Hank Jansen
Jeanpaul Jenack
Bill Kaiser
Frank Kappler
Frank Katzmann
Jan Wilson Kaufman
Kite Lines Magazine
Kiting Magazine
Nancy Knoble
Last Gasp
Len Lawson
Le Beastro
Craig Lerner
Marilyn MacGregor
Alan M. MacRobert
Magic Collectors Association
Make*a*Circus
Bob Malowney
William Manns
Owen Marecks
Jim McCoy
Patrice McFadden
Bob Mecoy
Elana Mingo
Nuna Mingo
Roger Mingo
Vera Mingo
National Circus Project
National Skateboard Association
Emily Netterfield
Tom "The Bubble Guy" Noddy
Michael O'Brien
Cal Olson
Muriel Owens
Pacific Bell Directory
Pacific Film Archive
Pan American World Airway
Louis "The Amazing Bubble Man" Pearl
Photolab
Piedmont Piano Company
Poweredge Magazine
Jef Raskin
RollerCoaster! Magazine
Sharyn Rosenblum
Rubberstampmadness
San Francisco Vultures
  Model Airplane Club

Sand Sculptors International
Santa Cruz Surfing Museum
Ted Schulz
Ron Schwarz
Scooby's Toys
The Scowrers and
  Molly Maguires Society
Susan Segal
Roger Sharpe
Sky and Telescope Magazine
Slot Dynasty
Anne Marie Spagnuolo
Roberta Sperling
Ivan Stang
Kelli Stanley
Eunice Stunkard
Oliver Sturtz
Susan Subtle
Leon Swerin
Ken Taylor
Kevin Thatcher
Don and Maggie Thompson
Thrasher Magazine
The 3-D Zone
Jim Tolbert
Roland Turner
Ron Turner
Tyco Toys
United States Forest Service
University of California/Berkeley
Mark Cotta Vaz
View-Master Ideal Group
Emma Watling
Wham-O Manufacturing Company
Bill Whelan
Tony Wuehle
Yo-Yo Times
Zon International Publishing Company
Ray Zone

Contributors

EDITOR-IN-CHIEF
Jack Mingo

EDITORS/SENIOR WRITERS
Barry Katzmann
Pat Katzmann

DESIGN & PRODUCTION MANAGER
Emily F. Douglas

ASSOCIATE DESIGN & PRODUCTION MANAGER
Libby Ellis

SENIOR WRITERS
Sandra Pungor
Carl Wells

WRITERS
Paul Axelrod
Michael Berry
Matt Berson
Dimitre Cavendar
Heather Garnos
Vida Maralani
Chris McKenna
Barbara Najjar Ramsey

CONTRIBUTING WRITERS
Karl Cohen
Stephen Ronan
Paul Rubens

DESIGNERS
Dale Brown
Jean Butterfield
Rachel M. Ellis
M. Kay Elmore
Kathleen Heafey
Jeanette Madden
Karen Marquardt
Marcia McGetrick-Cooney
Judy Sitz
Andrea Sohn
Laurie Wigham
Susan Wight

PRODUCTION
Peggy Mocine
Susan N. Putney
Joseph Stubbs

ELECTRONIC LAYOUT MANAGER
Dave McFarlane

ELECTRONIC LAYOUT
Julie L. Betts
Courtney Bowie
Jeffrey Clayton
Karen Einstein
Mike McGee

ADDITIONAL RESEARCH
Barry Gantt
Gary Handman
Penelope Houston
Betsy McGee
Peter Moore

Concept & Original Prototypes by John Javna
Book Design Based on Prototypes by Michael Brunsfeld

Photo by Dana Downie, at Scooby's Toys, Berkeley

Table of Contents

Bud ABBOTT AND Lou COSTELLO

This Bud's for Lou

Abbott was the tall, lean one — the dreamer, the plotter, the contriver of schemes to get rich quick. But to make his master plan work, he needed a patsy to do his bidding. That's where Costello, the short, pudgy one comes in. But he always bungled Bud's blueprint because he'd find some way to screw things up. Sometimes by accident. Sometimes on purpose because he was "a baaaad boy!"

Shut Up & Deal. In real life, the boys loved to gamble. So much so that they had a rule, "Nothing's funny after four o'clock!" because that's when they played cards. Their gambling became so consuming at times that they had to be carried to the set, while still sitting in their chairs, by crew members. And they hardly ever filmed more than one take.

A Real Knock Out. Born Louis Francis Cristillo, Lou became a prize fighter under the name Lou King.

He knocked out his wife when he first met her. Literally! In 1933 he was a comedian in burlesque and a mutual friend brought wife-to-be Ann to meet him. She was standing in the wings when Lou accidentally pushed over a prop tree, knocking her out cold.

Lou was a kleptomaniac, "appropriating" things from movie sets. No one confronted him, since he and Bud were making a lot of money for the studio. But sometimes he would take items before filming was completed, creating utter havoc. One director had to beg him to "lend" back a big clock needed for background shots.

Hey Abbott! William "Bud" Abbott was born in a circus tent. He was a heavy drinker and an epileptic. When he suffered a fit, Costello would punch his stomach in a certain way and it would stop.

Bud was a pallbearer at Lou's funeral, but he was said to have been so drunk that he was actually leaning on the coffin rather than helping to carry it.

Great Comedy...

Or annoying bickering? You decide. Abbott is explaining to Costello about his baseball team's funny nicknames:

Bud: On the bags...Who's on first. What's on second and I Don't Know's on third.

Lou: Who's on first?

Bud: Yes.

Lou: I mean the fellow's name?

Bud: Who.

Lou: The guy on first?

Bud: Who.

Lou: The first baseman?

Bud: Who.

Lou: The guy playing first?

Bud: Who's on first!

Lou: I'm asking you!

* * * * *

Lou: When you pay off the first baseman every month, who gets the money?

Bud: Every dollar of it.

Lou: All I'm trying to do is find out the fellow's name on first base?

Bud: Who.

Lou: The guy that gets the money?

Bud: That's it.

Lou: Who gets the money...

Bud: He does, every dollar. Sometimes his wife comes down and collects it.

Lou: Who's wife?

Bud: Yes...

And on and on and on...

Bud Abbott was born in a tent belonging to Barnum & Bailey Circus.

Outrageous Outtakes

Abbott & Costello Outtakes Video. Caution: geniuses at work. Fantastic lost footage of their film career. You'll marvel at how great these guys were when you watch them perform before the camera. They do some real long takes here before they make a mistake. Incredible what motivation a waiting card table can provide.

$24.95 + 3.95 shipping.
Video Resources N.Y. Inc.
220 W. 71st Street
New York, NY 10023

Who's On TV?

Back when TV was live, Abbott & Costello were the small screen's zaniest duo—quite different from their scripted feature films. These videos show their vaudevillian best, with lots of mugging, ad-libbing and horsing around!

• Vol. 1 features (sigh) "Who's On First," an opera spoof "Don Juan Costello" and their famous "Haunted House" sketch. #1705284.

• In Vol. 2, Bud and Lou welcome Charles Laughton. #1705292.

• Vol. 3 finds Abbott and Costello in swinging Paris. #1705300.

• In Vol. 4, Bud and Lou are guest stars with Keefe Brasselle and Sonia Henie in a visit to the set of *The Creature of the Black Lagoon.* #1705318.

Each 60 minutes, VHS only. $14.95 each + 4.50 shipping. Or all four volumes (#1705326) for $39.95 + 4.50 shipping.

Barnes & Noble
125 Fifth Avenue
New York, NY 10011
(201) 767-7079

Join the Club

Abbott & Costello Fan Club. Fanatic Bud & Lou fans dedicated to keeping the memory and memorabilia alive.

For more information, send SASE to P.O. Box 262, Carteret, NJ 07008

MOVIEHOUSE MEMORIES

The boys made 36 films between 1940 and 1956. Here are eight of their best full length movies available on video:

• *Buck Privates.* Their first starring vehicle includes the Andrews Sisters' "Boogie Woogie Bugle Boy."

• *The Naughty Nineties.* Features "Who's On First."

• *Abbott & Costello Meet Dr. Jekyll And Mr. Hyde.* Features Boris Karloff.

• *Who Done It?* As would-be radio writers the boys get involved in a real-life murder mystery.

• *The Time Of Their Lives.* Considered one of their best.

• *Abbott & Costello Meet Frankenstein.* They get to meet Dracula and the Wolfman here, too. Co-stars Bela Lugosi and Lon Chaney, Jr.

• *Hold That Ghost.* A haunted house, a rubbed-out mobster and the Andrews Sisters.

• *Hit The Ice.* Bud and Lou play newspaper photographers over their heads with underworld thugs.

$19.95 each (B & W, VHS). Or, buy a gang of four: #XMC002 *Classic Collection* (first four movies above) or #XMC001 *Abbott & Costello Favorites* (last four movies above). Each collection of four: $77.88 + 3.95 shipping.
Blackhawk Films
5959 Triumph Street
Commerce, CA 90040-1688
(800) 826-2295

Comics in Comics

Abbott and Costello: The Classic Comics Vol. 1. Abbott & Costello found themselves inside 40 comic book issues from 1948 through 1956 and again for another 22 issues from 1968 through 1971. These are 24 of their best. The cover says it's "a madcap collection of their wildest misadventures.!" We agree.

$14.95 + $3.00 shipping from Malibu Graphics, 1355 Lawrence Drive #212, Newbury Park, CA 91320. (805) 499-3015

ADVERTISING

History of the Hard Sell

For as long as people have had names to publicize and goods to sell, they have used advertising to spread the word. Babylonian kings imprinted their names on temple bricks. The early Greeks hung written curses on public statues in hopes of bringing divine vengeance on thieves.

After the fall of Rome, the use of written advertising declined because few people knew how to read. But that didn't stop advertising: easy-to-decipher symbols and "barkers" were used to drum up business. The commercial jingle of today, possibly America's only indigenous art form, is a direct descendent of the "Cockles and Mussels, Alive-Alive-O!" commercial chants of street vendors.

Taverns were marked by symbols which were immediately recognizable, especially bulls and lions and even angels. William Hogarth, who we know in our time as a painter and satirist, was better known in his own as a first class tavern sign painter. (Pop artist Andy Warhol continued in this "spiritual" tradition with his

Absolut Vodka ad.)

The First Freebies. French tavern keepers of the Middle Ages first used free street samples of wine to attract customers. In more literate 15th-century England, written ads were tacked up in public places to sell luxury items like tobacco, perfume, and coffee. Handbills, inexpensive to print and distribute, were another popular advertising format.

In the early days of printing, ads were sometimes bound directly into books at the printing press. As newspapers and magazines became more available to the average person, they were recognized as a venue for advertisement. National magazines like *Collier's*, *Liberty*, *Life*, *Look*, and the *Saturday Evening Post* were the major

advertising market. That is, until television came along.

A word from our sponsor. In the beginning, TV shows had a single sponsor for an entire show. As the world of television expanded, the cost of advertising grew and so did the number of sponsors for each show. Now they rarely sponsor a whole show or even part of one: they buy a "spot." Biggest cost for one? Over a million dollars during the Superbowl.

COKE WAS IT

In 1894 the Coca-Cola company painted its first billboard on a drug store in Cartersville, Georgia. It's now one of the biggest outdoor advertisers.

The 1950s Coke billboards featured the "Sprite Boy." He was originally sketched in 1942 by Walt Disney himself, but Walt's design was deemed "too fancy" and the company had artist Haddon Sundblom revise it. Sundblom used his own face as a model.

It's funny how something that was a blight in its own time gets considered picturesque decades later. Take this clock, a replica of a picturesque rural gas station with 1950s Coke billboard.

#8591, $36.98 + 3.95 shipping from The Lighter Side, 4514 19th St. Court E., P.O. Box 25600, Bradenton, FL 34206. (813) 747-2356.

OFF-THE-WALL APPRECIATION

Ghost Signs: Brick Wall Signs in America by William Stage. This book's haunting photos capture what's left of wall signs around the Midwest.

They were painted on the bricks of buildings, remnants of a time before billboards and TV spots. You still sometimes see them, faded and peeling, pitching obscure products and defunct businesses. Stage gives us photos and interviews with sign painters. He reports that some old signs are now being restored and preserved.

$21.45 postpaid. ST Publications, 407 Gilbert Ave., Cincinnati, OH 45202. (800) 543-1925.

Ads for Sale

Weber's Nostalgia Supermarket offers over 500 different sign reproductions, including these three. These are full-color replicas of classic advertising signs on pressed tin. Their catalog is free with order, otherwise $4.00, refundable with first order.

**#T-64 Osh Kosh B' Gosh tin sign
#T-27 Indian Motorcycles tin sign (shown)
#T-49 Popeye Soda tin sign
$9.95 each + 2.50 shipping per order (no matter how many signs). Weber's Nostalgia Supermarket, 1121 S. Main St., Dept WPC, Fort Worth TX 76104. (800) 433-7867.**

A REAL "BILLBOARD MAGAZINE"

Signs of the Times Magazine. This magazine is a lot more fun than it has a right to be. The ads and industry news in the back are clearly aimed at people in the business of outdoor ads, but the articles are not at all the usual dreary trade fare.

Recent issues have included ugly sign contests, a historical feature on the Burma Shave signs, and an interview with artist Mark Pauline who alters billboards in dead of night to make political and satirical statements about current events. *Signs of the Times* is surprisingly funny and hip, considering the subject matter.

**One year (13 issues) $30.00
407 Gilbert Ave.
Cincinnati, OH 45202
(800) 543-1925**

The first recorded singing commercial was for Moxie, that much hyped soft drink with a medicinal taste, released on disk in 1921.

AD FACTS

• In a 1985 Procter & Gamble poll, 93% of the people questioned recognized Mr. Clean, but only 56% of the same group could identify Vice President George Bush.

• More American kids age 3-5 recognize Ronald McDonald than Santa Claus or any other entity, real or mythical.

• The typical 30-second prime time TV commercial costs about the same to produce as the half program it interrupts.

• One man was responsible for the creation of some of America's most memorable ad icons. During fifty years of work in the entertainment business, animator Hal Mason created the Pillsbury Doughboy, Mr. Clean, the Frito Bandito, the Hamm's beer bear, and the Raid roaches.

• Advertisers spend about $400 a year on each newspaper subscriber and $300 a year on each television household.

It Costs to Advertise

Prices for a full-page color magazine advertisement:

People Magazine	$75,485
Ladies' Home Journal	$67,200
Rolling Stone	$40,035
Penthouse	$35,640
Scientific American	$26,102
The New Yorker	$25,985
Boys' Life	$17,650
Accounting Today	$ 4,100

Source: 1990 Literary Market Place

• The notorious "this is your brain on drugs" ad had an unintentional side effect: Small kids all over the country refused to eat fried eggs, believing they were somehow laced with drugs.

AD ICON-O-CLASTS

The ad artist folks at "The Chicken Boy Catalog" started creating Chicken Boy products after rescuing the 22-foot tall statue, left homeless when the Chicken Boy Restaurant in Los Angeles closed down.

The fowl man ("too tall to live, too weird to die") adorns a variety of items in their slick catalog which also features bizarre and funny products like the "pocket trout" flashlight and faux-fur computer cozies (Macintosh compatible only). A blurb on the back of the catalog states, "Just remember, this might be funny but it's not a joke."

Life is incomplete without official Chicken Boy accessories. Get the "Starter Bucket Gift Set" (t-shirt, lapel pin, floating action ballpoint, mechanical pencil and postcard) for $25 + $3 shipping. Catalog is $1 or free with order.

**Chicken Boy Catalog for a Perfect World
Future Studio
P.O. Box 292000
Los Angeles CA 90029
(800) 422-0505.**

What, no "Coke" Spoon?

Celebrated trademarks of yesteryear on hand-painted pewter spoons. 12 famous ad character spoons, with commentary, shipped one at a time every other month. Characters in the "Country Store Spoons Collection" include the Morton Salt girl (shown), the Fisk Tire boy, the White Rock nymphet, Elsie the Borden Cow, the Dutch Boy dutch boy, and the Hills Brothers Ayatollah. Includes a mirrored wall display at no additional charge.

**$37.50 each from:
The Franklin Mint
Franklin Center, PA
19091**

Mail Chauvinists

Advertising post cards were probably the most common form of advertising in the late 19th Century. This is a book of 24 full-color reprints from 1900-20 which you can mail to your friends, featuring the Campbell's Kids, Buster Brown, the Cracker Jack Bears, the Victor Dog, Flexible Flyer and others. Also available for the same price from the same source: *Antique Automobile Advertising Postcards*.

Advertising Postcards or *Antique Auto Postcards* . $3.95 each + 2.00 shipping from Dover Publications, 31 East Second St., Mineola, NY 11501.

YOU NEED MORE COMMERCIALS

Commercial Mania is a video featuring highlights from the weirdest, wackiest, wildest commercials of the innocent 1950s and '60s. See Ronald Reagan promote soap, and Lucy and Ricky push Phillip Morris cigarettes. Go to Tunaville for Breast O' Chicken Tuna, and then use Colgate with "Gardol" to fight bad breath. Sixty minutes of fun.

Available for $29.95 + 2.50 shipping from Rhino Video, 2225 Colorado Avenue, Santa Monica, CA 90404-3598. (800) 432-3670.

• Or, if that's not enough, Video Resources has 24 different one hour collections of vintage commercials. Each tape is by subject: *Toys Vol. 1 & 2, Dolls Vol. 1 & 2, Cigarettes, Cereal, Beer, Cars* and *Sport Star Endorsements.* Our favorites? *Classic TV Commercials of the Fifties and Sixties, Vols. 1-8.*

$24.95 each, + 3.95 shipping from Video Resources New York, Inc., 220 West 71st Street, New York, NY 10023. (212) 724-7055.

ROADSIDE ATTRACTIONS.
The Burma Shave Signs

The Verse By the Side of the Road: Burma Shave Signs & Jingles by Frank Rowesome.

We've Made Grandpa
Look So Thin
The Local Draft Board's
After Him
Burma Shave

Unless you traveled the highways before the mid-1960s, you may not know about Burma Shave signs. But for those of us who waited many boring miles for the 5 or 6 distinctive red signs placed sequentially along the road (even swiveling around to read them backward on the other side of the road) it was a sad day when they disappeared. The product itself did too, not long afterward.

Every Day
We Do Our Part
To Make Your Face
A Work of Art
Burma Shave

Allan Odell got the idea for the signs in 1925 while driving through the Midwest on sales calls. The yard-long pine signs were originally spaced 20 yards apart, aiming for 18 seconds of reading at 35 MPH. This was increased to 50 yards as speed limits and cars got faster.

If You Want
A Hearty Squeeze
Get Your Female
Anti-Freeze
Burma Shave

By 1938 there were more than 40,000 Burma Shave signs on the nation's highways, set by crews called by the company "PhDs" (post hole diggers).

Originally members of the Odell family wrote the verses, but this was

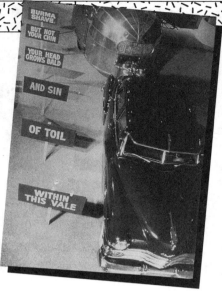

eventually augmented by a jingle contest which brought in 50,000 responses. Winners won $100 and a chance to see their words along the road.

This book, the definitive history of the Burma Shave company and signs, was reissued in a special 25th anniversary edition of its first printing in 1965. To put it succinctly:

Want More?
Don't Pout
Get This Book
It's All About
Burma Shave

$9.95 + 2.00 shipping from: Penguin USA, 375 Hudson St., New York, NY 10014.

Commercials for the Ears

TeeVee Toons: The Commercials.
• I'm Chiquita Banana
• No Matter What Shape (Your Stomach is In)
• I'd Like to Teach the World to Sing
• We've Only Just Begun

All of the above were first commercial jingles before hitting the Top 10 charts. And all but the last one are available on this collection of vintage ads. Plus 52 other memorable jingles like "Meow Meow Meow Meow", "Plop Plop Fizz Fizz", "Here's to Good Friends", and many more.

You'll be surprised, maybe even horrified, at the number of jingles you can sing along with. And speaking of crafty commercialism, the creators of this collection reportedly charged each advertiser $7500 to be on it!

#1400 $8.98 for LP or cassette, 14.98 for CD + 3.50 shipping. TVT Records, 59 W.19th St., New York, NY 10011. (212) 929-0570.

Old Time Radio Commercials.

These radio commercials from the 1930s and '40s are an entertaining novelty. Here are some of the best of the medium including Pepsi-Cola, Ovaltine and 98 other products, many of which don't exist any more. Buy both these tapes—they're a bargain at $3.98 + 1.35 shipping for each (7.96 + 2.70 for both).

#80097 (Vol. 1) and #80198 (Vol. 2), available from Johnson Smith Company
4514 19th Court East
P.O. Box 25500
Bradenton, Florida 34206-5500
FAX (813) 746-7896.

Pets of the Ad World
• *The Dog Made Me Buy It!*
• *The Cat Made Me Buy It!*
• *The Black Cat Made Me Buy It!*
by Alice L. Muncaster & Ellen Sawyer. Color reproductions of classic advertisements featuring dogs and cats, including Buster Brown's dog Tige and the Thomas' Inks black cat. Fascinating facts for people who love animals, or ads.

Each book costs $12.95 + 2.50 shipping from Crown Publishers Inc., 201 East 50th St., New York, NY 10022. (800) 733-3000.

Required Reading

ARCHIVE: *Ads, TV and Posters Worldwide* is a magazine consisting of literally nothing but ads—some of the best in the world, printed in color on quality paper. Non-English ads are painstakingly translated, explained and interpreted. A backstage view of the best ads of our time.

Subscription: $39.97 per year (6 issues). 724 Fifth Ave., New York, NY 10019. (212) 245-0981 / FAX (212) 265-2247.

IF YOU CAN'T JOIN 'EM

Lick 'Em, Stick 'Em: The Lost Art of Poster Stamps by H. Thomas Steele. Poster stamps were brilliantly designed little brothers of the great ad posters from 1890-1940, often designed by the same artists in the same styles.

Advertising everything from war bonds to corsets, they were treasured for their bold graphics and rich colors. This beautifully rendered hardcover shows them in full-color glory.

$39.90 + 2.00 shipping from Abbeville Press, 488 Madison Avenue, New York, NY 10022. (212) 888-1969.

I Write the Songs

Through the Jingle Jungle by Steve Karmen. Want to follow in the footsteps of such jingle giants as Barry Manilow and Randy Newman? Written by a pro ("I Love NY", "You Can Take Salem Out of the Country, But...", "This Bud's for You") this book tells you everything from matching song with product to handling production budgets. Highly recommended.

$22.95 + 2.50 shipping from Watson-Guptill Publications, 1515 Broadway, New York, NY 10109-0025.

MODERN MYTHOLOGY

Character Trademarks by John Mendenhall. There's something about those advertising characters that makes us want to buy the product— as if by doing so, we'd get to adopt the character as well. This book has page after page of character illustrations. Some are famous like the Reddy Kilowatt and Speedy Alka Seltzer; some just as appealing but unexplainably obscure like Top Tator, Mr. Flea and Señor Froggy. A great deal of fun all around, and a suitable companion to two other highly recommended Chronicle Books: *Trademarks of the '20s and '30s* and *Trademarks of the '40s and '50s.*

Each book $14.95 + 2.00 shipping. Chronicle Books, 275 Fifth St., San Francisco, CA 94103. (800) 722-6657.

AD COLLECTIBLES

A 1910 tin Campbell's Soup sign sold for $93,000 in 1990. To find out what your ad collectibles are worth, get a copy of *Kovels' Advertising Collectibles Price List.*

Crown Publishers, 201 East 50th St., New York, NY 10022. (800) 733-3000.

JOIN THE CLUB

National Association of Paper and Advertising Collectors
P.O. Box 500
Mt. Joy, PA 17552
717 653 1833/ 800 428-4211

These folks buy, sell and collect antique paper and advertising "ephemera". At last count, they have 3000 members and two publications, the *Paper and Advertising Collector* and the *Antiques and Auction News.* Send SASE for more information.

"In our culture most people don't know who Sisyphus was. But everyone knows Mr. Clean, Mrs. Olsen and Colonel Sanders. Commercial entities are the closest thing we have to the gods on Mount Olympus."

—Ed Zorn

Pilgrimages

The American Advertising Museum contains 6,000 square feet of advertising memorabilia, including print ads dating back to several hundred years ago. You can also learn about the advertising process and "The Evolution of the Logo". Next time you're in Portland, OR, stop in at 9 N.W. Second Street, near the Old Town District. Call (503) 226-0000 for operating hours.

Museum of Modern Mythology. As of this writing, the best ad character pilgrimage site doesn't exist. Alas, the earthquake in 1989 wrecked the Museum's building. Before this, the museum featured an earthshaking collection of ad icon memorabilia.

With an unexpected dearth of corporate funding (ad agencies tend to be embarrassed by the declasse nature of even their own characters), the museum still managed to put on some impressive displays of commercial entities and even Burma Shave signs.

If you're going to San Francisco, check the phone book. The Museum may be down for now, but, like the Doughboy, it will rise again.

TOP 10 AD CHARACTERS

According to an *Advertising Age* poll, these are the favorite ads characters of all time (Sorry, Charlie!)

1. The Pillsbury Doughboy
2. Morris the Cat
3. Frank Bartles
4. The Keebler Elves
5. Ed Jaymes
6. Life Cereal's Mikey
7. Ronald McDonald
8. Tony the Tiger
9. Snuggles Bear
10. California Raisins

Live Ad Gods

Some advertising icons who are, or were, real people may surprise you:

Orville Redenbacher
Colonel Harlan Sanders
Famous (Wally) Amos
Chef Boyardee (Hector Boiardi)
Jimmy Dean (the pork sausage man)
Laura Scudder
Paul Newman
Ben-Gay (Jules Bengue, a French pharmacist)

Not So Great Moments in "Product Placement"

You've paid $7 to get into a movie and suddenly you're seeing real-life brand names parading in front of your eyes. You whisper to your companion, "What is this, a commercial?"

You're exactly right. In most cases, somebody's paid good money for that casual appearance. It's called "product placement" and while it's sometimes unobtrusive—maybe somebody eating a particular brand of breakfast cereal—some are blatant enough to cause groans in theatres. Here are some low points in a pretty low practice:

• *Total Recall* contained 55 paid references to 31 products.

• *Ghost*: 23 references to 16 brands.

• *Home Alone*: 42 references to 31 brands.

• *Pretty Woman*: 20 references to 18 brands.

• *Star Trek* is set far enough into the future that they don't usually have the opportunity to engage in the practice. When they set *Star Trek IV* in present day San Francisco, they made up for lost opportunities, including a scene where Spock walked his fingers through the Yellow Pages to find spaceship parts, thanks to Pacific Bell.

• Quick: which brand of pizza was delivered to the sewer in *Teenage Mutant Ninja Turtles*? They also plugged 17 other brand names.

• Black & Decker sued the makers of *Die Hard II* for cutting a scene they had paid for.

• McDonald's actually put up money to produce an *ET* clone called *Mac & Me* (Get it? "Mac"?). This

embarrassing display is available on video if you want to point and hoot at all the McReferences. Note the kids wearing "McKids" clothes, and talking like this: "You know what I feel like right now?" "A Big Mac?" "What a genius!"

Matchless Friends

Close Cover: The Golden Age of Matchbook Art by H. Thomas Steele, Jim Heimann & Rob Dyer.

Matches were the biggest invention of 1827, and it didn't take long before somebody started selling ads on them. This fascinating book shows us colorful, exotic and strangely familiar designs from the late 1800s on.

$39.90 + 2.00 shipping. Abbeville Press, 488 Madison Avenue, New York, NY 10022. (212) 888-1969.

Light My Fire

Matchcover collectors ("phillumenists") are the second largest collecting group in the world, after stamps. But few are as dedicated as these folks. Send 'em a SASE for membership info.

Rathcamp Matchcover Society, c/o John Williams, 1359 Surrey Rd., Vandalia, OH 45377.

TRUTH IN ADVERTISING?

• In 1657, coffee was advertised as a cure for "miscarriage, hypochondria, dropsy, gout, and scurvy....makes skin exceeding clear and white....It quickens the spirits, and makes the Heart lightsome."

• A 1929 Lucky Strike ad touts "the modern common sense way—reach for a Lucky instead of a fattening sweet. Everyone is doing it—men keep healthy and fit, women retain a trim figure."

• Campbell's used to shoot ad photos with clear marbles in their soup to keep the meat and vegetables on top. Now, they get the same effect by using a wide, shallow bowl.

• Drops of "condensation" in that soft drink ad? Probably corn syrup or glycerine to avoid evaporation under hot lights. "Ice cream"? Most likely cold mashed potatoes.

ADS SUCK

"Oral gratification seemed to be the general theme of many of these salvaged treasures of advertising from the Fifties....there was a dominant 'suck it and see,' come-on in advertising."

Mark Burns and Louis DeBonis, Fifties Homestyle.

AIRPLANES

The Wright Stuff

Even before Icarus and Daedalus put on their ill-fated wax wings, people wanted to fly. And we continue to be fascinated by it. Let's face it, there's a certain excitement about looking down and realizing the ground is wa-a-a-y down there.

• The earliest record of a parachute being used was more than six hundred years ago, for a coronation celebration. Before balloons, parachutists jumped from tall towers and cliffs, providing an entertaining spectacle, sometimes even surviving to jump again.

• Ever heard the old expression "Pigs can't fly"? On November 4, 1909, a British pilot took a piglet on an early flight, specifically to prove it untrue.

• The first case of an airplane being used to commit a crime occurred on November 12, 1926, when a farmhouse in Williamson County, Illinois, was attacked with three small bombs (which did not explode). The raid was part of a Prohibition feud between two gangs over supplies of beer and rum.

• On March 23, 1944, Flight Sergeant Nicholas Alkemade jumped from his flaming British Lancaster bomber and fell 18,000 feet without a parachute. Reaching a speed of well over 100 mph, he bounced off a fir tree and landed in an 18 inch snow bank. He survived, didn't even break a bone.

• On December 14, 1986, the aircraft "Voyager" took off from Edwards AFB in California, and nine days later landed at the same base, having gone around the world *non-stop* without refueling—not a small achievement. The plane was designed to carry fuel and very little else. The cockpit was bathtub size, so cramped that the pilot and copilot needed about a minute to change places, squeezing by each other contortionist-style. After the trip of 25,012 miles, there were only 5 gallons of usable fuel in the tanks.

26

Aeroplanes on Video

"Happy landings to you, Amelia Earhart. Farewell, first lady of the air!" —Popular song recorded shortly after her disappearance

FREEDOM, NO LICENSE

This single seater doesn't require a pilot's license! Challenger cruises at 63 to 100 mph and flies 1-2 hours per 5 gallons of gas. Needs 200 feet of pavement to takeoff, 600 to land. Requires 60 hours assembly with basic tools.

$6995 + shipping from Quad City Ultra-lights, 3610 Coaltown Road, Moline, IL 61265. (309) 764-3515.

See By Your Outfit...

Who says you need to be a flier to look like one? Being a feet-on-ground poseur is safer than a real air-head. Here are fashion accessories for any Lindbergh wanna-be.

• Air Force classic lambskin leather bomber jacket. Rugged, comfortable and durable, just like you. S, M, L, XL.

#42914X, $349.00 + 9.50 shipping.

•Matching leather airman's backpack.

#47251X, $169.95 + 8.50 shipping.

• Bombardier's watch, stainless steel bezel and leather band, water resistant to 100 feet (down, presumably).

#45734X, $229.95 + 9.50 shipping.

All of the above from: Hammacher Schlemmer 9180 Le Saint Drive Fairfield, OH 45014 (800) 543-3366.

"Honey, Have You Seen My Aileron?"

Scores of people are building their own airplanes at home. At a cost of $5,000 to $10,000, it's a way to get a vehicle which can cruise at 180 mph while burning less gas than a Hyundai.

Some years back, the Federal Aviation Administration streamlined its certification process, so there's not a great deal of red tape to keep you from turning your garage into an aircraft factory. Construction is time consuming, so you have to be as crazy about building as you are about flying. Says one home plane builder, "It's about the same complexity as a model airplane kit, except you tend to pay more attention to the plans."

The Experimental Aircraft Association is for you if flying a few thousand feet above the ground in a contraption you built with your own hands sounds like a neat idea. The EAA publishes the monthly *Experimenter* magazine, a how-to publication for light plane and ultralight enthusiasts.

The club also sponsors the biggest aviation convention in the world every July in Oshkosh, Wisconsin. The "International Experimental Aircraft Association Convention and Sport Aviation Exhibition" draws almost a million visitors for hundreds of home-built and factory-built planes, "warbirds" (military aircraft), museums, air shows, the "fly market" (a flea market of the air), and a vast array of doodads and T-shirts.

Membership, $28.00. EAA, Aviation Center, P.O. Box 3086, Oshkosh, WI 54903-3086. (800) 322-2412 / (800) 236-4800 in Wisconsin.

Fear of Flying

The World's Worst Aircraft by Bill Yenne. Some of the most absurd and dangerous contrivances ever built, including one which was essentially three triplanes nailed to a houseboat. Lots of photos.

#1650068, $12.95 + 4.00 shipping. Barnes & Noble, 126 Fifth Ave., New York, NY 10011. (800) 242-6657.

ON-FLIGHT MOVIES

Only *some* of these films will put you in the mood to go shopping for a flight jacket.

• *Twelve O'Clock High* (1949). Plenty of B-17's as Gregory Peck does his part in World War II.

• *The High and the Mighty* (1954). John Wayne tries to make it over the ocean with serious engine trouble.

• *Those Magnificent Men in Their Flying Machines* (1965). Great old airplanes in this high-altitude tale of a London-to-Paris air race.

• *The Battle of Britain* (1969). Real Spitfires, Hurricanes, Messerschmitt 109s, and more for the confirmed air buff.

• *The Great Waldo Pepper* (1975). Wonderful flying in this epic about barnstorming, with Robert Redford.

• *Airport* (1970), *Airport 1975*, and *Airport '77*. Starring everybody in Hollywood. Would you fly with Dean Martin at the pilot's controls?

These Clubs Put on Airs

• **The Confederate Air Force.** The CAF has restored some 130 aircraft, many of which are in their museum in Midland, Texas. They also put on great air shows all over the country.

You don't have to be able to fly, just be interested in old military aircraft. Contact them for a membership application.

PO Box 62000. Midland, Texas 79711-2000. (915) 563-1000.

• **Antique Airplane Association.** "Keep the Antiques Flying" is the motto of this group. You don't need to fly to join—all you need is a liking for old airplanes.

The AAA operates the Airpower Museum at Antique Airfield in Blakesburg, Iowa where you can get a closeup look at over 40 working airplanes from before World War II. They hold a "fly-in" there during the Labor Day weekend each year.

Dues: $35 year, which includes subscriptions to three different quarterly publications about antique airplanes. Send $5.00 for three sample issues. Route 2, Box 172, Ottumwa, IA 52501. (515) 938-2773.

• **C.A.L. / NX211 Collectors' Society.** C.A.L. stands for Charles A. Lindbergh and NX211 was his plane, "The Spirit of St. Louis."

Formed in 1989, the organization holds an annual symposium about flyer Lindbergh. Members get together and swap Lindy-mania items like tapestries, photos, lithographs, coins, watch fobs, book-ends, and cigar labels.

Dues: $7 year, includes subscription to the *Spirit of St. Louis*. Richard Hoerle, Executive Secretary, 727 Younkin Parkway South, Columbus, OH 43207.

Art? I Nose What I Like

Vintage Aircraft Nose Art by Gary M. Valant. This entire book is filled with airplane "nose art"—custom paintings which personalized military aircraft in World War II. Although there's a uniformity of subject matter in this art—mostly women, some even with clothes on—there's a also a certain folk art charm to this stuff.

$39.95 + 4.75 shipping from EEA Catalog Sales, PO Box 3086, Oshkosh, WI 54903-3086. (800) 843-3612.

Spirit of St. Louis Model

Plastic and wood kit, for display or flying. Assembles in 40 hours (6 1/2 hours longer than Lindbergh's flight). **$19.95 + 4.50 shipping. Mason & Sullivan, 586 Higgans Crowell Rd., W. Yarmouth, MA 02673. (800) 933-3010.**

Man Will Never Fly

• *"Heavier-than-air flying machines are impossible."*

—William Thomson, president of the Royal Society (1893)

• *"God would never surely allow such a machine to be successful."*

—Francesco Lana (1670)

• *"Birds fly—men drink."*

—The Man Will Never Fly Society (1982)

The Man Will Never Fly Society holds an anti-flying gathering at Kill Devils Hills, NC (near Kitty Hawk) every year on December 16, the eve of the day in 1903 when the Wright Brothers allegedly did their thing. Hate flying? Join the club. $5 gets you a lifetime membership.

PO Box 1903, Kill Devils Hills, NC 27948.

Alloyed Forces

Why let Boeing and McDonnell Douglas have all the fun? Send for these plans for recycling your favorite aluminum cans into high flying art. Biplane propeller even turns in wind.

$14.95 + 2.25 shipping from AB Aluminum Airforce, #8 Hawthorne Ct., Independence, MO 64052.

Flying In Formation Age

There are some great computer flight simulations out there. Here are three of our favorites.

• **Microsoft Flight Simulator.** The first and maybe best. Buzz the Empire State Building (what, no King Kong?) and swoop under the Golden Gate Bridge. Fly coast to coast over accurately scaled landscape. Or try out crop-dusting or flying in formation (this being the In Formation Age, after all). You can even fly tandem with a friend connected by cable or modem. The only thing missing is Frequent Flyer points.

IBM or MAC, $32.99 + 4.00 shipping from Egghead Software, 22011 SE 51st Street, Issaquah, WA 98027-7004. (800) EGGHEAD / FAX (206) 391-0880.

• **Chuck Yeager's Advanced Flight Trainer.** Shatter sound barriers without incurring the wrath of your neighbors. Vertigo? Barf bag not included.

Apple, IBM—$29.99. MAC—$39.99. Add 4.00 shipping from Egghead Software (see above).

• **Battlehawks 1942.** Lucasfilm Games created this World War II Pacific naval air fight simulation featuring your choice of nationality and over 30 heart-pounding missions.

IBM. $38.99 + 4.00 shipping from Egghead Software (see above).

BADYEAR FOR THE BLIMP

In 1990, a radio-controlled model airplane ripped a 3' hole in the Goodyear blimp (it got home safely, despite our whimsical artist's rendering, right). You can re-enact this dramatic moment—or if you have hydrogen, the Hindenburg tragedy—with your own 4 1/2' battery-driven, tether-guided blimp. Flies for two months per helium dose.

#C737668 blimp, $39.95 + 5.50 shipping. #C738039 6 months of helium, $24.95 + 4.00 shipping. Sync, Hanover, PA 17333. (800) 722-9979.

SHOW YOUR METTLE

This 9 inch, all-metal Spitfire PRXIX kit is the most elegant we've run across, from a great source for classy classic models. Over 100 parts cast in mazak, a superior new alloy. Amazing detail, authentic decals. Construction time: about 40 hours.

#5917, $129.00 + 4.40 shipping. Mason & Sullivan, 586 Higgans Crowell Road, W. Yarmouth, MA 02673. (800) 933-3010.

Only Way to Spy

Sterling silver captain's wings from Air America, the CIA front reportedly used to flout those pesky little federal laws against gun-running, drug-smuggling, assassination, and terrorism.

$20. AAM, PO Box 6084, Albany, CA 94706.

Light Plane

Wooden biplane will light up your life.

#21-19224, $84.95 + 7.95 shipping. EEA Aviation Foundation, PO Box 3065, Oshkosh, WI 54903-3065. (800) 843-3612.

Heir Plane

Puddle Jumper handcrafted all-wood children's rocker. $229.95 + 8.95 shipping. EEA Aviation Foundation, PO Box 3065, Oshkosh, WI 54903-3065. (800) 843-3612.

Plane & Fancy

- B-17 pin—$9.90 ppd.
- Star/Airplane earrings—$28.65 ppd.
- Bar/Airplane pin—$33.65 ppd.

EEA Aviation Foundation, PO Box 3065, Oshkosh, WI 54903-3065. (800) 843-3612.

PROP PROP

63" solid mahogany propeller. $89.50 + 10.00 shipping from Mountain Star, Inc., 970 E. Main St., Suite 202, Grass Valley, CA 95945. (800) 428-7825.

"Lovers of air travel find it exhilarating to hang poised between the illusion of immortality and the fact of death." —Alexander Chase

BARF BAGS & SWIZZLE STICKS

• **The World Airline Historical Society.** Over 1,000 members worldwide collect commercial airline memorabilia like silver lapel pins, those little soaps, postcards, letterheads, mini drink bottles, swizzle sticks, coasters, headrest covers, even barf bags (a guy in the Netherlands claims the largest collection with 2,000). An annual convention offers a trading area, contests, and slide shows.

Dues: $15 per year. 3381 Apple Tree Lane, Erlanger, KY 41018. (606) 342-9039.

• *Commercial Aviation Collectibles: An Illustrated Price Guide* by Richard R. Wallin. Got an Aeroflot captain's helmet (above)? It's worth about a $100. Assorted swizzle sticks? 50¢ to $1. Airsickness bags? $1-2 in good shape, less (much less) if used.

Lots of information for aviation memorabilia collectors, including a list of airlines and dates of operation. What's collectible? Just about everything—coasters, cups, baggage labels, timetables, crew uniforms, wings, badges, and pillow cases.

$15.95 + 2.50 shipping. Wallace-Homestead Book Co., One Chilton Way, Radnor, PA 19089. (800) 695-1214.

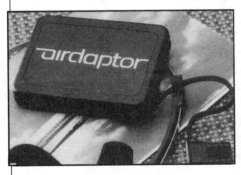

Better Sound, Free Movies

In-flight earphones are uncomfortable and not very good—for economy they are hollow tubes that channel sound to your ears like stethoscopes. This device plugs into aircraft arm seats and converts not-too-good aural quality of in-flight entertainment into better Walkman-like stereo sound. AAA batteries not included.

#WK100, $19.95 + 3.00 shipping from Markline, PO Box 13807, Philadelphia, PA 19101-3807. (800) 992-8600.

Scare Craft

Intended as a genuine warning for an amateur-built aircraft, but we like the practical joke possibilities: how about hanging it near the assigned seat of that "white-knuckle" flyer? Or sticking it on your car's dashboard?

#11-32540, $6.00 + 2.40 shipping. EEA Aviation Foundation, PO Box 3065 Oshkosh, WI 54903-3065. (800) 843-3612.

CIRCULATING FLIERS

• *Flying*. You get wide ranging features and columns about flying in this, the "World's Most Widely Read Aviation Magazine."

$17.97 per year (12 issues). Hachette Magazines, Inc., P.O. Box 51377, Boulder, CO 80321.

• *Model Airplane News*. This monthly magazine, founded in 1929, has been providing advice to several generations of modelers. Covers radio-controlled model aircraft with lots of how-to articles and product reviews.

$25 per year, 12 issues. P.O. Box 428, Mount Morris, IL 61054-0428. (800) 435-0715 / in Illinois, (800) 892-0753.

• *Model Aviation*. This is the official publication of the Academy of Model Aeronautics. All aspects of model aviation—remote control, models, free-flying, etc.—and coverage of competitions and other special events.

$18 per year, 12 issues. Model Aviation, 1810 Samuel Morse Drive, Reston, VA 22090. (703) 435-0750

Flying Tape Heads

This place will rent you aviation videos of all kinds by mail. About half are instructional; the others are entertaining, like air shows, historic footage, and "views from the cockpit" videos. Send $1 for catalog and membership information.

Atlanta Pilot Center 1954 Airport Rd., Suite 66W, Atlanta, GA 30341. (800) 344-1556.

"The airplane has unveiled for us the true face of the earth." —Saint-Exupery

Me & My R/C: Plane Facts

Some folks take their flying with their feet firmly on the ground by building and flying model planes. That way they can always be sure of walking away from their air disasters. Hey, it makes sense.

• A powered model airplane was built in 1647 by an Italian living at the

royal court in Poland. It was spring-driven and had four sets of wings: the two center pairs were fixed, the forward and rear pairs flapped up and down.

Not Everybody Loves that "Nyeeeeeeee!" Sound

Non-hobbyists relaxing on a Sunday hate the sweet sounds of gas-powered, radio-controlled model planes going all out in the open space nearby (and especially the few hot-shots who like to buzz their trees and rooftops).

Electric planes help—they're 50% quieter. This electric Aviator Plane with 34" wingspan is considered a good beginner's model, in part because of the 60 day "crash warrantee" which covers broken parts. Everything's included except an open field: radio, battery pack, charger, extra parts, tools, instructions.

**#CM009R (red) or #CM009BL (blue).
$249.95 + 6.00 shipping. Markline, PO Box 13807, Philadelphia, PA 19101-3807.
(800) 992-8600.**

• The Wright Brothers built models to test their flight designs first. Good plan!

• In 1930, a high school junior in Philadelphia named Bill Brown designed and built the world's first engine for model airplanes. It revolutionized the model airplane hobby, which had been based up to then on wind and rubber bands.

• Many ultralight model airplanes weigh less than a penny. They're launched with a gentle touch and only indoors—a gust of wind would tear them apart.

• Some ultralight enthusiasts have used houseflies for power. They trap the insects and put them in the refrigerator. In the cold, the flies become listless and their bodies can be glued to the models. When the flies recover, the insect-powered craft flies around for a minute or two. Pretty creepy.

• The world altitude record for a model aircraft is 26,922 feet. For distance, 314.96 miles.

Model Citizens

There are three kinds of model aircraft enthusiasts:

• **Radio controllers**, ("R/Cers" in the vernacular) fly powered planes that are directed by transmitters that move control surfaces that make the plane go up, down, left or right. The radio commands can also control engine speed, wheel brakes, landing gear, and parachutes.

• **Control liners** fly planes, mostly gas-powered, with wires or strings attached to a control handle manipulated by a pilot on the ground.

• **Free-flighters** use just enough power from rubber bands, towlines, catapults or engines to get the airplanes aloft to ride air currents on their own. They're considered the purists of model aviation. (Their first world championship was in 1928).

MODEL AIRPLANES
You'll Find These Books Elevating

• *The World of Model Airplanes* by William J. Winter. This is a very good introduction to the hobby, if you're just getting started, or fills in the gaps if you've been modeling for a while. Traces the history of model aviation and starts you off with accurate information and tips for building models. Good photos and illustrations.

$10.00 postpaid from the Academy of Model Aeronautics, 1810 Samuel Morse Drive, Reston, VA 22090. (703) 435-0750.

• *The Beginner's Guide to RC Sport Flying* by Douglas R. Pratt. All the information you need to enjoy radio controlled flying. Covers subjects in plain language like tools, materials, building techniques, radio systems, and engines; also offers aeronautic tips which are useful when flying your model on those glorious sunny weekends.

$9.50 postpaid from the Academy of Model Aeronautics, 1810 Samuel Morse Drive, Reston, VA 22090. (703) 435-0750.

Head Wind

With enough wind, you'll able to fly with this propeller beany.

#IPAC child size, #IPAA adult, $12.95 + 3.00 shipping. Markline, PO Box 13807, Philadelphia, PA 19101-3807. (800) 992-8600.

Dollars & Innocence

American Junior "Classics" Model Airplanes. Sure you can buy similar, updated planes in drug stores. But if you're on a nostalgic quest for your lost innocence ("*Rosebud!*"), it'll cost you. These are *exact replicas* of the airplanes you flew if you were a child in the 1930s, '40s or '50s: a catapult-launched "404" Interceptor and a rubber band-powered A-J Hornet. Hand-silkscreened on premium grade balsa.

#16943, $19.95 + $3.90 shipping. Wireless, P.O. Box 64422, St. Paul, MN 55165-0422. (800) 669-9999.

OH, CHUTE!

12 inch long Huey helicopter flies up 200 feet, its engine "stalls," the door opens, a tiny Marine bails out and the helicopter drifts gently back to earth. High-revving Cox engine takes two D batteries (not included).

**#CK4862, $49.95 + 4.50 shipping from Markline
PO Box 13807
Philadelphia, PA 19101-3807
(800) 992-8600**

J OIN THE CLUB

The Academy of Model Aeronautics. The AMA serves more than 2,500 chartered clubs and nearly 200,000 individual members, publishes *Model Aviation*, and sponsors the definitive National Model Airplane Championships with over 75 events for every major category of plane.

The club's museum in Reston, VA features hundreds of classic model airplanes covering the walls and ceilings, and computer-simulated remote control model flying.

**Dues: $40 year.
1810 Samuel Morse Drive
Reston, VA 22090
(703) 435-0750**

"In about three years commercial planes will fly from New York to California in about an hour." —Dr. Alexander W. Lippisch, 1948

PAPER AIRPLANES

Fold Your Wings

The favored toys of bored students everywhere, paper airplanes can be manufactured with available, expendable material and quietly sent sailing around the classroom when the teacher isn't looking.

Understandably, academia has long viewed paper planes with hostility. But that's changing. Paper airplanes have become popular as class projects, and in school hallways little kids can be heard discussing wing design and lift.

This shift comes from one critical event: The First Great International Paper Airplane Contest held by *Scientific American* in 1967.

The 12,000 entries from 28 countries gave paper airplanes a mantle of legitimacy. The Second GIPAC rolled around 18 years later, and the Third, in 1991.

*"Life is a game
You fly a paper plane
There is no aim..."*
—**Thunderclap Newman**

The planes are a marvel of engineering and design. Still, the professionally designed models sometimes get upstaged by upstarts, like in 1985, when a 12 year old, wielding the classic "schoolboy's delta wing" airplane we've all flown, beat thousands of embarrassed professional designers. The boy placed 2nd in the Distance category.

Fly This Catalog

Paper Airplanes From Around the World by Ray Roberts. This definitive book/catalog contains a selection of more than 3,000 paper airplanes from around the world in a variety of languages. You can buy one postage stamp size or over six feet wide. Descriptions include a photo and skill level required for assembly.

The catalog's a little expensive, but if you're into paper wings, it's worth the price. We haven't run into anything at all like it. The book's so complete that it promises: "If you find us a paper airplane that we don't have in this book, we will send you one of your own choice FREE!"

$18 (deducted from first order over $25)
Paper Airplanes International
433 Nihoa Street
Kahului, HI 96732
(800) 244-4667

A Simple Tip

"A real high-performance glider has a glide ratio of about 50 and a sinking speed around 0.5 meter a second. On the other hand, since the Reynolds number is smaller, the gliding ratio of a paper plane is only 6 or 7 due to heavy air drag. But a lightweight paper airplane can have a sinking speed of about 0.5 to 1 meter a second, almost the same as that of a real glider." —Dr. Yasuaki Ninomiya, the premiere paper airplane engineer

On a Wing & a Prayer

The Great International Paper Airplane Contests happen only irregularly. But if you're impatient to try out your paper engineering skills, check out these annual contests, open to the public:

• **Illinois Institute of Technology.** Two categories: Distance, and Flight Time, and paper is provided for you. There are no fees, but registration by phone is required for the contest held in February. **Contact: Ruth Sweetser, ITT Rice Campus, Wheaton, IL (708) 682-6000.**

• **Georgia Institute of Technology.** This one's been held for over 30 years, and prizes are awarded. **Dept. of Aerospace Engineering, c/o Sigma Gamma Tau, Atlanta, GA 30332. (404) 894-3000.**

Their Business is Folding

• *15 Excellent Paper Airplanes: Whitewings Assembly Kit.* Fifteen elegant and functional paper airplane gliders ready for cut-out and assembly, designed by amazing Dr. Yasuaki Ninomiya, Grand Prize winner in both Flight Time and Distance at the First International Paper Airplane Contest in 1967.

$16.00 + $3.50 shipping. Seattle Museum of Flight Museum Store, 9494 E. Marginal Way, Seattle, WA 98108. (206) 764-5704.

• *Classic Paper Planes.* 10 amazingly realistic, full-color flying models of craft from World War I and its sequel. Glide them or add a small motor for powered flight.

#06-J8427, $19.95 + 3.95 shipping. Bits & Pieces, 1 Puzzle Place, Stevens Point, WI 54481-7199. (800) JIGSAWS.

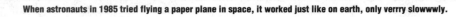

When astronauts in 1985 tried flying a paper plane in space, it worked just like on earth, only verrry slowwwly.

ANIMATION

Cartoon Heaven

It's Saturday afternoon at the movies. You grope your way down the dark aisle, having just made careful purchases at the refreshment stand. You slide sideways to your seat, making yourself as thin as possible so you won't step on every last person's toes. You finally make it, having only spilled a little bit from the top of your jumbo-sized bag of popcorn. You settle back in your cushioned chair, just as (before your innocent and delighted eyes) the first images of a color cartoon light up the screen. It's enchantment.

DAYS OF FUTURE PAST

The Flintstones Meet the Jetsons. Elroy's science project mixes up millennia and enables the Jetsons to meet their Stone Age counterparts, the Flintstones.

#HBV 1119-V/B, $19.95 + 3.50 shipping from The Whole Toon Catalog, P.O. Box 369, 1460 19th Ave N.W., Issaquah, WA 98027. (206) 391-8747.

A Dinosaur Leads the Way

Winsor McCay, a reporter, editorial cartoonist, and illustrator, is regarded as the father of American animation. His first animated film, *Little Nemo*, debuted in April, 1911, and *The Story of a Mosquito* followed soon after. But it was the 1914 *Gertie the Dinosaur* that astonished the public, which was still getting used to the idea of any kind of moving picture.

McCay put the animated film about Gertie into his vaudeville routine— he appeared on stage as her trainer, and she seemed to obey his commands and to react to what he said. As a finale, McCay appeared to walk into the screen and Gertie carried him away on her back. Posters for his show referred to it as "The Greatest Animal Act in the World" and called Gertie his "wonderful trained dinosaurus...She eats, drinks and breathes! She laughs and cries! Dances the tango, answers questions and obeys every command! Yet she lived millions of years before man inhabited this earth and has never been seen since!"

The public can be forgiven for being a bit confused about what was going on, but the show was an enormous hit. Even today, Gertie's charm is evident—she does seem to "live" and have a "personality."

Magoo, You've Done It Again

UPA Classics. Eight titles from the UPA studio (1948-56). Included in the selection are two Oscar winners: *Gerald McBoing-Boing* and a Mr. Magoo cartoon, *Magoo's Puddle Jumper.* 50 minutes.

#MGW 60809-V, $14.95 + 3.50 shipping The Whole Toon Catalog, P.O. Box 369, Issaquah, WA 98027. (206) 391-8747.

Cartoons, now thought of as only "kids' stuff" were aimed at adults in the old days.

THE EFFECT

"Persistence of vision." That's what makes your brain see motion when really there's only a series of still images. Animation can be created using a wide range of tools and techniques including the computer, acetate cels, clay, collage, 3-D models, cut-out figures, and so on.

When something is photographed a frame at a time and moved a little each time, the technique is called pixillation, or stop-motion photography.

The field of animation has enabled people to create their own animated worlds. There don't seem to be any limits to what can be imagined and put on the screen. And we've been enchanted for decades. A non-stop action parade of animated ducks, cats, birds, dogs, mice, and most every other kind of animal marches through the popular consciousness.

Many of the cartoon characters have been so believably given life that we feel like we know them— Donald Duck, Bugs Bunny, the Roadrunner, and the rest—better than we know the people around us.

Animation Magazines

• *Animato, The Animation Fan's Magazine*. Interviews, reviews, histories, and news about people in the business.

One year (4 issues), $10.00. P.O. Box 1240, Cambridge, MA 02238

• *Animation Magazine*. People in the animation industry. Also recent film releases, studio updates, and collecting news.

One year (4 issues), $15.00 from 6750 Centinela Ave., Suite 300, Los Angeles, CA 90230. (213) 313-9214.

Four-Finger Discount

Become the cartoon character you've always wanted to be. These four-fingered white gloves are like what all the hippest characters wear.

#T1439 Mouse Mitts, $8.98 + 3.50 shipping from Funny Side Up, 425 Stump Road, North Wales, PA 19454. (215) 361-5130.

Whole Toon Catalog

Our favorite source for classic cartoon videos is the Whole Toon Catalog, specializing in animated materials both famous and obscure. Send $2.00 for their catalog today, or live a life of unanimated regret.

Whole Toon Catalog, P.O. Box 369, 1460 19th Ave N.W., Issaquah, WA 98027. (206) 391-8747.

Who's That Tapping On My Tree?

Woody Woodpecker, with cartoons like *Born to Peck* and *The Coo Coo Bird*.

#MCA 81011-V, Vol. 1. #MCA 81012-V, Vol. 2. Each tape (4 cartoons, 30 minutes). $12.95 + 3.50 shipping. The Whole Toon Catalog, P.O. Box 369, 1460 19th Ave N.W., Issaquah, WA 98027. (206) 391-8747.

The first sound cartoons were produced by Max Fleischer between 1924 and 1927.

PILGRIMAGE

Disney-MGM Studios Theme Park Animation Tour. From the glass-walled walkway, it's one of the few places where you can look over the artists' shoulders and see how a new animated film is created. It's a great tour, but a little disconcerting watching them, almost like seeing a "Creative People in their Native Habitat" exhibit at a zoo.

P.O. Box 10,000, Lake Buena Vista, FL 32830-1000. (407) 824-4531.

Original Animated Art

A comprehensive selection of animation cels, both **production cels** (paintings on acetate that actually appeared in animated films) and **limited edition cels** (paintings created only for display). Choices span the range of animation, from Yogi Bear to the California Raisins to Peter Pan.

$3.95 for full-color catalog (refunded on first order) from Gallery Lainzberg, 200 Guaranty Building, 3rd Avenue & 3rd Street S.E., Cedar Rapids, IA 52401. (800) 553-9995 / (319) 363-6136.

Just Huck's Luck

Huck takes on the Dalton gang in *The Good, the Bad, & Huckleberry Hound.* His friends Quick Draw McGraw, Yogi Bear, Magilla Gorilla and Snagglepuss help him balance the odds.

#HBV 1135-V/B, $29.95 + 3.50 shipping. The Whole Toon Catalog, P.O. Box 369, 1460 19th Ave N.W., Issaquah, WA 98027. (206) 391-8747.

Strong to the Finich

Popeye Cartoons. These short films made by Fleischer Brothers in 1933-38 show our spinach-eating sailor man at his best.

90 minutes, black & white, #VR 012-V, $24.95 + 3.50 shipping. The Whole Toon Catalog, P.O. Box 369, 1460 19th Ave N.W., Issaquah, WA 98027. (206) 391-8747.

Name That "Toon"

Here's a concise compendium of cartoon characters' little-known names:

- Popeye's pal Wimpy's complete name: **J. Wellington Wimpy**
- Donald Duck's middle name: **Fauntleroy**
- Mr. Magoo's first name: **Quincy**
- Bullwinkle's pal Rocky's full name: **Rocket J. Squirrel**
- Their nemesis Natasha's last name: **Fatale**
- The Roadrunner's actual name: **Mimi**

Bill Hanna Joe Barbera

Telling Tales in Toontown

Want to know how to break into writing TV cartoon animation? Go to your local library and track down the August, 1989 issue of *Writer's Digest* (F & W Publications, 1507 Dana Avenue, Cincinnati, OH 45207) where you'll find an excellent article by David Wiemers titled: **Animated Debate: How to Write and Sell Animated Cartoon Strips.**

It's only a Paper Toon

One of the latest amazing developments in animation was *Who Framed Roger Rabbit?*, a combination of live-action and animation which is technically dazzling and very funny. It's a nostalgic look at some of the best-loved characters in cartoondom—over 250 of them from the major cartoon studios in an unprecedented display of cooperation (Felix the Cat and Popeye were two exceptions). Sheer heaven for the cartoon fan.

Righty-O Videos

Here are two video collections of Felix the Cat cartoons that will make you "laugh so much your sides will ache."

#VR 007-V/B (8 titles, 60 min.), $19.95 + 3.50 shipping; #V-YES 1431-V/B (12 titles, 88 min.), $29.95 + 3.50 shipping. The Whole Toon Catalog, P.O. Box 369, 1460 19th Ave N.W., Issaquah, WA 98027. (206) 391-8747.

Watch Felix...

Whenever you want at the flick of your wrist with a wonderful, wonderful Felix the Cat watch.

#17620, $45.00 + 4.95 shipping from Wireless, P.O. Box 64422, St. Paul, MN 55164-0422. (800) 669-9999.

Mixing cartoons and live action is an old idea. *Gertie the Dinosaur* was first. Disney's *Alice* series was another early one. Here are some others.

• *Anchors Aweigh* (1945). Gene Kelly dances with Jerry (the mouse of Tom & Jerry). One footnote: after drawing the sequence, the animators realized that they hadn't allowed for the highly reflective floor. They had to go back and draw in Jerry's reflection, frame by frame.

• *The Three Caballeros* (1945). Aurora Miranda (Carmen's sister) dances with Donald Duck, presumably after reading him his rights.

• *Song of the South* (1946). James Baskett sings *Zip-A-Dee-Doo-Dah* with a host of cartoon flora and fauna.

• *Mary Poppins* (1964). Extensive animated section includes penguin waiters and a fox hunt gone astray.

• *Pete's Dragon* (1977). Elliot the dragon renders himself invisible in a lot of the scenes, saving big bucks in animation costs.

Take A Spin

Hand-made zoetrope provides hours of fun. Spin the leather-covered slotted drum and you'll see a band of figures come to life! Includes 6 different bands.

#08-J8483, $39.95 + 5.95 shipping. Bits & Pieces, 1 Puzzle Place, Box 8016, Stevens Point, WI 54481-7199. (800) JIGSAWS.

Dr. Seuss designed the first animated color commercial in 1949, for Ford.

Play Cat & Mouse...

Tom & Jerry's 50th Birthday Classics. Three volumes of frenetic fun, with titles like the Oscar-winning *Yankee Doodle Mouse* (Vol. 1), *Cat Concerto* (Vol. 2), and *Mice Follies* (Vol. 3).

Vol. 1 #MGM 201664-V/B (7 titles, 57 min.), $14.95 + 3.50 shipping; Vol. 2 #MGM 202049-V (6 titles, 45 min.), $12.95 + 3.50 shipping; Vol. 3 #MGM 202050-V (6 titles, 45 min.), $12.95 + 3.50 shipping. The Whole Toon Catalog, P.O. Box 369, 1460 19th Ave N.W., Issaquah, WA 98027. (206) 391-8747.

Screwball Toons

Tex Avery was a master of loony surrealism. Enjoy 16 favorites like *Swing Shift Cinderella* (Vol. 1) and *Red Hot Riding Hood* (Vol. 2).

Vol. 1 #MGM 203852-V/B (8 titles, 59 min.), $14.95 + 3.50 shipping; Vol. 2 #MGM 201667-V/B (8 titles, 60 min.), $14.95 + 3.50 shipping. The Whole Toon Catalog, P.O. Box 369, 1460 19th Ave N.W., Issaquah, WA 98027. (206) 391-8747.

ORGANIZATIONS

• **The Animation Art Guild.** Members collects cels, backgrounds, concept sketches, drawings, and other items related to animation from all studios.

Membership: $49.00 per year from 330 West 45th St., Suite 9D, New York, NY 10036. (212) 765-3030.

• **ASIFA.** An international organization for animated film buffs, fans and scholars. Ask *them* what it stands for—it's in French.

—ASIFA East, c/o Dick Grauh, 11 Admiral Lane, Norwalk, CT 06851.
—ASIFA Central, c/o Dave Daruszka, 790 N. Milwaukee Ave., Chicago, IL 60622.
—ASIFA West, P.O. Box 14516, San Francisco, CA 94114.

Animation Firsts

• The principles of animation were demonstrated in a series of 19th century toys including the "zoetrope" (a rotating slotted metal drum which is cranked rapidly to animate a series of drawings inside) and "phenakistoscope" (two disks spinning rapidly together to match image with slots).

• The first film with drawn animation was James Stuart Blackton's *Humorous Phases of Funny Faces* in 1906.

• The first animated commercials appeared in movie theatres prior to World War I.

• The basics of cel animation, painting on transparent material so you don't have to redraw *every* part of *every* picture, were developed and patented by Earl Hurd and John R. Bray in 1914.

• The first feature-length cartoon was Disney's *Snow White*.

The first cartoon in 3-D was Disney's *Melody* in 1953.

Draw Upon Your Book Learning

• *Enchanted Drawings: The History of Animation* by **Charles Solomon.** An excellent coffee-table book with lavish, beautifully reproduced illustrations. It gives a fascinating overview of the industry and interesting anecdotes (like Betty Boop getting in trouble with the censors for wearing a garter).

Hardback, $74.95 + 3.75 shipping. The Whole Toon Catalog, P.O. Box 369, 1460 19th Ave NW, Issaquah, WA 98027. (206) 391-8747.

• *Of Mice and Magic: A History of American Animated Cartoons* by **Leonard Maltin.** A thorough reference work which is fun to read at the same time. Maltin traces the work of all the major American cartoon studios, with complete lists of their films.

$16.95 + 3.50 shipping. The Whole Toon Catalog, P.O. Box 369, 1460 19th Ave N.W., Issaquah, WA 98027. (206) 391-8747.

• *Cartoon Monickers: An Insight Into The Animation Industry* by **Walter M. Brasch.** This book is a fascinating account of how cartoon characters got their names. How about these names considered but not chosen for the Seven Dwarfs: Glick, Snick, Plick, Dirty, Dizzy, Hotsy, Jumpy, Neurtsy, Nifty, Snappy, and Thrifty? Learn about baseball player Yogi Berra's threatened defamation-of-character lawsuit over

Hanna-Barbera's Yogi Bear character. Interesting material on "forbidden" names and on WASP and ethnic names.

$10.95 + 1.00 shipping from The Popular Press, Bowling Green State University, Bowling Green, OH 43403. (419) 372-7865.

• *The Animation Book: A Complete Guide to Animated Filmmaking—From Flip-Books to Sound Cartoons* by **Kit Laybourne.** A how-to manual that is inclusive in scope and eclectic in spirit. With the illustrated plans provided, you can construct your own animation studio, equipped with everything from a zoetrope to a sophisticated animation stand for cels or clay.

Crown Publishers, Inc.—Out of print, but worth the search.

Adult Cartoons

Cartoons for Big Kids. The classic cartoon shorts for movie theatres were always drawn with an adult audience in mind (although kids could enjoy them, too). This is a selection of four with grown-up themes—*King Size Canary, The Great Piggy Bank Robbery, The Big Snooze* and *Red Hot Riding Hood.* The last one features the Big Bad Wolf as a tuxedoed playboy and Red as a sexy nightclub singer—reportedly the inspiration for Jessica Rabbit.

44 minutes, #TUR6031-V, $19.95 + 3.50 shipping from Whole Toon Catalog, P.O. Box 369, 1460 19th Ave N.W., Issaquah, WA 98027. (206) 391-8747.

Your Obedient Serpent

Now you can own all 80 color episodes of *The Adventures of Beany and Cecil.* They're collected in 13 volumes, each containing 6 or 7 titles and running 60 to 70 minutes.

Each volume $24.95 + 3.50 shipping. The Whole Toon Catalog, P.O. Box 369, 1460 19th Ave N.W., Issaquah, WA 98027. (206) 391-8747.

The first sound cartoon to become a hit with the public was Disney's *Steamboat Willie* in 1928.

ANT FARMS

MOUNTAINS OUT OF ANTHILLS

Nobody's done more PR for ants (since Aesop anyway) than Uncle Milton, and the ants have returned the favor. It's a fairly safe bet that Uncle Milton has made more money out of ants than anyone else in history.

"Uncle Milton," is the inventor of the Ant Farm. His real name is Milton Levine, also known as "Lord of the Ants " and "the man who made a mountain out of an anthill."

It was Independence Day, 1956, when the idea struck: "It just came to me in a flash," Uncle Milton says (he was 32 at the time, and looking to expand his line of mail order novelties). "I was at a Fourth of July picnic at my sister's house. I saw a bunch of ants around the pool. I saw a bunch of kids, and they were interested in the ants. And it came to me."

The first farms were six inches by nine inches, a solid-colored plastic frame holding two sheets of transparent plastic with a layer of sand in between. There was a plastic farm scene—barn, silo, farmhouse, and windmill. They sold for $1.98.

Levine bought a 2-inch ad in the *Los Angles Times*, inviting the curious to "watch the ants dig tunnels and build bridges" in their own Ant Farms. "I got so many orders, you wouldn't believe it." And that was just the beginning.

Not that selling ants was always a picnic. In the beginning, ants were dropping like flies—the result of either booze breath from the assembler (Levine's theory) or glue fumes (Levine's partner's theory). Whichever, the problem was eventually solved.

The Ant Farm has been an enduring product, to say the least. Sales began two years before the Hula-Hoop and are still going strong. Over 12 million Ant Farms have been sold, with more than 360 million ants. The company, now managed by Milton's son Steven Levine, reports getting about 12,000 letters each year from Ant Farm owners (often former childhood owners reporting they had bought one for

a child or grandchild). Not that there isn't an occasional complaint letter—one kid was mad that his ants weren't wearing top hats like on the box.

The product is just about the same today as back then, except for the price. You get the Ant Farm, which comes with a certificate you mail in to get your ants. You also get the *Ant Watchers Manual*, which gives you information about your new livestock (Do ants talk? Yes. Do they take baths? Yes). One improvement from the ant farms of our childhood: connectors for plastic tubes so you can string Ant Farms together and watch the ants crawl from one to another.

Why is he called "Uncle Milton"? "Everyone always said, 'You've got the ants, but where's the uncles?' So I became Uncle Milton."

Anty Monopoly

Ant farms are the flagship of Uncle Milton Industries, but they aren't the only culturally significant product the company has made. How about these?

- Plastic shrunken heads to hang from rear-view mirrors
- The Spud Gun, which fires potato pellets
- The once-popular insecticides Fly Cake and Roach Cake
- "100 Toy Soldiers for a Buck"
- The Sea Horse Corral
- The Bonsai Tree Kit

Anty Matters & Insect Asides

• Coincidence? You decide: The Ant Farm was invented in the same year as Raid insecticide.

• All the ants supplied for the Ant Farm are female. In the ant world, there aren't many males, and all they do is mate and die (an anty-climax, if you will). And since the company can't legally ship queen ants, your colony can't reproduce and will eventually dwindle to nothing.

• Out of thousands of varieties of ants, the harvester ant was chosen to work

"The ant farm I had as a child never worked…We may, in fact, have never sent away for the ants. That would do it."

—James Gorman

on the Ant Farm because it's big and is one of the few varieties that will dig in daylight.

• The leading cause of barnyard death is overfeeding. If you exceed the recommended ration of one birdseed or a single cornflake every two days, the food gets moldy, and your ants "buy the farm".

• The next leading danger is too much sunlight (baked ants). Shaking the farm has been known to cause mass death by shock (it's too darn frustrating to spend all those hours digging, only to have your work reduced to nothing in a few seconds).

• At a funeral, the ant graveyard detail always carries the dead ant to the northeastern corner of the farm. If the farm is rotated to a new direction, the pallbearers march into action again, digging up the dead ants and reburying them in the northeast. Why? Nobody knows.

• The technical name for an ant farm (or any ant habitat) is a formicarium.

• Every Ant Farm is entirely American-made; they are assembled and packaged in Southern California by disabled workers.

• Singer Linda Ronstadt once gave an ant farm to California's Governor Jerry Brown.

ANT FARM

I Want My Ant TV

Ant farms have been featured in a surprisingly large number of TV shows, including:

- *You Bet Your Life*
- *Roseanne*
- *Alf*
- *Pee-Wee's Playhouse*
- *The Cosby Show*
- *Punky Brewster*
- *Dr. Who*
- *The Wonder Years*
- *The Munsters*

Chinese farmers use ants against pests. A large colony can capture several million insects a year.

Thesis & Anty Thesis

The Ant Rancher's Handbook **by George S. Glenn, Jr.** The main problem with the Ant Farm is that all the information you get is in a tiny 12 page pamphlet. This book fills the gaps for anybody interested in ant language, society, species varieties and behavior.

$7.95 + 2.50 shipping. Running Press, 125 S. 22nd St., Philadelphia, PA 19103.

THE Ant Rancher's Handbook
George S. Glenn, Jr.

Movie Anty Heroes

Ant Farms have played bit parts in a number of films (not counting *THEM*, about giant radioactive ants):

- *Beetlejuice*
- *Parenthood*
- *When Harry Met Sally*
- *UHF*
- *Short Circuit*

Ant Queen

After answering an ad in the *Los Angeles Times* in 1959, Kenneth Gidney started digging ants. He taught his ten children early. One of them, Robin Brenner, is still doing it; 30 years later, one of only three diggers that supply the 15 million ants Uncle Milton sends out each year.

Not that it's an easy job. You get bitten a lot. "Sometimes when I'm sitting up late at night, I think 'People don't know how hard this is. They don't know where these ants come from. They don't know how much sleep I'm missing,'" she says.

Ant collecting techniques vary. Some take straws and blow into the hole, catching the ants as they run out. Brenner's invention is a car vacuum fixed to a Tupperware container, which she uses to suck up ants after digging up the tunnels.

It takes about 10 hours to gather 50,000 ants, for which Brenner earns about $550. Afterward, a half-dozen workers tediously fill little plastic vials with exactly 30 ants each, which are mailed out to Ant Farm owners.

Buy the Farm

The Ant Farm. "Be inspired," says this catalog, "by these miniature co-dependent workaholics as they slave within their plastic habitat." Uncle Milton's Ant Farms are available from almost any decent toy store. Or order by mail.

Standard Ant Farm, $9.95 + 4.00 shipping. Giant Ant Farm, $21.95 + 6.00 shipping. Ruby Montana's Pinto Pony, 603 2nd Avenue, Seattle, WA 98104. (206) 621-PONY.

The Ant's Pajamas

Every year Joe Boxer comes out with a new ant-motif line. This is 1991's model—1992 promises an ant farm design, available on PJs, socks and whatnots.

For prices and nearby retailer, contact Joe Boxer Hdqtrs., 984 Folsom St., San Francisco, CA 94107. (415) 882-9406.

Anty Materialism

Avoid the inevitable heartbreak of having all your ants die. These low-maintenance plastic ants will live forever in your Ant Farm, and you don't even have to feed them.

#3353, Dozens of Phony Ants, $1.98 + 1.35 shipping from Johnson Smith Company, 4514 19th Court East, P.O. Box 25500, Bradenton, FL 34206-5500. (813) 747-2356 / FAX (813) 746-7896.

Ants taste sweet. Some people eat them as a natural taste treat.

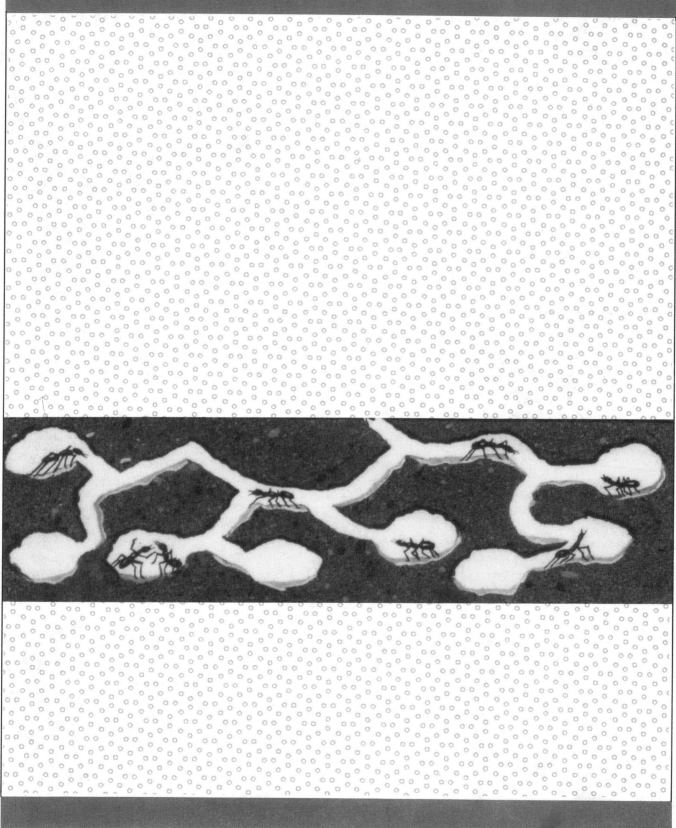

ATOMIC

A MEGATON OF FUN

Americans have always been better at cheerful denial than painful introspection. In a poll, 1 in 9 of us swore that the U.S. has never used a nuclear bomb in war. While that's a minority it's an indication that these things are so horrible many of us would rather not think about them, thank you.

Not that awareness of our own dark side doesn't leak out through our collective mental repression. A lot of the paranoia that has permeated our politics and popular culture has come from the realization that others may try to do unto us what we've been willing to do unto them.

People who grew up in the 1950s find it hard to explain to their kids about crouching under school desks and watching cheerful cartoon turtles telling what to do if the world collapses ("If you see the flash, duck into a ditch or behind a car…"). This generation's apocalyptic nightmare is slow death by environmental poisons. While just as dismal, that scenario is less nerve-jangling than thinking that evil Nikita's sneak attack may suddenly come at any time of day or night.

Bomb Blasts from the Past

• Scientists working on the first atomic bomb had a $1 betting pool on how big the explosion would be, ranging from 0 to 45,000 tons of TNT. Enrico Fermi predicted that the blast would ignite all available atmospheric oxygen. He took side bets on whether it would destroy the entire earth, or just most of New Mexico.

• Despite assurances to the president that only a military target would be hit, the Generals chose Hiroshima precisely because it had no military significance and therefore hadn't previously been hit with air raids. They wanted a "virgin" target so it would be easier to measure the effects of the Bomb.

• The bomb burned people's shadows onto pavement and walls as they were instantly seared into small, sticky, smoking black char. About 100,000 people died instantly, and the same number within the next five years from burns and radiation.

EXPLOSIVE QUOTES

"Perhaps two thirds of the people of earth might be killed, but enough men capable of thinking, and enough books, would be left to start again, and civilization could be restored." —Albert Einstein, 1945

"Hiroshima, Nagasaki paid a big price for their sin/When scorched from the face of earth, their battle could not win… Atomic power, atomic power was given by the mighty hand of God." —Buchanan Brothers, **Atomic Power**

"The atomic bomb is not an inhuman weapon. I think our best answer to anyone who doubts this is that we did not start the war, and if they don't like the way we ended it, to remember who started it." —Major General Leslie R. Groves of the Manhattan Project, 1945

"The atom bomb is shit. This is a weapon which has no military significance. It will make a big bang—a very big bang—but it is not a weapon which is useful in war." —J. Robert Oppenheimer, 1945

Atomic Cocktail

In typical American fashion, we dealt with the terror of the atomic age by making a few bucks from it. In the early 1950s "atomic" became a commercial metaphor for anything powerful or scientifically advanced. Hundreds of products and businesses proudly bore atomic names (even the bikini, named after a bomb test site).

Most of these names had a half-life of only a few years, but one is still hanging on like nuclear waste—the Atomic Fire Ball candy, released in 1954 and still selling megatons. Look for it in local stores, or call the Ferrara Candy Company (708) 366-0500.

Stage a Mini-Meltdown

Do-it-yourself nuclear power plant model is a near-replica of Three Mile Island! Scale model includes generator station, containment building and cooling tower. 14 inches high. Glue and operator errors not included.

#G36-718 Nuclear Power Plant, $13.95 + 4.25 shipping from Edmund Scientific Co., Barrington, NJ 08007-1380. (609) 547-8880.

Bomb Sha Bomb Sha Bomb

"Atom bomb baby, boy can she start / One of those chain reactions in my heart / A big explosion, big and loud / She mushrooms me right up on a cloud / Atom bomb baby, li'l atom bomb / I want her in my wigwam / She's just the way I want her to be / A million times hotter than TNT."

—The 5 Stars, Atom Bomb Baby

The Bomb's Greatest Hits

"Eve of Destruction"—Barry McGuire

"It's Good News Week"—Hedgehoppers Anonymous

"Political Science (Let's Drop the Big One)"—Randy Newman

"Jesus Hits Like an Atom Bomb"—Lowell Blanchard & Valley Trio

Give Me Shelter

A combination home fallout shelter and snack bar? We can get you plans.

The hinged canopy can be tilted down for filling with bricks, concrete blocks or even piles of books. (For fallout protection, 14" of books and magazines are equivalent to 4" of concrete).

Even in these budget-tight times, when dozens of worthy programs are being strangled, the Federal Emergency Management Administration (FEMA) will still send you a hefty free package of fallout and blast shelter information, including how to build, stock and manage them.

To get yours, call FEMA headquarters at (202) 646-3061. Now. When the air raid sirens wail, it'll be too late.

Movies to End All:

The Whole Pop Film Fest

• *The China Syndrome*: Prophetic drama about a nuclear power plant melt-down and cover-up.

• *Dr. Strangelove, or: How I Learned to Stop Worrying and Love the Bomb*: Probably the blackest of black comedies about a crazed general hell-bent on destroying the world.

• *Cafe Flesh*: Post-nuclear porno about live-sex shows patronized by mutants who become nauseated when touched, so can only enjoy sex vicariously by watching those not affected by this strange malady.

• *The Day After*: Post-nuclear melodrama that takes place in Lawrence but makes you feel it's not Kansas anymore.

• *A Boy and His Dog*: Post-nuclear black comedy that first saw Don Johnson's stud potential.

• *Fail Safe*: The U.S. accidentally bombs Moscow, and the guilty President decides the U.S. should call it even by bombing Manhattan.

• *Fat Man and Little Boy*: In the New Mexico desert, the people behind the bombs dropped on Japan test them.

• *On the Beach*: Beautiful people wait for the winds to bring fallout.

• *Red Dawn*: Teenage rednecks battle the Red Menace with native wits and pick-up trucks. Thank God for loose gun laws!

• *Deadline*: Pay the ransom in time or the terrorists will nuke you.

• *Def-Con 4*: Astronauts miss a nuclear holocaust while in space and return to face the aftermath. At least they're dressed for it.

• *The Day the Fish Came Out*: Atom bombs over the Aegean.

• *Wargames*: Teen hackers tap into NORAD computer and start playing games with real nuclear warheads.

• *The World, the Flesh, and the Devil*: The last people on earth form an interracial menage a trois with a white Eve and black and white Adams.

• *The Incredible Shrinking Man*: Radiation can make you feel mighty small.

For Your Shelter Library

Did you know that electrons from an atomic bomb blast, even if hundreds of miles away, would wreck the circuits in your electronic gear, and erase your video tapes? Better watch these now before the bombs start falling.

Federal Follies Videos. Government training films from 1934-1973, these collections of unintentionally hilarious shorts cover topics from atomic blast survival to avoiding hookworm. Four volumes to choose from.

$19.95 each + 3.90 shipping, or all 4 for $79.00 + 7.75 shipping from Wireless, PO Box 64422, Saint Paul, MN 55164-0422. (800) 669-9999.

Atomic Cafe. Funny, chilling look at the Bomb from newsreel footage and propaganda films from the 1940s and '50s. The soundtrack album features *Atom Bomb Baby, Atomic Love* and *Jesus Hits Like an Atom Bomb.*

• Video. $59.95 + 4.80 shipping, Home Film Festival, Box 2030, Scranton, PA 18501. (800) 258-3456. • LP or Cassette. #R1034, $9.00 + 2.50 shipping. Roundup Records, Box 154, N. Cambridge, MA 02140. (617) 661- 6308.

PLACES TO GLOW

Three Mile Island. Ironically, sightseeing here has more than tripled since its partial meltdown. Mugs, t-shirts and more available from the gift shop.

Route 441, Middletown, PA 17057. (717) 948-8587.

Titan Missile Museum. This former base was active from 1962 to 1984. On display are nose cones, rocket engines and the world's only public ICBM silo. The launch silo houses a "Peacekeeper" missile. Inactive, but don't push any buttons, just in case.

Duval Mine Road, Green Valley, AZ 85614. (602) 791-2929.

National Atomic Museum. See how your tax dollars have been spent for the past half-century. Put your hands on actual bomb casings, and see artifacts from the Manhattan Project.

Kirtland Air Force Base, P.O. Box 5400, Albuquerque, NM 87115. (505) 845-6670.

The Russians Are Coming

Survive the Coming Nuclear War: How to Do It by Ronald L. and Robert L. Cruit, MD. "Don't want to live through a nuclear war? Wouldn't want to be around after it's all over? That's a common attitude," say the authors with scorn. They offer preparations for surviving World War III, including shelter designs, food and first aid checklists, and survival skills for "the day after."

ISBN #6222-8, $8.95 + 3.00 shipping from Scarborough House, PO Box 459, Chelsea, MI 48118. (313) 475-1210.

What to Do When the Russians Come: A Survivor's Guide by Robert Conquest and Jon Manchip White. "Russians are not famous for their sense of humor... These are a mean people." Reads like a McCarthy era tract, but it was written in 1984. Straightfaced advice for different occupations and even ethnic groups about how to negotiate the best possible treatment from the occupying Russians.

The heroically-named authors advise the reader to "BURN THIS BOOK" after finishing it, but we say, why wait until then?

$6.95 + 3.00 shipping from Stein and Day, Scarborough House, PO Box 459, Chelsea, MI 48118. (313) 475-1210.

ALWAYS FOLLOW THESE OFFICIAL CIVIL DEFENSE
AIR RAID INSTRUCTIONS

↓ IF ATTACK COMES WITH NO WARNING	BE QUICK BUT CALM	↓ IF YOU HAVE WARNING
Drop to floor. Try to get under a bed or heavy table.	AT HOME	Turn off stove burners. Go to shelter room you have prepared.
Drop to floor and try to get under desk or bench.	AT WORK	Go to assigned shelter, follow warden's orders.
Drop to floor and bury face in arms. Get out of line with windows.	IN SCHOOL	Go to assigned shelter, follow teacher's orders.
Drop to ground. If cover is close by, dive for it. Bury face in arms.	IN THE OPEN	Get in nearest approved building or shelter, obey CD wardens.
Drop to floor and bury face in arms.	STOP CARS, BUSSES OR TROLLEYS	Get out and go to nearest approved building or shelter, obey CD wardens.

OBEY INSTRUCTIONS AND
STAY PUT UNTIL THE ALL-CLEAR SOUNDS

---

4 inches of concrete

5 to 6 inches of brick

6 inches of sand or gravel

7 inches of earth

8 inches of hollow concrete block

10 inches of water

14 inches of books or magazines

18 inches of wood

Visit A Blast from the Past

Trinity Site, White Sands Missile Range, Alamogordo, NM. Open House Tour: first Saturday in October.

The original Ground Zero, site of the first nuclear explosion on July 16, 1945. A black lava obelisk marks center of the 800 yard wide, 15' deep crater. See the radioactive blue-green "Trinitite" gems—sand melted by the intense heat. You can't take 'em home as souvenirs, you can't bring food and drink, and you have to leave after 90 minutes to minimize radiation exposure (1/15 of an average chest X-ray they say). For more info, call (505) 678-1134.

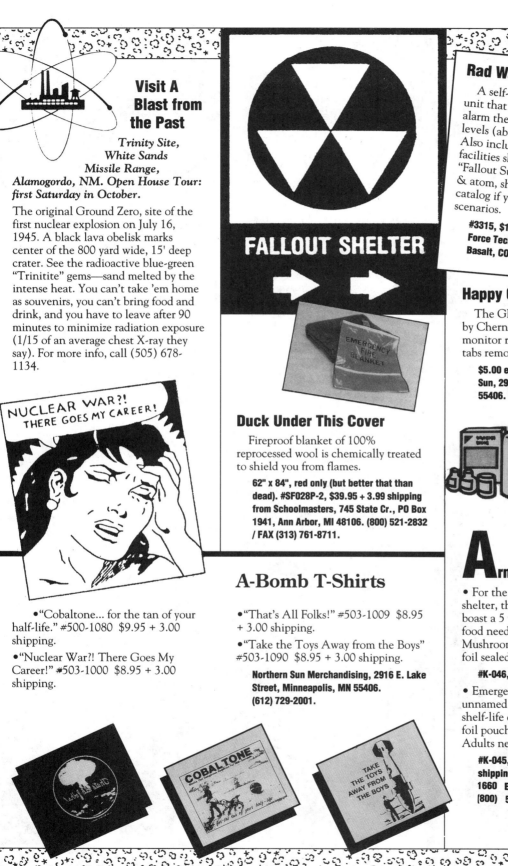

FALLOUT SHELTER

Rad Warning Device, Dude!

A self-contained, portable, solid-state unit that sounds an audible and visual alarm the instant radiation reaches unsafe levels (above 10 milliRADS per hour). Also included are maps of all nuclear facilities showing prevailing winds, and "Fallout Survival," a 180 page book. Up & atom, shoppers! Get this company's catalog if you're a fan of worst-case scenarios.

#3315, $175.00 + 4.25 shipping from Life Force Technologies LTD., P.O. Box 755, Basalt, CO 81621. (800) 922-3545.

Happy Glow

The GENUINE dosimeter pins worn by Chernobyl power plant workers to monitor radiation exposure (absorbent tabs removed).

$5.00 each + 3.00 shipping from Northern Sun, 2916 E. Lake St., Minneapolis, MN 55406. (612) 729-2001.

Duck Under This Cover

Fireproof blanket of 100% reprocessed wool is chemically treated to shield you from flames.

62" x 84", red only (but better that than dead). #SF028P-2, $39.95 + 3.99 shipping from Schoolmasters, 745 State Cr., PO Box 1941, Ann Arbor, MI 48106. (800) 521-2832 / FAX (313) 761-8711.

A-Bomb T-Shirts

•"Cobaltone... for the tan of your half-life." #500-1080 $9.95 + 3.00 shipping.

•"Nuclear War?! There Goes My Career!" #503-1000 $8.95 + 3.00 shipping.

•"That's All Folks!" #503-1009 $8.95 + 3.00 shipping.

•"Take the Toys Away from the Boys" #503-1090 $8.95 + 3.00 shipping.

Northern Sun Merchandising, 2916 E. Lake Street, Minneapolis, MN 55406. (612) 729-2001.

Armageddon on $7 a Day

• For the most discriminating fallout shelter, these compressed comestibles boast a 5 year shelf life, and fulfill adult food needs for 3 days. Great with Mushroom Cloud Sauce. Lightweight, foil sealed, waterproof package.

#K-046, Food, $9.95 + 3.95 shipping.

• Emergency drinking water of an unnamed vintage and an indefinite shelf-life comes sealed in heavy-gauge foil pouches, each containing 4.2 fl. oz. Adults need 2 pouches a day.

#K-045, Water (10 pouches), $6.95 + $3.95 shipping from Kaufman's West, 1660 Eubank NE, Albuquerque, NM 87112. (800) 545-0933 / FAX (505) 275-1441.

Super Star Barbie®

What a Doll!

She's glamorous, beautiful and rich. She stands 11 3/4" tall, yet in her world she's far bigger than anyone else.

Not that Barbie hasn't known controversy. She's been called a role model for anorexia and crass materialism, even an environmental nut. She's even been unfairly compared to Vanna White and Dan Quayle.

Despite all this, Barbie still manages a smile. It probably helps that she's got fans everywhere.

Preteen girls and even adult doll collectors have snapped up 500 million of the dolls since 1959, plus accessories. *Lots* of accessories.

From Dream to Dreamhouse. In the mid-1950s, Ruth Handler, co-founder of Mattel, noticed that her daughter Barbara preferred adult paper dolls to baby dolls. She decided that girls weren't interested in playing just mommy any more.

In 1957 Mattel designers began working on a prototype face, body and miniaturized Givenchy and Dior designs based on a German doll named Lilli. They named the doll after Ruth's daughter (son Ken would have to wait until 1961 for notoriety).

When introduced at the 1959 New York Toy Fair, toy buyers largely ignored Barbie. They thought parents wouldn't allow such a sexually-developed doll for their daughters.

They took notice soon enough, as initial shipments—500,000 dolls and one million outfits—sold out immediately. Barbies have been selling steadily ever since, with $590 million in sales in 1989.

Barbie has kept changing with the social trends of her times. Her makeup, hairstyle and fashions change year by year, yet her face is sweetly generic so that little girls can project their own fantasies onto the doll. That's also why Barbie and Ken never officially married, although wedding outfits leave that option open to each individual girl.

Barbie By the Numbers

- Barbie is a statuesque 11 3/4" tall. Ken is a manly 12 1/2".

- Barbie's measurements brought up to human scale would be an implausible 38-18-28.

- Most Barbies are bought for girls between the ages of 5 and 9. A typical girl has an average of 5 dolls.

- Mattel sews 5 million yards of fabric each year into Barbie fashions.

- Selling more than $20 million in Barbie fashions a year, Mattel could be considered one of the world's largest retailers of womens' clothes.

- Price of the original Barbie doll in 1959: $3.00.

- 1990 price of mint condition, 1959 Barbie doll in original box: $1,800.00.

- Barbie doll, new, 1990: $5.95 for basic doll in bathing suit, up to $14.95, dressed in various costumes.

The Barbie Fan Club has 8,500 chapters.

Required Reading

Barbie: Thirty Years of America's Doll by **Cynthia Robins.** Full of amusing facts, history, sociology and trivia, this book will charm Barbie fans.

$8.95 + 1.50 shipping from Contemporary Books, 180 N. Michigan Ave., Chicago, IL 60601. (312) 782-9181.

Barbie, Her Life and Times by **"BillyBoy."** Paris designer BillyBoy uses his own 11,000-piece Barbie collection to make an arty statement about the changing American standards of feminine beauty and social values. Interesting, but nostalgia-seekers won't find this book particularly useful, since Mr. Boy's dolls wear one-of-a-kind outfits that weren't part of Mattel's line.

$25.00 + 2.00 shipping from Crown Publishers, 201 East 50th St., New York, NY 10022. (800) 733-3000.

• ***The Collectors Encyclopedia of Barbie Dolls and Collectibles*** by Sibyl DeWein and Joan Ashabraner. A complete listing of dolls and accessories produced from 1957-1976. Some history, abundant photos, many in color. Detailed to the point of obsession: if you ever wanted to know, for instance, the difference between Barbie arms made in Mexico versus Hong Kong, this is the book for you.

$19.95 + 2.00 shipping from Collector Books, PO Box 3009 Paducah, KY 42001. (800) 626-5420.

The World of Barbie Dolls Illustrated Value Guide by **Paris and Susan Manos.** Prices for Barbie dolls, costumes, cases, furniture, gift sets and accessories. Brief descriptions, photos and prices, no history or anecdotes.

$9.95 + 2.00 shipping from Collector Books, PO Box 3009, Paducah, KY 42001. (800) 626-5420.

Your Mother Did WHAT With Your Old Barbie Dolls?

Flea market and attic finds are still possible, but getting scarcer. The best bet for finding collectible Barbies is a toy or doll collectors' publication.

Barbie Bazaar. Classified advertising section lists exclusively Barbie, her friends, clothes and accessories. This handsome, full color publication has intelligent articles that appeal to the nostalgic adult more than to children. We love the way the photo layouts treat Barbie as if she were a life-size fashion model, with Barbie-scale sets and props.

$23.95 / 6 issues, $4.95 single issue from Murat Caviale Communications, 5617 6th Ave., Kenosha, WI 53140.

Toy Shop. Lists all kinds of toys and dolls, wanted and for sale, including but not limited to Barbie. This is a great general-interest tabloid made up exclusively of dealer ads and classifieds.

12 issues / $17.95, single issue $3.50 from 700 E. State Street, Iola, WI 54990.

Barbie Fan Club

Barbie Magazine. Every member of Mattel's official Barbie Fan Club receives 4 issues of *Barbie Magazine* plus a special *Best of Barbie Magazine* each year. No meetings, no secret decoder ring, club handshake or password, just the satisfaction of belonging to a club and the thrill of receiving its members-only magazine in the mail. The magazine's aimed at 8-10 year olds, with simple stories and lots of photos of Barbie and her pals.

Membership / $9.45. PO Box 10798, Des Moines, IA 50340.

One of the three original Barbies was a brunette — the rest were blonde.

Barbie's Kith and Ken

Kinky Ken. A Tampa, Florida Toys R Us customer thought she had a valuable collectible when she bought a Ken doll dressed in a purple tank top and a lace covered skirt. It wasn't until Arsenio Hall, Joan Rivers and various wire services had fun with the news that the store clerk responsible for the switch confessed.

Barbie Plays Around. Ken wasn't the only contender for Barbie's little plastic heart. The 1961 Barbie "Queen of the Prom" board game included three other Barbie-besotted boys as well: Bob, a handsome, dark Romeo-type, Tom, a "brain," with horn-rimmed glasses and Poindexter, a classic red-haired nerd who probably now owns the company that makes Barbie's computers.

Who Could Hate Barbie?

Not everyone loves Barbie. Despite her cheerful inoffensiveness, she sometimes raises hackles:

- California child psychologist Dr. James Dobson called Barbie a role model for anorexia.

- Peace groups were upset when Mattel issued military Barbies last summer (see below).

- Despite all her careers, many women's groups believe Barbie to be a harmful role model.

- Northwest loggers demanded suppression of a "radical environmentalist" Barbie TV commercial in December of 1990. The problem? Barbie talks of a better world where "we could keep the trees from falling, keep the eagles soaring." The angry wood-choppers objected that she was giving deforestation a bad name. The same group also convinced Kmart to stop selling "Save the Trees" t-shirts.

Puzzle Out Barbie's Career

The many faces of Barbie, who can't seem to manage to keep a job for very long, are what you'll see when you put together this 550 piece puzzle. Ken and other friends join this multi-faceted look at Barbie as nurse, bride, ingenue, businesswoman and more.

#01-J0369, $8.95 + 3.95 shipping from Bits & Pieces, 1 Puzzle Place, Stevens Point, WI 54481-7199. (800) 544-7297.

Barbie's Employment History

1959 to present: Fashion Model
1961 to present: Ballerina
1961-64: Stewardess, American Airlines
1964: Nurse
1965: Teacher
1966: Stewardess, Pan American
1973: Flight Attendant, American Airlines
1973 to present: Medical Doctor
1976: Olympic Athlete
1984: Aerobics Instructor
1985: Corporate Executive
1987: Rock Singer
1988: Perfume Designer
1989: Animal Rights Volunteer
1990: Enlistee in All 3 Branches of Military

Wipe That Smile Off Your Face, Soldier!

Women made a contribution in the Kuwait war, but not just in their traditional roles as nurses, Red Cross volunteers and innocent victims. Since there's no reason why only little boys should learn that war is harmless and exciting fun, Barbie has decided to join the martial parade, enlisting as an Air Force pilot, Navy Chief Petty Officer, and an Army Captain with the cooperation of all three services. She's available through PX's for about $25.

GENUINE *Barbie* ® BY MATTEL

"She has the face of an angel, the body of Jamie Lee Curtis, the IQ of a lettuce leaf, but she's a real doll." —Lisa Anderson.

War Criminal Barbie???

Barbie fans were shocked day after day during the summer of 1987 when the headlines screamed:

ACCUSERS CONFRONT BARBIE IN COURT

VICTIM'S SON SAYS HE ALMOST KILLED BARBIE

TWO FORMER RESISTANCE MEMBERS IDENTIFY BARBIE BY EYES AND LAUGH

COURT TOLD OF BARBIE TIE TO U.S. SPIES

BEYOND IDEOLOGY BARBIE'S CRIMES WERE AGAINST HUMANITY

And, finally:

BARBIE CONVICTED AND JAILED FOR LIFE

The headlines were enough to strike terror. And were Ken, Midge and Skipper involved? But closer reading cleared our plastic heroine: the headlines referred instead to one Klaus Barbie, a former Nazi officer.

BARBIE POP QUIZ

1. How old are Barbie and Ken?

2. Did they ever get married? Have they ever been on an unchaperoned overnight outing together?

3. She has a lovely pair of these in the U.S., but in Japan they are even bigger and rounder. What are they?

4. For every Ken doll, how many Barbies are sold? (Hint: same ratio as in "Surf City").

5. The average American worker has to work about one hour to buy a Barbie. How long does it take the average worker in India?

6. What was Barbie's first car?

Answers: 1. Purposely left obscure: usually 7-8 years older than the girl playing with them, according to Mattel. 2. Despite all those wedding outfits, no. Yes, to Europe (tsk-tsk). 3. Her eyes. 4. Two Barbies for every Ken. 5. One month for 236 rupees ($18). 6. A pink 1962 Austin-Healy.

Big As Life But Still Not Anatomically Correct

Life-size retail mannequins play havoc with your sense of reality. They're 6' tall, and clothing is not included, but if your measurements are 38-18-28, your clothes will look fabulous on Barbie.

Goldsmith and Company, 15 West 20th Street, New York, NY 10011. (212) 741-5190. $495.00 + variable shipping.

BARBIE MUGGED

Barbie's been beheaded to bear beverages.

#1811, $16.00 + 3.50 shipping from Clay Art, 1320 Potrero Ave., San Francisco, CA 94110. (800) 252-9555.

Bas-Relief Barbie

Colorful plaque spotlights Barbie's chiseled features.

#1821 Mask $50.00 + 7.50 shipping from Clay Art (see above).

Pin the Ponytailed Barbie...

To your lapel for a touch of '50s nostalgia.

#1806, $7.50 + 3.50 shipping from Clay Art, 1320 Potrero Ave., San Francisco, CA 94110. (800) 252-9555.

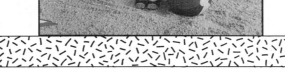

BASEBALL

Some Hits, Many Errors

Did Abner Doubleday invent our national pastime? Legend has it he did one day in 1839. But like many legends, this one seems to be completely wrong.

The Doubleday myth was created by a jingoistic sporting goods manufacturer, A.G. Spaulding, who set out to "prove" that baseball was completely an American invention without roots from any alien European games.

The "evidence" he presented was a letter from one of Doubleday's old Army buddies who said he was there 65 years earlier when Doubleday, in a flash of inspiration, sketched out a diamond and rules in Cooperstown, NY.

The fact that Doubleday was already famous as a captain in the Civil War warmed the cockles of Spaulding's patriotic heart. "It certainly appeals to an American's pride to have had the great national game of Base Ball created and named by a Major General in the US Army," he wrote. Spaulding spent a lot of time and money spreading the "official" story despite massive evidence to the contrary:

• Doubleday was a first year cadet at West Point when he was supposedly in Cooperstown. This was at a time when first year cadets were not allowed off-campus.

• No record before 1905 associated Doubleday and baseball, including his obituaries written in 1893.

• Doubleday was a prolific writer, yet in all of his writings (including two autobiographies and letters to friends) he never even mentioned baseball.

•Doubleday had numerous opportunities to see professional teams play baseball. So how many games did Abner see? Not one.

Conclusion? Just as football grew out of rugby and soccer, baseball was probably not created by anyone but evolved from earlier bat-and-ball games, including and especially the British game of rounders. In 1700, over 130 years before "Base Ball" was supposedly invented, Reverend Thomas Wilson in England wrote disapprovingly of "baseball" games played on Sunday. There are many other written mentions of the game that predate Doubleday.

One last note: even the Baseball Hall of Fame in Cooperstown seems to have doubts. Abner's not in it.

Take Me Out

• **The National Baseball Hall Of Fame And Museum.** Cooperstown is traditionally and probably erroneously believed to be the spot where baseball first began. It's a quaint old 19th century town that revels in its presumed historical significance, and it has a great baseball museum.

P.O. Box 590, Main Street, Cooperstown, NY 13326. (607) 547-9988.

• **Baseball City—Boardwalk and Baseball Amusement Park.** This is the site of the Kansas City Royals training camp. But that's not all—it's also a theme park with baseball-themed rides, games and other attractions.

Intersection of I-4 and U.S. 27, Haines City, FL 33844. (800) 826-1939.

Berra of Good News

Baseball quotes attributed to Yogi (Lawrence Peter) Berra by sportswriters of his time. Who knows, some of these things he might have even said.

• *"It's deja vu all over again."*

• *"You've got to be careful if you don't know where you're going, because you might not get there."*

• *"Baseball is ninety percent mental. The other half is physical."*

• *"You can observe a lot by watching."*

• *"The game's not over 'til it's over."*

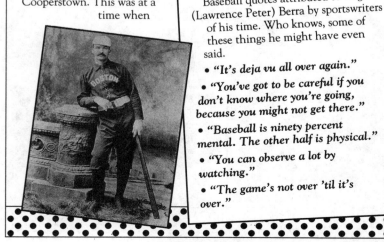

"Abner Doubleday didn't invent baseball. Baseball invented Abner Doubleday."—Harold Peterson

HOME RUN

FOR THE BOOK

- *The Whole Baseball Catalogue* Edited by John Thorn and Bob Carroll. The best overview baseball source around, covering the game and all the pop aspects of it. The business section talks about players' agents, the clubs, and how to get a job in baseball.

  $17.95 + 3.50 shipping. Simon & Schuster, 1230 Avenue of the Americas, New York, NY 10020. (212) 698-7541.

- *Baseball Hall Of Shame* by Bruce Nash and Allan Zullo. A chronicle of baseball's dumbest, foulest and most disgraceful acts. Includes the worst trades, plays, cheaters and scoundrels. Great fun.

  $6.95 + 2.70 shipping. Pocket Books, 1230 Avenue of the Americas, New York, NY 10020. (212) 698-7541.

- *The Physics Of Baseball* by Robert K. Adair. Hey, we wouldn't throw you a curve! This book gives you the inside pitch on why the ball behaves the way it does when it's thrown and batted.

  #10-J8291, $7.95 + 4.25 shipping. Bits & Pieces, 1 Puzzle Place, Stevens Point, WI 54481. (800) JIGSAWS .

- *Baseball Analysis & Reporting System—National League. Baseball Analysis & Reporting System—American League* by Bill Welch. Welch says forget batting average. What's important is how a specific hitter performs against, say, a lefty pitcher throwing low and inside when behind in the count. Number-crunching at its most extreme, for coaches, scouts and hardcore fans.

  $17.95 + 3.50 shipping for each volume from BARS, Box 50, Chillicothe, MO 64601.

Video Pop Hits

Gillette Blue Blade Newsreels. These three black & white videos capture 1950s and '60s excitement as once seen in movie theaters across the country. Hear the original crack of the bat and that memorable narrator's voice. All the heroes, the big plays, the historical moments. *Sports Illustrated* calls it "…baseball that drips with the wax of nostalgia." Let's assume that's a compliment.

#15189. Vol. 1, 1951-1955— Highlights include Joltin' Joe belting his last home run and the Dodgers finally taking a World Series from the Yanks.

#15188. Vol. 2, 1956-1960— Larsen's perfect game and the Dodgers leave Brooklyn.

#15190. Vol. 3, 1961-1967— Willie clubs four HRs in one game and the Cards trump the Yankees.

Each tape $29.95 + 3.90 shipping from Wireless, P.O. Box 64422, St. Paul, MN 55164-0422. (800) 669-9999.

Low Ball, High Ball

- St. Louis Browns owner Bill Veeck pulled a fast one on August 19, 1951, when he sent a 3'7" midget in to pinch hit against the Detroit Tigers. Eddie Gaedel, the shortest player to bat in the major leagues, wore uniform number 1/8. Having a strike zone measured in inches, he walked in four straight pitches.

- Pittsburgh Pirate Doc Ellis once pitched a no-hitter while tripping on LSD. On June 12, 1970 he took acid at noon, unaware that he was supposed to pitch that night.

"I can only remember bits and pieces of the game," he told a reporter 14 years later, "I was psyched. I had a feeling of euphoria." Still, he decided never to do it again. Years later he received treatment for drug-dependency and became coordinator of a Los Angeles anti-drug program.

Song Pitchers Of Record

Baseball's Greatest Hits, Vol. 1 & 2. *Take Me Out To The Ball Game* was written by Jack Norworth and Albert van Tilzer, before either had ever seen a baseball game. This compilation of baseball-related hits includes two versions of this classic (by Doc & Merle Wilson, and Bruce Springsteen) and lots more like Abbott & Costello's *Who's On First*; John Fogerty's *Centerfield*; Steve Goodman's *A Dying Cub Fan's Last Request*; Danny Kaye's *D-O-D-G-E-R-S* ; and *I Love Mickey* by Teresa Brewer (not related to the Milwaukee ball club).

- *Baseball's Greatest Hits: Vol. 1—***#R41H 70710 (cassette) $9.98 or #R21S 70710 (CD) $13.48 + 2.00 shipping.**
- *Baseball's Greatest Hits: Vol. II—***#R41H 70959 (cassette) $9.98 or #R21S 70959 (CD) $13.48 + 2.00 shipping.**

Rhino Records, 2225 Colorado Ave., Santa Monica, CA 90404-3598. (800) 432-0020.

DETROIT TIGERS

J. deBEER & SON, INC. DOUBLE HEADER EST. 1889 ®

Baseball Bloopers

• *Baseball Funny Side Up.* *Baseball Funnies.* Videos of baseball's best blunders, bumbles, battles and bungles. Crazy, wild…just plain fun.

#1371 *Baseball Funny Side Up.* #1285 *Baseball Funnies.* Each tape is $12.98 + 4.20 shipping from Johnson Smith Co., 4514 19th Court East, P.O. Box 25500, Bradenton, FL 34206-5500. (813) 747-2356.

BASEBALL FIRSTS

• First president to throw out a baseball was William Howard Taft.

• First major league night game—May 24, 1935, Crosley Field, Cincinnati.

• The earliest game on record under the Cartwright Rules was on June 19, 1846 in Hoboken, NJ.

• The Cincinnati Red Stockings, the first pro team, went 56-0-1 in their first year of existence in 1869.

Join the Club

National Baseball Fan Association. Members seek to preserve baseball as a sport, not entertainment or TV spectacular. The association represents the fans' point of view to the Commissioner's Office.

President, Robert Godfrey, P.O. Box 4192, Mt. Laurel, NJ 08054. (609) 235-4192.

What's In A Name?

• In Brooklyn in the early 1900s, pedestrians were constantly "dodging" trolley cars. Hence the name Brooklyn Trolley Dodgers, later shortened to just plain Dodgers.

• The Pittsburgh Alleghenies (after the Allegheny River) stole some players from a rival ball club in the 1890s. They were renamed the Pirates.

• When the early 1950s ushered in the McCarthy era and everyone equated "Reds" with "Commies," the Cincinnati Reds officially changed their name to Redlegs. When the patriotic panic died down, they quietly changed back to Reds.

Our Baseball Film Festival

• *It Happens Every Spring* (1949)—A screwball comedy of a mad scientist who develops a no-hit chemical.

• *Fear Strikes Out* (1957)—The Jimmy Piersall story rates as the best baseball film biography.

• *Damn Yankees* (1958)—Funny musical about a fan who deals with the devil to lead his team to the pennant.

• *Bingo Long & His Traveling All-Stars* (1976)—Bright comedy about a Negro Leaguer bucking the exploitive owners by starting his own team.

•*Bull Durham* (1988)—Not necessarily a great film, but one of the most realistic looks at the people and personalities involved in the game.

•*The Natural* (1984)—Robert Redford nearly ascends to heaven as a baseball saint in this fantasy.

• *Eight Men Out* (1988)—Baseball's worst scandals make for a great fact-based film.

• *Field of Dreams* (1988)—Man builds a field for the ghosts of the disgraced players from the previous movie.

• *Bang The Drum Slowly* (1973)—Both the TV play (from the 1950s starring Paul Newman) and the movie are great drama that use baseball as a backdrop.

• *Major League* (1989)—Irreverent look at the game makes this one a lot of fun.

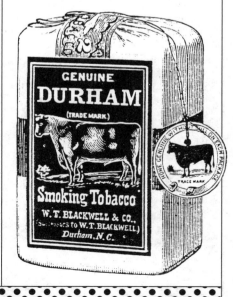

GENUINE DURHAM (TRADE MARK.) Smoking Tobacco W. T. BLACKWELL & CO., Successors to W. T. BLACKWELL, Durham, N.C.

HERE'S THE PITCH!

• The Sultan of Swat pitches cigs on a tin Old Gold advertising sign from the early '30s. "Not a cough in a carload," it says as it shows two poses of the Babe—one swinging, the other taking the "blindfold test." In glorious four color. (#TIN7).

• Or, how about a reproduction of a tin ad sign featuring notorious Shoeless

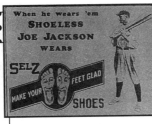

Joe Jackson as he sells Seltz Shoes? Red & black against a yellow background. (#TIN2).

Either tin just $18.00 + 3.50 from:
Kitchen Sink Press
2 Swamp Road
Princeton, WI 54968
(414) 295-6922
FAX (414) 295-6878

Drive You Batty

550 piece jigsaw puzzle crams every shred of baseball memorabilia into the dream room of every collector (and the nightmare of those he lives with).

#01-J0474, $8.95 + 3.95 shipping. Bits & Pieces, 1 Puzzle Pl., Stevens Point, WI 54481-7199. (800) JIGSAWS.

Flip Over Nolan Ryan

Flip Tipp flip book lets you see Nolan Ryan's record-breaking third strike to Ricky Henderson in full-speed, slow-mo, stop action or (if your thumb is fast enough) never-see-the-ball action! Features side view, rear view, stats, tips...even quotes from Ryan himself!

#3711, $8.98 + 2.70 shipping from Johnson Smith Company, 4514 19th St. Court East, P.O. Box 25500, Bradenton, FL 34206-5500. (813) 747-2356 / FAX (813) 746-7896.

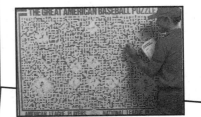

Call The Bullpen

Batting helmet mounted on solid oak base hides touch-tone phone and a miniature brass glove (ball not included.)

#T236 (specify team), $169.00 + 9.95 shipping from Herrington, 3 Symmes Drive, Londonderry, NH 03053. (800) 622-5221.

HEADS UP BALL!

Bobbin' Head Dolls — complete "Golden Era" series features Ruth, Gehrig, "Shoeless" Joe Jackson, Cobb and Wagner.

$174.00 (ppd). MinneMemories, 108 Warren Street, Mankato, MN 56001. (507) 387-6864.

Clap Your Hands... Stamp Your Letters!

Cuba's Fidel Castro actually played in our country's minor leagues—when he didn't get into the majors, he went home and started a revolution.

Throughout Latin America baseball is played and appreciated with a passion reflected in these postage stamps.

• Set of 80 baseball postage stamps from the country of (post-invasion) Grenada commemorates baseball's best including 30 Hall of Famers. Complete with 60 page hardcover album detailing the history of the game, its teams and its stars.

#3889, $29.98 + 4.95 shipping.

• First day cover Nolan Ryan stamp from St. Vincent.

#1790, $7.98 + 2.70 shipping from Johnson Smith Company, 4514 19th St. Court East, P.O. Box 25500, Bradenton, FL 34206-5500. (813) 747-2356 / FAX (813) 746-7896.

3 Up, 4 Across

Giant, wall-size crossword puzzle will challenge your knowledge of baseball with over 1450 clues about baseball's greatest plays, players and managers. 58" x 42".

#1626, $9.98 + 2.00 from The Lighter Side, 4514 19th Court East, P.O. Box 25600, Bradenton, FL 34206-5600. Phone: (813) 747-2356.

Fields of Dreams
Rotisserie Baseball & Fantasy Camps

What red-blooded American hasn't dreamed of playing in the majors? Or at least, as middle age sets in, of owning his or her own baseball team?

Well, you can live out your own field of dreams in organized fantasy. If you're a closet Willie Mays, there's a baseball camp where you can be coached by and play against some of the best pro ball players (see below). But for latent George Steinbrenners, there's Rotisserie Baseball.

Rotisserie Baseball? Named that because it began in a restaurant that no longer exists named *La Rotisserie Française* in New York. A group of baseball fanatics met there to lament that they could run a major league team much better than the real owners, except for one minor detail—buying a franchise costs close to $100 million.

They decided to do the next best thing. They invented their own game, played with real statistics on paper instead of a diamond.

The game took off like wildfire. About 2 million play, including such celebs as Mario Cuomo, Larry King, Bryant Gumbel and Wayne Gretzky.

How do you play? Here's the short version: You and your fellow league "owners" draft real baseball players onto your team, after which you trade, fire and otherwise act like boorish baseball tycoons. As the real baseball season gets under way, you keep track of your players' real-life statistics.

The better your players do in real-life, the better your fantasy team does in relation to the other fantasy teams. But if your players have a real-life injury, slump or return to the minors mid-season, you may find yourself at the bottom of the league and looking for a Billy Martin to kick around.

If you want to know more about the origin of the game as told by its inventors, read the bible of the sport: *Rotisserie League Baseball (The Official Rule Book)*, edited by Glen Waggoner & Robert Sklar.

$12.95 + 2.50 shipping. Bantam Books, 666 Fifth Ave., New York, NY 10103.

Fantasy Camps

Some ex-major leaguers (such as Jim Rice, Bucky Dent and Rod Carew) have their own baseball schools for serious students of the game. But if you're just a fan with a fantasy, check out a baseball camp.

At most camps you get instruction, training and games with some of baseball's best. You also get a team photo, room and board, uniform, autographed ball, and sometimes even a videotape of your best (and worst) moments on the field, all for the price of a good used car. Here are two of the better ones.

• **Sportworld.** Runs camps for the SF Giants, Milwaukee Brewers, Minnesota Twins, San Diego Padres and others.
5764 Paradise Drive, Suite 7, Corte Madera, CA 94925. (415) 924-8725.

• **Mickey Mantle/Whitey Ford Fantasy Baseball Camp.** How could you go wrong with those names?
P.O. Box 68, Grayson, KY 41143-0068. (606) 474-6976.

What's The Score?

If you do your own Fantasy League stats, there are a lot of sources like *USA Today*, or its *Baseball Weekly* ($35 a year from PO Box 4209, Silver Spring, MD 20914. (800) 872-1415).

If you have a computer, you can even purchase software that compiles team stats.

But if you want to avoid all that work (did you ever see *Steinbrenner* do his own stats?) there are companies that'll do it for you each week.

• **Rotisserie League Stats.** Owned by the guys who invented the game, this company sends weekly stats by mail or fax. Fee: $675 *per league* for the season.
211 West 92nd St., Box 9, New York, NY 10025. (212) 496-8098.

• **Compu-Stat Sports.** One of the biggest and best. Reports by modem or mail. Fee: $40 *per team* per season.
P.O. Box 1264, Solana Beach, CA 92075. (800) 456-3698.

Speed Thrills

Radar Gun. This'll clock a baseball (or any moving object) from up to 100 yards away. Displays speed on a digital readout up to 250 mph. But what if you throw faster than 250 mph? Call the Yankees!
33850H $650.00 from Hammacher Schlemmer, 9180 Le Saint Drive, Fairfield, OH 45014. (800) 543-3366.

Jose Canseco gets up to $60,000 to show up and sign his name for 3 hours at baseball shows.

10 OF THE WORLD'S BEST BASEBALL PLAYERS

1. BABE RUTH
2. LOU GEHRIG
3. TY COBB
4. WILLIE MAYS
5.
6. MICKEY MANTLE
7. JOE DIMAGGIO
8. HANK AARON
9. TED WILLIAMS
10. HONUS WAGNER

YOUR NAME HERE

You're Not Number One!

Nobody would believe that you're the best ball player of all time. But they might believe that you're number five! 7 x 5 inch plaque.

#P1727 Baseball Plaque (specify name for engraving), $7.98 + 3.50 shipping from Funny Side Up, 425 Stump Road North Wales, PA 19454. (215) 361-5130.

Capping It Off

Top off your baseball look with a traditional old-timers' 100% wool cap featuring embroidered team graphics. All your favorites: the St. Louis Browns, Washington Senators, Philadelphia Athletics, Boston Braves and others. Several sizes available to fit even the swellest of heads.

#B312 Old Timers Cap, $22.99 + 4.95 shipping from Athletic Supply Catalog 10812 Alder Circle, Dallas, TX 75238. (800) 635-GIFT or (214) 348-3600.

For Your Belfry

Personalize any name into the barrel of this authentic white ash Louisville Slugger, up to 20 characters (including spaces). Specify child size 28, 29, 30 or 31, or adult size 32, 33, 34 or 35 (inches).

#16096 Adult, $39.50 or #16097 Little League, $36.00. Add 9.95 shipping from Wireless, P.O. Box 64422, Saint Paul, MN 55164-0422. (800) 669-9999.

Virtual Baseball

• **Computer Game.** The Earl Weaver Baseball Game allows you to manage a team just like in the big leagues.

$29.99 + 5.00 from: Egghead Software, 22011 SE 51st Street, Issaquah, WA 98027-7004. (800) EGGHEAD / FAX (206) 391-0880.

• **VCR Game.** Manage your own team with Grand Slam VCR Baseball. All the excitement and unpredictability of a real game. Pick your team, change pitchers, bunt, steal, pinch hit! For 1 or 2 players. VHS only.

#1362 VCR Baseball, $22.98 + 4.95 shipping from Johnson Smith Company, 4514 19th St. Court East, P.O. Box 25500, Bradenton, FL 34206-5500. (813) 747-2356 / FAX (813) 746-7896.

New Jerseys

Exact replicas of old-time home jerseys worn by the White Sox, Cubs and N.Y. Yankees. Officially licensed.

• **#37711H. 1919 Chicago White Sox with three-quarter length sleeve.**

• **#37710H. 1952 Yankees with Mickey's #7.**

• **#37709H. 1969 Chicago Cubs with Ernie ("Let's Play Two") Banks' #14.**

Men's sizes: Medium (38 to 40), Large (42 to 44), Extra Large (46 to 48). 35% wool/65% acrylic. $179.95 each + 4.00 shipping from Hammacher Schlemmer, 9180 Le Saint Drive, Fairfield, OH 45014. (800) 543-3366.

Memorabilia, Cards and Collectibles

Did moms everywhere really throw away baseball cards and comic books? Or are they hoarding them, waiting for the right moment to dump them on the market and escape to a villa in Spain?

Time has a way of changing a hobby. Once people collected baseball memorabilia mainly for memories and as a way to get closer to the game. These days, greed has taken over: "investing" has replaced "collecting" for a lot of people, which means other greedy people have gotten involved too: card counterfeiters, signature forgers and worse.

It's easy even for experts to be taken in,

especially when they let their greed blind them to their own good sense. If the objects or prices are too good to be true, walk away.

Not to be outdone, sports magazines like *Sporting Life* and *Sporting News* jumped in, issuing cards as subscription incentives. Candy companies (even Cracker Jacks) joined in too.

In 1921 the cards moved from being a sales incentive to a product in its own right. You could now buy cards from vending machines.

Although we now think of cards and gum as natural companions, gum didn't rear its sticky head until 1939, when a company named Gum, Inc. introduced "Play Ball" brand, and became a major force in the marketplace.

World War II temporarily wiped out both cards and gum because the war effort had other uses for paper and rubber. Afterward, Gum, Inc. became Bowman and cornered the card market until 1952 when a new kid named Topps appeared. The two companies battled for a few years with Topps beating and eventually buying Bowman in 1955.

Post cereal issued cards on the backs of their boxes from 1961 to 1963. Also in 1963, Fleer issued a set of cards and Topps sued, claiming exclusive rights.

When a Federal court ruled against them in 1981, the floodgates were open. There are now plenty of card companies, most notably SportFlics (3D cards), Dunruss, Score and Upper Deck.

Baseball Card History

The first baseball cards didn't appear in bubble gum, but in packs of cigarettes with names like Gypsy Queen, Dog's Head and Old Judge, distributed by Goodwin & Co. This was back in 1887. The cards were so popular that a lot of the other cigarette manufacturers also jumped on the bandwagon.

Life was good for early card collectors until the leading tobacco companies merged. Since the new monopoly no longer needed gimmicks to stimulate sales, the cards disappeared.

Then some upstart cigarette companies started importing

Turkish tobacco to the American market, challenging the domestic monopoly. As competition heated up, someone got the bright (if not too original) idea to revive baseball cards to boost sales.

Between 1909 and 1912 dozens of different sets were issued in the tobacco wars. The most famous of these sets was the American Tobacco Company's T-206 series that included what has become the most valuable baseball card of all time—the Honus Wagner card.

PICK A CARD...ANY CARD

Investing in cards is like investing in the stock market—you gotta buy 'em low and sell 'em high. Most investors make only modest profits if any.

One strategy that works is to collect rookie cards and hope the players hang on long enough to prove their greatness. If you had gotten these for a few pennies way back when, look what you'd have now:

• **1954 Topps, Hank Aaron**: $1350

• **1968 Topps, Nolan Ryan**: $1200

• **1980 Topps, Rickey Henderson**: $180

• **1986 Donruss, Jose Canseco**: $125

• **1910 ATC, Honus Wagner**: one sold in early 1991 for $451,000 to a partnership that included hockey great Wayne Gretsky.

Why is the Wagner valued so highly? Because they were pulled from circulation almost as soon as they were issued. They had come from a tobacco company. Wagner didn't smoke and didn't want to endorse the filthy habit (besides, the company hadn't paid any royalties). So, there are probably fewer than 50 genuine ones (and plenty of copies) in existence.

BUCK MARTINEZ CATCHER

Brewers
BUCK MARTINEZ CATCHER

Errors Off The Field

Even baseball card companies make mistakes. Some of the most famous goofs include:

• Aurelio Rodriguez's 1969 card which really portrays the bat boy.

• Both of Claude Raymond's 1966 and 1967 cards show him with his fly open.

• Reversing negatives is a common mistake (see above). In 1982, Fleer did that on card #576 showing righty pitcher John Littlefield pitching lefty. It's now worth $150.

• In 1989, someone played a joke on Billy Ripken and caused a furor in the industry. Fleer's card #616 (left) showed an obscenity ("Fuck Face") scrawled on the bottom of Ripken's bat handle. Fleer made three attempts to correct the card. One variation (obscenity whited out) sells for even more than the original error card ($20-150).

BILL RIPKEN
SECOND BASE

Reading the Cards

• *Beckett Baseball Card Monthly.* If you want to know what most baseball card shops are going to charge you for a particular card, look it up in this monthly magazine. Dr. James Beckett also publishes an annual guide, but the magazine is better since market prices fluctuate regularly. This glossy guide also gives a reader's forum, storage tips and techniques, player profiles, errors and variations department and card show calendar.

$19.95 (12 issues). 4887 Alpha Rd., Suite 200, Dallas, TX 75244. (214) 991-6657.

• *Sports Collectors Digest.* Krause publishes excellent books and magazines—anything and everything for the memorabilia collector of any sport. The *Digest* has news and features, of course, but also a price guide, a convention calendar and an abundant ad section, which the magazine monitors for truthfulness, reliability and responsiveness to customers.

$32.95 (52 issues) from Krause Publications, 700 E. State St., Iola, WI 54990. (715) 445-2214.

GOOD REPUTATION

Buying cards is a risky business, so buy from someone who is reputable. Here are a couple we've consistently heard good things about.

• **The Score Board, Inc.** These folks average around 200 buyers a day. You can purchase cards, autographed bats and balls, used uniforms...practically everything for the serious collector. And you'll also get a Certificate of Authenticity they stand behind.

100 Dobbs Lane, Suite 206, Cherry Hill, NJ 08034. (800) 327-4145.

•Alan "Mr. Mint" Rosen is a noted hobbyist who collects, buys and sells a wide range of memorabilia materials— just about anything sports-related such as autographed balls, bats, jerseys, pins, plaques, programs, ticket stubs, etc.

70l Chestnut Ridge Road, Montvale, NJ 07645. (201) 307-0700 / FAX (201) 307-1653.

New Old Cards

Reproductions of 1888 tobacco cards originally produced by Allen & Ginter's, Old Judge and Gypsy Queen cigarettes are framed and ready for display. Set of 24 cards capture every detail of the original watercolor paintings and are mounted between panes of glass to exhibit the reverse sides. Hardwood frame.

#15420, $95.00 + 8.50 shipping from: Signals
P.O. Box 64428
St. Paul, MN 55164-0428
(800) 669-9696.

BATHROOMS

What do bathrooms have to do with popular culture? Plenty. Anything taboo becomes more powerful in the minds of the populace. Obsessions with bathrooms and what takes place there are as old as civilization. There is a whole secret culture that thrives inside that little room, so close the door, sit down, and let's get down to business.

First Flush of Civilization

Primitive man, aware that his body waste was a potentially toxic thing, did his business right into the rivers and streams that carried his pollutants away—at least to the next village.

Some historians believe that it was 10,000 years ago in Scotland that the first crude plumbing systems to carry waste away from dwellings appeared, allowing humans to safely relieve themselves indoors for the first time in history. This latrine-system was a series of drains that led from each village hut to the nearest running water source.

The oldest surviving toilet with running water was excavated at Mohenjo-Daro in India, dating back to the period 3250-2750 BC.

Queen Elizabeth in 1596 allowed her godson, Sir John Harrington, to install his own invention, a flush toilet, in her living quarters. Unfortunately, Harrington then wrote a small book

about it, turning it into the butt of local jokes. The incensed Queen banished her godson for several months; his invention, now a source of humiliation, fell into disuse.

In 1775, Alexander Cumming improved upon Harrington's design, creating a "stink trap" in the soil pipe to prevent waste odors from lingering in the room. Still, it was more than 100 years before it would replace the chamber pot and become a common fixture in British and American bathrooms.

Incidentally, the often-repeated story about a "Thomas Crapper" inventing the toilet is a hoax perpetrated by author Wallace Reyburn who wrote a mock biography in 1969. His next book was also a hoax—a biography of the supposed inventor of the bra, "Otto Titzling."

Bathroom Etiquette

The more "civilized" we get, the more complicated our etiquette about bodily functions becomes.

In the Middle Ages, it was sufficient to step "an arrow's flight" distance into the gardens before doing what had to be done. But royalty thought this unnecessary—one English noble was appalled that the visiting king and retinue defecated wherever they chose throughout his castle. During a conversation with a young noblewoman, he was surprised to hear tinkling water and see a puddle spreading across his floor from beneath her long dress.

One of history's earliest etiquette books, by Erasmus of Rotterdam (1465-1536), advised, concerning gas, "let a cough hide the explosive sound."

Though officially banned as early as 1395 in Paris, it was the centuries-long practice throughout Europe to empty bedpans from high windows into the street. Oft-ignored etiquette demanded that emptiers first shout the classic warning "Gardez l'eau!" In Edinburgh you could hire a guide to walk ahead and shout "Haud your hand!" to people in the windows above.

LIBERTY BELL TOILET

SUPERFINE WIRE HOOK
PURE MANILLA TISSUE

Bathology Thru the Ages

It wasn't long after humanity quit its nomadic ways that organized bathing began. By 3000 BC, terra cotta plumbing systems for bathtubs were common in the Near East, and by 2000 BC wealthy Minoans had hot and cold running bath water.

The Egyptians continued to perfect bathroom technology, with copper pipes carrying the water to their hot and cold taps. Bathing and general bodily cleanliness were an integral part of daily life, as well as a religious practice.

The Romans in the 2nd Century BC were the first to turn bathing into a social activity. The Baths of Caracalla, for example, would have rivalled today's most luxurious health clubs, with gardens, shops, libraries, exercise rooms and even recital lounges with hot and cold running poetry. The baths could pamper up to 2,500 people at a time.

By AD 500, Barbarians had invaded and destroyed most of the Roman Empire, including its luxurious baths. Even worse, Christianity was flourishing. Forget "cleanliness is next to Godliness"—the Church preached the mortification of the flesh. To uncover your festering skin, even to bathe it, was to invite sin.

The rich in Europe dowsed themselves in perfume and the poor stank. And nearly everyone died of sanitation-related diseases.

EUPHEMISMS

- the smallest room in the house
- the john
- the jane
- the privy
- the powder room
- the facility
- the necessary
- the throne room
- the bank
- the loo
- the W.C.
- "I'm gonna see a man about a horse..."
- the jake
- the hopper
- the can
- the throne
- the porcelain bus
- the toidy
- the potty
- the commode
- the library

Toilet Paper

The first packaged toilet paper in 1857, consisting of a packet of individual sheets, was the brainstorm of Joseph Gayetty, an American. It sold poorly and was soon removed from store shelves. After all, who needed newfangled bathroom tissue when everybody's privy was stocked with an ample supply of Sears catalogs?

In 1879, Englishman Walter Alcock invented the perforated toilet tissue roll, but marketing his unmentionable invention in the Victorian era was nearly impossible, and he struggled for over a decade to get it accepted by the public.

In the same year, brothers Edward and Clarence Scott began a paper products company in Philadelphia, and they started successfully marketing toilet paper due to lucky timing: it was a slightly less inhibited time.

It was an era when major American cities were busy laying down elaborate public sewer systems and most new buildings boasted complete indoor plumbing. Hotels wanted to offer their guests more luxury than newspapers and catalogs, and they welcomed the Scott brothers' new product.

Guests used the new product and wanted it for their homes. The Scotts' fortunes literally rolled in from their indispensable, readily disposable and totally unreusable commodity.

The Romans designed vomitoriums, rooms for publically practicing socially sanctioned bulimia.

History's first recorded toothpaste, applied to the teeth with frayed twigs, was an Egyptian mixture of ground pumice and wine.

The early Romans brushed their teeth with human urine, and also used it as a mouthwash. They particularly prized costly imported Portuguese urine for its strength—a factor more attributable to evaporation on the long, overland route to Rome than to any particular ethnic characteristics.

Urine was an active component in toothpastes and mouthwashes until well into the eighteenth century—the ammonia molecules were what gave it its cleansing power. Ammonia continues to be an ingredient in many modern dentifrices, though manufactured in the laboratory, not the lavatory.

Fluoride toothpaste is a modern invention, but the effect of fluoride on cavities was noted as early as 1802. The soil and water in Naples, Italy then had a very high fluoride content and dentists there noticed that while their patients' teeth appeared to be stained with curious

LOOK MA, NO CAVITIES

R   L

brown spots, they were almost cavity-free. By the 1840s, both Italians and French sucked honey-flavored fluoride lozenges to prevent tooth decay.

The United States began trials with fluoridated drinking water in 1915, although right-wing fanatics warned as late as the 1970s, that it was a communist plot to produce a generation of idiots.

In retrospect, maybe they were right?

The Toothbrush

"Chew sticks," twigs with one end frayed into soft bristles, have been found in Egyptian tombs dating from about 3000 BC.

The first modern bristled toothbrush originated in China around 1498. The bristles were plucked from hogs from China's colder regions, where the hairs grew firmer and stouter, and were set into handles of bone or bamboo.

A few fifteenth century Europeans, when they cleaned their teeth at all, used soft horsehair bristle brushes, but most preferred a quill or carved pick as the Romans had used.

The discovery of nylon by Du Pont chemists in 1938 revolutionized the toothbrush industry. Doctor West's Miracle Tuft Toothbrush was first marketed that year, but its stiffness was a hazard to the gums. It wasn't until the early 1950s that they developed a soft, safe nylon bristle.

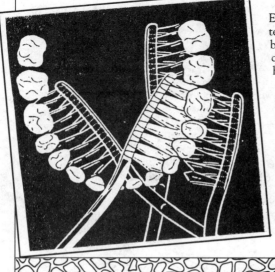

Float Alone

Soap has gone in and out of vogue depending on the prevailing religious climate, from the time the Hittites first washed their hands with the ashes of the soapwort plant four thousand years ago. In the 6th Century BC, Phoenicians boiled goat fat, water and ash. They let excess liquid evaporate, leaving a waxy solid "cake"—the first true soap.

The first floating soap was the result of an accident at the Procter and Gamble plant in 1881. The machinery that whipped air into the viscous mixture of Ivory soap was allowed to run too long. The worker in charge, either unaware or trying to conceal his negligence, sent the batch on to be packaged.

Almost immediately, the company

was deluged with letters from delighted customers who loved the soap that couldn't get lost at the murky bottom of the tub. Harley Procter and James Gamble decided to incorporate the accident into the design.

Procter said he received the name "Ivory" as a divine inspiration while reading Psalms 45:8—"All thy garments smell of myrrh, and aloes, and cassia, and out of the ivory palaces whereby they have made thee glad."

Toothbrushing was uncommon in the U.S. until World War II, when the armed forces issued toothbrushes to all new recruits.

RAZORS

Flint, shells, and hammered metal shaved our early ancestors. The Greeks shaved daily—the Romans thought it sissified. They shaved only when at war because a beard could be grabbed by the enemy.

In the colonial Americas, men plucked out their beard hairs one by one with clam shell tweezers. Yow! The French invented the safety razor, a metal guard placed along the blade to prevent it from mortally slicing flesh. The modern T-shaped razor was an American invention, appearing sometime in the 1880s.

King Gillette—yes, that was his real name—invented the disposable razor blade in 1895. When young,

he worked for William Painter, the inventor of the bottle cap, who shared the secret of his own success: come up with something that can only be used once before being thrown away. For years Gillette imagined disposable replacements for everything he saw.

One morning his eyes were opened—"I found my razor not only dull, but beyond the point of successful stropping…As I stood there with the razor in my hand, my eyes resting on it lightly as a bird settling down on its nest, the Gillette razor was born." By 1906, American men had purchased a half million blades, and Gillette's face on the package became one of the most familiar in the world.

Hair Today…

Shampoo, first commercially manufactured in Germany, was not widely available outside hair salons before the 1920s. The modern American shampoo industry was born because of John Breck's obsession with his impending baldness. His concoctions, designed to stop hair loss, became popular for their superb cleansing abilities even with consumers who still had their hair.

Kleenex

The disposable tissue has firmly found its place in our bathrooms (and, since the advent of "designer" packaging, any other room as well), but it was originally developed as a cotton surgical bandage substitute during World War I.

After the war, Kimberly-Clarke's warehouses were still heavily stocked with the stuff so the company set out to promote "Cellucotton" as a cold cream remover. The ads featured film celebrities and star-smitten women bought it.

Men discovered the "cellucotton" in the bathroom and just blew their noses on it. A confused and confusing influx of consumer inquiries prompted the manufacturer to run a test-marketing campaign in Peoria, Illinois. Consumers were exposed to alternative headlines: "We pay [a free box of tissue] to prove Kleenex is wonderful for handkerchiefs," and "We pay to prove there is no way like Kleenex to remove cold cream."

61% of the coupons redeemed were from the handkerchief ad. Kimberly-Clarke decided that the response was nothing to sneeze at, and Kleenex found its true calling as a disposable handkerchief.

The first electric toothbrush was developed and tested on dogs, who reportedly learned to enjoy the experience.

PITTED BATTLE

Every civilization since the dawn of history has left a record of its efforts to eradicate body odor, but none of the perfumed and spiced preparations smeared on underarms managed to zero in on the source of the problem until Mum antiperspirant came out in 1888. Its main ingredient, zinc, worked simply—it blocked the sweat glands, depriving underarm bacteria of the damp environment it needed.

Everdry, Hush and the melodiously named Odo-Ro-No debuted soon after Mum. These were marketed exclusively to women.

It wasn't until the 1930s that men became the focus of the advertisers' persuasion. As the product became gender diversified, the names evolved from demure terms of denial such as Hush and Secret, to aggressive acknowledgements like Ban and Right Guard.

Bathrooms on the Big Screen

• **The Tingler** (1959). Not even Mr. Clean could cope with the amount of blood spilled in this classic "man trapped in the bathroom" scene.

• **Psycho** (1960). This flick made many think twice about taking showers and staying in small motels.

• **They Came From Within** (1975). In a cheap play on the old "alligators in New York sewers" myth, director David Cronenberg's monsters come crashing up through commodes in an ill-fated condominium complex.

• **Fun with Dick and Jane** (1977). This may be the first American film to show someone actually using the bathroom for its intended purpose. Jane Fonda relieves herself matter-of-factly in this farce about middle-class American values.

• **The Shining** (1980). Shelly Duvall hides from her psychotic husband, Jack Nicholson, in the bathroom of the large hotel they're caretaking. He breaks the door down with an axe and an unforgettable: "Heeeeere's Johnny!"

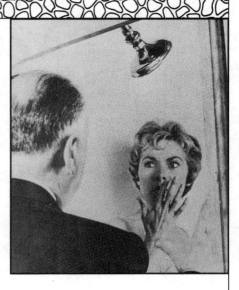

• **Arthur** (1981). While Dudley Moore is cavorting with a casual friend in the tub, his droll butler John Gielgud inquires solicitously: "Would you like me to hold your dick, sir?"

• **Lethal Weapon 2** (1989). A "piss or get off the pot" dilemma for the man poised on a toilet rigged to explode.

Bathrooms on the Tube

All in the Family got credit for breaking the tube toilet-taboo by incorporating the sound effects of a flushing toilet into the script. But the very first program really to "come out of the water closet" was *Leave It to Beaver.*

It took the network weeks to get up the nerve to air the episode about Wally and the Beav surreptitiously adopting a pet alligator and keeping him in their toilet's water tank. Network execs postponed it from the first show of the season to the fourth. Afterward, the execs were surprised that viewers didn't seem to mind.

Still, not much changed after this ground-breaking occurrence. Donna Reed never scrubbed her toilet bowl, Hoss Cartwright never got down off his horse to take a leak in the sagebrush, and advertising—even of toilet products—was typically as unreal as the Tidy Bowl Man floating in a tiny toilet boat.

A recent proctology study found that people who read on the toilet get more hemorrhoids.

Nothing Like a Good Bathroom Read

• *Uncle John's Bathroom Reader, Vols. 1, 2, 3, 4* by The Bathroom Readers' Institute. A grab bag of tidbits and essays arranged not only by category but by length.

Each volume $8.95 + 1.50 shipping. St. Martin's Press, 175 5th Ave. New York, NY 10010. (800) 221-7945.

• *The Specialist* by Charles (Chic) Sale. Originally written in 1929, this enormously funny story of Lem Putt, master privy builder, has sold over 2 1/2 million copies!

#A-66X, $5.00 + $2.50 shipping. Vestal Press, 320 N. Jensen Road, P.O. Box 97, Vestal, NY 13851. (607) 797-4872.

• *Vanishing American Outhouses* by Ronald S. Barlow. Lavishly photographed, the book covers lots of outhouse information and trivia.

#A-23X, $15.95 + 2.50 shipping. Vestal Press, 320 N. Jensen Road, PO Box 97, Vestal, NY 13851. (607) 797-4872.

Toity Tunes

"A musical novelty! Makes your toilet paper sing!" reads the colorful hang tag. And the battery is INCLUDED! This ingenious little electronic device slips inside the toilet paper roll. When you pull the tissue, a mosquito orchestra starts playing one of these selections: *Christmas Medley, Happy Birthday,* or *The Star Spangled Banner*— potentially a real mess since true patriots will leap to their feet.

#T2682 *Christmas*; #T2683 *Birthday*; #T2684 *Star Spangled Banner*, each $4.98 + 3.50 shipping from Funny Side Up, 425 Stump Rd., N. Wales, PA 19454. (215) 361-5130.

Kitschy Curios

Add a bit of wicker whimsy to your powder room with these plaques that feature bathroom fixtures. Ceramic flush box and pedestal sink actually have working parts, brass-toned fittings and chain pull. And, yes! The lid opens! 7 x 4-3/4-inches.

#5944 Blue Plaque Set or #8234 Pink, $9.98 + 3.99 shipping each from Taylor Gifts, 355 E. Conestoga Road, P.O. Box 206, Wayne, PA 19087-0206. (215) 789-7007.

Paeon to the Animal World

Each Tinkle Time Targets pack contains 45 colorful, flushable, non-staining targets. Just float one in the bowl and fire away. Only one complaint: the targets are all animals like kittens, puppies, tropical fish, ducks, cows—are they subliminally supporting violence against animals, or bestiality? The intention is to train kids to aim.

#G225, $4.95 + 2.50 shipping. The Right Start Catalog, 5334 Sterling Center Drive, Westlake Village, CA 91361. (800) 548-8531.

TALKING TISSUE

Well, no, the tissue doesn't actually talk. But with this thing and a 9-volt battery (not included), you can make your toilet paper holder say some pretty surprising things. Pop it in before you have guests (it'll wear thin with your family if you leave it on all the time). When they pull on the roll they'll trigger fire alarms and electronic voices saying cute things like "Stinky, Stinky," and "Yuk, Yuk."

#T2224, $19.98 + 4.95 shipping from Funny Side Up, 425 Stump Road, North Wales, PA 19454. (215) 361-5130.

KINDLY FLUSH TOILET AFTER EACH USE ~ EXCEPT ~ WHEN TRAIN IS STANDING IN STATION

Stop Station Stink

Reproduction of Pullman train car sign that politely reminds you to flush but not while train is "standing in station." Looks like brass, feels like brass, but it's just plain ol' metal. Measures 5 x 7-inches and has self-adhesive backing.

#A-99X, $4.75 + 2.50 shipping from Vestal Press, 320 N. Jensen Road, P.O. Box 97, Vestal, NY 13851-0097. (607) 797-4872 / FAX (607) 797-4898.

Bantam Bath Set

Perfect for doll houses or pint-sized pets, these miniature bath items are reminiscent of old-fashioned, turn-of-the-century "facilities."

#2869-1 Toothpaste/Brushes.......$3.29
#3173-1 Sink/Tub/Toilet............$11.98
#3276-1 Facial Tissue.................$0.98
#3294-1 Medicine Cabinet...........$3.49
#3066-1 His/Her Towels...............$2.98
#3228-1 Radiator.......................$2.19
#3267-1 Toilet Tissue..................$1.89
#3068-1 Tissue/Towel Rod...........$3.49
#3090-1 Towel Rack....................$7.98
#3273-1 Soap Dish......................$1.98

For orders up to $8.00 add $1.95 shipping; $8.01 to $15.00 add $2.95 shipping. ALL of the above items for just $40.25 + $4.95 shipping. Miles Kimball, 41 West Eighth Avenue, Oshkosh, WI 54906.

Talking Toilet

"Hey, I'm working down here!" is just one of the expressions your unsuspecting guests will hear from the deep recesses of your toilet when they sit down. Each phrase is accompanied by maniacal laughter. Fits all toilets and operates on 1 "C" battery (not included).

#T272 Talking Toilet, $12.98 + $3.95 shipping from Funny Side Up, 425 Stump Road, North Wales, PA 19454. (215) 361-5130.

Laughable Looks

Mirror, mirror in my hand...who's the ugliest in the land? Your friends are and this mirror'll tell 'em so because when they pick it up, it'll laugh at them! No longer will those laugh lines seem so funny!

#2320 Laugh Mirror, $14.98 + 4.20 shipping from Johnson Smith Co., P.O. Box 25500, Bradenton, FL 34206-5500. (813) 747-2356.

Pinko Paper Poster

Bolsheviks in the bathroom? Could terrible towels really lead to a Red revolt? That's what Scott Tissue would have you believe back in the '30s. This red, black and white ad urged companies to provide quality paper towels to keep workers happy and Republican.

#4, Reprint Poster, $7.00 postpaid. Northern Sun Merchandising, 2916 E. Lake Street, Minneapolis, MN 55406. (612) 729-2001.

PILGRIMAGE

The Unknown Museum. You can see the largest collection of toilet paper from around the world at this quirky museum. Call for an appointment because it never seems to stay in one place too long. Still, it somehow thrives as it moves from storefront to house to warehouse and back. A huge volume of stuff, most of which is not bathroom-related. Drop them a line and tell 'em you want to visit — they'll tell you where they'll be then.

The Unknown Museum, PO Box 1551, Mill Valley, CA 94942.

BATMAN

Lonely Days, Dark Knights

He had the coolest costume and car of all the superheroes. And even better, he was a bat-man, so he got to stay up all night long. So while kids played Superman during the day, at night they played Batman.

Artist Bob Kane and writer Bill Finger were both in their early 20s when D.C. Comics asked Kane to come up with a superhero crimefighter. Taking inspiration from Zorro, the Phantom, the Shadow, and Leonardo da Vinci's inventive drawings of human flight, Kane came up with the bat figure and Finger scripted the first stories.

Batman made his debut in Detective Comics #27 and became an instant hit. In subsequent issues, Robin and all the bizarre villains appeared.

In 1954, the comics industry set up the Comics Code Authority in reaction to criticism that comics were undermining the morals of youth. In *Seduction of the Innocent,* author Frederic Wertham claimed that Batman and Robin were "a wish dream of two homosexuals living together." The Dark Knight toned down his vigilante action and started fighting more aliens from other worlds.

In 1966, Batmania first reared its wings when Adam West and Burt Ward starred in the campy twice-weekly TV show that featured celebrity guests like Joan Collins, Vincent Price, Bruce Lee, Tallulah Bankhead, Milton Berle, Pierre Salinger, and Liberace. The Batman theme, recorded by dozens of groups, made the top 10.

Batmania faded away for a few decades. Then in 1986, Frank Miller's book, *The Dark Knight Returns,* set in the future with a middle-aged Batman, made the *New York Times* bestseller list and introduced another Robin— a young woman.

In 1988 DC Comics conducted a comic book phone-in poll to decide whether Robin survived a warehouse explosion. The vote was 5,343 to 5,271 against letting Robin live.

A year later, nobody ever had a bigger 50th birthday party. The hype of the $30 million movie sent Batman surfing on a wave of popularity again.

Batfacts

• In a survey taken just before the Batman movie's release, Americans rated their favorite cartoon and comic characters. Surprisingly, Batman was rated a real dud — about as popular as Moon Mullins, Beany & Cecil and the Incredible Hulk; slightly less popular than Deputy Dawg, Betty Boop, and Chicken Little; and *four times* less popular than the California Raisins.

• But it was a different story among hard core comics readers. Batman was voted "Favorite Character" by the *Comics Buyer's Guide* Fan Awards for three years in a row in the late 1980s.

• Michael Keaton was 37 when he played Batman in the 1989 movie — the same age that Adam West was when he began playing Batman on TV.

• Batman's world sometimes got a little crowded. Besides Robin there were also Batwoman, Bat-Girl, Ace the Bat-Hound, and Bat-Mite, a comic elf-like creature from another dimension.

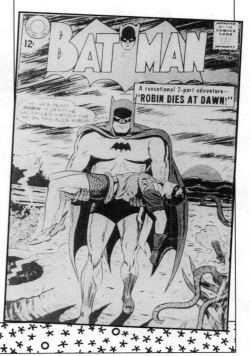

Batman has been published in more than 20 languages and in over 45 countries.

Batquotes

"The 'Batman,' a mysterious and adventurous figure, fighting for righteousness and apprehending the wrongdoer, in his lone battle against the evil forces of society…His identity remains unknown!"

— From Batman's debut issue, Detective Comics #27, May, 1939.

"Criminals are a superstitious, cowardly lot. My disguise must be able to strike terror into their hearts. I must become a creature of the night— dark, terrible…A BAT! That's IT! It's an OMEN! I shall become a BAT!"

— Batman, In Detective Comics #33, November 1939

"He's purely urban. The city is his playground, his theater. He gets down and dirty and patrols the back alleys. Superman is always flying above the crowd; Batman is down in it in the shadows and darkness."

— Mark Cotta Vaz, author of *Tales of The Dark Knight: Batman's First 50 Years.*

[Batman and Robin are hanging precariously over a cauldron of boiling wax.]

Robin: "Holy paraffin, Batman! This is going to be a close one!"

Batman: "Too close."

Riddler: "This is my dream come true! With the two of you out of the way, nothing can stand between me and the Lost Treasure of the Incas. And it's worth millions…millions! Hear me Batman? Millions!"

Batman: "Just remember, Riddler, you can't buy friends with money."

— From the TV show

The Movie's Batmobile

The Batmobile began in a London junkyard when two rusted 1968 Chevrolet Impalas were bought for $5,500 each. Three months and $250,000 later, two identical Batmobiles were ready for service. One was used for close-ups and routine scenes; the other was used whenever there was danger of damage.

On each car, the frame was stretched almost 3 feet and widened by almost 2 feet. The engine was lowered a foot to accommodate a low slung hood. Its basic dashboard gauges came from a Ferrari, with additional instruments from fighter aircraft.

Exhaust flames came from air and gasoline ignited under pressure. Though press releases boasted that the car had a top speed so impressive it was "not available to the public," it was actually slower than a Honda Civic.

FIRST SPRING OF ROBIN

Cartoonist Bob Kane says that he named the Boy Wonder after Robin Hood. "Both Robins were crusaders, fighting against the forces of evil…I even dressed Robin in the tunic, cape, and shoes of Robin Hood's era, and drew his trunks to look like chain mail."

Memorable Villains

- **The Joker.** Green-eyed, white-faced, red-lipped, with a preference for warning his victims in advance exactly where and when he intends to do them in.

- **The Penguin.** Waddling along in tails and top hat, armed with special deadly umbrellas.

- **The Catwoman.** Sensual, and partial to the wrong side of the law, but sweet on Batman.

- **Two-Face.** A district attorney of Gotham City, who went bad after half his face was scarred by acid.

- **The Scarecrow.** An ex-teacher who hires himself out to scare people, but resorts to murder if the scare tactics don't work.

- **The Riddler.** Leaves riddles at the scene of the crime to lure Batman into a game of wits.

Batman took crime so personally because he saw his parents gunned down by a hold-up man.

Game Enough For Batman?

The Batman Game board glows in the dark (because after all, Batman does his crimefighting at night, right?). It came out in 1989 to coincide with Batman's movie and 50th Anniversary hoopla, but it's still available, unlike most other bat-merchandise. The idea is to capture the villains and get back to the Batcave before your opponents do. Up to 6 players, ages 8 and up.

$16.95 + 3.00 shipping from The Funny Papers, 7253 Geary Blvd. San Francisco, CA 94121. (415) 752-1914.

BATBOOKS

• *Batman & Me: An Autobiography* by Bob Kane with Tom Andre. Here's the inside story of the Caped Crusader. Cartoonist Bob Kane tells how Batman and the great villains came to be. Includes reprints of three complete Batman stories in full color.

$15.95, postpaid. Eclipse Books, P.O. Box 1099, Forestville, CA 95436. (707) 887-1521.

• *Tales of the Dark Knight: Batman's First Fifty Years: 1939-1989* by Mark Cotta Vaz. This is a big book, tracing the changes of Batman through the decades. Lavishly illustrated

with fifty years of comic book art, including 48 color reproductions of Batman and Detective Comics covers.

$17.95 + 2.00 shipping from Ballantine Books, 400 Hahn Road, Westminster, MD 21157 (800) 733-3000.

• *The Official Batman Batbook* by Joel Eisner. Covering the Batman TV series with summaries of episodes, interviews with the celebrity guests, and many photos.

$9.95 + 2.00 shipping from Contemporary Books, 180 North Michigan Ave., Chicago, IL 60601. (312) 782-9181.

Catch A Hood

All rubber Batman hood covers head, shoulders and upper chest, too. Made by famous Hollywood mask and costume maker, Don Post Studios, to the exacting specifications of DC Comics and Paramount Studios.

#2184, $49.98 + 5.95 shipping from Johnson Smith Company, 4514 19th St. Court East, P.O. Box 25500, Bradenton, FL 34206-5500. (813) 747-2356 / FAX: (813) 746-7896.

BAT SIGNal

Five color tin sign with the art of '40s. 12 x 16".

#TINBAT, $18.00 + 3.50 shipping. Kitchen Sink, 2 Swamp Rd., Princeton, WI 54968. (414) 295-6922.

Batshirt

Shirt or sweatshirt.
Adult sizes L and XL. #10559 Sweat, $16.99 + 3.90 shipping or #10553 T-Shirt, $7.99 + 2.75 shipping. Wireless, Box 64422, St. Paul, MN 55164. (800) 669-9999.

Batmobile Has A Nice Ring To It

The headlights on this replica of the famous Batmobile flash every time the Commissioner (or anyone else for that matter) is calling to say hello. Why? Because it's really a phone! Just put the undercarriage to your ear.

#C738740, $49.95 + 5.50 shipping from Sync, Hanover, PA 17333-0042. (800) 722-9979.

LIFE'S A BEACH PRESERVER

Life's a Beach...

It seems like we secretly wish we all could be California girls or beach boys. The world has adopted the Southern Californian and Hawaiian ideal of tan and trim, sun-streaked and wind-blown. Even in Iowa and Kansas, you can almost hear the pounding surf rolling in, forming perfect cylinders for riding. Cowabunga!

"Aloha?" Read My Hips!

How to Hula Video. Slip into your grass skirt, slip this tape into your VCR and learn how to swing & sway from one of Hawaii's best dancers. Or forget the lessons and just enjoy the dancing against the exotic island backdrop of the Queen Liliuokalani Gardens.

#EL050, Hula Video, $29.95 + 4.95 shipping from Special Interest Video, 100 Enterprise Place, P.O. Box 7022, Dover, DE 19903-7022. (800) 522-0502.

Float Alone

Add a little turf to your surf (or to your portion of the public swimming pool) with a 6-foot in diameter floating inflatable island banana republic. Comes equipped with PVC palm tree and giant banana backrest.

#FOP440 $79.95 + 7.50 shipping from The Sharper Image, P.O. Box 7031, San Francisco, CA 94120-7031. (800) 344-4444.

No Tiki, No Party

Ye gods, what's a luau without Tikis? This place has over 30 handcarved deities, costing $9.00 for a 7" version to $2000 for a huge and elaborate one. The most popular Tiki is about 4" tall for $120 unpainted, or $155 painted. Shipping is extra. Call for details.

Oceanic Arts, 12414 Whittier Blvd., Whittier, CA 90602. (213) 698-6960.

Create a Lulu of a Luau

Oceanic Arts Rentals. Dying to experience a real Hawaiian feast but can't get away? Now you can bring the flavor of the Islands home with Polynesian party props. We found the greatest warehouse full of tiki gods, fish nets, dinghies, shells, dock pilings and Hawaiian thatched huts. You just need sand from your local building supply company and a pit for the pig.

Oceanic Arts rents to movie companies, restaurants and hotels and private parties all the time, and their stuff is first class, mostly handbuilt. Here are examples of 3 day rental charges (shipping's extra and, with large pieces, formidable). Call for info on shipping arrangements.

Wooden dinghy, $20.00
Old rowboat, $30.00
Boat oars, (pair),$ 6.00
Life preserver, $ 8.00
Dock pilings, $6.00-$9.00
Barrel (large), $6.00
Fish net, 7' X 24', $5.00
All the above are *rental prices*. Oceanic Arts, 12414 Whittier Blvd., Whittier, CA 90602. (213) 698-6960.

"I dig a French bikini on the wild island girls by a palm tree in the sand"—The Beach Boys

Sand Castles Don't Come Dirt Cheap

All thumbs when it comes to building a sand castle? If you've got the bucks, you hire a team of professional designers and contractors to create your custom-built fantasy fiefdom.

Sand sculptures by a professional run anywhere from $2000 to $600,000 in price. A standard castle can cost approximately $15,000, and typically last less than a week outdoors, but up to several months if housed indoors.

Sand sculpting has really caught on in Japan, which already has over 300 professional sand carvers, 2 sand museums, and an annual Sand Festival.

So who would pay that kind of money for a *sand castle*? Governments and corporations mostly, for various promotional purposes. For instance, a pharmaceuticals company commissioned a whimsical "Mt. Psychmore" of famous psychologists.

How big can they get? The beach is the limit—Sand Sculptors International, based in Solana Beach, California, recently made it into the Guinness Book of World Records for the largest castle ever—56 feet tall.

Interested in commissioning your own custom sand tribute? Contact the president of the World Sand Sculpting Association: Gerry Kirk, Sand Sculptors International, 304 Pacific Avenue, Solana Beach, CA 92075. (619) 481-0252.

Hawaiian Sounds

• **Real Surf Sounds.** Waves crashing against the shore, digitally recorded, live, on a genuine beach. Good for beach party backgrounds, meditative trances, or bittersweet nostalgia if you're stuck far from the sunny shores (New York's a lonely town, after all, when you're the only surfer boy).

$13.48 for CD or $8.98 for cassette (postpaid). Rhino Records, 2225

Colorado Avenue, Santa Monica, CA 90494. (800) 432-0200.

• **Genuine Hawaiian Music.** Not touristy Don Ho stuff (Aloha oy vey!).

Assorted tapes, $7.98 + 1.75 shipping. Oceanic Arts, 12414 Whittier Blvd., Whittier, CA 90602. (213) 698-6960.

Or Build Your Own

Here are a few secrets from the pros:

• If you're planning an elaborate sculpture, start with models and plans.

• Bring the proper tools: shovel, molds, spray bottle (keeps sand damp and workable) and flat blades to "shave" away sand.

• For freeform castle towers without a lot of work, dribble a mix of sand and water between your fingers for impressive 6" stalagmites.

• More ideas can be found in *Sand Castles* by Nicolas Freeling.

$4.95 + 2.00 shipping. Warner Books, PO Box 690, New York, NY 10019. (212) 484-3191.

New Waves in Literature

Making Waves: Swimsuits and the Undressing of America by Lena Lencek and Gideon Bosker. Gorgeously illustrated, with a narrative history of public bathing from the ancient Greeks to present. Some facts from the book:

• Until the 1850s in Western culture, men and women didn't swim together. What was worn in the water was an only slightly abbreviated version of street clothes, including cumbersome corsets for women.

• By the time swimming was accepted as a serious sport in the early Twentieth Century, designers for the first time began streamlining apparel for ease of motion in the water and reducing the weight of water-saturated fabric. Rubberized fabrics didn't come until much later.

• Men as well as women swam completely covered until 1932, when men's swimming suits first began offering an optional removable top. Some men took the option—and were promptly arrested for indecent exposure.

• Every era had its controversial "too-daring" swimsuit, revealing "forbidden zones" from ankles and bare arms early in the century, to women's breasts in the 1960s.

$19.95 + 2.00 shipping from Chronicle Books, 275 Fifth Street, San Francisco, CA 94103. (800) 722-6657.

A Magazine to Suit You

Sports Illustrated unwittingly launched what became its annual swimsuit issue in 1964, during a slow sports week between the Super Bowl and the start of basketball. Designed to lift the winter doldrums, this fantasy fluff issue featured models with the "California Look"— broad-shouldered, full-bosomed, trim-bottomed, long-legged, muscled and tanned.

If you want a more professional look at swimsuits, check out *Swimsuit International*, largely aimed at people in the industry. Serious articles about fashions, trends, materials and accessories.

$15.95 (9 issues). Swimsuit International, Swimsuit Publishers, 801 Second Ave., New York, NY 10017. (212) 986-5100.

The first "streamlined swimsuits" of the early 1900s were made of wool and could weigh upwards of twenty pounds when wet.

Great California Beaches

• **Malibu Colony.** The exclusive home to many show business celebrities. Multi-million dollar beachfront properties are still the province of entertainers like Johnny Carson. The surf is said to be better at Malibu Surf-rider State Beach, north of the Colony, but if you've got stargazing on your mind, the Colony is the place to be.

• **Venice Beach.** The antidote to rubbing shoulders with celebrities in Malibu Colony is to be panhandled at Venice Beach just down the shore on Santa Monica Bay. Funky, seedy, yet always colorful, this is another great spot for watching an endless parade of street performers, body builders, skimpy suits, and colorful roller skaters. Originally a salt marsh, the town was

outiftted with canals and authentic arched bridges from its Italian namesake. Riding in genuine gondolas with singing gondoliers didn't impress people as much as was hoped, and the town slid into near ruin.

Beatniks discovered its funky charms in the 1950s, followed by hippies in the 1960s and artists and musicians of various stripes since then.

• **Santa Cruz Beach Boardwalk.** Built in 1904, then rebuilt after a 1907 fire, the Boardwalk Amusement Park is the first and last such seaside attraction operating on the West Coast. An antique merry-go-round and a wooden roller coaster will transport you to a bygone era.

Gumshoes in Zoris: The 5 Best Beach Detective TV Shows

1. *Hawaiian Eye*
2. *Surfside Six*
3. *Hawaii 5-0*
4. *Magnum P.I.*
5. *Miami Vice*

DON'T GO NEAR THE WATER
Best Beach Horror Flicks

Jaws (1975)
Monster from the Surf (1964)
Horror of Party Beach (1963)
Ghost in the Invisible Bikini (1966)

Best Beach Love Scenes

• Burt Lancaster and Deborah Kerr's wave-washed clinch in *From Here to Eternity* (1953).

• Love at first breath when Lorelei the Mermaid rescues drowning surfer Bonehead with skillful CPR technique in *Beach Blanket Bingo* (1965).

• A surprisingly sexy Disney heroine wrapped in nothing but a sheet in *The Little Mermaid* nearly seduces a prince after saving his life (1989).

Riddle: Why need you never be hungry at the beach? Because of the sand which is there.

THE BEATLES

They were a phenomenon, affecting our hairstyles, our clothes, our ways of looking at popular music, our philosophies, even our attitudes toward drugs. Ladies and gentlemen, the Beatles!

Hair, There And Everywhere

While the Beatles weren't always the originators, they popularized many musical forms:

- The "Skiffle beat" (their early stuff)
- Classical rock (*Yesterday*)
- Psychedelic music (*Tomorrow Never Knows, Lucy in the Sky With Diamonds*)
- Indian "raga rock" (*Norwegian Wood* was first pop use of sitar)
- The "concept album" (**Sgt. Pepper's Lonely Hearts Club Band**)
- 1920s "retro-rock" (*When I'm 64*)
- Backwards tapes, synthesizers and other "new" sounds (they were always experimenting—John once tried recording while lying flat on his back on the studio floor. Another time he positioned the microphone behind his head. Neither method changed the sound much, but he tried).

Beatle Statistics:

- **The Beatles (The White Album)** sold nearly two million copies in its first week of U.S. release.
- According to the Guinness Book Of Records, the songwriting team of John Lennon and Paul McCartney was responsible for more No. 1 single hit recordings than anyone else ever.
- Also according to Guinness, The Beatles have the greatest sales of any group—well over a billion copies.
- Broadcast Music Inc. says that Paul McCartney's *Yesterday* is the most-played song of the last 50 years—over 5 million times. They estimate that at any given moment, some version of the song is playing on the radio somewhere in the world.
- More than one estimate has it that Yoko Ono is one of the world's richest women.

Bob Dylan was the one who first turned the Beatles on to marijuana.

WITH A LITTLE HELP FROM THEIR FRIENDS

Do you want to know a secret? A lot of uncredited people played on Beatles songs. In the beginning it was mostly just producer George Martin occasionally playing keyboard. Billy Preston was one who actually received credit for his work on *Let It Be.* But some notable musicians made contributions in between.

• It was September, 1964 and Ringo had only been with the group a short while. Unsure of Ringo's capabilities, Martin brought drummer

Andy White in for *Love Me Do.* Ringo played tambourine.

• Mick Jagger sang background on *Baby You're A Rich Man.* John and Paul returned the favor on the Stones' *We Love You* and *Dandelion.*

• A reluctant Eric Clapton played lead guitar on *While My Guitar Gently Weeps.*

• And, of course, the dozens of classical musicians who picked up a few pounds for their contributions to many songs.

Beatles Collectibles

• After Brian Taylor paid $18,000 for Paul McCartney's birth certificate, Beatle fans began asking Taylor for his autograph. "It's ridiculous," Taylor said.

"I'm ridiculous for buying it but wanting my autograph, that kills me."

• A promotional copy of Vee Jay Records' *Ask Me Why/Anna* issued free to DJs back in 1964 can sell now for between $4,000 and $5,000.

• That quickly suppressed cover of *Yesterday and Today* with cleavers, dolls, blood and butcher aprons could be worth as much as $4,000.

• Remember those nodding head Beatle figures from 1964? A set of four can be worth up to $400.

Collecting the Beatles?

Some good books for finding out what's out there, and typical prices. The first set is remarkably complete; the second gives you Elvis, too.

• *Collecting The Beatles Vol. 1 & 2* by Barbara Fenick. Hardcover, $34.50 each + 3.50 shipping from Popular Culture, Ink., PO Box 1839, Ann Arbor, MI 48106. (800) 678-8828.

• *Official Price Guide to Memorabilia of Elvis Presley & the Beatles* by Osborne, Cox & Lindsey. $10.95 + 1.00 shipping from House of Collectibles, 201 E. 50th St., New York, NY 10022. (800) 638-6460.

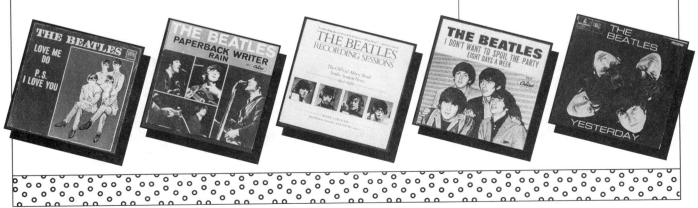

The working title for *Help* was *8 Arms to hold You.*

PAPERBACK WRITERS

Books on the Beatles

There must be close to a thousand books about the Beatles. Here are a few of our favorites and why:

• *The Beatles Recording Sessions* by Mark Lewisohn. Based on Abbey Road Studios documents and interviews, this book walks you through every Beatle recording session from 1962 to 1970: who was there, what they did and how they did it. This sounds like too much, we know, but the details are strangely fascinating.

For instance, *Strawberry Fields Forever* was actually two different versions, at two different speeds and keys, that George Martin glued together (listen for the splice 59 seconds into the song). And the bits of radio dialogue on *I Am the Walrus* are what actually happened to be broadcast on the BBC at the time.

$16.95 + 4.00 shipping from Harmony Books, 225 Park Avenue South, New York, NY 10003. (212) 254-1600.

• *All Together Now / The Beatles Again / The End Of The Beatles?* by Walter J. Podrazik and Harry Castleman. THE best reference source about the Beatles—three volumes worth of all their records from all over the world, movies, Beatles songs recorded by others, books, records by people related to the Beatles, and on and on.

All Together Now, $29.50. The Beatles Again, $29.50. The End Of The Beatles, $34.50. Add 3.00 shipping. Popular Culture, Ink., P.O. Box 1839, Ann Arbor, MI 48106. (800) 678-8828.

• *Nothing Is Beatle Proof* by Michæl J. Hockinson. A trivia book to end all.

$34.50 + 3.00 shipping from Popular Culture, Ink (see above).

Beatles For Sale

Who says you can't buy me, luv? For many years the only new Beatle products were unofficial "bootlegs." But in 1984, Yoko and the three remaining Beatles agreed to release new merchandise, partly out of fear of losing trademarks on the name. Here are two we like:

• **Not A Second Time... Until Now!** Time is on your side (oop, wrong group) with this black & white photo watch featuring the Fab Four in their famous Edwardian collarless jackets. Return to the '60s with this mechanical stem-wound (not quartz, not solar-powered or digital) watch. Includes "twisty" metal expansion band so you can twist and shout. Don't wait another minute, Mr. Postman.

#16281 Beatles Watch, $29.00 + 3.90 shipping from Signals PO Box 64428 St. Paul, MN 55164-0428 (800) 669-9696

• **Here Comes The Sun Shield.** Put an *Abbey Road* album replica sun shield and protect your interior from the good day sunshine. On the back is HELP! No, not the movie but an actual emergency sign in case baby, you can't drive your car.

$6.00 + 3.25 from: Beatlefest P.O. Box 436 Westwood, NJ 07675 (800) BEATLES / FAX 666-8687

Lennon got the phrase Goo Goo Ga Joob *(I'm the Eggman)* from James Joyce's *Finnegan's Wake* .

Rock Band With Nodding Heads

If they could talk they'd say yeah, yeah, yeah! These pre-fab fellows look like the Fab 4 but only if you squint at them in a dim room. 4" tall, and yes, their heads do move, but not very well. Not to be confused with the collectible version worth $400.

#9220 Set of four, $5.00 + 4.00 shipping from Archie McPhee, P.O. Box 30852, Seattle, WA 98103. (206) 547-2467 / FAX (206) 547-6319.

Fab Four Comic Capers

• **Rock 'N' Roll Comics** issued a series of comic books featuring the Fab Four. Numbers 1 & 2 are available, 2.50 each.

• Here's a soon-to-be collector's item. In issue No. 3 of **Honkytonk Sue**, the Queen of Country Swing gets the Beatles to reunite and convert to Country Western music! $1.75.

Add $2.00 shipping for 1- 4 comics. Last Gasp Comics, 2180 Bryant St., San Francisco, CA 94110. (415) 824-6636 / FAX (415) 825-1836.

FAN CLUBS

Come Together Over Me

Here are two of the best Fab Four Fan Clubs and their magazines:

• **Strawberry Fields Forever.** Dues: $6.00 annually. Members receive subscription to Strawberry Fields Forever, probably the best fan magazine available.

310 Franklin Street #117, Boston, MA 02110.

• **Good Day Sunshine.** Dues: $10 annually. Members receive subscription to club magazine (6 editions) plus membership card, updates and fan club benefits. GDS also produces fan conventions and packaged Beatle tours.

Liverpool Productions, Charles F. Rosenay, 397 Edgewood Avenue, New Haven, CT 06511-4013. (203) 865-8131.

PILGRIMAGE SITES

There's A Place

• **The Beatles Room.** Take a magical mystery tour to the room in Miami where John Lennon slept on a concert tour in 1964. In 1984, Jeff Walker of Vancouver paid over $36,000 for an 80 year lease on it to rent it out to Beatle fans. The room features Beatle portraits, Beatle wallpaper, even the same toilet seat used by Them. Guests get to keep a set of John Lennon pillowcases, phony Beatle money and a key chain.

Reservations: Jeff at (604) 685-8841. Room 1111, Deauville Hotel, 6701 Collins Avenue, Miami, FL 32141.

• **Beatlefest.** Held in major cities throughout the U.S. (including New York, Chicago and L.A.), this has been going since 1976, with Beatle flea markets , movies and videos , guest celebrities, Beatle sound-alike bands, contests and more. "A Splendid Time Is Guaranteed For All!"

For information: Mark & Carol Lapidos, P.O. Box 436, Westwood, NJ 07675. (800)

Compleat Beatles

Complete Beatles CD Library. A Beatlemaniac must. Great if you didn't save your original Beatles albums. Or even if you have them, you may want to consider getting the CDs anyway. They're in stereo, they're scratch-free, and they've been remixed by George Martin for CD-clarity (you can hear details, even mistakes you never heard on record: the boys whispering between verses while doing backups, the squeaking of the piano stool on the long fadeout at the end of **Sgt. Pepper**, etc.). And they're the British albums, as originally conceived by the lads, instead of Capitol's sometimes bizarre American lineups which added and subtracted songs at whim, giving 12 songs per album instead of 14. All the original British albums (12 single CDs and the double-disc **White Album**) plus two additional singles collections.

D1824X, All 16 discs $224.95 + 4.95 shipping from Postings, P.O. Box 8001, Hilliard, OH 43026. (800) 262-6604 / FAX: (614) 777-1470.

Everyone Knew Her as Norma

Not all the Beatles songs turned out exactly as originally conceived. For instance:

• Before words were added, the working title for *Yesterday* was *Scrambled Eggs*.

• *Hey Jules* which became *Hey Jude*, was written by Paul for John's son, Julian after his parents' divorce.

• *Come Together* was originally titled *Come Together Join the Party*. John wrote it for Timothy Leary's campaign for Governor of California in 1969.

• *For No One* was originally titled *Why Did It Die?*

• *Sexy Sadie* was originally called *Maharishi*. A disillusioned John wrote it about his Transcendental Meditation guru, but his advisors convinced him to change the words to avoid lawsuits.

The Pre-Fab Four

There have been dozens of Beatle spoofs, but one is incomparable (and no, we're not talking about the Monkees):

The Rutles! Thoroughly disassembling the documentary *The Compleat Beatles*, this parody group's video includes appearances by George Harrison, Mick Jagger and Paul Simon. Neil Innes wrote and produced the uncannily Beatle-sounding songs, and Eric Idle makes a convincingly wide-eyed McCartney. The music is funny yet completely authentic-sounding.

• **The video is $15.00 + 3.25 shipping from Beatlefest, P.O. Box 436, Westwood, NJ 07675. (800) BEATLES .**

• **The soundtrack CD (#R21Z 75760) is $13.98 + 2.00 shipping from Rhino, 2225 Colorado Avenue, Santa Monica, CA 90404-3598. (800) 432-3670.**

Novelty Records

Parody artists like Allen Sherman, Dickie Goodman and the Chipmunks jumped on the Beatles bandwagon. Scores of others tried as well. Here are a few of the more novel novelty songs:

• Beagles - *Deep In The Heart Of Texas,* 1964. Dogs wearing Beatle wigs, barking to slightly Beatlesque arrangements.

• Bon Bons - *What's Wrong with Ringo,* 1964. This song didn't make them stars so they changed their name to the Shangri-Las and had several hits including *Leader of the Pack.*

• Rainbo - *John You Went Too Far This Time,* 1969. A musical commentary about John appearing nude with Yoko on the **Two Virgins** album. Rainbo never made it as a singer, so she switched fields and became famous under her real name, Sissy Spacek.

Whole Pop Beatle Film Fest

Hard Day's Night (1964). Fast-moving "day in the life" of the Beatles.

• **Help!** (1965). Used as a training film by the Monkees.

• **The Beatles At Shea Stadium** (1966). TV special of concert footage.

• **Yellow Submarine** (1968). Animated undersea romp.

• **Let It Be.** They fall apart.

• **Compleat Beatles.** The Beatles from birth to breakup.

Available from Beatlefest, PO Box 436, Westwood, NJ 07675. (800) BEATLES.

Our Favorite "Paul Is Dead" Rumor Clues:

Out of the Midwest and across the world, rumors spread that Paul had died years earlier and that the clues were scattered throughout Beatles albums.

Thousands of albums were ruined as people tried to play them backwards. Paul *(or was it his evil look-alike Billy Shears?)* finally issued a statement that he was alive, admitting "...on the other hand, if I were dead, I'd probably be the last to know."

Of the hundreds of clues, here are some of our favorites.

• Paul always differs from the others: On the cover of **Abbey Road,** he's not wearing shoes. On **Magical Mystery Tour**, he's wearing a black rose instead of red. On **Help!**, he's not wearing a hat like his pals. On the back cover of **Sgt. Pepper**, he's turned his back on the camera.

• Play *Revolution Number 9* backwards and you'll hear the car crash that Paul "blew his mind out" in and a strange voice repeating "turn me on dead man." Play the end of *I'm So Tired* backwards and listen to John say "Paul is dead man, miss him, miss him." Listen to the end of *Strawberry Fields* and you can hear "I buried Paul."

• The graveside flower arrangement on the **Sgt. Pepper** cover is shaped like Paul's left-handed bass guitar. And the hyacinths spell out BE AT LESO, the underwater island where Paul is buried, or living as a vegetable.

• In the same picture, a hand can be seen hovering above Paul's head. Everyone knows that this is a Norse (or Tibetan or Indian or something) symbol of death.

• And when did Paul die? "Wednesday morning at 5 o' clock," of course. Because those are the lyrics George is pointing to on the back cover of **Sgt. Pepper.** The whole thing is described in the "He blew his mind out in a car" verse of *Day in the Life.*

• Hold your **Magical Mystery Tour** album cover up to a mirror and you'll see a telephone number in the stars of the words. Call the correct London exchange and ask for Paul's replacement, Billy Shears. He'll tell you everything. Shears, by the way, looks just like Paul. But he doesn't sound like Paul, so Paul's voice is done by an anonymous woman.

• Check out Ringo's drum set on **Magical Mystery Tour.** Doesn't his bass drum read "Love 3 Beatles?"

People removed at the last minute from the *Sgt. Pepper* montage: Bowery Boy Leo Gorcey, Gandhi and Adolf Hitler.

He's Leaving Home (Bye Bye)

When the Beatles broke up forever, Paul took the heat for being the one who walked. Ironically, all the others had quit or thought about it before him.

• John was thinking about quitting, starting in 1966. He was (as he put it in an interview) "...always looking for a reason...I didn't have the guts to do it."

• Ringo was the first actually to quit, during the tense **White Album** sessions in 1968. Paul temporarily replaced him on drums (that's him on *Back in the USSR).* Ringo returned to a flower-covered drum set several days later.

• George quit after Paul criticized his playing in January 1969. He returned in a few days, too.

• In 1970 Paul released his McCartney solo album and made it official.

REUNION? WE CAN WORK IT OUT

No sooner did the Beatles break up, when the "come together" talk began.

• George tried to get them back together for his Bangla Desh benefit concert in 1971. However, John wouldn't come because George wouldn't let Yoko perform. Paul would—but only if George dropped his lawsuit against him.

• In 1976, a promoter offered them $50 million for one concert.

• Also in 1976, *Saturday Night Live* jokingly made a public offer to the Beatles: perform just three songs on the show and take home $3,000. They could "even give less to Ringo if you want to!" the producer announced. John and Paul happened to be together watching the show and "nearly got into a cab" to head for the studio as a joke, before changing their minds.

• In May 1979 rumors were revived when Paul, George, Ringo, Mick Jagger and others jammed at the wedding reception of Eric Clapton and Patti (George's ex-wife) Boyd.

• Periodically, improbable rumors pop up about a reunion with Julian Lennon and/or even Michael Jackson (?) standing in for John. George's reaction: it's possible—but only when John returns from the dead.

Lennon intended *Please Please Me* as a parody of Roy Orbison's overblown style.

Minor Notes of the Beatles

• In 1973, George Harrison was caught fooling around with his best friend Ringo's wife, Maureen. When asked why, he shrugged his shoulders and said, "Incest."

• The Beatles all had their share of women, especially during the touring days. Even though John was the "married Beatle" he had several. Yoko you knew about. Joan Baez you probably didn't.

• John Belushi was paid $600 to perform the Joe Cocker imitation he perfected on **Saturday Night Live** at a birthday party for Paul.

• After the long chord ending *A Day In the Life*, the Beatles added a high-pitched whistle that only your dog will hear.

• According to "Official Fan Club" materials dating back to 1964, one of Paul's hobbies as a young lad was writing backwards.

• The Beatles' music publishers sued **Sesame Street** over two satirical songs which appeared on the show and an album: *Hey Food* (a parody of *Hey Jude*) and *Letter B (Let It Be)* .

• First official U.S.S.R. Beatle record release was a single (EP)

of Let It Be in 1972. First albums released were **A Hard Day's Night** and **A Taste Of Honey** in 1986.

• Recently an 8mm "home movie" of their 1965 U.S. tour was auctioned at Christies' for $40,000.

• The Beatles' first U.S. TV appearance was not their live appearance on **Ed Sullivan**, but a taped performance of *She Loves You* shown on the **Jack Paar Show** January 3, 1964.

• *Abbey Road*, released in September 1969, is really their last recorded album, not **Let It Be** (which was actually completed in May 1969, but not released until May 1970.)

• The song *L.S. Bumblebee* is not an unreleased Beatle song, but a parody by British comedians Peter Cook and Dudley Moore. A lot of people were fooled and it even erroneously appeared on several Beatle bootleg albums.

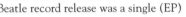

Beatnik

"Hey, Daddy-o!"

Most of us too young, too old, or too square to actually hang out on Bleecker Street knew the Beat scene only through caricatures on the screen and on the pages of *Mad Magazine*. Beat seemed to be nothing more than Bullwinkle reading poetry in a beret, Bob Hope making jokes in a goatee and the harmless eccentricity of Maynard G. Krebs.

Other media images were less flattering: Maynard's aversion to work was tame stuff compared to the diabolical stereotypes like the psychotic "Aspirin Kid" in the film classic *The Beat Generation*.

So what was with these guys, anyway? Well, the short version was that they were having a gut reaction to the materialist sterility of the 1950s. If you didn't like Ike and couldn't stomach Perry Como, you had only a few role models: the "juvenile delinquent" rock 'n' roller or the cool jazz bebopping beat. The alternative was bowties and poodle skirts. Squaresville, Dad.

The Beats were given a voice in 1955 when Allen Ginsberg began giving public readings of *Howl*, at the Six Gallery in San Francisco. Other Beat poets followed. Dylan and other folkies soon took some of that Beat sensibility, made it rhyme, and put it to popular music.

The Beats go on: The 1990s may turn out to be the Beats biggest decade since the 1950s. Jack Kerouac's three spoken word albums have been reissued on CD; his hometown of Lowell, Massachusetts has erected a monument in his honor and San Francisco has named an alley after him (fittingly, the little street between two Beat landmarks: Lawrence Ferlinghetti's City Lights bookstore and the Vesuvio bar). Allen Ginsberg and novelist William Burroughs have both released new albums in collaboration with contemporary musicians, and Burroughs has embarked on a hip new career as a cult film character actor.

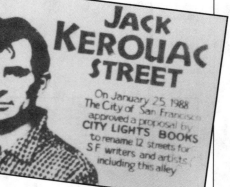

In his decline, Jack Kerouac loved the *Beverly Hillbillies*, sitting a foot from the TV and slugging whisky from the bottle.

The Beat Goes On

The Jack Kerouac Collection. Now you can take Jack Kerouac and friends on the road with you in your car cassette or CD player in this 1990 reissue of three LPs originally titled Jack Kerouac & Steve Allen: *Poetry For The Beat Generation;* Jack Kerouac With Al Cohn & Zoot Sims: *Blues And Haikus* and *Readings By Jack Kerouac On The Beat Generation.* Plus there's bonus material that includes previously unreleased recordings and a 40-page comprehensive booklet about the man and his times.

**#R23K 70939, CD, $49.98 postpaid.
#R44R 70939, cassette, $39.98 postpaid.
Rhino Records, 2225 Colorado Ave., Santa Monica, CA 90404. (800) 432-0020.**

Make the Scene, Man

The Beatnik. You'll need a beret, "dungarees," a black turtleneck sweater and a pair of sandals. Those striped boat-necked French fisherman shirts are cool, too. Don't forget the Ray-Ban shades, a pouch of tobacco and a good supply of rolling papers. If you can grow a goatee, start now.

The Beatchick. You'll need dark-rimmed eyes, black leotard, dark skirt, black stockings, and sandals or ballet slippers. Wear your hair long and straight —if it isn't naturally that way, then iron it (use the lowest setting, place a towel over the hair, and don't press for more than a few seconds). Wear hoop earrings, or any abstract shapes that dangle are a nice touch.

"*Who wants a living—I want a life.*"
—**Jack Kerouac**

"Beatniks" on TV

• *Peter Gunn*—Gunn often visited Beat coffee houses for espresso and leads in investigations.

• *Alfred Hitchcock Presents*—besides the host appearing in Beatnik attire, several episodes had a Beat theme.

• *Mr. Lucky*—the debonair Mr. Lucky had Beatniks among his informants and suspects.

• *Dobie Gillis*—Maynard G. Krebs was probably the most sympathetically portrayed Beat character.

• *The Dick Van Dyke Show*—Laura attends a Beat theatre with hilarious consequences.

• *The Rocky & Bullwinkle Show*—Natasha made the perfect Beatchick in one episode, and the Moose appeared several times in goatee and beret, spouting poems about the sponsor's wares.

• Cheerios and Kix cereals both used animated Beatnik characters as spokesters in the early 1960s.

• Also in the early 1960s Red Rose Tea dressed four chimpanzees in shades and berets and gave them saxophones, trumpets and drums. The chimps wailed to Charlie Parker and Dizzy Gillespie's *Salt Peanuts.*

Neo-Beats

The Washington Squares. *Neal Cassady* was the first hit from the group which adopted its name from the famous Beat Greenwich Village mecca. This neo-Beat group formed in the 1980s sports shades, goatees and berets, and are bringing back that classic Beat/folk, Peter Paul & Mary attitude.

The Washington Squares **album, $17.50 postpaid;** *Fair and Square* **cassette / CD, $22.50 postpaid from Gold Castle Records, P.O. Box 2568-L, Hollywood, CA 90078.**

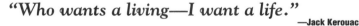

San Francisco Chronicle **columnist Herb Caen, following the lexicon fad inspired by the Soviet Sputnik, dubbed them "Beatniks."**

Where to get the props

• **Piccolo bongo.** The little ones Beatniks play. These are the deluxe model in that they can be tuned to whatever different drummer pitch you want.

$39.00 postpaid from Grant's Drum City, 411 E. Irving Blvd., Irving, TX 75060. (800) 247-3786.

• **Goatees.** Grow your own, or fashion your own realistic, false goatee with this stage hair. It comes in a variety of natural colors.

$30.00 + 3.75 shipping from Kryolan Corporation, 132 Ninth St., San Francisco, CA 94103-2603. (415) 863-9684/ FAX (415) 863-9059.

• **Berets.** Basic black wool beret. One size fits all.

$13.99 + 4.00 shipping from Abrams Sales Co., 1055 Market Street, San Francisco, CA 94103. (800) 234-2775.

• **Beat Blinders.** Cool Beatniks wore shades like these with heavy black frames.

#6595, $5.98 + 2.70 shipping from Johnson Smith Company, 4514 19th Court East, P.O. Box 25500, Bradenton, FL 34206-5500. (813) 747-2356 / FAX (813) 746-7896.

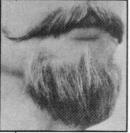

Dig These Books, Man!

Down and In—Life in the Underground by Ronald Sukenick. Slide into step with the American avant garde and follow it from the 1950s to the 1970s—from the Hipster underground that grew out of Greenwich Village Bohemianism to Rockers, and finally Punks. Everyone who was anyone makes an appearance: Jack Kerouac, Norman Mailer, Andy Warhol, Bob Dylan, William Burroughs, Jackson Pollock, the Fugs, Dylan Thomas, Joan Baez and many others.

$10.95 + 1.25 shipping from Macmillan Publishing, Front & Brown Streets, Riverside, NJ 08075. (800) 257-5755.

• *Heart Beat* by Carolyn Cassady. The book zeros in on the relationship between Kerouac and Cassady but the supporting cast of Beat characters is given honorable mention. The 1979 movie made from the book was a disjointed disappointment starring John Heard, Cissy Spacek and Nick Nolte.

$6.75 postpaid from Beat Books, P.O. Box 5813, Berkeley, CA 94705.

• *The First Third* by Neal Cassady. The companion of Kerouac and later, Ken Kesey, wrote about his cross country and other weird trips.

$7.95 + 1.50 shipping from Last Gasp, 2180 Bryant St., San Francisco, CA 94110. (415) 824-6636 / FAX (415) 824-1836.

• *Memoirs of a Beatnik* by Diane DiPrima. "She was beat, she was hip, she is now teaching metaphysics" and in this book she takes the reader back to where it all began.

$7.95 + 1.50 shipping from Last Gasp, 2180 Bryant St., San Francisco, CA 94110. (415) 824-6636 / FAX (415) 824-1836.

VIDEO BEATS

Fried Shoes, Cooked Diamonds. Allen Ginsberg narrates this film of a 1978 gathering of Beat poets who read their creations, reminisce and take part in an anti-nuclear demonstration. Features William Burroughs, Gregory Corso, and Diane DiPrima. Filmed at the Jack Kerouac School of Disembodied Poetics at Naropa Institute in Boulder, Colorado.

$29.95 + 4.00 shipping from Mystic Fire Video, Inc., P.O. Box 9323, Dept. C3, S. Burlington, VT 05407. (800) 727-8433.

Beat Catalogs

• *City Lights Booksellers & Publishers.* 261 Columbus Ave., San Francisco, CA 94133. (415) 362-8193. Free mail order catalog—new books.

• *Beat Books.* PO Box 5813, Berkeley, CA 94705. Send $2.00 for a catalog of new, used and rare books and recordings.

Cool Beatnik Movies

Some of these aren't readily available on video yet, so late night TV and rep theaters are your only hope of seeing these Beat classics.

• *The Beat Generation* (1959). Although most Beats were exceptionally non-violent, Beatniks were frequently cast as movie villains. In the 1950s, after all, anybody different was thought to be dangerous, possibly even a Communist. This film was directed by Albert Zugsmith, who owes gentle, poetry-loving Beats everywhere an apology.

• *The Beatniks* (1960). Loads of unintentional laughs in another film with Beatniks as criminals. *Big Valley's* Nick Barkley plays a hipster psycho.

• *The Subterraneans* (1960). Kerouac was justifiably embarrassed by this Hollywood version of his book which cast white Leslie Caron as his black girlfriend and a swishy Arte Johnson as Allen Ginsberg.

• *A Bucket of Blood* (1959). Roger Corman's black comedy about a nebbish who accidentally kills some folks and ends up becoming a big cat in the Beat scene when he decides to encase the bodies in plaster and pass them off as modern art.

$19.95 + 3.00 shipping from Mr. Dickens (see below).

• *High School Confidential* (MGM 1958). One of the earliest Beatnik exploitation movies complete with teen angst and reefers. Only has one major Beatnik scene, which focuses on a performance of an immortal jazz-poem, *Tomorrow is a Drag, Man*. A lot of fun, and it's available on video.

$39.95 + 3.00 shipping.

Mr. Dickens Books and Video, 5323A Elkhorn Blvd., Sacramento, CA 95842. (800) 228-4246.

PILGRIMAGE: X Marks the Scene

Now you can go on THE road with "The Beat Generation Map of America." This poster identifies the hip coffee houses, crash pads, jazz clubs and bars from coast to coast, from Sausalito's "No Name Bar" to Kerouac's Lowell, Massachusetts.

$5.75 folded, $9.70 rolled from Aaron Blake Publications, 1800 S. Robertson, Ste. 130, Los Angeles, CA 90035.

How to Talk Beat

bread: money

busted: to run afoul of the law

cat: a swinging nonconformist

chick: a cat who's female

cool: whatever sends you

cop out: to go conventional

crazy: something that meets with a cat's approval

dig: understand, enjoy

drag: a bore, disappointment

like: Beat equivalent of "um" or "you know?" as in "Like, that's YOUR reality, man."

man: general personal pronoun indicating whomever is being addressed, regardless of gender or quantity (i.e., you don't say "What's happening, Woman?" to a "chick" and you don't say "Hey, dig, Men!" to a group, despite size or gender)

pad: where a cat crashes or lives

square: anyone who's not with it, or cool; a conformist

wig: lose your mind, as in "I wigged out"

"A comedian knows just what he is saying but he doesn't mean it. A poet might not know what he is saying but he means every word."

—Whitman McGowan

"Grandma, what fantastic eyes you have!"

"The better to dig you with, my dear," said the Wolf.

—Steve Allen, *Steve Allen's Bop Fables*

Wail, Baby!

Dizzy Ratstein T-Shirt. From Bob Armstrong's *Mickey Rat* underground comics, comes Dizzy Ratstein, the coolest rodent from hipsville. The design's full color on white cotton.

Specify size. $12.00 + 2.00 shipping from Last Gasp, 2180 Bryant St., San Francisco, CA 94110. (415) 824-6636 / FAX (415) 824-1836.

The Foam of the Brave

While we have our own very high opinions about beer, the Beer Institute *really* views the world through amber-colored glasses. Some misguided folks may think that the quantum leaps of civilization were fire, the wheel,

"They who drink beer will think beer."
—Washington Irving

or math, but this trade group has discovered the true motivating force: beer. We couldn't argue with the logic nor match the eloquence, so we offer excerpts from their pamphlet:

"How the Discovery of Beer Led to Civilization. According to one prominent anthropologist, what lured our ancient ancestors out of their caves may not have been a thirst for knowledge, but a thirst for beer.

"Dr. Solomon Katz theorizes that when man learned to ferment grain into beer more than 10,000 years ago, it became one of his most important sources of nutrition. But in order to have a steady supply of beer, Man had to give up his nomadic ways, settle down, and begin farming. And once he did, civilization was just a stone's throw away."

"If The Mayflower Had Been Carrying More Beer, It Might Never Have Landed At Plymouth Rock. A journal by one of the Mayflower's passengers indicates that beer played a part in the Pilgrims' decision to land at Plymouth Rock, instead of sailing further south: 'we could not now take time for further search, our victuals being much spent, especially our beere.'

"The British Called the Taverns 'Hotbeds of Sedition.' Thomas Jefferson wrote much of the Declaration of Independence in Philadelphia's Indian Queen tavern..."

You want to know more? We're not surprised. Contact the Beer Institute, 1225 Eye Street, NW, Washington, DC 20005, and ask for a copy of their civilization pamphlet.

You Vill Like This Product ...OR ELSE!

Stereotypical jolly German gentleman wearing Lederhosen willkommens you to his home on this all-weather, durable rubberized vinyl doormat.

#E2145 German Mat, $12.98 + 3.95 shipping from Harriet Carter, North Wales, PA 19455, (215) 361-5151.

One for the Road

Use the breathalyzer the pros use (cops that is, not professional drinkers). Alcomax tests the blood alcohol concentration in your bloodstream by analyzing exhaled breath.

#AP008 Alcomax, $39.95 + 3.00 shipping from Markline, P.O. Box 13807, Philadelphia, PA 19101-3807. (800) 922-8600.

Roll out the barrel...there are 31 gallons of brew in every barrel, enough for 330 cans.

The Beer Facts

• In medieval times, taverns were rough. Glass-bottomed beer tankards were invented so you could keep a wary eye on fellow drinkers.

• The reason beer keeps you in the john: besides the flood of liquid, the alcohol acts as a diuretic, taking fluids out of your body and flushing them down the tubes. This dehydration also causes a lot of the hangover the next morning. Best prevention? Drink some water every time you visit the facilities.

• Sadder, Budweiser? About one out of four beers consumed in the United States is a Bud. Next most popular are Miller Lite, Coor's Light, Bud Light, Busch, Miller High Life, Milwaukee's Best, Old Milwaukee, Coor's, and Miller Genuine Draft.

• Northeasterners and westerners drink more imported beer than elsewhere—more than twice the national average.

• The first commercial beer cans appeared in 1935. The next major innovation occurred in 1962 with the introduction of the pop top. Church keys went the way of the slide rule.

• Tanked? In Pilsen, Czechoslovakia, residents filled a surplus military tank with their local brew to celebrate the 45th anniversary of the town's liberation in World War II. They drank a tankful of beer in one evening. Tanks for the memories.

"The beer that Rip Van Winkle drank made him sleep for twenty years. The beer we drink—Hamm's—makes us sleep soundly all night and creates a good appetite in old people like your grandmother!"

"I'm going to keep on setting here until I'm petrified
And then maybe these tears will leave my eyes
There's a tear in my beer
Cause I'm crying for you, dear
You were on my lonely mind."
—**Big Bill Lister**

Frontiers of Social Science

Anthropologist James M. Schaefer studied the effects of music on drinking in C & W bars. Some findings:

• Jukeboxes are "mood selection devices." There was a direct "tears-to-beers" correlation—sad, sentimental tunes leading to more drinking.

• Also, the slower the tune, the faster the drinking.

• Country music leads to alcohol abuse more than pop or rock.

• Factors contributing to moderation: a strict, posted dress code, an even man-woman ratio, and landscape paintings on the walls.

• Factors contributing to heavy drinking: dim lights, cheap drinks, a small dance floor, and action art on the walls.

Beer Belly?

"It isn't the beer that gives you the belly. Americans assume that winking at a bottle of beer will make your eyelids fat...but suicidal drinkers are gaunt. Beer drinkers are just poor (calorie) managers. The beer belly is really the nachos, cheese and bean dip belly."

—**Beer anthropologist Alan Eames.**

"Beer is not a good cocktail-party drink, especially in a home where you don't know where the bathroom is."
—**Billy Carter**

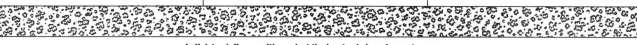

Short Hops

• **Oldenberg Brewery & Entertainment Complex.** Tour a working brewery and enjoy the Brew-Ha-Ha! revue. It's always "Suds Time" at the world's largest collection of beer and brewing memorabilia.

Just south of Cincinnati, the brewery boasts a huge collection of beer bottles, beer cans, coasters, tap knobs, photos, equipment, and more.

I-75 and Buttermilk Pike, Fort Mitchell, KY 41017. (800) 323-4917.

• **Museum of Beverage Containers & Advertising.** Tom Bates, started collecting roadside beer cans when he was 13. His father, Paul, also became fascinated and soon the items overflowed their home. So they began this amazing museum.

Ridgecrest Drive, Goodlettsville, TN 37072. (615) 859-5236.

I Said Bud Light

Bud sign. Light up the classic Budweiser "bowtie" neon sign to let the gang know the bar is open.

#N2302, $249.00 + 7.50 shipping. Anheuser-Busch Catalog, PO Box 14309A, St. Louis, MO 63178-1309. (800) 553-1987.

Don't Worry, Be Hoppy!

American Homebrewers Association. Brewing beer is fun and not too hard. Drink in a copy of *Zymurgy* and you'll be brewing your own before you know it.

This friendly, readable magazine offers up plenty of technical information, gadgets, and procedures, recipes, and special tips for the new brewer. Also they sell the classic beermaking guide, *The Complete Joy of Home Brewing*, $8.95 plus 3.00 shipping.

Dues: $21 a year. Includes sub to *Zymurgy*, The Magazine for the Homebrewer and Beer Lover. PO Box 287, Boulder, CO 80306-0287. (303) 447-0816.

The Libation Library

• *Beer and Bar Atlas* by Pat Baker. A beer drinker's pick of the country's outstanding beers, bars, and breweries.

$4.50 + 3.00 shipping from American Homebrewers Association, P.O. Box 287, Boulder, CO 80306-0287. (303) 447-0816.

• *The Complete Book of Beer Drinking Games* by Andy Griscom and Ben Rand. Fifty guzzling games (ever played "Beer Hunter" or "Slush Fund"?). Enjoy its beer trivia between swigs.

$7.25 + 1.50 shipping from Beer Drinkers Intl., PO Box 566402, Oceanside, CA 92058. (619) 724-4447.

• *Beer USA* by Will Anderson. This is truly an "all about beer" book, with facts, folklore, photos, and fun.

$20.75 + 1.50 shipping from Beer Drinkers Intl., PO Box 566402, Oceanside, CA 92058. (619) 724-4447.

Hold the Foam

Budweiser Telephone. This phone doesn't ring, it plays Bud commercial jingles like "This Bud's for You."

$100.00 + 7.50 shipping from Anheuser-Busch, P.O. Box 14309A, St. Louis, MO 63178-1309. (800) 553-1987.

Checkered Pabst

No, actually Budweiser again. Bud versus Bud Light checker set. You crown kings with bottle caps.

#N2084, $12.50 + 3.50 shipping from Anheuser-Busch, P.O. Box 14309A, St. Louis, MO 63178-1309. (800) 553-1987.

It's a Gas

Electronic Burp Mug. Looks like a beer mug, sounds like a beer hog.

$16.98 + 4.20 shipping from Johnson Smith, 4514 19th Court E., Bradenton, FL 34206. (813) 747-2356.

In Cedar City, Utah, citizens over 50 aren't allowed to drink beer if their shoe laces are untied.

Beer Nuts

• **American Breweriana Association.** This organization is for beer enthusiasts historians, and collectors of brewery advertising and antiques (signs, cans, bottles, trays, etc.). They have conventions and a lending library of books, catalogs and periodicals for members. Their journal is a cut above most.

Dues: $20 year, includes subscription to *The American Breweriana Journal.* PO Box 1157, Pueblo, CO 81001. (719) 544-9267.

• **Beer Can Collectors of America.** Open to anyone who has an interest in collecting beer cans and breweriana. It offers "the opportunity to meet and make friends with people around the world who have the same strange obsession." The organization hosts an annual "CANvention."

From their literature: *How to Grade Cans.* **Excellent**—has top and bottom, but may have "church key" holes. No rust, scratches, fading, dents or easily noticeable imperfections; **Average**—In good shape but some easily noticeable light rust, scratches, nicks, "dimples," fading. **Poor**—Rusted or faded and label is undistinguishable or almost so. Recycle it!

Dues: $27 year. Includes subscription to *Beer Can Collectors News.* 747 Merus Court, Fenton, MO 63026-2092.

Stein Collectors International. An interest in antique beer steins is what brings these folks together. Covered steins first appeared in Europe in the 1500s to protect the beer from flies that were thought to carry the plague. Most of the early steins were made of stoneware (*stein* means stone in German), but later ones were made of glass, wood, porcelain, pewter, and even leather.

Dues: $20/year. Includes subscription to *Prosit.* PO Box 661125, Los Angeles, CA 90066. (213) 837-9734.

Hold Your Head Up High

Half a Yard of Ale Glass. When they ask for "a tall one," you'll be ready. The handsome walnut stand holds a tall glass beaker that can handle 18" of the foamy brew.

$14.98 + 3.95 shipping from Funny Side Up, 425 Stump Rd., North Wales, PA 19454. (215) 361-5130.

Beer Necessities

Beer Mugs on Boxer Shorts. These look too cool to hide them away as underwear. Show your foamy beer mugs to the world! 100% cotton in sizes 30-32, 34-36, 38-40, and 42-44.

$11.98 + 3.95 shipping from Funny Side Up, 425 Stump Rd., North Wales, PA 19454. (215) 361-5130.

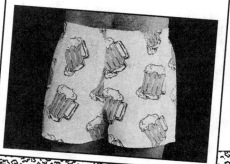

"Rhapsody in Brew"

Love that great beer advertising from the past? Here are connections you'll want to make:

• **National Association of Breweriana Advertising.** Quarterly journal, conventions, trading opportunities.

Dues: $20 year, includes subscription to *Breweriana Collector.* 2343 Met-To-Wee Lane, Wauwatosa, WI 53226.

• **Rhapsody in Brew.** TV beer commercials from the 1950s and '60s. All your favorite brands, plus regional brands you've never heard of.

$24.95 + 3.95 shipping. Video Resources, 220 W. 71st St., New York, NY 10023.

• *The Paws of Refreshment: The Story of Hamm's Beer Advertising* by **Moira F. Harris.** The history of the popular Hamm's Bear from "The Land of Sky Blue Waters." Lots of black and white photos for Hamm's fanatics.

$15.95 + 2.50 shipping from Pogo Press, Four Cardinal Lane, St. Paul, MN 55127. (612) 483-4692.

BETTY BOOP

"Don't Take My Boop-Oop-A-Doop Away"

Betty Boop started out as a dog. Literally. When she was first drawn in 1930 by Fleischer studio veteran Grim Natwick, she had floppy ears and a pug snout and served as Bimbo the Dog's girlfriend in the Talkartoon series. She shed her doggy image in *Betty Coed* and her long ears became earrings.

Betty was a popular combination of sweet and saucy. Her figure was modeled after Mae West's and her singing was a direct imitation of Helen Kane's (who unsuccessfully sued the Fleischers about it). Because of objections from the guardians of morality, her wardrobe became less daring as time went on, with more cloth added to hide her garter belt on one end and shoulders on the other.

As the song has it, "Made of pen and ink, she can win you with a wink, ain't she cute, boop-oop-a-doop, sweeeeeet Betty."

Betty made more than 100 films before retiring after *Yip, Yip, Yippy!* in 1939. She had a small cameo in *Roger Rabbit* in 1988.

Bop Outta Bed With Boop

1930s-style alarm clock features Betty and Koko plus Bimbo, who acts as the "second hand" by running around the face of the clock with each ticking second.

#2635, $26.98 + 3.50 shipping. The Lighter Side, 4514 19th Court East, P.O. Box 25600, Bradenton, FL 34206-5600. (813) 747-2356 / FAX (813) 746-7896.

Boop Box

Let Betty keep track of your trinkets, coins, candy, paper clips, whatever!

#4542, $10.98 + 3.50 shipping from The Lighter Side, 4514 19th Court East, P.O. Box 25600, Bradenton, FL 34206-5600. (813) 747-2356 / FAX (813) 746-7896.

She's Got A Great Mug

And you can have it, too. Large ceramic mug is safe for dishwashers and microwaves.

#2412, $13.98 + 3.50 shipping. The Lighter Side, 4514 19th Court East, P.O. Box 25600, Bradenton, FL 34206-5600. (813) 747-2356 / FAX (813) 746-7896.

You Must Have Been A Boopiful Baby

Baby Boop is all dolled up in pink plaid bonnet and dress, both trimmed in eyelet lace.

#2412, $13.98 + 3.50 shipping. The Lighter Side, 4514 19th Court East, P.O. Box 25600, Bradenton, FL 34206-5600. (813) 747-2356 / FAX (813) 746-7896.

Show Off Your Boops

Bouncy, bubbly Betty struts her stuff on the front and back of this colorful cotton Bet-T-shirt.

#B3756 Small; #B3757, Medium; #B3758, Large; #B3759 XLarge. Each $14.98 + 4.75 shipping from Harriet Carter, North Wales, PA 19455. (215) 361-5151.

Betty's voice was performed by the amazing Mae Questel, who was also the voice for Olive Oyl.

Baggers & Choosers

Shoop 'til you droop with the Betty Boop Bag.

#1498, Set of two, $7.98 + 2.50 shipping. The Lighter Side, 4514 19th Court East, P.O. Box 25600, Bradenton, FL 34206-5600. (813) 747-2356 / FAX (813) 746-7896.

Out of the Inkpad

Set of two rubber stamps will liven up letters and more.

#1540, $10.98 + 3.50 shipping. The Lighter Side, 4514 19th Court East, P.O. Box 25600, Bradenton, FL 34206-5600. (813) 747-2356 / FAX (813) 746-7896.

LIVEN UP YOUR LOBE LIFE

Boop Earrings for pierced ears.

#2621, $5.98 + 2.50 shipping. The Lighter Side, 4514 19th Court East, P.O. Box 25600, Bradenton, FL 34206-5600. (813) 747-2356 / FAX (813) 746-7896.

Keychain Kicks

Boop in the right key.

#2613, $8.98 + 2.50 shipping. The Lighter Side, 4514 19th Court East, P.O. Box 25600, Bradenton, FL 34206-5600. (813) 747-2356 / FAX (813) 746-7896.

Toon Up Your VCR

Betty Boop Collector's Edition. Here are some of the original Betty Boop cartoons from the 1930s. These are well-recorded from good-quality, cleaned up prints, and are not colorized.

84 minutes long, #REP 7066-V, $19.95 + 3.50 shipping from The Whole Toon Catalog, P.O. Box 369, Issaquah, WA 98027. (206) 391-8747 / FAX (206) 391-9064.

Mask Confusion

Confound friends and process servers with the Betty Boop rubber mask.

#3424, $24.98 + 3.50 shipping. The Lighter Side, 4514 19th Court East, P.O. Box 25600, Bradenton, FL 34206-5600. (813) 747-2356 / FAX (813) 746-7896.

Framing the Scorecards of History

Bowling may be the most played sport in the world with 71 million bowlers worldwide, rolling billions of frames a year. And did you know that this sport may also be the oldest?

Bowling with Fred and Barney. Historians believe that bowling of sorts may date back to when cavemen roll rocks at a standing target for hunting practice. Pins and balls were found in the tomb of an Egyptian youth who

died in 5,200 BC. And an ancient Polynesian society used to bowl with round stone discs from a distance of 60 feet, coincidentally the exact length of bowling lanes today.

When in Rome, Bowl-O-Roma. Bocci, an outdoor bowling game without pins was extremely popular in Imperial Rome. Caesar's troops conquered the

world, and left bocci behind everywhere they went. In England, bocci evolved into lawn bowling. Even Henry VIII played on his private palace grounds between feasts and beheadings.

Sir Francis Drake was in the middle of a game when he was told of the Spanish Armada's approach. "Play out the game," he said, "there's time for that and beating the Spanish after." We don't know how he bowled, but he beat the Spanish.

A Devil of a Game. Bowling indoors originated in German monasteries where they bowled at a "kegel", a bottle-shaped club. Martin Luther was an enthusiast and used bowling metaphors in speeches.

We'll Bowl Manhattan. The game spread to America by way of Dutch and/or British settlers. One early bowler was William Penn, founder of Pennsylvania. The Bowling Green area of Lower Manhattan was once exactly that; then the game spread into the Catskills, site of Washington Irving's famous 9-pins story, *Rip Van Winkle*.

The 1800s saw a 9-pin boom, with Abraham Lincoln an alley regular. But it also saw a backlash. Associated closely with gambling, 9-pins was outlawed in many cities, but was deftly rescued by a sly aficionado who simply added another pin, sidestepping the "9-pin" prohibition completely.

PEGGING THE PINBOY

Pinboys used to reset the pins after each frame. This was a dangerous job, and slowed the games. Automatic pinsetters were introduced in 1952 and the popularity of the game expanded rapidly.

BOWLING BIMONTHLY

Bowling Digest comes out every two months to keep you informed and bowling-literate. $22 for 6 issues.

German monks used bowling proficiency as a proof of godliness.

Reading to Spare

Bowl-O-Rama; the Visual Arts of Bowling by H. Thomas Steele. Alley artifacts from architecture to awards, postcards to pinups. Exploring the bowling arts from middle high culture to pure kitsch, this visual feast features everything vaguely related to the sport, even ashtrays and salt shakers.

Highly recommended.

$19.95 + $2.50 shipping from Abbeville Press, 505 Park Ave., New York, NY 10022. (800) 227-7210.

> *"In ordinary life many a person thinks he can defeat others by knocking down all nine pins and then misses all of them."*
> —Martin Luther

Zen Bowling

The Mental Game: The Inner Game of Bowling by George Allen. That whole Zen thing comes to the middle class. This book promises to teach you how to handle pressure, psyche yourself up or down, develop a winning attitude and reach that state of relaxed concentration while bowling that the Zen masters normally reach only after years of grueling meditation.

$14.95 + $1.50 shipping from Bowling Digest, Dept B, 990 Grove Street, Evanston, IL 60201

No-Handicap Bowling

With the help of guide rails and Braille score-keeping, blind and wheelchair-bound bowlers have established leagues and tournaments, opening the world's most popular sport to even more enthusiasts. "You could say these bowlers opened my eyes, they showed me you don't have to roll over and play dead," says a bowler with multiple sclerosis.

- **American Blind Bowling Assoc.**
  67 Bame Ave.
  Buffalo, NY 14215
  (716) 836-1472

- **American Wheelchair Bowling Assoc.**
  N54 W15858 Larkspur Lane
  Menomonee Falls, WI 53051
  (414) 781-6876

YOUR OWN TROPHY

Trophyland USA features hundreds of ego-stroking trophies in a myriad of styles, and they don't even ask for proof that you deserve it. So you can have it engraved "1st Place—Interplanetary Bowling Competition—(Your Name Here)" and only you will know how empty your achievement really is.

For info or catalog, contact Trophyland USA, 7001 W. 20th Ave., P.O. Box 4606, Hialeah, FL 33014. (800) 327-5820.

Self-righteous militant anti-bowling prohibitionists in the 1800s busted up bowling alleys.

PINNING DOWN THE FACTS

• If you throw ten strikes, you can achieve the perfect bowling score of 300. But the highest score possible in a game where no strikes are thrown is 190.

• 25% of all Americans interviewed in a 1990 survey said that their dream house would include a built-in bowling alley. Only 9% would have a tennis court.

• According to the *Guinness Book of World Records*, the largest bowling center is Fukuyama Bowl in Osaka, Japan, featuring 144 lanes under one roof. America's grandest alley is Showboat Lanes in Las Vegas (where else?) with 106 lanes.

• There were 8,025 bowling centers with a total of 153,163 lanes in 1990, down from 11,476 alleys and 163,323 playing lanes in 1962.

• It's usually not a big deal when your score is equal to your age doubled. When Mollie Marler did just that, though, it was: she rolled a 202 game at the age of 101.

• The oldest operating certified bowling center is the Elks Bowling Lanes in Fond Du Lac, Wisconsin.

• On April 30, 1988, Audrey Gable scored a perfect 300 point game.

She was eight months pregnant at the time.

• Other notable perfect games: Youngest: Richard Daff Jr., age 11, April, 1990. Oldest: Leo Sites, age 80, April, 1985.

> "Having children is like having a bowling alley installed in your brain."
> —Martin Mull, American cultural commentator

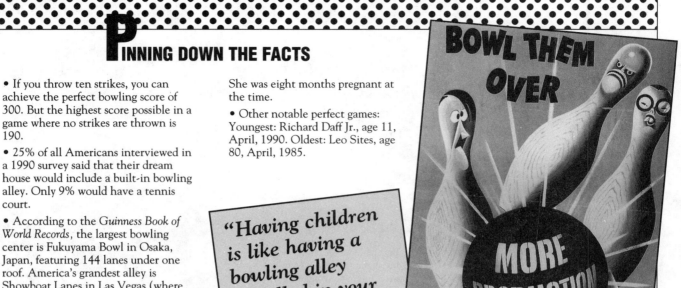

A Lobe of the Game

Bowling ball and pin earrings certainly make a "striking" impression. Keep your mind in the gutter with these pierced ear accessories. One earring is a 2" pin; the other, a 3/4" ball.

#B3161 Bowl Earrings $5.98 +$3.50 shipping from Harriet Carter, North Wales, PA 19455. (215) 361-5151.

STRIKING SHIRT

Like every sport, bowling has its uniform. Unlike most, bowling wear is also a fashion statement. Those in the know favor the '50s style shirts, complete with two-tone pleats and built-in belts, which ushered in a colorful era in bowling wear. And the alley elite wear a cool logo stitched on their chests—either their name or something like the Flintstones (below).

"Fifties Forever" bowling shirt with Modern Stone Age Family stitched above pocket. Sizes 30-46, women and S, M, L, XL, XXL and (Fred's size) XXXL for men. Your choice of red & white; peacock blue & yellow; tan & brown; or raspberry & winter white. $36.20 + 2.75 from King Louie International, 13500 15th St., Grandview, MO 64030. (800) 521-1212.

There's a bowling alley in the White House basement, installed by Harry S Truman.

BOWLingo

Apple—a bowling ball

Barmaid—a pin hiding behind another

Bedposts—7-10 split; a.k.a. telephone poles, snake eyes, mule ears, or goal posts

Body English—an instinctual attempt to change an already thrown ball's course through body contortions

Cherry—downing only the front pins when going for a spare

Christmas Tree—3-7-10 or 2-7-10 splits

Dead Apple—a ball with no power when it reaches the pins

Dutchman—alternating strikes and spares for a 200 score

Golden Gate—4-6-7-10 split

Grasshopper—a ball that sends the pins leaping

Grandma's Teeth—a random, gap-filled group of pins left standing

Jack Manders—a roll right between the "bedposts"

Mother-In-Law—the 7 pin

Poodle—a roll right into the gutter

Schleifer—a suspenseful domino-like strike

Turkey—three strikes in a row

Never Get Another Gutter Ball

The latest thing for novices are bumpers which fit in each gutter and bounces your ball back to the center. If you have trouble handling failure your bowling center may already have 'em. Otherwise, bring your own.

#46E-362, $395.00 + 16.00 shipping from Saunier-Wilhem Co., 3216 Fifth Ave., Pittsburgh, PA 15213. (412) 621-4350.

THIS ALLEY'S A ZOO

For some reason, animals like bowling balls. The balls break up the boredom and give them something to play with. But sometimes there are problems, just like with people. The Washington National Zoo used to buy chipped balls for the bears before they were moved to a new exhibit area. Curators were afraid the bears might try rolling a strike at the new glass windows.

The Brookfield, Illinois zoo even got some bowling balls without holes so the animals wouldn't break their teeth on them. The polar bears thought they were terrific, but curators had to take them away when they discovered the balls were the perfect size for plugging the drains in their moat.

There was a problem with the lions, too. The big cats took to batting the balls against the walls, which left holes. One male liked a ball so much he adopted it and refused to let any other lions near it.

IF THE SHOE FITS

There is nothing more evocative of the bowling experience than rented bowling shoes. They are always sort of musty, with funny colors and the size emblazoned on the back. So why not invest in your own pair for sliding up to the foul line, or just being extremely cool at sock hops?

Newer models feature the latest leaps in footwear technology, but if you have any sense of tradition you can opt for the old reliable rental type, silly lookin' but extremely sturdy.

In all men's and women's sizes, red & green combo only. $21.75 + 3.50 shipping. Saunier-Wilhelm Co. 3216 Fifth Ave. Pittsburgh, PA 15213 (412) 621-4350

Step Out in Style

Mount these personalized metal plates on the heels of your shoes and you can show the world that you have a name. Choice of 6 colors (raspberry red, blue, green, violet, black or gold).

$6.95 ppd. from Awards to the Wise, 28 Abbott Ave., Milpitas, CA 95035

BUBBLES

Pucker Up & Blow

When soap is added to water, it weakens the water's surface tension, which makes the invisible filmy "skin" on top of the liquid more stretchable. When you dunk your dipper in the soapy solution and blow gently, the liquid skin stretches until it leaves the dipper and floats away as a bubble. Bubbles are colorful, enchanting, beautiful—and brief, first here and then suddenly gone, a fragile film destined to dissolve into thin air.

Why are we so fascinated by them? It may be because we were once liquid ourselves. We evolved from the sea, so we were likely blowing ocean bubbles eons ago, and before that we probably **were** bubbles.

Bubbles are definitely part of—poof!—pop culture, and they are also a big business. There are all manner of bubble wands, bubble hoops, bubble trumpets, a "Swiss army bubble knife," bubble pipes, bubble-blowing toy lawn mowers, bubble jewelry for adults, bubble bears and even bubble festivals featuring professional bubble demonstrators. Not bad for something that's 97% air.

Inflationary Facts

• The skin of a bubble is only a few millionths of an inch thick.

• Though heat and dryness are enemies of bubbles, sharpness is not. According to attorney and bubble stuntman Sterling Johnson, "If it's really soaked, you can even stick a knife through a bubble and not pop it."

• The colors that swirl around the surface of bubbles are caused by the interference of light waves. Some are reflected from the outside surface and some from the inside surface of the bubble. The colors change as the soap film gets thinner from evaporation.

• Scientists who study changes in climate consider bubbles good friends. Bubbles trapped in the ice of glaciers are filled with Ice Age air—unbreathed by anyone for 12,000 years. The bubbles are clean samples of ancient air that can tell scientists the way it was back then before civilization reared its ugly head.

• The late Eiffel Plasterer (his real name) holds the record for the oldest "breath-blown" bubble: 364 days (It was protected inside a bell jar).

Bubbly Personalities

• Louis Pearl of Sausalito, California, known as "The Amazing Bubbleman" and "The Pope of Soap," has sold hundreds of thousands of his Bubble Trumpets which produce huge bubbles.

• Bernie Zubrowski puts together museum exhibits and has written a book about bubbles for a science-for-children series (he says both Einstein and Newton were enthusiastic bubble blowers).

• Myron B. Shur, is chairman of the board of the Strombecker Corporation of Chicago, maker of the nation's biggest line of bubble soap and toys (Mr. Bubbles, Wonder Bubbles). They sell 50 million bottles of bubble soap each year.

bubble up

Bubble-Head Philosophy

"Bubbles are like love; impossible to describe, and constantly new."

—Louis "The Amazing Bubble Man" Pearl

"A soap bubble is the most beautiful thing, and the most exquisite in nature…I wonder how much it would take to buy a soap bubble, if there was only one in the world."

—Mark Twain

"Bubble magic is no illusion. It's real magic!"

—Tom "The Bubble Guy" Noddy

Bubbliography

• *Professor Bubble's Official Bubble Handbook* by Richard Faverty. Shows you to how make unusual bubble wands, how to do tricks like barehanded bubbles and bubbles inside bubbles, and lots of other great bubble ideas from a bubble pro.

$5.95 + 1.50 shipping. Greenleaf Books, Depot Street, Schenevus, NY 12155.

• *Tom Noddy's Bubble Magic* by Tom Noddy. An upbeat guide to the world of bubbles and bubble-blowing from a professional bubble demonstrator (Want him for your next party? PO Box 1576, Santa Cruz, CA 95061. (408) 423-1021).

$8.95 + 1.50 shipping. Running Press, 125 S. 22nd Street, Philadelphia, PA 19103. (800) 345-5359.

• *The Unbelievable Bubble Book* by John Cassidy with David Stein. This is a package deal: an odd-looking, stringy plastic "Bubble-Thing" and a guide on how to get humongous bubbles out if it—we're talking several feet in diameter! A one-trick device, but what a trick it is.

$9.95 + 2.00 shipping. Klutz Press, 2121 Staunton Ct., Palo Alto, CA 94306. (415) 424-0739.

Chic Bubble Bauble

At first glance people will think you're wearing a sterling silver perfume bottle pendant. But when you uncork the flask, pull out the attached 1/4 inch wand and blow, your little clique will break into amazed applause.

It's the '90s alternative to the coke spoon. Madonna's got one, and so have Whoopi Goldberg, Larry Hagman, Ron Howard, and Debra Winger.

Created by New Mexico jewelry maker Ted Cutter who has also designed a sterling silver pea shooter that comes with 10 jade peas.

The Bubbler comes with gift box, leather pouch, satin cord, bubble solution, and miniature funnel.

$65 from Tops Malibu, 23410 Civic Center Way, Malibu, CA 90265. (213) 456-8677.

Foaming at the Mouth

• Special wand lets you blow bubbles inside other bubbles. Bubble fluid included.

#4255 Pocket kit, $3.98 + 1.35 shipping. #4263 Giant kit (8" tray & wand), $5.98 + 2.70 shipping. Johnson Smith Co., 4514 19th Court E., PO Box 25500, Bradenton, FL 34206. (813) 747-2356.

• **Magic Wands.** Set of three plastic wands includes Sun, Heart, and Bubble in Bubble Wand. What shape are the bubbles, you ask?

#90503, $16.50 + 3.25 shipping from Discovery Corner, Lawrence Hall of Science, University of California, Berkeley, CA 94720. (415) 642-1016.

Bubbling Basics

• There are commercial bubble solutions that do a good job, but you can make a better one cheaper. Mix 1 oz. of dishwashing liquid like Dawn and Joy, 1 oz. of glycerin (available at drug stores— promotes bubble longevity), and two cups of water. You're in business.

• You can use just about anything with a hole through it as a bubble dipper—a juice can with ends removed, a plastic straw, a pipe cleaner, wire patio furniture, or a wire hanger twisted into a circle.

• If you're blowing a lot of bubbles, stay off the lawn. Any quantity of bubble stuff can turn patches of grass brown.

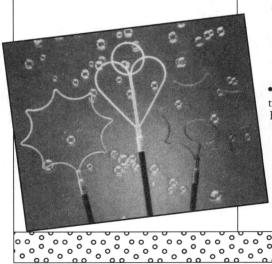

Bugs Bunny and Friends

Warner Bros. cartoons asked viewers to go on a wild ride of impossible gags, playful visual tricks, and outrageous, irreverent characters. These masterpieces of comic timing may have been the funniest animation ever.

• **Bugs Bunny.** The brash rabbit became one of the world's favorite characters. The first "true" Bugs appeared in *A Wild Hare* in 1940. In 1960, he became the host of his own prime-time TV show.

Bugs' trademark was the wisecrack delivered while chomping on a carrot. The Utah Celery Company and the Broccoli Institute of America both tried to get Bugs to switch vegetables, but Bugs remained true to the carrot even though his voice, Mel Blanc, would've been happy to switch. He claimed that carrots made his throat tighten so that he didn't sound like the character anymore. He taped the carrot-crunching parts last, and had them spliced into the right places.

• **Daffy Duck.** He first appeared (with Porky Pig) in a cartoon released in 1937. He often played against arch-rival Bugs, who always outwitted him, leaving Daffy muttering, "You're dethpicable!"

• **Porky Pig.** Shy, good-natured and simpleminded, Porky had his own cartoons, but he was most famous for the "Th-Th-Th-That's All Folks!" closing line. He first appeared in 1935 in *I Haven't Got a Hat*, and later married Petunia.

• **Tweety & Sylvester.** The baby-talking but ruthless Tweety made his debut in *A Tale of Two Kitties* in 1942, uttering his famous line "I tawt I taw a puddy-tat!" The forever-hungry cat, Sylvester, first appeared, without Tweety, in *Life With Feathers* in 1945. Sufferin' succotash! The fateful collision of Tweety and Sylvester was in *Tweetie Pie* in 1947, when Tweety became a yellow canary. (He had been pink, but censors had objected that he looked naked.)

• **The Roadrunner & Wile E. Coyote.** These two speeding adversaries were introduced to the world in the 1949 *Fast and Furry-ous*. Animator Chuck Jones developed fifteen years of those backfiring schemes concocted by the Coyote to catch the beeping bird. This in spite of (actually, *because* of) the unlimited gadgetry of the ACME company, items like Rocket Powered Roller Skates and Do-It-Yourself Tornadoes. "When I was a kid," Jones says, "we called everything the ACME Corporation. I adored the idea that there was a factory someplace that supplied nothing but things for coyotes."

• Some other Warner Bros. favorites include Elmer Fudd, Pepe Le Pew, Foghorn Leghorn, Speedy Gonzales, and Yosemite Sam.

"Eh, What's Up, Doc?"

When the animators were thinking up lines for Bugs in 1940, Tex Avery remembered "Hey, what's doin', doc?" from a kid at high school in Taylor, Texas and revised the phrase a little.

Bug's greeting is famous around the world—"What's up, Doc?" is "Do shi ta no da ro?" ("What's happening?") in Japanese, "Che sucede, amico?" ("What happens, friend?") in Italian, and "Quoi de neuf, docteur?" ("What's new, doctor?") in French.

Mel Blanc's Porky Pig characterization, just one of a series of speech-impeded characters, provoked protests from a stutterers' rights organization.

Can You Control Taz?

Pick up his remote control and take Taz out for a spin. He goes forward, backward, and spins around, just like the pint-sized, growling Tasmanian Devil cartoon character.

#6063, $49.95 + 5.04 shipping from The Warner Bros. Collection, 4000 Warner Blvd., Burbank, CA 91522. (800) 223-6524.

Dynamite Alarm Clock

Wake up with a bang with this "ACME" dynamite alarm clock, just like Wile E. Coyote might use to wake up the Roadrunner. When the alarm goes off, a voice says, "All right, you have ten seconds to get up!" There's a countdown, followed by "OK. One more chance" and then another countdown that ends with an explosion sound.

#6065, $49.95 + 3.28 shipping. The Warner Bros. Collection, 4000 Warner Blvd., Burbank, CA 91522. (800) 223-6524.

Silly Sylvester Slippers

Pussy-foot around in these cushiony black, white and ruby slippers.

#5025 Children's, $14.95. #5024 Adults', $22.95. Add 2.87 shipping. The Warner Bros. Collection, 4000 Warner Blvd., Burbank, CA 91522. (800) 223-6524.

Music for the Savage Bunny

The Carl Stahling Project. Imagine those classic cartoons without voices and sound effects—you'd still get a sense of what was going on, thanks to the splendid soundtrack music. Carl Stahling wrote virtually all of the music from the classics, and amazing stuff it was: starting, stopping and changing directions on a dime. Lie back with headphones on and let the cartoons play in your mind.

Available for $15.98 + 3.65 from Bose Express Music, 50 West 17th St., New York, NY 10011. (800) 233-6357 / FAX (212) 627-2613.

Beep Beep!

You're the Road Runner against Wile E. Coyote's hate and rockets.

Nintendo compatible game, #7032, $49.95 + 2.04 shipping. The Warner Bros. Collection, 4000 Warner Blvd., Burbank, CA 91522. (800) 223-6524.

Sufferin' Succotash! Tweetie Pie was the first Warner Bros. cartoon character to win an Oscar, in 1940.

Bugs for Your Friends' Phones

Have that special bunny deliver a message for you: your choice of Happy Birthday, Happy Anniversary, Get Well, or Congratulations. Bugs will address your friend by name, if it's among the more than 1300 first names he knows. Just call the 900 number, answer some questions, and pick the time and day you want Bugs to call (order 9 minutes to 90 days in advance). You can also add a recorded message of your own to Bugs', if you like.

1-900-VIP-BUGS ([900] 847-2847). $6.95, charged to your phone bill.

Creature Feetures

Sock it to your tootsies. Specify size.

#7017 Sylvester and Tweety; #7020 Taz. $5.95 + .95 shipping. The Warner Bros. Collection, 4000 Warner Blvd., Burbank, CA 91522. (800) 223-6524.

War on the Warner Bros. Set

Looney Tunes characters as chessmen. The royal couples are played by Bugs & Honey Bunny and Porky & Petunia Pig. Sylvester and Daffy star as opposing bishops. Road Runner and Wile E. Coyote are rival rooks. Yosemite Sam and Tasmanian Devil play fierce armed knights. And tiny Tweety and Speedy Gonzalez are pawns, of course. Hand-painted pewter figures come with a walnut-finished chessboard with a clear raised lid for displaying the cartoon court.

#6014, $495.00 + 19.95 shipping from The Warner Bros. Collection, 4000 Warner Blvd., Burbank, CA 91522. (800) 223-6524.

Warner Bros. Limited Editions

American Royal Arts Corp. features hand-painted art derived from classic animated films. Sold with museum quality framing and matting, ready for you to hang.

• "Ducklaration of Independence," featuring Pepe Le Pew, Bugs Bunny, Daffy Duck, Porky Pig, and Yosemite Sam, signed by award-winning animator Chuck Jones, framed size 21 x 21". $895.

• "That's All Folks!" with Porky Pig in the classic end-of-cartoon pose, framed size 16 x 18", $695.

Free catalog.

American Royal Arts Corp., 70 East Old Country Road, Hicksville, NY 11801. (800) 888-9449.

Not 14 Carrots?

Watch has 1¹/₄" champagne dial, "gold-tone" face, and grey faux lizard leather strap.

#5030, $39.95 + 2.87 shipping from The Warner Bros. Collection, 4000 Warner Blvd., Burbank, CA 91522. (800) 223-6524.

Quote from a Master

"A small child once said to me: 'You don't draw Bugs Bunny, you draw pictures of Bugs Bunny.' That's a very profound observation because it means that he thinks that the characters are alive, which, as far as I'm concerned, is true. Animation isn't an illusion of life. It is life."

—Chuck Jones

The character and speech of Daffy Duck were modeled after the cartoonists' much-despised boss.

THE ACME OF ANIMATION

That's All Folks: The Art of Warner Bros. Animation by Steve Schneider. The first part of this colorful volume takes you inside the Warner Bros. studio where they made the cartoons that are so funny they can still bring down the house at university film festivals. The second part gives you a close-up look at the cartoon character stars: Porky Pig, Daffy Duck, Elmer Fudd, Bugs Bunny, Tweety and Sylvester, and many more. Informative text and plenty of illustrations, many in color.

$39.95 + 3.00 shipping. Funny Papers, 7253 Geary Blvd., San Francisco, CA 94121. (415) 752-1914.

That's Not All Folks! My Life in the Golden Age of Cartoons and Radio by Mel Blanc and Philip Bashe. The king of cartoon character voices tells his story. He was the voice of nearly all of the Warner Bros. characters. Lots of photos and animation art in this book about "the man of a thousand voices" who had an astonishing comic ability.

$4.99 + 2.00 shipping. Bud Plant Comic Art, P.O. Box 1689, Grass Valley, CA 95945. (800) 242-6642.

Chuck Amuck: The Life and Times of an Animated Cartoonist by Chuck Jones. Here's a readable and entertaining look into the life of animator Chuck Jones, winner of three Oscars, and recipient of a tribute by The Museum of Modern Art in 1985.

A perceptive observer, Jones takes you on an insider's tour of the Warner Bros. studio where talent and creativity were busting out all over (despite top management's efforts to squelch it), resulting in some of the world's finest cartoons. Lots of photographs and drawings (Bugs, Daffy, Roadrunner, many more), tied together with Jones' amusing and informative commentary.

$24.95 + 3.00 shipping from Funny Papers, 7253 Geary Blvd., San Francisco, CA 94121. (415) 752-1914.

Talking Book

It honks, it beeps, it says "What's up, Doc?" Toddlers love the push-button sound effects in this electronic book.

#5036, $21.95 + 2.87 shipping. The Warner Bros. Collection, 4000 Warner Blvd., Burbank, CA 91522. (800) 223-6524.

Tawt You Taw a Puddy Tat?

You did! You did! Sylvester chases Tweety Bird on this watch. Specify "men's" (1 1/4" across face) or "women's" (7/8").

#16945, $39.95 + 4.95 shipping from Wireless, P.O. Box 64422, St. Paul, MN 55154-0422. (800) 669-9999.

Mel Blanc was also a regular on the *Jack Benny* radio show, both as a character actor and as the noise of Jack's ancient Maxwell car.

Buttons

Labels for Your Lapels

Political campaign buttons, as we know them, have been around since the 1896 presidential campaign, which pitted William Jennings Bryan against William McKinley. Other political memorabilia, such as flags and banners, preceded buttons, appearing earlier in the 1800s.

Recently, though, campaign buttons have lost their zip. The bountiful colors and causes of past elections have deteriorated to the simple red, white and blue names of the candidates. Worse, election committees are turning away from true pins and instead issuing disposable lapel stickers because they cost only about a penny apiece.

Political bumperstickers have also seen a decline. More people can be reached for the dollars with a 60-second radio spot, and in these politically apathetic times fewer people are willing to gum up their chrome to wear their hearts on their bumpers.

BUTTON POETRY

- "Friendly, Dependable, Resourceful"? FDR, of course.
- "Dewey or Don't We?" was the button question of its day (and mentions of "Dewey buttons" became automatic laugh lines on radio and early TV).
- "I Like Ike" spawned reply buttons of "Ike Likes Me" and "I Like Adlai Better."
- Recycled buttons: "Nixon's the One" was used as a campaign slogan in 1968—the buttons reappeared shortly after Watergate with a whole new meaning.

Button Knows

- Although most campaign buttons are reasonably priced (as collectors' items go) a Cox-Roosevelt button from the 1920 presidential campaign sold in 1981 for $33,000, at an auction where labor lawyer Joseph Jacobs outbid Malcolm Forbes for the item.
- In 1983, a Highland Park, Michigan woman was sent to jail for 13 hours for refusing to remove a button supporting the judge's political foe while in his courtroom.
- The 1988 GOP campaign produced a blank, white button, meant as a satirical representation of the Democratic Platform, which they claimed "lacked substance." It's probably a collectors' item, but we're stymied about how you can tell if you've got an original.
- Peace buttons can be found as early as the 1890s, but they became the symbol of a later generation in the 1960s. It is the most recognizable non-corporate symbol worldwide.

Who's Got the Button?

The Political Gallery. Not surprising from the name, the Gallery features campaign buttons from the past, as well as an ever-changing supply of other political materials.

Quarterly catalogue $5.00, or subscription, $15.00 per year. 1325 W. 86th Street, Indianapolis, IN 46260. (317) 257-0863.

Dan Quayle: A Risk of Failure

The Quayle Quarterly. "If we don't succeed, we run the risk of failure." It seems every time Dan Quayle opens his mouth he offers us a quotation worthy of a button or T-shirt.

While it's not clear that J. Danforth Quayle could be any worse as president than what we've grown accustomed to, it's good to know that the *Quayle Quarterly* is keeping an eye on him. Besides scathing satire, it's loaded with Quayle books, calendars, doormats, watches, T-shirts, even satirical ditties. (*"Five foot ten, Looks like Ken…"*)

The Quayle Quarterly, P.O. Box 8593, Brewster Station, Bridgeport, CT 06605. $12.95 per year (single issues, $3.95 each).

JOIN THE PARTY

American Political Items Collectors Club. The APICC publishes two newsletters, *Keynoter* and *The Bandwagon*, and gives a support group to the people who collect everything from buttons to banners to bumperstickers. Local branches hold swap meets and seminars.

Send SASE for information.
P.O. Box 340339
San Antonio, TX 78234

Pinning Down Historical Events

Most buttons from the past century are not political. Advertising buttons used to be given as freebies with the purchase of candy, gum or tobacco. They commemorated holidays, clubs, expositions, circuses, comic strips, sports, tourism, religious crusades, even movies and radio shows.

Collectors value these buttons for their view of times gone by. Individual pin fiends often fixate on a few specific topics like sports heroes, commercial messages, cowboy stars or World Expositions.

JUST SAY NYET!

Genuine designs from the Evil Empire.

• **Soviet Tank Corps** (chest pin medal).

• **Baby Lenin** (picture inside red star).

• **Grown-up Lenin.**

• **Hammer & Sickle.**

Each button $1.00 + 3.00 shipping. Northern Sun, 2916 E. Lake Street, Minneapolis, MN 55406. (612) 729-2001.

Required Reading

• *Political Buttons: Book I, 1896-1972*

• *Book II, 1920-1976*

• *Book III, 1789-1916*

Breathtakingly in-depth information about campaign buttons from years gone by, with thousands of B&W photographs. Author Ted Hake is a noted expert on pin-back buttons (and, it seems from the number of books he's published, nearly everything else collectible). Each reference has accompanying updated price guides.

Each volume $30 postpaid from Hake's Americana and Collectibles Press, PO Box 1444, York, PA, 17405. (717) 848-1333.

Pushing Your Buttons

The 1960s and '70s brought a proliferation of "cause" buttons. Although "Votes For Women" appeared in the late l9th Century and Prohibition had its share of buttons, the early days of the Civil Rights Movement revived the cause button trend.

The 1970s were a decade of self expression. The button and its sibling the bumpersticker became an ideal way to subject strangers to the urgency of your message, whether it concerned religion, race or cultural identity, feminism, work, hobbies, politics, drugs, sex, self-growth or born-again cynicism.

Following the cryptic "Au H2O" Goldwater campaign bumpersticker came an influx of figure-it-out slogans like "I ♥ New York" followed by spinoffs like "I ♥ My Truck," "I ♥ My Cat" and on and on ad infinitum. Gallagher, the comedian, suggested variations on this theme with "I ♠ My Dog" and "I ♣ My Wife."

PINHEADS UNITE!

Bill Nelson Newsletter. All newsletter issues feature news on collectible pins, information for collectors, ads and display tips. Write Bill Nelson and he'll send you information on subscribing plus a free copy of a booklet for collectors just starting out called *Pins By Mail, Second Edition: An Introduction to the Hobby of Collecting Pins.*

The Bill Nelson Newsletter
P.O. Box 41630
Tucson, AZ 85717-1630

Start a Discussion...Or a Fistfight

This self-described catalog of "Products for Progressives—Have Propaganda Will Travel " is chock full of topical "cause" material on topics like war, capital punishment, animal research, capitalism, Central America, politics, labor, or (as they put it) "Something to offend everyone." Try out these buttons for size:

Ecology. "Stop Treating Our Soil Like Dirt," "Recycle or Die!" and "Live Simply That Others May Simply Live."

Nuclear. "Nuclear Weapons— May They Rust in Peace," "You Can't Hug a Child With Nuclear Arms," and "Better Active Today Than Radioactive Tomorrow."

Feminism. "Men of Quality Respect Women's Equality," "Uppity Women Unite," and "Women Make Policy, Not Coffee."

Quantity: 1-10 $1.00 each; 11-50 40¢ each; 51+ 30¢ each. Grab Bag Buttons (assorted close-outs) 15¢ each. Add 3.50 shipping *per order.* Northern Sun, 2916 E. Lake St., Minneapolis, MN 55406. (612) 729-2001.

Between the Buttons

Ephemera. This company offers a self-described "world's most outrageous button catalog."

Recent buttons in the "clean" category: "Elvis is dead—give it up," "Coffee is God," "i feel like e. e. cummings at a punctuation festival," "Prejudice is a mental handicap," "If God wanted us to vote, he would have given us candidates" and "I'm not really happy—it's a chemical imbalance."

We won't reprint any of their "rude" sayings—get their catalog. Their inventory is original, intelligent, very funny and ever-changing. Send four first class stamps for their latest catalog.

Ephemera, 275 Capp Street, San Francisco, CA 94110. (415) 552-4199.

Required Reading

Collectible Pin-Back Buttons: 1896-1986 by Ted Hake & Russ King. A unique visual record of American life since the year 1896. A remarkably sweeping look at over 5,000 non-political buttons, identified by age, color and value. The buttons are clearly photographed, some in color.

$48.00 postpaid from American Collectibles Press, PO Box 1444, York, PA 17405. (717) 848-1333.

CANDY

HISTORY OF CANDY

The word "candy" comes from a sweet reed called kand that was brought from India to Macedonia by Alexander the Great's troops about 340 B.C.

Candy has always been special to kids of all ages. Cocoa seeds once even served as currency. A Mayan could buy a rabbit for only eight seeds, a slave for 100. Mexican natives had been cultivating the cocoa bean for 2500 years before Hernando Cortéz "discovered" it and took chocolate back to Spain in 1528. Spanish royalty drank chocolate as a beverage but kept the delicious secret to themselves for the remainder of the century.

It wasn't until 1840 that a British firm molded the first commercial solid chocolate bar.

American Milton Snavlely Hershey, already a successful manufacturer of caramels, saw a German chocolate-making machine at the 1893 Chicago World's Fair. He bought one and began turning out the first mass-produced chocolate bars, kisses and chocolate cigars. By 1911, the Hershey Co. was making a sweet five million dollars a year.

World War I made candy bars a big industry, as the manufacturers were pressed into service supplying the doughboys with blocks of chocolate to boost their energy and morale.

World War II made the candy bar an internationally recognized symbol of America. American GIs overseas used chocolate bars as international wartime currency for barter, while back home an anxious American public bought new concoctions of peanuts and marshmallows as domestic chocolate supplies dwindled.

After the war, the profusion of colorful local wartime candy brands began to disappear. Big companies like Hershey and Mars began taking over the market.

There have been over a hundred thousand different brands of candy manufactured in the United States in the last hundred years. Their wrappers reflect the personalities and events that shaped history, like Little Orphan Annie, the Charleston Chew, the Astro-Nut and the Reggie Bar.

Baby Ruth?

The Baby Ruth bar was named for President Grover Cleveland's daughter, not the baseball star. Not that Babe Ruth didn't eventually have bars named in his honor, but the Bambino and Big Champ bars, made by the George Ruth (his real name) Candy Company, thrived only briefly.

It's a Chocolate World

Hershey Park and Hershey Botanical Gardens. Remember the thrill of a field trip where you visited an actual manufacturing plant, spent an hour on the bus, and most of a day on their hokey but fascinating tour? You got to take home a free sample of the company's product as well as the memory that you'd just been blessed with a rare peek into "how things work."

Now we get Chocolate World — a "replica" of the factory that must have cost more to build than a working plant itself. The good part is that the 20 minute trolley tour is free. The bad part is that you have to buy admission to the amusement park to get in to a factory that isn't even real — no delicious smells, no thrill of seeing actual products being made. Still, the amusement park rides are fun.

Located at 300 Park Blvd., Hershey, PA 17033. (800) 437-7439.

Oldies But Goodies

Pearson's Nut Goodies, a Midwest favorite, disappeared from the candy scene for awhile. But now they're back, just the same as they were back in 1912 when they were first produced from real milk chocolate, fresh unsalted peanuts and a creamy maple center. 24 bars to a box.

#13989, $14.95 + 2.75 shipping from Wireless, P.O. Box 64422, St. Paul, MN 55164-0422. (800) 669-9999.

Americans now consume over 20 pounds of candy per person every year.

Perfect For Home Movies!

Authentic movie candy...Goobers, Raisinets and Snowcaps! Plus fresh "Butter 'n' Salt" popcorn. Even has a movie concession price!

#35400, 1 lb. Movie Tin (15.8 oz.), $42.50 + 5.95 shipping from The Chocolate Collection, P.O. Box 310, One Chocolate Collection Blvd., Camanche, IA 52730. (800) 654-0095.

MARS

Candy From Mars

• The original script for *E.T. the Extraterrestrial* called for M&M's in the scene where the children lure the space visitor into their house with a trail of candy. But Mars, a privately owned family company so secretive it is sometimes called the "Kremlin of Candy," mysteriously turned down the offer of a tie-in. There's no doubt they eventually regretted it. Hershey had to keep two factories open around the clock to keep up with the 65% increase in the demand for Reese's Pieces, generated by their appearance in the film.

• The Mars Company is owned by one of the richest families in the world, invariably showing up in the Forbes top ten list. And yes,

their real name is Mars.

• When the Snickers bar was born it weighed 2.5 ounces, and sold for a nickel. By 1968, it still cost a nickel, but it had shrunk to 1.16 ounce. One year later the price doubled and its bulk swelled back up to 2.3 ounces. Between 1969 and 1980 the price rose up to 25 cents while the weight went up and down nearly a dozen times.

• The original Three Musketeers bar, which debuted in 1932, got its name because it divided into three pieces — chocolate, vanilla and strawberry. By the 1940s, it had become all one piece, chocolate throughout, but kept the name.

• "Forever Yours"? Unfortunately nothing is forever. The so-named Mars candy bar disappeared years ago.

3 MUSKETEERS

There's a Sucker Born Every Minute

The crafty marketers of the one cent Zero bar sent sales soaring when they promised children a free steam engine if they saved enough wrappers. Profits soared as well, because they neglected to tell them where to send the wrappers they'd saved, explaining the name of the bar.

QUICK! THROW ME A LIFE SAVER

Sweet Little Newsletter

The Candy Bar Gazebo, edited by Ray Broekel. A spin-off from *The Great American Candy Bar Book,* the world needs more like this newsletter, which explores the names, the wrappers and the stories behind some of these classic and obscure products.

Best of all, there's no collector "attitude" here — in fact, no collectors' ads, a refreshing change from most of these fanzines. Editor Ray loves his subject, which makes for fun reading.

Six Edge Street, Ipswich, MA 10938. (508) 356-4191. Subscription to the quarterly newsletter is $15.00 / year.

ATOMIC FIRE BALL

Cheap Childhood Memories

You never saw them on TV and they didn't have fancy wrappers, but the truly significant candies of childhood usually only cost a penny or a nickel.

Licorice laces
Root beer barrels
Jaw breakers
Boston Baked Beans
Indian necklaces
Candy lipstick
Candy dots on paper strips
Jolly Rancher watermelon candies
Atomic Fire Balls
Cherry Chan
Pixie Stix
Sugus
Nik-L-Nips
Necco Wafers

Why do Life Savers have a hole in the middle? Candy manufacturer Clarence A. Crane wanted to develop a line of hard mints to sell in the summertime when his chocolate sales fell off, but he had no room in his own factory to make them, so he jobbed out the mints to a pill manufacturer. The pill maker's machine was malfunctioning, and despite all efforts kept punching a hole in each mint's center.

The pill manufacturer presented the first batch apologetically to Crane. Crane hadn't named the candy yet but when he saw them, the marketing possibilities became clear, "Life Savers" became an irresistible choice for a name.

Crane advertised his "Crane's Peppermint Life Savers" as a cure for "that stormy breath."

Life Savers is the candy world's best seller, with 33,431,236,300 rolls sold between 1913 and 1987. Unfortunately Crane didn't make any money from all those rolls—he sold the brand to a New York ad salesman for $2,900 in 1913 before the candies had begun showing their real worth.

Sparking Violations

Some people got it at summer camp or at slumber parties. Some of us were weird enough to stand in front of a dark mirror and discover it all by ourselves. But one of the three best in-the-dark revelations of adolescence is that if you crack a Wint-O-Green Life Saver between your teeth, tiny blue and green lights will flash in your mouth.

RJR Nabisco, the maker of Life Savers, averages three or four phone inquiries a month about the phenomenon. "Triboluminescence resulting from crystal fracture" is the technical explanation. What that really means is that when the candy is cracked, negative and positive electrical charges separate, then quickly recombine like miniscule lightning bolts. Excited nitrogen molecules produce the blue-green glow.

Thomas Syta of Van Nuys, CA set the world's record for a Life Saver in his mouth, with hole intact—7 hours, 10 minutes.

A voice of Pezzimism

The Optimistic Pezzimist. This fascinating 36 page magazine, complete with Pez history, interesting facts and an active Pez collector's trading section, is a must-have for any appreciator of the fliptop candy.

$18 per year (6 issues). The Optimistic Pezzimist, c/o Mike Robertson, P.O. Box 606, Dripping Springs, TX 78620. (512) 858-7720.

Big and Small Screen Sweets

• Scrunch Bar, Gobstoppers and Oompas are all named after confections created by Roald Dahl's character Willy Wonka, in the book *Charlie and the Chocolate Factory*. They came out after the popular movie.

• **"Do you want a Walnetto?"** Arte Johnson mumbled the phrase into Ruth Buzzi's ear each week on *Rowan and Martin's Laugh-In* during the late 1960s. Viewers adopted the insinuating phrase and the caramel and walnut candy, first manufactured in the early 1920s, enjoyed a brief renaissance—before disappearing again, presumably forever.

KISS' GREATEST HITS

Hear a sweet tune from this silver-plated porcelain Hershey's Kiss music box, 4 1/2 inches high.

#7601, $28.98 + 4.75 shipping from Johnson Smith Company, 4514 19th Court East, P.O. Box 25500, Bradenton, FL 34206-5500. (813) 747-2356 / FAX (813) 746-7896.

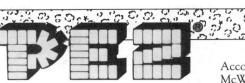

"What's the Pezword?"

• Pez was originally only available in peppermint. It was developed in Vienna in the late 1920s and the name is condensed from peppermint in German: "Pfefferminz."

• The little automatic dispensers were invented in 1950, and on the strength of those and Pez's new fruit flavor, the candy reached America in 1952.

• The first dispensers had no novelty head at all (in fact they looked a little like plastic cigarette lighters), but soon the Disney characters appeared, shooting Pezzes out of their necks.

• The strangest Pez dispenser?

According to company president Scott McWhinnie, it was a plastic hand with an eyeball in it. '60s surrealism, or some kind of Masonic thing? Either way, it didn't sell too well. Since then, they've stuck to the tried and true—Disney, Smurfs, the Peanuts Gang and Muppets—eschewing the controversial, weird or trendy.

• One billion Pez candies are ejected from those little plastic dispensers every year. That's in the US alone—Pez also sells in eighty other countries.

• In *E.T.*, the little alien is also offered, in addition to Reese's Pieces, some Pez candies by his Earth host, Elliot.

• *The Big Picture* (1989) features a rooftop band called "The Pez People."

HAVE YOUR PEZ DELIVERED BY A FEDERAL EMPLOYEE

• **Fez 'N' Pez Gift Set.** This fine set includes six different Pez dispensers and one plastic shriner figurine all nestled in a one-size-fits-all red fez. Put together just for sake of the irresistible rhyme, or is this still another clue in the secret Loyal Order of the Mystic Pez?

$13.50 + 4.00 per order shipping from Archie McPhee, P.O. Box 30852, Seattle WA 98103. (206) 547-2467 / FAX (206)-547-6319.

• **Postbox Pez.** Red metal mailbox with 4 different Pez dispensers inside. To keep 'em safe, mailbox comes with a tiny padlock and two keys. 5 1/8" long x 3 3/4" tall.

$10.95 + 4.00 per order from Archie McPhee (see above).

"If I could only have one thing to eat for the rest of my life? That's easy. Pez. Cherry-flavored Pez." —Teen boy, *Stand By Me* (Alas, cherry's no longer made)

Milked Chocolate

A carton of cows! A whole herd (7 oz.) plus a digital Hershey watch with plastic cow-skin band.

#16931, $16.95 + 3.90 shipping from Wireless, P.O. Box 64422, St. Paul, MN 55164-0422. (800) 669-9999.

Chocoholic Cookbook

There are over 150 sweet, savory chocolate creations including cakes, candies, pies, puddings, frostings and more, developed by the Hershey Kitchens. A delicious, delectable digest of dessert ideas.

#B2413, Hershey Chocolate Cookbook, $5.98 + 3.50 shipping from Harriet Carter, North Wales, PA 19455. (215)361-5151.

COCOA LOCO

The Cocoa Babe canister with candy. *Tin #1* (#6054) contains 19 oz. of Hershey's Kisses, Miniatures and Reese's Miniature Peanut Cups. *Tin #2* (#6001) features 22 oz. of just Kisses.

Each: $12.95 + 3.95 shipping from Hershey's Mailorder, P.O. Box 801, Hershey, PA 17033-0801. (800) HERSHEY.

M & M's— Melt in Your Mind

The original M&M's, invented in 1942, were larger, came only in brown and were 'M'-less for their first ten years on the market. They were developed by Alfred Stern, a Jewish scientist who fled Nazi Germany and was asked to develop a candy that wouldn't melt in heat and could be manipulated when wearing gloves. They weren't available to the public until after the war.

Why M & M's don't melt in your hand: the chocolate has air whipped into it to give it someplace to go when it melts and the candy coating is slightly expandable to prevent cracking from the pressure.

Mr. Plain and Mr. Peanut don't really dive into a pool of candy coating like the old TV ads suggested. Instead, the chocolate bits get their hard candy shell by rotating in a revolving pan as the coating is added. The 'M' is applied in a process similar to offset printing.

If you think that the government's nutritional standards were higher prior to the 1980s when ketchup was officially declared a vegetable, remember that a substantial portion of a WWII GI ration was a bag of plain M&M's.

In 1976, Red Dye No. 2 was linked to the development of malignant tumors in laboratory rats, and the FDA moved quickly to ban its use. When red M&M's subsequently disappeared, the public assumed it was because they had been colored with the evil dye. Not so. Red M&M's had always been colored with Red Dye Nos. 3 and 40, colors which still enjoy official FDA sanction. According to M&M/Mars, they removed the red candies from production "to avoid any consumer confusion and concern."

After the banning, letters poured in from angry mothers who had used the candies to teach their children about traffic lights and broken-hearted devotees who swore that the reds tasted better than the brown or green M&M's (there is no scientific basis for this — the formula is identical for all M&M's and the colored coatings are unflavored). After eleven years of "bring 'em back" fan mail, the red returned, without fanfare or explanation, in 1987.

200,000,000 M&M's are sold every day.

The ratio of colors in an M&M's batch? **Plain:** 30% brown, 20% each red and yellow, and 10% each orange, green and tan. **Peanut:** 30% brown, 20% each red, yellow and green, and 10% orange.

Violet was once a part of the M&M's rainbow, but was dropped after nine years for being "too way out."

Garbage Can Full O' Candy

That's what this red tin looks like. But it's full of your favorite Nestlé treats: mini Milk Chocolate, Crunch and Alpine White bars.

#22694 (5 lb. tin), $29.50 + 3.95 shipping. The Chocolate Collection, P.O. Box 310, One Chocolate Collection Blvd., Camanche, IA 52730. (800) 654-0095.

Ga Ga For Goo Goos

Maybe it's all those trips to Graceland, but the rest of the country is finally discovering this Nashville tradition since 1912. Goo Goo Clusters are made with milk chocolate, peanuts, marshmallows and caramel. Goo Goo Supremes are the same, except with pecans instead of peanuts.

#G0169, 2 boxes of 6 Clusters, $8.00 + 3.50 shipping. #G0172, 2 boxes of 6 Supremes, $10.00 + 3.50 shipping. Country Music Hall of Fame, 4 Music Square East, Nashville, TN 37203. (800) 255-2357.

Great Candy Bar Names

- *Vegetable Sandwich*
- *Rumor Bar*
- *Log Jam*
- *Love Nest*
- *Best Pal*
- *Tummy Full Peanut Bar*
- *Cold Turkey*
- *Baby Lobster*
- *Amos 'N' Andy*
- *Fat Emma*
- *Chicken Dinner*
- *Idaho Spud*

Movie Concessions

- Film critic Gene Shalit complained on the radio in the mid-1980s about the distraction of crackling paper candy wrappers in darkened movie theatres. An executive at Hercules, Inc. heard Shalit's broadcast and realized that a soft plastic they had in development would be perfect for silent wrappers. Theatre-size Baby Ruth, Butterfinger, and Hollywood Bars now come in the new material.

- Moviegoers buy more than $650 million worth of refreshments every year. Here are the best and worst selling candies:

BEST:	WORST:
Jujubes	Jordan Almonds
M&M's	Sno-Caps
Red Licorice	Gummi Bears
Raisinets	SweeTarts
Milk Duds	Good & Plenty
Reese's Pieces	Milky Way
Goobers	3 Musketeers
Whoppers	Starbursts
	Dots

Cows in Space

Hey Diddle Diddles™— cows and moons are 10 oz. of delicious diversion.

#5853, $11.95 + 3.95 shipping. Hershey's Mailorder, P.O. Box 801, Hershey, PA 17033-0801. (800) HERSHEY.

Fudge Your Answers

It looks like chocolate. Even smells like chocolate. But don't crunch this Hershey bar. It's really a solar-powered calculator, even comes in a Hershey wrapper.

#1295, $14.98 + 2.50 shipping. The Lighter Side, 4514 19th St. Court East, P.O. Box 25600, Bradenton, FL 34206-5600. (813) 747-2356 / FAX (813) 746-2356 ext. 5.

The Goo Goo Cluster was the first combination ingredient candy bar ever.

HALLOWEEN!

These candies seemed to appear in stores only right before Halloween:

- Candy corn
- Pumpkins, black cats and witch hats made from the same stuff as candy corn
- Wax whistles, vampire teeth and lips
- Wax pumpkins, tubes and barrels filled with sugar syrup
- Double Bubble Gum in taffy-like wrapping
- Dum Dum suckers
- Smarties

These are the ones you'd go back twice for, even lie and say you needed an extra one for your sick brother:

- Tootsie Roll Pops
- Brand-name chocolate candy bars, especially ones in tiny sizes: Snickers, Butterfingers, Baby Ruths, Three Musketeers, Milky Ways, Hershey bars

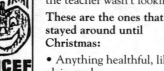

- Bonomo Turkish Taffy
- B-B-Bats
- Kraft Caramels
- Red Hots
- Snaps
- SweeTarts
- Anything grape or cherry flavor
- Anything small you could palm in class while the teacher wasn't looking

These are the ones that stayed around until Christmas:

- Anything healthful, like plain apples
- Anything lemon or lime flavored
- Anything hard on the outside, soft on the inside
- Taffy pumpkin faces
- Sour balls
- Jellied fruits
- The black Chuckles
- Sen Sen

America's Nose for Culture

(On a gummy new candy called Boogers): *"The name really strikes people. It's so exciting when the product and concept come together, and with Boogers, we've hooked into something culturally significant."*

— **John Sullivan, President, Confex, Inc., makers of Boogers**

Required Reading

- *The Great American Candy Bar Book* by Ray Broekel.
- *The Chocolate Chronicles* by Ray Broekel. Satiate your intellectual sweet tooth with these wonderful books by the editor of *The Candy Bar Gazebo* newsletter.

Both books are liberally sprinkled with mouth-watering photos and tasty trivia. The only flaw in *The Great American Candy Bar Book* is the lack of an index (we should talk!), but we can't complain too much because it was so much fun leafing through every page. How else would we have discovered there really was a candy bar called "Chicken Dinner?"

Candy Bar. $11.95 postpaid. *Chronicles:* $15.00 postpaid. From Ray Broekel, 6 Edge Street, Ipswich, MA 01938. (518) 356-4191.

Tootsie Bank Roll

It's a bank. No, it's a candy. Stop! It's both. 2 ft. x 3 in. faux Tootsie Roll comes with 50 bite-size candies and doubles as a bank for your coins.

#16935, $10.95 + 2.75 shipping from Wireless, P.O. Box 64422, St. Paul, MN 55164-0422. (800) 669-9999.

"Charlie Says..."

Remember Choo-Choo Charlie? He'd shake a full Good & Plenty box in a rail-rocking rhythm, and blow on an empty one for the whistle, which gave us a reason to wheedle in the store for two boxes.

Alas, the licorice train doesn't come here any more—product tampering fears killed the loosely folded box which made the train whistle sound. They're now glued shut, and the decline of the American railroad continues.

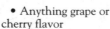

Candy of Death?

Will candy kill you? Some anti-white sugar activists believe so. But that's slowly. Luckily, other rumors, probably engendered by our Puritan heritage ("If it feels or tastes good, it must be bad for you"), have proven false.

• **Halloween Poisoning Deaths.** Hysterical urban myths. The only such fatality reported in recent times was false—a boy poisoned by his own father the day after Halloween. Ironically, the father thought he could get away with it because of all the rumors.

• **Pop Bang.** Rumor had it in kiddy cliques that chewing Fizzies would asphyxiate you or make you explode like a cheap balloon. Pop Rocks later inspired similar rumors, including one that "Mikey" of the Life Cereal commercials had exploded from eating them.

Pilgrimages: Take the Good Ship Lollipop

• **Candy Museum.** The Candy Museum makes for a savory little side trip through Lancaster County. Chocoholics, beware, though. The aroma alone, which can be detected from the street, is enough to render you helpless. Once inside you'll have to exercise super-human control to make it past the six-foot chocolate bunnies to the museum proper, three rooms filled with boxes, wrappers, molds and other pieces of unusual candy memorabilia. The collection is small, and could be more completely documented (One object on display was described only as "A Very Old Wooden Candy Mold").

Still, the sensory experience more than makes up for any lack of detailed scholarship.

Located in the Wilbur Chocolate Factory, 46 N. Broad Street (Rte. 501), Lititz, PA 17543. (717) 626-1131.

Kiss Kids Candy Box

Vintage design goes way back to the roaring '20s. Oh, the Kisses? 16 oz. worth.

#5834, $8.95 + 2.50 shipping from Hershey's Mailorder, P.O. Box 801, Hershey, PA 17033-0801. (800) HERSHEY.

PRINCIPLES OF FIZZIE-OLOGY

Whatever happened to Fizzies? We'd give up TV for a year to find a pack. They tried to placate us when they brought out Pop-Rocks and Volcano Rocks, but there's nothing that will ever replace the sickening sizzle of a root beer flavored Fizzies tablet on the tip of your tongue.

Fizzies weren't candy, really, they were a trial by carbonation. If you could hold a Fizzies on your tongue until it was gone, you could join the club, be part of the gang, deserve the respect of your peers.

Only nerds actually followed the directions and put Fizzies in water to drink.

CARNIVAL

CARNIVALS, FAIRS AND AMUSEMENT PARKS

A lot of people remember the childhood visits to carnivals with mixed excitement: the sugar rush from taffy apples and cotton candy, the scary look of the thrill rides and the people operating them.

Until Disney figured out a gentler way of separating people from their money, amusement parks featured the same midways as carnivals, staffed by tattooed ex-cons ready to rip you off with crooked games. Some of that genuine surreal scariness can still be found out there, especially in the traveling shows, but most amusement parks have followed the Disney "clean-cut college kid" model of staffing. Unreformed psychopaths have had to go into other lines of work, like S & Ls, politics and TV ministries.

FAMOUS PLAYLAND ON THE BEACH
SAN FRANCISCO, CALIF.
M-405

CARNY LINGO

Alibi agent: midway game operator who refuses to give legitimately won prizes based on previously undisclosed "rules": player touched the rail, leaned over the foul line, etc.

Burn the lot: cheat outrageously because of no intention of returning to that location

Chump: naive player

Circus candy: cheap candy in an impressive box

Donniker: toilet

Fixer: handles payoffs ("patch money") to local police

Gaff: Rig a game so a player can't win

Gig: Take all of a player's money in one try

"Hey Rube": a join-the-melee call for help when in trouble with non-carnies

Ikey Heyman: rigged wheel of fortune

Joint: a midway concession

Lot lice: carnival-goers who don't spend money

Marks, Tips: players

Mitt camp: palm reader area

Plaster, Slum: cheap prizes

Shill: accomplices who are allowed to win games to encourage others to play

Two Way Joint: A game which can be quickly converted from a dishonest to an honest one in case unbribed police come to visit

"With it": a carny, as opposed to the "marks" on the outside

Own Your Favorite Ride

Got some land, money and want your own favorite ride? Used carnival rides can be had for a fraction of what they'd cost new, yet can still get you just as nauseated as new ones. Recent classified ads in *Amusement Business* (see next page) offer a used Rock-O-Plane for $49,500, a Hurricane for $75,000, a 40' high rollercoaster for $125,000, a 10 seat ferris wheel for $2,500 and a Zipper for $35,000.

Or forget this piecemeal approach: how about an entire carnival with 10 month prebooked season ("gross over $800,000") for a mere $100,000?

Amusement Parks From the Past

• *San Francisciana Photographs of Playland* by **Marilyn Blaisdell.** A photo collection of Playland at the Beach, a classic, now extinct San Francisco amusement park. And it's all here: Laughing Sal, the Bobsled Dipper and the racially ignorant Topsy's Roost.

$12.50 postpaid from Marilyn Blaisdell Publishing, Box 590955, San Francisco, CA 94159.

• *Coney Island* (videotape). The greatest and most famous early amusement park in the world. Filmed in its heyday (1917 to 1936), this video includes a silent comedy featuring Fatty Arbuckle and Buster Keaton, newsreels and a film of a monkey's visit. Funny, with lots of shots of the rides.

$29.95 + 3.00 shipping from Encore Entertainment, PO Box 25, Frankenmuth, MI 48734.

More people are injured on merry-go-rounds than rollercoasters each year.

HOW TO WIN AT CARNIVAL GAMES

Carnival Secrets by Matthew Gryczan. Not all carnival games are crooked, but even the honest ones are nearly impossible to win. You can increase your chances of winning that big prize if you choose your game carefully and practice before it starts costing you money.

This book tells the odds for each game (any with halfway decent prizes are well above the "thousand-to-one against"

range), how to recognize dishonest set-ups, how to succeed (toss that dime to the *far* edge of the plate) and how to set up your own practice games at home (see below). A must-have item unless you want to spend the rest of your life spending big bucks for "slum" (cheap prizes).

Gryczan's Laws:

1. Don't be afraid to ask questions.

2. Make sure you understand all the rules before you play.

3. When in doubt, ask the carny to demonstrate the game. If he can't win, you can't. Then ask to play with the same equipment, and make sure the setup is *exactly* the same.

$9.95 + 1.25 shipping from Zenith Press, Box 230104, Grand Rapids, MI 49523.

A MAGAZINE THAT'S FAIR TO MIDWAY

Amusement Business. This magazine's been reporting fair and carnival news for over ninety years since splitting off from *Billboard*. Casual readers will be bored by the business stories generally, but there are some interesting bits like which rides produce the highest revenues, or what show is coming to your town next.

We love the ads. Want to know where to buy a Sno-Cone machine, a circus tent, a concession stand or a shooting gallery? You've come to the right place.

Subscription, $75; single issue, $3.75 from PO Box 24970, Nashville, TN 37202. (615) 321-4250.

HOW TO *AVOID* HAVING TO WIN

If you really crave those carnival prizes, it is much cheaper to just buy them than try to win them. In fact, you'll be amazed how little these things really cost: stuffed toys for $1 each (in quantity, of course), whoopee cushions, plastic hoohas and doodads, and everything else you've seen on the midway.

This company also sells the special carny supplies that Gryczan warns about (above)—the extra heavy milk cans, extra light softballs, reduced size basketball hoops and near-impossible hula hoop toss blocks—in case you want to practice at home or start your own "joint."

For catalog, contact:

**Acme Premium Supply Corporation
4100 Forest Park
St. Louis, MO 63108
(800) 325-7888**

BIG WHEELS

Introduced at Chicago's World's Columbian Exhibition in 1893, the first Ferris Wheel was huge: 250 feet high with 36 cars, each holding as many as 40 people. It was designed by American engineer George Washington Gale Ferris, age 33.

Carnivals as we know them are derived from pre-Lenten festivals, like Mardi Gras.

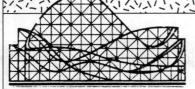

Rollercoasters:
From Gravity to Levity

• Rollercoasters were invented by an enterprising Russian showman, who built elaborate ice slides in St. Petersburg during the 15th Century. Catherine the Great so enjoyed the ice slides that she ordered tiny wheels added to the sleds so she could ride in the summer.

Americans perfected the rollercoaster as we know it today, at Coney Island in 1884. The device was such a hit it inspired imitators throughout the US. Despite their origin, the Russians now call them "American Mountains."

• Amusement parks don't like to let it get out (bad for business, you know), but rollercoasters are statistically much safer than merry-go-rounds. One reason is that people rarely decide to jump off or on a rollercoaster while the ride is moving. Also, the safety restraints work better.

• Despite that, twenty-seven people died on rollercoasters between 1973 and 1988. "If a coaster's paint is peeling or the operator looks sloppy, pass it by," says one safety expert who laments the laxity of safety standards.

• Designers purposely create the illusion that your head is in danger of being chopped by a low overhang at the bottom of a hill. Actually there's always at least 9' clearance.

• A researcher says that rollercoaster addicts often have an abnormally low level of the chemicals that signal fear, so that it takes an unusually high level of stimulation to make them feel "normal."

• In case you're one of those "afflicted" folks, here's a group for you: **The American Coaster Enthusiasts.** Membership includes conventions and a subscription to *RollerCoaster!*

For information, send an SASE to: ACE, PO Box 8226, Chicago, IL 60680.

OUR TOP TEN FAVORITE ROLLERCOASTERS

Wood

1. Georgia Cyclone
6 Flags Over Georgia
Atlanta, GA

2. The Beast
Kings Island, OH

3. Thunderbolt
Kennywood
West Mifflin, PA

4. LeMonstre
LaRonde Parc
Montreal, Quebec

5. Cyclone
Riverside Park
Agawam, MA

6. Cyclone
Astroland
Coney Park, NY

7. Twister
Elitch's
Gardens
Denver,
CO

8. Predator
Darien Lake
Darien Center, NY

9. Texas Giant
Six Flags Over Texas
Arlington, TX

10. Hercules
Dorney Park
Allentown, PA

Steel

1. Magnum XL-200
Cedar Point
Sandusky, OH

2. Viper
Six Flags Magic Mountain
Valencia, CA

3. Mindbender
Fantasyland
Edmonton, Alberta

4. Great American Scream Machine / 6 Flags Great Adventure
Jackson, NJ

5. Shock Wave / 6 Flags Great Adventure
Gurnee, IL

6. Big Bad Wolf
Busch Gardens
Williamsburg, VA

7. Dragon Mountain
Marineland
Niagara Falls, Ontario

8. Mind Bender
6 Flags Over Georgia
Atlanta, GA

9. Vortex
Kings Island, OH

10. SkyRider
Canada's
Wonderland
Maple,
Ontario

Amusement Park Fans

Hardcore appreciator of old amusement parks? Contact the **National Amusement Park Historical Association** (NAPHA), PO Box 83, Mt. Prospect, IL 60056.

Americans took 214 million rollercoaster rides last year.

CARNIVAL CUISINE

There is nothing quite like carnival cuisine. You can do it in your own home like the professionals do, if you're willing to pay the price. Gold Medal Products is the best provider we've seen of the machines, mixes, and display cases, all designed in "carnival motif" styling. They've got a big catalog, but how about these to whet your appetite?

Prices subject to change. For further information, contact:

Gold Medal Products Co.
2001 Dalton Avenue
Cicinnati, Ohio 45214
(513) 381-1313

Cotton Head

#3012, 10 Paper Caps. Also available: caps that say Sno-Kones, Popcorn, Candy Apples. $5.50 ppd.

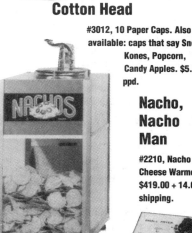

Nacho, Nacho Man

#2210, Nacho Cheese Warmer, $419.00 + 14.00 shipping.

Blue Sugar Blues

#3017, Econo-Floss Cotton Candy Machine, $549.00 + 14.13 shipping.

Small Fry

Cook up to 14 corn dogs at a time. Also does cheez-dogs, fries, shrimp rolls or taco shells. #8047, $555.00 + 14.00 shipping.

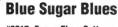

An Ice Device

#1006, Shavette Little Shaver Sno-Cone Maker $369.00 + 19.00 shipping.

Pop Art

#2014, Gay 90s Whiz Bang Popper, $1195.00 + 23.00 shipping. #2129, Wagon, $795.00 + 23.00 shipping.

For a realistic glimpse of seamy midway hustling, rent the video *Carny* (1980).

MERRY GO ROUND
EACH PERSON 50¢

THE INSIDE STORY

The name comes from a 12th century Arabian horseman's game called carosellos or "Little wars." Teams rode in circles throwing perfume-filled clay balls from one rider to another. You lost if the ball of perfume broke; worst of all, you carried the sickly smell of defeat with you for days to come.

Spread to Europe by the Crusades, the game evolved into elaborate, colorful tourneys called "carrousels."

In the 17th century, the French developed a training device for these carrousels: legless wooden horses upon which young nobles would lance rings as they rode around a center pole (this later evolved into the "catching the brass ring" tradition).

This device evolved into a popular form of entertainment. The peasants rode on barrel-like horses; the nobles, in elaborate chariots and boats.

Until the 1860s, these carrousels, which had spread all over Europe, were powered by horses, mules and even people. This changed when Frederick Savage, an English engineer, designed a portable steam engine which could power up to four rows of horses on a 48' diameter wheel.

Savage later patented designs for the overhead camshafts and gears which move the horses up and down. His "round-abouts" were an enormous success throughout Europe.

Ads for carousels appeared in the U.S. around 1800. Offering fun was not enough—they also claimed that the rides aided physical and mental health.

Merry-go-rounds became fine pop craft starting in the late 1800s. Hand-carved wooden horses from the G.A. Dentzel Co. (founded 1867), and the A. Herscell Co. (founded 1882) are among those most prized by collectors and have sold for tens of thousands of dollars.

Horses are now made of fiberglass. There are now fewer than 300 wooden-horsed carousels in the U.S., down from more than 4,000 in their heyday.

Most popular U.S. carousel? The one at Disneyland made by the Dentzel Co. at the turn of the century. It was in ruins in 1955 when Walt Disney bought it from New York's Central Park for $22,000. Now 2 million people ride it every year.

Music Goes Round

Catch Another Brass Ring. #E-191X, CD only, $22.48 ppd. Vestal, PO Box 97, Vestal, NY 13851. (607) 797- 4872.

CATALOG

Carousel Shopper: A Catalog of Resources. One-stop shopping for dealers, miniatures, supplies, reproductions, publications, and blueprints for carving your own animal! Send $2 to Zon International Publishing Co., PO Box 47, Milwood, NY 10546. (914) 245-2926.

POP ANALYSIS

"Originally they were not considered works of art, just a seat on a ride. In the late 1950s, you could pick one of them up free if you'd haul them off. The most you'd pay for one was, maybe, $200. Now they're called 'sculptures' and they cost anywhere from $5,000 to $75,000."

—Wilba Wilcox, carousel animal restorer

TRUE FACTS

• Amusement parks don't publicize this, but merry-go-rounds cause more injuries than any of the thrill rides. The main reason is that people know better than to step off a roller coaster while it's still moving.

• Some of the hand-carved animals are more than art, they're also political satire. Lincoln and Teddy Roosevelt, among others, were immortalized on the flanks of animals (Teddy's, no doubt, was a particularly rough rider).

• The first carousel in Central Park mystified riders because it would start and stop when the operator tapped on the floor. They didn't know it was powered by a horse under the platform which took its cues from the tap.

• You can tell American horses from European by seeing which side is more elaborately carved. The craftsmen showered extra attention on the side facing viewers. In America most of the carousels went counterclockwise, so the right side has all the detail. In Europe, the reverse is true.

• Horses were most popular with merry-go-round riders, so many more of them were carved than other animals. As a result, the other animals are now more valuable to collectors.

• Some Mexican and European carousels featured unauthorized replicas of Mickey, Donald, Goofy and other cartoon favorites–even that rodent Rambo "Mighty Mouse."

Good Organization, But Their Meetings Just Go Around in Circles...

The National Carousel Association works to protect carousels still in existence, provide restoration and historic information, and promote public awareness of the art form.

Dues $25 per year. Send SASE to:
The National Carousel Association
PO Box 8115
Zanesville, OH 43702-8115

REPRODUCTIONS

• **Chance Rides.** Authentic fiberglass reproductions of historical carousel animals cost much less than originals. Chance Rides, a well-known manufacturer of carnival rides, sells replicas for $2500 to $7500 per animal. Each represents about 110 hours of hand-finishing and painting.

Send $2.50 for two full-color poster catalogs to: Chance Rides, Inc., Box 12328, Wichita, KS 67277-2328. (316) 942-7411.

• **Cavolt's Classics.** Featuring 48 different reproductions to choose from, priced from about $1000 and up, Cavolt will paint your reproduction to your specifications.

Send $2.00 + SASE for color catalog to: Cavolt's Carousel Classics, 216 Ponoma Mall E., Pomona, CA 91766. (714) 622-5653.

BOOKS

These are the three best books we've found on Carousel art and history. All are beautifully photographed in full color. *Painted Ponies* and *Art of the Carousel* tell where to find working restored carousels in each state and Canada, as well as dealers, restorers, museums and organizations. *The Carousel Animal*, while also good looking, is a less ambitious "coffee-table" book.

• *Painted Ponies: American Carousel Art* by William Manns, Peggy Shank and Marianne Stevens. $43.45 ppd., or send SASE for free color brochure. Zon Publishing Co., PO Box 2511, Springfield, OH 45501.

Art of the Carousel by Charlotte Dinger. This is the source used by the U.S. Postal Service when it designed its carousel animal stamps in 1988. $42.00 ppd. from Carousel Art, Inc., Box 150, Green Village, NJ 07935. (201) 966-5252.

• *The Carousel Animal* by Tobin Fraley and Gary Sinick. Paperback, $16.95 ppd.; hardcover, $26.95 ppd. from Chronicle Books, 275 Fifth Street, San Francisco, CA 94103.

HECK, CARVE YOUR OWN

Carving Your Own Carousel Animal by Gene Bass. This book is a step-by-step plan, filled with practical advice all the way through, like where to get glass eyes (plastic ones scratch too easily) and how to make the eyes rest symmetrically. A great challenge to take on for anybody going through midlife crisis or otherwise needing a heavy-duty escape from reality.

$12.45 ppd. from Vestal Press, PO Box 97, Vestal, NY 13851. (607) 797-4872.

Chance Rides, Inc. recently built a 50' carousel and a mile long railroad for Michael Jackson's backyard.

CARS

Auto Biography

Cars are, for better or worse, part of the American identity, starting with Henry Ford, and his Model T (affectionately called "Tin Lizzy ").

In 1913, Ford began producing the Model T with conveyer belt technology he learned from Midwestern meat-packing factories. From disassembling hogs of the farm to assembling hogs of the road, the system turned out 1000 cars a day. By 1927, Model T Fords made up 68% of the world's cars—15 million total.

One reason why the Model T was so popular was its rugged, no-frills design and flexibility. People could use the Model T as a plow and harvester, or prop the back wheels off the ground to run farm and household implements like butter churns and flour grinders.

One man who must have hated Henry Ford was a sharp Philadelphia lawyer named George B. Selden. Seeing where auto manufacturers were headed, the lawyer patented a very basic blueprint of a simple motor car before anybody else. He then used that patent to bully payment from manufacturers of any and all automobiles.

By 1895, automobile manufacturers were paying Selden $5 for every car produced. But in 1911, Ford refused and sued, and the patent was voided.

People would have bought cars anyway. But manufacturers didn't trust the marketplace—they launched unrelenting lobbying to undermine public transportation. Sometimes they took even more direct steps. A holding company called National City Lines (made up of GM, Firestone, Standard Oil and Mack Trucks) bought and destroyed street car systems in 47 cities. When found guilty of unlawful conspiracy, the individual defendants were fined a whopping $1 each, the corporations $5,000.

Ironically, taxpayers are now spending billions of dollars to replace those lines, often on the exact same routes.

"When you reach two-tenths of a mile at Middle Street and the library, turn left. At one and one-tenths miles there is a fork in the road. Bear right. Take the first right at the trolley tracks and continue out of town..."

—A 1920s New Hampshire map giving instructions to Providence, RI

Car Pilgrimage

74th Street and Central Park, New York, NY. Drive out to this corner but don't get out of your car. There's no monument here yet, but it was at this corner in 1889 that Arthur Smith drove his car over pedestrian Henry Bliss, killing him—the first pedestrian ever killed by a car.

Cars By the Numbers

- In 1900, there were only 8000 cars on American roads, but by 1905, that multiplied nearly ten-fold, and by 1915, it had reached 2,491,000.

- Today, we own about 35% of the world's 400,000,000 automobiles.

Large Club, Small Cars

The **Model Car Collectors Association** says it's the oldest, largest, and "most influential" model car club in the U.S.

An aim of the association, says its president, is to reach out to "closet collectors"—adults who are embarrassed about building and collecting models. He says "We are an adult group, ages 20 through grandfathers. I'm 46 myself."

One year membership, $12.00 from MCCA, 5113 Sugar Loaf Drive SW, Roanoke, VA 24018.

Vincent's Van Goes

Art on the Road by Moira F. Harris. You think you've seen great van decorations, but it's nothing compared with the "chivas" of Colombia, the "Tap-Taps" of Haiti and the converted school buses of Panama: they don't stop at painting the sides and back of a van—they'll do everything including hubcaps, door handles and bumpers. Some of the artwork is kitschy, but some is quite stunning in its folk art renderings, and all is presented in this book.

$16.95 + 3.00 shipping from Pogo Press, 4 Cardinal Lane, St. Paul, MN 55127.

IH8PL8S....

Vanity License PL8S: How to Code and Decode Personalized License Plates by John F. Mahoney. The first book to tell all about vanity plates and their popularity, including strategies for making your message decipherable. Best of all, the author is willing to help decipher any obscure message you've had trouble with. Write to him at P.O. Box 1271, South Pasadena, CA 91030. Until then, "XLR8 & DV8!"

$6.95 + 2.50 shipping from Motorbooks International, 729 Prospect Avenue, Osceola, WI 54020. (800) 826-6600.

Cars for Stars

Star Cars by Beki Adams. Want to see what James Dean's car looked like before and after? Ever wonder what Jeff Beck, Paul McCartney, James Garner, Paul Newman, David Lee Roth, ZZ Top and Sylvester Stallone drive? Well, this is your vehicle for finding out. Includes the cars from TV and movies from *The Dukes of Hazzard* to James Bond to *American Graffiti*.

$19.95 + 4.50 shipping. Motorbooks International, P.O. Box 2, 729 Prospect Avenue, Osceola, WI 54020. (800) 826-6600.

Field and Street

Flattened Fauna: A Field Guide to Common Animals of Roads, Streets and Highways by Roger Knutson. This is a guide for identifying the birds and animals you see lying in and by the side of the road. Knutson, a biologist, plays it completely straight with straightforward descriptions, photos, drawings and even Xerox copies of flat dead things. Highly recommended.

$5.95 + 2.00 shipping from Ten Speed Press, PO Box 7123, Berkeley, CA 94707. (510) 527-1563.

Classic Cars to Buy

Some people would love to show off a classy '50s or '60s car but don't know how to find one. Two good sources for buying these beautiful monsters are from the same publisher:

- **Hemmings Motor News, P.O. Box 100, Bennington, VT 05201**
- **Special Interest Autos, P.O. Box 196, Bennington, VT 05201**

There are 3.6 million miles of paved roads in the U.S. In 1900, there were 150 miles.

Flop Goes the Edsel

The 1958 Edsel. You either loved it or…sadly, most people hated it. Even today, the very mention of that name brings to mind an enormous marketing catastrophe—sort of the "New Coke" of its generation.

In the beginning, the car seemed to be on a road to success. It was named after Henry Ford's son (who died in WWII) and was given its own division in the Ford empire.

Touted as Ford's "quarter-billion dollar baby," the Edsel was simply left out on the doorstep of the American public, and nobody bothered to pick it up. Why was is such a non-seller? Hard to say. Maybe because its modest technological advances were vastly oversold. Maybe it was introduced in the middle of the 1957 recession. Or maybe because it was pretty darned ugly.

From its vertical, "toilet-seat" grille to the "drum-like speedometer that glows a menacing red when the car exceeds a preset speed" (Ford's description), the Edsel was well endowed with tasteless excess and a lack of common-sense standards.

Consumer Reports said at the time "Edsels offer nothing new in passenger accommodations. Edsel's handling represents retrogression rather than progress in design and behavior. The 'luxury-loaded' Edsel will certainly please anyone who confuses gadgetry with true luxury." Get the picture? Ford did. They discontinued the monster after two years.

But a few people bought them, and they're getting the last laugh now. Because of the Edsel's relative rarity, it is worth far more among collectors than any comparable 1958 model.

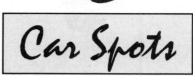

Show Us Your Woodie

The National Woodie Club. Aims to "promote interest in the wooden car, its beauty, usefulness and uniqueness…

"The wooden car is a special kind of car and it deserves special recognition. This club will work toward that goal."

One year membership, $20.00 (includes monthly *Woody Times*). 29 Burley Street, Wenham, MA 01984.

Other names considered for the Edsel: Mongoose Cigique, Pastelogram, Pluma Piluma, and Utopian Turtletop.

Beetle Mania

The **VW Bug** was designed and first manufactured in 1938 in Nazi Germany. Volkswagen, which means "people's car," was meant to be Nazism's Model T. It was Hitler's greatest (and perhaps only) contribution to the counterculture 1960s lifestyle.

The Bug had been introduced to the US in 1949, but really didn't start taking off until after a brilliant ad campaign in the early 1960s, which played off its being the opposite of what car companies were offering in that era: it was small and cute instead of macho, practical not expensive, functional not stylish. In advertising jargon, it was the steak, not the sizzle. The Bug became the car of preference for young intellectuals, students, hippies and fun-in-the-sun West Coasters, who customized them into dune buggies—as well as everyone else who wanted a great car for a little money.

But American production of the car stopped in 1977. Now Beetles are only made by the Mexican government. They've licensed the rights to make them (or "bochitos") for its domestic population at a plant in Cuautlancingo, about 75 miles southeast of Mexico City.

THE PEOPLE'S CAR

Vintage Volkswagens, photographed by Flat 4 Project. No words in this book, instead we see hundreds of lovingly photographed VWs—Bugs mostly, but a few VW buses and even some Karman Ghias. Beautifully done by the "Flat 4 Project" a group of VW aficionados and photographers from Tokyo.

If you've ever owned a VW, the photos will bring a cry to your throat ("Why did I ever get rid of it?") and start you dreaming of making a VW run to Tijuana.

$14.95 + 2.50 shipping from Chronicle Books, 275 Fifth St., San Francisco, CA 94103. (800) 722-6657.

Bug Screening

Herbie, the cute and laughable Volkswagen Beetle appeared in such classic Disney films as *The Love Bug* and *Herbie Goes Bananas.* The films went through about 30 VWs made from 1966 to 1969. The original Herbie is now on display at the VW factory in Wolfsburg, Germany, and the movies are all on video.

Bug Paper

VW rear end is both a toilet paper dispenser and AM radio.

#T1997, $16.98 + 4.85 shipping from Funny Side Up, 425 Stump Road, North Wales, PA 19454. (215) 361-5130.

SMALL WORLD

The Catalog for Car Lovers. When you're ready to come out of your model-car collecting closet, contact Accent Models, Inc. Their catalog offers hundreds of model cars at very reasonable prices, from a slew of manufacturers—Vitesse, Brooklin, Corgi, Solido, Eligor.

P.O. Box 295, Denville, NJ 07834. (201) 887-8403.

Pick Up a Bug From Mexico

Hungry for a Beetle? The good news is that you can go buy a no-frills one for about $5300 in Mexico. The bad news is you have to go there in person (they can't sell them to sources outside the country) and that it'll cost another $3000 to bring it up to U.S. safety and emissions standards (there are shops near the border that specialize in doing just that).

For more information, try the Mexican Embassy (202) 728-1600.

More than 30 million cardboard sunshades were sold in the US in 1988.

> ## "What do these things do, anyway?"
> —Soviet Premier Nikita Krushchev, on seeing car fins

1959
The Fin Again Wakes

The year 1959 will always be known for the greatest useless gift to car gaudiness: the tail fin. The rule for tail fins quickly became "the bigger, the better." Chevrolets, De Sotos, and Cadillacs all adopted a twin shark-fin rear.

Sometimes tail fins did not simply go up: on the 18-feet long 1959 Chevy Impala, the fins went sideways, projecting from the middle of the trunk. This "gull-wing" effect made it one of the all-time American classics, even though it looked like it could do damage to pedestrians.

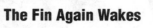

1958   1948   1949
1957   1950
1956   1959   1951
1955   1952
1954   1953

PINK CADILLAC

This 10 in. long x 3 1/2 in. wide replica of the legendary '55 Eldorado has workable doors and steering and is constructed in metal and high impact plastic.

#K5108, $34.95 + up to 4.39 shipping from Mason & Sullivan's Classics In The Making, 586 Higgins Crowell Road, West Yarmouth, MA 02673.

'57 Chevy Cassette Player

This red Chevy is an AM/FM stereo cassette player.

#1720, $89.00 + 6.00 shipping from Car's The Star, 8236 Marshall Drive, Lenexa, KS 66214. (800) 833-3782 / FAX (913) 599-2441.

Chevy Car Seat

Black and white '57 Bel Air loveseat is sophisticated, silly and expensive at the same time. Actually started out as a vintage Chevy and was turned into an elegant piece of furniture. Includes AM/FM stereo cassette player (hidden in tailfin chrome), power antenna and tail lights.

$18,000 postpaid from Car's The Star, 8236 Marshall Drive, Lenexa, KS 66214. (800) 833-3782 / FAX: (913) 599-2441.

Pink Caddy Bar Lets You Drink & Drive

Perk up your rec room with a genuine, pink, original '59 Caddy front end, custom adapted into a bar on wheels. The laminated wood housing carries a compact refrigerator, Alpine AM/FM stereo cassette player, speakers, power antenna and, of course, working headlights.

$22,000 postpaid from Car's The Star, 8236 Marshall Drive, Lenexa, KS 66214. (800) 833-3782 / FAX (913) 599-2441.

Half Scale Model Ts

Always wanted a Tin Lizzy? How about a Thin Lizzy? These folks sell terribly cute half-scale motorized replicas. Engine sizes vary from the crank-starting 3 horsepower engine to a 7 horsepower electric start model. Color of your choice, holds one adult and child maximum. Guaranteed to turn heads. Prices begin at $1695.00.

James Minicar Co., 624 W. Main St., Gardner, KS 66030. (913) 884-6242.

GET READY TO PONY UP

Mustang Restoration Book by Don Taylor and Tom Wilson. This book covers a little bit of everything: buying a Mustang, rebuilding its functional parts, fixing rust and body damage, replacing electrical equipment, restoring its interior trim and vinyl or convertible top, and so on.

More than 450 photos, drawings and charts for getting your little pony out back into stable condition.

$14.95 + 3.00

shipping from HP Books, 360 North La Cienaga Boulevard, Los Angeles, CA 90048.

Get a Mustang, Sally

Mustang Club of America. If you own a Mustang, or are one of the 250 million Americans who wish they did, join the Mustang Club of America. It's a great place to meet similarly obsessed people, in case you ever want to buy, fix or find parts for one.

Send SASE to MCA, P.O. Box 447, Lithonia, GA 30058-0447, and they'll get you in touch with a local chapter.

Pilgrimage: Edison's Ford

Not everyone can make it to Michigan for the great auto museums (notably the Henry Ford Museum in Dearborn, Michigan), so if you happen to be near Fort Myers, Florida, you're in luck—you can see the hand-made 1907 Model T prototype that Henry Ford gave to his friend and sometime neighbor Thomas Edison.

The car is one of only three or four of its kind, and was one of Edison's favorites. The story goes that in 1925, Ford tried to get Edison to accept a new Lincoln. Edison refused, saying that the "Tin Lizzie" was the most convenient car he'd ever driven. And to explain, the inventor turned his head and spit a huge gob of tobacco juice directly out the open cab. Ford let Edison keep the Model T.

The gob has since dried up, but the car is still on Edison's estate. The home is open daily for guided tours.

2350 McGregor Boulevard, Fort Myers, FL 33901.

The Mustang

Any list of classic American autos would have to include one in particular: the Mustang. The Mustang began its illustrious history as the original "pony" car—small, sporty and named after a horse. The first ones were the 1965 model year introduced on April 17, 1964 (following the custom of the time of introducing each year's models months early).

The Mustang was created by teams of engineers and designers under Lee Iacocca when he was General Manager at Ford. The great thing about the Mustang was that it came with more than 35 standard items, 40 different options, a zippy engine, and a low price tag to boot! The car quickly captured the public's imagination, inspiring many to utter memorable words in its honor. Quoth one Mustang enthusiast at the Ford Motor Company: "This car is the greatest thing since the erector set."

More highbrow kudos were also given to the Mustang: It became the only automobile ever to receive the Tiffany Award for Excellence in American Design.

More than 30 million cardboard sunshades were sold in the US in 1988.

Countdown

Twin Turbo Lamborghini Countach claims to be 39% faster than any other radio-controlled car.

#C736306, $169.00 + 10.00 shipping. Sync, Hanover, PA 17333-0042. (800) 722-9979.

Freedom, Not License

Stanford philosophy graduate Mike Wilkins designed, collected, and assembled "vanity" plates from all fifty states and the District of Columbia for a patriotic license plate art piece commemorating the U.S. Constitution's bicentennial.

All fifty-one plates put together read, in "PL8-ese," the Preamble of the 200 year old document: "WE TH P PUL, OF TH U NI DIDD ST8S…"

TWO FOR THE ROAD

• *The American Automobile: Advertising from the Antique and Classic Eras* by Yasutoshi Ikuta.

• *Cruise-O-Matic: Automobile Advertising of the 1950s* by Yasutoshi Ikuta. You can find out a lot about an era by its advertising, like these colorful vintage car ads. You want to know a lot about the mentality of the 1950s? See the smug suburban couple in an ad looking out their window and saying "My, the neighbors sure like our New '52 Dodge!".

The earlier art deco ads are even more fun, flogging brands that disappeared long ago like the Winton, Columbia, Haynes-Apperson, Lozier, Pope-Hartford, Oakland, and the Whippet.

American Auto, $27.50 + 2.50 shipping. Cruise-O-Matic, $14.95. + 2.50 shipping. Both from Chronicle Books, 275 Fifth St., San Francisco, CA 94103. (800) 722-6657.

High Speed Simulation

Test Drive by Accolade puts you in the driver's seat of five world class road cars, including the Ferrari Testarossa and the Porsche Turbo. You don't even need a license, but you will need an IBM 256K RAM, CGA, EGA, Hercules MGA; or an Apple 128K, PRO DOS 8, IIE, IIC.

$28.99 + 4.00 shipping. Egghead, 22011 S E. 51st Street, Issaquah, WA 98027-7004. (800) EGGHEAD / FAX (206) 391-0880.

Mean Muscle Machines

• '69 Camaro Z-28, plastic model kit, 1/12 scale.

• '69 Camaro SS, 1/25 scale.

'69 Z-28, #0380 A, $42.50 + 4.00 shipping; '69 SS, #0380 B, $9.50 + 3.00 shipping. Car's The Star, 8236 Marshall Drive, Lenexa, KS 66214. (800) 833-3782 / FAX (913) 599-2441.

Spring for this, Little Cobra

The Illustrated Discography of Hot Rod Music 1961-1965 by John Blair and Stephen J. McParland. When the surf fad started fading, some surf bands shifted gears and steered into hot rod music. This book will help you identify all those great and not-so-great tunes, covering not just the legendary bands like Jan & Dean, the Surfaris, and the Beach Boys but hundreds more, some with unforgettable music, and some with unforgettable names. Remember Bucky Walter and the Jukes? Sir Frog and the Toads? And what about the Vibra-Sonics? Well, neither do we, but the *Discography* has them all.

Also lists all the period race car movies, a valuable resource when draggin' your GTO down to the video store.

$29.50 + 3.00 shipping from Popular Culture, Ink., P.O. Box 1839, Ann Arbor, MI 48106. (800) 678-8828.

"Never lend your car to anyone to whom you have given birth." —Erma Bombeck

Car Talk

• Did you ever wonder where the word "doozie" (as in "it's a doozie") comes from? Well, if you ever saw a 1933 Deusenberg SJ "Twenty Grand," with its 153.5-inch wheelbase and 320-horsepower supercharged engine (the most powerful production engine in the world at the time), you would know. It was a real doozie!

• While Henry Ford and Walter Chrysler got rich from their car empires, David Dunbar Buick was not so lucky. He sold his company for cheap when it was on the skids in 1908. The buyer, William Durant, turned it around and it became General Motors. It is said that Buick died "so poor that he could afford neither a telephone nor a Buick."

• Road kill. Al Capone was the first to order a General Motors V-16 Cadillac, complete with bullet-proof doors. The car weighed in at four tons.

• TV's Batmobile was actually five different Ford Lincoln Futuras—each one 21-feet long and powered by a Thunderbird 428-inch V-8 engine, costing $234,000 in 1967 dollars.

• In 1925 only 12% of farm families had indoor plumbing, but 60% had a car. Asked why, a farm woman responded, "Why, you can't go to town in a bathtub!"

• More than 80% of Americans commute to work every day in a car.

> *"The ordinary 'horseless carriage' is at present a luxury for the wealthy; and although its price will probably fall in the future, it will never, of course, come into as common use as the bicycle."*
>
> —The Literary Digest, 1908

"Car Phone"

It's a phone that looks like an antique car. Solid wood with brass accent. Top lifts off to talk into.

#C733303, $69.95 + 8.75 shipping from Sync, Hanover, PA 17333-0042. (800) 722-9979.

They Do Their Parts

Not everybody can afford an entire classic car. That's where "automobilia" comes in, the collecting of car pieces. To quote one collector: "Automobilia is what's left after a Duesenberg and a Model T meet head-on."

The Hubcap Collectors' Club. Ever wonder where all the hubcaps went that juvenile delinquents used to steal? There have been over 2500 makes of autos made in this country, each with its own distinctive caps.

Sens SASE to P.O. Box 54, Buckley, MI 49620.

The Automobile License Plate Collectors Association. The ALPCA Newsletter can tell all about upcoming swaps and shows in your area.

One year, $16.00. P.O. Box 712, Weston, WV 26452.

The Spark Collector's Club of America. There have been over 4000 brands sold since 1895, many featuring "odd and unusual designs."

One year, $15.00 (includes subscription to The Ignitor). P.O. Box 2229, Ann Arbor, MI 48106.

Play Shop Teacher...

With the same model (1/4 scale) motorized V-8 engine used in auto mechanic classes. Valves open and close, pistons move up and down, spark plugs fire and the crank shaft revolves once you assemble all 350 parts. Manual included.

#7571, $59.98 + 6.95 shipping. Johnson Smith Co., 4514 19th Court East, P.O. Box 25500, Bradenton FL 34206-5500. (813) 747-2356.

CHEX, NOT SEX

Cereal's Flaky Beginnings

Believe it or not, modern ready-to-eat cereal was invented to reduce the sex drive.

Fruits & Nuts. It began at the Western Health Reform Institute at Battle Creek, Michigan. Founded in 1866 by Seventh Day Adventist Sister Ellen Harmon White, the Institute was dedicated to idea that "purity of mind and spirit" could be attained by eating the right foods—vegetables, fruits and bread from Graham flour.

The Institute survived without a doctor on staff for ten years. In 1876 White hired a med-school graduate, Dr. John Harvey Kellogg, who hired his brother William as chief clerk.

Precious bodily fluids. Dr. Kellogg believed that good health depended not only on good food and exercise, but also on complete sexual abstinence. He was a true believer, reportedly writing **Plain Facts for Old**

and Young, an anti-sex tract, on his honeymoon. His marriage was never consummated.

He believed that certain foods would "cure" sexual desires. First he used zwieback until a patient broke her dentures on it and demanded $10 compensation. He began looking for a softer alternative.

Nocturnal Mission. The answer came in a dream in 1885 which showed him how to flake cereal. His attempts at wheat flakes flopped, but in 1902 he came up with a crowd pleaser: corn flakes flavored with barley malt.

Realizing the commercial possibilities, the brothers set up a separate corporation and began selling cereal.

In their first year they sold 100,000 pounds. But the success wasn't easy. Sister White was furious that Dr. Kellogg had desecrated the divine with commercialism, and competitors jumped on the bandwagon.

Porn flakes. Worst of all, William Kellogg, pushing to widen the product's appeal, added sugar to the flakes, which the horrified Dr. Kellogg believed reversed the cereal's sex-suppressing effects. Brother sued brother in a series of court battles.

William took control of the company (although his brother was still a major stockholder) and it grew

into the mammoth Kellogg Company.

Post Partum. In 1895, Charles W. Post, a patient at the sanitarium, began hanging around the kitchens when the Kelloggs were perfecting whole-grain "coffee" (the real thing also "excited sexual urges").

Dr. John H. Kellogg

After a few months of convalescence, Post's funds ran out. He appealed to Dr. Kellogg to let him pay his bill by marketing the coffee. The doctor said no. In response, Post began marketing his own version of grain coffee under the name Postum Cereal Food Coffee.

Cure-All. Post claimed Postum "makes blood red," and cured previously unknown ills like "coffee neuralgia, coffee heart, and coffee-induced blindness." He sold $250,000 worth of the stuff the first year and 3 times that 3 years later. (Decades later, it was still being touted as the answer to "coffee nerves").

Post came up with a cereal which he called Grape Nuts, even though it contained only baked wheat. His ads said it would cure appendicitis, malaria and tuberculosis, feed the brain and even tighten loose teeth. By 1901, he was netting a million dollars a year.

That's a lot of Frosted Flakes! The average child consumes 15 pounds of cereal in a year.

SUGAR-COATED FACTS

• **What's the raisin?** Why don't all the heavy raisins in Raisin Bran end up at the bottom of the box? The flakes pack together, so the raisins can't move.

• **Cereal monogamy.** In commercials, TV's Clark Kent often ate Corn Flakes with Jimmy Olson but never Lois Lane. Why? Because Kellogg's didn't want us to think that Clark and Lois had spent the night together (but it was OK to think that Clark and Jimmy had?).

• **What's in a name?** C.W. Post came up with a cereal in 1904 that he named Elijah's Manna. But the government refused to register the trademark under that name, so he renamed it Post Toasties.

• **Sugar Blues.** Some cereals seem to be ashamed of their sugary roots. Super Sugar Crisp has become Super Golden Crisp; Sugar Pops became Corn Pops; and Sugar Smacks are now Honey Smacks. Despite name changes, some cereals are still half sugar.

• **Bang!** Puffed wheat really is "shot from guns," of a sort. The sudden change in pressure is what "puffs" it.

• **Cartoon characters** used to merely *sell* cereal. Now they have their own brands. Flintstones, Batman, Ghostbusters, GI Joe, Barbie, E.T., Ninja Turtles and Nintendo characters have all been flaked and boxed.

• **Just whistle.** Legend among "phone phreaks" in the 1960s had it that a "free-inside" premium whistle from Cap'n Crunch was exactly the right frequency for triggering free long distance calls if blown into the phone.

Bowlful of Memories

Cereal Commercial Tapes, 3089C Clairemont Dr. #202 San Diego, CA 92117. $22 each, 2 for $40, 3 for $55.

If you had an average childhood, you saw about 12,000 TV ads. These three volumes of lovingly selected old TV spots will help you relive those happy video-besotted times. Each is about an hour.

Volume 1: "Soggy Celebrities" includes Superman, Space Patrol, The Monkees, Jimmy Durante, Danny Thomas and more.

Volume 2: "Famous Animated Flakies" stars Rocky & Bullwinkle, Bugs Bunny, Top Cat, Yogi Bear, Quisp & Quake and more.

Volume 3): "Snap, Crackle, Poppourri" stars the weirdest, most obscure, TV cereal spots.

Classic Recipe

Rice Krispies Treats

1/4 cup butter or margarine
1/2 pound (about 32 large) marshmallows
5 cups Kellogg's Rice Krispies

1) Melt butter in 3-quart saucepan. Add marshmallows and cook over low heat, stirring constantly, until marshmallows are melted and mixture is well-blended. Remove from heat.
2) Add Rice Krispies and stir until well-coated with mixture.
3) Press warm mixture lightly into buttered 13 x 9 inch pan. Cut into squares when cool. Makes 24 2-inch squares.

TOSS THE CEREAL, KEEP THE BOX

Flake Magazine, PO Box 481, Cambridge, MA 02140. $20 / year.

Contains decent photography, well-written articles, reviews and informative display ads. Editorial focus is on the odd idea of saving cereal boxes *as investments*, with less emphasis placed on history, premiums, advertising or the product itself. Still, if you just look at the pictures, years of your early morning life will pass before your eyes.

Box Top Bonanza, 153-1/2 15th Avenue, East Moline, IL 61244. $20 / 6 issues.

"Free Inside!" No, not a New Age philosophy but a phrase that gladdens the hearts of kids everywhere. In a world of narrow editorial niches, this one beats most: it's dedicated to the toys that came inside the boxes or in the mail when you sent in box tops. This collectors' magazine focuses especially well on radio-TV premiums, comic, western and adventure characters.

Each year nearly 2.5 billion boxes of cereal (both hot and cold) are eaten in the United States.

Unforgettable Cereal Characters

Sonny the Cuckoo Bird
"CUCKOO FOR COCOA PUFFS!"
As if to confirm that sugared cereals can make you hyper, this manic bird inspired breakfast table imitation, accompanied by parental muttering: "Never again!"

Snap, Crackle & Pop
"Snap Crackle Pop, Rice Krispies."
Who are these guys, and why is my cereal clicking?

The Quaker Quaker
"Nothing is better for thee than me."
A Ben Franklin look-alike, he's been selling Quaker Oats since the 1880s.

Tony the Tiger
"He's G-R-R-R-EAT!"
The most popular cereal spokes-animal of all time.

Mikey
"He likes it!"
Twenty years later, Mikey again appeared on the Life Cereal box as an adult, squelching bizarre but widespread rumors that he had exploded from eating Pop Rocks.

Where to Get Collectibles
All of these memorable characters were available on a lot of premiums and prizes. A great source for making bids by mail on these and other original collectibles is: *Hake's Americana & Collectibles*, PO Box 1444, York, PA 17405. (707) 848-1333. $20/4 quarterly issues.

Sam Toucan
"Oot-Fray Oops-Lay!"
Who says Pig Latin's a dead language?

Marky Maypo
"I want my Maypo!"
This cereal-hating little buckaroo's line burrowed its way into the consciousness of an entire generation.

Trix Rabbit
"Silly rabbit, Trix are for kids!"
Given the chance in a much-ballyhooed election, over 99% of the vote granted the rabbit his own bowl of "raspberry red, lemon yellow and orange orange" in 1976.

Pilgrimage

BATTLE CREEK, MIGHICAN
If you want to see and even smell where it all began, Battle Creek's the place. Unfortunately, none of the plants give tours any more because of "industrial espionage" fears. Still, the dedicated pilgrim can find enough cereal sites to make the trip eventful.

• First of all, stop anywhere and sniff. The heady essence of Froot Loops and Chex wafts continuously through the city.

• Kellogg's World Headquarters. Historic photo and memorabilia display open to public. Downtown at 1 Kellogg's Square, (616) 961-2000.

• Tony the Tiger and Tony, Jr. Statues. High point of the defunct Kellogg's tour, you can see them now only through a fence at 235 Porter St.

• Where it all started: The Battle Creek Adventist Hospital (165 N. Washington, (616) 968-8101) has exhibits and a tour of the first cereal factory. Across the street, now housing federal offices, is the original Sanitarium building.

COMMERCIAL ART: ANIMATION CELS

Cels are the individual hand-painted pictures on acetate that are used when animating cartoons. Two companies sell them from TV cereal commercials.

**Just Kids Nostalgia
5 Green Street
Huntington, NY 11743
(516) 423-8449
$3 for catalog**

Just Kids sells original animation cels from some of our favorite cereal commercials: Sugar Crisp, Alpha Bits, Cocoa Pebbles, and more. The stock on hand varies, so send for a current catalog. Prices range from $45 to $125.

**Carey Ward Gallery
126 East 19th St.
Costa Mesa, CA 92627
(714) 631-2242**

Carey Ward is the son of Jay Ward, who brought to life Bullwinkle, Rocky, George of the Jungle, Super Chicken and other cult cartoon classics of the 1960s. He also animated three of the best of the cereal

commercial characters of the time: Cap'n Crunch, Quisp and Quake.

This gallery is the source for these commercial cels. Prices range from $300-$475.

They are all that's left of Jay Ward's art—the original paintings from his TV shows were erased and recycled at a time when the acetate was considered more valuable than the artwork.

Cap'n Crunch

A Triumph of Marketing

When Quaker was considering marketing a new cereal in the 1960s, they chose Jay Ward, creator of the popular Rocky and Bullwinkle cartoons, to come up with a character to sell it.

His idea was a sea captain with a zany crew: Cap'n Crunch. Quaker loved the idea and had him film a series of commercials. It was only after approving these that they got around to actually coming up with a cereal to go along with the commercials.

The cereal was a big success. So they did exactly the same thing with Quisp & Quake.

Freeze-Dried Flop

NASA-inspired freeze-dried fruit in cereal seemed like a great idea in 1964, so Post made "Corn Flakes & Strawberries."

Kellogg's saw what was happening and jumped into the shelf-space race with "Corn Flakes With Instant Bananas." Unfortunately, it was about that time people started seeing that the product didn't work.

The fruit was supposed to regain its original shape, color and flavor in milk. It didn't. It stayed crunchy for at least 10-15 minutes—long enough to render the cereal terminally soggy. Most people bought exactly one box out of curiosity, and never bought another.

CEREAL BOX PRICE GUIDE

Complete Cereal Boxography and Price Guide by Scott Bruce. Mr. Cereal Box Press, PO Box 481-F, Cambridge, MA 02140. $22.95 postpaid.

This obsessive but handsomely designed guide covers cereal from 1890 to the present — over 10,000 boxes made by more than 300 manufacturers. Indexed by character so it's easy to look up your favorites.

CEREAL SURREALISM

Turn On, Tune In, Snap, Crackle, Pop?

In the late 1960s psychedelic artist Peter Max designed a cereal box for a Swiss cereal called LOVE. Perhaps other cereals should feature psychedelic packaging as well, because large doses of cereal may contain enough natural LSD to induce mild euphoria.

According to Dr. David Conning, director of the British Nutritional Foundation, eating a large bowl of shredded wheat or bran flakes in one sitting may be enough to set you off. This is because LSD is produced by ergot, a common fungal infestation of wheat that can survive food processing. A high-bran diet could result in a daily consumption of 100 micrograms of LSD, four times the minimum dose needed to produce an effect.

We just want to know: was cereal actor "Mikey" naturally spacy, or did he get high on LIFE?

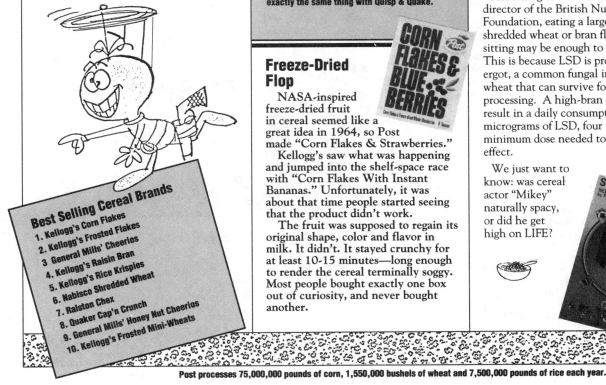

Best Selling Cereal Brands

1. Kellogg's Corn Flakes
2. Kellogg's Frosted Flakes
3. General Mills' Cheerios
4. Kellogg's Raisin Bran
5. Kellogg's Rice Krispies
6. Nabisco Shredded Wheat
7. Ralston Chex
8. Quaker Cap'n Crunch
9. General Mills' Honey Nut Cheerios
10. Kellogg's Frosted Mini-Wheats

BARNUM'S BABY

The modern circus is an American invention. It was P.T. Barnum who first brought us the 3-ring, "more is better," circus extravaganza. Say "circus" and what most of us visualize are hundreds of animals and performers in three rings set up in a coliseum.

Yet, of the 121 active touring circuses in America, only a few live up (or down) to the Barnum model. The rest? Some are just scaled-down versions of the same thing, traveling through smaller towns with enough acts to support maybe only one or two "rings." But others are from a different heritage, drawing from older and richer European and Asian circus tradition.

These "New Circus" troupes like the Pickle Family Circus, Big Apple Circus and the Cirque du Soleil, are actually an old idea: exhibitions of human skills on a scale small enough to let you see the sweat droplets. The intimacy and audience interaction are two of its biggest charms—the performers are more than a tiny dot way over there.

Each performer is by necessity multi-faceted—the trapeze artist may also help set up equipment and later join the clowns in some comic bit; the juggler may juggle swords on stage and then the books in the business office.

Best of all, most New Circuses forego animal and "death-defying" acts. Watching humans humiliate animals may have been satisfying when they were a threat to human survival, but now it's just embarrassing. And netless acts where a small professional mistake could mean serious injury or death seem less a thrill than an unconscionable work hazard.

I remember being taken to Barnum's circus. The exhibit which I most desired to see was 'The Boneless Wonder'." —Winston Churchill

Ladies & Gentlemen! Presenting Circus Facts

• The first known circus school was established in China during the T'ang dynasty (612-907 AD). Curriculum included "Duel Sword Dancing", "Seven-Ball Jumping", "Rope Walking" and "Long Pole Tricks."

• Leotards were named after Jules Leotard (1838-70) inventor of the flying trapeze. He also invented the safety net, sort of—while at the Cirque Napoleon he worked with a pile of mattresses underneath him.

• The circular shape of the Roman Coliseum was the model for modern day circus arenas ("circus" means "round" in Latin). The Coliseum was also the site of a sad piece of circus history. The first giraffe ever seen in Europe, caught by the Romans in Africa, was exhibited there. The Romans thought it was a cross between a camel and leopard and capable of fighting gladiators. The harmless creature was quickly killed, as the crowd cheered.

• The Clyde Beatty - Cole Bros. Circus is nicknamed "The I-95 Circus" because it doesn't venture far from that freeway stretching from Ft. Lauderdale, Florida to Portsmouth, New Hampshire.

• Traditionally, the calliope would appear only at the end of a circus parade. This was done for safety reasons, since the boilers in those steam-powered contraptions would occasionally blow up.

• Military logistics during World War I owed less to Washington and Napoleon than to Barnum & Bailey. By the turn of the century circuses had become such outstanding examples of organizational efficiency—being able to unload, perform and reload all in one day—that military officers were routinely dispatched to observe and learn.

Big Top 10

Tears of a Clown—Smokey Robinson.

Send in the Clowns—A Stephen Sondheim song sung by millions.

Goodbye Cruel World (I'm Off to Join the Circus)—James Darren.

Be a Clown (later recycled into **Make 'Em Laugh**)—Fred Astaire and Judy Garland, from Easter Parade.

The Man on the Flying Trapeze—A turn of the century heartwringer about local women having their hearts (and whatever else) stolen by traveling circus performers.

March of the Gladiators—The tune everybody associates with the circus but nobody knows the name of. You know: "Doo Dit DiDiDiDi DOO Dit DOO Dit…"

Gladiators is to the calliope what **Lady of Spain** is to the accordion and what **Louie Louie** is to electric guitar.)

A Little Bitty Tear ("Let me down / Spoiled my act as a clown…") —Burl Ives.

Cathy's Clown—Everly Brothers.

Tightrope—Leon Russell.

Everybody Loves a Clown (So Why Don't You?)—Gary Lewis & the Playboys.

TO THE CIRCUS
MAIN ENTRANCE

Circus acts dangerous? More performers are killed traveling to performances than during them.

CIRCUS WORLD MUSEUM
BARABOO, WISCONSIN

Pilgrimages

• *Circus World Museum, Baraboo, WI 53913 (608) 356-0800.* The world's largest circus museum, Circus World is housed in the original Ringling Bros. headquarters (used from 1884 until 1918, when they wimped out to the balmy climes of Sarasota, Florida). Boasts the largest collection of restored circus wagons (170 and counting), magic shows, calliope concerts, elephant rides and live circus acts every day of the year. The town is something of a circus curiosity itself: for some reason, six different circuses got started there.

• *Woodlawn Cemetery, Forest Park, Illinois.* Look for the five granite elephants marking the mass grave of 86 performers and roustabouts from the Hagenbeck-Wallace Circus who died in a train-wreck in 1918.

WORLD'S BIGGEST CIRCUS PARADE

Every year in mid-July a colorful 75-car circus train travels from Circus World Museum in Baraboo, Wisconsin to downtown Milwaukee. People line the 222 mile route to watch the antique cars go by.

The tons of elephants, hundreds of horses and dozens of bands march through town in the Great Circus Parade, the world's largest. Fireworks, circus acts and antique circus wagons round out the week's festivities.

For more information, contact Circus World Museum, Baraboo, WI 53913. (608) 356-0800.

Calliope Music

While calliopes rarely explode any more, they are still shrill enough to cause dogs to bark all over town.

You can do the same with this genuine calliope music played on an antique Tangley Air Calliope.

• *Calliope Capers*
• *Kallyope*
• *Calliope on Parade*

Records or tapes, $8.95 each postpaid, or 20.85 for all 3. Taggart Enterprises, 323 Logan St., Rockford, IL 61103. (815) 964-2789.

Posters

Official set of beautiful full-color posters from six years of Milwaukee's Great Circus Parades, printed on glossy enamel paper.

$40.05 postpaid from: Spectrum Creative, Inc., 7709 W. Lisbon Ave., Milwaukee, WI 53222 (414) 442-1367.

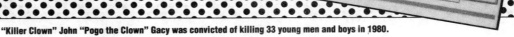

"Killer Clown" John "Pogo the Clown" Gacy was convicted of killing 33 young men and boys in 1980.

Goodbye Cruel World, I'm Off to Join the Circus

Okay, so you're ready to run away and join the circus. Well, hold on a minute. Not many circuses out there are eager to let you perform unless you have some incredible skills.

Unfortunately, odds are that you don't have these skills— most successful circus performers started learning from their circus families as toddlers and starting out now, the odds against you are daunting (it can take several years of practice and training just to learn the standing somersault or to how to hold a handstand for two long minutes).

Still there are a couple of possibilities. The first is to become a "roustabout" unskilled laborer, if you have the stamina and strength, a willingness to live and work in deplorable conditions for low pay, and at least one tattoo for every 1.5 square feet of skin.

CELEBRATING CLASSIC CLOWNING!

The second choice is easier. Larger circuses are continuously filling openings for semi-skilled people: dancers, extras, clowns, and ticket and concession sellers. Want to perform? Learn to be a clown. Here are two schools for the circus-skill impaired:

Clowns of America International. This organization of clowns and wanna-bes offers circus skills workshops. Local chapters around the country called "alleys" sponsor seminars for members. For information, write:

> **Clowns of America International**
> **PO Box 570**
> **Lake Jackson, TX 77566**

Ringling Bros. and Barnum & Bailey Clown College. This nine-week course begins each September with students recruited at stops of the Ringling circus. The curriculum includes clowning skills and makeup, gymnastics, mime, props, and elephant riding.

Some say the Clown College is actually a "Clown Boot-Camp"— a grueling orientation to the RB/B&B way of doing things.

The preselected students must sign binding contracts beforehand that they'll join the circus if asked. About one in ten is picked, which means a few years of exciting, exhausting, spartan, badly paid but resume-enhancing servitude. Still, it sounds like fun.

> **For free information, write to:**
> **Ringling Bros. and Barnum & Bailey**
> **Clown College**
> **P.O. Box 1528**
> **Venice, FL 33595**

Recommended Reading

Ringmaster! by **Kristopher Antekeier and Greg Aunapu.** If you've ever considered running away to join the circus, better read this first. Antekeier left a career as an actor and became the ringmaster for Ringling Brothers and Barnum & Bailey and shares the excitement, as well as the tedium and tension, of circus life.

Particularly vivid is his account of working conditions: few health or other benefits, and having to pay management for everything from your cramped living space to transportation to the arena. Cruelty to animals? Maybe what we need is an organization to prevent cruelty to clowns.

$19.95+$2.50 shipping from Penguin Books, 120 Woodbine Street, Bergenfield, NJ 07621. (201) 387-0600.

Most younger kids find clowns very scary.

"CLOWN CORRESPONDENCE COLLEGE": The WPC Home Study Course

If your ultimate dream is to put on makeup and act foolish, we've put together a clown curriculum for you. Exams, diploma and elevator passes will cost you extra.

General Clowning 101

Creative Clowning by Bruce Fife, et al. Java Publishing, PO Box 25203, Colorado Springs, CO 80936. (719) 548-1844. $16.95 + 1.25 shipping.

Eight professional clowns provide instruction on props, jokes, comedy, magic, unicycling, character development, and making a living as a clown.

Mime

The Mime Book by Claude Kipnis. $10.95 + 1.50 shipping from Meriwether Publishing, PO 7710 Colorado Springs, CO 80933. (800) 93-PLAYS.

Teaches the international language of pantamime. But what are these words doing in here?

Makeup

FRESHMAN
Face Painting by the editors of Klutz Press. $14.95 + 2.50 shipping from Klutz Press, 2121 Staunton Court, Palo Alto, CA 94306, (415) 424-0739.

Although more aimed at kids than adults, this book has the advantage of coming with a palette of washable, non-toxic facepaints.

SOPHOMORE
Strutter's Complete Guide to Clown Makeup by Jim Roberts. $14.95 + 1.25 shipping from Java Publishing (see above).

A proper clown face is not a mask, but a complement to the natural features of the wearer's face and personality, says Roberts. Instructions and photos explain how to bring out the bozo within.

Juggling

FRESHMAN
Juggling Made Simple by Dr. Dropo. $4.95 + .90 shipping from Java Publishing (see above).

This 16 page book comes with "slow-motion" juggling scarves to get that "toss-catch-toss" hand movement.

SOPHOMORE
The Klutz Book of Juggling by John Cassidy and B. C. Rimbeaux. $9.95 + 2.00 shipping from Klutz Press (see above).

THE classic beginning juggling book. Comes with soft juggling balls and clear instructions.

JUNIOR
How to Be a Goofy Juggler by Bruce Fife. $6.95 + .90 shipping from Java Publishing (see above).

Now that you know how to juggle, this book helps with gags, jokes, stunts, and even recovery lines when you drop something.

SENIOR
Dr. Dropo's Juggling Buffoonery by Bruce Fife. $7.95 + .90 shipping from Java Publishing (see above).

More tricks and gags, but also entire routines you can use in professional performances. Also balancing tricks and cigar box manipulation.

Balloon Sculpture

Dr. Dropo's Balloon Sculpturing for Beginners by Bruce Fife. $7.95 + .90 shipping from Java Publishing (see above).

Hats, toys, airplanes, dachshunds, giraffes, and dozens of other shapes can be carved out of latex and air. Includes a supply of those long balloons.

Performance

Clown Act Omnibus by Wes McVicar. $9.95 + 1.50 shipping from Meriwether Publishing (see above).

Over 150 stunts and skits for clowns, classified as to difficulty, physical ability and number of actors.

Clown Theology

• *Clown Ministry Handbook* by Janet Litherland. $7.95 + 1.50 shipping.

• *Send in His Clowns* by Stephen Perrone &James Spata. $8.95 + 1.50 shipping.

• *Mime Ministry* by Susie Toomey. $8.95 + 1.50 shipping. Available from Meriwether Publishing, PO 7710 Colorado Springs, CO 80933. (800) 93-PLAYS.

The Bible says to be "fools for Christ's sake" and these Born-Again Bozos take the command literally, being clowns to get a theological point across. While these books are aimed at Christians, there's no reason the basic idea can't be adapted to any religion, philosophy or political belief. Why not a koan-spouting clown battalion from the Zen Buddhist ministry? ("What is the sound of one mime talking?").

Then there were the two circus performers who got married in a three ring ceremony...

P.T. ■ Barnum—Hokum & Humbug

Phineas Taylor Barnum was not only the father of the American circus, but of Public Relations as well. A keen student of human nature and media behavior, he was able to parlay stunts and humbuggery into billions of dollars worth of publicity.

Consider these examples of harmless mind manipulation:

• He was the first to shine spotlights into the sky to attract attention. Three years before the electric light, Barnum wowed crowds with calcium lights on top of his American Museum in New York City.

• Barnum advertised free concerts and kept a band playing on the balcony of his museum. However, the musicians were purposely so bad that people hurried into the museum to escape the noise. "Of course the music was bad," shrugged Barnum. "When people expect something for nothing, they are usually cheated."

• He presented a number of hoaxes to the willingly gullible, including "The Fejee Mermaid" (the top of a mummified monkey sewed to a fish's hindquarters) and a woman who was supposedly 161 years old and George Washington's childhood nurse. When interest in the latter started falling off, he wrote an anonymous letter to the editor accusing himself of displaying a fake—that the lady was really a machine made of whalebone, molded rubber and hidden springs. That dramatically rekindled public interest, even generating repeat business from those who wanted to see if they had been fooled the first time.

• He coined the phrase "siamese twins" for his presentation of Chang and Eng, who were joined at the chest. Barnum also singlehandedly made famous "General" Tom Thumb, "Grizzley" Adams, and Jenny Lind, "the Swedish Nightingale."

• Crowds would come to his museum and not leave, forcing Barnum to turn other paying customers away. He solved the problem by putting up signs saying "This Way to the Egress." Thinking it some kind of exotic creature, people followed the signs out a self-locking exit door into the alley.

Required Reading

There are hundreds of great Barnum stories. Two biographies we can recommend:

P.T. Barnum: The Legend and the Man by A. H. Saxon. A thorough and scholarly work, drawing from newly unearthed sources, including 4,000 letters. Effectively contrasts the complexity of the man with the simple genius of his schemes.

$32.95 + 3.00 shipping from Columbia University Press, 136 South Broadway, Irvington, NY 10533. 914/591-9111.

The Greatest Showman on Earth by Ann Tompert. Less scholarly than the above. Nearly as entertaining, but cleaned up slightly for the "youth market."

$12.95 + $1.00 shipping, Dillon Press, 242 Portland Avenue S., Minneapolis, MN 53415. (800) 962-0437.

Barnum Pilgrimage

The Barnum Museum, 820 Main St.
Bridgeport, NY 06604
(203) 331-9881

For fans of P.T. Barnum in particular and circuses in general, the Museum offers history and artifacts which cannot be seen elsewhere, including some of Barnum's biggest "humbugs."

In Your Soup

Full-color replica ceramic sign from 1902, advertising Barnum animal crackers. 11 by 9 inches.

$21.95 + 3.90 shipping from: Wireless, P.O. Box 64422, St. Paul, Minnesota 55164-0422. (800) 669-9999.

Despite legend, there's no evidence Barnum ever said "There's a sucker born every minute."

FREAKS!

Once, every circus and carnival had its freak show exhibiting giants, midgets, dwarfs, pinheads, dog-faced boys, siamese twins, bearded ladies and wildmen. Today few such shows exist, legislated out of existence by laws against exhibiting "deformities." Generally, the intentions for passing for the laws were good ones. But there was an unintended downside, too.

Years ago, people born grossly abnormal would be hidden out of view by their family. Some, if given the chance, joined freak shows. Suddenly they were with people, traveling and earning a living. Their long-hidden deformities became assets. Many made a comfortable living. Some even got rich.

Today, many with the same handicaps—if allowed to live beyond infancy—spend their lives locked away from view in institutions. True, the shows were degrading—and so are the alternatives.

Freaky Reading

Freaks: We Who Are Not As Others by Daniel Mannix. A fascinating and intimate view of freaks and freak shows throughout history, with scores of photos. One interesting fact of many: In 1890, Dr. Martin Courney, inventor of the baby incubator, couldn't interest institutions in funding the device, so he exhibited his "incubator babies" at a freak show on Coney Island. People were shocked, but he saved babies.

Re/Search Publications, 20-B Romolo Pl., San Francisco, CA 94133. $14.00 postpaid.

Freak Show by Robert Bogdan. A scholarly but fascinating account of freak shows and how they were presented (including information on the large number of phonies in the business).

University of Chicago Press 11030 S. Langley Ave., Chicago, IL 60628. (800) 621-2736. $14.95 + $1.75 shipping.

"Ladies and Gentlemen…"

"…For the insignificant sum of one dime, two nickels, ten coppers, one-tenth of a dollar—the price of a shave or a hair ribbon…The greatest, most astounding aggregation of marvels and monstrocities gather together in one edifice.

"Looted from the ends of the earth. From the wilds of darkest Africa, the miasmic jungles of Brazil, the mystic headwaters of the Yan-Tse Kiang, the cannibal isle of the Antipodes, the frosty slopes of the Himalayas, and the barren steppes of the Caucasus!

"Sparing no expense, every town, every village, every nook and cranny of the globe has been searched with a fine-tooth comb to provide this feast for the eye and mind. A refined exhibition for cultured ladies and gentlemen. No waiting, no delays. Step up, ladies and gentlemen, and avoid the rush! Tickets now selling in the doorway!"

—Freak show barker, transcribed by Felix Isman, 1924

"Gooble Gobble, One of Us"

Freaks. The cult classic film by Tod Browning starred actual freaks from the Barnum & Bailey Circus in sympathetic roles—they're the good guys, the bad guys are "normals".

You'll be amazed at what people without arms and legs can do. The story line—about a treacherous "normal-sized" woman marrying a midget for his money—is somewhat based on a true story, although the movie has a happier ending (in real life, both killed themselves with poison).

Mr. Dickens, Books & Tapes, 5323-A Elkhorn Blvd., Sacramento, CA 95842. 800/228-4246. Video, $59.95; laserdisc, $34.95, + $3.00 shipping.

Before Zippy the Pinhead there was Zip the Pinhead in Barnum's freak show.

Clown Accessories

Juggling Chicken

Aerodynamic and weight-balanced plastic juggling devices. $6 each or 3 for $15. Add $3 shipping. From Klutz, 2121 Staunton Ct., Palo Alto, CA 94306. (415) 424-0739.

Fool's Cap

Satin cloth, hand-sewed—jest the thing for any silly occasion where you want to be there with bells on! $20 + $3 shipping from Klutz (see above).

Emmett Kelly: Elvis of the Circus

Like Elvis, this famous clown seems to be making more money dead than alive.

• The hobo clown depicting various professions in 4 1/2 inch bisque. #3606 executive; #3607 accountant; #3608 doctor; #3611 dentist; #6907 fireman; #6908 policeman; #8247 lawyer. $12.98 each +3.99 shipping from Taylor Gifts, 355 E. Conestoga Road, P.O. Box 206, Wayne, PA 19087-0206. (215) 789-7007.

• Framed print, Kelly reads Wall St. Journal (but what's with the middle finger?) #6078, $19.00 + 4.95 shipping from Post Scripts, PO Box 21628, Ft. Lauderdale, FL 33335-1628. (800) 327-3799.

• Jigsaw Puzzle, 550 pieces. #4615 $8.50 + 2.50 shipping from The Lighter Side, 4514 19th St. Court East, P.O. Box 25600, Bradenton, FL 34206-5600, (813) 747-2356.

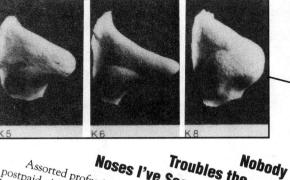

Nobody Troubles the Noses I've Seen

Assorted professional foam noses each $11.20 postpaid. Also available: bald wigs, professional makeup, beards and much more. Kryolan Corporation, 132 Ninth St., San Francisco, CA 94103-2603. (415) 863-9684 / FAX (415) 863-9059.

Like snowflakes, no two clown faces are alike, thanks to a face registry which precludes some other clown from copying.

CLOTHES

Threads of History

Who knows when and why people started wearing clothes?

The biblical account has it that Adam and Eve sewed fig leaves into aprons for modesty's sake after eating from the Tree of Knowledge of Good and Evil. Some anthropologists second that idea, sort of, suggesting that clothing was the first step toward sublimating sexuality; otherwise societies found that they never got any work done.

Protection from cold and rain, of course, were also reasons for clothing, but it's significant nearly every culture has had clothes, no matter how hot the climate.

As civilization advanced, clothes became more complicated, progressing (if you can call it that) from body covering to structure for molding, displaying and simulating whatever figure was deemed ideal at the time. This reached its apex of absurdity in the 19th century with whalebone corsets which sometimes caused internal injuries to fashion victims in pursuit of the 16 inch waist.

Clothing, strangely enough, is used simultaneously to both hide the body and display it. In wearing it, we express that universal tension between the impulses of concealing and revealing.

Victorian Secrets

Past Patterns: Meticulous Patterns of Fashion Rages Between the Victorian and Supersonic Ages. Do you yearn for a more romantic time, when courtships lingered in part because corsets were so difficult to remove? Love the look of layered petticoats over bloomers? There's an entire subculture of people who like to dress up Victorian. Joining this subculture takes an avid interest and willingness to give your sewing skills a good working over. Past Patterns offers catalogs of old patterns for your own past life regression. We liked the *Victorian & Edwardian Catalogue*, but for slightly more modern styles, try *The Teens Attic Copies* or *The Twenties Attic Copies*.

Middle Class Duds

Everyday Fashions of the Thirties: As Pictured in Sears Catalogue, **edited by Stella Blum.** Our impressions of an era's styles are often distorted, nothing at all like what the normal folks were wearing at the time. But what could be more normal than the Sears-Roebuck catalog? This book features page after page of typical catalog spreads for women's, men's and kids' clothes and accessories. Even though the fashions are pretty basic (this was Sears after all, and the Depression to boot) the pages are interesting not just for the clothes but for the art, the marketing and even the prices (dresses and hats for $1.98, Mickey Mouse and Buck Rogers watches for $1.29 and 98¢, men's suits with 2 pairs of pants for $25).

Keep Up With Last Century's Fashion Trends

Vintage Fashion Magazine. A wide mix of articles about clothes from a lot of different eras. A recent issue included articles on 1920s flapper dresses, art nouveau beaded purses, crinoline dresses from the 1840s, and buttoned shoes.

How about this useful tidbit from an article on storing vintage clothes? "A vacuum cleaner with a piece of screening or net fastened over the end of the wand can be used to pick up loose dust or insect cases, using care to avoid actually touching the fabric."

Subscription: $19.95 for one year (6 issues)

LOVELY COLORS GORGEOUS SATIN TRIMMING $2.98

from Hobby House Press, 900 Frederick St., Cumberland, MD 21502. (301) 759-3770 / FAX (301) 759-4940.

Yes, No Bandannas?

The American Bandanna: Culture on Cloth from George Washington to Elvis by Hillary Weiss. Martha Washington is credited with creating the first American bandanna ("little banner") a souvenir commemorating her husband and the 1776 revolution.

Since then, bandannas have commemorated world's fairs, political candidates, pop stars, magazines, books, movies, TV shows and airlines. This book shows hundreds, in color.

$16.95 + 2.00 from Chronicle Books, 275 Fifth Street, San Francisco, CA 94103. (800) 722-6657.

Escher Sketches

M.C. Escher sketched six notebooks of symmetrical patterns featuring birds, lizards, and mythical creatures. Found by his estate's curators, they were used for these Italian silk tie designs.

#18202, Lizards or #16434, Geometric. Each $28.50 + 3.90 shipping from Wireless, PO Box 64422, St. Paul, MN 55164-0422. (800) 669-9999.

Pilgrimage: Threads of Time

Clarkson Watson House, 5275 Germantown Ave., Germantown, PA. You'll find 7,000 articles of antique clothing dating from as early as the 1700s. Categories of clothes like wedding gowns and hats take up entire rooms. Especially evocative are such treasures as 18th century silk brocade shoes with wooden heels, Victorian era women's parasols and hand embroidered men's vests.

Fabrications

Changing Trends In Fashion: Patterns of the Twentieth Century, edited by Past Patterns. This book goes decade by decade from 1900-70, discussing the connection between styles of clothing and social trends. Undergarments are also covered (as they should be, Madonna take note); so are popular colors, proper accessories, and even authentic retro hairstyles. The fashion illustrations are accompanied by patterns for casual clothes, suits, and evening wear for both men and women.

$25.00 + 3.00 shipping from Past Patterns, PO Box 7587, Grand Rapids, MI 49502-1014.

Living in the Dark Ages

For a catalog of Medieval costumes, send $1.00 to **Medieval Miscellanea, 7006 Raleigh Road, Annadale, VA 22003.**

GOOD CLOTHES for MEN

Capper n Capper

Tie These On

The Tie: Trends and Traditions by Sarah Gibbings. Most men consider them useless, even uncomfortable, but in a traditional work environment, the tie is the only accessory that allows him to show any individuality. From the early continental cravat to the cowboy bandanna, bolos to bowties, this book takes a good and thorough look at each. A very thorough look at a colorfully trivial subject. **$21.95 + 2.00 shipping from Barron's Educational Series, Inc., 250 Wireless Blvd., Hauppauge, NY 11788. (800) 645-3476.**

Fit to be Tied: Vintage Ties of the Forties and Fifties by Rod Dyer and Ron Spark. Way-out illustrations of the wide, wild ties that followed World War II. We defy you to find a collection louder than these surreal specimens. Wearing the particularly gaudy hand-painted ones, depicting everything from buckaroos to buck-naked pin-up girls, would make anyone think you'd "tied one on." Jumping fish? Hula girls? Palm trees? Horses? Flying ducks? They're all here in lots of photos, but if you want analysis, get the other book.

$19.95 + 3.00 shipping from Abbeville Press, Inc., 488 Madison Avenue, New York, NY 10022. (800) 227-7210.

Fit to be Tied

36" Jumbo Tie is as loud as it is long.

#3147, $7.98 + 2.70 shipping from Johnson Smith Co., 4514 19th Court East, PO Box 25500, Bradenton, FL 34206. (813) 747-2356.

Big Bucks Bowtie

Dress for Excess, '80s style, with this pre-tied $100 bill bowtie.

#F11, $15 00 + 3.25 shipping from The Daily Planet, P.O. Box 1313, New York, NY 10013. (212) 334-0006 / FAX: (212) 334-1158.

"I love my ties, partly out of respect, partly out of fear."—Harry Anderson

Hat Pilgrimage

The Brown Derby, 3427 Wilshire Blvd., Los Angeles, CA. Visit the world's most famous oversized hat. The good news: unlike so much of great early Los Angeles architecture, it survived the wrecker's ball. The bad news: it's no longer at street level, but stuck two stories up on top of a strip mall (the price of preservation). This picture was taken before the mall—your photos will not be as impressive.

Some Like It Hat

The Hat: Trends and Traditions, **by Madeleine Ginsburg.** "If you want to get ahead, get a hat," said the ad campaign in the 1950s. This amazing book, the companion piece to the tie book mentioned on the other page, is exhaustively

researched and entertainingly illustrated.

Covers the gamut from brimless turbans, cowboy hats, picture hats, bowlers and top hats. What becomes clear with this book is that each one has a particular personality, a fantasy that can be

entered by simply putting it on. Excellent coverage of the subject through four centuries and several continents.

$21.95 + 2.00 from Barron's Educational Series, Inc., 250 Wireless Blvd., Hauppauge, NY 11788. (800) 645-3476.

Clubs: Capping It Off

The National Cap and Patch Association (CAP). If you're a John Deere cap aficionado, or are in the habit of collecting baseball-style hats that sport advertisements or patches, this is the club for you. Members learn about other collectors, like Bucky Legried who boasts hundreds of caps. Members also share information on how to get hard-to-find caps.

Contact Gene Dittman, Founder, 2216 200th Avenue, Deer Park, WI 54007. $15.00 annually gets a membership cap and quarterly newsletter.

Panama Hats Are *Not* From Panama

Panama hats originated in Peru. This one's made in Ecuador. So why are they called Panama hats? Because Panama became a major distribution center for them. This one's made of soft paja toquilla straw.

S, M, L & XL, #155510, $28.00 + 4.50 shipping from The Nature Company, PO Box 2310, Berkeley, CA 94702. (800) 227-1114.

Seams Like Old Times

Heels: In the 1600s, King Louis XIV of France tried to camouflage his shortness by having the heels of his boots made higher. His courtiers thought it a fun fad, and in turn raised the height of their heels. The King raised his heels higher. The escalation of elevated heels got out of hand—and foot—until men's heels eventually settled down again. Women's heels, however, stayed high. By the 1800s, American women got around to copying the high "French heels," which quickly became a mainstay of feminine fashion.

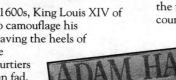

a better word for hat

Neckties: Croatian soldiers of the mid-1600s sported linen scarves around their necks. The French loved the look and called the neckwear "cravats." Charles II of England adopted the fashion, causing his countrymen to do likewise. The fashion spread, mutated and became that symbolic male appendage, the modern necktie.

Tuxes: In 1886, when suits with tails were fashionable, trendsetter Pierre Lorillard, of Tuxedo Park, New York, paid his tailor to design a tail-less suit. Considered extreme at its debut, the tuxedo nevertheless caught on, and is currently a clothing industry unto itself, fetching a half billion dollars annually.

Sneakers: The modern sneaker debuted in 1917, with brown canvas tops and black rubber soles. Its manufacturer, the National India Rubber Company, first called the creation Peds, but that name was already registered for another product, so the "P" was traded for a "K" (for "kids"), making Keds.

Shoelaces: A revolutionary concept introduced in England in 1790 as an alternative to buckles.

Shades: Invented in Philadelphia in 1885, sunglasses didn't catch on as a fashion accessory until the Jazz Age, when they caught on with flappers and were popularized by movie stars.

Collectible Celebrity Clothing

In recent auctions, collectors paid big bucks for rock star clothes, according to auction house Sotheby's:

• $4,400 for Michael Jackson's *Bad* tour jacket, autographed by the Great Weird One Himself.

• $8,800 for an Elvis Presley stage cape.

• $9,900 for Madonna's bustier from her *Gonna Dress You Up in My Love* video.

• $13,200 for Jimi Hendrix's Nehru jacket.

Gowns

Mini & Me

Designer Mary Quant introduced the mini skirt in 1965. Immediately its unprecedented popularity caused controversy all over the world.

• Women in minis were banned from entering Vatican City.

• Wearers were subject to jailing in Greece.

• In Egypt, women in minis could be charged with indecent behavior.

• Churches in Caracas, Venezuela erected signs telling women to renounce their mini-skirts or "be condemned to hell."

• Mini-skirts were even outlawed in the American duchy of Disneyland. Women wearing the offending garment could, however, gain admittance if they ripped out their skirt hems (and if the new length came close to the knee).

Formali-T

You say you hate to dress up? Now you can go to the most formal affairs dressed as informally as you wish! Authentic looking 100% cotton T-tux is pre-shrunk and won't fade on you even if your date does.

Sizes M, L & XL. #99966, $14.98 + 4.20 shipping from Johnson Smith Co., 4514 19th Court East, P.O. Box 25500, Bradenton, FL 34206. (813) 747-2356 / FAX (813) 746-7896.

KEEP YOUR COOL

Solar-powered safari hat keeps you comfortable when the heat is on. Electric motor-driven fan runs on batteries. A hi-tech beany!

#6584, $54.98 + 6.95 shipping from Johnson Smith Co., 4514 19th Court East, P.O. Box 25500, Bradenton, FL 34206-5500. (813) 747-2356.

Hemline Harbingers

For about 90 years, from 1897 to 1987, when the pattern broke, women's hemlines were considered to be a reliable barometer of stock market trends. Shorter skirts forecasted bull markets, while falling hemlines indicated bear markets.

What's That Garbage You're Wearing?

Recycle with this serape woven from the fashion industry's waste products.

#D04, $35.00 + 4.50 shipping from The Daily Planet, PO Box 1313, New York, NY 10013. (212) 334-0006 / FAX (212) 334-1158.

Even a Princess Down Under

Princess Diana & Prince Charles Fashion Paper Dolls in Full Color by Tom Tierney. According to the *Harper's Index*, Princess Diana spent $26,460 on underwear between marrying Prince Charles and the end of 1990. We don't get to see more than a few hundred dollars worth of it here on this paper doll, but we do get dozens of scrumptious gowns based on ones Di has worn.

Charles gets just a few boring suits and one silly Admiral Halsey uniform, but wins the prize for looking even more absurd than she in his underwear (estimated by the *Whole Pop Catalog Index* as costing, oh, maybe £7 tops).

Other politicians, presidents and celebrities in their underwear are available from Dover as well (our favorite is the set of Nancy Reagan Fashion Paper Dolls which includes dresses, so you don't have to "borrow" them from designers). Ask for their catalog for an impressive assortment of retro fashion books from all eras.

Prince/Princess (or Queen Nancy) doll book $3.95 + 2.50 shipping from Dover Publications, 31 East 2nd St., Mineola, NY 11501. (516) 294-7000.

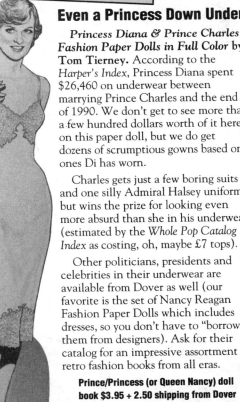

Platform shoes caused thousands of injuries in the 1970s.

COMICS

"Oh, no, Mom, you didn't really throw out all my old comic books!" Alas, Mom did—it happened to lots of us. In one toss of musty old newsprint she succeeded in obliterating part of our childhood and in providing the comic book market with justification for the fancy prices now paid for those same issues that went to the dump. Thanks, moms everywhere.

Except for the occasional supermarket or drug store rack, comic books today are pretty much found in two places: traditional newsstands and comic book specialty shops. Newsstands have sold comics since the 1930s; comics shops have been around only for a decade or two.

The biggest comic-book publisher today is Marvel Comics, with characters like The Hulk, The X-Men, Spider-Man). The second-biggest is DC Comics (Batman, Superman, Flash). But smaller publishers are also producing outstandingly entertaining material.

What sorts of things? Mostly comparatively small print runs of a wild spectrum from racy "undergrounds" to stuff too irreverent or odd for the mainstream. But they've also been responsible for material which sometimes crosses into mainstream culture like Fritz the Cat, Zippy the Pinhead, Howard the Duck, and The Teenage Mutant NinjaTurtles.

But it's not just the small press comics that make it onto TV and movie screens. Others that have spawned on-screen adventures include The Green Hornet, Dennis the Menace, Little Orphan Annie, Blondie & Dagwood, Charlie Brown, Dick Tracy, Batman, The Rocketeer and The Flash.

I'M DA YELLOW KID. BUT I DON'T KNOW WHO DESE OTHER GUYS IS.

Comic Book Facts

• The oldest comic strip is *The Yellow Kid*, first published in 1896. The most durable comic strip has been *The Katzenjammer Kids*, created by Rudolph Dirks in 1897. It's still being syndicated by King Features.

• As recently as 1961, a comic book cost only 10 cents. Now, the lowest price is about 10 times that.

• Clean-up artists work for comic strip syndicates and one of their chores is to white out hands the artist has drawn too close to a breast or crotch, and redraw them in neutral positions.

• Comics have spawned "graphic novels"— book-length serious tales told in comic-book format. Two best-sellers are *Maus*, a story of survivors of the Holocaust, and Frank Miller's *Dark Knight*, featuring a revisionist view of Batman.

• Speaking of caped crusaders, Marvel Comics published one of the most unusual issues in its long history in 1982: a comic book called *The Life of Pope John Paul II*.

• The popular *Gasoline Alley*, which started off in 1918 as a comic strip about a group of back alley car fans, added a new concept to the funnies: real time. In 1921, character Walt Wallet found an abandoned baby on his doorstep and took him in. Over the next six decades readers watched baby Skeezix grow up, become a teenager, go off to World War II, get married, have children, and eventually become a grandfather.

Reprints: *Nostalgia Reading*

Little Orphan Annie in the Great Depression, by Harold Gray. Aw, quit worrying about money! Annie got through hard times and so can you. 231 strips from 1931 detail the collapse of Daddy Warbucks' financial empire.

$3.95 + 2.50 shipping. Dover Publications, 11 East 2nd St., Mineola, NY 11501.

Zorro: The Complete Classic Adventures, by Alex Toth. Based on Disney's TV series, this swashbuckler will get your blood racing.

$9.95 + 1.00 shipping (for each of 2 vols.) from Eclipse Comics, P.O. Box 1099, Forestville, CA 95436. (707) 887-1521.

Krazy & Ignatz, by George Herriman. These five volumes reprint in color all the Sunday adventures of Krazy Kat, the prototype of all those cat 'n' mouse cartoons, from 1916 on. Artist George Herriman's strip has been likened to Chuck Berry's contribution to rock 'n' roll: It defined and set the standard.

$9.95 + 1.00 shipping (each vol.). Eclipse, PO Box 1099, Forestville, CA 95436. (707) 887-1521.

The Complete Pogo Comics, by Walt Kelly. Tales of the Okefenokee Swamp have been favorites for nearly 50 years for their satire of American culture, combined with the funniest animals since Orwell.

$8.95 + 1.00 shipping (for each quarterly volume) from Eclipse Comics, P.O. Box 1099, Forestville, CA 95436. (707) 887-1521.

The Complete Color Polly and Her Pals by Cliff Sterrett. Gorgeous early Sunday color strips showcase this major artist's surreal and stunning artwork.

$34.95 + 1.50 shipping from Kitchen Sink Press, #2 Swamp Rd., Princeton, WI 54968. (414) 295-6922. Also available from Kitchen Sink (get their catalog!): Alley Oop, Batman, Fearless Fosdick, Li'l Abner, Nancy & Sluggo, and Terry and the Pirates.

The Comics Code

In 1954 Frederic Wertham published *Seduction of the Innocent,* in which he charged that comic books corrupted youth and undermined American values.

Hysteria mounted. Comics were banned in some areas, even burned. Publishers were dragged in front of congressional hearings, and some comic book companies went under.

Under pressure, the industry set up a Comics Code to assure parents of their adherence to standards of "morality and decency." Comics became blandly non-controversial for many years.

It wasn't until the late 1960s that publishers broke through the self-imposed censorship and artistic sterility of the Code.

Bloom County Line

Three full-color posters (22" by 28") printed on heavy stock. Two Opus designs and "Bill the Cat for President," for $16 (postpaid). Cartoonist Berke Breathed's original *Bloom County* artwork is also available: $450 for a daily strip, $950 for Sundays.

Guy Glenn Graphics, PO Box 90933, Austin, TX 78709. (512) 261-3484.

COMIC BOOK TIMELINE

Some significant dates in comic book history:

• **May, 1934**: The first monthly comic book, *Famous Funnies #1.*

• **June, 1938**: First Superman, the Man of Steel, in *Action Comics #1.*

• **May, 1939**: First Batman, in *Detective Comics #27.*

• **February, 1940**: Captain Marvel, in *Whiz Comics #2.*

• **October, 1941**: *Classic Comics,* covering great works of literature, debuts to the applause of parents and educators.

• **November, 1941**: Wonder Woman, in All-Star Comics #8.

• **October, 1952**: *Mad Magazine,* early issues in comic book format.

• **February, 1968**: *Robert Crumb's Zap Comix #1,* the first influential "underground" comic book.

• **August, 1975**: X-Men's first comic book.

• **Spring, 1984**: *Teenage Mutant Ninja Turtles'* first appearance.

The biggest selling comic book of all time was a Spider-Man comic published by Marvel in August, 1990. Its total sales were 2.7 million copies.

Required Reading

The Comic Book in America: An Illustrated History by **Mike Benton.** Trace the history of the comic book year-by-year from 1933 to the present, with glossy color photos of over 500 comic book covers. An excellent overview of comic genres from Animals to Superheroes.

$29.95 + 2.00 shipping. Taylor Publishing, 1550 W. Mockingbird, Dallas, TX 75235. (800) 275-8188.

America's Great Comic Strip Artists by Richard Marschall. The folks who've made the Sunday funnies

so much fun—artists like Al Capp (Li'l Abner), Winsor McCay (Little Nemo in Slumberland), Walt Kelly (Pogo), George Herriman (Krazy Kat), Harold Grey (Little Orphan Annie), and Charles Schulz (Peanuts). Includes dozens of strips, including gorgeous color plates of Sunday pages.

$39.55 + 3.00 shipping from Abbeville Press, 488 Madison Avenue, New York, NY 10022. (800) 227-7210.

The Lexicon of Comicana by Mort Walker. Mort Walker, creator of Beetle Bailey, reveals hidden secrets of cartooning in this exploration of the symbols of an American art form.

$4.95 + 1.00 shipping from Brian Walker, 34 Old Forge Rd., Wilton, CT 06897. (203) 966-6066.

Cartooning: The Art and the Business, by Mort Gerber. This is the definitive "bible" of cartooning, about making both art and money in the field.

$14.95 + 1.50 shipping: William Morrow & Co., 39 Plymouth St., Fairfield, NJ 07004 (800) 843-9389.

Top 10 Comic Strips

The comics section is the most widely read part of the newspaper. Here are the strips that appear in the largest number of Sunday papers, according to Feature Research of Garland, Texas.

1) Peanuts
2) Garfield
3) Blondie
4) Beetle Bailey
5) Hagar the Horrible
6) The Family Circus
7) Andy Capp
8) B.C.
9) The Wizard of Id
10) Dennis the Menace

"Like the Coke bottle, Kodak, and Cadillac, the comic book is much more than a commodity; it is a universally recognized symbol of our culture, one of Uncle Sam's most potent icons."
Harold Schechter, comics historian

Cartoonist Jargon

• Speech balloon: Used to hold cartoon character's words.

• Idea balloon: Shows a character's thoughts.

• Maladicta balloon: Holds symbols (like stars, exclamation points, pound signs) to indicate cursing or pain. (Curse words of various configurations are called jarns, quimps, nittles, and grawlixes.)

• Sphericasia, or swalloop: Shows a complete swing at an object.

• Oculama: little plus signs drawn in place of eyes, used to indicate drunkenness or unconsciousness.

• Solrads: squiggly lines to indicate heat.

• Boozex: X's drawn on a bottle of liquor instead of a brand name.

—(from Mort Walker's *The Lexicon of Comicana*)

Steve Canyon

Knotted Nancy

Nancy necktie, available in blue or red.

$19.95 + 2.00 from Kitchen Sink Press, #2 Swamp Road, Princeton, WI 54968. (414) 295-6922.

The Phantom

COMIC VIDEO

The Masters of Comic Book Art Video. Harlan Ellison introduces ten of the world's greatest comic book artists, in living color, featuring Will Eisner (The Spirit), Harvey Kurtzman (Mad Magazine), Steve Ditko (Spider-Man), and Art Spiegelman (Maus). Interviews reveal the philosophy and creative process behind comic characters and stories.

$19.98 + 4.20 shipping from Johnson Smith Company, 4514 19th Court East P.O. Box 25500 Bradenton, Florida 34206-5500. (813) 747-2356.

Comics Collecting

• A recent survey by a leading comics publication, **Comics Buyer's Guide**, found that collectors are relatively affluent and educated. And nearly 96% are male.

• It's an odd fact that sales of comic books have shrunk over the years, but the number of collectors has increased. Some comics rack up good sales figures merely by selling to the collectors market. Must be frustrating to artists, knowing that most buyers of your work are not ever going to see it.

• Comics collectors are to be pitied, truth be told. Most other pop culture items can be enjoyed even when collected. Comics, though, are so fragile that reading them even once downgrades your "investment."

• Here's what you have to do if you're going to save for investment purposes: buy comics when they're first published, never open the cover (watch those paper-degrading fingerprints!), and immediately store them upright in acid-free plastic bags, supported by cardboard in a specially designed box. Park the box in a dry storage area (no mothers allowed!), and wait for decades. Finally, hope that there's some kind of demand for those particular comics after all that time, that age hasn't deteriorated them into yellow pulp, and that a million other collectors haven't done exactly the same thing.

• While a relative handful of comic titles may sell for outrageous prices, there's a good chance that most of the titles you bag away now won't be worth the space, the cost of moving them to new living quarters, and the fights with your spouse or housemates about them in the coming years.

FEATURE FUNNIES

Funny Pages

Comics Buyers Guide. A weekly newspaper of the comics field, covering both current comics and classics of earlier years. Full of reviews, columns, cartoons, collectors' information, ads and feature articles. Free copy available to Whole Pop readers on request.

One-year subscription, $33.95 from 700 E. State Street, Iola, WI 54990. (800) 258-0929.

POP QUIZ

Match the comic strip character...
1. Wimpy
2. Dagwood Bumstead
3. Zippy the Pinhead
4. Garfield
5. Pappy Yokum
6. Jiggs

...With his favorite food:
a. Sandwich
b. Corned beef and cabbage
c. Hamburger
d. Kickapoo joy juice
e. Taco sauce
f. Lasagne

(ANSWERS: 1-c; 2-a; 3-e; 4-f; 5-d; 6-b.)

The most collected comic books are those featuring superheroes.

POGO

PILGRIMAGE SITES

• **Pogo's Place.** Waycross, Georgia is on the edge of the Okefenokee Swamp, the home of Pogo, Albert the Alligator and the rest. The city sponsors an annual "Pogo Fest," including games, panels, buying and selling and multiple choruses of *Deck Us All With Boston, Charlie.* For details contact Lynda Lee, Tourism Director, PO Box 137, Waycross, GA 31501. (912) 283-3742.

• **Cartoon Art Museum, 665 Third Street, San Francisco, CA 94107.** Recent exhibits of original comic art have included underground comix and *Mad* magazine. Sells original art and autographed books in its gift shop.

• **Museum of Cartoon Art, Comly Avenue, Rye Brook, NY 10573. (914) 939-0234.** This museum boasts a collection of over 60,000 original works of cartoon art. Regularly features top cartoonists presenting chalk talks about their work.

THE SPIRIT

Get Into The Spirit

Now you can become Will Eisner's comic noir character, The Spirit. Just don this cardboard mask and go solve a case. Complete with holes for eyes and nose! Elastic band, too.

SPMASK, $4.95 + .50 shipping. Kitchen Sink Press, 2 Swamp Road, Princeton, WI 54968. (414) 295-6922 / FAX (414) 295-6878.

Comics Convention

San Diego Comics Convention. There are plenty of conventions all over the country, but this may be the biggest and wackiest. Fans from around the country meet and mingle. A highlight is a costume ball where you dress as your favorite character.

For info: San Diego ComiCon, P.O. Box 17066, San Diego, CA, 92117. (619) 442-8272.

DR. MIDNITE

ATOM

Guides to Comic Books

• *The Comic Book Price Guide*, by Robert M. Overstreet. Got old comics squirreled away? Find out their value in this commonly accepted annual price guide. The guide also includes a directory of comic book dealers. Here are some sample prices for items in "good" condition (well-read copies, slightly soiled, but complete): *The Count of Monte Cristo*, Classics Illustrated, 1st printing, 1940s, $71.00; *Howdy Doody*, 1950s, $14.00; *Mighty Mouse*, 1950s, $45.00.

$14.95 + 2.50 shipping from Bud Plant Comic Art, PO Box 1689, Grass Valley, CA 95945. (800) 242-6642.

• *The Photo-Journal Guide to Comic Books*, by Ernst W. Gerber. This two-volume monster edition comes at you with 856 pages and close to 22,000 comic book covers spanning the years 1933-1965 pictured in full color. Ernst and Mary Gerber lovingly performed a mind-boggling research job and created a beautiful reference work.

$145.00 + 10.00 shipping from Gerber Publishing Co., Inc., P.O. Box 906, Minden, NV 89423. (702) 883-4100.

Movies That Have Featured Cartoonists

• **How to Murder Your Wife** (1964) — Jack Lemmon is a comic strip artist accused of sketching out the murder of his wife, Virna Lisi.

• **The Hand** (1981) — Michael Caine stars in this preposterous tale of a cartoonist who loses his drawing hand in an auto accident. The disembodied hand returns, intent on murder.

• **Slamdance** (1987) — This one starred Tom Hulce as a cartoonist for an alternative Los Angeles weekly.

• **Cellar Dweller** (1987) — Vince Edwards and Yvonne DeCarlo starred in this yarn about comic book artists who create monsters that wreak havoc on the world after being unleashed from the inkwell.

• **Funny About Love** (1990) — Gene Wilder is a popular syndicated cartoonist who falls for a caterer (Christine Lahti) at a book-signing party in his honor. Lahti wants to beat the biological clock to conception, but Wilder's not totally convinced he wants to create any little characters outside the cartoon frame.

I Say It's Spinach

Did you know that Popeye had his own soft drink? No, it was not made from spinach and neither is this four-color tin sign. Measures 9 x 16".

#TINPOP, $18.00 + 3.50 from Kitchen Sink Press, 2 Swamp Road, Princeton, WI 54968. (414) 295-6922 / FAX (414) 295-6878.

Turtles in a Nutshell

In the early 1980s, two comic book creators, Kevin Eastman and Peter Laird, decided to spoof the comics industry. They created some odd characters as a parody of mainstream comic superheroes, self-published a comic book, and distributed it thinking what a great laugh folks would have. Their characters? Teenage Mutant Ninja Turtles.

What happened was that the joke blew up in their faces, and they got covered with money. The Turtles became superheroes to kids, who took their bizarre adventures to heart.

A copy of that first black-and-white book, which sold for just $1.50—originally meant by the authors to be the only book—is now worth between $175 and $250. The joke is now worth millions. At the end of summer 1990, as reported by Variety, the first Turtles movie had grossed $132 million, pulling in around $400,000 per month. Cowabunga!

Original Comic Art

Museum Graphics sells original artwork from comic strips.

Two year subscription of 12 price lists, $5.00 to Museum Graphics, Box 10743, Costa Mesa, CA 92627.

There are about 3500 comics shops in America.

Underground Comics

BY MARK JAMES ESTREN

Revolution in the Air

In the 1960s, rebellion was in the air. For many people the mainstream, "Establishment" comic books were out of touch with the cultural revolution that was taking place. Young rebel cartoonists didn't want to grow up drawing innocuous fantasies under the Comics Code of 1954. And students, anti-war activists and women's liberation activists couldn't relate to the malt shop malaise of Archie and Veronica anymore.

The first volley came from the infinitely imaginative R. Crumb. In February, 1968, his *Zap Comix #1* appeared on Haight Street in San Francisco, hawked by street vendors. Resembling a traditional comic book but containing Crumb's acid-inspired art, *Zap* immediately and unexpectedly set off an art movement and a cottage industry.

Other hippie comic books soon began to appear, drawn by young artists who seemed to show up out of nowhere. Printed by a few small companies, most of them in and around San Francisco, they were sold in "head shops," poster stores, record stores and on the street. Complete freedom of expression was the order of the day. Favorite themes were sex and drugs. Still are.

Some major talent emerged. In addition to Crumb there were Gilbert Shelton (Furry Freak Brothers), S. Clay Wilson, Spain Rodriguez, Rick Griffin, Bill Griffith (Zippy the Pinhead), Dan O'Neill, Art Spiegelman, Justin Green, Kim Deitch, and many others. Their work was a breakthrough for comics as expression, even serious art.

More recently younger artists began producing work that continued to chart new ground. The magazine *Raw* is a major venue for their work. Fantagraphics, Last Gasp and Kitchen Sink are among the most active publishers.

Sources for Undergrounds

For information and catalogs, contact:

Fantagraphics Books, 7563 Lake City Way, Seattle, WA 98115

Last Gasp Publications, 2180 Bryant Street, San Francisco, CA 94110. (415) 824-6636.

Kitchen Sink Press, No. 2 Swamp Road, Princeton, WI 54968. (414) 295-6922 / FAX (414) 295-6878.

Many observers have noted most cartoon artists resemble their characters.

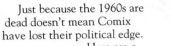

the CHIEF of the SECRET POLICE SAYS: COMIC BOOKS LEAD TO DEGENERACY.

T YOUR LOCAL HEAD HOP OR BOOKSTORE

DEALERS WRITE BOX 14158, SAN FRANCISCO 94114.

A History of UNDERGROUND Comics
BY MARK JAMES ESTREN

$17.95

Comic Cause

Just because the 1960s are dead doesn't mean Comix have lost their political edge. Here are a few recent progressive anthologies.

• *Choices: A Pro-Choice Benefit Comic,* edited by Trina Robbins. This anthology, created to benefit the National Organization for Women, addresses the topic of abortion. Art was donated by 37 cartoonists like Garry Trudeau, Jules Feiffer and Nicole Hollander. .

$4.00 + $1.00 shipping from Angry Isis Press, 1982 15th Street, San Francisco, CA 94114.

• *Strip Aids USA,* edited by Trina Robbins, Bill Sienkiewicz, and Robert Triptow. This collection features some of the biggest names and hearts in comics, all to benefit the Shanti Projects' AIDS education efforts. Contributors include Sergio Aragones (*Mad Magazine*), Mary Kay Brown (*National Lampoon*), Bill Griffith, Trina

CHOICES *A Pro-Choice Benefit Comic*

OH NO! I'M PREGNANT!

WOW! PREGNANT AT LAST!

Robbins, and the Hernandez Brothers.

$11.95 postpaid from Last Gasp Publications, 2180 Bryant Street, San Francisco, CA 94110. (415) 824-6636.

• *Slow Death Funnies, The Journal Of Eco-tastrophy.* This long-running series appears in graphic novel format, with a sci-fi look and adult themes.

$4.50 postpaid from Last Gasp Publications (see above).

Strip AIDS U.S.A.

Required Underground Reading

• *A History of Underground Comics,* by Mark J. Estren. This book has the most lavish collection—over 1,000 drawings—of these comics to ever appear in one book.

**$17.95 + 4 00 shipping from Ronin Publishing, P.O. Box 522, Berkeley, CA 94701.
(800) 858-2665 / (800) 992-2665.**

• *Comix Wave,* edited by Clay Geerdes. This highly regarded newsletter covers the underground and new wave comix scene; also provides commentary on comics and trends in popular culture.

$9.00 for 12 issues, P.O. Box 7094, Berkeley, CA 94707.

FRITZ the CAT

EP. COMICS

HARRY BARRY DIXON

CHIEF: DIS THING IS GETTING OUT OF HAND

THE END

© 1984 by Kim Deitch

LAST GASP

Some Actual Titles of Underground Comix

• *Insect Fear*
• *Barbarian Women*
• *Fleshapoids from Earth*
• *Bent*
• *Pork*
• *Commies from Mars*
• *Checkered Demon*
• *Young Lust*
• *Slow Death*
• *Gothic Blimp Works*

Send $1.00 for a current catalog of these and other titles in their original printings to Don Donahue, P.O. Box 3199, Berkeley, CA 94703. (415) 843-4342.

COMPUTERS

Hello, Mr. Chips

The whole world's gone computer-crazy. And aren't computers great? They're fast, they're efficient, and they're a convenient scapegoat for almost any foul-up you can imagine.

Most people who work with computers have a love-hate relationship with them. Working with a computer is often much better than the alternative, but they can drive you bonkers in their stubborn, silicon-brained, machine's way of fouling things up. Like 2 year olds, they take things so *literally*.

Computers Through Time. The abacus was a forerunner of the modern computer, and its hardware was successfully debugged around 500 B.C. But it was English visionary Charles Babbage (1793-1871) who laid out the basic concepts for the modern computer. But although he had the theoretics down to build a working computing machine, he kept thinking of improvements and hatching new designs—and died without ever completing a full working model.

His 1833 design was for a huge "analytical engine" covering the area of a football field with a locomotive engine as its power source. Think of how the world might have been changed if he had built it. (In fact, novelists William Gibson and Bruce Sterling *have* thought

about it. Their sci-fi book *The Difference Engine* is about how Victorian society would have been altered by Babbage's steam-driven computer.)

In 1843, Lady Ada Augusta Lovelace suggested the idea of using punched cards with Babbage's engine, earning consideration for the title of

computing's first programmer.

Coming to Our Census. The tabulating machine was invented by Dr. Herman Hollerith, who tried it out at the U.S. government's expense for the 1890 census. It saved Uncle Sam $5 million and five years—while the 1880 census had taken eight years to complete, Hollerith did it in just three years. In 1896 Hollerith founded the Tabulating Machine Company, which later evolved into International Business Machines—IBM.

CAINE Backwards? The first fully operational electronic digital computer was the ENIAC (Electronic Numerical Integrator and Computer) in 1946. Built at the University of Pennsylvania, it weighed 30 tons and took up 1,500 square feet of floor space. When first turned on, its 18,000 vacuum tubes drew so much electricity that all the lights in Philadelphia dimmed.

Computer development is often described in stages or

"generations" of the base technology used: **1st generation**, 1951-59 (starting with the Univac I, the first commercially viable electronic digital computer), vacuum tubes; **2nd generation**, 1959-64, transistors; **3rd generation**, 1964-71, modest use of integrated circuits; **4th generation**, 1971, large-scale use of integrated circuitry.

In 1977, 26-year-old Steve Wozniak and 21-year-old Steven Jobs launched the Apple II computer from a garage into the marketplace. In 1981, IBM introduced its PC. You know the rest.

Mega-Bite Diskette

When the computer work begins to go a little sour, go for the sweet. This 3.5 in. milk chocolate diskette is completely incompatible with either Macintosh or DOS.

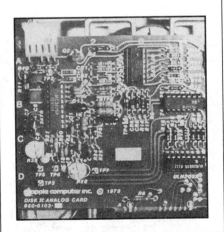

Words & Nerds

- The word "nerd" first appears in *If I Ran the Zoo* by Dr. Seuss (Theodor Geisel).

- *"Silicon Valley is to nerds what Hollywood is to actors."*—Stephen G. Bloom

- *"The Nerd's Credo: the precision of technology is more appealing than the uncertainty of social culture."*
Paul Saffo, founder of "Nerds Night Out," a club in San Jose, California

Terminally Funny

Computer Cartoons compiled by **Sebastian Orfali.** Computer humor by many of your favorite cartoonists.

$5.95 + 4.00 shipping from Books-by-Phone, (800) 858-2665.

Mac Attack!

14 inch vinyl Stress Club is just the thing for harmlessly clobbering your computer when it's driving you nuts.

#2327, $14.98 + 3.50 shipping from The Lighter Side, 4514 19th St. Court East, P.O. Box 25600, Bradenton, FL 34206-5600. (813) 747-2356.

Computer Screenings

- *Metropolis* (1926). This silent German film features a cyborg—a robot in human form—in a mechanized 21st century totalitarian regime.

- *Colossus: The Forbin Project* (1970). A huge computer with defense responsibilities teams up with its Russian counterpart to sabotage humanity.

- *The Computer Wore Tennis Shoes* (1970). In this Disney comedy, college student Kurt Russell gets an electric shock while repairing a computer (should've been wearing a surge suit). The jolt goes to his head, and suddenly he's an instant genius. Kids, don't try this at home.

- *Westworld* (1973). Yul Brynner plays a western bad-man robot that goes crazy and begins attacking tourists in a computerized adult amusement park where the wealthy play out fantasies.

- *Tron* (1982). Jeff Bridges is a computer genius who winds up inside the operating system and must win a video-game competition to keep from being permanently debugged.

- *WarGames* (1983). Teenage hackers accidentally set off a real-life doomsday scenario. Oops.

- *Electric Dreams* (1984). A guy and his computer fall for the same girl.

A Few Interesting Bits

• HAL was the computer that turned against the ship's human crew in the movie *2001*. HAL supposedly stood for "Heuristically programmed ALgorithmic computer," but observant film buffs noted that shifting each of HAL's initials one letter to the right gives you...IBM.

• The computer revolution caused the emergence of a new type of human, the "hacker"—an expert in the art of subverting computer system security.

• An early computer outlaw who earned legendary status was John Draper, known by the nickname of Captain Crunch. His most famous escapade: in the early 1970s he discovered that the free whistles from Cap'n Crunch breakfast cereal would fool AT&T's computers, which used the same frequency to connect lines with long-distance circuits. This trick gave Draper free calls. He reached out and touched a heckuva lot of people, and later served time for his escapades.

• In the spring of 1990, federal, state and local police, with the help of private security personnel, went on a witch hunt for teenage hackers in 14 cities; they seized 43 computers and 23,000 floppy disks.

• On a typical day in the U.S., your name is transmitted between computers five times. It's listed on average in about 40 government and 40 private-sector databases, which are used by thousands of different corporations and agencies to track everything from your buying habits to your economic status.

Crunching Numbers

• A 1989 Census Bureau study indicated that nearly a third of Americans (about 32%) have a computer at work, home, or school.

• The proportion of households with a home computer jumped from 8% in 1984 to 15% in 1989.

• 62% of owners use the computer for word processing.

• 84% of kids with home computers play computer games; 44% of the adults do.

• 23% of the home computers had a modem.

Hacker's Holiday

Hand-painted, wooden Christmas tree ornament features VDT holiday design display.

#H530-1, $4.98 + 1.95 shipping from Miles Kimball, 41 West Eighth Avenue, Oshkosh, WI. 54906.

Spread Sheets

Dubbed "The User Friendly Bedtime Program for Computer Lovers," SpreadSheets will take your bed into high-tech territory. Horizontal blue and white striping and vertical borders to simulate traditional computer printer paper in no-iron percale.

• Queen set (flat sheet, fitted sheet, two pillow cases), $79.95 + 7.50 shipping.

• Twin set (flat sheet, fitted sheet, one pillow case), $59.95 + 6.50 shipping.

• Set of two "HeadCrashers" pillow cases, $19.95 + 4.50 shipping.

Order from The Computer Museum Store, 300 Congress Street, Boston, MA 02210. (617) 426-2800, Ext. 307.

Chocolate Microchips

Take a "byte" out of these 54 grams of rich Belgian chocolate molded into a computer board shape.

#6598, $8.49 + 2.95 shipping from Miles Kimball, 41 West Eighth Avenue, Oshkosh, WI. 54906.

Panic!

This self-adhesive panic button looks like a regular key, except it's red and says "PANIC." Totally non-functional, but it may be just what you need during those moments of crisis.

#T2044, $2.98 + 3.50 shipping from The Lighter Side, 4514 19th St. Court East, P.O. Box 25600, Bradenton, FL 34206-5600. (813) 747-2356.

Computer Talk

Most computer jargon is boring, humorless and unnecessarily obscure—for instance, why not say "send" and "receive" instead of "upload" and "download" (or is it vice versa)? Still, there a few coinages which show some wit. Here are two we like:

- **The Potty Effect.** Unanticipated effects in man-machine undertakings. The name comes from Apollo 11 scientists, who pondered why the craft landed at the wrong lunar location. They discovered that toilets flushing during eleven lunar orbits added enough thrust to change the spacecraft's trajectory.

- **Vaporware.** Exciting new computer product widely ballyhooed as imminent by a manufacturer, but never delivered.

RAM Riot

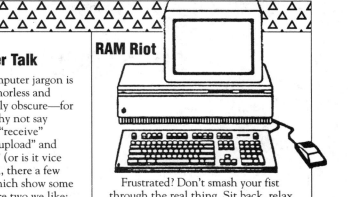

Frustrated? Don't smash your fist through the real thing. Sit back, relax and enjoy a cup of coffee from this smashed computer.

#5505, $12.98 + 4.20 shipping. Johnson Smith Co., 4514 19th St. Court East, P.O. Box 25500, Bradenton, FL 34206-5500. (813) 747-2356 / FAX (813) 746-7896.

"Read Only" Material

The Devouring Fungus: Tales of the Computer Age by Karla Jennings. Anecdotes about the "cybernetic gods," eccentric geniuses who gave birth to the computer age, of computers gone haywire, computer crime, computer wisdom and computer culture. Says Jennings: "Though it may look imposing, the computer is surprisingly fragile, resembling less a Goliath than that scrawny kid in fifth grade with smudged glasses and numerous allergies who was always sneezing."

$10.95 + 2.00 shipping from W.W. Norton & Company, 800 Keystone Industrial Park, Scranton, PA 18512-4601. (800) 233-4830.

PILGRIMAGES

- **The Garage.** Generically named in honor of the multimillion-dollar Silicon Valley companies started in garages, this new hands-on technology museum involves you in interactive exhibits. You can design a bicycle with computer-aided equipment, solve a crime using DNA fingerprints, make a low level flight over the surface of Mars by laser disc, commission a robot to do your portrait, and create your own earthquake. Called "a cross between *Star Wars* and high school physics," the Garage is the predecessor to the colossal $90 million Technology Center of Silicon Valley scheduled to open in a few years.

  The Garage, Technology Center of Silicon Valley, 145 West San Carlos Street, San Jose, CA 95113. (408) 279-7150.

- **The Computer Museum.** Here's a museum that demystifies computers and makes them fun. Reversing the trend of making computers and their components smaller and smaller, it features a gargantuan exhibit, *The Walk-Through Computer*, that's two stories high. It's a working model of a desktop computer that you can actually run programs on, enlarged 50 times—there's a 108 square foot screen, 6' high floppy disk, 10' trackball and a 25' keyboard (kids can hop around on the keys like literate cockroaches).

  One tip: In case you need to "download," restrooms are in the computer's Power Supply.

  Other museum attractions include a fine collection of "antique" computers, robots, and an award-winning Animation Theater.

  300 Congress Street, Boston, MA 02210. (617) 426-2800.

CONSTRUCTION TOYS

There are three rules of construction toys that every kid should know. Had we known them, we would've had a much nicer childhood. The three rules are:

1. It is awfully hard to build anything recognizable. The only way you're going to get a moving Ferris wheel out of your Erector set or a space ship from Legos is if you're willing to follow about four hours worth of tedious instructions. This is play? It's not worth it.

2. The pictures on the box lie. Those grinning kids didn't build any of those things. They came in for the photo shoot after a team of engineers sweated and cursed their way through the aforementioned four hours of tedious instructions.

Also, the most interesting things shown on the box always take more and different pieces than are provided in the box.

3. Construction toys are most fun when used for something other than what they were designed for. Although one museum claims to have made a model of the Empire State Building out of Lincoln Logs, that's improbable. Lincoln Logs have only one function besides building cheesy little log huts: as missiles in war with your friends.

Legos are most fun as dominoes to stand up in lines and knock down.

Erector sets were never fun. Maybe that's why they aren't made any more. The best trick was making a bunch of Xs and attaching them to make one of those things you see on cartoons, usually made by the Acme company, which often have a boxing glove attached. Closing the first X makes the device spring out like a snake, so you can hit your friends from a safe distance.

And as far as Tinker Toys go, there's not much you can do with them except use them as back-up missiles when you run out of Lincoln Logs. Still, if used correctly, those little round things can raise a welt.

LEGO BOOKS

Lego Brick: Where Does It Come From? **by Diane Tippell.** Aimed at young kids, this is a book telling the origins of those multicolored pieces of plastic, from oil underground to bricks underfoot.

$6.95 + .75 shipping from Silver Burdette Publishing Company, P.O. Box 2649, Columbus, OH 43216. (800) 843-3464.

The World of Lego Toys, **by Henry Wiencek.** Aimed at an older audience, this is more of a "coffee table" book. Especially good are the photos of Legoland (see Pilgrimages).

$17.95 + 2.00 shipping from Harry Abrams, 100 Fifth Avenue, New York, NY 10011. (800) 345-1359.

The name "Lego" is from the Danish phrase "leg godt" which means "play well."

Pilgrimages

• **The Cooper Hewitt Museum, 2 E. 93rd Street, New York, NY. (212) 860-6868.** This museum boasts a six foot tall replica of the Empire State Building made of Lincoln Logs. If you go, send us a photo. This we gotta see.

• **Legoland, Billund, Denmark. Contact the Danish Tourist Board, 655 Third Avenue, New York, NY 10017. (212) 949-2333.** Granted, it's a little unreasonable to recommend that you go to Denmark for a pop culture pilgrimage, but be assured that this is worth the trip. Legoland is a

—Egypt's Abu Simbel temple (265,000 bricks)

—Brussels Town Hall (195,100 bricks and 325 human hours)

—A room-size castle (276,000 bricks, yellow and blue only)

Wait, there's more: the Acropolis, London Bridge, the Eiffel Tower, the US Capitol, the Statue of Liberty, a monument to Sitting Bull, a Thai temple, Rodin's The Thinker, an entire menagerie of nearly lifesize African animals, and much more. At last count, the park contained 35 million Legos and attracts about 900,000 people a year. Purists will be shocked to know that the Legos are held together by glue.

Statue of Sitting Bull made out of hundreds of thousands of Legos. Legoland, Denmark.

Lego fantasia of mythic proportions about 100 miles from Copenhagen, part amusement park and part Legomaniac obsession. What's there? Hundreds of mostly 1:20 scale models, built completely out of Legos. Popular attractions include:

—Mt. Rushmore (made from 1.5 million bricks)

—The Space Shuttle Columbia (410,000 bricks)

—The Port of Copenhagen, with working ships, drawbridges, shipyards, ferries and water (3 million bricks)

LEGO Goes Hi-Tech

LEGO® Technic I is much more advanced than the LEGO sets of old. Physics actually becomes fun with 179 pieces including gear wheels, beams, axles, turntables, a piston head...even a universal joint! Plus instructions on how to build over 50 different models such as a windmill and tower crane.

$49.00 + 5.50 shipping from The Computer Museum Store, 300 Congress Street, Boston, MA 02210. (617) 426-2800 .

Lincoln Log Facts

• Lincoln Logs were designed by John Lloyd Wright, the son of renowned architect Frank Lloyd Wright, in 1916.

• Unlike most toys, Lincoln Logs have not gone the way of petroleum byproducts. They are still made of real wood cut from Oregon national forests, then sanded, stained and waxed to withstand years of play.

• Building sets range in price from about $10.99 for 72 pieces to $26.99 for 212 pieces, including roofs, signs ("Lincoln Grand Hotel," "Bank"), stands and gables.

LINCOLN GRAND HOTEL

Lincoln Logs For Real

Ready to graduate from toy Lincoln Logs? How about building your own house from real logs? A do-it-yourself house kit company, also called Lincoln Logs, offers a choice of over eighty designs. Provided are blueprints, sills, the logs for walls, twelve inch spikes, polyfoam sealer, caulking, trusses, roofing materials, vents, double-glazed windows and steel insulated doors. Also a 250 page step-by-step instruction manual.

Kits cost $13,000 to $60,000, depending on size and complexity. What are the benefits, beyond having the hippest house in your neighborhood? Great wall insulation, low-cost construction and a warranty on the logs for 100 years. And who knows, your kid may grow up to be president some day.

For information, contact The Original Lincoln Log Company, Riverside Drive, Chestertown, NY 12813. (800) 833-2461.

Tinker Toy Facts

• Tinker Toys were invented by a stonemason from Evanston, Illinois named Charles Pajeau and introduced at the American International Toy Fair in 1913.

• They sold well at first, then sales lagged. As a sales promotion stunt, Pajeau hired midgets to play with them in a show window at New York City's Grand Central Station. Sales took off again.

• When the $1.5 billion Hubble Space

Erector Set Facts

• The Erector Set was designed in the early 1930s by Alfred C. Gilbert, MD, a man who was a lot more interesting than the toy ever was. Besides being a physician and head of a toy company, Gilbert was a big-game hunter and Olympic Gold Medalist in the pole vault.

• Erector sets are no longer made. The ones that still exist are somewhat more valuable as a result.

• Most adolescents today don't even know what an Erector Set is. Too bad — the name was the source of many great adolescent jokes and double-entendres in the past.

Erectors for Sale?

Check in with expert Al Sternagle.

• His Erector Notes appears in *Yesterdaze Toys Magazine.* **One year subscription. Yesterdaze Toys, Box 57, Otisville, MI 48463.**

• *Greenberg's Guide to Gilbert Erector Sets* by Al Sternagle. **$29.95 + 2.50 shipping. Greenberg Publishing Co., 7566 Main St., Sykesville, MD 21784. (301) 795-7447.**

Telescope's antenna system snagged after its launch in 1990, engineers solved the problem on an impromptu model hastily assembled from a piece of lamp cord and set of Tinker Toys. "The model was a big help in visualizing the problem," said a deputy project manager.

Unfortunately, even Tinker Toys couldn't solve the lens flaws still plaguing the telescope. Maybe if they'd also had an Erector set...

It's Motor-iffic!

Invented in 1901, the Meccano Steel Construction Set lets latent engineers (ages 7 and up) design and build cars, boats, cranes, buildings and more. Includes 290 parts, battery-operated motor, wheels and illustrated instructions for nearly 40 projects.

#G39-079, $65.00 + 9.15 shipping. Edmund Scientific Co., 101 E. Gloucester Pike, Barrington, NJ 08007. (609) 547-8880.

Goo-Goo For Googolplex!

1988 Parents' Choice Award winner! In math, a googol is the number 1 followed by 100 zeros, and that's about how many variations and possibilities this architect-designed construction set allows. Basic pieces snap together to create flexible objects, from geometric shapes to space stations and skyscrapers. 244 pieces, for ages 5 and up.

#91403, $46.00 + 5.75 shipping from the Discovery Center, Lawrence Hall of Science, University of California, Berkeley, CA 94720. (510) 642-1016.

For Blockheads

Nothing fancy here. Classic wood blocks come in 7 shapes and varying sizes, all 1-in. wide for creations limited only by the imagination. Blocks are painted with non-toxic primary colors — red, blue, green and yellow. 80 pieces in all.

#202751, $24.98 + 4.95 shipping from Lillian Vernon, Virginia Beach, VA 23479-0002. (914) 633-6300.

It's Gear!

Lunapark Gear Set, a 100 piece construction set from Italy, lets kids create their own circus with plastic interlocking plates, gears and animals. Demonstrates the principles of cause and effect, simple mechanics and spatial relationships. Sounds complicated, but it's fun.

#90405, $18.95 + 4.75 shipping from the Discovery Center, Lawrence Hall of Science, University of California, Berkeley, CA 94720. (510) 642-1016.

Thick As A Brick

But weighs a heckuva lot less! Building blocks made of heavy, corrugated cardboard provide hours of fun for kids of every age. Set of 24, red, blue and green. Assembly (folding the cardboard) required.

#4667-1, $11.98 + 2.95 shipping. Miles Kimball, 41 W. 8th Ave., Oshkosh, WI 54906.

"If you have built castles in the air, your work need not be lost; that is where they should be."—Henry David Thoreau

Country

RUSTIC LIFE

Despite what Hollywood and Madison Avenue might have you believe, not all Americans live in Southern California and Manhattan. There are still places in this nation where the pace is a little slower, the pleasures a bit simpler, and people less concerned with nouvelle cuisine and the latest in compact disc technology.

Rural America may get short shrift from demographers, but that doesn't mean it doesn't play a large role in our collective imagination. The U.S. was built by farmers, and the folklore of life in small towns and farm communities still permeates popular culture, from *Green Acres* reruns to country music to farm decorating accents sprucing up Manhattan apartments.

So put on your best overalls, slop the hogs and hitch up the wagon. We're goin' country.

As The World Churns

Here's a better way to better butter. Old-timers claim that this Cedar Dasher-Style Churn is the best.

#6-DBC, $79.00 postpaid from Lehman Hardware and Appliances, P.O. Box 41, Kidron, OH 44636. (216) 857-5441 / FAX (216) 857-5785.

Talk as Purty as a Sow's Ear

Handy as Hip Pockets on a Pig by **Donald Chain Black.** Study this book and you'll be able to pepper your everyday conversation with picturesque phrases from rural America. A few cases in point— practice these with the right twang and you'll be the life of your next hoedown.

• When asked how you are, you can respond as they sometimes do in Arkansas: "Fine as frogs' hair" or "I'd have to get better to die" or even "If things was any better, I'd think they was lyin' to me."

• Next time you fold a hand in poker, impress your buddies by announcing that your luck "has gone

where the woodbine twines and the whangdoodle mourneth for its mate."

• For attracting the attention of livestock, try these variations on the old, tired calls. Pigs respond to "Wutzi!" while turkeys favor "Pee!" Horses prick up their ears at "Cope!" And Louisiana Cajuns soothe restless cows by murmuring "La!"

• When you're ready to depart an intimate gathering at a friend's house, you can announce, as did the coon hunters of yore, that it's "time to piss on the fire and call in the dogs."

• Just don't overdo the countryisms, or they'll think you were vaccinated with a Victrola needle and that your tongue is tied in the middle and flappin' at both ends.

$8.95 + 1.50 shipping from Taylor Publishing, 1550 W. Mockingbird Lane, Dallas, TX 75236. (214) 637-2800.

Half Cocked, Gotta Blow

This one has a crowing rooster perched on its directional arrow, but there are over 31 different hand-made sculptured weather vanes to choose from. How 'bout a "Ewe're So Vane" or a "Fawn With The Wind" vane? 30" high with pewter finish ornament.

$75.00 + 8.50 shipping from Holst, Inc., 1118 West Lake, Box 370, Tawas City, MI 48764. (517) 362-5664.

"Early to rise and early to bed, makes a male healthy, wealthy and dead." —James Thurber

Deere John Letters...

On a yellow and green metal sign. Collectors and farmers will dig this salute to the company that means tractors.

#8136, $24.98 + 5.99 shipping from Taylor Gifts, 355 E. Conestoga Road, P.O. Box 206, Wayne, PA 19087-0206. (215) 789-7007.

JOHN DEERE
THE TRADE MARK OF QUALITY MADE FAMOUS BY GOOD IMPLEMENTS

JOHN DEERE
TWO CYLINDER **TRACTORS**
BURN LOW-COST FUEL

SOLD HERE

TILTING AT WINDMILLS

Here's somethin' to tilt at—a miniature windmill kit that takes about an hour to piece together. Galvanized steel mind you—no plastic parts! There's even a tiny ladder for any tiny Don Quixotes you may have running around. 16 3/4" tall with 5" windwheel.

#540-043, $19.95 postpaid from Lehman Hardware, P.O. Box 41, Kidron, OH 44636. (216) 857-5441 / FAX (216) 857-5785.

Not For Tractor-Pull Contests

You can't enter these in your local tractor pull because you'd be lucky if they could drag a toothpick an inch! Authentic miniature replicas of vintage tractors are made of die-cast metal in 1/43 scale, with removable rubber tires. Models to choose from include Allis Chalmers D-21, Case 500 F-1, International 300, Massey Harris and seven others from farm history.

Each $7.95 + 3.95 shipping from Holst, Inc., 1118 West Lake, Box 370, Tawas City, MI 48764. (517) 362-5664.

Start A Chorus

You can be a blacksmith singing in the dead of night with this Enders 10 lb. bench anvil.

#110210, $33.95 ppd. from Lehman Hardware, P.O. Box 41, Kidron, OH 44636. (216) 857-5441 / FAX (216) 857-5785.

For Your Deere Child

A sandbox toy for kids. These tractors are exact replicas of historic John Deere vehicles that have become legendary. The Model A is also known as "Poppin' Johnny." The Waterloo Boy was a forerunner to the Deere tractors of today. Both are quality made, die-cast in metal.

#1518, Model A , $17.50 + 4.50 shipping and #1532, Waterloo Boy, $29.00 + 4.50 shipping from John Deere Catalog, 1400 3rd Avenue, Moline, IL 61265. (800) 544-2122.

WATERLOO BOY

Kid A Tractor

A real riding "Generation II" scaled down to tyke-size tractor. Both the easy-pedaling tractor and the easy-pulling trailer feature chassis of steel and rubber tires finished with child-safe baked enamel. Some assembly required.

#1515, Tractor, $165.00 + 12.75 shipping and #1517, Trailer, $35.00 + 6.00 shipping from John Deere Catalog, 1400 3rd Avenue, Moline, IL 61265. (800) 544-2122.

JOHN DEERE

"My mother's a little embarrassed to admit she likes to eat squirrel brains." —Dwight Yoakam

Goin' Up the Country

Most of these United States have museums devoted to our agricultural heritage. Here are our favorites:

• **Midwest Old Settlers and Threshers Heritage Museum.** Home of "America's Largest Steam Show," it has exhibits about steam traction engines, antique farm implements, rural electricity and the role of farm women.

Mount Pleasant, IA 52641. (319) 385-8937.

• **Old Cowtown Museum.** Features more than 35 exhibit areas, including a general store, a working blacksmith shop and Wichita's first jail.

1871 Sim Park Drive, Wichita, KS 67203. (316) 264-0671.

• **John Deere Historic Site.** Includes Deere's restored pioneer home and a special archaeological exhibit of the original blacksmith shop, all in Ronald Reagan's hometown.

8393 South Main, Village of Grand Detour, Dixon, IL 61021. (815) 652-4551.

• **Old Sturbridge Village.** Re-creates a rural New England town of the 1830s. Includes more than 40 restored buildings.

1 Old Sturbridge Village Road, Sturbridge, MA. (508) 347-3362.

PUMPING IRON

Pitcher perfect pump for shallow wells is cast iron (3 inch ID cylinder) made by Myers. Painted green with Myers logo (in raised lettering) finished yellow.

#HP1, $49.00 postpaid from Lehman Hardware and Appliances, P.O. Box 41, Kidron, OH 44636. (216) 857-5441 / FAX (216) 857-5785.

Spin A Yarn While You Spin Your Wheels

Many a sheep dreaded the original. Now you can own a reproduction of an early colonial spinning wheel. Fully functional from distaff to pedal. Durable lacquer seal and oil base stain. Stool included. Some assembly required.

#61555, Spinning Wheel and Stool, $369.99 + 19.95 shipping from Sturbridge Yankee Workshop, P.O. Box 4000, Westbrook, ME 04098-1596. (800) 343-1144.

Country Clubs

• *Cast Iron Seat Collectors Society.* Cast iron seats were made for horse-drawn farm implements from about 1850 through 1900, and many were intricately rendered with designs and lettering. The members of this collectors society view them as a form of Agrarian Art.

Membership $10.00. Charolette Traxler, Secretary-Treasurer, RFD 2 Box 40, Le Center, MN 56057.

• *American Gourd Society, Inc.* Organized for "promoting and encouraging the raising and use of gourds for decorative and useful purposes." Publishes a quarterly, *The Gourd.* Probably starts each meeting with a few choruses of *Nearer My Gourd to Thee…*

Membership $5.00. John Stevens, Secretary, P.O. Box 274, Mt. Gilead, OH 43338.

Texas Date Nail Collectors. Publishes the bi-monthly *Nailer News.* What's a date nail? They were used in railroad ties, posts and sometimes fences and the nail heads were inscribed with the year they were made.

Membership $14.00. Jerry Waits, 501 W. Horton, Brenham, TX 77833. (409) 830-1495.

"When tillage begins, other arts follow. The farmers therefore are the founders of human civilization." —Daniel Webster

COUNTRY SIT-COMS

Country Sit-Coms

Rural America has provided inspiration for several television situation comedies, especially in the golden age of rural TV. The accuracy of their depictions of life on the farm and in small towns has varied wildly, but the homespun humor rings true.

• ***The Real McCoys***. First aired in 1957 and ran for six seasons. Set on a small San Fernando Valley ranch owned by a transplanted family of West Virginians, the show starred Walter Brennan as Amos McCoy, Richard Crenna as his son Luke and, for a time, Kathy Nolan as Luke's wife Kate, who was killed off in 1962 when the actress demanded more money and more control of the scripts. As the cantankerous Grandpa, Brennan dispensed homespun wisdom and endlessly bullied his family and hired help, shouting "Little Luke! Little Luke!"

• ***The Beverly Hillbillies***. After dirt-poor mountaineer Jed Clampett discovered oil (while shootin' at some food), he became an overnight millionaire. So "they moved to Beverly...Hills, that is... Swimmin' pools, movie stars." Much to their stuffy neighbors' chagrin, the nouveau riche Clampetts stuck to their rustic ways, cooking squirrel stew and making lye soap out by the "cement pond."

• ***Petticoat Junction***. This spin-off of *The Beverly Hillbillies* debuted in 1963 on CBS and ran for seven seasons. Set in the farming communities of Hooterville and neighboring Pixley, it gave viewers a glimpse into the goings-on at the Shady Rest Hotel, run by widow Kate Bradley (Bea Benaderet) and the self-proclaimed manager, Uncle Joe Carson (Edgar Buchanan). Many episodes revolved around the problems of Widow Bradley's lovely daughters: Billie Jo, Bobbie Jo and Betty Jo.

• ***Green Acres***. Also set in the aforementioned Hooterville, this has to have been the dumbest farm comedy of them all, sort of a reverse *Beverly Hillbillies*. Eddie Albert and Eva Gabor starred as attorney Oliver Wendell Douglas and his wife Lisa. Oliver wanted to leave the urban rat-race, but Lisa stayed only out of wifely duty and because she couldn't bear the thought that their cow, Elinor, and their chicken, Alice, would be slaughtered if they left. *Green Acres* lasted six seasons and featured in its supporting cast character actors Pat Buttram, Frank Cady, Hank Patterson and the pigs that portrayed Arnold Ziffel.

• ***The Andy Griffith Show***. Easily the gentlest and most ingratiating rural comedy, this show was actually a spin-off of *The Danny Thomas Show*, where Andy Griffith had once guest-starred in an episode where he arrested Danny Thomas for speeding through his small Southern town. Set in Mayberry, North Carolina (Pop. 1200), it featured Don Knotts, Ronny Howard, Jim Nabors and Frances Bavier. It later spawned *Gomer Pyle, U.S.M.C.* and *Mayberry RFD*, starring Ken Berry.

"Farming looks mighty easy when your plow is a pencil and you're a thousand miles from the cornfield." —Dwight D. Eisenhower

Mayberry Mania

Mayberry, My Hometown by **Stephen J. Spignesi.** For more than you will ever want to know about *The Andy Griffith Show*, dip into **Mayberry, My Hometown.** This compendium of Mayberry factoids features a 4,000-entry encyclopedia of the show, as well as an 800-name character/actor index, maps and floor plans, interviews with the stars and even a year by year "character appearance frequency" bar chart (in case you need to know which years Floyd the Barber appeared on more shows than Otis the Town Drunk). Downright scary in its thoroughness.

Hardcover, $34.50 + 3.00 from Popular Culture, Ink., P.O. Box 1839, Ann Arbor, MI 48106. (800) 678-8828.

Join the Club

Two clubs, no less, for Mayberry Fans. Send SASE for membership information.

• **The Andy Griffith Show** Rerun Watchers Club, 27 Music Square East, Suite 146, Nashville, TN 37203.

• **The Andy Griffith Show** Appreciation Society, PO Box 330, Clemmons, NC 27012.

Mayberry, My Home Video

The Best of Barney, The Best of Ernest T. Bass, and **Love Life of Barney Fife?** They're just three of 14 available video tapes of the original shows. Each tape features four complete episodes—commercials edited out.

#12839 Barney; #12849 Ernest; #12872 Love Life. Each $39.95 + 4.95 shipping from Wireless, P.O. Box 64422, St. Paul, MI 55164. (800) 669-9999.

COUNTRY CATALOGS

• An easy, although expensive, source if you want country-related direct mail is Great Catalogs. They'll charge you a fee of $2 -5 each to get you on mailing lists of country catalogs like Laura Ashley, Kountry Krafts, Now & Then and Goose on the Loose.

• *Country Source Book* by Elaine Hawley. Lists nearly 300 shops and companies that do the country thing— many "well-crafted, authentic items" available.

#87-50293, $19.95 postpaid, from Chilton Book Company, One Chilton Way, Radnor, PA 19089. (800) 345-1214 / FAX (215) 964-4745.

Trade
You a Barney for a Floyd

Would you believe *Andy Griffith Show* trading cards? Available in individual packs, or an entire series of 110 cards housed in special collectors' box.

#6-NP90-04, Complete Series #1; #6-NP91-02, Series #2; or #6-NP91-03, Series #3, Each set $9.95 + 3.00 shipping from Pacific Trading Cards, 18424 Highway 99, Lynnwood, WA 98037. (206) 774-8473.

What killed the family farm: *Green Acres, Mayberry RFD, The Beverly Hillbillies, Gomer Pyle, Hee Haw* and *Lassie* were all canceled by CBS on the same day in 1971.

COUNTRY MUSIC
Fiddlin' With History

Surely you remember *The Little Old Log Cabin in the Lane* and *The Old Hen Cackled and the Rooster's Going to Crow.* Country music's commercial life began in 1923, when Fiddlin' John Carson became the first southern white folk musician to have his records professionally recorded and distributed.

But Country was kicking around before that. It began as a synthesis of two separate traditions, the Celtic-influenced music of the southeastern states and the music of the southwest (Texas in particular).

The first true country singing star was Jimmie Rodgers, also known as "The Singing Brakeman," who at the height of his popularity in the late 1920s introduced "the blue yodel" to the tradition.

In the 1930s, western swing, a blend of Texas fiddle music and jazz/pop, became the rage, thanks to Bob Wills and the Texas Playboys and others.

Singing cowboys like Roy Rogers and Gene Autry brought the western side of country music to an even wider audience through their

"Wait a minute. Sound more hillbilly. More Husky in the Ferlin."

—Stan Freberg,
Dear John

Hollywood films in the 1940s.

The Grand Ole Opry started in 1925 as a weekly program of "hillbilly" music on WSM in Nashville and began broadcasting nationally through NBC radio during the 1940s. *The Opry* reached the peak of its success in the 1950s for six years when Hank Williams was its biggest star until his death at the age of 29.

Rockabilly, as practiced by Elvis Presley and Jerry Lee Lewis, became a dominant country style in the youth-crazed 1950s. The 1960s saw the ascendency of stars like George Jones, Merle Haggard, Tammy Wynette and Loretta Lynn. In the 1970s, country rock/pop crossed over to the mainstream audience, best exemplified by Willie Nelson's phenomenal success.

Today, country encompasses a variety of performers with a variety of different styles. Many stars from the 1950s and 1960s are still going strong, while relative newcomers like Randy Travis, k.d. lang and Garth Brooks are pushing in new directions.

Aural History

The best way to learn the history of country music is to sit down and listen to a whole mess of the stuff. Here are some collections we took a hankerin' to:

• **Country*USA.** The "no fuss" method of building a country music library. Every six weeks, you get by mail 24 big hits from one particular year in country music. The initial offering covers 1961 (Patsy Cline's *I Fall to Pieces*, Tex Ritter's *I Dreamed of Hillbilly Heaven,* etc.), and subsequent issues span the 1950s through the 1970s.

LPs, $14.99 + 3.46 shipping; cassettes, $14.99 + 2.44 shipping; or compact discs, $16.99 + 2.99 shipping from Time-Life Music, P.O. Box C-32350, Richmond, VA 23261. (800) 832-8944.

• **Hankerin' For Hank?** Four studio sessions and 17 demos including three previously unreleased tracks. 84 tracks in all plus a booklet of rare pictures.

#D01487, 3-CD set, $54.95 + 4.95 shipping or #K00805, 3-cassette set, $44.95 + 4.95 shipping from Postings, P.O. Box 8001, Hilliard, OH 43026. (800) 262-6604.

• **Prime Patsy.** Cline was a classic. Her songs are legendary, and here are 22 of the best. Included are *Crazy, I Fall To Pieces, Your Cheatin' Heart, Love Letters In The Sand, I Can't Help It (If I Am Still In Love With You),* and more.

#PAR, 2 Records, $12.98 + 3.95 shipping; #PAC, 2 cassettes $12.98 + 3.95 shipping; #PAK, 1 Compact Disc, $16.98 + 3.95 shipping. Songbooks Unlimited, 352 Evelyn Street, P.O. Box 908, Paramus, NJ 07653- 0908. (800) 527-6300.

Pick, Grin & Rewind

• This video teaches you how to play the type of music that gets "everybody stompin', clappin' and whistlin'."

#TXV004, Bluegrass Banjo, $29.95 + 4.95 shipping.

• But why stop there? Learn Bluegrass Mandolin, Nashville Electric Guitar, Blues Style Harmonica, Country Piano, Chord & Finger Picking Guitar, and Bluegrass Banjo.

#TXV105, $189.65 + 6.95 shipping from Special Interest Video, 100 Enterprise Place, P.O. Box 7022, Dover, DE 19903-7022 (800) 522-0502.

I Said Dance, Pilgrim!

Hot Country Dancing lets you step lightly with the good ol' boys! Master the 2-step, Country Swing, Schottische and the Country Polka!

#BF201, $34.95 + 4.95 shipping from Special Interest Video, 100 Enterprise Place, P.O. Box 7022, Dover, DE 19903-7022. (800) 522-0502.

COUNTRY WESTERN WARES

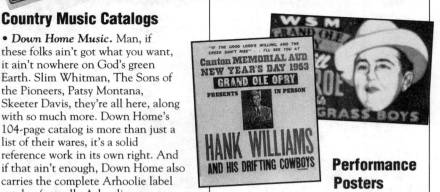

Country Cards

Cartoonist and music lover R. Crumb has created **Pioneers Of Country Music Trading Cards** featuring 40 greats like Jimmie Rodgers, the Carter Family and Dr. Humphrey Bate & His Possum Hunters.

#TCCOUN, $9.98 + 1.50 shipping from Kitchen Sink Press, 2 Swamp Road, Princeton, WI 54968. (414) 295-6922.

Country Music Catalogs

• *Down Home Music.* Man, if these folks ain't got what you want, it ain't nowhere on God's green Earth. Slim Whitman, The Sons of the Pioneers, Patsy Montana, Skeeter Davis, they're all here, along with so much more. Down Home's 104-page catalog is more than just a list of their wares, it's a solid reference work in its own right. And if that ain't enough, Down Home also carries the complete Arhoolie label catalog (actually Arhoolie owns Down Home Music, but that's a whole 'nother story) which includes everything from Country Blues to Zydeco to Cajun to Tex-Mex! Gospel, too. By the way, "Arhoolie!" is a corn field holler.

Down Home Music, Inc., 10341 San Pablo Avenue, El Cerrito, CA (510) 525-1494 / FAX: (510) 525-1204.

• *The Country Music Catalog.* Offers some exceptional recordings from the Country Music Foundation. Typical titles include **Elvis in Nashville 1956-1971, Buck Owens and the Buckaroos: Live at Carnegie Hall, Sixty Years of Grand Ole Opry and Hank Williams: The First Recordings.**

The Country Music Hall of Fame and Museum, Mail Order Department, 4 Music Square East, Nashville, TN 37203. (800) 255-2357.

Performance Posters

One of America's oldest poster shops, Hatch Show Print of Memphis, has done country music's earliest and most famous posters. These prints are hand-printed from the original wooden type. The Hank Williams poster is from one of his last performances, and the Bill Monroe poster is a limited edition print.

#H007, Hank Williams Poster, $10.00 + 3.50 shipping. #H004, Bill Monroe Poster, $18.00 + 4.50 shipping. Country Music Hall of Fame and Museum, Mail Order Dept., 4 Music Square East, Nashville, TN 37203. (800) 255-2357.

LOVE THAT COUNTRY MUSIC

Show 'em you care by what you wear. Like this 14k gold pendant on a chain that's 18 inches long.

#3805, Country Music Necklace, $49.95 + 5.95 shipping from The Music Stand, Rockdale Plaza, Lebanon, NH 03766-1585. (802) 295-7044.

COUNTRY MUSIC FILM FESTIVAL

Given country music's wide appeal and its frequent emphasis on sex, death, violence and substance abuse, it's no wonder that it has served as the basis for lots of films, many currently available on videotape. Here are some of our favorites.

• *Payday* (1973). Virtually ignored at the time of its release, this sleeper has slowly earned a strong reputation among discerning viewers. Directed by Daryl Duke, it details 36 hours in the life of Maury Dann (Rip Torn), an amoral and ambitious country singer. Cartoonist, author and songwriter Shel Silverstein contributed several original songs.

• *Nashville* (1975). Directed by Robert Altman, this masterful mosaic epic follows, count 'em, 24 characters as they meander through and around a Nashville political rally. They each manage to make an impression, and the music is memorable too. Cast includes Henry Gibson, Lily Tomlin, Barbara Harris, Ned Beatty, Jeff Goldblum and Keith Carradine, who won an Oscar for his song, *I'm Easy.*

• *Coal Miner's Daughter* (1980). Sissy Spacek did her own singing and copped an Academy Award for her portrayal of Loretta Lynn.

• *Honeysuckle Rose* (1980). William Nelson plays a country star (surprise!) who gets into trouble when he starts fooling around with his musical sidekick's daughter. According to Leonard Maltin, the film is officially based on *Intermezzo,* the 1939 violinists-in-love sudser starring Ingrid Bergman. Go figure.

• *Urban Cowboy* (1980). Everybody expected this John Travolta vehicle to be the down home follow-up to the phenomenal *Saturday Night Fever,* but the picture, a story of a hardhat trying to be macho in Pasadena, Texas (site of Gilley's), never really clicked with the movie-going public. Signalled the beginning of the end for Travolta and the rise of co-stars Deborah Winger and Scott Glenn. Responsible for the many unused mechanical bulls now gathering dust in honky-tonks across the land.

• *Tender Mercies* (1983). Robert Duvall won an Oscar for his starring role in this low-key story of a country singer attempting to put his life in order. Duvall wrote his own songs.

• *Sweet Dreams* (1985). Jessica Lange portrays Patsy Cline and wisely opts to lip-sync her original vocals. Ed Harris is her not-good-for-much husband.

• *Great Balls of Fire* (1990). Dennis Quaid stars as the carousing Jerry Lee Lewis and Winona Ryder as his child-bride Myra in this energetic biography that concentrates on the "Killer's" phenomenal early career.

Time To Watch *Hee Haw*

That's the *Hee Haw* donkey peering out at you from the watch face that features a quartz movement, genuine leather band and 3-year guarantee.

Our Favorite TV Country

Country was never well represented on network TV. Except for an occasional guest shot of Homer & Jethro on *Beverly Hillbillies*, the pickins were slim.

• *Ranch Party*. Great old early 1950s musical variety show hosted by Tex Ritter.

• *Hee Haw*. The country variety show, half modeled on *The Grand Ole Opry*, half on *Laugh-In.*

Johnny Cash Show. Summer show, 1969, featured first post-accident TV appearance by Bob Dylan.

YOU'LL SEE RED...

...if you watch The Nashville Network, country's answer to MTV. Shotgun Red is their music-loving mascot. (We've always thought Red was a "wrong side of the blanket" cousin of Yosemite Sam).

"What do you mean, 'peasant music,' you goddamn son of a bitch?" —Faron Young to Zsa Zsa Gabor

I Fall to Pages

If you want to know the inside story behind your favorite country hits and stars, here are a few choice tidbits for your edification.

• **Country: *The Music and the Musicians.*** With nearly 600 pages and over 700 photos, this big volume covers "pickers, slickers, cheatin' hearts and superstars." Includes the floor plan of Dolly Parton's tour bus, **Time Magazine**'s review of *Hee Haw*, memories from Garrison Keillor on *The Grand Ole Opry* and a concise discography of country's greatest recordings.

#B111, $65.00 + 7.50 shipping. Country Music Hall of Fame and Museum, Mail Order Dept., 4 Music Square East, Nashville, TN 37203. (800) 255-2357.

• *Nashville Babylon: The Uncensored Truth and Private Lives of Country Music's Stars* by Randall Riese. More than you want to know about sex, drugs, alcoholism, murder, mayhem, racism and D-I-V-O-R-C-E among country stars. Typical chapter titles include **Grand Ole Orgy** and **Big Balls in Cowtown.** Sleazy, but fascinating.

$12.95 + 3.50

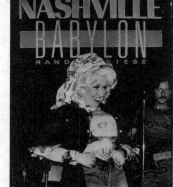

The Uncensored Truth and Private Lives of Country Music's Stars
NASHVILLE BABYLON
RANDALL RIESE

shipping. **Contemporary Books, 180 North Michigan Ave, Chicago, IL 60601. (312) 782-9181.**

• *Your Cheatin' Heart* by Chet Flippo. Hank Williams' life is put under the microscope.

#B0141, $3.95 + 3.50 shipping from the Country Music Hall of Fame and Museum, Mail Order Dept., 4 Music Square East, Nashville, TN 37203. (800) 255-2357.

• *Cooking with Country Music Stars*. Includes more than 200 recipes from the likes of the Judds, Barbara Mandrell, Dolly Parton, George Strait and Hank Williams, Jr.

$10.95 + 4.50 shipping from the Country Music Hall of Fame and Museum, Mail Order Dept., 4 Music Square East, Nashville, TN 37203. (800) 255-2357.

Pilgrimage: *Nashville Skyline*

If you want to spend your vacation contemplating the meaning and majesty of country music, then Nashville, Tennessee is definitely the place to go. Listed below are but a handful of the metropolitan area's major points of interest. Call them for information. All phone numbers are in the (615) area code.

• *House of Cash*. Remington bronzes, antique pistols and other Johnny Cash memorabilia on display. 824-5110.

• *Waylon's Private Collection*. Devoted to mementos of Waylon Jenning's illustrious career. 256-7923.

• *Barbara Mandrell Country*. Visit an actual replica of Ms. Mandrell's bedroom. 242-7800.

• *Minnie Pearl's Museum*. Stop by and say "HOW-DEE!" 889-6700.

• *Opryland*. Ride the wild rides.

Country Up-To-Date

Country America, The Magazine of Country Life and Entertainment. Published 10 times a year, this magazine features profiles of fan favorites and up-and-coming new country talent, also travel articles, recipes, trivia contests and complete monthly listings for The Nashville Network. Pleasant, laid-back and respectful of its subject, without being fawning.

One year subscription $14.97 to P.O. Box 10830, Des Moines, IA 50336. (800) 678-2666.

Watch the goings-on behind the scenes at The Nashville Network. Tour the Grand Ole Opry. The fun never stops. 889-6700.

• *Twitty City*. Features stuff once owned by Conway Twitty. 822-6650.

• *Country Music Hall of Fame*. The name says it all. 255-5333.

• Finally, once you've had your fill of country music, there's always the *Museum of Beverage Containers and Advertising*. 859-5236.

COUNTRY CRITTERS

How Do I Get Out Of This Chicken Outfit?

A chicken suit for every occasion. #8192, $110.00 + 7.95 shipping. Johnson Smith Company, 4514 19th Court East, P.O. Box 25500, Bradenton, FL 34206-5500. (813) 747-2356.

Cute Little Peckers

These lawn ornaments are pretty fowl. #8596-5 Rooster, $8.98. #8995-5 Hen & 3 chicks, $9.98. Add $2.95 shipping. Miles Kimball, 41 West Eighth Avenue, Oshkosh, WI 54906.

"FOWL PLAY"

Take a Gander

24" snow goose wind sock.

#8207-1, $9.98 + 2.95 shipping. Miles Kimball, 41 West Eighth Avenue, Oshkosh, WI 54906.

LOVE IN VANE

Weather vane with John Deere deer!
#1513 $75.00 + 8.50.
John Deere, 1400 3rd Avenue, Moline, IL 61265.
(800) 544-2122 / FAX (309) 765-4584.

WHAT DO YOU GET WHEN YOU CROSS...

Heavy cast iron, finished in antique verdigris.
#2420 Bunny. #2421 Duck. #2422 Squirrel. $22.50 each + 4.50 shipping. John Deere, 1400 3rd Avenue, Moline, IL 61265. (800) 544-2122.

Horsing Around

Wind 'em up...head 'em out! 2 1/2" jumping horse. Have a stable home.
(12) for $16.50 + 4.00 shipping. Archie McPhee, P.O. Box 30852, Seattle, WA 98103-0852. (206) 547-2467.

Out Like a Lamb

Sheepishly cute cartoony lamb. Put this on your front lawn and make your neighbors sick.

#F3138, $3.98 + 3.50 shipping. Harriet Carter, North Wales, PA 19455. (215) 361-5151.

The record for chicken plucking is held by four women who defeathered 12 in just 32.9 seconds.

PIGS

Pig Face

Silly wall masks.

#6322, "Rosie," and #6321, "Sophie," $50.00 each + 7.50 shipping. Clay Art, 1320 Potrero Avenue, San Francisco, CA 94110. (800) 252-9555.

The Proverbial Piggy Bank

Plays music with each coin.

#2686, $32.98 + 3.50 shipping. The Lighter Side, 4514 19th Court East, P.O. Box 25600, Bradenton, FL 34206-5600. (813) 747-2356.

TOWER O' PIGS

Ceramic bookends.

#6040X, $40.00 + 6.45 shipping. Postscripts, P.O. Box 21628, Ft. Lauderdale, FL 33335. (800) 327-3799.

Pig Pitcher

Pour little piggie.

#7401, $37.50 + 7.50 shipping. Clay Art, 1320 Potrero Avenue, San Francisco, CA 94110. (800) 252-9555.

Shake a Pig's Tail

Salt & pepper shakers.

#18395, $14.95 + 3.90 shipping. Wireless, P.O. Box 64422, St. Paul, MN 55164-0422. (800) 699-9999.

HOG *Wild*

Curly Tail Wind

Pink and black nylon windsock.

$18.00 + 3.00 shipping. Klutz, 2121 Staunton Court, Palo Alto, CA 94306. (415) 424-0736.

This Little Piggie

Pig Slippers. #5506, $24.98 + 3.50 shipping. The Lighter Side, 4514 19th Court East, P.O. Box 25600, Bradenton, FL 34206-5600. (813) 747-2356.

In a Pig's Tie

Hog-tied over you.

#16187, $16.50 + 3.90 shipping. Wireless, P.O. Box 64422, St. Paul, MN 55164-0422. (800) 699-9999.

PORK BUNS

Shorts for male chauvinists.

#16186, $14.00 + 2.75 shipping from Wireless (see above).

The heaviest hog ever was "Big Bill" from Jackson, Tennessee—2,552 pounds and 9 feet long.

COWS

Moo Mania

Collecting cute cat and dog items is almost understandable. But cows? Perhaps it's just carnivore guilt or a longing for the simple rural life, but for some reason cows are udderly hip.

COW BELLS

4" hand-painted ceramic cow wind chimes.

#CW-213, $9.95 + 3.95 shipping from Holst, Inc., 1118 West Lake, Box 370, Tawas City, MI 48764. (517) 362-5664.

Bathing Beauty Bossy

Salt & pepper shaker set.

#2550, $14.98 + 3.50 shipping. The Lighter Side, 4514 19th Street Court East, P.O. Box 25600, Bradenton, FL 34206-5600. (813) 747-2356.

String 'Em Up!

Ten 3-inch cow lights on a 14-foot wire.

#2666, $24.00 + 3.50 shipping. The Lighter Side, 4514 19th Street Court East, P.O. Box 25600, Bradenton, FL 34206-5600. (813) 747-2356.

Black Board Angus

Cow Blackboard.

#010679, $26.00 + 5.35 shipping. Casual Living USA, 5401 Hangar Ct., P.O. Box 31273, Tampa, FL 33631-3273.

Tip The Cow Game

Udder Madness!

Decipher, Inc.
P.O. Box 56
Norfolk, VA 23501
(804) 623-3600

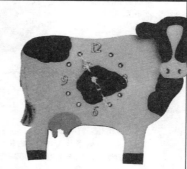

Cow Clock

Solid wood clock.

#HCC-15, Cow Table Clock or #CC-15 3D, Wall Cow Clock. $29.95 each + 4.95 shipping. Holst, Inc., 1118 West Lake, Box 370, Tawas City, MI 48764. (517) 362-5664.

COWSTUME

Udderly amoo-sing.

#T2193 (S) , #T2194 (M) , or #T2195 (L). $39.98 + 6.75 shipping. Funny Side Up, 425 Stump Road, North Wales, PA 19454. (215) 361-5130.

Udderly Delicious

Hershey's Chocolate Cows in a milk carton, plus a matching digital watch with plastic cow-skin band.

#16931, $16.95 + 3.90 shipping from Wireless, P.O. Box 64422, St. Paul, MN 55164-0422. (800) 699-9999.

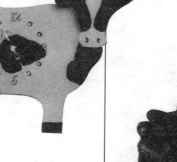

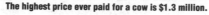
The highest price ever paid for a cow is $1.3 million.

Moo-ving Pitcher

Ceramic milk pitcher.

#7402, $37.00 + 7.50 shipping. Clay Art, 1320 Potrero Avenue, San Francisco, CA 94110. (800) 252-9555.

MOO Wave Fashion

Simply bovine!

#3437 Cow Earrings or #3486 Cow Tie Loop. $6.98 each + 2.50 shipping. The Lighter Side, 4514 19th Street Court East, P.O. Box 25600, Bradenton, FL 34206-5600. (813) 747-2356.

Bum Steer

Cow Design Deck Chair. #17628, $21.50. Matching Floor Mat. #17622, $18.00. Add $3.90 to each for shipping. Wireless, P.O. Box 64422, St. Paul, MN 55164-0422. (800) 699-9999.

For Your Cow-a-bungalow

19 inch tall cow lawn ornament, out standing in field.

#F8997, $6.98 + 3.50 shipping. Harriet Carter, North Wales, PA 19455. (215) 361-5151.

Grooming a Cow

Salt and pepper shakers.

#7504, $13.50 + 3.50 shipping from Clay Art, 1320 Potrero Avenue, San Francisco, CA 94110. (800) 252-9555.

IN COWS WE TRUST
E·PLURIBUS·MOO

COW SHIRT

Trust what you herd, but don't get bilked.

#16199, T-shirt, $15.00 + 2.75 shipping. #16200, Sweatshirt, $25.00 + 3.90 shipping. M, L, XL. Wireless, P.O. Box 64422, St. Paul, MN 55164-0422. (800) 699-9999.

Huge Heifers

Ceramic wall masks.

#6301R with glasses, #6301S without. $50.00 + 7.50 shipping. Clay Art, 1320 Potrero Avenue, San Francisco, CA 94110. (800) 252-9555.

Cow Sillies

Ceramic magnets, same designs as Wall Heifers, above.

6 for $27.00 + 3.50 shipping. Clay Art, 1320 Potrero Avenue, San Francisco, CA 94110. (800) 252-9555.

Constant Cow Mitt

Prevents kitchen cattle-clysms.

#M454, $10.95 + 2.75 shipping. Wireless, P.O. Box 64422, St. Paul, MN 55164-0422. (800) 699-9999.

Come again? A 0.5 cc unit of Holstein bull semen costs up to $75. Of human semen, about $48.

Cracker Jack

Popcorn, Peanuts, Candy &...

The prize came later. Like the Ferris Wheel, Cracker Jacks were born in Chicago's Columbian Exhibition in 1893. Brothers F.W. and Louis Rueckheim had whipped up a special mix of popcorn, peanuts and molasses at their popcorn specialties factory. It was such a success at the fair that they decided to continue manufacturing it.

It wasn't until 1896 that a snack-munching salesman's offhand remark "That's a cracker jack!" gave the stuff its name. A customer provided the slogan: "The more you eat — the more you want." Within a few years Cracker Jacks became immensely popular—

Cracker Jack Pilgrimage

The Center of Science and Industry. Contains a permanent exhibit of over 10,000 pieces of Cracker Jack memorabilia, including advertising ephemera, prizes and premiums.

280 East Broad St., Columbus, OH 43215. (614) 228-2674.

they were immortalized in the big 1908 hit *Take Me Out to the Ballgame*.

The box used to feature premium coupons, but that proved to be too unwieldy, so in 1912 the Rueckheims decided to provide immediate gratification instead. Little books, magnifying glasses, beads, miniature trains and animals, tops, whistles and other toys were the treasures to be found buried among the golden kernels. Since the beginning, more than 16 billion toys have been given away in Cracker Jack boxes.

During World War I, the package gained its patriotic red, white and blue stripes. Probably inspired by Buster Brown and his dog, the company also introduced the now-familiar boy sailor Jack and his little dog Bingo.

Time hasn't changed the product, but it has changed Jack, Bingo, the packaging and—alas—especially the prizes.

The Best Prizes

The intricate toys that went into Cracker Jack boxes during the decade of 1930 - 1940 are the ones now most popular with collectors. Elaborate hand painted charms, trinkets, even a complete train set came in the boxes.

During 1940 - 1950, you found toy soldiers and artillery. After the war, the prizes were plastic TVs, cars and rockets. Economics, child safety concerns and high speed packaging now dictate the type of toys that can be put into the box: cheap, flat and boring.

A Real Prize

Cracker Jack Prizes by Alex Jaramillo. This is an entire book about those great Cracker Jacks toys, and it's a delight. The deliciously photographed illustrations show you just about every prize there ever was since 1912.

Best if read during snacktime reading because otherwise, the Pavlovian cravings for "popcorn, peanuts and candy" may distract.

$19.95 + 2.00 shipping from Abbeville Press, 488 Madison Ave., New York, NY 10022. (800) 227-7210.

Cracker Jack is the world's largest user of popcorn.

Crayola®

Pigments of Your Imagination

Crayola wasn't the first crayon in the world. But for most American kids there isn't anything else. A lot of it is the mysterious smell and distinctive markings—the organ-pipe precision of new crayons in the yellow and green box and the trademarked serpentine borders on the label. It's been that way for nearly a century.

In 1885, Joseph W. Binney founded the Peekskill Chemical Co. in Peekskill, NY, and began producing lampblack, charcoal and red iron oxide barn paint. In 1900 his son and nephew, Edwin Binney and C. Harold Smith, took over the company, renamed it "Binney and Smith," and added schoolroom slate pencils to the line.

They learned that teachers were unhappy with the chalk and crayons available. The chalk was too crumbly and dusty, the imported crayons too expensive and anemic.

Binney and Smith went to work, developing first a "dustless" chalk and then a better quality crayon. Further research went into finding non-toxic pigments when they discovered that kids then, as now, thought the colors look good enough to eat.

In 1903, the first boxes of Crayolas rolled off the line, priced at 5¢ and offering eight colors: red, blue, green, yellow, orange, brown, violet and black.

Waxing Poetic

• "Crayola" comes from combining the French word "craie" meaning a stick of color with "ola" from the word "oleaginous," referring to the oily paraffin wax in the crayons. It was Binney's wife Alice (a schoolteacher, incidentally) who coined the term.

• The stubs of crayons can be melted down and "recycled" into new ones.

• A survey showed that the evocative smell of crayons is in the top 10 most recognized smells in America (the top two are peanut butter and coffee). Don't tell your vegetarian friends, but that distinctive smell comes from stearic acid—also known as beef fat.

• Waxing & waning—Binney and Smith uses petroleum-based paraffin as a major ingredient. But don't worry about disruptions of oil supplies destroying America's ability to color in our next Gulf War: the company says it is sitting on a secret contingency formula that requires no paraffin.

Colorize My World

The Colorization Movie Coloring Book by Ron Hauge. Have you always wanted to be Ted Turner? This book (crayons included) lets you colorize 30 black & white classics like *Citizen Kane, Psycho, The Grapes of Wrath* and *The Seventh Seal*.

$6.95 + 2.50 shipping. Workman Publishing Co., 1 West 39th St., New York, NY 10018. (212) 254-5900.

These Colors DO Run

Leave your crayons on your car seat on a hot day? Binney & Smith gives phone advice on how to get its products out of hair, furniture, carpets and the like. To save you a phone call, here's how to get molten crayon stains out of carpeting and car interiors. Try on an inconspicuous area first.

"Scrape excess crayon off the carpet with a dull-edged knife. Spray with WD-40® (lubricant) and let stand a few minutes. With a small, stiff bristle brush, work crayon stain and wipe with paper towels. Respray with WD-40 and apply liquid dishwashing detergent on the sprayed area; work in with the brush and wipe stain away with a damp sponge. If stain remains, repeat the procedure."

Other questions? Contact:
The Stain Removal Guidance Department
Binney & Smith
1100 Church Lane
PO Box 431
Easton, PA 18044-0431
(800) 272-9652

A "Rose" By Any Other Name

Crayons, although ageless, are not exempt from the changing world.

• In 1958, with Cold War xenophobia in full bloom, the company changed the name of "Prussian Blue" to "Midnight Blue."

• In 1962, heightened consciousness brought on by the civil rights movement led Binney and Smith to change the name of "Flesh" to "Peach," recognizing, as the company put it, "that not everyone's flesh is the same shade." (On the other hand, the color "Indian Red" still exists).

CRAYON PILGRIMAGE

Visit either of the two plants that make Crayolas. During the one hour tour, you'll see the mixing, molding, labeling and boxing operations, an amazing multi-color mechanical fantasy. Reservations are necessary, preferably months in advance. The factories are in Easton, Pennsylvania (50 miles north of Philadelphia), which includes a Silly Putty tour as well, and Winfield, Kansas (45 miles south of Wichita). Contact:

Crayola Product Tours
1100 Church Lane
PO Box 431
Easton, PA 18044-0431
For the Pennsylvania tour: (215) 559-2632.
For Kansas, call (316) 221-4200.

A typical child will wear down 730 crayons between ages 2 and 8.

Coloring By the Numbers

- Four out of five crayons sold in this country are Crayolas.

- Each year Binney and Smith manufactures more than 2 billion Crayola crayons, enough to produce a giant crayon 35 feet in diameter and 410 feet tall, towering 100 feet taller than the Statue of Liberty. If you laid them end to end on the Equator... you're right, they'd melt. But anyway, the multicolored mess would circle the Earth over 4 1/2 times.

- American children spend 6.3 billion hours coloring each year.

- Extensive research indicates that crayons typically don't get used beyond the halfway point on the label.

- 65% of all American children between the ages of 2 and 7 will pick up a crayon at least once today.

- Average parents of young kids buy crayons three times a year.

- Kids average 27 minutes per coloring session, longer if the crayons are brand new.

- It takes about four minutes to make one batch of 2,400 crayons.

- The number of colors available has risen several times since the basic eight in 1903. Crayolas were up to 48 colors in 1948; 64 in 1958; and 72 in 1972 (eight fluorescent colors were added just in time to aid the cultural transition from psychedelia to disco).

- Apparently deciding that 72 was a nice number, they've stuck with it since. To introduce new ones they've had to retire some, most recently in 1990 (see below, left).

Local Color

For many years restaurants have given crayons to kids to keep them quietly entertained. *Les Auteurs* in the Detroit suburb of Royal Oak takes that one better. They provide crayons to keep *adult* patrons quietly entertained as well.

The restaurant's tables are covered with butcher paper for drawing on. A "crayolier" with sharpener strolls from table to table ("Sharpen your Royal Purple, sir?"). Several hundred regulars, including the governor of Michigan and a vice chairman of Ford Motor Company, pay $5.50 a year for on-site crayon storage in the restaurant's special climate-controlled vault. Reservations are recommended, and, if you prefer, you may BYOC without extra charge.

Les Auteurs, 222 Sherman Drive, Royal Oak, MI 48067. (313) 544-2887.

STRIKE THE COLORS

In 1990, with much ballyhoo, Binney and Smith discontinued eight of their less popular colors in order to replace them with the brighter colors their marketing research indicated that kids wanted.

After Binney and Smith announced the changes, a small knot of protesters picketed the company's headquarters, carrying signs like "We Take Umber-age" and "Save Lemon Yellow." As a sop, the company promised to place a five foot replica of each retired color in its new "Crayon Hall of Fame."

The retired colors (if you want to hold on to them for their collectible potential):

Blue Gray	Green Blue
Lemon Yellow	Maize
Orange Red	Orange Yellow
Raw Umber	Violet Blue

The new colors, with names sounding more like an interior designer's vocabulary than a kid's:

Cerulean	Dandelion
Fuchsia	Jungle Green
Royal Purple	Teal Blue
Vivid Tangerine	Wild Strawberry

Crayons on the Wall

"Box of..." by Mickey Myers. Who says you should keep crayons off the wall? This colorful poster will please art lovers of all ages.

The first and second crayons to get used up in a box are usually the black and red.

James Dean

Forever Young

"Live fast, die young and leave a good looking corpse."—James Dean

His life and movie career were brief. Dean died at 24 after some TV appearances and only three motion pictures. Still, his legend and image have lasted for decades.

More than one cynic has suggested that his death at the time was a very good career move. What kind of roles would he have been playing if still alive in the 1980s and '90s? *The Godfather?* Superman's father?

Dean was born in Marion, Indiana on February 8, 1931 to Winton Dean, a dental technician and Mildred Wilson, his wife. When Jimmy was 9 his mother died of breast cancer, scarring him for his remaining fifteen years and propelling him to Fairmount, Indiana, where he was raised by his aunt and uncle through high school. Eventually he took off for California, bound for UCLA and eventual stardom.

He'll Mug For You!

Have a cup of coffee with James Dean every morning. In fact, have a couple of cups because these hand-painted ceramic mugs are available in two distinctive styles.

#1711, $15.00 + 3.50 shipping from Clay Art, 1320 Potrero Avenue, San Francisco, CA 94110. (800) 252-9555 / FAX (415) 285-3017.

QUOTES: The Water Method Man

"I'm a Method actor, I work through my senses. If you're nervous, your sense can't reach your subconscious and that's that—you can't work. So I figured if I could piss in front of those 2,000 people, man, and I could be cool…I could get in front of the camera and do just anything, anything at all."

—**Dean after urinating in public on the *Giant* set.**

"He really wanted to look uptight. So to get himself really uncomfortable, he told me he didn't pee all day until they did the shot."

—**Dennis Hopper on Dean's *East of Eden* performance.**

Pilgrimage: Fairmount, Indiana

Fairmount is where Dean grew up and is buried. After years of ambivalence about him, the citizenry finally began catering to the Dean pilgrims. Here are some of the sights:

- **Museum Days.** Held on the weekend nearest the anniversary Dean's death, the event attracts Deanophiles from the world over. Most of the festivities take place at or near the Fairmount Museum on Washington Street.

- **Park Cemetery.** That's where Jimmy's grave is, if you can find it. Faithful followers have chipped off pieces of his tombstone and even been caught sleeping on top of his grave. In 1983 the entire headstone was stolen. We hope its replacement is still there when you visit.

- **James Dean Gallery.** Displays various Deanabilia as well as a gift shop which sells Dean products both old and new. They'll also do business by mail and phone, so contact them for information about what's available.

425 N. Main Street, Fairmount, IN 46928. (317) 948-3326.

Magnetic Personality

James Dean is not only more popular in death than he was in life, but more useful, too. He can hold notes and newsclips on your refrigerator door. Not to mention the fingerpaintings by your little rebel without a cause.

#1708 Set of six, $39.00 + 3.50 shipping from Clay Art, 1320 Potrero Avenue, San Francisco, CA 94110. (800) 252-9555.

DEAN FACTS

• Jimmie didn't have any front teeth and had to wear a special bridge to fill in the gap. He liked to startle people by smiling at them with his teeth out.

• Irony: At the time of his death, Dean was slated for a role in *Somebody Up There Likes Me*.

• Dean avoided the draft by registering as a homosexual. Whether just a dodge or the truth isn't completely clear. Still, Dean had several gay roommates and his response to being asked about being bisexual was reportedly "Well I'm certainly not going through life with one hand tied behind my back!"

Rebel Without a Club?

• James Dean Fan Club
   3924 St. John's Terrace
   Cincinnati, Ohio, 45236

• We Remember Dean International
   Box 5025
   Fullerton, CA, 92635

Dean's List

James Dean in His Own Words by Mick St. Michael. St. Michael devotes only two pages to commentary on Dean. The remaining 94 pages consist entirely of black and white photos and quotes by and about Dean.

Arranged in loose themes, you can read what Dean thought about life, death and himself, as well as what others — his family, classmates, co-stars — thought of him.

$14.95 + 3.00 shipping from Music Sales Corporation, 225 Park Avenue South, New York, NY 10003. (212) 254-2100.

Auto Safety

In late 1955, Dean made a highway safety spot with Gig Young to promote better driving among teens. When Young asked Dean to give his opinion about fast driving on the highway to the young listening audience he said:

"I used to fly about quite a bit, you know, took a lot of unnecessary chances on the highways. Then I started racing, and, uh, now I drive on the highways, and, uh, extra cautious... I don't have the urge to speed on the highway. People say racing is dangerous but I'd rather take my chances on the track any day than on the highway... Drive safely, the life you save may be mine..."

Not long after filming, Dean died in a car crash on the highway, only two hours after receiving a speeding ticket.

Busted!

Park this hand-painted ceramic bust on your piano instead of Beethoven and help perpetuate the general confusion over whether he was the same person as Jimmy Dean the musical sausage maker.

#1502, $100.00 + 7.50 shipping from Clay Art, 1320 Potrero Avenue, San Francisco, CA 94110. (800) 252-9555.

While filming *Giant*, Dean annoyed his co-workers by walking around with unfurled pastry hanging out of each nostril.

The End

"You know something? I never figured I'd live to see 18. Isn't that dumb? Each day I'd look in the mirror and say, 'What, you still here?'" —**James Dean.**

Dean was always fascinated with death. "Death. It's the only thing left to respect," he said. "It's the one inevitable, undeniable truth. Everything else can be questioned."

During a trip to his home town, Dean had himself photographed in a casket of a local funeral parlor. He wrote poems about dying and produced drawings of himself hanging by a noose from his ceiling in his apartment.

Dean was also obsessed with race car driving and was always seeking faster cars. In the end, he even predicted his crash. When told of his friend Bob Francis's car accident, he said, "Well, Francis makes two...Don't worry — I'll be the third."

Last Words. "That guy up there has got to stop, he's seen us..."

Book of the Dead

Death of James Dean: What Really Happened on the Day He Crashed? by **Warren Newton Beath.** Most Dean fans know the general details of his life and death. But some Deanophiles want to get down to the exquisite details.

Ever wonder: What was Jimmy drinking when he stopped at Tips Diner outside of Newhall at 3 o'clock on the day of his death? (Milk). Or, what was the occupation of the father of Donald Gene Turnupseed, the young Cal Poly student whose 1950 Ford Tudor collided with Dean's Spyder? (An electrician who installed automatic telephone exchanges).

Using inquest transcripts and other previously unpublished material, author Beath reconstructs the minutes and seconds before and after Dean's death, from the contortions of Dean's twisted body after the crash to a minute-by-minute replay of Dean's 20-minute ambulance ride. A book for hardcore Deanophiles.

$8.95 + 1.50 shipping from:
Grove Press
920 Broadway
New York, NY 10010
(800) 937-5557

Stand-Up Stand-In

Make your own James Dean film. Doesn't matter that he's dead, because you've got the perfect stand-in—this life-size (when he was alive, of course), sturdy, die-cut photo with attached easel.

#4251J, $29.95 + 5.25 shipping from Enticements, PO Box 4040, New Rochelle, NY 10802-4020. (800) 243-4300 / FAX (800) 244-4591.

Cool Cats

• Brat Cat Garfield's creator, cartoonist Jim Davis, also graduated from Fairmount High, Dean's alma mater.

•This is the special recipe Dean fed Marcus, his little Siamese cat. The recipe had been given to him by Elizabeth Taylor:

Mix and chill:
1 teaspoon white Karo Syrup
1 big can evaporated milk
1 egg yolk
equal part boiled or distilled water

DETECTIVES

"Who Are These Guys?"

He's got a face that looks like it's been run over by a Buick. He's got so many holes in him he could strain pasta. He's in a trenchcoat under the streetlight, talking in a boozily cynical tongue. He's the classic detective.

He owes a lot of what he is to Francois-Eugene Vidocq, a real-life reformed forger, smuggler, and pickpocket who used his knowledge of the Paris underworld to create a detective force staffed entirely by ex-convicts in the 1800s. Vidocq became known for the importance he attached to tiny, seemingly irrelevant clues, and his ability to get inside the criminal mind. He laid the foundation for modern criminology, and spawned thousands of detective stories starting with the first ever—Edgar Allan Poe's *Murders in the Rue Morgue* (1841).

Allan Pinkerton founded the United States' first detective agency in 1851 after finding his job as Sheriff of Cook County (Chicago) unchallenging. Pinkerton's played a major role in the development of crime detection throughout the country and even acted as presidential guards before the Secret Service was formed (In *Butch Cassidy & The Sundance Kid*, Paul Newman keeps asking Robert Redford: "Who are those guys?" In the movie as well as in history, they were from Pinkerton's—tired of being held up, bank owners had hired them).

Some historians believe Pinkerton's gave detectives the "private eye" name, based on their logo—a large, staring eye under the slogan "We Never Sleep" (others say the name is just short for "private investigator").

Fictional Gumshoes. Dashiell Hammett has been called the Hemingway of detective fiction; Raymond Chandler—tough, cynical, and lyrical—the Fitzgerald. Chandler's detective Philip Marlowe has been played by Humphrey Bogart, Robert Mitchum, Dick Powell, Robert Montgomery, George Montgomery, and Elliott Gould.

Mickey Spillane introduced his violent detective Mike Hammer in the gruesome 1947 psychodrama *I, The Jury*. A critic once criticized the writer and public taste at a time when Spillane had 7 books on the top 10 paperback best-seller list. "Shut up," said Spillane, "or I'll write three more."

These days the fictional detective field is notable for the diversity of the characters in it. Agatha Christie was responsible for opening up the field to women, cerebral Belgians and others outside the tough male model.

Recent popular gumshoes have included a Grey Panther, a gay antique dealer working with a lesbian cop, a female college professor, a civic foundation executive, and a Navajo Indian.

Two currently popular fictional women "shoes" are Sara Paretsky's V.I. Warshawski, and Sue Grafton's Kinsey Millhone, both lively characters who see just as much action as their hard-boiled male counterparts, albeit with less booze and a better sense of humor.

One out of every four fiction books sold in the U.S. is a mystery or suspense novel.

True Detectives

There are at least 45,000 private investigators in the U.S. But they aren't all what most people think: burly ex-cops with brush cuts and pot bellies, their shoulder holsters bulging through cheap double-knit polyester suits.

• **Women and minorities.** Over 40% of private detectives are female. Some women say it's a natural match—they've got good communication skills and are seen as less threatening than men, so people open up to them more easily, which is a big part of the job. And many detectives are black or Hispanic.

• **Team players.** No longer a solo act, the modern detective works with a back-up team of support personnel.

• **Corporations.** Firms are turning to private detective agencies in big numbers. With police departments overburdened with work, and some jobs too delicate to perform in-house, detective agencies take on background investigations, employee theft, and industrial espionage countermeasures.

• **Appearance.** Detectives dress to fit the assignment—it's necessary to fit in. Working corporate locales, detectives wear three-piece suits.

• **Job qualifications.** The ability to beat the truth out of bad guys is not

"At night nothing comes between you and your subject. No massive traffic jams to get in the way. And the cops are all in the dough-nut shops."

—**Gil Lewis, Private Investigator, on why he likes night work**

so much in demand—you're better off with a degree in law, accounting, or computer science.

• **Weapons.** Modern detectives carry guns less frequently than in the old days (and much less than fictional detectives). Although they say it's not a dangerous job, most have some interesting stories to tell.

• **Assignments:** Tracking down the spouse's secret lover is still part of the gumshoe's caseload and there are still some messy divorce cases, but no-fault divorce legislation has made this far less common. (One new type of client, though, is people who want to size up their dates, as in "Is he really an

unmarried astronaut like he says?") These cases are most typical:

—**Missing persons.** Vanished spouses, abducted children, runaways, missing heirs, debtors who have disappeared, even old friends who have drifted away. Most of this kind of work can be done in an office using computer

databases and a telephone.

—**Criminal investigations.** A lot of PI s work for attorneys—playing Paul Drake to the country's Perry Masons.

—**Process service.** It can be a challenge to track down an unwilling participant in the legal process.

—**Insurance fraud.** Why is that guy who filed the claim for a back injury playing tackle football in the park with his friends?

• **Pay.** About $8 to $15 an hour at the rock bottom entry level is common; $55 an hour and more for established professionals (up to $250 an hour isn't unheard of).

Detective Quotes

"Down these mean streets a man must go who is not himself mean, who is neither tarnished nor afraid…He must be, to use a rather weathered phrase, a man of honor."

—Raymond Chandler (from the preface to a Dashiell Hammett collection called *The Simple Art of Murder*, Houghton Mifflin, 1950)

"Nobody reads a mystery to get to the middle. They read it to get to the end. If it's a letdown, they won't buy any more. The first page sells that book. The last page sells your next book."

—Mickey Spillane

FROM SARTRE TO SAM SPADE

***Gumshoe: Reflections in a Private Eye*, by Josiah Thompson.** Thompson was a Kierkegaard scholar and tenured professor of philosophy at Haverford College when he broke from the academic ranks and became a private investigator—making, in the words of one book reviewer, "the decade's biggest career jump-cut." A good read, with an interesting look at learning the ropes (Thompson confesses that he once accidentally asked directions from the person he was assigned to tail), what it's like to be a working detective, and how reality plays against the legacy of Sam Spade.

$17.45 postpaid from Little, Brown and Company, 200 West Street, Waltham, MA 02254. (800) 343-9204.

A Real Police Detective's Tool Kit

The Boston Globe reported recently on what a working police detective takes to the scene of the crime:

- **Tape measure**
- **Rubber gloves** (keeps the detective's fingerprints from contaminating the crime scene)
- **Tweezers** (for picking up small items at the scene, such as a hair)
- **A penlight**
- **Chalk** (for making outlines of the body)
- **Small manila envelopes** (for holding evidence)
- **Stenographer's notebook**
- **Jar of Vicks Vap-O-Rub** (rubbing it under your nose masks the aroma of decomposing bodies)

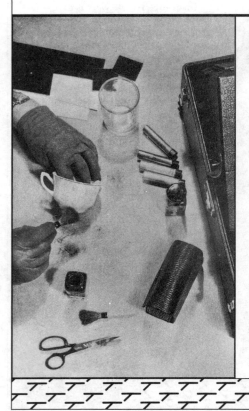

Schools of Hard Knocks

- **The Nick Harris Detective Academy.** Founded in 1907, it claims the title of "the world's oldest investigation academy." It's run by Milo Speriglio, a detective involved with many headline cases. (One was the death of Marilyn Monroe. He believes it was murder, not suicide, and he's written two books about it.)

Would-be gumshoes can take mini-courses in missing persons, skip tracing, background investigations, record searching, surveillance, insurance fraud, undercover work and process serving. The most intensive course is the seven week "Master" course, which Speriglio claims is the equivalent of more than 4 1/2 years of on-the-job training.

"Master" course, $3,875 from The Nick Harris Detective Academy, 16917 Enadia Way, Van Nuys, CA 91406. (818) 343-6611.

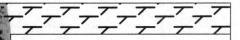

- **The Rouse School of Special Detective Training.** Rouse offers at-home private investigation courses in subjects like Special Surveillance and Undercover Techniques, Electronics Eavesdropping Detection, Automobile Repossession, and High-Speed Pursuit Tactics. Rouse also offers a catalog of equipment for detectives, including leg holsters, bullet-proof vests, and thumbcuffs.

The Basic Course costs $260, both Basic and Advanced are $459.95, or you can start with the first 5 lessons of the basic course for $69.95. All from The Rouse School, P.O. Box 25750, Santa Ana, CA 92799-5750. (714) 540-9391.

VICKS® VapoRub® Decongestant/Cough Suppressant VAPORIZING COLDS MEDICINE NET WT. 1.5 OZ.

Famous Fictional Detectives

Ya gotta wonder why there's so much crime around when we've had so many super·sleuths on the job so much of the time. Here are our favorites from books, TV, radio, movies and even comic strips (Perry Mason, although technically not a detective, gets honorable mention):

- Nero Wolfe
- Nick and Nora Charles
- Simon Templar, "The Saint"
- Dick Tracy
- Charlie Chan
- Sam Spade
- Philip Marlowe
- Lord Peter Wimsey

- Miss Jane Marple
- Sherlock Holmes
- Hercule Poirot
- Inspector Clouseau
- Columbo
- Kojak
- Charlie's Angels
- The Hardy Boys
- Nancy Drew
- Encyclopedia Brown

- Father Brown
- Gideon Fell
- Mike Hammer
- Travis McGee
- Lew Archer
- V.I. Warshawski
- Toby Peters
- Spenser
- Kinsey Millhone

Watching the Detectives

- **The Thin Man** (1934). This movie, based on Dashiell Hammett's novel, ushered in that famous detective couple, Nick and Nora Charles, in a sophisticated murder mystery-screwball comedy hybrid.

- **The Big Sleep** (1946). Bogie and Bacall, directed by Howard Hawks in the William Faulkner adaptation of Raymond Chandler's first novel. It doesn't get any better than this.

- **The French Connection** (1971). One of the most exciting car chases ever filmed in New York City keeps your attention riveted in this Academy Award winner. Gene Hackman is lawman Popeye Doyle.

- **The Long Goodbye** (1973). Robert Altman's updating of Raymond Chandler's novel borders on black comedy, but it still works. Elliott

Gould's Marlowe is a shabbier semblance of Bogie's version.

- **Chinatown** (1974). Set in a 1930s Chandleresque Los Angeles, it's an homage to the noirish Chandler/ Hammett mysteries it evokes. Stars Jack Nicholson and Faye Dunaway.

Our Favorite Spoofs

- **Dead Men Don't Wear Plaid** (1982). Carl Reiner directed Steve Martin, playing a detective who interacts with clips from vintage '40s noir films. The editing is surprisingly seamless.

- **The Black Bird** (1975). George Segal spoofs Sam Spade in this take-off of *The Maltese Falcon*. Elisha Cook, Jr. and Lee Patrick reprise their roles from the 1941 classic.

- **Murder By Death** (1976). Neil Simon has Truman Capote bringing together caricatures of detectives like

Charlie Chan, Miss Marple and Sam Spade to solve this comedic whodunit.

- **The Cheap Detective** (1978). Neil Simon's at it again in this parody that takes off where Bogie's screen detectives began. Stars Peter Falk.

- **Young Sherlock Holmes** (1985). Engaging film speculates about Sherlock as a sleuthing shaver, his first meeting with an adolescent Dr. Watson.

The Story Behind *The Maltese Falcon*

Dashiell Hammett invented the hard-boiled detective story (as fellow writer Raymond Chandler put it) by taking murder away from the little old ladies and giving it back to the folks who were really good at it.

Warner Bros. paid Hammett's publisher, Knopf, $8,500 for all movie rights to *The Maltese Falcon.* Hammett earned nothing from its success. In fact, Warner Bros. even sued him for selling ABC Radio the rights to produce a series called *The Adventures of Sam Spade.* Hammett had to fight a three-year court battle to affirm that he still owned the rights to his own hero.

Warner's officials debated abandoning the book's title for the 1941 movie, even coming up with *Men on Her Mind* and *The Gent from Frisco* as working titles before coming to their senses.

Humphrey Bogart came to define the character, but the detective was portrayed differently in the book: "Samuel Spade's jaw was long and bony, his chin a jutting V under the more flexible V of his mouth...His yellow-gray eyes were horizontal...He looked rather pleasantly like a blond Satan." And Hammett's Sam Spade was more verbal and vulnerable than Bogart, who played him as cynically taciturn.

Bogart wasn't the producers' first choice for Sam Spade. They wanted George Raft, but he turned down the part.

Despite all impressions, Bogart was the son of a well-to-do New York physician. He attended private schools: Trinity, an Episcopalian school on New York's Upper West Side, and Andover, which was to prepare him for college at Yale. But he flunked geometry, chemistry, French,

English and Bible Studies, and decided it was time to go into acting.

It is still possible to see various San Francisco locations where action in *The Maltese Falcon* took place. At the corner of Bush and Burritt streets in downtown San Francisco, a bronze plaque reads: "On approximately this spot Miles Archer, partner of Sam Spade, was done in by Brigid O'Shaughnessy."

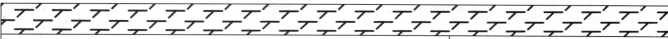

SHERLOCK HOLMES

He was a reasoning and observing machine with a passion for justice, yet beset by some human frailties like arrogance, pettiness and an addiction to cocaine. Sherlock Holmes, what a detective! Since Arthur Conan Doyle set him loose in the world in *A Study in Scarlet* over 100 years ago, the hawk-nosed sleuth has captured imaginations far and wide.

Holmes is said to be the second most famous name in world literature, bowing only to Shakespeare's *Hamlet*. But that great Dane doesn't get mail like Holmes does. The "world's greatest consulting detective" receives—and answers—5,000 letters a year at his 221-B Baker Street address in London. The answers are provided as a whimsical public service by the

company that resides at the address. Holmes has also inspired over 80 movies. Can the Prince of Denmark claim anything comparable?

Arthur Conan Doyle nearly called him Sherrinford Homes or Mordecai Sherlock. His stories established the whodunit's conventional characters: the eccentric detective who has it one up on the police (to their embarrassment) and the constantly amazed narrator/sidekick.

In the 1890s, tired of his creation, Doyle killed off his character. Holmes had been written so skillfully, however, that readers thought of the detective as a real person. Thousands of people wore black armbands in mourning, and there was weeping in the streets, as if a national hero had been taken from them.

Sounds of Sherlock

These radio episodes of *The New Adventures of Sherlock Holmes*, with Basil Rathbone as Holmes and Nigel Bruce as his faithful Dr. Watson, were broadcast in the 1940s, only to disappear for 40 years. They come complete with original commercials and wartime public service messages ("...and keep on buying more and more and more war bonds!").

> **Audiocassettes, #17947, Vol.1-4, $24.95 + 3.90 shipping. #16496, Vol. 5-8, $39.50 + 4.95 shipping. Wireless, P.O. Box 64422, St. Paul, MN 55165-0422. (800) 669-9999.**

Elementary Reading

Sherlock Holmes Scrapbook by Peter Haining. This is a far-ranging collection of the most illuminating and amazing items to appear about the world's most famous detective.

> **$5.99 + 2.00 shipping from Random House, 400 Hahn Rd., Westminster, MD 21157. (800) 733-3000.**

A Tall Cool One...

Authentic reproduction of the famous **Sherlock Holmes Pub** sign (8 x 12 inches), or a set of four coasters.

> **#M688 Pub Sign, $16.95 + 2.00 shipping. #M690, Pub Sign Coasters, $14.95 + 2.00 shipping from What On Earth, 25801 Richmond Road, Cleveland, OH 44146. (216) 831- 5588.**

Holmes Delivery

The Baker Street Journal. This quarterly comes to you from the Baker Street Irregulars, the foremost Holmes society in this country. Columns and articles cover everything about the master detective and his world.

> **$15.00 for one year. Single copies $5.00. The Fordham University Press, University Box L, Bronx, NY 10458-5172.**

Holmes, Where You Hang Your Hat

Put on this cap while working on your income tax and you'll come up with an amazing number of brilliant deductions. 100% wool, ear flaps and poplin lining. Sizes: S, M, L, XL.

> **#9762, $14.98 + 4.20 shipping. Johnson Smith Co., 4514 19th Court East, P.O. Box 25500, Bradenton, FL 34206-5500. (813) 747-2356, FAX/(813) 746-7896.**

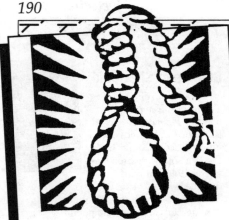

A Dark & Stormy Night

La Jolla Festival Mystery Writers Contest. Want to make fun of famous mystery writers for fun and profit? Each year a different writer becomes your victim. Prizes? Recognition and cash: $500 first place, $250 second place, $150 third place. Interested? Start practicing phrases like "He had a face that looked like it should be wearing a cheap shoe" and "The bullet hit like the first blush of puppy love and I felt my knees turn to overcooked macaroni."

Send self-addressed, stamped envelope for current guidelines to Pat Schaelchlin, Friends of La Jolla Library, 7545 Drape Avenue, La Jolla, CA 92037. (619) 459-8409.

MYSTERY TOURS

• *The Dashiell Hammett Tour.* "No reservations taken. Just show up. Look for the mug in snapbrim hat and trenchcoat." The tour guide is Don Herron, ready to take you from the steps of San Francisco's main public library into a hard-boiled world created by the city's most renowned mystery writer. The Dashiell Hammett Tour ("gumshoeing up and down Frisco's mean streets since 1977") will clue you in on the legendary locales of *The Maltese Falcon* and other stories, and all the places where Hammett is known to have hung out. The 4-hour, 3-mile walking tour costs $5.00 and begins Saturdays at noon.

BRILLIANT DEDUCTION, SHERLOCK

Here are some ways you can become the next Nick or Nora.

• **The Mystery Train.** A murder's been committed, and all the passengers become part of the mystery—as sleuths, and suspects. There's a 3-day jaunt to San Francisco for $598.00, a 1-day trip to Santa Barbara for $198.00, and a ferry ride to Balboa Island for $98.00.

For more information, contact: Pickwick Productions, Case 007, Laguna Beach, CA 92652. (714) 494-6800.

• **Kill Your Boss.** If you've got a large group to entertain, whether social or business, these folks can create a custom murder mystery for you in any setting. Meet with the writers ahead of time for special requests, like having your company's president bumped off (plenty of motives here!). For groups up to 250 people, costs are in the $2,500 to $5,000 range, plus expenses.

Blyth & Co., 68 Scollard Street, Toronto, Ontario, Canada M5R 1G2. (800) 228-7712.

• *How To Host A Murder.* The world's best-selling murder mystery game gives you an unsolved murder and the usual amount of intrigue, blackmail, larceny and sabotage. Ten different games, for eight adult players.

$28.00 each + 3.00 shipping. Decipher Inc., P.O. Box 56, Norfolk, VA 23501-0056. (800) 654-3939.

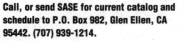

Call, or send SASE for current catalog and schedule to P.O. Box 982, Glen Ellen, CA 95442. (707) 939-1214.

• *Showbus "On Location" Tours.* San Francisco's been the background for dozens of movie crimes, and the Showbus returns you to the scene of most of them. Two show-biz veterans run this bus tour for movie buffs, visiting sites of numerous movie scenes, including non-detective ones. Movie locations include those of several Hitchcock films, *Foul Play, Bullitt* and *Dirty Harry.*

For groups of 25 at $37.50 per person, includes refreshments. Showbus Tours, 2065 California Street, San Francisco, CA 94109. (415) 775-SHOW.

• *Raymond Chandler Mystery Map.* Embark on a do-it-yourself tour of the Marlowe mysteries in Los Angeles.

$5.00 + 2.50 shipping from Sherlock's Home Mystery Store, 4137 E. Anaheim, Long Beach, CA 90804. (213) 494-2964.

"When in doubt, have two guys come through the door with guns." —Raymond Chandler

Mystery Magazines

• *Ellery Queen's Mystery Magazine.* Focuses on crime short stories, suspense and mystery; includes book reviews, plays, films, radio & TV programs, and puzzles.

> One year subscription, 15 issues, $31.97 from P.O. Box 7052, Red Oak, IA 51591. (800) 333-3053.

• *True Detective.* This magazine has existed since 1924, with lurid stories about actual crime cases on file, crime facts and nothin' but the facts, ma'am.

> One year subscription, 9 issues, $13.00 from P.O. Box 53393, Boulder, CO 80322. (800) 525-0643.

• Similar glimpses of the rotten underbelly of crime can be obtained through other magazines published by the same company:

> *Inside Detective*
> *Master Detective*
> *Official Detective*
> *Front Page Detective*

Sleuth Spoof

In *Li'l Abner*, Al Capp parodied *Dick Tracy* with his famous strip-within-a strip character, *Fearless Fosdick*. This book brings you five great spoofs in which you'll meet Anyface, the Atom Bum, Sidney the Crooked Parrot and criminal mastermind Chippendale Chair.

> #FEARSC, $9.95 + 1.50 shipping. Kitchen Sink Press, 2 Swamp Road, Princeton, WI 54968. (414) 295-6922 / FAX (414) 295-6878.

A PUZZLING CASE

Put on your ragged raincoat and help Columbo solve the case of *A Death Foretold*. Read the booklet and assemble the 550 piece jigsaw puzzle to piece together the hidden clue to this baffling case.

> #04-J0366, $10.95 + 3.95 shipping. Bits & Pieces, 1 Puzzle Place, Box 8016, Stevens Point, WI 54481-7199. (800) JIGSAWS.

Required Reading

The Dime Detectives by Ron Goulart. Trace the history of the "dime detectives" like Spade, Marlowe, and Race Williams, a model for Mike Hammer.

$17.95 + 2.00 shipping from Random House, 400 Hahn Rd., Westminster, MD 21157. (800) 733-3000.

Give Someone The Bird

The bird of mystery. This Maltese Falcon replica is 7 lbs. of plaster, painted black.

$27.95 + 2.50 shipping from Sherlock's Home Mystery Store, 4137 E. Anaheim, Long Beach, CA 90804. (213) 494-2964.

Frame Up Job

The film poster about the bird of mystery, framed. It measures 22 x 30 inches.

#M02769, $69.99 + 8.95 shipping from Postings, P.O. Box 8001, Hilliard, OH. 43026. (800) 262-6604.

Mystifying Sounds

Great Radio Mysteries. Six audio cassettes from radio's Golden Age. Listen to original radio shows from the 1940s: *The Green Hornet Drops a Hint*, *The Big Slug* from **Dragnet**, *Nora's Night of Mystery* from **The Thin Man**, and more. Six hours.

> #16727, $24.95 + 3.90 shipping from Wireless, P.O. Box 64422, St. Paul, MN 55165-0422. (800) 669-9999.

Big "Dicks" on Video

• **Peter Gunn Videos.** Two episodes from TV, *Death House Testament* and *Rough Buck*, both 55 minutes, in black and white. "Hot jazz, hot women, hot action. And the coolest private eye ever," according to *TV Guide*.

> $14.95 each postpaid from Rhino Video, 2225 Colorado Avenue, Santa Monica, CA 90404. (800) 432-0020.

• **The World's Best Known Dicks.** Murder, mystery and mayhem here, featuring the world's greatest super sleuths in highlights of Sherlock Holmes, Charlie Chan, Dick Tracy and others from TV and films. Approximately 60 minutes, black and white.

> #RNVD 2926, $29.95 postpaid from Rhino Video, 2225 Colorado Avenue, Santa Monica, CA 90404. (800) 432-0020.

• **Cartoon Crook Chaser.** Dick Tracy's animated adventures from the 1961 TV cartoon series. Tracy basically sat behind a desk and dispatched his colleagues Joe Jitsu, Go Go Gomez, Heap O'Callory, Hemlock Holmes and the Retouchables to do the dirty work. 13 episodes available.

> Each is $12.95 + 3.50 flat rate shipping for up to 3 tapes; for 4 or more, add $1.00 per tape instead. From The Whole Toon Catalog, P.O. Box 369, Issaquah, WA 98027. (206) 391-8747 / FAX (206) 391-9064.

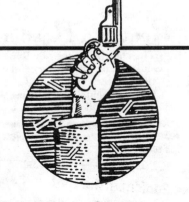

Mystery Loves Company

Bouchercon. Mystery writers and mystery lovers get together every October at an encampment called "The Bouchercon" (named after the late mystery writer-critic-anthologist Anthony Boucher). If you like mysteries, this is the place to rub gummed shoes with writers and fans.

> For info, send SASE to Bouchercon c/o Len & June Moffatt, Box 4456, Downey, CA 90241.

ORGANIZATIONS

• **Mystery Writers of America.** This group of fans and writers was founded in 1945 and has very famous authors as members. Presents the annual Edgar Allan Poe Literary Award.

> Membership, $65.00 to Priscilla Ridgway, 236 W. 27th St., New York, NY 10001. (212) 255-7005.

• **Sisters in Crime.** Works to support women writers and reverse the trend of violence toward women in the mystery genre.

> Membership, $15.00 to c/o Kate's Mystery Books, 2211 Massachusetts Avenue, Cambridge, MA 07140. (617) 491-2660.

• **Mystery Readers International.** Dedicated to "enriching the lives of mystery readers everywhere." Local chapters feature guest speakers and writing workshops.

> Membership, $22.50 to Janet A. Rudolph, P.O. Box 8116, Berkeley, CA 94707. (415) 339-2800.

DINER

Origin of the Diner

The year was 1872. The city, Providence, Rhode Island. The problem: every restaurant in town closed promptly at 8:00 pm, and late-shift factory workers couldn't get anything to eat after work.

The solution was provided by an enterprising pushcart peddler named Walter Scott.

Scotty outfitted a horsedrawn wagon with a stove, painted Walter Scott's Pioneer Lunch on the side, and trundled through the factory district late at night, selling sandwiches, boiled eggs, and coffee for a nickel.

Although it wasn't a restaurant, it was a welcome service and an instant success. Before long, after-hours lunch wagons were operating all over town.

A decade later, an unemployed laborer named Sam Jones had an inspiration while shivering on a chilly night: Why make people stand outside in bad weather to eat? Why not build a lunchwagon big enough to accommodate people inside?

Jones started saving his money. In 1887 he finally had the $800 he needed to build a custom walk-in lunchwagon, complete with a kitchen, a counter, and stools for four to five people.

When Jones hit the street, it created a sensation, and walk-in lunchwagons

"Let's go down to the diner—where the coffee's five, the donut's five, coffee & donut's ten."

—Kay Kyser & his Orchestra

caught on all over the Northeast. By 1910 dozens of lunchwagons—many of them decrepit eyesores—were roaming the streets of most New England cities. City ordinances permitted them to operate only between dusk and dawn, but many were skirting the law and staying on the streets until after the noon lunch break. Outraged "respectable" citizens (and many restaurant owners) started a clamor over being aesthetically assaulted by the ramshackle lunch wagons. So many cities began a crackdown, forcing the wagons off the streets by 10 am.

Lunchcart owners didn't like the idea of closing up when there was obviously plenty of business around. They came up with a way around the rules—they simply picked a good site,

off the road, where they could set up their lunchcarts permanently. Some left the wheels on their carts to avoid having to deal with building codes. But others removed the wheels and hooked up to power, water, and gas lines.

Now they were officially "street cafes," and they could operate night and day. And so the 24-hour diner was born.

In 1937, one million people a day ate at a diner.

On Video

Diner (1982), directed by Barry Levinson. Starring Mickey Rourke, Ellen Barkin, Steve Guttenberg.

A four-star flick about American teenagers in transition. At Christmas vacation, 1959, a group of Baltimore teenagers gather over burgers and fries to discuss where they're headed in life and whether Mathis or Sinatra is better to neck to. Some are in college, some are dropouts, but they renew the bonds of friendship at the same diner they frequented in high school. For director Barry Levinson, the diner is an American shrine. As one character says, summing it up, "We'll always have the diner."

AVAILABLE FROM VESTRON VIDEO, $39.95

GUEST CHECK

TALK THAT TALK

CHECK NO. 309500

- "Adam & Eve on a Raft" (two poached eggs on toast)
- "Bossy in a bowl" (Beef Stew)
- "Burn the British" (toasted English muffin)
- Burger "on the hoof" (very rare)
- "Frog sticks" (french fries)
- "MD, hold the hail" (Dr. Pepper, no ice)
- "Nervous pudding" (Jell-O)
- "Noah's boy with Murphy carrying a wreath" (ham, potato & cabbage)
- "Splash of red noise" (tomato soup)
- "Radio sandwich" (tuna)
- "Wrecked hen fruit" (scrambled egg)
- "Drag one through Georgia" (Coke with chocolate syrup)

THE DINER CLUB

Sean Hill and his gang at the Diner Appreciation Development Association (DADA) are wonderfully obsessed. Since 1987, they've published *Counter Culture* magazine ("The Journal of Diner Appreciation") which is a crazy quilt of news clippings, diner lore, intense treatises like "Co-opting Reality and Dinertude" and even poetry about french fries ("Those fries keep a-rollin'..."). An absolute must for any diner fanatic, membership and subscription can be had for $8 a year from: DADA / Counter Culture 2730 Monroe-Concord Road Troy, OH 45373.

4 CLASSIC DINERS

- **The Blue Benn, Bennington, Vermont.** An unbelievable find for diner lovers: a completely authentic, untainted late-1940s dining car beauty. Food ranges from traditional burgers & fries to health food. Sonny, the owner, is most proud of his falafels and "Havarti Cheese Melt."

- **Joy's Diner, Eureka, California.** Located in this Northern California town since the 1950s, Joy's is owned by Joy Moseby, a 5-foot 6-inch, 275 pound fry cook. "I eat the mistakes—that's why I'm so fat," she says. Feeling adventurous? Try "Joy's Grey Poupon Swiss Pastrami Burger," a toasted bun smothered with mustard, pastrami, melted Swiss cheese, grilled onions, a 1/4-pound hamburger patty, dill pickle, tomato, and lettuce.

- **Mickey's Diner, St. Paul, Minnesota.** So famous, it's in the National Register of Historic Places. A beautiful streamliner erected in 1937 and maintained in its Art Deco glory.

- **Joe's Diner, Lee, Massachusetts.** Nestled in the Berkshires, run by ex-Army cook Joe Sorrentino since 1955. Their motto: "We make friends, not money." Prices are rock-bottom—$4-5 tops. Specialty: "We make the best corned beef dinner in the world," Joe says proudly.

"The diner is like everybody's kitchen." — David Slovic

DINER FACTS

• The term diner originated with manufacturer Patrick J. Tierney, who in the early 1900s called his pre-fab restaurants "dining cars." Salesmen shortened the name to "diners."

• Tierney's other claim to fame: his company built the first diner with an indoor toilet in 1911.

• Contrary to popular belief, diners were never converted railroad dining cars. Rather, manufacturers of the late '30s were so impressed by the streamlined look of modern loco-motives that they imitated the style and called the diners "Streamliners."

• Diners through the years of their manufacture reflect the technological advances of the day. When materials like stainless steel, Naugahyde, and Formica became available, dinermakers quickly found uses for them. So what we think of as a "classic" diner was actually "state of the art" in its time.

• Diner or dinersaur? At their peak in the late 1940s, there were some 10,000 diners. Today there are only 3,000.

5 DINER MOVIE SCENES TO WATCH

• *Five Easy Pieces* (1970). Jack Nicholson instructs a waitress on diner etiquette.

• *The Brink's Job* (1978). Peter Falk and pals plan their heist at the Kitchenette Diner in Cambridge, Massachusetts.

• *The Blob* (1958). The creature attacks and swallows the Downington Diner in Downington, Pa. Great scene.

• *Dreamchild* (1985). Wow. Inside diner: waves of food, color, and sound. Outside diner: giant billboard of Jean Harlow.

• *Dark Passage* (1947). Humphrey Bogart stops for a quick bite while he's on the lam.

RECOMMENDED READING

American Diner
By Richard J. S. Gutman
and Elliott Kaufman
Harper & Row
154 pp., quality paperback. $15.95

This is THE diner bible—a perfect blend of pop history and diner photos, some in color. There's nothing like the vision of sunshine glimmering on ceramic floor, or reflections in stamped stainless steel. And the text is well-done. With astute attention to detail, Gutman traces the diner from its lunchwagon infancy, serving up a menu of architectural details, historical context and a full plate of dates, names, and diner "firsts" (first booths for the ladies, first in-house toilets, and so on). The last third of the book is a photo essay "Diners and Diner People" showing off Kaufman's great eye for atmosphere, for faces and diners' best details…as well as the pathos of their decay.

◆ ◆ ◆

"To see a diner's development," Gutman writes, "is to understand something important about the country's development and the American idea of what looks and feels good."

LIKE MOTHER USED TO MAKE

P.J. Tierney, father of the modern diner, died in 1917 of acute indigestion after eating at a diner.

POP POETRY

Jack Nicholson: "I'd like a plain omelette—no potatoes on the plate—a cup of coffee, and a side order of wheat toast."

Waitress: "I'm sorry, we don't have any side orders here."

Nicholson: "No side orders. You've got bread and a toaster of some kind?"

Waitress: "I don't make the rules."

Nicholson: "Okay, I'll make it as easy for you as I can. I'd like an omelette—plain—a chicken salad sandwich on wheat toast—no mayonnaise, no butter, no lettuce, and a cup of coffee."

Waitress: "A Number Two, chicken salad sandwich—no butter, no mayo, no lettuce, and a cup of coffee. Anything else?"

*"All night diners
Keep you awake
On black coffee
And a heart of gold."*

—James Brown,
"Livin' in America"

◆ ◆ ◆

Nicholson: "Yeah. Now all you have to do is hold the chicken, bring me the toast, give me a check for the chicken salad sandwich, and you haven't broken any rules."

Waitress: "You want me to hold the chicken, huh?"

Nicholson: "I want you to hold it between your knees."

—*Five Easy Pieces*

THE DINER STORE

If you've always wanted to own a classic diner, but only have a Blue Plate Special budget, Jerry Berta's Diner Store is perfect fare. Jerry makes and sells ceramic diner replicas that range from 7" salt and pepper shakers ($17.95 a pair) to elaborate 2-foot models that come complete with interior lighting and neon signs flashing "EAT" and "Dinerama" ($185.00). The Diner Store actually is a 1949 diner, restored to its original splendor (complete with pink formica ceilings and stainless steel sunburst patterns). Visit, or write for a mail order catalog.

The Diner Store
4500 14 Mile Road
Rockford, MI 49341
Ph: 616-696-CLAY

"BLUE PLATE SPECIAL?"

Everybody's heard the phrase, but few people knew where it came from.

During the Depression, a manufacturer started making a plate with separate sections for each part of a meal—sort of like a modern-day TV dinner tray. At first, for some reason, they were only available in blue.

Because they were inexpensive and saved on dish-washing, diners began using them for their low-priced daily specials.

Other colors eventually became available, but the name stuck.

DINOSAURS

A Mark of Extinction

Dino might! Kids love dinosaurs because they are big and fierce and more powerful than daddy. Toy marketers love dinosaurs because they don't have to pay any royalties for using them, and they're good for about $50 million worth of business every year. Is this a marriage made in heaven, or what?

Something old, something new. This is an exciting time for lovers of dinosaurs. There are new species being discovered every year (in fact, 40% of all known species have been discovered in the last twenty years).

Even the old species are being revised. The brontosaurus, for instance. No such thing any more. That was an embarassing mistake—the wrong head was attached to the wrong body and given the wrong name. Even the post office got it wrong on its famous dinosaur stamps. Any kid can tell you its now called an Apatosaurus, and they take great glee that we pitiful,

giant, soon-to-be-extinct adults don't know this.

Still, it's reassuring that dinosaurs continue to be hip after all these eons, the hippest oversized dead things to stomp through popular culture (not counting Elvis). Reassuring, because long after Homo Sapiens kills itself off, maybe cockroach children will carry bookbags sporting little cartoon pictures of us. We can only hope.

Pop Poetry

"I am real now don't you know
Born 10 billion years ago.
But you don't love me enough and so
I'm planning to go away.
I'm a little dinosaur
I'm a little dinosaur
I'm a little dinosaur
And I'm planning to go away."
—Jonathon Richman & the Modern Lovers

ULTIMATE DINOSAUR MODELS

These are the incredible half-scale moving models you've seen in museum exhibits, designed with the assistance of Dr. Jack Horner, leading new wave paleontologist. They bellow, they bite, they care for their young, they fight, they move their heads, mouths and tails. You can have one in your home or office for between $85,000 and $115,000 (air compressor not included). Dinosaurs currently available include T. Rex (pictured below), Stegasaurus, Apatosaurus, Ankylosaurus, Pachycephalosaurus, Corythosaurus, Pteranodon and the newly discovered "good mother lizard" Maiasaura, with offspring. For more information, contact:

Kokoro
22900 Ventura Boulevard, Suite 225
Woodland Hills, CA 91364
(818) 992-8918

Dinosaur Duds

Toothsome T. Rex t-shirt design. Also available: T. Rex swallowing another dinosaur ("Lunch!").

Child sizes $12.95. Adult sizes $14.95. Add $3.50 shipping. Zoobooks, 930 West Washington Street, Suite 14, San Diego, CA 92103-9908. (619)299-5034.

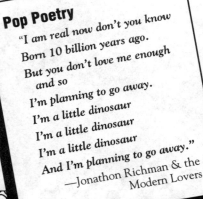

There were probably 150-250 species of dinosaurs.

We Ask the Experts:
Why Did Dinosaurs Go Extinct?

Climate got too hot. —Disney's Fantasia

From smoking cigarettes. —Gary Larsen, The Far Side

"High insurance rates." —David Letterman

"God killed off the dinosaurs with hydrogen bombs. There is no doubt about it." —Peter Gerits, Dutch Paleontologist, quoted in a supermarket tabloid

"I don't give a shit why the dinosaurs went extinct. I want to know what they were like when they were alive. We really don't know a damned thing about the dinosaurs. But they were around for 140 million years, and we've only been here for 4 million. So you'd think we'd want to know why they were successful, instead of always concentrating on why they died."

—Jack Horner, Montana State University

From a six-mile wide asteroid hitting Earth with an explosive force equal to 100 million tons of TNT.

—Walter Alvarez, Univ. of California

The dinosaurs were slaughtered for sport by big game hunters from Mars.

—Story from the tabloids

"It wasn't a death star. It was death by diarrhea. Triceratops were immigrants and they brought diseases with them. Dinosaurs were already weakened by environmental pressures, it didn't take much to finish them off."—Robert Bakker, Univ. of Colorado

Inflatable Party Dinosaurs

These inflatable creatures come with their own educational videos.

#75 — 55 inch Tyrannosaurus Fun Pack includes "Dinosaurs, Dinosaurs, Dinosaurs" video.

#76 — 60 inch Stegosaurus Fun Pack comes with "More Dinosaurs" video.

Both $29.95 + $4.50 shipping from Zoobooks, 930 West Washington Street, Suite 14, San Diego, CA 92103-9908. (619) 299-5034

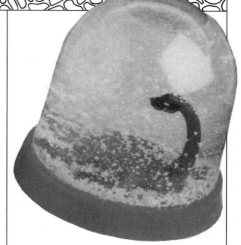

Sno-Domes Killed the Dinosaurs

Ice Age killed off the dinosaurs? This bucking bronto in a snow-dome illustrates the beginning of the end.

#612200 Snow-Globe Brontosaurus from Bully Toys. Call for a local retailer (800) 289-2855.

TOKYO BEWARE!

Giant, furry Godzilla-like dino slippers go "boom" and roar with each step you take. Acrylic plush feet, vinyl claws. Six AA batteries for sound effects (not included).

Adult size S (3-5) (fits most children), M (6-8), L (9-11). #471X, $35.00 + $6.45 shipping from Post Scripts, 3200 S.E. 14 Avenue, P.O. Box 21628, Ft. Lauderdale, FL 33316. (800) 327-3799

Boom!
Bam!
Boom!
Bam!

Dinosaurs ranged in size from nearly 100 feet long and 3 stories high to about the size of a small turkey.

Dino Want a Cracker?

- Is little Petey Parakeet a dinosaur? Many scientists believe dinosaurs were more related to birds than lizards. They think some had feathers, bright colors and even birdlike songs.

- Shakespeare never mentioned dinosaurs. Neither did anybody else until 1841, which was the year the term was coined, the result of fossils found 20 years earlier in Tilgate and Stonesfield, England. A few dinosaur bones were discovered before then, but nobody quite knew what to make of them (a dinosaur thigh bone discovered in the 1600s was mistakenly assumed to be from a giant human wiped out by Noah's Great Flood).

- Even latter day paleontologists make mistakes. Besides the (literally) wrongheaded brontosaurus fiasco, a renowned early scientist even put the head on the wrong end of a skeleton he assembled. And in 1930 a scientific mission in Tehran thought they had discovered the ribs and vertebrae of an unusual dinosaur. Instead they turned out to be pieces of an abandoned haymaking machine that had been caught in a landslide.

- Only two states have official state fossils, unless you count elected state representatives. South Dakota (the Triceratops) and Utah (the Allosaurus).

Improve Your Sex Life

Huge and startling! This eight foot Pteranodon hung over your marital bed can rekindle a clinging level of closeness with your loved one; hung over the kids' bed can keep them from bothering you in the night.

Dinos, Bigfoot, LBJ & Elvis Still Alive!
Actual Stories From the Tabloids

- Pterodactyls have been terrorizing Peruvian villages in the Andes Mountains, carrying away llamas and eroding the villagers' property values and quality of life.

- Soviet scientist, working with frozen dinosaur eggs in Siberia, have detected heartbeats. They're trying to hatch them for use as battlefield weapons.

- But not to worry: US scientists, in a sort of Stegasaurus Defense Initiative, are experimenting with sophisticated cloning techniques to bring the dinosaurs back. Again, as battlefield weapons.

- Not that all dinosaurs are violent, say scientists who have found that some of the smaller breeds are trainable, to the point of making halfway decent household pets. Still, we're not buying one until we're sure they've licked that diarrhea problem (see *What Killed the Dinosaurs?*).

- In related news, scientists have found a Stone Age tribe in Papua, New Guinea that worships a faded photograph of former US President Lyndon B. Johnson as the image of a god-king. "One of the most bizarre situations I've ever encountered," said anthropologist Dr. Ulrich Ritterfeldt, who witnessed their rituals, which presumably involved beagle-torturing, long-winded speeches, funny hats and balloons.

CHOCO-VORES

Inside each chocolate dinosaur egg created by the renowned Cocolat are ten chocolate dinosaurs. Foil wrapped and raffia tied.

CARTOONASAURUS BOOKS

ALLEY OOP

A classic comic about a time-travelling caveman called Alley Oop. In this first collection from 1946, Alley can be found hanging out with Napoleon, fighting pirates and stagecoach robbers, even thwarting Cro-Magnon kidnappers.

#ALLESC, $13.95 + 1.50 shipping, Kitchen Sink Press, 2 Swamp Road. Princeton, WI 54968. (414) 295-6922 / FAX (414) 295-6878

Cadillacs & Dinosaurs

Here's the premise: it's 2490 AD. Natural disasters and marauding dinosaurs are commonplace and the human race is reduced to a desperate struggle to stay alive. Will humanity survive?

#CADDSC Softcover $12.95 + $1.50 shipping from Kitchen Sink Press, 2 Swamp Road, Princeton, WI 54968. (414) 295-6922 / FAX (414) 295-6878

Dinosaurs For Hire: Dinosaurs Rule!

"Three walkin', talkin' gun-toting' reptiles fight crime and injustice the only way they know how: with brute force and guns the size of imported cars!"

$5.95 + 1.50 shipping from Malibu Graphics, 1355 Lawrence Dr. #212, Newbury Park, CA 91320. (805) 499-3015

Hey, Dino Brain!

Dinosaur Brains by Albert Bernstein and Sydney Craft Rozen. This book says that people in corporate settings devolve back several hundred million years. According to the authors, dinosaur brains "are the foundations on which our own brains are built," so you must manage your own and others' reptilian responses if you want to survive in the corporate swamp. Full of scientifically dubious advice like: "The people at the bottom have to do what the head dinosaur says if they want to stay in the herd."

$19.95 + 2.50 shipping from: John Wiley & Sons Publishing 1 Wiley Drive Somerset, NJ 08875 (800) 225-5945

"How long had it been since I had seen a little Dinosaur, so perfect, so full of his own Dinosaur essence?" — Italo Calvino

The Land of the Fiberglassosaurus

Sure, we could send you to great museums—the Smithsonian in Washington, DC, the American Museum of Natural History in New York, or the excellent Tyrell Museum of Palaeontology in Alberta, Canada. But why bore you to death with facts, bones and excruciatingly accurate exhibits, when there's a plethora of scientifically dubious fiberglass imitations available? These are fun dinosaurs, pop dinosaurs—and all they want to do is entertain you. Best of all, you can see them all in one day.

• *Wall Drugs, Wall, South Dakota. (605) 279-2175.* Your fiberglass dinosaur odyssey begins near the Badlands, a place where real dinosaurs would feel at home. Follow the endless signs to Wall Drugs near the interchange of I-90 and State Highway 240. Get your picture taken with the 80-foot high dinosaur while you sip your loss-leader free ice water and 5¢ coffee. Next stop, Dinosaur Park.

• *Dinosaur Park, Skylight Drive, Rapid City, SD. (605) 343-8687*

From Wall, mosey over to Rapid City, 52 miles due west on I-90, and head for the hills. Dinosaur Park, overlooking Rapid City on Skylight Drive, allows you to hang out with dozens of full-scale fiberglass dinosaur replicas. Bring a silly attitude and a camera—there are photo opportunities aplenty.

Next head 45 miles south on Highway 16 to The Flintstones' Bedrock City.

• *Flintstones' Bedrock City, Highway 16, PO Box 649, Custer, SD 57730, (605) 673-4079.* This modest theme park and RV campground features six acres of furnished lifesized Flintstone houses, a dinosaur slide, Mt. Rockmore (with a Flintstones parody of nearby Mt. Rushmore) and prehistoric train. Photo opportunities include Dino, Fred, Barney, Wilma and Betty themselves. Incidentally, there's also one near the Grand Canyon on Grand Canyon Highway (Highway 64 and 180),Williams, AZ 86046 (602) 635-2600.

False Teeth

These replica fossil teeth look just like the ones old dinosaurs left in glasses near their beds some 400 million years ago. Each tooth is shaped and etched in tough "polystone," handstained and wrapped with parchment information card.

• SC-12301 Tyrannosaurus Tooth (3 1/2")
• SC-12302 Camarasaurus Tooth (2 1/2")
• SC-12303 Allosaurus Tooth (2 1/2")
• SC-12304 Megalosaurus Tooth (2")

$9.00 each + 2.50 shipping from:
Safari Limited
P.O. Box 630685
Miami, FL 33163
(800) 554-5414 / FAX (305) 621-6894

"Dinosaurs have edged out flamingos as icons of kitsch. I even saw dinosaur toilet paper with a different creature on each perforated segment."

—Stephen Jay Gould,
Natural History Magazine

TO BEDROCK CITY FAMILY FUN!

Prehistoric Poster

6-foot long poster reproduction from Yale University's Peabody Museum features realistic reptiles on a romp 'round prehistoricville. Comes with 40 page guide. Item #90804 — $12.95 + $3.25 shipping from:

Discovery Center
Lawrence Hall of Science
University of California at Berkeley
Berkeley, CA 94702
(415)642-1016

Puffy Dinosaur Stickers

$1.50 per pack of 4+ $3.00 shipping per any size order. California Pacific Designs, PO Box 2660,Alameda, CA 94501 (415) 521-7914.

"Everybody do the Dinosaur"— Was/Not Was

Grumpy Paleontologist Hates Pop Dinosaurs

On **Dino Riders**, made by Tyco Toys: "They've juxtaposed dinosaurs with science fiction. On the package it says 'scientifically accurate.' Does the accuracy include spacemen? The proportions and posture are pretty awful. I think they used a rather fat elephant model."

On **Definitely Dinosaur** (Playskool), which includes cavemen: "C'mon. Humans arose on the scene about 60 million years after the last dinosaur died."

On *The Land Before Time* **animated movie:** "They should've made it with possums or something. Instead they made a baby triceratops look like Elmer Fudd with a frill on his back."

—**Dr. David Weishampel**
John Hopkins University
Interviewed in
the *SF Chronicle*

60 Million Years in the Making!
The WPC Dinosaur Film Festival

- Gertie the Dinosaur, by Windsor McKay. (1914). The very first animated movie ever.
- The Lost World (1925)
- One Million, BC (1940)
- Unknown Island (1948)
- Godzilla (1956)
- The Land Unknown (1957)
- Teenage Caveman (1958)
- The Lost World (Remake) (1960)
- Dinosaurus (1960)
- One Million Years BC (1966)
- Women of the Prehistoric Planet (1966)
- A Man Called Flintstone (1966)
- Destroy All Monsters (1969)
- When Dinosaurs Ruled the Earth (1970)
- The Land That Time Forgot (1975)
- At the Earth's Core (1976)
- The People That Time Forgot (1977). Sequel to "The Land..."
- The Day Time Ended (1980)
- Baby—Secret of the Lost Legend (1985)
- The Land Before Time (1988)

Why Do Kids Love Dinosaurs?

- "Big, fierce, and extinct."
  —Shep White, Child Psychologist

- "Bigness and power is something for a young child to conquer. He animates the dinosaur to gain control over his anxieties and can project onto them the biting he'd like to do to his baby sister.

  "Dinosaurs become something to emulate, a source of awe and admiration. If you're a dinosaur, you're bigger than anything. By associating with powerful things, you take on power."
  —Sebastiano Santostefano, McLean Hospital

Dinosaurs... You Dig?

If you like dirty, painstaking labor and you're willing to pay to do it, a dinosaur dig may be just the ticket for you (or for that matter, we have a few choice projects around the Whole Pop offices...).

The payoff? Being involved in scientifically important work, finding fossils millions of years old, and earning a really unusual resume entry. Expeditions travel to sites in the US and around the world; you pay your own travel expenses plus fees in the range of $500-$1600.

For information, contact:

- **Denver Museum of Natural History**
2001 Colorado Blvd.
Denver, CO 80205
(303) 370-6304

- **Earthwatch**
Box 403
Watertown, MA 02272
(617) 926-8200

- **Research Expeditions, Univ. of California, Berkeley, CA**
93720 (415) 642-6586

- **Museum of Science & Industry,** 4015 SW Canyon Road, Portland, OR 97221.
(503) 222-2828

Disco

The 1970s:
Winter of Our Disco Intent

The discotheque—the word means "record library" in French—appeared during the early 1970s in the primarily black, Latino and gay neighborhoods of New York City. But it didn't take long before uptown Manhattanites were hailing Yellow Cabs to Fire Island for a night of dancing on the wild side.

And wild it certainly was. The disco experience was a voyage into a far-out world of outrageous costumes and gyrating flesh, dancers high on cocaine and flying on the magic carpet of a relentless beat. Polyester shirts, glittering mirrored balls, flashing strobes and mystifying fog machines hustled and bumped their way into the mainstream of American consciousness.

Discomania. By 1977 over 15,000 discos were thump-thump-thumping all across the United States. The newly energized record industry cranked out ready-to-play vinyl in a rate and manner comparable to McDonald's fast-food. Clothing designers like Yves St. Laurent and Halston jumped on board with wide collars and platform shoes, while the power of the trend catapulted new stars like John Travolta and the Bee Gees onto the covers of *Time* and

Newsweek. Disco was a music, a place, a fashion, an attitude, and—to use the word of the 1970s—a lifestyle.

Death Of Disco. The mega-million dollar disco movement stayed at the top of a high plateau until about 1980. Amid a backlash of punk rock, New Wave and neo-puritanism, *Rolling Stone* announced what was becoming obvious: the death of disco.

Disco now spins restlessly in its shallow grave, dormant in the collective consciousness of the nation, waiting to come alive again. And why not? This year's trend usually mirrors what was happening two decades ago.

And say, isn't it about time for another Nixon revival?

IT'S BAAAAAAACK!

Club 1970 is a disco revival society. Each week they rent regular venues around Los Angeles and San Francisco, hang up clusters of mirrored balls and pump out the boogie beat. "All '70s, all the time."

Interested? Dust off your platform shoes and polyester shirt and contact these retro-revolutionaries.

- **In Los Angeles, write: Ground Zero Inc., P.O. Box 292047, Los Angeles., CA 90027.**
- **In San Francisco, call: (415) 541-5010.**

The Whole Pop Catalog Disco Top 10

Never Can Say Goodbye—Gloria Gaynor

Love To Love You Baby—Donna Summer

Le Freak—Chic

I Need A Man—Grace Jones

The Hustle—Van McCoy

Funkytown—Lipps Inc.

That's The Way I Like It—K.C. & the Sunshine Band

That's Where The Happy People Go—Trammps

YMCA—Village People

Celebration—Kool & the Gang

"The bottom line is that disco is here to stay." —Ray Cavino of Warner Bros. Records

Disco Discovery

You want to see where it all began? Here are some spots of former famous discos to check out in New York City. Just follow the echo of that incessant thump-thump-thump.

• **2001 Odyssey** was the disco where *Saturday Night Fever* was filmed. Located at 64th Street and 3rd Avenue in Brooklyn, this neighborhood disco with its flashing illuminated dance floor soon became the place for droves of Tony Manero look-alikes. Take a (reckless) drive across the Verrazano Bridge and see if you can find it. Last time we looked, it was still there.

• **Studio 54**—America's most exclusive and controversial club was located at 244 West 54th Street, in what was once the baroque Fortune Gallo Opera House and later a CBS studio for TV shows like *The $64,000 Question*. Throngs gathered outside every night to see who would be hand-picked for admittance by Napoleonic gatekeeper and owner Steve Rubell.

DISCO HELL—THE WHOLE POP MARATHON FILM FEST

Hollywood went Disco in a big way, only to crash and burn. These flicks (with one or two notable exceptions) were failures at the box office. Most are available on video.

Car Wash (1976). Comedy for the disco crowd from the Dee Luxe Car Wash. Starring Richard Pryor, George Carlin.

Saturday Night Fever (1977). This blockbuster movie changed John Travolta from a TV Sweathog into an international sweetheart and made the white suit a disco garb de rigueur. The soundtrack album by the Bee Gees, K.C. and the Sunshine Band, and Kool and The Gang was all time best-seller at 25 million copies until Michael Jackson's *Thriller*.

T. G. I. F. (1978). Donna Summer and Jeff Goldblum star in this wacky discotheque adventure.

Can't Stop the Music (1980). The Village People movie starring the Indian, the Construction Worker, the Policeman, the Biker, the GI and Bruce Jenner. "... A hype disaster...peopled by butch gay stereotypes of both sexes pretending to be straight. The pervasive tackiness is unrelieved."—**Time Out**

Roller Boogie (1979). Linda Blair of *Exorcist* fame straps on some skates and hits the rink in this throw-away roller disco movie.

Xanadu (1980). Inspired by the poet Coleridge, this fantasy features Olivia Newton John as the muse of disco who falls in love with a nightclub owner while the great Gene Kelly, wearing too much eye shadow, tries to dance his way into the disco decade. Music by Electric Light Orchestra.

The Spirit of '76 (1991). Starring '70s teen-idol-grown-old, David Cassidy, as an adventurer from the year 2176 who travels back in time for a raucous romp through America circa 1976. Also features Leif Garrett and tons of disco culture.

BEE GEES

The disco beat was set at about 125 beats a minute to simulate an excited heart rate.

Mood Rings

Instead of asking "What's your sign?" first glance at his or her mood ring. This fad item from the disco era changes colors depending on the wearer's mood.

#F08, adjustable size, silver band. $9.00 + 3.25 shipping from The Daily Planet, P.O. Box 1313, New York, NY 10013. (212) 334-0006 / FAX (212) 334-1158.

Kiss My Smiley Face

What generic icon could better reflect the disco years than a bright yellow, unflaggingly perky and thoroughly impenetrable smiling face? On these glow-in-the-dark boxer shorts, they prompt the question: "Are those smiley faces on your shorts, or are you just glad to see me?"

#T2133, size 30-32; #T2134, size 34-36; #T2135, size 38-40; #T2136; size 42-44, $12.98 + 3.95 shipping from Funny Side Up, 425 Stump Rd., North Wales, PA 19454. (215) 361-5130.

Great Disco Dance Names

Taxi Driver

The Bump

The Freak

Ride-a-Bike

The Freeze

L.A. Lock

The Funky Glide

Bonaparte's Retreat

The Disco Duck

The Mule Dig

NY Bus Stop

COMPACT DISCO

Most of disco hits you'd ever want to hear are available as reissues on recent CD offerings:

• *Saturday Night Fever*, a double disc collection of mainstream hits. Check your local record store.

• Rhino Records' 15 volume collection, *Have A Nice Day: Super Hits Of The '70s*, is an encyclopedic compendium of 1970s songs , including a generous smattering of disco. Rhino also offers *The Village People's Greatest Hits*.

Each CD $12.95 postpaid. Rhino, 2225 Colorado

Fashion Passion

Disco denizens worked to look their glitziest 24 hours a day. Here are some of the hottest numbers.

Bell Bottoms — Tight in the thighs and butt and wide at the hem to accentuate the swing of the hips and beat of the feet.

Shorts — Tight and tiny hot pants or gym-style boxing shorts; both looked steamy in satin and let you flash your legs as you sweated the night away.

Shoes — High platform shoes, from three to ten inches tall, defied nature in their very design, becoming an icon of the daredevil disco attitude.

Shirts — Polyester, worn open to show your chest hair, cleavage, gold medallion and/or coke spoon, preferably with bright reproductions of the Great Masters' paintings.

Suits — The double-knit leisure suit was a favorite, always worn with a vest and your shirt collar on top of the lapel like Travolta.

Avenue, Santa Monica, CA 90404. (800) 432-0020.

• Other hit-oriented collections: *Those Fabulous '70s*, *Those Funky '70s*, and the dynamic *Disco '70s*.

Cassettes, $14.99 each, CDs, $18.99 each. Add 4.00 shipping   From the '70s Preservation Society. (800) 666-1972.

Skirts and Dresses — Spaghetti straps and a slit past the hip to show skin; wrap-around skirt to show movement (looked great with a halter top.)

Headwear — A popular "pimp" hat in a variety of colors. Barrettes, in leather or with feathers, kept your hair out of your eyes.

Where to get some? The best bet for disco fashion is your local thrift store or vintage clothing boutiques. There are only a few stores specializing exclusively in '70s wear, including:

• **Screaming Mimi's, 22 East 4th St., New York, NY 10003. (212) 677-6464.** Call for information; they handle mail order but have no catalog.

• **The New Government, 1427 Haight St., San Francisco, CA 94117. (415) 431-1830.** They don't handle mail order, but if you're in the neighborhood…

Have a Ball

Mirrored balls were (literally!) fixtures in every 1970s disco. Shine a spotlight on this 8" ball, covered with mirrored facets. Rotates continuously via a small motor.

#6977 ball, $29.98 + 4.95 shipping. #6978 motor, $14.98 + 4.20 shipping. Johnson Smith Co., 4514 19th Court East, P.O. Box 25500, Bradenton, FL 34206. (813) 747-2356 / FAX (813) 746-7896.

The Man in the White Suit

The original disco White Suit in *Saturday Night Fever* was selected by Travolta himself at the Leading Man clothing store in Brooklyn.

A parody copy of The Suit appeared in the movie *Airplane*. In *Staying Alive*, a thoroughly 1980s and depressed Tony Manero dresses up in his old threads and hits the streets. In his own brave and poignant words, "I wanna strut."

Whatever happened to the actual suit from the 1977 movie? Movie critic Gene ("the tall thin one") Siskel owns it.

You Lite Up My Life

Have a nice decor! Buy a string of these happy folk and color your world! Seven light-up heads in green, red and yellow in each set.

$15.95 + 5.00 shipping from Ruby Montana's Pinto Pony, 603 Second Ave., Seattle, WA 98104. (206) 621-PONY.

SAVE THE SEVENTIES

A few years back, two disco fans started the **'70s Preservation Society,** part club and part merchandising effort. They now claim a roster of over 80,000 happy-faced members. Yearly parties for members are also the sites of the annual Lava Lamp Awards.

Initiation fee is appropriately $7.70, and the perks include special merchandise offers. To join, and/or for a catalog of merchandise, contact '70s Preservation Society, P.O. Box 585, Cooper Station, New York, NY 10276. (800) 666-1972.

Dance 'Til You Drop

Never be a wall flower again. Learn how to disco with this 60 minute video. It teaches you other dances, too, including slow ones.

#6452, $29.98 + 3.50 shipping. The Lighter Side, 4514 19th St. Court East, P.O. Box 25600, Bradenton, Florida 34206-5600. (813) 747-2356.

Required **R**eading

• *The Seventies: From Hot Pants To Hot Tubs* by Andrew J. Edelstein and Kevin McDonough. This fun guide to the decade includes film, fashion, personalities and, of course, disco.

$13.95 + 1.50 shipping from Penguin Books, Box 120, Bergenfield, NJ 07621-0120. (800) 526-0275 / FAX (800) 227-9604.

• *It's A Wonderful Lifestyle* by Candi Strecker. A three-volume publication focusing entirely on the 1970s, from both a personal and encyclopedic point of view. Definitely worth a spin, and you can't beat the price.

Vol. 1: fashion, hair, cars, TV and movies.

Vol. 2: The Bicentennial, furniture, crafts, food, sex, drugs, books and comix.

Vol. 3: Pop Music: rock, disco, top 40 and more.

3 issues, $3.00 per volume to Candi Strecker, 590 Lisbon, San Francisco, CA 94112.

Disney

Of Mice And Man

Walter Elias Disney was just 22 years old when he arrived in Hollywood in 1923. He was a cocky young animator from the Midwest when he first developed a cartoon character, Oswald the Rabbit. The cartoon bunny was so well-received by the public that people wrote the studio, not for the artist's autograph, but for Oswald's.

And manufacturers began offering money for merchandising rights. Unfortunately, the character contractually belonged to Universal Studios so Walt didn't

share in these profits. When contract negotiation came up with Universal unwilling to cut him in, Walt plopped an Oswald the Lucky Rabbit badge on his distributor's desk in Kansas City and exclaimed, "Here, you can have the little bastard! He's all yours."

Birth of a Notion. Legend has it that Disney was riding the train back to Hollywood from that fateful meeting in 1928 when he happened to take particular note of the whistle blowing: it seemed to sound like "a m-m-mowaouse." Before he knew it, he had drawn a quick sketch of a mouse. His wife, Lillian, talked him out of calling the new character "Mortimer," and suggested Mickey.

Ub Iwerks, a talented animator and friend of Walt's (and too often the butt of Walt's sometimes cruel practical jokes) redesigned Mickey and became his chief animator (some say that, despite legend, Iwerks originated Mickey as well).

Though Mickey appeared in two silent cartoons, it wasn't until the studio's first sound cartoon, *Steamboat Willie* in 1928, that the public went crazy for him. When the jaunty little mouse played *Turkey in the Straw* on a cow's teeth, animation's silent era was stone cold dead.

By 1931, more than a million children had become members of the original Mickey Mouse Club. Walt had learned a few things from the Oswald Rabbit affair, so all manner of Mickey Mouse toys and other licensed products began to scamper off the assembly line.

Soon, Mickey was joined by a supporting cast: Minnie, Donald, and the rest. But Mickey continued to be the mainstay of Disney productions. For some 20 years (with Walt first supplying the mouse's high squeaky voice and, more recently, Wayne Allwine) he was the focus of the entire operation and eventually became the Disney corporate symbol.

Today, Mickey's image is the number one most-reproduced in the world, with over 7,500 items bearing his cheerful little image. Jesus is number two, and Elvis is number three.

The name "Mortimer Mouse," discarded in favor of Mickey, was later used for an obnoxious college-kid rival for Minnie's affections.

THE DONALD

Popular as Mickey was, it wasn't long before he was upstaged by one of his co-stars. Donald Duck was less sweetly lovable and more prone to all-too-human attributes like greed, jealousy and vindictiveness, making him more interesting than that predictably goody-goody mouse.

In 1933 Walt Disney signed on Clarence Nash, who gave Donald Duck the voice that would stay with him for more than 50 years. "Ducky" Nash also vocalized for the Nephews and Daisy by raising his Donald voice up an octave.

"Unca" Donald's nephews—Huey, Dewey, and Louie—first appeared in 1938, Daisy, in 1940, and the miserly millionaire Scrooge McDuck, in 1947. Gyro Gearloose, the screwball chicken scientist, invented himself onto the scene in 1952.

While Mickey appeared on thousands of products, Donald Duck carved a niche for himself by becoming the only major Disney cartoon character who ever shilled for food products—Donald Duck orange juice, bread, rice, coffee, popcorn, and soda pop.

3 Faces of Walt

Understanding the highly complex man who created on the back of a mouse is apparently difficult. Walt Disney is somebody who excited great passions—people who worked with him either loved or hated him (sometimes both simultaneously). That's why we're recommending three different biographies, ranging from the adoring to the bitterly rancorous. Where lies the truth? We don't know, but from sweet to sour, here they are:

• *Walt Disney: An American Original* by Bob Thomas. Disney often changed the fairy tales he made into movies to make them more appealing. Thomas' book doesn't go as far as changing history, but his book manages to cast the best possible light on some of the more disturbing facets of Walt's life and times.

$5.95 + 4.00 shipping from Pocket Books, 200 Old Tappan Road, Old Tappan, NJ 07675. (800) 223-2348.

• *Walt Disney And Other Assorted Characters* by Jack Kinney. Sure, everyone employed by Disney worked hard. But they played hard, too. This fun book is an unauthorized account of the early years that gives you a behind the scenes look, through uncensored anecdotes, at the Disney you never knew.

#1688431, $5.98 + 4.00 shipping. Barnes & Noble, 126 Fifth Ave., New York, NY 10011-5666. (800) 344-2470.

• *Disney's World* by Leonard Mosley. The untold story of the animation film mogul, a complex and lonely man, perfectionistic visionary, genius, and ruthless authoritarian. This book tells all—perhaps more than you care to know.

$18.95 + 3.00 shipping from Stein & Day, Scarborough House, Briarcliff Manor, NY 10510.

Carl Barks was the man responsible for giving the Donald Duck comic books an unusually high level of artistry and creativity.

"Disneyana" Collectors

- **Storyboard.** Bi-monthly collectors' memorabilia magazine focuses on materials.

  One year, $18.00. 2512 Artesia Blvd., Redondo Beach, CA 90278. (213) 376-8788.

- **The Mouse Club.** Over 1000 collectors of Disney memorabilia. Club distributes information (through correspondence and a bi-monthly newsletter) about available items both old and new. Provides advice, answers to questions and lots of background information. Free ads, conventions, Disney shows.

  Yearly membership $22.00 to 2056 Cirone Way, San Jose, CA 95124. (408) 377-2590.

- **National Fantasy Club for Disneyana Collectors.** Boasts over 1000 Disneyana diehards in nearly all 50 states and three foreign countries.

  P.O. Box 19212, Irvine, CA 92713. (714) 241-8104.

Mickey Memorabilia

In 1929, Disney needed money. As a matter of fact, he always needed money, because whenever he did make a profit he would pour it right back into another new idea. In 1929, he sold the use of Mickey's likeness for $300 to a man who wanted to print the character on writing tablets for school children. That was only the beginning.

In 1933, Walt granted a license to the Ingersoll-Waterbury Company which began manufacturing the first Mickey Mouse watches. At the time, they sold for somewhere between $2.95 and $3.75 each. Today, housed in their original boxes, they'd sell for around $400.

Every Disney character item is worth something to someone, because so many people have such fond memories of their youth spent with Disney entertainment. Here are some typical dollar figures:

- A 6-inch ceramic bank of Happy from Snow White from the early 1960s—$60.
- Mattel's Mickey, Donald and Goofy Skediddlers toys from the early '60s. All three in their original boxes—around $50.
- That Mickey Mouse Magic Kit you got as a premium from Mars Candy in 1955 can fetch as much as $45.
- Got any Donald Duck cars lying around? The Paperino Polytoys (Italy) car with Huey, Dewey and Louie in the rumble seat is valued at $75 in top condition. The wind-up car originally made of tin by Marx in 1955 is worth $125.
- In the late 1950s, Linemar (a subsidiary of Marx) sold a battery-operated Mickey the Magician. It's now worth about $250.

For more information about what your memories are worth in dollars and cents, check out *Stern's Guide to Disney Collectibles Vols. I and II* by Mike Stern.

Each volume $14.95 + 2.00 shipping from: The House of Collectibles 201 East 50th Street New York, NY 10022 (800) 733-3000

SNOW WHITE

When Disney proposed a feature-length animated movie, the conventional wisdom was that Disney was completely reckless to attempt it. "Nobody could sit through a whole 90 minutes of that stuff," they said.

Disney argued that his cartoons had become so popular that exhibitors were showing up to six of the short films back-to-back. Once again, over the "better judgment" of his brother/partner Roy, Walt risked complete financial ruin and launched full-steam ahead into a feature-length cartoon.

Snow White and the Seven Dwarfs was made for a record cost of $2.6 million, requiring over 2 million drawings. But Walt was right. When it was released in 1937, it was a smash.

Viewers were astonished to see the level of character development and emotional depth never before seen in the slapstick world of cartoons. The characters seemed real and the soundtrack gave the world such song hits as *Heigh Ho, I'm Wishing,* and *Whistle While You Work.*

Much Too Grimm

Maybe it's a good thing that Disney changed the stories and fairy tales he adapted. The originals were scary and pretty darned morbid.

♥ In Grimm's *Snow White,* for instance, the Queen ordered the hunter to bring back Snow White's liver and lungs as proof of her death. The hunter brought back a boar's organs instead, which the Queen, believing them to be Snow White's, promptly boiled and ate.

♥ Happy ending: the Queen was later invited to a wedding where she discovered that Snow White was the bride! The newlyweds forced her to put on red hot iron shoes and dance in them until she died.

♥ In the original story of *Pinocchio,* the un-named cricket didn't last long. The puppet squashed him with a mallet.

♥ *Cinderella's* slippers? In Grimm, they weren't made of glass, but of gold. When one step-sister realized that her foot was too big for the shoe she cut off her toes. The second step-sister cut off her heels.

♥ In Hans Christian Andersen's original *Little Mermaid,* the unlucky heroine gets turned into sea foam. The end. Great story, huh?

Classic After Classic After Classic

• *Alice in Wonderland.* Everybody's first choice as the best visual adaptation of the Lewis Carroll classic. VHS #704218 (75 min.)

• *Dumbo.* State-of-the-art animation for its time. The film has been a favorite for millions of children throughout the world and still stands the test of time. VHS #743639 (63 min.)

• *Bambi.* Maybe the most beautiful animated film ever made. And what a supporting cast! Thumper, Old Prince and the rest live forever in this film that runs the gamut of emotions. VHS #925575 (69 min.)

Each video, $26.95 + 4.95 shipping. Postings, P.O. Box 8001, Hilliard, OH 43026. (800) 262-6604 / FAX (614) 777-1470.

• *Cinderella.* Disney's adaptation of this fairy tale filled with romance, fantasy and music is one of his most brilliant! Comes with a Little Golden Book with photos from the film.

#WD005 Cinderella Video and Storybook, $26.95 + 5.95 shipping from Special Interest Video, 100 Enterprise Place, P.O. Box 7022, Dover, DE 19903-7022. (800) 522-0502 / FAX (302) 678-9200.

More people saw *Snow White* in its first run in 1937 than saw *Star Wars* in its first release in 1977.

Inkers Do It With Great Animation

Disney Animation: The Illusion of Life by Frank Thomas and Ollie Johnston. Nearly 600 pages (including 489 full-color plates and thousands of B&W illustrations) analyzing the art of animation from the Disney point of view. A monumental, comprehensive and visually stunning work by two veteran Disney animators. More than a mere coffee table book (although it is beautifully put together)—it provides in-depth details on how Disney animators portray personality, motion and lifelike effects. For any serious appreciator or student of animation.

#64827X, $39.95 + 4.95 shipping from Postings, P.O. Box 8001, Hilliard, OH 43026. (800) 262-6604 / FAX (614) 777-1470.

DISNEY FACTS

• Walt Disney decided to give his overworked staff a reward after *Snow White*: an all-expenses paid weekend at a plush, posh Palm Springs resort. Walt was determined that they be given the royal treatment. The usually well-behaved and reserved Disney staff really relaxed; in fact, according to those present, they had a virtual orgy. Walt was appalled, and he and Lillian left early. He never mentioned the incident to anybody afterward. Ever.

• **Hello, Dali!** In the early 1950s, Salvador Dali and Walt Disney considered doing an animated film together, but the discussion stage is as far as the project got. Too bad!

• In 1985, Donald Duck received nearly 300 write-in votes in the

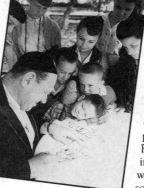

Swedish parliamentary elections.

• How many spots does a Dalmatian have? If it's Disney's papa dog Pongo, it's 72. Mama Perdita had 68. Each of the 99 pups had 30. Fortunately for the inkers, all the dogs weren't in every frame, so the grand total came to just 6,469,952 spots over the 113,760 drawings for the movie. Whew!

• It was none other than the "Big Mooseketeer" Roy Williams who designed the original Mickey Mouse beanie. Disneyland alone has sold more than 13 million sets of these "ears" since it opened.

Lock Up These Cels

A cel? It's short for celluloid. It's the final step in the creative development of an animated character for film. Cels are hand-painted on clear acetate. The Cricket Gallery is a great place to find cels, if you've got the bucks and inclination. Their inventory is changing continuously, but here are some typical recent offerings of Disney production cels. Hard to believe at these prices that Walt used to stand by the front gate at Disneyland and give away cels for free.

• *Lady & the Fish* (1955) —Hand-inked production cel of Lady and overturned fish bowl scene. $15,000.

• *Tigger* (1968)— Our favorite character in *Winnie the Pooh and the Blustery Day*. Original production cel on master watercolor background. $3,700.

• *Sneezy* (1937)—From *Snow White and the Seven Dwarfs*, seen waist up on a wood veneer background. $2,500.

For more information and latest catalog, contact The Cricket Gallery, 529 Covington Place, Wyckoff, NJ 07481. (800) BUY-CELS / FAX (201) 891-9095.

101 Dalmatians was the first Disney film where they used Xerox technology instead of laborious hand-inking.

Disney Firsts

Walt Disney was an innovator and would jump into any new technology which would help him tell a story better:

• The first sound cartoon to hit it big with audiences was Disney's *Steamboat Willie* in 1928 (although prior sound cartoons were produced by Max Fleischer and Paul Terry several months before Disney released his).

• The first full-color cartoon: *Flowers and Trees* in 1932. It had been half-finished in black & white when word of the new color process came out, so they started over again.

• The first use of the multiplane camera (several levels of drawings moving at different speeds to give the illusion of depth): *The Old Mill*, 1937.

• The first full-color animated feature: *Snow White* in 1937.

• The first stereo movie soundtrack: *Fantasia* in 1940.

• The first stereo TV show, *The Peter Tchaikovsky Story*, broadcast by Disney in 1959. The TV audience had to put an FM radio next to the TV set and tune in to a radio station that was simultaneously broadcasting the second channel.

MUSIC FACTS

• *The Ballad of Davy Crockett* was composed on the spot when it was discovered that the first episode of the show was a couple of minutes short. It went on to sell over 10 million records and was number one on the Hit Parade for thirteen weeks.

• *Zip-a-Dee-Doo-Dah* won an Academy Award for Best Song in 1946.

• The Sherman brothers who wrote *It's A Small World* and a lot of other Disney music (**Mary Poppins, Jungle Book,** etc.) also wrote the rock 'n' roll classic *You're 16 (You're Beautiful, and You're Mine).*

Even After Donald Sang Der Fuhrer's Face?

• Mussolini's favorite cartoon character was Donald Duck.

• Emperor Hirohito of Japan wore a Mickey Mouse watch.

• One of Franklin D. Roosevelt's favorite movies was the *Three Little Pigs*. (*Who's Afraid of the Big Bad Wolf* was the country's unofficial anthem during the Depression.)

De Tails of Fashion

Just before Christmas 1957, ABC presented Disney's first installment of *Davy Crockett, Indian Fighter*. The response was phenomenal. Crockett guns, lunchboxes, pencil cases, and anything else became the rage; a lot of raccoons died to supply the de rigueur coonskin caps.

It had been pretty much chance that the Disney folk had chosen Crockett for their "American heroes" series. They had also considered Daniel Boone, Johnny Appleseed, Mike Fink and others.

They wanted James Arness for the role but he had just signed to play Matt Dillon on *Gunsmoke*. While viewing an Arness film, Walt liked another actor, Fess Parker. Parker was underwhelmed. Westerns were the dregs of the film business, he was allergic to horses, and he hated the fringed jacket and coonskin cap.

We agree about the jacket, but think maybe Parker was wrong about the cap.

There's something about that tail hanging down your back that makes you irresistible. Best of all, we've tracked down a 1957 "King of the Wild Frontier" look that comes in 1990s "Save the Raccoons" fake fur.

#9373, Adult sizes L & XL; #9361, Kids' sizes S & M. Each $7.95 + 4.00 shipping from Archie McPhee, Box 30852, Seattle, WA 98103. (206) 547-2467 / FAX (206) 547-6319.

MEESEKA MOUSEKA MOUSEKETEERS

Do you remember Circus Day, Fun With Music Day, Anything Can Happen Day and Round-Up Day? It's the original *Mickey Mouse Club*, of course. All together now: "Meeseka mooseka mouseketeer, Mousekartoon Time now is here!"

You may be wondering whatever happened to…

• **Cubby O'Brien.** He became a drummer for the Carpenters, Andy Williams, Carol Burnett and Bernadette Peters.

• **Tommy Cole.** Now an Academy Award-winning makeup artist for TV shows such as *Designing Women* and *Evening Shade*.

• **Johnny Crawford.** Went on to *Rifleman* fame. He had four Top 40 recording hits in 1962-63.

• **Dick Dodd.** Danced in *Bye Bye Birdie*, sang in the Belairs surf band and later the Standells, with whom he recorded the hit *Dirty Water*. Founded an oldies band, the Dodd Squad.

• **Sherry Alberoni.** She has a swimming pool shaped like Mickey.

• **Sharon Baird.** Still going strong within the Disney organization. She's a real character—a live action animal character, that is—for Disney TV productions.

• **Bobby Burgess.** Went on to fame with Lawrence Welk as a singer/dancer for 21 years. He actually proposed to his wife on the Skyway ride to Tomorrowland.

• **Darlene Gillespie.** The only Mouseketeer to ever sue Disney, claiming the organization had falsely promised to make her a star.

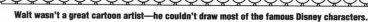

Walt wasn't a great cartoon artist—he couldn't draw most of the famous Disney characters.

Dogged Realism

The 6 1/2 inch tall plush stuffed animal is designed to look just like one of Pongo and Perdita's pups. And 101 can be had for less than $1000!

#10013 1 Dalmatian Puppy, $9.00 + 3.25 shipping. 101 Dalmatian Puppies, $909.00+ 18.50 shipping from The Disney Catalog, Inc., P.O. Box 29144, Shawnee Mission, KS 66201-9144. (800) 237-5751 / FAX (913) 752-1095.

Ducking Home

The Duckburg Dream House. Collect Mr. Duck himself along with Daisy, Uncle Scrooge, the nephews and all the rest, including their furniture! Yes, even the kitchen sink. There are thirty-six pieces in all, including the dream house itself.

Each piece is just $19.95 + 1.69 shipping from The Duckburg Dream House Collection, Groiler Collectibles, Ltd., P.O. Box 1797, Sherman Turnpike, Danbury, CT 06816.

Comrade Mickey

Mickey T-shirt has Mickey written all over it. In Russian, that is. It depicts our hero in a traditional Russian hat and you can see the Kremlin in the background. The shirt's color? Red, of course! And, like the Russia we used to know, you don't get a choice. There is only one—oversize. 100% cotton.

#R21T, Moscow Mickey. #R42T Paris Mickey and #R43T London Mickey also available. Each $24.95 + 2.00 shipping from What On Earth, 25801 Richmond Road, Cleveland, OH 44146-1486. (216) 831-5588 / FAX (216) 831-5788.

A COMPUTER WITH MOUSE

Cartoons can be educational. Computers, too! Four Disney games featuring Mickey are an intriguing and fun way to learn.

• *Mickey's Colors & Shapes: The Dazzling Magic Show.* (Ages 2 to 5). Colors, shapes and drawing program all rolled into one.

• *Mickey's Crossword Puzzle Maker.* (Ages 5 to 8). Word and picture clues help youngsters to learn language.

• *Mickey's 123s: The Great Surprise Party.* (Ages 2 to 5). A numbers game.

• *Mickey's ABCs: A Day at the Fair.* (Ages 2 to 5). Alpha-bet your kids'll like this one!

Each game $38.99 + 5.00 shipping from Egghead Software, 22011 SE 51st Street, Issaquah, WA 98027-7004. (800) EGGHEAD / FAX (206) 391-0880.

One Goofy Watch

That's why it runs backwards, just like the first Goofy watch ever made. Swiss quartz, silvery case, black leather band.

#10196 Goofy Watch, $75.00 + 8.50 shipping from The Disney Catalog, Inc., P.O. Box 29144, Shawnee Mission, KS 66201-9144. (800) 237-5751 / FAX (913) 752-1095.

To Keep Your Pants Up

That's why Mickey Mouse is pictured on these red suspenders. Not only functional, they make a fashion statement! Quality made with leather connecting tabs and sturdy clip-on clasps. One size fits all men, not mice.

#T2674, $19.98 + 4.95 shipping from Funny Side Up, 425 Stump Road, North Wales, PA 19454. (215) 361-5130.

I'm Late, I'm Late!

One of several styles available, this Mickey Mouse is an exact replica of the original watch made by Ingersoll in 1933 and features a rhodium-plated chain-link bracelet. This time around, though, it has a precision quartz movement. Numbered, limited edition of 25,000 watches come in a replica of the original box, too.

#10199, $95.00 + 8.50 shipping from The Disney Catalog, Inc., P.O. Box 29144, Shawnee Mission, KS 66201-9144. (800) 237-5751 / FAX (913) 752-1095.

PUT YOUR MONEY WHERE THE MOUSE IS

Limited collector editions and Disneying prices. Here are some very upscale Disney products.

• **Sorcerer Mickey** is perched on top of a train conducting the Broom and three flatcars of *Dance of the Hours* characters from *Fantasia*. Broom actually pumps the handcar and the train actually moves! Sequentially numbered, limited edition (1,500) train is all-metal with 22-kt. gold and operates on any "0-27" gauge track. Figures are hand-painted resin.

#10440 Train w/ Wood Base, $595.00 + 18.50 shipping.

• **Limited edition sculpture** by Ron Lee captures a magic moment—Snow White kissing the bald head of Grumpy. Hand-painted 24-kt. gold plate on white metal with onyx base. Stands 5 1/2 inches tall and each is signed and numbered by the artist. Edition limited to 2,750.

#10439 Snow White & Grumpy, $140.00 + 10.50 shipping.

• **Mickey's Animated Studio** depicts Mickey, Minnie, Goofy and Pluto making a cartoon—the process from sketch to painted cel. Capodimonte

porcelain, limited edition of 1,000.

#10438 Mickey's Animation Studio, $1,450.00 + 18.50 shipping.

• Hand-painted ceramic collector's plates showing Mickey's career highlights.

#10448 Steamboat Willie (black & white)

#10449 Panic Mickey (full-color)

#10450 Two-Gun Mickey (full-color)

$30.00 each + 5.75 shipping.

All items above from The Disney Catalog, Inc., P.O. Box 29144, Shawnee Mission, KS 66201-9144. (800) 237-5751 / FAX (913) 752-1095.

Mouse Bytes

The Mouse Ears Bulletin Board. If you have a computer with a modem, you can tune in to this electronic club. Members contribute information and opinions on Disney movies, products and the amusement parks, ask questions, play trivia games and advertise for collectible items. Set up your computer and call (714) 992-5341.

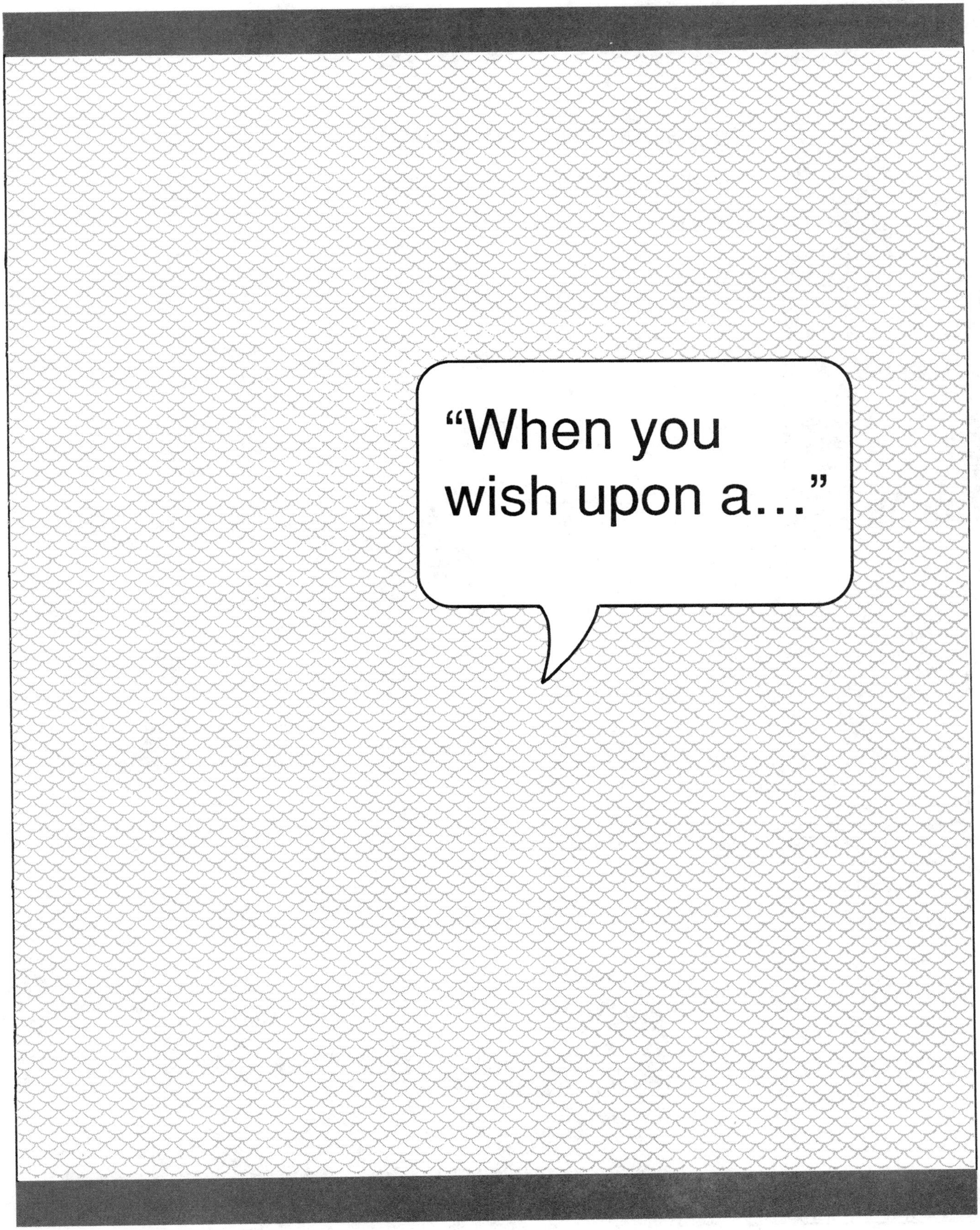
"When you wish upon a…"

Disneyland

THE HAPPIEST PLACE ON EARTH

DISNEYLAND AND DISNEYWORLD

How It All Began

Disneyland has been defined by one wag as "the biggest people trap ever built by a mouse." But do you know where it all began?

Some of Walt Disney's top animators got him interested in miniature trains. He built a layout around his house and gardens with a train big enough for people to ride. Noting that his friends were getting a great kick out of one ride, Walt got the idea that an entire amusement park might lure the tourists that were streaming to Hollywood.

Walt proposed the idea to his brother Roy and his stockholders. They hated the idea. You could hardly blame them, though. At the time, amusement parks were tawdry side-shows, rip-off games and rides staffed by dangerous-looking guys sporting tattoos.

Treasure hunt. On his own, Walt went on a relentless search for financing. He sold his Palm Springs home and cashed in his $100,000 life insurance policy to make his fantasy(land) come true.

He recruited other "imagineers" who shared his dream and they set off to amusement parks throughout the world, measuring, calculating and observing. After months of exhaustive reconnaissance they came to the conclusion that nobody was doing it right. So Walt tried another way:

• Unlike most parks, Walt designed Disneyland with only one grand entrance and a logical layout.

• Instead of the standard fare of ferris wheels and roller coasters, he decided to make each attraction—big or small—unique to Disneyland.

• Disney was determined that the park would be hyperclean and wholesome. He hired college kids and trained them to be courteous and friendly.

• Disregarding all amusement park operators' advice that people would not walk up a flight of stairs, he built an elevated railway that eventually became one of the parks most popular rides. They also told him he couldn't hope to make a profit without running the rubes through a gauntlet of rip-off "win a stuffed animal" games.

• Disney insisted that the park be open every day, all year long. This despite all advice that the rides would break down constantly and that there wouldn't be enough customers to even pay for the maintenance staff, much less turn a profit.

Walt finally struck a deal with ABC-TV for the financing he needed. Roy and the stockholders also eventually came to their senses and jumped on the bandwagon. In 1954 ground was broken in an Anaheim orange grove.

Disasterland

When the park eventually opened in July, 1955, it wasn't quite ready. Nearly 33,000 people—twice as many as invited—packed the park with the help of forged tickets and ladders over walls. Some of the rides weren't ready. The restaurants ran out of food and drink early on. The asphalt hadn't hardened properly and women's high heels got stuck. Also, there had been a plumbers strike during the construction phase and there weren't enough drinking fountains. The press thought it was a ploy to get visitors to buy soft drinks. What they didn't know was that in order to be ready for opening day, Walt had a choice of installing either toilets or drinking fountains.

Within two months, Disneyland had welcomed its millionth visitor, and within a year paid off its $4 million debt.

Disneyland has the fourth-largest navy in the world.

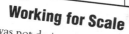

Working for Scale

Disneyland was not designed to any one particular scale. The designers used whatever size worked to create the illusion they wanted.

The Lilly Belle train, for example, was built to 5/8 scale. The first floors of buildings on Main Street are about 90% normal, the second floors, about 80% and so on, giving the illusion of added height. Look carefully at Sleeping Beauty Castle and you'll notice that with each level the bricks get a little bit smaller.

INSIDER TIPS

• The best time of year to avoid crowds at a Disney park is from after Thanksgiving weekend until the week before Christmas.

• The best day to visit is Friday.

• Arrive early. Like an hour before official opening time. You have a few hours before the multitudes arrive. Take a break during the busy midday, come back after and stay late.

• Avoid the horrendous lunch rush. Plan to eat before 11:00 AM and buy food in Critter Country because it's usually less crowded. Grabbing the Monorail to a Disneyland or Disney World hotel restaurant can actually save time and get you better food. Or skip lunch—eat a huge breakfast and then snack throughout the day at various vendors and food carts.

"That's a real E ticket ride!"
—Astronaut Sally Ride after the space shuttle launch.

"What's an E ticket, Mommy?"

In the earliest days, Disneyland visitors paid an admission fee at the main gate and then had to dig into their pockets again and again for each ride. There were big lines at the better attractions and none at the lesser rides.

After some thought, Disney devised the ticket book, with different grades of tickets attached. "A" tickets were for the smaller, less expensive fun spots. "B" rides were a little better, "C" better still, up to the "E" tickets, which were reserved for the best rides in the park—Space Mountain, Matterhorn, Haunted Mansion and so on.

Having already paid for a booklet that contained at least one of each ticket denomination, people were inclined to use them rather than throw them away. Even the "A tickets," which gave admission to the lamest possible things—rides down Main Street on a barely-moving fire engine, for instance.

On the other hand, "E tickets" were hoarded and traded like gold. The phrase became Southern California slang for anything superlative.

Our Favorite Disney Rides

• **"Star Tours"**—A video and a flight simulator are combined to give you the feel of zooming through space—the entire room moves.

• **"Splash Mountain"**—A strange hybrid ride that looks like it's been put together by a committee. Cute little animals singing and dancing, punctuated by terrifying drops.

• **"Space Mountain"**—Real dark, lots of careening. They blow air in your face to feel like great speed, but you never go faster than 37 MPH.

• **"Pirates of the Caribbean"**—Yo-Ho-Ho and no bottles of rum. The cast is composed of 119 "audio-animatronics."

• **"Haunted Mansion"**—Haunted house? Never. Disney does things on a grand scale. So this scary abode is a mansion. Great illusions.

Disneyland sold 8.5 million Donald Duck hats, with eyes and plastic bill, the first year they sold them.

Small World

Ten years after opening Disneyland in Anaheim, the company secretively started buying up property near Orlando, Florida until they had a spread of 27,500 acres. The idea was to avoid the clutter that had sprung up around the entrance to Disneyland: cheap hotels and tourist traps. They wanted to try again with plenty of land and complete control. Walt Disney World opened in October of 1971 and today is the most famous resort in the world.

Testing the Disney System

We knew Disney employees are picked for and trained in both cleanliness and public contact skills, no matter what their job. On a recent visit, we tested the system:

• We purposely littered in the parks with stopwatch in hand. Average time before our small scraps were picked up: 2 minutes, 33 seconds.

• We wandered the grounds looking for workers to bother. One painter working intricate trim on a building cheerfully answered our questions as he worked (Yes, they strip the hydrants and light poles down to the metal before repainting to avoid buildup…), even giving the youngest member of our party a unique Disney character "Wet Paint" sign.

PARADISE LOST

Disney had an idea for a futuristic, self-enclosed community where everything worked smoothly, a laboratory for engineering human living spaces, EPCOT ("Experimental Prototype Community of Tomorrow").

EPCOT was supposed to be a real city with a real purpose, not a futuristic amusement park. As Walt put it, "It will be a planned, controlled community; a showcase for American industry and research, schools, cultural and educational opportunities. In EPCOT there will be no slum areas because we won't let them develop. There will be no landowners and, therefore, no voting control. People will rent houses instead of buying them, at modest cost. There will be no retirees, because everyone will be employed according to their ability. One of our requirements is that the people who live in EPCOT must help keep it alive."

As always, his vision was far ahead of its time. EPCOT would recycle (long before it was popular) most of its waste. It would feed itself and keep its residents healthy in a kind of beehive utopianism.

But after Walt died, the plans fell into other hands. The corporation decided to abandon Walt's pet project, the one above all that he wanted to leave to posterity. Instead we have another theme park, this one with a slight medicinal whiff of "open your mouth, this'll be good for you" education.

Still, most of the rides are fun if you can ignore that bland and annoyingly optimistic Disney Futurism ("And in the future, everybody will be happy all of the time thanks to technology and corporations like [sponsor's name here]").

Disney Data

• At Disneyland alone they use up about 3,000 mops, 1,000 brooms and 500 dustpans a year.

• 50 percent of people living in Japan claim that Disneyland brings "the most happiness into their lives."

• According to Kodak, 3.6% of all snapshots taken in America are snapped at one of the Disney theme parks.

Underneath Disney World is a massive subterranean world where all the deliveries and backstage action happen.

DRAWN, AND QUARTERLY

Disney News. Great place for official behind-the-scenes news about new rides, hotels, movies, and products and articles about things like Disney history, cels, in-park landscaping and food prep. Great for Disneyphiles of all ages.

2 years / 8 issues — $12.95 from Walt Disney's Magic Kingdom Club, P.O. Box 3310, Anaheim, CA 92803.

Politics in the Park

• In 1959, Nikita Khrushchev was denied a visa to Disneyland. Too much security risk said the U.S. government. He was peeved and disappointed.

• In 1970, Yippies took over Tom Sawyer Island and hoisted the Viet Cong flag. The police were called in not only to roust them but also to provide protection *from* the other 30,000 or so upset visitors. The park closed early that day and thereafter began enforcing a stringent dress, hair and attitude code.

Mickey Mouse Classes

Everyone who sees Disney parks wonders how they do what they do. Here are some backstage peeks available to the general public, all at Disney World in Florida.

• For adults, **Cultivating the Gardens of the World**, where you'll learn how they shape shrubs into animal shapes or **Culinary Arts**—classroom cooking plus a look at the Food Distribution Center where kitchen professionals create the meals served throughout Disney World. Cost: $15.00.

• If you're with a group of 15 or more, you can take a 3 1/2 hour **Innovation in Action** course, which brings you into the subterranean tunnels, wardrobe rooms, computer rooms and parade rehearsal rooms.

• If you're 10 to 15 years old you get a choice of three different 6 1/2 hour programs, which many schools recognize for credit: **Creative Arts** (drawing and sketching), **Exploring Nature** and **Entertainment** (behind the scenes looks at the Disney performing arts). $70 each.

For information: WDW Seminar Productions, PO Box 10000, Lake Buena Vista, FL 32830. (407) 828-1500.

Theme Parks By the Book

• *Steve Birnbaum Brings You the Best of Disneyland* and *Steve Birnbaum Brings You the Best of Walt Disney World* by Steve **Birnbaum.** These are official Disney-sanctioned guides to the parks, but Birnbaum says the company didn't interfere editorially. Birnbaum is a well-known travel guide author and his advice is sound when it comes to telling you, as the subtitle says, "How to get there, when to go, where to stay, what it will (and should) cost, how to see and do it all." Also includes non-Disney attractions in the immediate area.

#1679901 Disneyland, $8.95 +

4.00 shipping; #1679828 Walt Disney World, $10.95 + 4.00 shipping. Barnes & Noble Bookstores, 126 Fifth Avenue, New York, NY 10011-5666. (201) 767-7079.

• *The Unofficial Guide To Disneyland* and *The Unofficial Guide to Walt Disney World & EPCOT* by Bob Sehlinger. Buy this book, even if you're going back for the tenth time. Extremely valuable for dealing with the realities of the Disney parks— chronically overcrowded with frustratingly long lines everywhere. Sehlinger's strategy for avoiding the lines, he says, can save you up to *two hours* of waiting on a busy day.

The system requires timing—getting up early, and being at the right rides at the right time of day. We tried the system, and, to our surprise, it actually worked!

Each book $7.95 + 2.50 shipping from Prentice Hall, 15 Columbus Circle, New York, NY 10023. (800) 223-1360.

Despite recurrent rumors, there's no evidence that Walt Disney is cryogenically frozen in Sleeping Beauty's castle.

Dolls

Hello, Dolly!

As homo sapiens developed myths to explain the world, we began to fashion gods in wood, wax, stone and bronze. Dolls made the transition from idols to toys when kids started wanting to play with the household gods. Parents, to save themselves from the wrath of vengeful deities and the whining of little voices, created toy dolls to look like ordinary people. At the time these toys didn't take the form of infants but resembled adults, sexually mature and often with prominent genitalia.

Even 2,500 years ago, behavioral distinctions between the sexes were reflected in toys. Early Greek children played with ancestors of Barbie and G.I. Joe — girls' dolls dressed in the fashions of the day and boys' dolls outfitted as soldiers.

Recently, dolls have gone from being playthings to household gods again — collectibles that kids are forbidden to touch.

Dolling for Dollars

• *Blue Book of Dolls & Values* by Jan Foulke. The "Bible" of doll collectors, it has 100 color and 500 black and white photos to help identify and price dolls from all eras. This business-like tool reads rather like your mother's high school yearbook, but it is very useful to collectors.

$15.95 + 4.00 shipping from Hobby House Press, Inc., 900 Frederick St., Cumberland, MD 21502. (301) 759-3770 / FAX (301) 759-4940.

• *Doll Fashion Anthology* by Glenn Mandeville. Almost as much fun as shopping. This illustrated guide to modern doll fashions covers all the best dressed dolls, including Barbie, Tammy and Tressy. Complete value guide for the fashion-minded collector.

$9.95 + 3.50 shipping from Hobby House Press, Inc., 900 Frederick St., Cumberland, MD 21502. (301) 759-3770 / FAX (301) 759-4940.

Doll Magazines

• *Doll Reader Magazine*. It's a regular *Vogue* for dolls, full of luscious photos, features, profiles and projects covering a broad range of interests.

One year (8 issues) $24.95, single issue $4.95, from Hobby House Press, 900 Frederick St., Cumberland, MD 21502-1289. (301) 759-3770.

• *Dolls — The Collector's Magazine*. Attractive layouts, quality photography and great resources.

1 year (8 issues), $24.95 from Collector Communications, 170 5th Ave., 12th Fl., New York, NY 10010. (800) 347-6969.

Doll Pilgrimages

• **Doll-Fan Attic Museum**. Located above a funky paper memorabilia store, the Attic contains an inviting, overcrowded jumble of dolls. A real mannequin melting-pot, the collection features dolls from all over the world, and of many different types of construction. Straight-laced china-faced ladies sit cheek to jowl with dolls made from old prunes, loofa sponges and cow bones. Monica Owens, proprietor, Rte. 175, Ashland, NH 03217. (603) 536-4416.

• **Doll Hospital.** Does your doll have a broken arm? Need a hair transplant? The "doctors" at Auntie Clare's Doll Hospital (shop and museum), will fix them up and treat them with more respect than most humans get at hospitals. Clare Erickson, proprietor, 22 Greenway Ave. N., Oakdale, MN 55119. (612) 739-1131.

Join the Club

The United Federation of Doll Clubs, Inc. This clearinghouse for doll collectors' clubs will forward letters or requests for membership to local or regional organizations. Membership entitles your club to receive their newsletter and participate in their annual convention.

$18.00 a year to P.O. Box 14146, Parkville, MO 64152. (816) 741-1002.

A Bush in the Hand

George Bush and His Family: Paper Dolls in Full Color by Tom Tierney. Ever wanted to see George and Barbara Bush in their underwear? Here they are, with 24 dresses and boring suits the two have worn. The grandchildren are represented, but not son Neil — apparently his doll is down at the savings and loan stuffing his little paper pockets. George even has a guitar with "the Prez" written on it from that wildly incongruous moment he pretended to jam with Lee Atwater at the 1989 Willy Horton Memorial Blues Festival.

Other politicians (and their families) can be bought for the same price: the Kennedys, Lincolns, Roosevelts, Ronald and (separately) Nancy Reagan, with the best of borrowed evening wear anywhere. Just don't get kinky cross-dressing them unless you want the Secret Service barging through your door.

$3.95 + 2.95 shipping from Dover Publications, 31 E. 2nd St., Mineola, NY 11501. (516) 294-7000, ext. 118.

Tom Tierney

STRANGE DOLLS

All of these were manufactured in the past few years. Some may even still be in stores.

- **Mr. Gameshow.** The Wink Martindale look-alike doll humiliates the losers of this electronic game with snappy comments like: "Dig a hole and crawl in!"

- **Dozzzy**, a $50.00 pajama-clad doll, organizes your bedtime ritual. Squeeze Dozzzy's hand and she'll ask: "Did you remember to brush your teeth? Is the light turned out?" More like sleeping with your crabby old nanny than a trusty pal.

- **Talking Cabbage Patch Kids** gurgle when they drink from a special cup, giggle when they're tickled, recognize and talk to members of their own species and even sing together, if you can afford any others at $100 each.

- **Oopsie Daisy** is a klutz. Flick on the switch and she crawls, falls down, cries and then gets up just to do it all over again. Priced at $45.00, but her medical insurance is very steep.

- The **Special Blessings** doll is the first doll to profess a belief in a higher power. She kneels and prays, her hands held together by little Velcro pads.

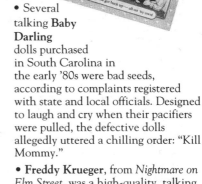

- **Several** talking **Baby Darling** dolls purchased in South Carolina in the early '80s were bad seeds, according to complaints registered with state and local officials. Designed to laugh and cry when their pacifiers were pulled, the defective dolls allegedly uttered a chilling order: "Kill Mommy."

- **Freddy Krueger**, from *Nightmare on Elm Street*, was a high-quality, talking doll that sold 40,000 clones at $29.99 before parents' groups pressured the makers to cease production. They felt a murderer was not an appropriate role model. Freddy now fetches about $75 in the current collectibles market.

- **Ronald Reagan**: Vinyl, molded hair and painted face, just like the original. First priced at $62.49, then marked down to $39.88, now hard to find.

P aper Doll Magazine

Midwest Paper Dolls and Toys Quarterly. This 30 page market and calendar newsletter fills the need for a national paper doll enthusiasts forum, with regional and national show information.

Send $3.50 for a sample copy to Janie Varsolona, P.O. Box 131, Galesburg, KS 66740.

Women Progress— At Least On Paper

Precious Paper Dolls and *Celebrity Paper Dolls*, both by Cynthia Musser. These books look at historic paper dolls as a reflection of the changing ways society sees women's roles.

Each $14.95 + 4.00 shipping. Hobby House Press, 900 Frederick St., Cumberland, MD 21502-1289. (301) 759-3770.

Bloody **B**aby

• "Injure" Boo Boo Baby with a special marker, then apply a bandage (with "just a drop of magic lotion"). The injury disappears when you take the bandage off. Includes bandages, marker and lotion.

#299917, $50.00 + 7.80 shipping from FAO Schwarz, P.O. Box 182225, Chattanooga, TN 37422-7225. (800) 426-TOYS.

• Help the hurt with Boo Boo Baby Accessory Carry Case. Comes complete with dressing gown for long hospital stays, extra bandages, comb, brush, mirror, cream box and bottle for milk.

#299909, $25.00 + 5.80 shipping from FAO Schwarz (see above).

Fast Delivery

Forget Lamaze...the easiest, fastest delivery is by Federal Express. Baby In Valise arrives overnight with 2 outfits, accessories, and birth certificate. Just barely cheaper than a real baby's delivery.

#363820, $270.00 + 26.50 Federal Express from FAO Schwarz, P.O. Box 182225, Chattanooga, TN 37422-7225. (800) 426-TOYS.

Gorby, Not Ken

In 1989, the Society of Ukranian Designers invited Mattel representatives to meet them in the USSR. Mattel created a Mikhail Gorbachev doll for the occasion, with a body by "Ken." Gorby's "mature" silhouette came from padding the suit.

Not the original Gorby Doll, this 10 in. version looks fairly realistic.

#M278, $26.95 + 3.00 shipping from What On Earth, 25801 Richmond Road, Cleveland, OH 44146. (216) 831- 5588.

> *"I want to buy a paper doll that I can call my own, One the other fellas cannot steal..."*
>
> **—Mills Brothers**

Made for Playing Doctor

Zaadi Dolls. Child-size dolls created to explain medical procedures and offer comfort to hospitalized children.

These dolls are anatomically correct both outside and inside. Each contains 16 soft-sculpture cloth internal organs plus major veins and arteries.

The female dolls come with removable hair and a scarf to explain the effects of chemotherapy. The male has an eye patch, a breakable arm, and a removable hernia. Both have a transplantable kidney and a broken lower leg.

Available for $269.00 for one, $495.00 for both from The Zaadi Company, 836 Chelmsford, Lowell, MA. 01851. (508) 453-6508.

Wouldn't It Be Great If All Babies Behaved This Well?

Pull the pacifier out of her mouth and she doesn't cry...she walks or crawls away (depending on her mood) to the tune of *It's A Small World*. Better yet, when you put the pacifier back in, she instantly falls asleep!

#B3034, $15.98 + 3.95 shipping from Harriet Carter, North Wales, PA 19455. (215) 361-5151.

MUSICAL BABY CRAWLS & WALKS

ARMS & LEGS BEND

Doll counterfeiters have been known to soak new dolls in tea to "age" them.

As Seen on TV!

The Hamilton Collection features individually handcrafted 17" porcelain dolls. Favorites are Lucy & Ricky Ricardo, Fred & Ethel Mertz, the Three Stooges and the *Wizard of Oz* foursome. Authorized by Lucille Ball, this "Lucy" wears an ensemble by *I Love Lucy* costume designer Elois Jenssen.

"Lucy" doll, $95.00 + 3.00 shipping from The Hamilton Collection, 9550 Regency Square Blvd., P.O. Box 44051, Jacksonville, FL 32231.

Doll For The Write Occasion

Pencil-top dolls keep youngsters amused as they learn how to do the write thing.

#C517573, $4.98 postpaid from Hanover House, Hanover, PA 17333-0002. (717) 633-3377.

The Video Doll Shoppe

This sixty-minute video is a collection of doll-related commercials, promo pieces and sales films. A tour of the Betsy Wetsy Doll assembly line. A sales film for stores on how to display Shirley Temple dolls, dishes and coffee cup sets. TV commercials for Patty Play Pal and brother Peter, Betsy Wetsy, Betsy McCall, Bye Bye Baby, Tiny Tears, Little Miss Echo, Thumbelina and many more. And a doll fashion show produced for a toy convention.

$24.95 + 3.95 shipping from Video Resources New York, Inc., 220 W. 71st St., New York, NY 10023. (212) 724-7055.

Mommy, Where Did I Come From?

Spawning a fad even bigger than hula hoops, a young Georgia sculptor named Xavier Roberts created the first Cabbage Patch baby in 1977. He formed a company to manufacture the dolls by hand in a converted medical clinic where the employees wore hospital gowns while working.

The ingenious "adoption ritual" marketing scheme brought Roberts' company regional success, eventually selling 250,000 dolls at $125 each.

Coleco Industries, having ridden a fad of their own in 1955 with Davy Crockett moccasin kits, obtained the rights to manufacture a mass-produced 16" $25 version of Roberts' handmade dolls, retaining the adoption ploy. Names were chosen from a 1938 Georgia birth register, using colorful Southern monikers such as Clarissa Sadie and Cornelia Lenora.

Consumers went crazy, even rioted. Cabbage Patch "parents" even sent their "kids" to Camp Small Fry, a "summer camp" started by Dr. Sanford Stein in Rumson, New Jersey. After the fad went bust, Coleco went out of business.

East and Nest

• Nesting dolls are synonymous with Russia. The classic Semenov Matryoshka dolls (not shown) are hand-crafted, hand-painted works of art.

#S26, Semenov Matryoshka (6 nests, 5 in.), $29.00 + 4.50 shipping or #S27, Big Matryoshka (9 nests, 11 in.), $135.00 + 9.95 shipping from Russian Dressing, P.O. Box 1313, New York, NY 10013. (212) 334-0006 / FAX (212) 334-1158.

• This U.S. / U.S.S.R. nesting set pits Bushes, First Dog Millie, the White House and Coke against Gorbachevs, Misha the Bear, Red Square, and vodka.

#R26, $252.00 + 9.95 shipping from Russian Dressing (see above).

Singer Belinda Carlisle collects troll dolls outfitted in punk fashions.

Drive-Ins

NEVER HAVE TO LEAVE YOUR CAR AGAIN

America's love affair with the automobile is well documented. One of its strangest permutations has been drive-in movies and restaurants. While both seem to be on the road to extinction, there will always be something magical about the idea of never having to leave your car for food or entertainment.

The History of Drive-in Movies

Richard M. Hollingshead Jr. knew he was onto something when he saw people's reaction to his car movie system. For informal parties, he would stick his home-movie projector on the hood of his Model A and screen films onto the white wall of his garage. His guests sat on the car's comfy upholstery while they watched. They loved it, and Hollingshead started looking for a way to make money from the idea.

He first tried to sell the idea to gas stations, figuring they could keep their patrons amused while filling their tanks. But his idea was met with great indifference, so he abandoned it and came up with a winner.

"The World's First Automobile Theater" opened on June 6, 1933 in Camden, New Jersey—a screen at one end of a parking lot flanked by huge raised loudspeakers. Customers paid 25 cents per car plus 25 cents per person ($1.00 tops) to see *Wife Beware*, starring Adolph Menjou. Six hundred people paid to see the movie; plenty more heard it as the tower speakers blasted dialog for miles around.

Before long Hollingshead began improving his invention. First, he sloped the parking area to allow better viewing. Individual car speakers and heaters came next.

The idea caught on and all over the country acres of cow pastures were paved over. Many theatres even erected playgrounds and miniature golf courses at the foot of the screen to amuse patrons' children.

The timing was right. The post-war baby boom of the late 1940s was also an automobile boom,

fueled by cheap gas and a thriving consumer market. Roomy back seats provided a place for kids, or an arena for love's wrestling matches.

Unfortunately, the dream was not fated to last. Encroaching suburbia drove up once-cheap rural land prices, cars got smaller, TV reared its ugly screen, and the quality of drive-in films declined to B-minus at best. Drive-ins began dwindling and finally disappearing across the landscape.

"The first rule of drive-in moviemaking: Anybody can die at any moment." — Joe Bob Briggs

Making Drive-In Movies

"For decades, I've heard film makers malign drive-ins, but to my mind they're a direct connection with mainstream America, and that's the film audience for whom my pictures are made."
—**Roger Corman, drive-in film auteur**

If you went to a drive-in in the 1950s or '60s, the odds are pretty good that the movie was made by American International Pictures.

Over 25 years, AIP cranked out over 500 titles with low (under $100,000) budgets, launching careers of directors Martin Scorsese, Roger Corman, and Francis Coppola, and actors like Jack Nicholson and Charles Bronson.

AIP had a unique marketing strategy. First, come up with a catchy title like *I Was a Teenage Werewolf* and produce a rough poster and ad. Then send the ad proposals to exhibitors. Only if the package received a positive reaction would a script be written and the film shot, usually in a couple of weeks. Soon another zombie, biker or beach blanket bimbo movie would be ready for the drive-in screens.

DRIVE-IN THEATRE
MOTION PICTURES UNDER THE STARS

Starlite DRIVE-IN

Drive-In Restaurants

The forerunner of the modern fast food restaurant was the 1950s drive-in restaurant, which evolved from the 1930s style diner. So you'd never have to touch pavement, the best drive-ins featured servers (usually young women, although only rarely on skates, despite what you've seen in movies).

They'd take your order and hang a custom-designed tray on your half-closed car window. A & W was one chain that did it well—foamy, frosty cold mugs and food with themes ("Give me a mama burger, a papa burger and a coupla baby burgers...").

The early McDonald's drive-ins were the other end of the spectrum. You actually had to leave your car and walk up to a window to place your order. The young man (McDonald's didn't hire any other age or sex at the time) gave you your order in a sack and you ate it in your car, or on the restaurant's picnic table if the weather was nice (McDonald's didn't offer indoor seating until years later).

SPEAKERS FOR YOUR HOUSE

Remember the drive-in speakers that you hung on your car window that sounded like ducks quacking? These *look* like that, but are mercifully silent. Your choice: a clock or a nightlight, in yellow, red, pink or baby blue.

#7032, clock. #7033, nightlight. Your choice $49.00. Add 4.00 shipping from Car's the Star, 8236 Marshall Dr., Lenexa, KS 66214. (800) 833-3782.

Drive-In Facts

• In their heyday—late 1950s and early 1960s—over 4,000 drive-ins operated across the U.S.

• There are so few drive-ins now (just over 1,000) that the National Association of Drive-In Operators is defunct.

• Several drive-in theatres offered drive-in church services on Sunday morning. You didn't have to dress up and you said "amen!" by honking your horn. The Antioch Baptist Church in the San Francisco area went the idea one better—they erected a Gospel Drive-In and snack bar on its grounds and showed films like *Angel Alley, The Cross and the Switchblade,* and *Image of the Beast,* while strolling field ushers maintained "godly" behavior among patrons.

• In 1989, the Norwegian National Opera staged a drive-in production of the classic opera *The Barber of Seville.* The sound was blasted from huge loudspeakers and closeups were projected onto a huge screen. 1300 people attended in 300 cars and on foot. And no, Rossini's 1816 opera wasn't updated to match the automotive ambiance, say to *The Barber of the Cadillac Seville.*

One expert estimates that fewer than half the people at a drive-in movie actually watch the entire movie.

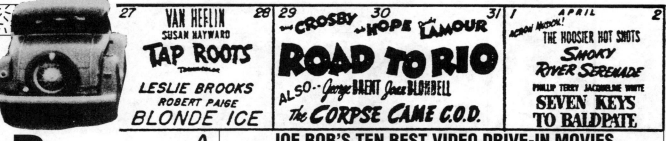

JOE BOB'S TEN BEST VIDEO DRIVE-IN MOVIES

DRIVE-INS AND DRIVE-THROUGHS

Everyone is familiar with drive-through fast food restaurants and drive-through banking, but the following are some of the more noteworthy drive-in innovations.

• **Drive-Through Newsstands,** selling newspapers, magazines, maps, soft drinks, sweets and snacks, lottery tickets and film processing.

• **Drive-Through Groceries.** Runners fetch your selections.

• **Drive-Through Immigration.** The Houston office of the Immigration and Naturalization Service opened a drive-through window in May 1988. On an good day, over 300 green-cards served.

• **Jack in the Box?** Several mortuaries have installed windows allowing for a drive-by view of the deceased, but Gatling's Funeral Home on Chicago's South Side has gone one better. It has a 24-hour drive-through service using video cameras, a monitor and a sound system. A head shot of the loved one resting in a coffin appears on a 25-inch screen for approximately three seconds, but another button allows visitors to call up the image repeatedly.

Shogun Assassin (1981). Contains many severed heads and also features a demon-possessed ninja.

Bolero (1984). Top contender as Bo Derek's worst film.

Basket Case (1982). Another severed head, this one formerly belonging to a Siamese twin, kept in a basket by his grieving brother.

The Brood (1979). "Slime glopola" movie about mutating DNA.

Pumping Iron II. The Women (1985). "Their legs look like the road map of the Mexico City subway system."

Make Them Die Slowly (1985). Anthropologists meet hungry cannibals in the jungle. Best line: "No! Don't eat that! It might be Rudy!"

The New Kids (1985). Features vigilante high school kids.

I Spit On Your Grave (1977). Joe Bob gives it a "94 on the vomit meter."

The Dean Martin Show (1965). Dated, definitive '60s routine, plus 15 drunk jokes in the opening two minutes.

Never Pick Up a Stranger (1979). A psycho killer stalks Times Square hookers.

These and other great films are reviewed in this anthology of Joe Bob's columns from the last few years: *Joe Bob Briggs Goes to the Drive-In* by Joe Bob Briggs.

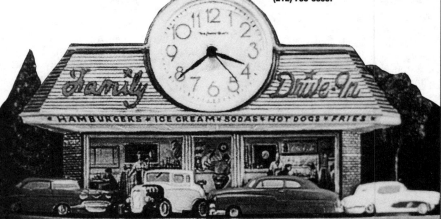

Turn Back the Hands of Time

1950s Drive-In Restaurant Clock. Travel back in time to the Fabulous Fifties when a Coke or fries set you back a dime. Miniature fast food joint captures all the essential nostalgic details: classic cars outside, classic customers inside the authentically outfitted interior scene. If you squint, you can even read today's special on the blackboard. 21 x 10 1/2" quartz clock runs on 1 AA battery.

Best 3 minute drive-through show? Riding through an automatic car wash.

Caddy for Your Shack

If you like the "drive-through" decor of cars bursting out of walls at trendy spots like the Hard Rock Cafe, you can achieve a small-scale version at home. This replica of the back end of a pink '59 Cadillac houses an AM/FM stereo radio and recording cassette deck in its trunk. Its twin-finned tail lights flash to the beat.

#CAD-PINK, $179.00 + 9.00 shipping. The Scope Catalog, 260 Motor Parkway, Hauppauge, NY 11788-5134. (800) 695-4848 / FAX (516) 435-8079.

Write Joe Bob Briggs

Joe Bob Briggs is the patron saint of drive-in movies. His syndicated column has consistently been a voice of reason against the "communists" who want to close down the theaters, and his reviews cut right to the meat of the drive-in experience. Contact him at: **Joe Bob's Mail Bag, P.O. Box 2002, Dallas, TX 75221. FAX (214) 368-2310.**

Video Trash

Joe Bob Briggs Presents. The world's foremost authority on drive-in movies hosts this video series of bawdy, bodacious buffoonery and bad taste from the big screen. Joe Bob says check it out.

#VHS 7623, *Blood Feast*; #VHS 7620, *Nude On The Moon*; #VHS 7622, *Suburban Roulette*. Each $19.95 + 3.95 shipping from Walden Video, P.O. Box 305188, Nashville, TN 37230-518. (800) 322-2000.

"They can burn us up. They can knock us down. But they can't close the drive-in in our heart."

—Joe Bob Briggs

Drive-in Restaurants on the Screen

- *American Graffiti* (1973)
- *More American Graffiti* (1979)

Hanging around the local drive-in burger joint was the center of these two nostalgic films. The first was about coming of age in the innocent early 1960s, and its sequel about hitting early adulthood in the less-innocent late 1960s. Captured the era as it was lived in small-town California.

Want to visit the drive-in from the movie? Funny thing—three drive-ins in Modesto, Petaluma and San Francisco have each claimed that the drive-in scenes were filmed there. Either two are mistaken, or Lucas filmed individual segments in each.

The first movie launched director George Lucas' phenomenal career, and proved to be the big break for Richard Dreyfuss, Harrison Ford, Ron Howard, Cindy Williams, Paul LeMat, Mackenzie Phillips, Suzanne Somers, Candy Clark and Charles Martin Smith.

- *Happy Days*. The sitcom that wouldn't die owes much to *American Graffiti*, including the talents of Ron Howard, but the show's setting was pushed back a few years to ride Fab Fifties nostalgia. Its huge cast eventually spun off into other sitcoms like *Laverne and Shirley*, *Mork and Mindy*, and *Joanie Loves Chachie*, giving employment to producer Garry Marshall's entire family.

Drive-in restaurants were often traumatic for kids—nothing like spilling a milkshake on the new car's upholstery to stir up the grown-ups.

ELVIS

Always On My Mind

According to *Rolling Stone* magazine, Elvis' "achievement was to remake American popular culture with music of passion, humor, adventure and desire by drawing on more sides of the American character than anyone, with the exception of Mark Twain (Samuel Clemens) and Abraham Lincoln, had ever done before." Sam and Abe, eh? Good company.

Since Elvis' death we've learned more than we probably want to know about him. Some say he was lucky. Some say he is a legend. Some even worship him as if he were a god.

Early Elvis Step By Step

• January 8, 1935—At 4:35 a.m. in Tupelo, Mississippi, Elvis struggled from the womb. His twin brother Jessie didn't survive.

• January 8, 1946—Elvis received a guitar for his eleventh birthday.

• Summer, 1953—Elvis paid to record his first songs for his mom at Memphis Recording Service. The songs were *My Happiness* and *That's When Your Heartache Begins.*

• January 4, 1954—While recording another two songs at Memphis Recording, Elvis met Sam Phillips, head of Sun Records.

• June 1954—Elvis' first recording session with Sun didn't go very well. Sam had him sing several songs including *Without You* but wasn't pleased with the results.

• July 5, 1954—Teamed with Scotty Moore and Bill Black, Elvis recorded another batch of tunes.

• July 7, 1954—A DJ named Dewey Phillips was the first to broadcast an Elvis record to the world, *That's All Right, Mama,* recorded two days earlier.

• Sam Phillips sold Elvis' contract to RCA because he thought that Carl Perkins would be the bigger "star" of the two.

Read All About It

• *Long Lonely Highway* by Ger Rijff. Snapshots and news clippings from the early days capture Elvis Mania in scrapbook form. The spectacle and the hysteria are all chronicled in this hardcover keepsake.

$24.50 + 1.75 shipping from Popular Culture, Ink, P.O. Box 1839, Ann Arbor, MI 48106. (800) 678-8828.

• *All Shook Up* by Lee Cotten. On December 8, 1960, "Pop Singer Fabian (Fabiano Forte) visited Elvis at Graceland. While Elvis was demonstrating karate, he tore his pants. Fabian kept them as a souvenir." Find out all the events of Elvis' life in this daily diary covering 1954 to 1977.

$34.50 + 3.00 shipping from Popular Culture, Ink (see above).

Bruce Borders of Jasonville, Indiana is the first known professional Elvis impersonator to hold the office of mayor.

I REALLY DON'T WANT TO KNOW

• Elvis sold one billion records. He had 18 Number One hits and 31 Top 40 hits. Yet, although he received co-writing credits, Elvis never wrote a song. The credits were just another of Col. Parker's cheap tricks: he told songwriters that Elvis wouldn't record their song unless Elvis got credit (and half the resultant royalties).

• More Americans saw the 1973 TV special *Elvis—Aloha From Hawaii* than saw Neil Armstrong walk on the moon. Worldwide, 1.5 billion people in 40 countries tuned in to the broadcast.

• Where Elvis first shook: July 30, 1954, Overton Park, Memphis. He was opening for Webb Pierce and really just flapping his legs to keep from fainting of stage fright in front of the large crowd, but people seemed to like it, so he kept doing it.

• Nothin' But Hound Dogs: 50 dogs named Elvis are registered in Los Angeles county. Just for comparison, only 37

canines are registered as Zsa Zsa (probably pit bulls, dahling).

• A poll taken by The Amusement and Music Operators Association found that the best jukebox record of all time was Elvis' 1956 two-sided hit, *Hound Dog/Don't Be Cruel.*

• *White Noise*, a darkly satirical novel by Don DeLillo, features a Professor of Elvis Studies.

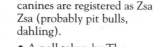

How Great Thou Art

• *"He can't sing a lick."* —**The New York Journal American**

• *"There's no way to measure his impact on society or the void he leaves. He will always be the King of Rock & Roll."* —Pat Boone

• *"Elvis Presley had nothing to do with excellence, just myth."* —Marlon Brando

• *"Without Elvis none of us would have made it."* —Buddy Holly

• *"The fact that someone with so little ability became the most popular singer in history says something significant about our cultural standards."* —Steve Allen

• *"The only possibility in the United States for a humane society would be a revolution with Elvis Presley as leader."* —Phil Ochs

• *"Nothing really affected me until Elvis."* —John Lennon

• *"I wouldn't have Presley on my show at any time."* —Ed Sullivan

• *"And now, here is Elvis Presley!"* —Ed Sullivan

• *"He's that fella we see ever' now and then on television, shakin' and screamin' kinda like somebody's beatin' his dog."* —Sheriff Andy Taylor, *The Andy Griffith Show*

Elvis Fan Club President: "You haven't mentioned Elvis Presley."
Groucho Marx: "I seldom do unless I stub my toe."
—*You Bet Your Life*

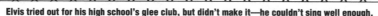

BIG BOSS MAN

If Elvis was The King, what would he have been without Colonel Tom Parker? Probably Master of the Universe because "the Colonel" (a meaningless honorary title from Louisiana state) held Elvis back as much as he promoted him. Also he grabbed 50% of Elvis' income as his cut (an unusually high management fee).

Most people don't realize, as music critic Mick Farren explains, "every career decision that was made about Elvis, generally by the Colonel, was the wrong one." Part of the blame goes to Elvis, of course. He hated business and laid it all in Parker's lap.

Parker in turn played it safe. He sold Elvis' services for less than what they were worth, even less than lesser talents of the day. And he put him in those godawful movies, which may have been a good short-term business move but crippled Elvis' career.

More than anything

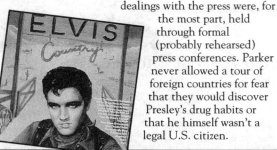

else, the Colonel's best skill was keeping Elvis in the public eye while keeping Elvis away from the public. He seemed to believe that if fans were to get close to the real Elvis, they wouldn't like what they saw. Elvis' dealings with the press were, for the most part, held through formal (probably rehearsed) press conferences. Parker never allowed a tour of foreign countries for fear that they would discover Presley's drug habits or that he himself wasn't a legal U.S. citizen.

Parker never pushed Elvis to broaden his musical boundaries and so, when the 1960s came along, Elvis' exceptional voice was out of tune with society's changing musical and political tastes. He was so square, but Elvis didn't really care. What for? He was a millionaire and had all the time in the world to redecorate Graceland.

Puppet On A String

• "Colonel Tom Parker" was an illegal Dutch immigrant named Andreas Cornelis van Kuijk.

• Parker had a dancing chicken show on the carnival circuit. No great trick—he set the chickens on an electric hot plate "stage" and the birds jumped and wiggled for the gawking crowds. Is there a metaphor here?

• Col. Parker also used to sell "canaries"— sparrows painted yellow.

• Thanks to Parker's questionable business acumen, Elvis received only half the amount of royalties from RCA that other major recording artists received, and Parker took half of that.

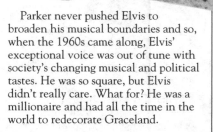

Number 1, With a Bullet

Elvis was fond of shooting his gun indoors, once even at the TV set because Robert Goulet was on. Another time, the story goes, he wanted to turn off the light but was too lazy to walk across the room to flick the switch, so he shot it out instead. The bullet slammed through the wall and narrowly missed his girl friend in the next room. After that, The King set some new rules for indoor gunplay. "We're in the penthouse," he told his trigger-happy entourage. "Nobody's gonna get hit long as you shoot straight up."

Colonel Tom Parker once earned the distinction of being both Tampa, Florida's dogcatcher and top pet funeral director.

Memories of Elvis

Sotheby's Auction Catalog lists these prices received for Elvis mementos:

- Elvis' guitar—$27,500
- Elvis' stage boots—$6,050
- A pair of size 14 underwear thrown by a Presley fan—$440
- Meanwhile at another auction house, Elvis' driver's license, issued when he was 17 years old, fetched $7,400.

Check Your Attic

- Elvis Presley Doll (1957)—18 inches high, plaid shirt, blue suede shoes. Value: $1500-2000.
- Elvis Bubble Gum Card—$20-30.
- Elvis (Army) Dog Tag Keychain (1958)—$20-40.

- Elvis Hound Dog (1956)—10 inch dog with "Hound Dog" hat, $200-300.
- Elvis Jeans with "Elvis Presley Jeans" tag (1956)—$100-150.
- Elvis Sideburns Machine Label (1956)—Yup! Someone actually thought they'd make a killing by selling Elvis Sideburns out of a vending machine. A complete machine would be valued at several hundred dollars, however none are known to exist. The only thing left is the machine's label—$50-60.

ELVIS PRESLEY *Lipstick*
Keep me always on your lips!
Elvis Presley

ONLY $1.00 each
Plus 25c for tax and postage

- Elvis Teddy Bear (1957)—24 inch bear with "Elvis Presley" and "Teddy Bear" ribbons—$200-300.
- *Don't Be Cruel/Hound Dog*—RCA Victor Recording #47-6604 issued in July, 1956—$25-30.
- Got anything Elvis you want to sell or buy? Before you do, consult:

The Official Price Guide to Memorabilia of Elvis Presley and the Beatles, by Jerry Osborne, Perry Cox and Joe Lindsay.

$11.95 postpaid from House of Collectibles, 201 E. 50th Street, New York, NY 10022. (800) 638-6460.

Sign Here

Elvis autographs? This place gets them now and then. Recently, they had one, matted with photo, for $750. Get in touch to see what they have.

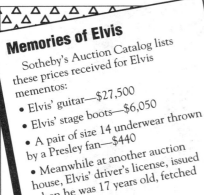

R eturn to Sender

The Citizens' Stamp Advisory Committee meets every two months to suggest stamp subjects to the US Postal Service. Nearly all of their recommendations have been approved, except one: Elvis.

Not a day goes by that the Postal Service doesn't receive a letter about an Elvis stamp, running 6 to 1 in favor. Still it balks, apparently because of Elvis' history of drug abuse and the rumors that he's still alive (which would disqualify him).

But that hasn't stopped other countries from issuing their own Elvis stamps, now for sale:

- **New Guinea.** 300 franc stamp, $1.98; same stamp on specially designed first day cover $4.00.

- **The Republic of Central Africa.** Mint 70 franc stamp 99¢; 485 franc stamp $2.94.
- **Germany.** First day cover with flexible record of *Return To Sender.* Framed, $25.00.

Add $3.00 shipping. Marlen Stamps, 156B Middle Neck Rd., Great Neck, NY 11021. (516) 482-8404.

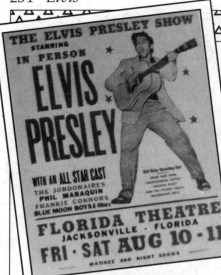

Wanted Posters

Posters from Elvis' foot-stomping, show-stopping performances in the early 1950s. The posters are hand-printed from the original lead and wood type to ensure the closest reproduction possible.

#H008 Elvis Poster, $10.00 + 3.50 shipping from The Country Music Catalog, 4 Music Square East, Nashville, TN 37203. (800) 255-2357.

The Elvis Clean Plate Club

From his 1968 comeback special, it's Elvis wearing black leather on a ceramic plate.

#5451 Elvis Collector's Plate, $24.75 + 2.89 from The Bradford Exchange, 9345 Milwaukee Avenue, Chicago, IL 60648. (800) 842-2300.

W hat a Face

Just like Elvis, this watch has "fine movement," only this one's quartz. Comes with tan leather band and card authenticating it as the "official" Elvis watch. Accept no substitutes!

#5867, $49.95 + 5.95 shipping from The Music Stand, 1 Rockdale Plaza, Lebanon, NH 03766-1585. (802) 295-7044 / FAX (802) 295-5080.

Olden Goldies

Gold-plated LP of Presley's *The Number One Hits* album, to look at, not to listen to. Album cover and commemorative plaque are beautifully mounted in a black matte, framed in solid oak and covered in unbreakable glass, in case things get out of hand in your rec room (but it's *not* bullet proof).

#T674, $250.00 + 7.95 shipping from The Lighter Side, 4514 19th St. Court East, P.O. Box 25600, Bradenton, FL 34206-5600. (813) 747-2356.

Elvis Clock

This alarm clock has twin alarm bells.
#8648, $34.98 + 6.99 shipping. Taylor Gifts, 355 E. Conestoga Road, Wayne, PA 19087. (215) 789-7007.

Elvis Xmas Ornament

Let him be your little good luck charm, or he'll have a blue Christmas without you.

#1612, $6.98 + 2.50 shipping. The Lighter Side, 4514 19th Court East, P.O. Box 25600, Bradenton, FL 34206-5600. (813) 747-2356.

Elvis In Concert!

Stage lights flash on Elvis as *Hound Dog* plays through "concert-sound" speakers in the stage. 20" tall.

#G206, $200.00 + 10.00 shipping from The Country Music Catalog, 4 Music Square East, Nashville, TN 37203. (800) 255-2357.

Wrap Singer

Full-color photos of Elvis adorn this festive all-occasion gift wrap.

#D271, $4.50 + 2.50 shipping from Chicken Boy Catalog, P.O. Box 292000, Los Angeles, CA 90029. (800) 422-0505.

On Spoons, Elvis!

Silver-plated collectible spoons feature Elvis in 3 different striking poses and outfits. 4 1/2" ornamental spoons make one-of-a-kind gift for collectors and fans.

#B9069 Set of 3 spoons, $19.98 + 4.95 shipping from Harriet Carter, Dept. 30, North Wales, PA 19455. (215) 361-5151.

ELVIS DEAD?

"Elvis Presley is dead. As dead as any door implement, as lifeless as a lug nut. He is deceased, defunct, departed, extinguished, spent, insensate; he is, to paraphrase an old Monty Python bit, a past Presley. He died on August 16, 1977, and, as **Saturday Night Live** *used to delight in telling us about Generalissimo Francisco Franco, he is still dead today."*

—**Steve Johnson,** *Chicago Tribune* **(1990)**

Too Much

The day before he died, Elvis had a few prescriptions filled: 250 tablets of Amytal and Quaalude (depressants), 275 of Dexedrine and Biphetamine (stimulants) and 150 tablets plus 200cc of Percodan and Dilaudid (painkillers.)

How many pills did Elvis take? Medical records show that "Dr. Nick" (George C. Nichopoulos) prescribed more than 11,000 "uppers," "downers," and other narcotics to The King during the final fifteen months of his life. That means an average of 24 mood-altering pills a day. Still, the jury (after deliberating over four hours) found the good doctor innocent of over-prescribing drugs for Elvis, Jerry Lee Lewis and seven other patients.

At least ten different drugs were found in Elvis' body during the autopsy. Heart failure was ruled the official cause, caused by "straining at stool." (This is the cause of 1 in 20 of all natural deaths, including Judy Garland's. Eat your fiber!)

So sure, you can go to Graceland, but afterward, why not also visit Elvis' drug store? After all, it indirectly helped make Elvis what he is today (dead).

Prescription House, 1800 Union Avenue, Memphis, Tennessee.

WE ARE NOT CROOKS

Astoundingly, in 1970, Elvis wanted to become an undercover narcotics officer and inform on drug-users in the entertainment business! He made a special visit to President Nixon's Oval Office to secure a drug-agent badge.

Twenty-eight different photos of this historic meeting were taken, featuring various Nixon and Elvis shots. You can buy a very reasonably priced copy from the federal archives (an 8 x 10" of Photo #5364-19 pictured here is $6.25 — larger sizes are also available). Send a check for this one (made out to NLNP), or ask for the free Presley photo description and price list.

Administrator, Trust Fund Board, P.O. Box 100793, Atlanta, GA 30384. (703) 756-6498.

He's Alive!

Do you believe he's alive? About 7% of all Americans do. And some have even seen him:

• One of the first sightings was at the drive-in window of the Kalamazoo Burger King at 3015 South Westnedge Avenue. He was in a red Ferrari.

• A woman named Sunny from Jonesboro, Georgia swears she received a bag of Cheetos and a bologna sandwich from The King while visiting the Air Force Museum in Dayton, Ohio ten years after his death.

• Alton, a service station attendant near Nashville, says Elvis got gas at his station.

• Author Gail Brewer-Giorgio says Elvis revealed in a message on her answering machine that he hangs out in Washington, D.C.

• Still not convinced? A man from the "Show Me" state of Missouri says he saw Elvis on the second floor of the Graceland mansion in 1987.

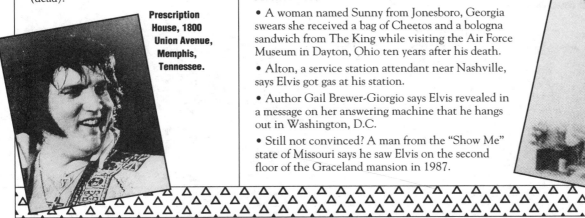

Some associates believed Parker literally hypnotized Elvis—one of the skills he picked up touring with carnivals.

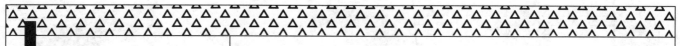

Is He Alive Or Is He Memorex?

• *The Elvis Files—The Video*. Was Elvis' death an elaborate hoax? You bet it was! This film proves it with never-before-seen footage plus interviews with people who have actually spoken with Presley since his death!

#1777, $19.94 + 4.95 from Johnson Smith Co., 4514 19th Court East, P.O. Box 25500, Bradenton, FL 34206. (813) 747-2356.

• *Elvis— The Final Years* by Jerry Hopkins. Describes The King as a "white trash druggie in decline, until he ended up kissing the Graceland bathroom tiles with his sweatpants around his ankles." Elvis, we hardly knew ye.

#0829, $4.50 + 2.00 shipping. AMOK, P.O. Box 861867, Terminal Annex, Los Angeles, CA 90086-1867. (213) 665-0956.

• *Elvis After Life— Unusual Psychic Experiences Surrounding the Death of a Superstar* by Raymond A. Moody, Jr., MD. Okay, so Elvis *is* dead, but lately he's been coming back to warn people about the dangers of drugs. Dr. Moody analyzes "psychic" experiences that have involved Elvis.

#0272, $3.95 + 2.00 shipping from AMOK (see above).

ELVIS LIVES EVILS

"An Elvis Presley impersonator who was described as 'Satan personified' was executed by injection early today for one of five slayings he was accused of committing."

—*Los Angeles Times, September 20, 1989.*

Presley Performs

• *Elvis: The Great Performances Vol. 1—Center Stage.*

• *Elvis: The Great Performances Vol. 2—The Man and His Music.*

The greatest rocker of all cuts loose in a new, definitive videography. *Volume 1* highlights his smoldering, sexy performance style from a rare first screen test to his very last filmed performance. *Volume 2* gives you his recently discovered first recording *My Happiness*, home movies with friends and family, and more brilliant performances. Bonus full color booklet included with each.

Each video volume, $19.95 + 4.95 shipping from Postings, P.O. Box 8001, Hilliard, Ohio 43026. (800) 262-6604 / FAX (614) 777-1470.

Over 1 Billion Sold

• *The Complete Sun Sessions*. Two discs of Elvis' earliest and maybe best recordings, including mistakes and alternate takes.

#R898 (CD only), $18.98 + 4.50 shipping. Country Music Catalog, 4 Music Square East, Nashville, TN 37203. (800) 255-2357.

• *Elvis' Top Ten Hits*. Big recordings from 1956-1972 like *Love Me Tender*, *Burning Love*, and more.

#R598 (LP or Cassette only), $14.98 + 4.50 shipping. The Country Music Catalog (see above).

Elvis Impersonators: The Many Who Would Be King

• **Li'l Elvis.** 4 year old Miguel Quintana of Englewood, Colorado is the youngest Elvis impersonator. He lip-syncs to The King's records.

• **Black Elvis.** Backed by the "White Trash Band," Clearance Giddens has gained national exposure on such TV shows as Arsenio Hall.

• **Doctor Elvis.** Nazar Sayegh, M.D., also nicknamed "Hindu Elvis," is an anesthesiologist from Yonkers who regularly trades in his white coat for a white jump suit. He's even been known to sing to surgery-bound patients.

• **Mexican Elvis.** "El Vez" performs his campy act mostly in the L.A. area, where he has achieved popularity for such hits as *Huaraches Azules*.

• **Lady Elvis.** When Lincoln, Nebraska native Janice K. "gets her Elvis feeling," she does her impression of The King — or is it The Queen?

These and 60 other imitators are in *I Am Elvis — A Guide to Elvis Impersonators*, edited by Bill Yenne, which gives a profile on each impersonator, including booking information and astrological sun sign.

$8.95 + 2.00 shipping from Pocket Books, 1230 Avenue of the Americas, New York, NY 10020.

PRESLEY'S PICS

Elvis made more than 30 films, most of them within a 14 year period. That may have been a mistake. Not monetarily, but career-wise. First, because it kept him away from performing in public, which was what he did best. But worse

was the fact that the movies were too innocuous. The rebellious rock 'n' roller's charismatic qualities did not transfer to the "sanitized for your protection" roles he played.

Too bad. Because early on, Elvis was serious about an acting career and worked hard at it. And he even had the raw talent. But the studio insisted on cranking the movies out quickly so they could cash in on the Elvis fad before it came to an end.

You'd think after a few dozen movies they might've figured out that they could slow down and do it right.

Elvis was offered starring roles in *Midnight Cowboy* and opposite Barbra Streisand in *A Star is Born*, but Colonel Parker torpedoed both offers. So instead Elvis is remembered for his awful "singing race car driver" self-parodies.

As time wore on, Elvis began apologizing for his films. Back in Memphis, he used to reserve the Orpheum Theater for private midnight film screenings with his friends. He never, *ever*, requested to see one of his own.

"He can't last. I tell you flatly, he can't last."
—**Jackie Gleason**

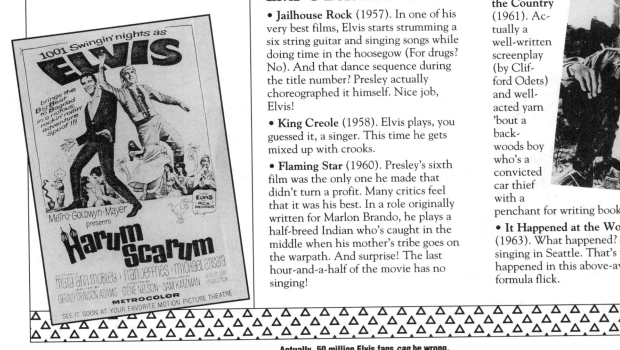

Elvis' 5 Best Bad Movies

• **Jailhouse Rock** (1957). In one of his very best films, Elvis starts strumming a six string guitar and singing songs while doing time in the hoosegow (For drugs? No). And that dance sequence during the title number? Presley actually choreographed it himself. Nice job, Elvis!

• **King Creole** (1958). Elvis plays, you guessed it, a singer. This time he gets mixed up with crooks.

• **Flaming Star** (1960). Presley's sixth film was the only one he made that didn't turn a profit. Many critics feel that it was his best. In a role originally written for Marlon Brando, he plays a half-breed Indian who's caught in the middle when his mother's tribe goes on the warpath. And surprise! The last hour-and-a-half of the movie has no singing!

• **Wild in the Country** (1961). Actually a well-written screenplay (by Clifford Odets) and well-acted yarn 'bout a backwoods boy who's a convicted car thief with a

penchant for writing books.

• **It Happened at the World's Fair** (1963). What happened? A lot of singing in Seattle. That's what happened in this above-average formula flick.

ELVISYCLOPEDIA

Elvis: His Life From A to Z by Fred Worth & Steve Tamerius. Truly *the* Elvis encyclopedia of events, information and trivia. More than 2000 entries, alphabetically arranged by key words, which provide the ultimate glimpse into the life of Elvis Presley. The book is divided into sections of the man, music, discography and filmography. Many photos.

$35.00 + 5.50 shipping from Contemporary Books, 180 N. Michigan Avenue, Chicago, IL 60601. (312) 782-9181 / FAX (312) 782-3987.

A State of Graceland

Elvis World by Jane & Michael Stern. Advertised as "the most lavish book ever created for the most spectacular star there ever was."

Okay, so maybe that's a bit of an overstatement, but *Elvis World* offers over 300 pictures and commentary about everything Elvis in a candy-box package, including reprints from fanzines, amusing anti-Elvis literature, an inside look at Graceland and much more. Another for your coffee table.

#1628, $17.95 + 3.00 shipping. Chicken Boy Catalog for a Perfect World Future Studio P.O. Box 292000 Los Angeles, CA 90029 (800) 422-0505

Pieces Of My Life

Mondo Elvis, The Real-Life Rites and Rituals of The King's Most Devoted Fans, video produced and directed by **Tom Corboy.** You'll meet an Elvis impersonator who says Elvis visited him in a dream. Also the twin sisters who claim that Elvis was their father (they *do* resemble him). Last is the woman whose husband divorced her on the grounds of "excessive devotion to Elvis."

This award-winning video's been described as "disturbing yet entertaining, haunting yet hysterical." You'll laugh, you'll cry—definitely a must-see.

#RNVD 1440, $29.95 + 2.00 shipping from Rhino Video, 2225 Colorado Avenue, Santa Monica, CA 90404-3598. (800) 432-3670.

Flaming the Fans

• **Elvis International Forum.** Stories, articles, interviews, magic moments and more! Lots of pictures and a column in which Joe Esposito ("the man closest to Elvis") answers your personal questions about The King!

One year subscription (4 Issues), $19.95 to P.O. Box 3373, Thousand Oaks, CA 91359. (818) 707-9014.

• **Elvis Forever TCB Fan Club.** TCB ("Taking Care of Business") was Elvis' motto and the name of this fan club that harbors a serious interest in the King. They keep an archive of material and stats for research purposes. They also issue the *Elvis Presley TCB Newsletter* six times a year. The club is currently 1200 strong.

P.O. Box 1066, Pinellas Park, FL 34665. (813) 521-1970.

Elvis' favorite sandwich: grilled peanut butter and banana.

Find an Etch Market & Scratch It

From the TV screen proportions to the difficulty of drawing anything more complicated than perpendicular straight lines, there is something unsettlingly postindustrial about Etch A Sketch. It's a Rube Goldberg machine that actually makes an easy task—creating a one-color line drawing—infinitely difficult.

It's a triumph of form over function: people are so fascinated by *how* it does what it does, they don't seem to care that *what* it does is pretty unspectacular. They draw on it because it is a challenge. There's genuine satisfaction in drawing something, *anything* even vaguely recognizable on it, knowing that it's not only difficult, but fragile—

it'll all disappear if dropped, tipped or shaken.

Hard to believe that Ohio Arts has sold more than 60 million of the damned things.

Sketchy beginnings. Etch A Sketch was invented in France by Arthur Granjean, who called it "L'Ecran Magique" (The Magic Screen). Representatives of the Ohio Art Company saw it at the Nuremberg Toy Fair in 1959 and decided the toy had possibilities. They purchased the rights to market it in the US.

Meanwhile, back in the States, Ohio Art management decided to introduce the new toy at the New York Toy Fair in 1960. The rush to create workable

prototypes was hampered because the instructions from Granjean were in French and metric, both about equally foreign to Americans at the time.

The company still had no idea that the toy would become a big success. Their first inkling was on the plane flight to the New York show when company officials started bickering about who would get to play with the prototypes next.

Etch A Sketch was officially released to the public on July 12, 1960. It was a smash.

How It Works

The Etch A Sketch is really pretty simple. In case you never laboriously scraped away enough silver powder to see this for yourself, here's what's inside.

The glass window on front looks into a compartment filled with powdered aluminum so fine that it sticks to everything it touches, including the window. Also in there are little plastic beads to agitate the powder and keep it from clumping together.

Each knob controls nylon strings attached to a moveable metal bar, one vertical, the other horizontal. Turn the knob and the strings pull a cone-shaped brass stylus either left-right or up-down against the window. The stylus point scrapes away a line of the aluminum powder, revealing

the darkness of the inner compartment. It's easy to draw straight perpendicular lines, but takes coordinated, simultaneous movement of the two knobs to draw curves or diagonals.

When you shake the Etch A Sketch, the powder re-covers the glass, and you're back where you started. The manufacturer says that the dust is non-toxic, but for added safety the glass has been protected with a plastic sheet on any made after 1973.

The New Breed

Esher-Sketch

"Frustrated, I broke my Etch A Sketch open and dumped the powder into my aquarium. Now my fish only swim up, down and sideways."—Mark Klein

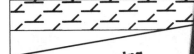

An Exposure to Impulse by David Sosalla

Make Your Drawing Permanent

Say you've drawn a masterpiece on your Etch A Sketch and can't bear to have it erased. Here's how to make it permanent:

• Drill holes in the bottom of the frame without disturbing the drawing. This is not easy.

• Gently shake out all the aluminum powder and plastic beads. Be careful not to mess up your drawing and keep it off the furniture and out of your eyes.

• Spray a fixing agent throught the holes you drilled, covering the inside of the screen.

• Glue the knobs to keep them from turning.

Etch A Sketch Elite

The Executive Model. What makes this special? A brushed sterling case with silver trim, each knob decorated with your choice of topaz or sapphire, and a handcarved "Etch A Sketch" signature. Available on a custom order basis for $3750 (shipping free).

**The Ohio Art Company
One Toy Street
Bryan, OH 43506.
Phone (419) 636-3141.**

Come Up & See My Etchings

Only a few artists have picked up the artistic gauntlet posed by the extreme limitations of Etch A Sketch as an art medium: You can't erase, your canvas is always the same size and you have no control over line width or color.

On the other hand, Etch A Sketch has some benefits, as well: It's relatively cheap, you can easily start over, and the frame is free.

• **Michael Angelo Vidal, Jr.** has exhibited his Etch A Sketch art at public libraries across Southern California. It's exhibited in glass cases, propped up just slightly to allow viewing without erasing. It takes him about 15 minutes for a portrait sketch , although his more complicated works—wildlife, dragons, celebrities— can take up to 25 hours.

• "This is baby boom art," says Colorado artist **Jeff Gagliardi**, who has Etch A Sketched

Michelangelo's Sistine Chapel creation scene, the Mona Lisa and the corner of a five dollar bill.

• **Jeff Gosline** from San Diego has escaped the toy's size limitations. Two of his pieces are murals, both of guru Sri Chimnoy playing musical instruments. "Child's Play" is made of 72 Etch A Sketches arranged in a multi-screen, mosaic tile effect. "Battle of Kurukshetra" is 36 screens large.

"Drawing with an Etch A Sketch is spiritual in a way," he says. "Your drawing is just going to be erased. You know it won't be permanent. But how permanent is anything?"

Belying that, Gosline has figured out a way to make his etchings last a heck of a long time (see above). Good thing, too. His murals can take forty hours of work, first on paper and then on each of the magic screens. His room is so small that he doesn't get to see the completed murals until they're hung up in the gallery.

OFFICIAL ETCH A SKETCH CLUB MEMBER

ANDREA SOHN IS AN OFFICIAL *Etch A Sketch*® CLUB MEMBER

To Etch His Own

The Etch A Sketch Club. This club offers products not available anywhere else like Etch A Sketch t-shirts, patches and calendars. The triennial newsletter features stories, news, drawing contests and even poetry. Membership is a bargain: $4 for 3 years. Any age can join (10% of the members are adults).

**Send name, address and check to:
Etch A Sketch Club Membership Committee
Ohio Art Co.
One Toy Street
Bryan, OH 43506**

"Etch A Sketch's wonderfully forgiving message is that a fresh start and a brand-new canvas are always just a shake away." — Diane diCostanzo

FAST FOOD

In 1936 Charlie Chaplin's *Modern Times* suggested the idea of a machine that would feed the laborers without losing any work time. Less than two decades later, fast food pioneers like Harlan Sanders and the McDonald brothers married the efficiency of the auto assembly line to the architecture of the diner, and fast food was born.

The idea was a hit as soon as the first meat hit grease. The needs of busy families, harried working folks and weary travelers were perfectly matched by places where the food was exactly the same no matter where, and quick.

Even the interior decor was designed to move customers through quickly: over-stimulating colors, cacophonous acoustics and anti-lounging seats designed to be comfortable only as long as you're sitting forward and eating.

Fast food kitchens also work as a metaphor for the American economy: unskilled workers working for minimum wage in service to $70,000 computer-driven food prep machines.

CLOCK

TWICE AS BIG   TWICE AS GOOD

14 CONVENIENT LOCATIONS TO SERVE YOU

SEE ADDRESSES ON INSIDE COVER

Speed Reading

• *McDonald's—Behind the Arches* by John Love. Love, a former *Business Week* correspondent, investigates America's most successful fast food purveyor. The book is engaging and informative, although his scrutiny sometimes turns to a love-sick gaze. The image Love projects of McDonald's is too burnished to be real.

$22.45 postpaid from Bantam Books, 414 E. Golf Road, Des Plaines, IL 60016. (800) 223-6834.

• *Ronald Revisited— The World of Ronald McDonald*, Edited by **Marshall Fishwick**. A scholarly and thought provoking collection of essays on the ritual, the psychology, and the sheer wonder of this fast food empire.

$12.95 postpaid. Bowling Green State University Popular Press, Pop Culture Center, Bowling Green, OH 43403. (419) 372-7865.

• *Orange Roofs, Golden Arches— The Architecture of American Chain Restaurants* by **Philip Langdon**. Burger Chef, Denny's, Red Barn, Dairy Queen, Whataburger—even the offensive Coon Chicken Inn, with its 10-foot high, grotesque caricature of a black waiter—they're all here, as well as the HoJo's and McDonald's of the title.

Many wonderful old photos such as the original White Castle built in 1921 (Hamburgers—5¢) in Wichita, Kansas, and an early '60s Burger King with rooftop "handlebars" in Miami.

Langdon begins with the diner's history, charts the rise and fall of the drive-in with its spiffy carhops, and serves up McNuggets of information about the development of the "get 'em in, feed 'em fast, and get 'em out" fast food philosophy. Better than a degree from Hamburger University.

Unfortunately it's out-of-print, but well worth tracking down.

HOWARD **Johnson's** FAMOUS ICE CREAM 28 FLAVORS

ICE CREAM SHOPS - RESTAURANTS

Real American Food

Based on numbers consumed, the hamburger has replaced Mom's apple pie as the American food icon. And thanks to McDonald's world conquest, the rest of the planet is adopting our greasy gastronomy of ground beef grub— originally a naked export to the U.S. from Hamburg, Germany, America added the bun.

I'M "SPEEDEE"

"The [first] hamburger was probably a case of spontaneous combustion."—Nancy Ross Ryan, Food Writer

The First Name in Burgers

• First McDonald's location: 400 Lee St., Des Plaines, IL.

• In 1990, the Soviet Union suffered its first Big Mac Attack. Your order in Russian: "Big Mak," kartofel-fries, koktel—5.5 rubles (more than 1/3 the average Muscovite's daily wage).

• Richard and Maurice McDonald are the fathers of fast food, because they automated the burger business. Ray Kroc earns kudos for knowing enough to buy a brilliant idea when he saw one.

• In 1964 a McDonald's hamburger cost 15¢. At a recent price fixing, here's what a Big Mac cost around the world:

• *Norway 28 Kronen—$4.21*
• *Finland 16.6 markkaa—$3.84*
• *Switzerland 4.50 francs—$2.99*
• *France 17.2 francs—$2.81*
• *Japan 370 yen—$2.78*
• *Italy 3500 lire—$2.60*
• *U.S. $2.19*
• *England 1.04 pounds—$1.78*
• *Australia 2.00 dollars—$1.59*
• *Yugoslavia 2,300 dinars—$1.47*
• *Hong Kong 7.60 dollars—97¢*
• *Turkey 1,300 liras—95¢*
• *Hungary 43 forints—74¢*

• The McDonald's in Tupelo, Mississippi promotes an Elvis theme with the King's face etched right into the glass booth dividers, and memorabilia on all the walls.

• Coke Spade—McDonald's changed the shape of their coffee stirrers from spoon to flat paddle in the early '80s when it was reported that the spoons were popular with cocaine users.

• McDonald's employs over 8 million people. That's 1 in 15 American workers. McDonald's has overtaken the Army as the number one job training organization in the U.S.

• McDonald's, exclusive owner of "Mc" as it applies to restaurant services, in 1987 served the owners of Santa Cruz vegetarian restaurant to a court order. McDharma's eventually accepted an undisclosed sum from McDonald's to change their name.

• In 1987 Etna Huberty filed suit, claiming her husband had overdosed on Chicken McNuggets when he killed 21 and injured 19 others in a shooting spree at a Southern California McDonald's.

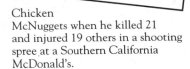

Moon Your Friends

It's that fabulous Mac Tonight Cheese Head Guy, complete with grey tux, red bowtie and cummerbund. Plus sunglasses, of course.

Available in a set of 3, each about 3 inches tall. $3.25 + 4.00 shipping per order from Archie McPhee, P.O. Box 30852, Seattle, WA 98103-0852. (206) 547-2467.

McDONALD'S MECCA

McDonald's Museum. It's all here, almost: the huge arches, the candy-stripe tile and the little man on the sign. This restoration of the world's first McDonald's franchise has everything as it was in 1955 when it first opened— except the burgers. If you actually want to eat, you have to go to the typical, bland, modern McDonald's across the street.

400 Lee St., Des Plaines, IL 60016. (708) 297-5022.

Wendy's Way

- First Wendy's location: 257 E. Broad St., Columbus, Ohio, in 1969.
- Most Memorable Advertising Campaign: "Where's the Beef?" featuring Clara Peller, Mildred Lane and Elizabeth Shaw.
- R. David Thomas made it from busboy to millionaire entrepreneur without a high school diploma. Thomas and a restaurant partner met Colonel Sanders and bought a franchise, where Thomas learned all he needed to know to start Wendy's.
- Wendy's 1984 "Where's the Beef?" campaign made advertising history by registering the highest-ever

consumer awareness levels. It swept the Clios, winning three of the ad industry's highest honors. Wendy's experienced a 31% increase in revenue during the campaign, and the phrase even became a campaign taunt in the presidential primaries.

BURGER KING

He Had It His Way

Elvis' Favorite Posthumous Burger King. Eleven years after he died, this was Elvis' favorite place to grab a quick flame-broiled bite. The King was allegedly sighted at this Burger King Restaurant in 1988 by the off-spring of the same Kalamazoo, Michigan housewife who'd "spotted" him twice before in her local mall. Shopping for a new disguise, we hope.

3015 South Westnedge Ave., Kalamazoo, Michigan.

Have It Your Way

A Whopper with squeaky pickles and rubber cheese, please!

#9030, Fake Swiss Cheese with whitish-yellow, oily look. Six slices for $2.95 + 4.00 shipping. And #8877, 4 inch long Squeak Pickles (10 of 'em) that even have those little knobby things on the sides, $3.50 + 4.00 shipping from Archie McPhee, P.O. Box 30852, Seattle, WA 98103-0852. (206) 547-2467.

EXPLODING CLOWNS

In 1980, Jack-in-the-Box quit clowning around and dynamited its long-time spokes-figure on network TV to usher in its new "No more junk-in-the-box" image.

Further Fare

Have A Light Lunch. This gooseneck hamburger lamp'll light up your life and your leftovers.

#242B, $65.00 + 7.50. Clay Art, 1320 Potrero Ave., San Francisco, CA 94110. (800) 252-9555 / FAX (415) 285-3017.

For Small Fries

Tyco's Super Dough Snack Shop. Cones, burgers, dogs, pizza. Fries, too!

About $25.00 at your local Toys 'R' Us store, or contact Tyco Toys, 540 Glen Ave., Morristown, NJ 08057. (800) 257-7728.

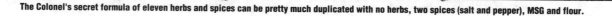

The Colonel's secret formula of eleven herbs and spices can be pretty much duplicated with no herbs, two spices (salt and pepper), MSG and flour.

White Castle SYSTEM, INC.
A NATIONAL INSTITUTION
ESTABLISHED IN 1921
Buy 'em by the Sack

"They taste like sin would taste, if you could eat it..."
—Glenn Savan, *White Palace*

SQUARE SLIDERS

"The bun was very soft, and when he pulled it away, bits of bread stuck to the meat, which was a flatdead-looking gray, scored with holes and sprinkled with translucent onions."

—Glenn Savan, *White Palace* (a novel about a love affair between a yuppie and a fast food waitress)

• First White Castle location: 110 West First Street, Wichita, Kansas (opened in March, 1921).

• Most Memorable Advertising Campaign: "Buy 'em by the sack."

• The average order placed by a man is 4-10 burgers; by a woman, 2-3.

• Edgar "Bill" Ingram borrowed $700 to start the first White Castle, and repaid the loan in only 90 days. Three generations later, the Ingrams still run White Castle.

• The burgers are known as Sliders, Belly-Bombers, Gut-Busters, Beef Cookies and Whiteys, depending on where you live.

• Why are they square? No esoteric reasoning here—you can fit more square burgers on a grill with less wasted space. Also, they look bigger on a bun because the corners stick out. The five holes are equally practical, enabling burgers to cook through without being flipped.

• If you're a White Castle fan living west of the Mississippi whose friends are sick of schlepping burgers every time they visit, look for frozen Bombers in your local grocery store's frozen food case. Microwave 'em and, except for the missing pickle (they don't freeze well, according to W.C. sources), they taste exactly like you remember 'em.

Before Going On Duty

White Castle BELLY BOMBERS

• White Castle burgers rank in the top ten foods that are "better than sex," according to Albert B. Gerber's *The Book of Sex Lists.* Among its worthy peers: caviar from Caspian Sea sturgeon and raspberries with creme fraiche.

• In 1980, Transplanted Ohioans of Fountain Hills, AZ craved some White Castles, so they placed a phone order for 10,000. The burgers only cost 50¢ apiece, but the delivery charge ran $2500. W.C. picked up the delivery tab, and everybody was happy.

WHITE TOWER HAMBURG
PUBLIC TELEPHONE
2 CABS
KELLY TIRES
DRINKS

Icon to Icon

Colonel Sanders on White Castle hamburgers:

"Now, I'd eat that hamburger. Holes make it cook faster, and it won't warp. I like the onions, too. It's a tasty little thing. See, there's a lot of bread, but it's spongy. It's just air. They've got a special formula."

—[From an interview by Ira Simmons in *Junk Food.*]

" I like to compare them [White Castle burgers] to a good scotch. It's a taste one has to acquire."—Gail Turley, Director of Public Relations, White Castle.

THE PIZZA PRINCIPLE

• Birthplace of Domino's Pizza: DomiNick's, 507 West Cross Street, Ypsilanti, Michigan (opened December, 1960).

• Most Memorable Advertising Character: The Noid.

• Tom Monaghan borrowed $900 to start Domino's with his brother James. Tom eventually bought James' half of the business in exchange for a Volkswagen Beetle.

• Domino's Pizza used more than 132 million pounds of cheese in 1989, enough to feed 1000 mice for 104 years.

ParaNoid?

Convinced that the Domino's Pizza "Avoid the Noid" campaign was aimed at him personally, Kenneth Laram Noid took revenge on this Georgia Domino's store. He held the employees hostage at gunpoint while they prepared and then watched him eat a pizza. He was found not guilty of robbery or kidnapping by reason of insanity.

Domino's Pizza—Site of the Noid attack, 4763 Buford Highway, Chamblee, Georgia.

Panned Pizza Movies

• *Splendor in the Grass* (1961). Warren Beatty, drunk, is encouraged to eat some so he won't get sick. Whatever happened to black coffee?

• *The French Connection* (1971).Gene Hackman scarfs a slice while he waits for gangsters.

• *Fast Times at Ridgemont High* (1982). Sean Penn alleviates a munchies attack by having a pizza snack delivered to his classroom.

• *Mystic Pizza* (1988). Nothing New Age about these slices of life and love concerning three Mystic, Connecticut pizza parlor waitresses.

• *Do the Right Thing* (1990). Danny Aiello's pizzeria sets the stage for violence in Spike Lee's controversial film.

• *I Love You to Death* (1990). Tracey Ullman tries to kill the pizza man, her husband, for making too many unauthorized deliveries.

• *Teenage Mutant Ninja Turtles* (1990). Rad Reptiles' food of choice.

Pizza Points

• Every day, Americans eat 75 acres of pizza.

• In 1984, U.S. pizzerias out-numbered ham-burger joints.

• The largest non-prank pizza order ever placed: 2,000 pies Youth for Christ ordered from Kansas City, Missouri's C&L Pizza for their regional youth rally.

• Red herring is the most popular pizza topping in Moscow, where there are now over 30 pizzerias. Indians require curry in the sauce. And in Costa Rica they like coconut!

Chicken Bits

• Home-made fried chicken is a chore. You've got to cut the bird into pieces, dredge them in flour, dip them in batter and breading, deep-fry them in boiling oil (taking care not to spatter yourself or start a grease fire), and drain them on paper towels before serving. Hot, time-consuming, messy work that the Colonel knew people would rather leave to somebody else.

• First Kentucky Fried Chicken location: Corbin, Kentucky, 1939.

• Colonel Sanders started KFC with a $125 Social Security check and a pressure cooker in his gas station's kitchen.

• Harlan Sanders was made a Kentucky Colonel in 1935 when Governor Ruby Laffon honored him with the title for his outstanding contribution to the state's cuisine.

• In 1964, Colonel Sanders appeared on *What's My Line?* He stumped the panel.

• The Colonel sells in one year, world-wide, 541,000,000 chickens.

• While a guest on a Dallas talk show, Gloria Pitzer, the "food detective," received an on-the-air call from the Colonel, who said all his chicken coating ingredients could be found in one stop at the local market. When the plucky food sleuth concocted a facsimile of the Colonel's secret 11 herbs and spices with: 3 cups flour, 1 table-spoon paprika, 2 envelopes Lipton's Tomato Cup-A-Soup and two envelopes Seven Seas Italian Dressing, the Colonel said "Now you're cookin'."

• Three who tried to do chicken right and failed: *Fats Domino, Mahalia ~kson, and Minnie Pearl.*

Colonel Sanders Museum

See the Colonel's personal favorite National Restaurant Association's Restaurateur of the Year Award: a wire sculpture of a hen laying a golden egg. The hen turns and flaps her wings at the touch of a button. This is a small museum of exhibits like plaques, city keys, honorary titles and other civic gestures of appreciation. The late Colonel's presence is vividly brought to life by details such as the real Masonic pin stuck into the plaster lapel, and working Timex watch on the wrist of his life-size Colonel statue.

Kentucky Fried Chicken International Headquarters, 1441 Gardiner Lane, Louisville, KY 40232-2070. (502) 456-8300.

Real Lookin' But Not For Cookin'

This Kentucky Fried Chicken Dinner is a fake! It arrives in a compartmentalized plastic tray (we're not sure if it's original recipe or extra crispy). Also included is a biscuit, fries, "buttery" corn on the cob, ketchup, margarine and honey, plus something that looks like a cross between gravy and chocolate pudding. And, of course, the plate, napkin and "spork" (the hybrid eating utensil).

Only $14.50 per serving. Add 4.00 shipping per order. Archie McPhee, P.O. Box 30852, Seattle, WA 98103-0852. (206) 547-2467.

Colonel Sanders' Final Resting Place

The Colonel died at the age of 90 in 1980. His body lay in state in the Kentucky state capitol rotunda before retiring to its final resting spot at Cave Hill. Once you find the cemetery, just follow the yellow painted line to the Colonel's grave.

Cave Hill Cemetery, 710 Baxter Ave., Louisville, KY 40204. (502) 584-8363.

One Clever Cookie

Ice Cream And Cookies. Looks like the world's largest ice cream cone, but looks are deceiving. This ceramic strawberry treat is really a cookie jar.

#030979, $16.95 + 4.25 shipping from Casual Living USA, 5401 Hangar Court, P.O. Box 31273. Tampa, FL 33631-3273. (800) 843-1881 / FAX (800) 882-4605.

Dairy Queen

• First Dairy Queen location: Joliet, Illinois, 1940.

• J.F. McCullough and son Alex came up with the soft-serve ice cream device and built an empire around it.

• There are only 4 Dairy Queens in Kuwait, where the average daily temperature ranges from 56° to 99°, but there are 2 in Iceland where the average daily temperature only ranges from 34° to 56°.

• Around 1978, Dairy Queen attempted to introduce frozen yogurt, but it was a concept ahead of its time, and the idea melted down in the pre-health conscious market.

Get Your McCollectibles

Hake's Americana & Collectibles. Ted Hake is the man the Smithsonian goes to when they need a Colonel Sanders doll or a Ronald McDonald nightlight. His mail and phone auction is probably the best source anywhere for fast food—or almost any other—collectibles. McDonald's "Happy Meals" toy premiums, character drinking glasses and other promotional items are featured with up to three thousand items, each described in detail and sometimes illustrated.

$20.00 U.S. / Canada $30 foreign for 4 bi-monthly catalogs to P.O. Box 1444, York, PA 17405. (717) 848-1333 / FAX (717) 848-4877.

A Brawny Lad, Please

Who hasn't been embarrassed by reading aloud these items while ordering:

• *Yumbo*
• *Big Foot*
• *Brawny Lad*
• *Whaler*
• *Whopper*
• *Biggie Fries*
• *Fajita Pita*
• *McNuggets*
• *Poacher's Platter*

W.C. FIELDS FOREVER

His raspy voice, another trademark, was the result of a long series of colds. He slept outside from age 11, when he ran away from home, till age 15, when he became part of a vaudeville troupe.

Possibly the funniest man in movies was born Claude William Dunkenfield in Philadelphia in 1879, but he eventually reversed his first two initials and streamlined his last name.

W.C. Fields ran away from home at age 11 and started a career as a circus hand, then a juggler. He added misanthropic patter to his juggling act and, through sheer discipline, became the greatest juggler of his time, using eggs, canes and cigar boxes.

Although popular myth has it that his bulbous red nose was a testament to tippling, its monumental size really came from beatings Fields took from toughs during his childhood.

His talent at juggling and comedy made him a star in the Ziegfeld Follies for a decade before jumping over to radio and film.

In a career beginning in 1915 and spanning 31 years, Fields appeared in 42 films, many of which he wrote and directed as well. Of these, almost a third—12—have vanished or are otherwise unavailable for viewing. Fields died in 1946 on a day he absolutely detested—Christmas.

Fields Studies

• *"Anyone who hates dogs and children can't be all bad."*

• *"Twas a woman who drove me to drink, and I never had the courtesy to thank her for it."*

• *"Reminds me of my safari to Africa. Somebody forgot the corkscrew and for several days we had to live on nothing but food and water."*

• *"Women are like elephants to me. I like to look at them, but I wouldn't want to own one."*

Fields of Dreams & Vice Versa

While an alarming proportion of Fields' work is "lost," that which remains is pretty damned good. Here are some of our favorites of what is available on video:

The Best of W. C. Fields. Three early classics: "Golf Specialist," "The Dentist," and "The Fatal Glass of Beer." 58 min. B&W, RP7058 $19.95 + $3.95 shipping.

The Bank Dick. One of his best, in which Fields accidentally stops a bank robbery and is hired to be the bank's detective. 73 min. B&W (1940), MC80019 $29.95 + $3.95 shipping.

International House. Starring Fields and Burns and Allen, with cameos by Bela Lugosi, Cab Calloway, Sterling Holloway, Rudy Vallee and Baby Rose Marie as a motley crew of tourists quarantined in a Shanghai hotel. 73 min. B&W (1933) MC80512 $29.95 + $3.95 shipping.

David Copperfield. Atypical Fields vehicle, a result of Universal loaning his talents to MGM. Director George Cukor unexpectedly brought out Fields' considerable ability as a character actor in this classic Dickens tale. 132 min. B&W (1934) MG300649 $24.95 + $3.95 shipping.

All of the above titles available from:

Blackhawk Films
5959 Triumph Street
Commerce, CA 90040-1688
1-800-826-2295

"A thing worth having is a thing worth cheating for."—W. C. Fields

ANECDOTAL FIELDS EVIDENCE

• "W. C. Fields practiced juggling with his feet till his legs bled, and he didn't bring one change into his act without weeks of rehearsal." — Joe Adamson

• Early in his career, when Fields was just a juggler on the vaudeville circuit, he followed the Marx Brothers' act, which at that time had 20 additional performers. Tired of closing the show to half a house, he made up an imaginary affliction, telling the manager he had to leave for New York: "You see this hand? I can't juggle any more because I've got noxis on the conoxis and I have to see a specialist right away." It worked.

• According to Groucho Marx, Fields had about $50,000 worth of booze stored in his attic. Groucho: "Don't you know that Prohibition is over?" Fields: "Well, it may come back!"

• Fields' claimed dislike of humanity was legendary. Whenever tourists came to gawk at his San Fernando Valley home, he was known to sit in the bushes and shoot spit balls at them.

• His misanthropy carried over to his sponsors as well. During Fields' radio show the executives at Winston Cigarettes smiled along with the nation at stories about Chester, his fictitious son—until one day when they realized that the son's full name was the same as a rival cigarette's.

• Fields opened hundreds of bank accounts under scores of unlikely names. Much of the money remained unclaimed, but what was found, he willed to the establishment of a non-denominational orphan's home.

Fields on Radio

A classic Fields radio routine on audiocassette, "The Day I Drank a Glass of Water." Perish the thought!

W.C. Fields' Patented Cigar Boxes

Fields' skills as a juggler were legendary. The tricks he did with three cigar boxes became a kind of trademark and he used to slip the routine into his act whenever possible, including a great bit in his movie *The Great McGonigal*.

You can own Fieldsian cigar boxes. Using them is like stop-action juggling, keeping three boxes moving with only two hands. These boxes are specially designed for tricks, and each has a caricature of Fields on the side.

Great Godfrey Daniels! Read These Books

W.C. Fields: His Follies and Fortune by Robert Lewis Taylor. First published in 1949, the New York Times called this classic bio "a hilarious history of the fabulous comedian." We agree.

Three Films of WC Fields: Never Give a Sucker an Even Break, Tillie and Gus, The Bank Dick. There is no substitute to seeing and hearing Fields in action. Still, reading the complete scripts of three of his best movies shows off his comic writing skills as well.

Fields wrote the original story and/or screenplay for two of these under the improbable pseudonyms of Otis Criblecoblis and Mahatma Kane Jeeves. The compilers have carefully noted differences between written script and what appeared in the movie's actual soundtrack.

Cat In The Hatfish

It comes in two styles, bass or trout, and adjusts to all sizes. Hat is 100% cotton, fish is 100% weird.

#B3044 Blue Trout Cap or #B3045 Red Bass Cap, each $11.98 + 3.95 shipping from Harriet Carter, Dept. 30, North Wales, PA 19455. (215) 361-5151.

Calling Cods

Automatic Fish Call comes in a convincing package so your unsuspecting fishing buddy'll fall hook, line & sinker. When he sees that it's a kazoo attached to a funnel he'll know he's been had. Great gag.

#4331K, $4.50 + 1.35 shipping from Johnson Smith Company, 4514 19th Court East, P.O. Box 25500, Bradenton, FL 34206-5500. (813) 747-2356

Fish to Be Tied

Don't flounder around trying to figure out what to wear. Try this Yellowtail Tie which is, like the fish, actually blue with a hint of pink. Goes great with 100% cotton art-quality Coral Shirt, also available.

#L02 Shirt (L, XL) $24 + 4.50 shipping. #L03 Tie $19 + 3.25. Daily Planet, PO Box 1313, New York, NY 10013. (212) 334-0006.

A Trout No Doubt

9" of rubber fun! Dark green with light green belly and white eyes.

5 fish for 9.95 + 3.00 shipping. Archie McPhee, P.O. Box 30852, Seattle, WA 98103-0852. (206) 547-2467.

We Fish You a Merry Xmas

Wooden replicas of your favorite fish suitable for hanging on your Christmas tree or wherever your heart desires. Each fish is a tad over 3 inches long.

#H480-1 Coho Salmon, #H481-1 Northern Pike, #482-1 Walleye Pike, #483-1 Rainbow Trout and/or #H484-1 Largemouth Bass. Each $5.95 + 1.95. Miles Kimball, 41 West Eighth Avenue, Oshkosh, WI 54906.

Nice Catch

Oven mitt looks like a fish. Apron looks like a fisherman's outfit complete with lures and escaping worm.

#G0269, $19.99 + 4.50 shipping from Country Music Hall of Fame and Museum, Mail Order Dept., 4 Music Square East, Nashville, TN 37203 (800) 255-2357.

"Go Fish" Cards

In 1910, Will's Tobacco Co. of Bristol and London issued a set of 50 fish and bait cards as a premium with their cigarettes. These authorized reproductions show popular fresh water sport fish and the best bait for catching them. Cards are displayed in hardwood and matted between glass to reveal both sides.

#16298, $185.00 + 8.50 shipping from Signals, P.O. Box 64428, St. Paul, MN 55164-0428. (800) 669-9696.

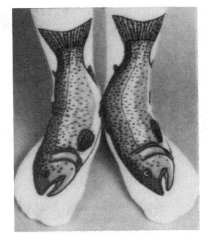

Filet of Sole

Fish socks—maybe these will stop those complaints about the smell of your feet.

#7403, Trout Socks, $9.98 + 3.99 shipping from Taylor Gifts, 355 E. Conestoga Road, P.O. Box 206, Wayne, PA 19087-0206. (215) 789-7007.

Reading on the Fly

The Art of the Trout Fly by Judith Dunham & photos by Egmont Van Dyck. "If all the fish in the waters of the world were to disappear tomorrow, I would still continue to tie flies," says fly artist Jack Gartside. Tying flies that will fool the fish is difficult. but that's almost beside the point. The folk art finished product is beautiful as well. This book shows the artistry and skill involved in combining feathers, fur and tinsel into eye- (and fish-) catching designs.

$29.95 (hardcover) or $18.95 (paper) + 2.50 shipping from Chronicle Books, 275 Fifth St., San Francisco, CA 94103. (800) 722-6657.

What's The Password?

Swordfish. The Marx Brothers could have used this in *Horsefeathers!* Picture Harpo pulling four of these 18-inch airbrushed, realistic-looking, plastic swordfish out of his coat.

#D272 four fish, $12.00 + 3.00 shipping from Chicken Boy, P.O. Box 292000, Los Angeles, CA 90029 (800) 422-0505.

Bag 'O Fish

Here's a new angler on shoulder bags. Fish-shaped!

#8298, Trout Bag. #8299, Bass Bag. $29.98 + 5.99 each from Taylor Gifts, 355 E. Conestoga Road, P.O. Box 206, Wayne, PA 19087-0206. (215) 789-7007.

String 'Em Up!

Mess-O-Trout is a light set of ten 6" plastic trout. Perfect if you're fishing for compliments.

#930073, $24.90 + 5.35 shipping. Casual Living USA, 5401 Hangar Ct., PO Box 31273, Tampa, FL 33631-3273. (800) 843-1881.

Bass Ackwards

Realistic looking 16-in. large-mouth bass is mounted on a wood trophy plaque but it's still alive! Any sudden noise (telephone, voice, hand-clap, etc.) activates hidden mechanism and fish squirms and wiggles as if it were freshly caught.

#T2574, It's Alive Fish, $49.98 + 6.75 shipping from Funny Side Up, 425 Stump Rd., North Wales, PA 19454. (215) 361-5130.

Flamingos

Mingo Madness

• Flamingos, looking pretty much as they do today, were roaming the earth almost 47 million years before humans came along.

• They were well known in Egypt, during the "pyramid and Sphinx" period. One played a prominent role in Aristophanes, 414 BC play *The Birds*.

• The flamingo phenomenon as we know it probably had its origins in the 1920s Florida land and tourist boom. Scores of wealthy speculators and tourists swarmed to the semi-tropical state and brought back souvenirs of the odd pink bird, native to the southern tip of the peninsula. The flamingo became a status symbol in the north, displayed by those folks rich enough to travel to such exotic places.

• By the 1950s the flamingo had been adopted by the great middle class as an icon proving their attainment of the suburban American dream.

• Don Featherstone designed the first plastic lawn flamingo in 1951 when he was a 21 year old art student. Don's first flamingo was flat, and somewhat bland in contrast to the 3-D model soon to come. In its next incarnation, his lawn flamingo was made of construction foam, but it fell apart too quickly, and dogs loved to chew it. But the third attempt was the charm, and the bright pink hollow, molded plastic bird proved durable, dog-proof and popular. Featherstone later became vice president of Union Products of Leominster, Massachusetts, the company for whom he originally designed the bird. It continues to be the world's largest flamingo manufacturer.

Plastic Classic

Bring down local property values with these 34" birds with steel legs.

#UP101, $9.95 + 3.00 shipping. The Cat's Pyjamas, 20 Church St., Montclair, NJ 07042. (201) 744-3896.

Flamingo Shades

See things through black or white flamingo frames.

#UX294, $19.50 + 4.00 shipping. The Cat's Pyjamas, 20 Church Street, Box 1569, Montclair, NJ 07042. (201) 744-3896.

People buy 450,000 plastic flamingos every year in the United States.

FLAMINGO MOVIES

• *Pink Flamingos*. A cult classic that pushes the limits of bad taste from Baltimore filmmaker John Waters and starring the inimitable and late Divine. Gangster film *Goodfellas* gives this film a plug.

• *Flamingo Road*. The original 1949 production starred Michael Curtiz, Joan Crawford and Zachary Scott. Crawford plays a tough carnival dancer stuck in a small Florida town. Wonderfully seedy. The 1980 remake was average, and the TV spin-off degenerated further still.

• *The Flamingo Kid*. Starring Gary Marshall, Matt Dillon, Richard Crenna, *Kid* is a decent coming-of-age story about a Brooklyn kid who works at a beach club.

• Flamingos also make cameo appearances in lots of films including *Earth Girls are Easy* and *Beaches*.

Not A Stool Pigeon...

...but a flamingo stool! Hand-carved maple legs and poplar seats finished in pink enamel. 29" tall.

#V529, $136.00 + 8.00 shipping from The Cat's Pyjamas, Box 1569, Montclair, NJ. (201) 744-3896.

Indoor Flamingos

House-trained, 10" tall flocked flamingo sits quietly anywhere you wish! All you have to do is say, "stay!"

$5.00 + 2.00 shipping from Klutz, 2121 Staunton Court, Palo Alto, CA 94306. (510) 424-0739.

Say It Loud, Pink & Proud

Flamingo Collectors' Society. When you join, you get not only a newsletter for your membership fee, but also a canvas flamingo tote bag and an official certificate of membership, too.

The newsletter is full of flamingo trivia, collections for trade, import items, and unique handmade items. In case you're the only one on your block who loves the tropical birds, you can correspond with flamingo aficionados all over the world.

Membership: $15 per year, includes tote bag and 6 newsletters
P.O. Box 346
Cross River, NY 10518
(914) 763-3845

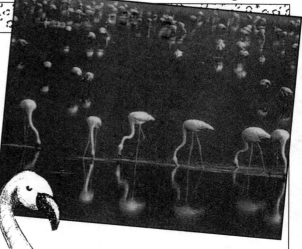

PRETTY IN PINK

Out of Africa and onto your wall! 24" x 36" poster of African flamingos at their favorite watering hole, Lake Nakuru.

#AN8501, $5.99 + 2.99 shipping from Flamingo Collector's Society, P.O. Box 346, Cross River, NY 10518. (914) 763-3845.

For Flamingo Fans

A Pink Flamingo by Susan Segal. Los Angeles commercial photographer Segal actually conceived this book one night in a dream. When she awoke she lit out travelling from Mulholland Drive all the way to Nassau, snapping pix of every flamingo she could find along the way. An introduction by Alexander Sprunt IV of the National Audubon Society gives the reader a fascinating look at flamingos from the scientific side — the perfect complement to Segal's quirky photo essay. A fine tribute to everybody's favorite spindly-legged pink bird.

$8.95 + $1.25 shipping from Ten Speed Press, PO Box 7123 , Berkeley, CA 94707. (800) 841-2665 / (510) 845-8414.

FLAMINGO FACTS

• The American Flamingo is extinct in the wild—the only ones left are in captive flocks (most with wings clipped so they don't fly away) at zoos, bird sanctuaries, casinos and race tracks.

• Flamingos' knees don't really bend backward. But their legs are so long that the joint you see where it seems the knee ought to be is really the flamingo's ankle, and it bends the same way yours does. The knee is hidden, high up inside the body.

• The flamingo is the only bird that eats with its head upside down—even while it is standing up.

• While flamingos are known to sometimes eat small fish, shrimp and snails, they are primarily vegetarians. They consume vast quantities of algae,

and this is what gives them their characteristic color. Flamingos in captivity are, as a result of algae deprivation, quite a bit paler than their wild cousins.

• Zoos keep their flamingo flocks in the pink by feeding them a natural food coloring, carotene.

• Why should your plastic flamingo be invisible in the dark? Drill a hole in your flamingo's bottom, add a light (twisting lamp wire up its legs), and brighten the night's decor.

FAMOUS FLAMINGO HANG-OUTS

• **Hialea Race Track and Park— "Home of the Flamingos."** You will find the pink birds here—about 800 of them—the world's largest "free flight" flock, in fact. Every March the track runs "Flamingo Stakes" with $250,000 to $500,000 in prize money.

   21st Street & E. 4th Ave., Hialea, FL (305) 885-8000.

• **Flamingo Republic Ardastra Gardens and Zoo.** The flamingo is the national bird of the Bahamas, and this preserve features a daily performance by the famous "Marching Flamingos"— kind of a Busby Berkeley with birds affair. The birds have been performing since 1954 with Carlton Briscoe, who is often called "Mr. Flamingo."

   Nassau, Bahamas. (809) 323-5806.

• **The Flamingo Hotel.** You might not find any real flamingos hanging out here but this is some of the best flamingo neon to be found anywhere. Of course it is. This is Las Vegas.

   3555 Las Vegas Blvd. S., Las Vegas, NV 89109. (702) 733-3111.

Placido Flamingo?

Hand-crafted flamingo soft sculptures made of natural fabrics with interior frame so they stay in shape without exercising!

#B705, 32", $59.99 + 6.99 or #B926, 24", $48.99 + 5.99 shipping from Flamingo Collector's Society, Box 346, Cross River, NY 10518. (914) 763-3845.

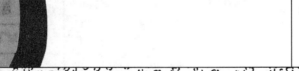

There are more plastic flamingos in the world than there are real ones.

FLAMINGOS *TO GO*

Enlist In The FAF

You get this fun T-shirt plus a membership card that entitles you to show it to anyone who cares!

#FAFIWY, $12.99 + 3.99 shipping. The Cat's Pyjamas, 20 Church Street, P.O. Box 1569, Montclair, NJ 07042. (201) 744-3896.

Flamingo Toilet Paper

Wipe that smile off your face. Flamingo toilet paper is for humans, not flamingos!

#CP756, $4.95 + 5.00 shipping for one roll, $42.00 + 5.00 shipping for 10. The Cat's Pyjamas, 20 Church Street, P.O. Box 1569, Montclair, NJ 07042. (201) 744-3896.

Shake Your Tail Feathers!

Salt & pepper shakers.

#SD5057, $14.50 + 4.00 shipping. The Cat's Pyjamas, 20 Church Street, P.O. Box 1569, Montclair, NJ 07042. (201) 744-3896.

Shower Curtain

Shower with 6 fine feathered friends!

#SK817, $24.00 + 4.00 shipping from The Cat's Pyjamas, 20 Church Street, P.O. Box 1569, Montclair, NJ 07042. (201) 744-3896.

SHORTS

#JB462, $16.00 + 3.00 shipping. The Cat's Pyjamas, 20 Church Street, P.O. Box 1569, Montclair, NJ 07042. (201) 744-3896.

Our Favorite Flamingo Store

The Cat's Pyjamas. Over one hundred flamingo items to choose from: inflatable flamingos, neon flamingos, flamingo clocks, mugs, bedroom slippers, toilet plungers, towel bars, TV trays, ash trays—we could go on, but you get the idea. More flamingos than you can shake a long, pink stick at. To stay in the pink, give 'em a call!

20 Church Street
P.O. Box 1569
Montclair, NJ 07042.
(201) 744-3896.

Rhinestone Pin

#PLSP165, $17.50 + 4.00 shipping. The Cat's Pyjamas, 20 Church Street, P.O. Box 1569, Montclair, NJ 07042. (201) 744-3896.

Football

A 100-YARD TIMELINE

English football, soccer, rugby and something played at Harvard called the "Boston Game"—these are the parents of modern football. From the murky past certain dates emerge:

1869. After years of making up rules and variations, Princeton played Rutgers in a game many consider to be the first football contest.

1880. At Yale, Walter Camp began modifying and codifying football rules. He cut the on-field team size down to 11 and replaced the circular chaos of the "scrum" with a line of scrimmage. Players kept looking for loopholes in the new rules. Princeton players discovered that nothing specified that the kickoff had to go to the other team, so the quarterback kicked to himself and ran inside an arm-linked wedge of teammates. Princeton also invented the "block game" and held the ball for an entire half,

forcing the invention of downs.

1895. The first professional game was played between two small town teams—Latrobe vs. Jeannette, Pennsylvania.

1906. The first forward pass was thrown by St. Louis University against Carroll College in Waukesha, Wisconsin.

1909. Football was nearly banned because so many players were getting killed—27 players that year, and hundreds more seriously injured. Even boxer John L. Sullivan, no stranger to brutal sports, observed "There's murder in that game!" after watching a Harvard-Yale game.

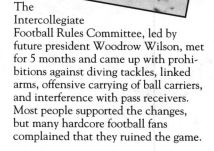

The Intercollegiate Football Rules Committee, led by future president Woodrow Wilson, met for 5 months and came up with prohibitions against diving tackles, linked arms, offensive carrying of ball carriers, and interference with pass receivers. Most people supported the changes, but many hardcore football fans complained that they ruined the game.

Football Facts

• George Halas coached more seasons than any other coach in history — 40 and all of 'em for the Chicago Bears.

• Paul Horning scored the most points ever in a season — 176. That's because he was not only the star halfback of the Green Bay Packers, but its field goal and extra-point kicker, too.

• More women report physical abuse from spouses and boyfriends during the Super Bowl than at any other time of the year.

From the Pigskin's Mouth

• "Football is not a sport in any sense. It is a brutal and savage slugging match between two reckless opposing crowds. The rougher it is and the more killed and crippled, the more delighted are the spectators, who howl their heads off at the sight of a player stretched prone and unconscious on the hard and frozen ground." —Gunfighter turned sportswriter Bat Masterson

• "Tackling is more natural than blocking. If a man is running down the street with everything you own, you won't let him get away. That's tackling." —Vince Lombardi

• "There are two types of coaches: them that have just been fired, and them that are going to be fired." —Bum Phillips

• "I left because of illness and

fatigue. The fans were sick and tired of me." —John Ralston (ex-coach, Denver Broncos)

• "Coach, some day when the going gets rough, tell the boys to win one for the Gipper." —Ronald Reagan, *Knute Rockne: All American*

• "I never made the team...I was not heavy enough to play the line, not fast enough to play halfback, and not smart enough to be a quarterback." —Richard M. Nixon

• "Vince Lombardi never really thought about winning; his trip was not losing." —Hunter S. Thompson

It's In The Cards

And you thought baseball was the only game in the trading card hobby. Wrong. There are no less than a dozen football card manufacturers. Here are some hot old football cards and their values.

• 1935 National Chicle — **Bronko Nagurski**, $6,500

• 1935 National Chicle — **Knute Rockne**, $2,000

• 1933 Sport Kings — **Red Grange**, $1,000

• 1957 Topps #119 — **Bart Starr** (Rookie), $425.00

• 1957 Topps #138 — **Johnny Unitas** (Rookie), $500.00

Looking for any particular old football cards? Contact the Chicago Card Company, P.O. Box 1135, Dundee, IL 60118. (708) 426-0556.

Football Card & Memorabilia Price Guides

• *Allen Kaye's Football Card News*. Allen Kaye wraps it all up in a large glossy magazine four times a year. Gives you an informative, easy-to-read price guide section plus feature stories and editorials about the game, the cards and the players.

One year (4 issues) $15.00, single issue $3.95 from 225 Stevens Avenue, Suite 104, Solana Beach, CA 92075. (619) 755-2811 / FAX (619) 755-5241.

• *Tuff Stuff.* Not only one of the best sources for football collectibles, but also baseball, basketball and hockey. Besides a comprehensive guide to card and memorabilia values, there's autograph info, a hobby dealer directory and a sports show calendar.

One year (12 issues) $24.95, single issue $3.95 from 2309-A Hungary Road, Richmond, VA 23228. (804) 266-0140 / FAX (804) 266-6874.

NEW JERSEY?

• **New, Genuine NFL Game Jerseys.** Remember they're cut large in order to take shoulder pads. Customize yours with up to 12 characters and any number between 0-99.

#F185 (dark) Authentic NFL Jerseys, $86.99 + 8.95 shipping; #F186 (white) Authentic NFL Jerseys, $86.99 + 8.95 shipping. Athletic Supply Catalog, 10812 Alder Cr., Dallas, TX 75238. (800) 635-GIFT or (214) 348-3600.

• **"Game-Worn" NFL Jerseys.** These were actually worn by your favorite stars in games. Here are some typical products and prices; call to see what's currently available.

—Walter Payton's Bears road jersey (with George S. Halas memorial patch), $2,750.

—Fran Tarkenton's Vikings home jersey with number on back, $2,350.

—Dick Butkus' Bears home jersey, $4,500.

—Alex Karras' Lions home jersey, $1,500.

Get in touch with what you want and maybe he's got it.

Mark Friedland 402 S. Galena Street, Aspen, CO 81612. (303) 920-2287.

Phoney Helmet

You might not be able to call the plays on the field, but you can call your mom. Inside the real Riddell helmet is a high-quality touch-tone phone with illuminated keypad. Comes mounted on a solid oak base, in the colors and logo of the pro team of your choice (some college teams, too).

#T235, $269.00 + 12.95 shipping from Herrington, 3 Symmes Drive, Londonderry, NH 03053. (800) 622-5221.

Paper Lions

Make your next Super Bowl party memorable with action-packed football invitations and settings.

#B2740 Paper Plates, $10.98
#B2741 Invitations, $5.50
#B2742 Cocktail Napkins, $1.98
#B2743 Luncheon Napkins, $2.99
Add $4.95 shipping. Harriet Carter, North Wales, PA 19455. (215) 361-5151.

REAL HELMET

Authentic NFL Helmet made by Riddell. Complete with cage-style face mask, inside lining, jaw pads, chin strap, and team logo.

Adult large only. #F189, $189.99 + 8.95 shipping. Athletic Supply Catalog, 10812 Alder Cr., Dallas, TX 75238. (800) 635-GIFT.

Tray Chic

No way is he leaving that chair in front of the TV merely to eat dinner. Don't fight it. Get this durable lacquered wood table tray with favorite team logo.

#7765 NFL Snack Table, $34.98 + 6.99 shipping from Taylor Gifts, 355 E. Conestoga Road, P.O. Box 206, Wayne, PA 19087-0206. (215) 789-7007.

Buckin' Bronko

Hall of Famer Bronko Nagurski is the first issue of the new Gridiron Greats Series of bobbin' head statues.

$25.00 + 3.50 shipping from MinneMemories, 180 Warren Street, Mankato, MN 56001. (507) 345-4246.

DECK 'EM ALL WITH BALLS OF FOLLY

Show your holiday and team spirit! Choose your favorite NFL or college tree ornament. Over 300 college and all 28 NFL teams.

#T690 School Ornament, $8.98 + 2.00 shipping; #T691 NFL Ornament, $9.98 + 2.00 shipping from The Lighter Side, 4514 19th St. Court East, P.O. Box 25600, Bradenton, FL 34206-5600. (813) 747-2356.

Leave Your Mark on Pedestrians

Make your car a real "sports" car with a chrome-finished, solid zinc ornament that'll fit your car, truck, van, RV or—if you're a true fan—motorcycle.

#F909 NFL Hood Ornament, $28.99 + 4.95 shipping from Athletic Supply Catalog, 10812 Alder Circle, Dallas, TX 75238. (800) 635-GIFT or (214) 348-3600.

INSTANT REPLAYS

Want a Divorce? *Nine hours* of Super Bowl highlights—exclusive NFL footage on 6 VHS tapes. From Green Bay's first win in 1967 through the whole splendid spectacle.

#FX051 (6 VHS Tapes), $129.70 + 8.95 shipping from Special Interest Video, 100 Enterprise Place, P.O. Box 7022, Dover, DE 19903-7022. (800) 522-0502 / FAX. (302) 678-9200.

• **Football Funnies.** Check out some of the stumbles, fumbles and bumbles from Sundays past. Crazy plays and stupid stuff that'll have you doubled over in laughter. 30 mins. each on VHS only.

#1284 *Football Funnies*, $12.95 + 4.20 shipping; #1370 *Pro Football Bloopers*, $12.95 + 4.20 shipping; Or buy both at $11.98 each + 4.20 shipping from Johnson Smith

Company, 4514 19th Court East, P.O. Box 25500, Bradenton, FL 34206-5500. (813) 747-2356 / FAX (813) 746-7896.

• *Knute Rockne & the Fighting Irish.* From the Four Horsemen to the famous "Gipper" speech, the story of Notre Dame's legendary coach. 45 minutes of an all-American hero.

#VHS 5609, $19.95 + 3.95 shipping. Waldenvideo By Mail, P.O. Box 305188, Nashville, TN 37230-5188. (800) 322-2000.

> *"When in doubt, punt."*
>
> — Knute Rockne

Screen Plays: The Whole Pop Football Film Festival

- College (1927)
- Horse Feathers (1932)
- Paper Lion (1968)
- Knute Rockne, All American (1940)
- Brian's Song (1970)
- Longest Yard (1974)
- North Dallas Forty (1979)

RAMs Versus the DOS Cowboys

NFL Challenge Computer Game. Nearly 50 offensive plays, 26 defensive, skill ratings for every NFL player...even slow motion instant replays. You control your game with three different philosophies: conservative, aggressive or existential. A real game of strategy.

IBM, $79.99 + 5.00 shipping; MAC, $89.99 + 5.00 shipping from Egghead Software, 22011 SE 51st Street, Issaquah, WA 98027-7004. (800) EGGHEAD.

out and hands it off instead. (See Figure 41.)

Figure 41. The power sweep against the 4-3 defense

BLITZ

MAN-TO-MAN MAN-TO-MAN MAN-TO-MAN

MAN-TO-MAN

MAN-TO-MAN

Have an Offensive Kid

Offensive-Defensive Football School. Two one-week sessions for boys 8-18 who want to learn the advanced version of football from folks like Ronnie Lott, Roger Craig, John Taylor, Matt Millen, Bubba Paris and others. Just a warning: be in shape because there's a lot of contact involved.

$450.00 per week. For more information contact Menlo College, Business Office, 100 El Camino Real, Atherton, CA 94027. (800) 243- 4296.

FOOTBALL
for the Books

• *How To Watch Football* by John L. Johnson. "What used to seem like a random 22 man pileup will be revealed as an intricately orchestrated design of finesse, guts and strategy," says the introduction. If you have a limited knowledge of football and want to start with the basics, this is the book for you.

$5.95 + 3.00 shipping from Accent Communications Company, Slawson Communications, Inc., 165 Vallecitos de Oro, San Marcos, CA 92069. (800) SLAWSON.

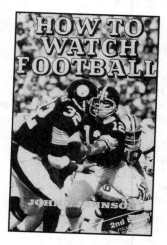

• *Football's Greatest Quotes* by Bob Chieger and Pat Sullivan. More than 1500 quotes from players, coaches, sportscasters, celebrities and others. How about this from Dandy Don Meredith? "The higher you climb the flagpole, the more people see your rear end." Really a lot of fun!

$8.95 + 4.00 shipping from Simon & Schuster, Inc., 1230 Avenue of the Americas, New York, NY 10020. (800) 223-2348.

• *Sports Babylon — Sex, Drugs and Other Dirty Dealings in the World of Sports,* by Mark Sabjak with M.H. Greenberg. Enough juicy stuff about a variety of sports figures (not just football) to keep you amused even during the halftime shows.

$7.95 + 2.80 shipping from AMOK, P.O. Box 861867, Terminal Annex, Los Angeles, CA 90086-1867. (213) 665-0956.

Mondays Will Never Be The Same

As if Saturday and Sunday weren't enough, football went prime time on September 21, 1970 thanks to ABC and Roone Arledge. People said it couldn't be done, But Monday Night Football has lasted over 20 years.

Rights to broadcast the first season cost ABC $8.5 million for the 14 game schedule. In 1990, the rights cost $12 million...per game!

• *Strange Sight #1 —* During a particular boring game, as a camera focused in on a dozing fan, the man woke up and flipped the "middle finger greeting" to the national audience. Explained Don Meredith, "I think he's just trying to tell us that he thinks his team is number 1!"

• *Strange Sight #2 —* Unfortunately only the announcers were able to witness this scene one Monday night in the broadcast booth: Ronald Reagan (Governor of California at the time) with his arm around John Lennon, explaining the game of football.

FRISBEE

Watch Your Head!

There was a time when you couldn't walk a college campus or go to a rock concert without getting conked on the head by a plastic flying saucer. Frisbees were especially popular in the late 1960s through 1970s, when they were seen as a non-competitive, non-violent counterculture answer to sports like football. That distinction eventually wore down, to a point now where some of the Frisbee sports—Ultimate, Guts—are at least as competitive as the others.

Most people use Frisbee as a generic term, despite the best PR efforts of the Wham-O Corporation, which is understandably touchy about any misuse of their trademarked term. We will try to keep everybody happy by capitalizing "Frisbee," and using the officially generic term "flying disc" when a non-Wham-O product is specified.

Frisbee History

The flying disc appeared in the late 1950s, a time of fascination with UFOs. Inventor Fred Morrison called his product "Morrison's Flyin' Saucer," because it looked so much like an invading alien space craft. When Wham-O bought the rights, they sold the discs for 59 cents each and called them "Pluto Platters."

In 1958, Wham-O changed the name to Frisbee. This was in honor of the Frisbie Baking Company in Bridgeport, Connecticut, whose pie plates were the original flying discs. Students at Yale and elsewhere had been flying them since the 1920s, shouting "Frisbie!" right before impact. A company spokesman estimated that the company lost about 5,000 pie plates in the late 1940s to the sport, and the company's now out of business. If only they'd gotten smart and started selling the tins instead of pie...

Although Frisbees have always been peaceful things, the military tried to change their character. In 1968, the Navy spent $400,000 of taxpayers' money to see if Frisbee-like discs could keep flares or other payloads aloft when launched from planes. But no go. The payloads were too heavy and the discs wouldn't work right. So Frisbees continue to maintain their peaceful nature.

Over-"Whelmed" by Jargon

In 1957, Frisbee fanatics developed a special vocabulary for the new toy. Try this: "If a wrimpleplat misses the sprovit, it is blort, but it might fall with the vit and be a grunde." (Translation: when a disc is badly thrown onto the playing field, it will be out of bounds or it might fall short.) Other terms to describe the stages in a Frisbee's flight were "whelm, wedge, well, wax, waft, wane, waste, warp and was." For some reason, the jargon never really caught on.

FRISBEE FACTS

• In 1982, the New England Journal of Medicine warned of a syndrome called Frisbee Finger, an injury to the middle finger of your throwing hand. Symptoms include blisters, cuts, abrasions and calluses. All seem to be caused by friction from the repeated throwing of Frisbees, especially older ones that have developed rough edges from being bounced along concrete surfaces and chewed by dogs.

• The exact number of Frisbees is a mystery, even to the company that makes them. According to a Wham-O spokesman: "Our archivists have not been very accurate and we have no count on how many are currently on people's roofs."

More flying discs are sold each year than baseballs, basketballs and footballs combined.

PILGRIMAGE

The Frisbee Statue. Yale, Princeton and Dartmouth have all claimed that their students were the first to borrow a pie tin from the Frisbie Baking Co. and start tossing it. But dark horse Middlebury College says it *really* started there and did something to commemorate its claim: in 1989 the college unveiled a bronze statue of a dog catching a Frisbee.

Just south of Munroe Hall. Middlebury College, Middlebury, VT.

Frisbee Science

"Like an airplane, a Frisbee flies because of two forces: lift and thrust. Your toss provides the thrust. Lift comes from air pressure underneath the Frisbee. Because the top of the Frisbee is curved, the air on top travels a greater distance as the Frisbee goes by. So the top air must go faster. And faster air doesn't have time to push down on the Frisbee as hard as the slower air underneath is pushing up. The spinning of the Frisbee is what keeps it from wobbling."

—Catherine O'Neill, *Washington Post*

Frisbee Sports

In late 1990, a Wham-O publicist was quoted by the *Washington Post* as saying that freewheeling, non-competitive Frisbee throwing—"Berkeley Frisbee," he called it—is like "talking to George Washington; it's history." He was explaining that Frisbee is now a serious competitive sport device (we wouldn't know; being from Berkeley, we still play catch, usually in Birkenstocks). Here are the hot Frisbee games, and their rule-making entities:

• **Ultimate.** Ultimate is a soccer-like game in which teams try to score goals against each other.

Ultimate Players Association, 1852 Old Country Road, Riverhead, NY 11901. (516) 369-0097.

• **Freestyle.** This is the arty, gymnastic aspect of Frisbee. Teams toss and juggle discs to music and are scored on grace, accuracy and difficulty.

Freestyle Players Association, P.O. Box 2412, Fort Collins, CO 80522. (303) 484-6932.

• **Golf.** There about 500 public Frisbee Golf courses nationwide, but the game can be played almost anywhere. Very much like real golf, including water traps and natural obstacles, but with Frisbees.

Professional Disc Golf Association, P.O. Box 240363, Memphis, TN 38124-0363. (901) 323-4849.

• **Guts.** Guts Frisbee, legend has it, was first played with a circular saw blade instead of a Frisbee. And that's how Guts players like to imagine themselves, even when playing with relatively harmless plastic. You get points by throwing discs at your opponents so hard and fast that they can't catch them one-handed. Many Guts players get themselves incapacitated by mild concussions or the dreaded "Frisbee Finger."

Guts Players Association, 5841 Haverhill, Lansing, MI 48911. (517) 882-1187.

• **Dogs.** Every year hundreds of local dog & owner competitions culminate in the national "Carnation Come 'N' Get It Canine Frisbee Tournaments." Competitions center around accuracy, speed, jump height and "grace."

Irv Lander, Executive Director, Come 'N' Get It Canine Frisbee Tournament, P.O. Box 16279, Encino, CA 91416. (818) 780-4915.

• **Everything else:** There are new Frisbee games being developed all the time, even faster than new clubs can spring up to foster them. How about "Double Disc Court" (a game likened to playing tennis with two balls)? How about "43-Man Disc Squamish" (a game so new that it doesn't exist yet)?

United States Disc Sports Association, c/o Jim Palmari, 1090 South Avenue #3, Rochester, NY 14620. (716) 271-6546.

CHAMPIONSHIP MATERIALS

Over-the-counter Frisbees are perfectly fine, for amateurs. But would the Cubs use a wiffle ball in the World Series? "It's like the difference between a Chevy and a BMW," says Dan Roddick, sports marketing director of Wham-O, explaining why his company and others make lines of discs that you won't find in your local Kmart.

A serious Disc Golfer, for instance, may carry fifteen or more different discs in a game, including a "driver" for long distances, two others that curve predictably either left and right, an into-the-wind special, and a "putter" for short shots. About fifty manufacturers make discs for extraordinary hovering or distance or maneuverability, available only from specialty shops. Here are our two favorite mail order flying disc outlets:

- **DISCovering the World.** Their free 48 page catalog offers over 150 different flying discs, ranging in price from $1.00 to $9.00.

   6272 Beach Blvd., Buena Park, CA 90621. (714) 522-2202.

- **The Wright Life.** Another source for acutely specialized discs. Or how about a Gumabone® dog Frisbee for $8.50 + 3.00 shipping?

   Free catalog. 200 Linden, Ft. Collins, CO 80524. (800) 321-8833.

Toss Away Reading

Frisbee Players' Handbook by Mark Danna and Dan Pointer. This book is full of tips and wonderfully helpful photos, plus official rules for a lot of the disc games. A good source if you've got the basics and want to take the next steps. Actually packaged with a Frisbee, so you can immediately begin trying out the throws and neat stunts that'll impress your friends, and confound your enemies.

Book and disc set available for $9.95 postpaid from Para Publishing, P.O. Box 4232, Santa Barbara, CA 93103. (805) 968-7277.

Make an Aerobie Acquisition

- *The Aerobie Book* by John Cassidy. Buy the book, get an Aerobie ring, the farthest flying thrown object ever made (see next page). Then go set some records of your own.

   Book and ring in a convenient package deal. $12.95 + 3.00 shipping from Klutz, 2121 Staunton Ct., Palo Alto, CA 94306. (415) 424-0739.

Beautiful Streamer

The Klutz Comet flying disc comes with a mylar streamer so if you miss the disc as it passes you by, you have a second chance by grabbing its tail. You can even use the tail to twirl it back. A unique twist to a popular sport.

$10.00 + 2.00 shipping. Klutz, 2121 Staunton Ct., Palo Alto, CA 94306. (415) 424-0739.

A Record Far and Away

The farthest distance a flying disc has ever been thrown is 1257 feet—four football fields plus tax—thrown by Scott Zimmerman.

Not only was this the greatest distance for a *disc*, but for *any* heavier-than-air object tossed by a human, according to the *Guinness Book*.

Zimmerman used an Aerobie disc, designed by Alan Adler of Stanford University. Adler created the Aerobie with the help of a simulation computer, with a design calculated to balance the center of lift with the center of gravity, which minimizes flight instability.

A SOUND DESIGN

Toss this Sonic Saucer and it shrieks like a banshee. Electronic chip creates digital sound effect that'll clear the beach. 10 inch diameter.

#2729, $12.98 + 4.20 shipping from Johnson Smith Company, 4514 19th Court East, P.O. Box 25500, Bradenton, FL 34206-5500. (813) 747-2356 / FAX (813) 746-7896.

Feel Like Orson Welles

Your UFO-phobic neighbors will panic and run amok when they see this green and red blinking saucer sailing overhead. It actually appears to hover; flashing lights make it look like it's changing spin directions.

#4463, $16.98 + 4.20 shipping. Johnson Smith Co., 4514 19th Court East, P.O. Box 25500, Bradenton, FL 34206-5500. (813) 747-2356 / FAX (813) 746-7896.

Some Official Special Edition Frisbees

• Glow in the dark

• Goldplated (for trophies)

• Chocolate and Vanilla scented for dogs (a postman-scented model was suggested and rejected)

• Gumabone Dog Chew Frisbee

• Frisbee Dog Biscuits, licensed by Wham-O and manufactured by Kennel Ration. Design for "maximum hang time" (in other words, hovering ability).

Frisbee Free Verse

The first Frisbees from Wham-O had this molded onto them.

"Play catch, invent games.
To fly, flip away backhand.
Flat flip flies straight.
Tilted flip curves."

GAGS

The Gift Of Gags

Gag can mean a joke or getting ill. So, is the joke called a gag because it's sort of sick? Gags are usually more mean-spirited than the joker is willing to admit to. They're funny only unless you're the hapless victim.

It was probably a cave person who pulled the first practical joke by coming up with fake mastodon poop. Not long after, we suspect, were variations on the ol' "pocketbook on a string" trick that has had folks foolishly chasing up and down the sidewalk for years. And no doubt there were "kick me" signs in the earliest Sumerian cuneiforms.

Yes, you can't trust anybody except us, and why don't you sit down on this cushion here? You want some gum? How about peanuts? Wanna sniff my flower? What's this on your tie?

What's the matter, don't you have a sense of humor, buddy?

A Real Blow Out!

Blow all you want, these birthday candles won't go out.

#3724 Crazy Candles $1.35 from Johnson Smith (see end of Gags section).

Cajun Bubble Gum

Looks real. Tastes horrendous. After the first few chews they'll never want to blow a bubble again.

#2069 Hot Bubble Gum $1.60
#2073 Garlic Bubble Gum $1.60
Available from Johnson Smith (see end of Gags section).

Watch Out for Kryptonite

X-Ray vision isn't just for Superman. These X-Ray Glasses are rated as one of the best gags ever—at least on the buying public. It's an optical illusion which, under optimal conditions, gives the illusion, sort of, of being able to see the bones in your fingers. Look through clothes? Nope, sorry. Trivia note: the guy who came up with this gag is the same who made millions by convincing generations of children that insect-like brine shrimp are really cute little "Sea Monkeys."

#3762 X-Ray Glasses $2.75 from Johnson Smith (see end of Gags section).

Stupid But Classic

The Whoopee Cushion—sophisticated humor at its finest.

#2953 Whoopee Cushion $1.75 from Johnson Smith (see end of Gags).

Find An Itch

What can be funnier than watching other people in physical discomfort? To itch his own.

#3581 Itching Powder (2 pkgs.) $1.25 from Johnson Smith (see end of Gags section).

CHATTERING TEETH

Toothsome fun, with a bite.

#2167 Talking Teeth $4.98. Available from Johnson Smith (see end of Gags section).

Peanut Envy

This peanut brittle canister on the table yields two spring snakes. It'll surprise anybody who doesn't get out much.

#2924 Candy Can Snakes (two, 5 ft. each) $8.98 from Johnson Smith (see end of Gags section).

The Real Thing's Cheaper

Do a double whammy! Hand-held squeeze device makes a farting sound that'll turn heads. Stench Spray'll send 'em running for the exits.

#2530 Whoopee Device $3.98
#4778 Stench Spray $3.98
Available from Johnson Smith (see end of Gags section).

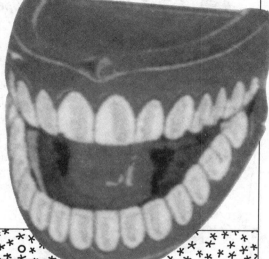

Psychiatrists observe that practical jokers tend to be hostile and slightly sadistic.

The Backstroke

Waiter! What's this fly doing in my soup?

#2007 Phony Flies (6) $1.98 from Johnson Smith (see end of Gags section).

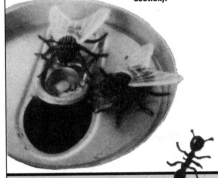

Anty Matter

Next July 4th picnic potluck, offer to bring the ants!

#3353 Phony Ants (dozens of 'em) $2.25 from Johnson Smith (see end of Gags section).

Save the Roach for Me

One, giant (4 1/2" long) roach. Full-featured, looks like the real thing.

#8879 Giant Deluxe Cockroach $1.85

Gross O' Roaches lives up to its name in appearance and in sheer numbers. Great for parties in the kitchen at 3 a.m.

#8599 Gross O' Roaches (144 2" long cockroaches) $23.00.

Both products available from Archie McPhee (see end of Gags section).

Hot Rats

Not just one but two, count 'em, two rubber rats that'll disgust even the bravest of souls.

#3109 Big Daddy Rat (5" long) $1.98.
#3886 Mashed Rat (looks like it's just been run over) $3.98. Available from Johnson Smith (see end of Gags section).

Come to Doggy, Do!

The classic phony dog poop.

#2999 Pre-formed Dog Mess $1.25

Can Doo! Aerosol dog mess so you can "doo" your own designs.

#3941 Instant Dog Mess $5.98

Both available from Johnson Smith (see end of Gags section).

The Yolk's on You!

Raw, raw! Egg on your friends. You can't beat this trick—plastic broken egg will crack everyone up.

#3918 I'm the Eggman $3.98 from Johnson Smith (see end of Gags section).

For That Little Squirt

The ancient Squirting Nickel trick gives unsuspecting victims a much needed shower.

#2032 Squirt Nickel $2.98. Available from Johnson Smith (see end of Gags section).

Kids today don't care about a piddling little nickel. But a pocket size Squirting Video Game is guaranteed to make your victim cry "Nintendo!"

#2364 Squirt Game $3.98. Available from Johnson Smith (see end of Gags section).

The Trouble with Dribbles

The dribble glass looks like an ordinary glass but drips beverage all over the drinker. Use grape juice to leave a permanent memory.

#3312 Dribble Glass $5.98 from Johnson Smith (see end of Gags section).

Cookie Toss

Another rubber classic "gag."

#1296 Fake Vomit $7.98 from Johnson Smith (see end of Gags section).

Shaked, Not Baked

• Chicken moves and shakes when you start talking. Noise-activated, 16" long chicken works great on a platter.

#8258 Wiggling Chicken $30.00 + $5.45 shipping from:
Post Scripts
P.O. Box 21628
Ft. Lauderdale, FL 33335
(800) 327-3799

Throw Your Voice

You'll never be lonely again because you bought this book on ventriloquism. You can impress your friends. Or at least when you talk to yourself you'll have a different second voice.

#1984 Secrets of Ventriloquism $1.25 from Johnson Smith (see end of Gags section).

Here's Tie In Your Eye

Tie one on and you'll be a real knockout! Pop-up tie device works with any tie.

#2867 Pop-Up Tie $3.98 from Johnson Smith (see bottom of page).

Black Eye Please

•Better than a poke with a sharp stick. Your friend looks into this eyepiece and emerges with a black eye!

#2531 Black Eye Joke $1.59 from Johnson Smith (see bottom of page).

If Your Nose Runs

...and your feet smell, then you're built upside down! Okay, that's an old joke. But so is the running nose gag. Wind-up fun that's nothing to sneeze at.

#2137 Wind-Up Nose $3.50 from Johnson Smith (see bottom of page).

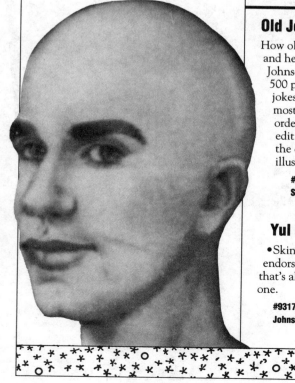

Electrifying Reading

It's a shocker of a book! Not like a Kitty Kelley exposé but readers will get a real jolt when they open it up to read the "World's Greatest Jokes."

#2709 Shocking Book $13.98 from Johnson Smith (see bottom of page).

Take 'Em For Granite

Fake and fun! Grapefruit size grey foam rubber rock is light enough to throw at your TV set or friend.

#8390 Fake Rock $2.50 each from Archie McPhee (see bottom of page).

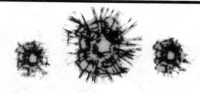

Number One With A Bullet

•Fake bullet hole decals. Really realistic!

#2246 Bullet Holes (15 per pkg.) $0.98 from Johnson Smith (see bottom of page).

Old Jokes Never Die

How old are these jokes? Pretty old, and here's proof—the reprint of the Johnson Smith 1929 catalog. Over 500 pages and filled with over 7,000 jokes, tricks and gadgets including most on these pages. You can't order from this reprinted collector's edition, but you'll get a kick out of the entertaining copy and illustrations.

#1929 Reprint Catalog $8.98 from Johnson Smith (See bottom of page).

Yul Go Wild

•Skinhead O'Connor doesn't endorse this bald head "wig" and that's all the more reason to buy one.

#9317 Bald Head $2.95. Available from Johnson Smith (see bottom of page).

Rabid Eye Movement

Move your head and your eyes drop outta their sockets. Bouncing eyeballs attached to glasses will make you the life of the party. Goes great with a lamp shade, too!

#2059 Bug-out Glasses $3.95 from Archie McPhee (see below).

You'll Get A Bang Out Of This

Comic pistol says "Bang!"

#2909 Joke Pistol $3.49 from Johnson Smith (see below).

How to Order

Johnson Smith and Archie McPhee are far away the two very best sources for gags old and new. Both have amazing catalogs filled with the "back-of-the-comic-book" products you coveted as a kid. It's not too late! For a catalog, or to order the products in this chapter, contact:

Johnson Smith Company

4514 19th Court East
P.O. Box 25500
Bradenton, FL 34206-5500. (813) 747-2356/ FAX (813) 746-7896
Add shipping charges:
Up to $5 add $1.35
$5.01 - $10 add 2.70
$10.01 - $20 add 4.20
$20.10 - $30 add 4.95
$30.01 - $40 add 5.95

Archie McPhee

P.O. Box 30852
Seattle, WA 98103
(206) 547-2467 / FAX
(206) 257-6319
Add $4.00 shipping per order.

Gambling

GAMBOLING THRU HISTORY

- Ancient Greeks gambled with "astragals," the ankle bones of cloven-hooved animals (like sheep and goats). In Greek mythology, the universe had been divided by a throw of astragals: Zeus won the heavens, Hades took charge of the underworld (tough luck, Hades, but what the hell), and Poseidon got the sea.

- One of Johannes Gutenberg's first orders for his newly invented printing press was not for Bibles, but for playing cards.

- The French, in the 15th century, began to play with a 52-card deck, one card for each week of the year. The four suits stood for the four seasons, the 13 cards in each suit stood for the 13 lunar months, and the 365 spots or pips in a complete deck represented the days of the year.

- The great lover Casanova was a heavy gambler, obtaining his stakes from his mistress of the moment. The piles of winnings he claimed are in doubt, though he certainly made money when he persuaded the King of France to open a national lottery, for which Casanova himself sold tickets.

- Benjamin Franklin was one of America's first printers of playing cards, which he supplied to customers of his post office in Philadelphia.

- In 1850, about 500 steamboats operated on the Mississippi River, offering floating opportunities for about 1,000 flashy-dressing, smooth-talking riverboat gamblers. They regularly fleeced passengers of their money, sometimes acting in cahoots with the ships' officers.

- Wild Bill Hickok played his last poker game the day he broke his own rule of never sitting with his back to the door. When drifter Jackie McCall came through the door and shot Wild Bill from behind, his poker hand included the two black aces and two black eights (the fifth card was either a jack or queen of diamonds). Since then, pairs of aces and eights have been known as a "dead man's hand."

- English gambler Charles Wells was immortalized in song as *The Man Who Broke the Bank at Monte Carlo*. In 1891, he broke the 100,000 franc banks at three roulette tables, subsequently draped in black by casino management. He left with a million francs and returned a few months later to win another million. His luck broke in a third visit when he lost money, was caught taking part in a scam, and sentenced to eight years in prison. After his release, he died a poor man.

- Actor Sean Connery tried his luck in 1963 at the roulette table in an Italian casino. He bet number 17 and won. He let his money ride, and again the wheel stopped at 17. He bet once more on 17 and won a third time, successfully bucking odds of over 40,000 to 1 against three consecutive wins, and collected $30,000. Maybe that's why Connery looked so relaxed playing James Bond taking his chances at the gaming tables.

Ante-Americanism

Place your bets while you can. According to I. Nelson Rose, a professor of law at Whittier College in California, legal gambling activity will be outlawed by the year 2029.

Rose says that Americans are now in the midst of the third large wave of gambling activity in our country's history. There were more lotteries in colonial America than there are today, but by the 1820s and '30s, they were banned almost everywhere. A second wave of gambling flourished during the Civil War and the Western frontier expansion, but scandals and Victorian morality brought it to a close—New York closed its race tracks in 1910.

The third wave started in the 1930s and is sweeping the country now. But Rose says that it will crash in turn, its demise fueled by scandals.

"Money won is twice as sweet as money earned." —Fast Eddie Felton in *The Color Of Money*

A SUCKER BITE

A music-hall joke has it that Van Gogh once bet a Parisian 100 francs that he could bite his own ear. The artist then pulled his ear from his pocket and bit it. The Parisian then offered a 200 franc wager that he could bite his own ear. Van Gogh accepted, and the man took out his false teeth and bit his ear with them.

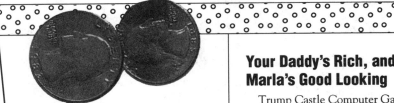

Heads I Win, Heads You Lose

You May Already Be a Loser

There are an estimated 80 million gamblers in the U.S. who play lotteries, bingo, slot machines, cards, or bet on sports or races for entertainment. About 6 million of these are "out of control" gamblers.

According to Washington D.C. psychiatrist Robert Custer, in his book *When Luck Runs Out*, pathological gamblers tend to be highly intelligent, highly energetic and easily bored in social situations. Most (80%) are men, 84% are married to a spouse who supports their addiction, 5% borrow money from illegal sources, 75% brag about winning even when they are losing, and 90% say they feel like "big shots."

Your Daddy's Rich, and Your Marla's Good Looking

Trump Castle Computer Game. It's billed as the "ultimate casino gambling simulation," where you can choose among Blackjack, Craps, Keno or Roulette. Buy it and help Mr. Trump out from HIS gambling mistakes in real estate. Great graphics and 3-D animation help recreate the seedily opulent atmosphere of Atlantic City.

This One-Armed Bandit Has A Gun!

Hand-painted, solid wood, 6 foot tall one-armed bandit is a reproduction of a '40s slot machine. So good a replica that it really works! So real, in fact, that it's not legal for sale in some states.

When Your Chips Are Down

Suppliers to give your home that casino ambiance:

• **Gambler's Bookstore**. Their 64-page "magalog" (part magazine, part catalog), *The Gambler*, features poker books and stuff for your rec room Las Vegas Night. And if you're actually in Vegas, waiting for your luck to change at the tables, this is a great place to browse. It's a gaming emporium that's also a small museum, with one of the world's largest collections of casino chips dating back to the 1920s, and other historical materials.

• **Gamblers General Store**. Get your green plastic visor here. Also poker tables, cards, chips and dice.

More than $3 billion of illegal bets were riding on the outcome of the 1990 Super Bowl.

Games of Chance

Gamblers have been known to bet on which side a falling leaf would settle, which raindrop would reach the bottom of a windowpane first, and which sugar cube a fly would light on.

The idea of getting something for nothing has intrigued many people throughout the centuries. After all, hard work is okay—in its place.

It's exciting to test your luck, and despite the odds, people continue to make all manner of wagers. There's horseracing, dog racing, jai alai, bingo, lotteries, casino games like poker, blackjack, craps, keno, baccarat, and roulette, and those ever-ready one-armed bandits, the slot machines. Sure, it's tough to win, but as Damon Runyan said, all life is 6-5 against.

How To Win In Las Vegas

John Patrick has an answer...money management. And that's what he emphasizes in this Casino Survival Kit video that teaches you the basics of popular casino games.

#JJ025, $39.95 + 4.95 shipping from Special Interest Video, 100 Enterprise Place, P.O. Box 7022, Dover, DE 19903-7022. (800) 522-0502.

SPORTS BETTOR'S BIBLE

The Gold Sheet. Published by Mort Olshan for over 30 years, this weekly advises you on college and pro football teams "With the kind of edges I give you in *The Gold Sheet*, winning 60% of your bets is possible," claims Olshan. "With luck, you might win 65%. If you win more than 65% you might want to consider starting your own church."

On the other hand, if he's so good, where's the church of Saint Mort? And why is he publishing a newsletter instead of living off his winnings?

$105 (23 issues) to 9255 Sunset Blvd. #200, Los Angeles, CA 90069-9959. (800) 798-4653.

The Real Thing

Authentic slot machine. Pull the handle. The lights flash while real casino sound effects, but no payoff, make you feel as if you're right in the heart of the action.

#36770H, $369.00 + 12.50 shipping from Hammacher Schlemmer, Midwest Operations Center, 9180 Le Saint Drive, Fairfield, OH 45014. (800) 543-3366.

A GUIDE FOR SUCKERS

Read 'Em and Weep

• *Old and Curious Playing Cards* by H.T. Morley. Lots of illustrations, some color plates of cards showing subjects from Aesop's fables to the Spanish Armada. Learn why the knave of clubs is historically significant and why the nine of diamonds is called the curse of Scotland.

$14.98 + 3.50 shipping from Book Sales Inc., 110 Enterprise Ave., Secaucus, NJ 07094. (201) 864-6341.

• *A Guide for Suckers,* by *Night Court's* Harry Anderson. "Harry shows you games, tricks, bets, stunts, cons and bald face lies that you can perpetrate for yuks and bucks."

$6.95 + 2.70 shipping from Johnson Smith Co., 4514 19th St. Court East, P.O. Box 25600, Bradenton, FL 34206-5600. (813) 747-2356.

Gamblin' Magazines

• *The Card Player.* Subtitled "The Magazine for Those Who Play to Win," this publication covers a variety of card games (lots on poker) and also some sports betting. News about the Nevada gambling scene and California card clubs.

One year subscription (26 issues) $47.00 from 1455 E. Tropicana, Suite 450, Las Vegas, NV 89119. (702) 798-5170.

• *Win Magazine.* Articles and columns on casino gambling, sports betting, horse racing, dog racing, lotteries, and the gaming industry.

One year subscription (12 issues) $36.00, single copy $3.95 from 16760 Stagg St. #213, Van Nuys, CA 92406. (818) 781-9355.

Las Vegas' green felt gaming tables cover more ground than the grassy green NFL football fields.

Slot Speculation

Since 1839, when the first mechanical gambling devices appeared, the public has been in love with equipment that promises a payoff to the lucky. Coin-operated gambling machines flourished in Europe during the mid-1800s, but American firms didn't really get heavily involved until the late 1800s. The automatic paying-wheel machine and a three-reel device known as the Liberty Bell came into being in 1896, invented by Charles Fey in San Francisco (a historical marker marks the exact spot on Market Street). Within 30 years there were a million slot machines throughout the world.

As the popularity of a wide array of "nickel-eaters" grew, so did a backlash of opposition from members of the clergy, women's clubs, police, politicians, and newspapers. Many classic slot machines located in saloons were destroyed by zealous crusaders such as Carrie Nation and publicity-minded district attorneys during the prohibition era. The anti-gambling movement was largely successful, and it spawned the development of "trade stimulators"—countertop devices similar to slot machines but with payoffs in cigars, perfume, aspirin, soap or gumballs. These machines became highly popular as a way of getting around the prohibition against gambling devices.

After gambling became legal in Nevada in the 1940s, the population of slot machines began to increase again. Antique machines, along with jukeboxes and other arcade favorites, have become hot collectibles.

Because of the difficulty in getting parts for vintage slot machines, restoration work often requires a specialist. High-priced vintage slot machines cost upwards of $40,000, but classic counter gumball machines can be under $200.

Coin-Op Odds

• Most visitors to both Las Vegas and Atlantic City pour their money into slot machines.

• Some casino managers are arranging slot machines in circular layouts these days to make the one person-one machine pattern seem less anti-social and to create "an atmosphere of frenzy." They use aluminum trays to maximize "clatter" so that gamblers anywhere in the area will start salivating at the sound. "It sounds like a million dollars," says a casino executive.

• Much of the research effort expended by slot machine manufacturers goes toward offsetting new cheating techniques. Cheaters have used all manner of slugs to fool the machines, they've attacked with drills, wires, and various prying tools, they've slapped magnets on the sides of machines, and even wrapped automobile coils around their waists to try to zap machines with a 40,000 volt electric shock, hoping to somehow knock loose a jackpot.

A Random House Advantage

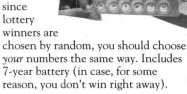

• **Pocket Lottery Computer.** It only takes 2 seconds to generate random numbers, and you might live the rest of your life as a rich, snooty person. Based on this alarmingly logical idea: since lottery winners are chosen by random, you should choose *your* numbers the same way. Includes 7-year battery (in case, for some reason, you don't win right away).

WHOLE LOTTO LOVE

Winning the lottery means your problems are over, right? Wrong.

Gussie DiBenedetto, a $5.7 million winner in the New York State Lottery, claims that winning large amounts of money causes lots of problems: winners get taken in by scams, they don't put enough away for taxes, and they get guilt and sympathy trips from friends and family. She started the Millionaire's Circle Club to teach fellow lottery winners how to avoid losing it all. One club member, a former financial planner, estimates that "about 40% of lottery millionaires are in debt."

Poker

5¢ Limit

SHUT UP & DEAL

Some call it "The Great American Game" — it's played in rec rooms, dining rooms and dens across the country. With "dealer's choice," you can choose from colorful names like Draw Poker, Seven Card Stud, High/Low Split, Hold 'Em, Low Ball, Around the World, Lame Brain Pete, and Spit in the Ocean. Through it all, as Kenny Rogers tells us, "You've gotta know how to hold 'em, know where to fold 'em, know when to walk away, know when to run."

Prominent Poker Players

- ♥ Richard Nixon
- Franklin D. Roosevelt
- Groucho Marx
- Calamity Jane
- ♣ General Custer
- General MacArthur
- Judge Robert Bork
- Justice Thurgood Marshall
- ♦ Angie Dickinson
- Telly Savalas
- ♠ Red Foxx
- Ed Koch
- Miz Lillian, Jimmy Carter's mother

Poker Pics

- **The Cincinnati Kid** (1965). This flick is aces, with young Steve McQueen learning lessons about life and poker from wily old Edward G. Robinson, in a New Orleans setting. The finale's winning hand is every poker player's fantasy.

- **Big Hand for the Little Lady** (1966). Joanne Woodward plays homesteader Henry Fonda's wife, who is forced to take over his poker hand when he falls ill in the middle of a game. Jason Robards and Kevin McCarthy are among her opponents, who don't know a good bluff when they see one.

- **Five Card Stud** (1968). Dean Martin is a gambler-turned-sleuth trying to discover who's causing the other players in a high-stakes poker game to fold—permanently! Robert Mitchum plays a priest with a fast draw, and a secret revenge motive.

- **The Sting** (1973). Robert Redford and Paul Newman take down gangster Robert Shaw using a rigged poker game on the night train to Chicago, and the hook for the whole film involves an elaborate con.

- **House of Games** (1987). Writer-Director David Mamet's intricately plotted psychological drama about a psychologist in a nightmare world of professional gamblers and con men. Excellent sequence as she learns about poker players' habits and give-away secrets ("tells").

Prescribed Poker Perusal

The Biggest Game in Town by A. Alvarez. This book will take you inside the world of high-stakes poker players, including the championships. It's good reading about character, about Las Vegas, about America, and about the characters who are the best at what they do.

$7.95 + 1.50 shipping from The Gambler, P.O. Box 14827, Las Vegas, NV 89114. (702) 734-6089.

Poker Pet Names

It seems like all top players have got lots of savvy, full-house egos, and nicknames.

- Walter "Puggy" Pearson
- Doyle "Texas Dolly" Brunson
- Johnny "The Grand Old Man" Moss
- David "Chip" Reese
- Johnny "Orient Express" Chan
- Stu "The Kid" Ungar
- Thomas "Amarillo Slim" Preston
- Bobby "The Owl" Baldwin
- Brian "Sailor" Roberts
- Jack "Treetop" Strauss
- Bobby "The Wizard" Hoff

Seven imperfect shuffles are necessary to mix a fifty-two card deck randomly.

POKER PILGRIMAGES

The World Series of Poker

The world's biggest poker shootout, the green felt playing fields where gold and fame are waiting for somebody who's got what it takes to take it. Every spring you've got four days of drawing, passing, folding, raising, reading 'em and weeping.

Anybody with the $10,000 entry fee can compete for world champ, so if you call a stack of five $100 chips "a nickel," $1,000 a "dime," and $10,000 "a big dime," contact Binion's Horseshoe Hotel & Casino, 128 E. Fremont St., Las Vegas, NV 89101. (800) 727-SLOT.

Research Jackpot

Maybe your accountant feels you'd be better off just reading about the World Series of Poker. The Gaming Resource Center, a part of the University of Nevada–Las Vegas library, is amassing a serious collection of everything ever published on the subject of gambling.

Gaming Resource Center, University of Nevada, Las Vegas, 4505 Maryland Parkway, Las Vegas, NV 89154-7032. (702) 739-3252.

Face Up Poker

You might not be playing with a full deck, but now you can have your face pictured on a full deck! Custom photo playing cards, bridge-size, finished in b&w. Send any photo (color or b&w).

Deck, $30.00 + 3.50 shipping from FaceCards, P.O. Box 1304, Yakima, WA 98907. (509) 453-2904.

Bluffin' and Woofin'

Ya gotta love those poker-playing dogs. You've seen 'em everywhere. They're kitsch classics! Five full-color posters: *Poker Sympathy, Bold Bluff, Sitting Up With a Sick Friend, A Waterloo,* and *Pinched with Four Aces.* Size: 12 x 16".

All five for $11.92 + 3.95 shipping from The Gambler, P.O. Box 14827, Las Vegas, NV 89114. (702) 734-6089.

Used Cards

These cards weren't owned by a little old lady who only used them to play canasta. These like-new playing cards were actually used in Las Vegas and are imprinted with the casino's name. Set of two decks.

#1294, $4.98 + 1.35 shipping from Johnson Smith Co., 4514 19th Court East, P.O. Box 25500, Bradenton, FL 34206-5500. (813) 747-2356.

Tell-Tale Hearts

Mike Caro's Book of Tells, by Mike Caro. Everybody knows you've gotta have a "poker face" but veteran players know you've got to control your whole body, or there'll be "tells" that other players can read. Some dead giveaways are:

• Pulse in the neck: Some veteran players wear turtlenecks because their pulse starts throbbing when they have a real good hand.

• Tapping feet and knocking knees: Top player Johnny Moss used to drop a cigarette on the floor and check under the table to see who was bluffing.

• A bead of sweat, a flickering eyelid, or a change in how the chips are pushed in, may indicate insincerity.

Over 150 photos explain how to read your opponents. Find out what you may be revealing about yourself and seal the leaks.

$19.95 + 3.95 shipping from Gambler's Bookstore, 4460 W. Reno St., Las Vegas, NV 89118. (702) 365-1400.

Card Clubs

• *National Poker Association.* Membership includes a subscription to the quarterly *NPA News,* discounts at gaming supply houses, and coupons for use at casinos. Over 1,500 members.

One year membership $20.00 to Steve Fox, President N.P.A., P.O. Box 17187, Colorado Springs, CO 80935.

• *International Home & Private Poker Players' Association.* Provides news of tournaments, tips on poker strategy, and helps members secure discounts on poker products. Membership includes subscription to newsletter and *Poker Tips* publication.

One year membership $7.00 to Tony Wuehle, Rt. 2, Box 2845, Manistique, MI 49854. (906) 341-5468.

GOLF
A Long Drive Through History

No one knows for sure who was the first person to pick up a stick and hit a rock into a hole. There have been reports of golf-like games reaching back into pre-history (including one vivid story about early golfers using heads of vanquished enemies). The Dutch swear golf's birthplace is Holland. Still, the most widely accepted version is Scotland's insistence that modern golf originated at St. Andrews in Scotland.

In 1467 the Scottish parliament decreed against playing both "fute-ball and golfe," but that prohibition was eventually repealed. St. Andrews Golf Club was founded in 1552. Later that same year, Mary, Queen of Scots, became the first woman golfer. It's unknown whether she played in moderation, or completely lost her head over the game.

St. Andrews, Scotland

originally had 19 holes (no, we're not including the bar). They decided to get rid of one so that they could lengthen the others. The rest of the golf world followed suit.

Golfers didn't always get teed-off. Instead of wooden tees, they used to hit their drives off small mounds of wet sand.

Way back when, the best golf clubs were made of hickory. Best of all, they sported great names, not numbers. What we call a "five iron," for example, was called a "mashie;" our "nine iron" was a "niblick."

Golf has spread around the world with interesting cultural variations. In Japan, golfers buy insurance policies for fear of getting a hole in one—the ritual parties, receptions and gifts that are expected afterward can cost upwards of $30,000 and in some cases mean financial ruin.

AN ACE IN THE HOLE

• Most people think a hole in one is a once-in-a-lifetime dream. Not Scott Palmer. According to *Guinness*, Scott had 100 aces, all on holes measuring 100 yards or more. In one year alone he had 33 (between June, 1983 and 1984). Good thing Scott didn't live in Japan.

• The longest hole in one? 480 yards on the 5th hole at Hope Country Club in Arkansas by Larry Bruce on November 15, 1962.

Popular Image of Golfers

The popular image of golf isn't completely fair. It isn't true that there are certain prerequisites:

• Being over 50 years old, wealthy, white, male, Protestant and somewhat overweight.

• Holding a public office, especially (since you have unlimited time on your hands) Vice President.

• A proclivity toward wearing plaid clothes and white shoes.

• The ability to tell people, without irony, that it's a great form of exercise before riding around in an electric cart.

• Knowing 200 jokes, each of which includes at least a talking animal, an ethnic of your choice, a rabbi, a priest or nun and either a crashing plane, a sinking boat or a bar.

COLLECTIBLES OFF COURSE

For decades, golf has had the schlockiest accessories and novelties of all known sports, even including bowling. Because of that, some of the more bizarre are actively sought after by both serious collectors and those who have a highly developed sense of irony.

Where to find old golf things? Check your attic or local garage sales for trophies, postcards, collectors plates, mugs, even scorecards.

Other much-valued items include golf club-shaped cocktail stirrers and bottle openers, walking sticks that conceal golf clubs, golf-design watches and flasks. But the following are among the most sought-after by golf collectors:

• Kenlock Ware unglazed black basalt and terra cotta-colored pottery pieces from the early 1900s by Josiah Wedgwood & Sons, decorated with a fashionably-dressed woman golfer with matching golf bag.

• A Japanese bank from the 1950s featuring a golfer putting a penny.

• An *Arnold Palmer Golf Game*, also from the 1950s.

Want to know more? Check out: *The Encyclopedia of Golf Collectibles* by John M. and Morton W. Olman.

$14.95 + 2.00 shipping from Vestal Press, 320 N. Jensen Road, P.O. Box 97, Vestal, NY 13851-0097. (607) 797-4872 / FAX (607) 797-4898.

Golf Club

The Golf Collectors Society. If you're interested in niblicks, mashies and other old golf equipment, or mementos, tees, cocktail napkins, souvenirs and schlock, this is the club for you. Their newsletter includes articles on collecting and the usual want ads. Back issues are available.

$25.00 annual membership. P.O. Box 491, Shawnee Mission, KS 66201. (913) 649-4618.

Illusions: Golf Figure It

• Wasn't that green a lot closer yesterday? The 14th hole at Coeur d'Alene (Idaho) Resort Golf Club has a computerized floating golf green on the surface of Lake Coeur d'Alene. Players are shuttled back and forth to it. Best of all, it can be anchored anywhere from 100 to 200 yards out.

• Don't bother trying to visit the National Association Of Left-Handed Golfers Hall Of Fame because, even though there are over a dozen inductees, "there's no building, no pictures, no anything like that," admits the head of the association.

"I'd like to join a club...and hit you over the head with it!"
—Groucho Marx

"I'm afraid I lack the temperament required to chase a little ball over acres of what should be animal pasture."
—Professor Kingsfield, *The Paper Chase*

"We're playing a game where the aim is to be below par. It's so wrong for me."
—Stephanie Vanderkellen, *Newhart*

The Theory Of Evolution

Nicely mounted table-top display of the development of the ball and club, with informative booklet. 10" x 3" x 3".

#49017, $279.00 + 14.45 shipping from W.M. Green & Company, P.O. Box 278, Highway 64 East, Robersonville, NC 27871. (800) 482-5050 / FAX (800) 232-9296.

Trading Cards For Golf!

Just like baseball cards, golf cards were given away as premiums with tobacco products in the old days. Set of 50 reproductions of these early 1900 cards come mounted between glass for viewing both sides, and framed in antique gold.

#13722, $185.00 + 8.50 shipping from Signals, P.O. Box 64428, St. Paul, MN 55164-0428. (800) 669-9696.

VIRTUAL REALITY

Australian Don Curchod spent nine years and close to $1 million perfecting and developing this indoor simulation. Just hit the ball against a huge protected video screen. A computer figures out the ball's path, spin and distance, and your ball actually continues "through" the screen and onto the computer-driven picture, reflecting the distance, speed and even hook or slice you would have gotten on a real course. You get an ever-changing view of a 7,000 yard pro course, with putting green on the side. If you've got a passion for golf, 250 square feet and a chunk of money to spare, you can play year-round without worrying about crowds or bad weather.

$30,000 + variable shipping from InGolf, 2010 Fortune Dr., Suite 102, San Jose, CA 95131-1823. (408) 954-1253.

Putter Around Your Backyard

Plant 'N' Putt Backyard Golf Course Green. Create your own personal, professional putting surface. The kit contains Penncross Creeping Bluegrass seed, a 31" flagstick and a 4" deep cup. Plant it, mow it, and putt it there, pal!

$49.95 postpaid from Clyde Robin Seed Co., 3670 Enterprise Avenue, Hayward, CA 94545. (510) 785-0425.

Greening of America

3 ft. x 9 ft. kidney-shaped green lets you putt or chip at home just like on the course. Simulated grass surface green has four holes with plugs so you can vary the target. Plugs double as risers so you can give yourself a downhill or uphill lie. Removable backstop and flap pole included. Green has non-skid rubber backing.

#169-000, $39.95 + 4.95 shipping from Golf Day, 395 Beecham Street, Chelsea, MA 02150. (800) 669-8600.

Pinehurst, North Carolina has the highest density of golf courses per capita: one for every 341 people living there.

A Green on Your Screen

Jack Nicklaus' Greatest 18 Holes of Major Championship Golf. Boot up and tee off. To make the transition from being a mere hacker to a *computer* hacker, play along with Jack Nicklaus on some of the most spectacular golf courses in the world—Pebble Beach, St. Andrews, Riviera, Royal Lytham, Muirfield, Augusta National and more, complete with roughs, sand traps, water hazards, wind gauges, even golf-cart paths. Offers 360-degree overhead and behind-the-tee perspectives. Random pin placement makes every hole play a little bit different every time.

$30 to $50 depending on computer (Amiga, Apple IIGS, Commodore, Mac, IBM) + 5.00. Egghead Software, 22011 SE 51st Street, Issaquah, WA 98027-7004. (800) EGGHEAD.

S illy Putters

These oddball clubs conform to USGA rules, believe it or not, and are actually balanced and functional. This company makes more than a dozen novelty head designs like a banana, beer bottle, water pipe, pickle, fish, corn cob and hot dog on a fork (you never sausage a thing!).

$36.00 + 5.00 shipping from Matzie Golf Company, 112 Penn St., El Segundo, CA 90245. (800) 722-7125.

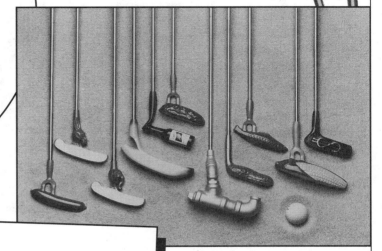

Putt Away Your Money

Antique replica cast iron bank keeps you on the money. You can bank on it!

#B7838, $19.98 + 4.85 shipping. Funny Side Up, 425 Stump Rd., North Wales, PA 19454. (215) 361-5130.

Game In The Toilet?

Three hole design on the toilet cover with "drop-in" printed on the underside...just above the big hole!

#156-003, $29.95 + 4.95 shipping from Golf Day, 395 Beecham Street, Chelsea, MA 02150. (800) 669-8600.

CALL THE CLUB

Not just another golf phone. This one doesn't ring...it hollers "FORE" instead! You talk through the club head and listen through the shaft.

#8067, $59.98 + 8.49 shipping from Taylor Gifts, 355 E. Conestoga Road, P.O. Box 206, Wayne, PA 19087-0206. (215) 789-7007.

Putt it Anywhere, Pal

There's a hole in your pocket! But only when you're carrying Perfecta-Putt—the shape-retaining silicone putting cup that folds easily for transport.

#4318, $14.95 + 3.25 shipping from Enticements, P.O. Box 4040, New Rochelle, NY 10802-4040. (800) 243-4300 / FAX (800) 244-4591.

Get the Shaft

Is That A Golf Club In Your Pocket...? You can take this travel putter with you, too. Because it folds to 12" then springs open to a full-size 36" shaft. Aluminum with black satin finish and molded rubber grip.

#4317, $26.95 + 5.25 shipping from Enticements, P.O. Box 4040, New Rochelle, NY 10802-4040. (800) 243-4300 / FAX (800) 244-4591.

"Fore!"

Okay, So It's Not A Caddie!

You're never too young to learn to drive. Or even putt. This kiddie cart comes with miniature bag, club and balls in case the kid wants to play a few rounds.

#359752, $38.00 + 6.80 shipping. FAO Schwarz, P.O. Box 182225, Chattanooga, TN 37422-7225. (800) 426-TOYS.

Give It A Shot

Golf Digest. Articles by and about some of golf's premiere players, useful tips from tee to green, equipment tests.

One year subscription (12 issues), $23.94. $2.95 single issue. Golf/Tennis Inc., 5520 Park Avenue, P.O. Box 395, Trumbull, CT 06611-0395. (800) 862-1200.

GREAT BALLS O' FUN

• **Screaming Ball.** Electronic ball shrieks like a banshee when you putt it.

#3675, $12.98 + 3.50 shipping from The Lighter Side, 4514 19th St. Court East, P.O. Box 25600, Bradenton, FL 34206-5600. (813) 747-2356 / FAX (813) 746-7896.

• **Exploding Ball.** This is the joke George Bush used on General Scowcroft once to get him to "lighten up," with only limited success (but you should have seen the Secret Service agents' faces).

#394 (set of three), $9.98 + 3.50 shipping from The Lighter Side, 4514 19th St. Court East, P.O. Box 25600, Bradenton, FL 34206-5600. (813) 747-2356 / FAX (813) 746-7896.

AAAUGH!

Reading the Greens

• *Downhill Lies And Other Falsehoods, Or How To Play Dirty Golf* by Rex Lardner. Can't beat 'em? Trick 'em! Psych out your opponents through creative misdirection. Humorous book teaches you how to win any way you can.

#C7761 Downhill Lies Book, $5.95 + 3.50 shipping from Harriet Carter, North Wales, PA 19455. (215) 361-5151.

• *Golf—The Golden Years* by Sarah Baudiel. This lavishly illustrated coffee table book leads you through the history of golf. Great gift.

#167-211, $34.95 + 4.95 shipping from Golf Day, 395 Beecham Street, Chelsea, MA 02150. (800) 669-8600.

• *Golf Gadgets: The Ultimate Catalog of Golf Equipment and Accessories* by Bill Hogan. This book proves that golf has more gewgaws than any other known sport.

How Great Thou Aren't

No one is gonna believe you're better than Bobby Jones. No way you're better than Nicklaus either. But would they believe that you're number five? Maybe if they saw it engraved on this official walnut grain wood plaque.

#D5919, $12.98 + 3.95 shipping from Funny Side Up, 425 Stump Rd., North Wales, PA 19454. (215) 361-5130.

THE ALL TIME TOP 10 OF GOLF

1. BOBBY JONES
2. JO ANNE CARNER
3. JACK NICKLAUS
4. MICKEY WRIGHT

YOUR

Golf Balls Overboard!

Golf Ball In A Life Jacket. A great golf gag gift for those who can't stay out of the water hazards. Actually floats!

#B7913 Golf Ball, $3.98 + 3.50 shipping from Harriet Carter, North Wales, PA 19455. (215) 361-5151.

From devices to improve your swing to novelties and desk ornaments. Need a solar-powered, self-ventilating golf hat? A parachuting gag golf ball? Exotic clubs, tees or balls? Aerosol "Slice Repellent"? This is the place to shop.

$12.95 + 1.30 shipping. Collier Books, 866 Third Avenue, New York, NY 10022. (800) 323-7445.

GOLF BY ASSOCIATION

A Long Drive

World Golf Hall Of Fame.
Dedicated in 1974 by golfer and president Gerald Ford, this 17-acre complex attracts over 30,000 visitors a year and features everything from two 1690 hand-crafted clubs to the signed scorecard of golf's best tournament round—a 59 by Al Geiberger.

See the Golf History Wall that extends 92 feet, exhibiting the evolution of golf from antique wooden clubs to today's high-tech graphite metal "woods." Or how about the collection of over 10,000 scoring pencils from clubs all over the world? Great stuff, and lots of golf courses nearby.

P.O. Box 1908, Pinehurst, NC 28374. (800) 334-0178.

• **United States Golf Association.** Founded in 1894 to promote the best interests of the game, the USGA writes the rules you play under and conducts the U.S. Open and National Amateur Championships. Even sponsors research, like finding turf grasses that need less water and maintenance.

Various memberships available—an Associate Member, the lowest general membership, receives a sub to *Golf Journal, U.S. Open Magazine* and more.

$25.00 from USGA, P.O. Box 746, Far Hills, NJ 07931-0746. (800) 233-0041.

• Laid Back Golfers Association. Their ritual greeting is "How many strokes?" answered by "Who cares?" It's an organization dedicated to the proposition that you don't have to be good at golf to have a good time on or off the course. The official membership kit includes LBGA golf cap, golf thongs ("flip-flops" with spikes), membership card and laissez-faire rule book.

$19.95 + 4.95 shipping from Las Vegas Discount Golf, 5325 South Valley View Blvd., Suite 10, Las Vegas, NV 89118. (800) 933-7777.

The Great Ones

• *The Golf Classics.* I Love Lucy *and* The Honeymooners. Two of TV's best 1950s shows lampoon golf (51 mins.).

#167-022, $14.95 + 4.95 from Golf Day, 395 Beecham Street, Chelsea, MA 02150. (800) 669-8600.

• *Outrageously Funny Golf.* An educational but hilarious videotape. 30 minutes of fun taught by Paul Hahn Jr., trick shot specialist, teaching pro and stand-up comedian.

#3760, $14.95 + 3.25 shipping. Enticements, P.O. Box 4040, New Rochelle, NY 10802-4040. (800) 243-4300.

Murphy's Laws Of Golf. Golfers aren't immune to Murphy's Law. Tom Poston is the perfect example as he stars as the victim of every imaginable mishap. If anything can go wrong, it's bound to go wrong on the golf course (30 mins. VHS or BETA).

$24.95 + 3.50 shipping from Frie's Home Video, 6922 Hollywood Blvd., Los Angeles, CA 90099-2453. (800) 321-6839.

Two Great Catalog Sources

From the first tee to the 19th hole, we think that if these two catalog companies don't have what you're looking for, it doesn't exist:

• **Austad's, 4500 East 10th Street, P.O. Box 1428, Sioux Falls, SD 57196-1428. (800) 759-4653 / FAX (800) 444-1234.**

• **Golf Day, 395 Beacham St., Chelsea, MA 02150. (800) 669-8600.**

Traps, divots and other unavoidable duffer's dilemmas! **MURPHY'S LAWS OF GOLF**

"If you drink, don't drive. Don't even putt."—Dean Martin

GONE WITH THE WIND

Frankly, My Dear…

A rose by any other name…would it smell so sweet? *Bah! Bah! Black Sheep*, *Milestones*, *Jettison*, *Not in Our Stars* and *Bugles Sang True* were some of the titles Margaret Mitchell considered naming her Civil War epic. Mitchell also originally called her gutsy heroine Pansy O'Hara; the demure Melanie, Permalia; and Tara, Fontenoy Hall. She wrote the manuscript in longhand on yellow legal pads. She finally got the courage to submit the ten-year effort to a publisher because she was in a blind fury after a "friend" told her she wasn't the type to successfully write a book. By the way, Mitchell wrote the book's last chapter first.

Reluctant Rhett. Clark Gable offered this reply when *GWTW* producer David O. Selznick and Louis Mayer of MGM prodded him to accept the role of Rhett Butler: "I don't want the part for money, chalk or marbles."

Gable was adamant, but in a vulnerable position. Still legally married to second wife Ria Langham Gable, Clark was in love with actress Carole Lombard. Mayer shrewdly encouraged Mrs. Gable to ask for an exhorbitant divorce settlement. Gable paid over $286,000 and was suddenly receptive when MGM added a $100,000 bonus to take the "role he was born to play."

Cruel hoax. The 2-year "search" for Scarlett was a PR move that raised MGM's profile and the hopes of 1,400 secretaries, housewives and aspiring actresses nationwide.

$5,000 word. Producer Selznick gladly paid a Hays Code profanity fine so that Rhett could say what he *damn* well pleased.

Clark Goebbels?

Hermann Goering, Air Marshall of the Nazi Luftwaffe, put a price on Clark Gable's head during his stint with the Eighth Air Force in World War II. When his boss, Adolf Hitler, heard about it, he created a furor and rescinded the order—Gable was his favorite movie star.

"And the Winner is…"

The 12th Academy Awards banquet in 1940 was significant —GWTW was nominated in 13 categories and won 8—an unprecedented number, especially notable since it was up against other worthies like *The Wizard of Oz*, *Mr. Smith Goes to Washington*, *Ninotchka*, *Of Mice and Men*, *Stagecoach*, *Wuthering Heights* and *Dark Victory*.

1940 was also the last year that Oscar results were routinely released to the press before the envelopes were opened. That year, *The Los-Angeles Times* prematurely splashed *GWTW*'s winning sweep across their early edition's front page. Since then, the Academy has kept the secret safely tucked away in vaults of the CPA firm of Price, Waterhouse and Company.

In 1987, *GWTW* won an even more impressive award when the 350,000 member American Film Institute voted it the greatest American film ever made.

Rogue Rhett Woos Widow

The oh-so-charming Rhett Butler proposes marriage to the Widow Kennedy in this fine china salute to *GWTW*. Artist Paul Jennis re-created this magic moment for plate collectors. Plate measures 8 1/2 inches and is rimmed with 22k gold.

Gone With The Wind in Russian is translated as "Carried Out With the Wind."

Clark Gable— Toothless Slob?

Gable was voted the reigning "King of Hollywood" by the movie-going public in the 1930s. Many of his fellow stars were equally enamored: "People can't understand it now, but we were in awe," said co-star Olivia de Haviland, who played Melanie. "Clark Gable didn't open supermarkets."

But those intimate with MGM's megastar sang a different tune.

Toothless wonder. "His false teeth were just too much," said Grace Kelly after shooting *Mogambo*. During the filming of *GWTW*, Vivien Leigh threatened to stop shooting love scenes with Gable until he took care of his denture breath.

Lousy kisser, etc. "My God you know I love Pa (Gable)," said Carole Lombard, "but I can't say he's a helluva lay."

But self-aware. "...this 'King' stuff is pure bullshit. I eat and sleep and go to the bathroom like everyone else. There's no special light that shines inside me and makes me a star. I'm just a lucky slob from Ohio."—Clark Gable

> ## "No movie has a right to be that long!"
> — Franklin D. Roosevelt after falling asleep at a White House screening

Push 'Em Back North

"For Christ's sake, let's get a good look at the girl's boobs," Victor Fleming ordered. Vivien Leigh's naturally side-sliding breasts had to be retrieved from her armpits and tightly taped to give adequate cleavage to fit into the décolleté burgundy velvet gown at Ashley's birthday party.

Some Tomato

Despite the death of Mitchell and her husband, the rights to *GWTW* are being zealously guarded by three Atlanta lawyers who prevent copyright infringements such as the California seed company which tried naming a new tomato the "Scarlett O'Hara."

JOIN THE CLUB

• **Tara Collectors Club**, PO Box 1200, Jonesboro, GA 30236.

• **GWTW Collectors Club**, 8105 Woodview Rd., Ellicott City, MD 21043.

Betty In Bloomers

Betty Boop doesn't give a boop on this double-screen printed T-shirt that's available in adult sizes M, L & XL.

#99634. $14.98 + 3.50 shipping from The Lighter Side, 4514 19th St. Court East, P.O. Box 25600, Bradenton, FL 34206-5600. (813) 747-2356.

WIND STATS

• Time Margaret Mitchell spent writing *Gone With the Wind*: 10 years
• Book advance she received from Macmilllan: $500
• Number of published works before: 1 locally published magazine article
• Number of books she wrote afterward: 0
• Copies of the book sold: 25 million in 27 languages
• Amount Mitchell received for GWTW movie rights: $100,000
• Total movie production time: 5 months and a day
• Total film shot: 85.1 miles (449,512 feet)
• Percentage used in final version: 4.5% (20,300 feet)
• Total estimated gross earnings from GWTW ticket sales, foreign rights, rentals and sales of the videocassette: $2.5 billion

Gone With the Wind **is the only Civil War epic ever filmed without even one battle scene.**

Black & White & Rhett All Over

• *The Complete Gone With the Wind Trivia Book* by Pauline Bartel. A quintessential *GWTW* guide, this book not only offers behind-the-scenes tales of the casting, production and promotion of the film but is also chock full of anecdotes of pranks and boo-boos. It even offers advice on how wanna-be Scarletts can control their hoops when dashing off to *GWTW* balls in their Toyotas ("To go through a doorway, push the sides of the dress in. When exiting the car, hold the gown down around you…").

The subtitle of the book is "The Movie and More" and *The Complete GWTW Trivia Book* gives much more than trivia. Author Bartel, a self-described "Windie" since age 16, keeps readers on their toes with novel quizzes and "Who said it?" match-up games.

$9.95 + 2.00 shipping from Taylor Publishing Co., 1550 W. Mockingbird Lane, Dallas, TX 75235. (214) 637-2800.

• *Gone With The Wind: The Definitive Illustrated History of the Book, the Movie and the Legend* by Herb Bridges and Terryl C. Boodman. Lavishly illustrated, this book is heavy on the visuals — movie clips, never-before-published photographs and even souvenir programs from the movie's premiere. Author Herb Bridges is a world-renowned expert on *GWTW* who has published three other books about the film.

$15.95 + 4.00 shipping from Simon & Schuster, 1230 Avenue of the Americas, New York, NY 10020. (800) 223-2348.

Rhett & Scarlet Together Again

800 piece puzzle depicting movie-posteresque scenes from *GWTW*. Can you put it together? Frankly, my dear, we don't give a damn.

#01-J4067, $10.95 + 3.98 from:
Bits & Pieces
1 Puzzle Place
Stevens Point, WI 54481-7199
(800) JIGSAWS / FAX (715) 341-5959

Southern Comfort

Cashing in on the *GWTW* phenomena, Southern Comfort Corporation introduced these toddies (below) in 1939 with the warning not to drink more than two "lest you be Gone With the Wind."

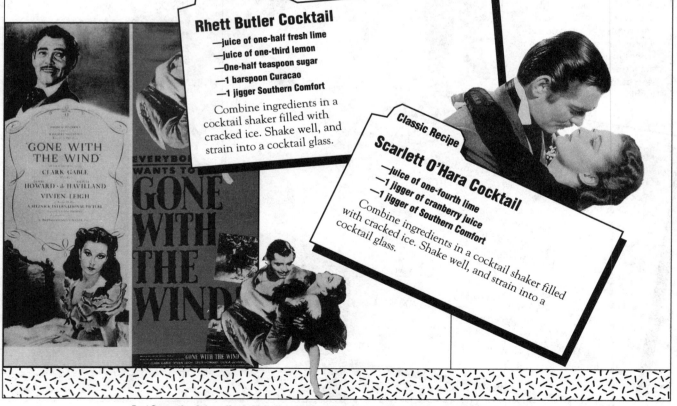

Classic Recipe

Rhett Butler Cocktail

—juice of one-half fresh lime
—juice of one-third lemon
—One-half teaspoon sugar
—1 barspoon Curacao
—1 jigger Southern Comfort

Combine ingredients in a cocktail shaker filled with cracked ice. Shake well, and strain into a cocktail glass.

Classic Recipe

Scarlett O'Hara Cocktail

—juice of one-fourth lime
—1 jigger of cranberry juice
—1 jigger of Southern Comfort

Combine ingredients in a cocktail shaker filled with cracked ice. Shake well, and strain into a cocktail glass.

Chewing Gum

Chicling Your Fancy

The discovery of well-chewed wads of tree resin, unearthed along with bones and other prehistoric artifacts, leads archaeologists to believe that even our primitive ancestors engaged in recreational chewing. Man has chewed everything from human gristle to synthetic rubber; a good chew has been touted as teeth-preserving, nerve-soothing, digestion-aiding, seasickness-preventing, mind-refreshing and even sex-appeal-enhancing.

Our more recent forebears enjoyed chewing home-made spruce resin and beeswax gum, and the first commercial batch of spruce resin chewing gum was manufactured by John Curtis in 1848. Sales were slow at first, but at two chaws for a penny, the gum became an overwhelming success within a year. By 1852, the Curtis Chewing Gum Company of Portland Maine employed over 200 in its new three story factory.

In 1871 inventor Thomas Adams, Sr. received the first patent on a gum-making machine and began mass producing a chicle-based gum. To enhance the appeal of his product, he began adding a licorice flavoring and called his invention Black Jack, the first flavored gum in America. It was sold until the 1970s when production was halted because of slow sales. Warner-Lambert reintroduced the 100 year old Black Jack, Beemans, and Clove gums in October, 1986 as a part of their "Nostalgia Gum Program."

Beeman's was originally invented in 1898 as a cure for heartburn. Clove gum got a boost during Prohibition when it was handed out as a breath freshener in illegal liquor houses.

By the turn of the century, new products such as Frank V. Canning's Dentyne "dental gum" and Henry Fleer's candy-coated Chiclets were gobbled up by the chewing public. The first bubble gum came along in 1906. Invented by Henry Fleer's brother Frank, Blibber-Blubber bubble gum never made it to market—it was so sticky that the only way to remove it from skin was with vigorous scrubbing and turpentine. Walter Diemer, a Fleer employee, achieved the breakthrough in August,

1928—and he wasn't even a chemist. Diemer was working as Fleer's cost accountant when he discovered, through trial and error, the magic mix of ingredients. Bubble gum even owes its characteristic pink hue to serendipity, pink being the only coloring left on the shelf for the first commercial batch. Soon after its introduction, Fleer's Dubble Bubble became the largest selling penny candy.

The next major innovation in gum making came in the early 1950s, when Harvey's chemically-sweetened sugarless gum was introduced. Suddenly, gum was deemed safe to chew, and its popularity surged again as dentists began recommending sugarless gum "to their patients who chew gum."

This Smacks of the Truth: Gum Facts

• Gum made from the resin of the mastic tree was popular in Greece as early as 50 A.D.

• Native Americans introduced European settlers to chewing spruce resin in the 1600s.

• In an attempt to raise money to fund his army, exiled Mexican president Santa Ana tried to sell chicle to the United States as a rubber substitute. New York inventor Thomas Adams, Sr., failed to transform the General's chicle into rubber, but he got the idea to market the gooey stuff as a chewing gum instead. Even though it was unflavored, his chicle gum was an instant success.

• Gum manufacturers voluntarily rationed their product at home during World War II so that supplies of it could be shipped to our fighting forces around the globe.

• Liquid gum base (it hardens into gum as we know it only after cooking and cooling) has been used as an organic pesticide—insects drawn to its sweetness find their jaws stuck together and they soon starve to death.

• "Save this wrapper for disposal after use " and "Close cover before striking" are the most often read sets of instructions in the world.

• New York Central Railroad once employed a full-time gum removal man to clean discarded gum from Grand Central Station. He harvested an average of seven pounds a night with the wad growing to fourteen pounds on holiday weekends.

WORKIN' ON THE CHAIN GANG

Gum Wrapper Chain. Remember spending all your allowance on gum so you could have the longest wrapper chain in the whole neighborhood? It takes 50 wrappers to make a chain one foot long. Long Island, New York teens Randi Grossack and Barbara Malkin assembled a chain that's 196 feet, eight inches long and still growing—that's over 9,800 wrappers. In case you want to beat them, here's how to make one:

• *Get a pack of flat stick gum like Wrigley's Juicy Fruit or Doublemint.*

• *Remove and fold the individual paper wrapper lengthwise into thirds.*

• *Fold it again, in half, crosswise.*

• *Fold each end in toward the center— this becomes the first link in the chain.*

• *Repeat with remaining wrappers to create many links.*

• *To assemble the chain, slip the ends of the second link into the "V" of the first link.*

• *Add to the chain by feeding the ends of link three through the ends of link two, and so on, in a zig-zag pattern (see above).*

Pick 'n' Chews Pilgrimages

• Sculptor Les Levine immortalizes gum in 18-kt gold. He's cast tiny sculptures from actual pieces of chewed gum and displayed them in his Greenwich Village **Museum of Mott Art** in New York City.

• **Gum Alley.** It has no official name, but it's the alley right next to 733 Higuera Street in San Luis Obispo, California. People have been depositing their chewed gum on the side of the old brick building there for over a decade. A wonderfully tacky— in all senses of the word—mural.

"Who Wants Gum?"

• Prince Edward VII nearly fainted when he was first given some and told what to do with it.

• Legendary boxer Jack Dempsey chewed it to strengthen his jaw.

• Jeremy Boob, Ph.D., used it to repair the Beatles' yellow submarine.

Mint is the most popular flavor for modern chewing gum.

A Gallon Of Gum

It's a real gallon paint can that's been cleaned and filled with 2 1/2 lbs. of bubble gum balls—in a "rainbow of colors."

#616, $14.98 + 4.20 shipping from Johnson Smith Company, 4514 19th Court East, P.O. Box 25500, Bradenton, FL 34206-5500. (813) 747-2356 / FAX (813) 746-7896.

Sex and Gum

• Sharing someone's ABC (already-been-chewed) gum is a sign of true love, as Tom Sawyer proved when he shared a piece with Becky Thatcher.

• One hot time, guaranteed—Frenchie's Spanish Fly Chewing Gum was marketed at $1.00 a stick by Swingers, Inc., of Gary, Indiana. The so-called aphrodisiac's main ingredient was cayenne pepper, and contained none of the dangerous Spanish Fly (cantharides).

• In Korea, at least one brand of gum is laced with ginseng, which is believed to increase sexual potency.

• Long gone Love Gum, Passion Gum, Forbidden Fruit and Kis-Me gum all promised romance, for just a penny.

Teach An Old Dog A New Trick

Gumball machine for dogs has bone handle so Fido can dispense his or her own biscuit!

#4135A, Dog Dispenser, $55.00 + 7.95 shipping from Post Scripts, P.O. Box 21628, Ft. Lauderdale, FL 33335-1628. (800) 327-3799.

Bubble Gum Music

• *Chew Chew Chew (Your Bubblegum)* (1939)—Sung by Ella Fitzgerald

• *Goody Goody Gumdrop* (1968)—The 1910 Fruitgum Company

• *Chewy Chewy* (1968)—The Ohio Express

Gumball Saturday Night

Chew, Chew, Baby. Bronze finished design looks like old time malt shop juke box.

#3213-13, $29.95 + 4.50 shipping from Golds', P.O. Box 1968, Des Plaines, IL 60018. (800) 828-9990.

Vintage Gumball

Not the gum...the machine. Antique treasures from the '40s and '50s. Actual machine may vary.

#18306, $74.95 + 7.25 shipping from Golds', P.O. Box 1968, Des Plaines, IL 60018. (800) 828-9990.

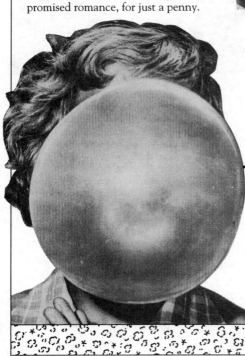

Duck! It's A Gumball Machine!

#3400-04, Painted Brown Mallard Markings, $29.95 + 4.50 shipping, or #3413-13, Antique Bronze Plated Duck Gumball Machine, $39.95 + 6.00 shipping from Golds', P.O. Box 1968, Des Plaines, IL 60018. (800) 828-9990.

GUMBALL LAMP

#3323-01, $19.95 + 3.50 shipping from Golds', P.O. Box 1968, Des Plaines, IL 60018. (800) 828-9990.

Bubble Gum's a Gas...

When it comes out of an "Olde Tyme" gas pump gumball dispenser. Red metal base with battery-lit Gilmore or Supertest logo. 21 in. high.

#1517, $55.00 + 4.00 shipping. Car's The Star 8236 Marshall Drive Lenexa, KS 66214 (800) 833-3782 / FAX (913) 599-2441

Phone & Gumball Machine

Dials numbers *and* dispenses gum. **#3020-01, $29.95 + 4.50 shipping from Golds', P.O. Box 1968, Des Plaines, IL 60018. (800) 828-9990.**

BRASS CLASS

Authentic cast metal reproduction of a 1920s Columbia machine.

#3032-16, $49.95 + 7.25 shipping from Golds', P.O. Box 1968, Des Plaines, IL 60018. (800) 828-9990.

Chewing Gumption

The Wrapper. This non-sports gum card collectors newsletter is the place to find buyers, traders and sellers, articles and show announcements for non-sports cards without searching through thousands of baseball and football card ads.

One year (8 issues) $22.00, sample copy $2.00 + 2 first class stamps to 1903 Ronzheimer Ave., St. Charles, IL 60174. (708) 377-7921.

Reading That Sticks With You

The Great American Chewing Gum Book by Robert Hendrickson. Fascinating, scholarly and complete, yet humorously written, this is definitely a book for those who can chew gum and read at the same time. Covers history, sociology and manufacturing.

From the section about gum etiquette: "Don't chew gum in the streetcar, bus, or any other public place. You look disgusting and are repugnant. Just gaze at the chewing brigade every day and notice the type of person who does it. Do you really wish to be of that class?" For curious kids or adults, we don't know of a more satisfying gum book anywhere.

$10.95 postpaid from Independent Publishers Group, 814 N. Franklin, Chicago, IL 60610. (800) 888-4741.

The Chewing Gum Book by Robert Young. This photo-illustrated children's book is fun for grownups, too. Learn about making gum, chewing it, swallowing it, getting it out of your hair, and more. Interesting black and white photographs, wads of facts.

$11.95 postpaid from Dillon Press, Inc., 242 Portland Ave. S., Minneapolis, MN 55415. (800) 962-0437.

GUMBY

FEATS OF CLAY

Gumbasia. In the early 1950s, Art Clokey was making Coke bottles fly and vegetables dance for animated television commercials. He spent his spare time animating his own private fantasia using plasticine clay. Setting his geometric and amorphous shapes moving to a jazz score, Clokey created a quirky feature "Gumbasia" in 1953.

In a turn of fate straight out of a Hollywood movie, film producer Sam Engle saw the film and proclaimed it "the most exciting film I have ever seen in my life!"

Kid Vid. With Engle's financial backing, Clokey created the Gumby character, put together a pilot and took it to the networks. NBC executives were charmed by the plucky green boy and signed Clokey to produce a series. *The Adventures of Gumby* was first introduced on *The Howdy Doody Show* in 1956 but Gumby soon graduated to a show of his own, hosted by Pinky Lee.

Clokey bought back the syndication rights, and, after six years of limited success selling the films, he decided,

Pokey's Polkas

Gumby (The Green Album)
Buena Vista Records, 2600 W. Olive Ave., Burbank, CA 91505. (818) 560-1000. $15.95
This pop/rock/reggae/zydeco/polka/jazz tribute to everybody's favorite clay boy holds such memorable tunes as "(In Love) With You Gumby," by Dweezil and Moon Unit Zappa; "Pokey's Polka," by Brave Combo, and the TV theme "The Gumby Heart Song," sung by Frank Sinatra, Jr. Our favorite is Flo & Eddie's irresistible satire of the Sgt. Pepper era Beatles called "We All Are Gumby." The music's good enough to stand by itself whether you're a Gumby fan or not.

"*Gumby is claymation on hallucinogens.*"

—Shep Stern

reluctantly, to market a Gumby toy. It was an immediate success. But just as Gumby's star was rising, things began falling apart for his creator.

Crash. A painful divorce and the ensuing legal battles all but crushed Clokey, who didn't bounce back as readily as his clay boy. By the late 1970s, the show had been dropped by station after station, the doll was no longer being manufactured, and the royalties from both were just about dried up.

Guru-vy Gumby. Then in 1979 Clokey and his new wife, Gloria, took a trip to India to see a Guru they'd been following from afar. Satya Sai Baba walked through the assembled crowd sprinkling holy ashes from his fist. Some of it fell on the Gumby doll Clokey held aloft for blessing.

When the Clokeys returned to the United States, things miraculously began to turn around. He gave a guest lecture at the Art Center in Pasadena, and he found the students who had loved Gumby as children regarded him as he had regarded Sai Baba.

A new surge of Gumby worship began to roll through the nation and culminated in an $8 million contract with Lorimar-Telepictures for an all new Gumby series which began in late 1988.

THE CLAY BOY CLUB

The Gumby Fan Club, PO Box 3905, Schaumburg, IL 60168 Dues: $5.00
Say it loud, you're green and proud. Join the Gumby Fan Club and here's what you'll get: membership certificate and card, The Gumby Newsletter, an autographed photo of Gumby, the official song lyrics, an iron-on t-shirt transfer, Gumby bookmarkers and stickers, and a door knob sign that says "Don't even think of disturbing this Gumby fan."

POP POETRY

"*You're bendable, dependable /
Most of all befriendable /
Gangly and green, you're tall and you're lean…/
Show me the stuff /
That you're made of /
'Cause I think I'm in love with you Gumby!*"

—*"(In Love) With You Gumby,"*
Dweezil and Moon Unit Zappa

GUMBY FACTS

• "Gumbo" is oil-driller lingo for the sedimentary layer of clay on top of a petroleum field.

• "Gumby" is the Latin diminutive of "Gumbo," his father's name. The clay boy's Mother is named "Gumba." Creator Clokey admits that after seven years of Latin in school, that's the only time he ever put the language to good use.

• The trademark bump on Gumby's head came from an old photograph of Clokey's father in which a cowlick appears to give him an unnatural bump, or as Clokey puts it, "the bump of wisdom that the Buddhists have."

• To produce each show requires 60 artists and technicians turning out approximately two minutes of film every eight working hours. Gumby and his pals may be moved up to 9,000 times in a 6-minute episode.

• Good thing Gumby characters are so simple. Because he's made of plasticine which disintegrates quickly, animators go through five or six Gumby's per scene.

• Cartoon characters of the gods? Valleys and fault lines created a 40 mile formation on Venus that looked just like the green boy to scientists watching pictures come in from the Magellan spacecraft. In 1990, they nicknamed the formation "Gumby."

• A few years ago rap fans were sporting the Gumby, a hairstyle with the sides shaved (a "fadeaway") and a tilted bump on the top.

Gumby to Go

Gumby and Pokey Dolls
Hand-painted, non-toxic molded gum rubber. $1.50 each + shipping (see below).

Gumby Polo Shirt
Cotton/polyester knit with embroidered logo. All men's and women's sizes, various colors. $15.+ shipping (see below).

Stationery
Green paper, of course, with full-color Gumby & Pokey imprint. 40 sheets with 20 envelopes. $2.95 + shipping (see below).

All of the above, and more (ask for their catalog) available from: Official Gumby Products, Box 3921 Schaumburg, IL 60168-3921. Add shipping: $2.50 for orders up to $10, $3.00 for orders up to $19.50, and $3.50 for anything above.

Gumby's Neighborhood

Prickle Dinosaur & Goo Mermaid
Based on a remark by the late Zen philosopher Alan Watts that there are two kinds of people in the world, prickly (uptight and rigid) and gooey (easygoing and flowing).

Gumbo, Gumba & Minga
Gumby's father, mother and little sister.

The Blockheads
Mostly seen racing around in their car.

BOOKS

Gumby: The Authorized Biography of the World's Favorite Clayboy
by Louis Kaplan & Scott Michaelson, Harmony Press
$12.95, out of print

While this book may be out of print by now, we felt it required a mention, since it's the only Gumby book around, and it's good. A lengthy introduction by Art Clokey himself covers the historical background surrounding the creation of Gumby and his relation to Clokey's search for spiritual enlightenment. The second half of the book gives you synopses for all the original episodes. Wonderful photos, worth hunting down.

GUMBY ON YOUR SCREEN

Classic Gumby Video. The 32 classic episodes produced from 1958 through 1969 are all here on this video series. From your local video store or: Live Home Video, 2030 E. University Dr., Rancho Dominguez, CA 90220. (800) 752-9343. $14.95 + $4.00 shipping.

Art Clokey's Favorite Episodes

1. The Grooby. W.C. Fields sells our pal a troublesome pet.

2. Gumby Crosses the Delaware. Gumby saves George Washington.

3. Robot Rumpus. Cybernetic housepainters wreak havoc.

4. Moon Trip. The very first Gumby adventure.

HAIR

The Long & Short of It

Hair's important. Think of Lady Godiva, who made up for the deficiencies in her total fashion look with a stunning array of hair. Or Samson—when he lost his hair he lost his strength, mirroring many men's middle-aged fears.

Hair has long been used as a way of signalling conformity (the military or corporate haircut) or rebellion (Elvis' "D.A." in the 1950s, "I'm going to let my freak flag fly" in the '60s).

Hair obsession is evident in the thousands of shampoos, conditioners, gels, mousses and sprays to dyes, wigs, and hair extensions. Men buy monoxidil to encourage hair on top and Gillette to discourage it below. Women pamper their crowning glory, and torture the rest with razors, depilatories and waxes.

HAIRLINE FRACTIONS

• The average woman says she spends about $32 on her hair every month.

• If under 50, she visits her hairdresser about 12 times a year. If over 50, about 18 times a year.

• Southern women, regardless of age, income bracket, marital status or educational background, spend more time and money on their hair than those of any other region.

• At the average growth rate of a little more than a half inch every two months, a man can expect his beard and mustache to grow between 13 and 20 feet during a span of 55 years.

Fuzzy Logic

• The ancient Greek poet Aeschylus died soon after an eagle mistook his bald head for a rock and dropped a tortoise on it to break the shell.

• A sudden fright actually *can* make your hair stand on end. Each hair on your body is attached to its own tiny muscle and nerve fiber, and a strong stimulus can cause a simultaneous reaction.

• The longest hair attached to a living head: 26 feet long, belonging to an Indian swami, according to the Guinness Book of Records.

• Russian Tsar Peter the Great, in another sweeping attempt to Westernize medieval Russia, actually taxed by the inch anyone wearing a long beard.

• Hair today, gone tomorrow? A term of the divorce settlement between Vidal and Beverly Sassoon stipulated that Beverly could launch a cosmetics business, as long as she didn't manufacture hair products.

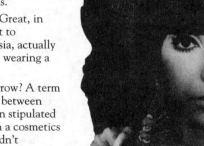

Hairy ears are considered a sign of virility in India.

Hair-trigger Responses

- "*It would probably be the end of the act.*"

  —John Lennon, on what would happen if the Beatles trimmed their mops into crewcuts.

- "*He hit my hair!*"

  —Tony Manero's (John Travolta) wounded cry after his father assaulted his perfect blow-dried hair helmet in *Saturday Night Fever*.

- "*I'm in Special Ed because of my hair!*"

  —Tracy (Ricki Lake) the "hair-hopper," busted for her bi-color bouffant in *Hairspray*.

- "*Five inches of hot-buttered yak wool.*"

  —*Time* magazine's description of Elvis Presley's famous Fifties 'do.

- "*Oh, Murray, you're so lucky. Other men get dandruff. You get waxy yellow buildup.*"

  —Sue Ann Nivens, *The Mary Tyler Moore Show*

- "*I was afraid if they cut my hair too much they would cut my talent.*"

  —Tony Curtis

- "'*Tis not the beard that makes a philosopher.*"

  Thomas Fuller, MD (1732)

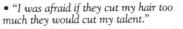

- Art Linkletter: "*What makes a man bald?*"

  Preschooler: "*They eat too much. It fills them up so much that it pushes the hair right through the top.*"

  —House Party

- Buddy Sorell (to Mel Cooley): "*I wish you'd kept your hair and lost the rest of you.*"

  Sally Rogers: "*Watch it, Buddy, he'll turn on you.*"

  Buddy: "*What's the difference? He's the same on both sides.*"

  —*The Dick Van Dyke Show*

Close Shaves in the Corporate World

- Gillette's Boston Headquarters razor research division goes through a daily shaving ritual involving nearly 300 volunteer employees, all male. Researchers watch them shave, after which the men rate quality of the shave. The products tested could be a new, experimental Gillette prototype or something made by a competitor.

- Hair may take the place of urine in employee drug tests because minute quantities of whatever substances the body ingests are always present in hair.

A COLLECTIBLE TO LEAVE TO YOUR HAIRS

The Only Authentic Beatle Wig. In 1964, once the British Invasion gained a steady foothold, the Beatles licensed NEMS to manufacture black synthetic mop-tops so any fan could look like a Beatle. Thousands were produced, but since no one knew then that the Beatles would be more than a flash-in-the-pan, the wigs' relative scarcity brings in top dollar—$40-45 if in its original packaging.

Mock Locks

Skimpy hair? Get an extension! Human hair extensions are sewn into your own tresses for added length and volume, and are easy to wash and wear. Prices start at around $200, and go up into the thousands if you want to look like Rapunzel, or even Diana Ross. The service is advertised by salons who specialize in this time-consuming technique, so don't try this at home.

Don't want to spend $200 for a human hair extension? How about a 24 inch long black or blonde wig made of man-made fiber instead?

#T1561, Blonde Wig, or #T1562, Black Wig. Each $17.98 + 4.85 shipping from Funny Side Up, 425 Stump Road, North Wales, PA 19454. (215) 361-5130.

STERLING SHAVER

For the boy born with a silver spoon in his mouth. When it's time to graduate to shaving, get him Gillette's Sensor Razor sheathed in a sterling silver handle. $225, only at Tiffany's, of course. Or, if platinum's okay, pick up this plated edition of the Gillette Sensor Razor.

#43104W, $79.95 + 6.50 shipping from Hammacher Schlemmer, Midwest Operations Center, 9180 Le Saint Drive, Fairfield, OH 45014. (800) 543-3366.

We Call Ours Marie Antoinette

When others all about you are losing their heads and blaming it on you, at least you'll have an extra.

Perfect for displaying your wigs, these mannequin heads are made of firm yet fair, fleshy-feeling rubber with hand-painted eyes, eyebrows and lips.

#M514, Male, $24.95. #M539, Female, $21.95. Add 4.00 shipping from Archie McPhee, P.O. Box 30852, Seattle, WA 98103-0852. (206) 547-2467.

Salon Sweets

This chocolate will make your hair curl. Only your hairdresser will know for sure what a sweet gift this is—boxed chocolates shaped like a blow dryer, comb and pink curlers.

#B2592, $7.98 + 3.50 shipping from Harriet Carter, North Wales, PA 19455. (215) 361-5151.

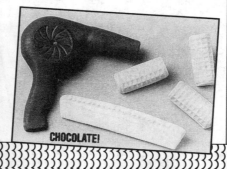

CHOCOLATE!

Don't Spite Your Face

Safety Trimmer. Tired of negotiating nail scissors up your nasal passages to cut nose hairs? Compact, cordless cylindrical trimmer is safer because protected steel blades are recessed, so there's no risk of nicking. AA battery not included.

#B1528, $5.98 + 3.50 shipping from Harriet Carter, North Wales, PA 19455. (215) 361-5151.

Superstition holds that witches can harm or even kill someone if they acquire strands of their hair.

HAIR-RAISING BOOKS

• *Haircults: Fifty Years of Styles and Cuts* by Dylan Jones. From crewcuts to conks, bobs to beehives, shags to skinheads, Jones records a half-century of hair history. Did you know that wire armatures were sometimes used to prop up beehives? Did you know that it was Warner Brothers staff hairdresser Joe Cirello who invented the D.A., short for Duck's Ass? Photos galore.

$14.95 + 1.50 shipping. National Book Co., 800 Keystone Industrial Park, Scranton, PA 18512. (800) 233-4830.

• *The Chadwick System: Discovering the Perfect Hairstyle for You* by John and Suzanne Chadwick. Hairstyling is less art than science, according to the Chadwicks. They help you choose the most attractive 'do for you, based on your TFQ (Texture, Formation, Quantity) quotient. A perfect opportunity to use dormant high school algebra skills.

Out of print, but worth tracking down.

• *Bald Like Me: The Hair-Raising Adventures of Baldman* by Richard

Hair Magazines

PASSION International Hair Magazine. PASSION is the umbrella title of four very pricey magazines (one on video) from Japan aimed at professionals. Each contains approximately 64 huge, full color photos of really exotic creations in women's hair by stylists from all over the world. How exotic? Things like "topiary tresses"— tree shapes and other freeform designs you wouldn't necessarily wear to the office.

Published quarterly, extra large format. No ads. One year, $110.00, single issue $32.00 from Intra-American Beauty Network, 14 Commerce Dr., New Branford, CT 06471. (800) 634-8500.

Black HairCare. Probably the most comprehensive fashion magazine on the market about trends in hairstyles for black women, including fantasy styles based on braiding techniques from Africa, celebrity looks, a special hair-and-makeup color section and step-by-step how-to guides. Also extensive product ads for buying human and synthetic hair, books on braiding and weaving techniques, and an array of treatments to promote healthier hair.

Published quarterly at $3.95 per issue from Beauty Secrets, Inc., 1115 Broadway, New York, NY 10010.

Sandomir. No hair apparent? Be like bald-is-beautiful activist Sandomir who insists that the coming trend is to enjoy the free, nude, natural look, like "patron saints of baldness" Joe Garagiola, Willard Scott and Yul Brynner. Sandomir also pulls the rug out from famous names who think their hairpieces look natural (Howard Cosell and Charlton Heston), and doesn't split hairs over how many they own (Frank Sinatra and Burt Reynolds, roughly 20 apiece).

$7.95 +.80 shipping from Macmillan & Co., 100 Front St., Riverside, NJ 08075. (800) 257-5755.

Perennial big-hair capital Baltimore holds an annual Hair Ball featuring huge hair-dos.

PILGRIMAGE: WISH YOU WERE HAIR

Cowlicks. One trend in the hair biz is the kiddie salon, specifically designed for children. Los Angeles area salons set the pace with child star pix on the walls, piped-in pop music, arcade games, and comfort food, like peanut butter-and-jelly sandwiches. Cowlicks offers an interesting bonus: a video of each hair cut. Also a kiddie cafe next door for after-cut schmoozing.

Average price (including video) $17 for boys, $19 for girls. 4774 Park Granada Blvd. Suite #8, Calabasas, CA 91302. (818) 992-3333.

For Aspiring Hairstylists

It's never too early to start training for a career in the beauty business. This kiddie salon table features a closed circuit water system, stool, cosmetics, soap, sponge and battery-operated blow dryer. Kids and their dolls love it—their pets don't!

#359919, $165.00 + 19.50 shipping. FAO Schwarz, P.O. Box 182225, Chattanooga, TN 37422-7225. (800) 426-TOYS.

Hair Plugs

- *"A Little Dab'll Do Ya"* —Brylcreem
- *"Because I'm Worth It"* —L'Oreal
- *"Does She Or Doesn't She?"* —Clairol
- *"If I Have Only One Life, Let Me Live It As A Blonde"* —Clairol
- *"If You Don't Look Good, We Don't Look Good"* —Vidal Sassoon
- *"Is It True Blondes Have More Fun?"* —Clairol
- *"It Lets Me Be Me"* — Clairol
- *"Look Sharp, Feel Sharp, Be Sharp"* —Gillette
- *"No More Tears"* —Johnson & Johnson

SCALPS FOR SALE

Remember O. Henry's story *The Gift of the Magi*, where a woman sells her hair so she can buy a Christmas gift for her husband? There's still a market for long, thick hair. These human hair extensions come in swatches measuring 10" long. Colors range from black to brown to auburn shades, and are wavy in texture. Specify color.

Each swatch $27.95 + 3.00 shipping. El Shaddai, P.O. Box 2644, Newport News, VA 23609. (804) 874-8684.

Which Twin has the Toni?

(see answer below)

- *"Only Her Hairdresser Knows For Sure"* —Clairol
- *"Take It Off, Take It All Off"* — Noxema
- *"Take That Gray and Wash It Away"* —Clairol
- *"The Wet Head Is Dead"* — Mennen
- *"Which Twin Has the Toni?"* — Toni

Not All of Our Presidents Were Bald-faced Liars

- Five U.S. presidents had beards: Lincoln, Grant, Hayes, Garfield, and Harrison. All were elected in the 1800s, and two were assassinated in office.

- Four U.S. presidents had mustaches: Arthur, Cleveland, Teddy Roosevelt, and Taft. The first two were elected in the 19th century, the last two in the 20th.

- The last serious mustachioed presidential candidate was Thomas Dewey, who lost to Franklin Roosevelt in 1944. He lost in part because his mustache made him look like "the little man on top of a wedding cake," as one widely circulated observation put it.

Blondes may not have more fun, but they do have more hair follicles per square inch.

Do-It-Yourself Hairstyle Trends

wire or plastic and lots and lots of hair spray—the cheaper the better, hole in the ozone layer be damned. Legend has it that the biggest, stiffest beehives were those least washed, with the most lacquer build-up. Then there were those urban legends about colonies of insects living inside them…

• **Corn-Row.** If you don't have the big bucks, gather some friends with nimble fingers who might enjoy pulling your hair. It will take hours, but you won't have to fuss with your hair for over a month, and the tension of the pulled-back hair adds the benefit of a natural face lift.

• **Dreadlocks.** The name means exactly what it says: the snaky, Medusa-like look is meant to inspire fear in enemies and non-believers (known as "baldheads" regardless of hair quantity) among Rastafarians.

• **Beatle Bangs.** Don't own a Beatle wig, yet always felt

• **Punk.** The hair industry owes a debt to the punks for creating a market for gels, mousses and temporary coloring. Before that, punks used butter, lard, shortening, glue, toothpaste, dish detergent or egg whites to stiffen hair into Mohawks and stegosaurus silhouettes, and food coloring to tint it.

• **Beehive.** For this you need teasing, extra hairpieces, structural frames of

you were the true Fifth Beatle? Get a friend to put a bowl on your head and cut everything that sticks out. Remove bowl, give your head a shake, and you've got yourself a fab gear mop top. Yeah, yeah, yeah!

Get It By Hair Mail

For gels, colors and other theatrical hair effects, send $3.00 for a great catalog to California Theatrical Supply, 132 Ninth St., San Francisco, CA 94103. (415) 863-9236.

George Harrison   Ringo Starr   Paul McCartney   John Lennon

"A hair on the head is worth two on the brush." —Oliver Herford

FROM HAIR TO ETERNITY: THE WHOLE POP HAIR FILM FESTIVAL

• *The Boy With Green Hair* (1948). This story hinges on an embarrassing shampooing accident. Who knew then that the boy was just ahead of his time?

• *Shampoo* (1975). Warren Beatty casts himself as a playboy hairdresser who really services his clients.

• *10* (1979). Bo's corn-row is the most memorable image of this mid-life crisis comedy.

• *Hairspray* (1988). John Waters' reminiscence of early '60s Baltimore's big hair heyday complete with "hair hoppers" bopping on the local teen dance show.

• *Earth Girls Are Easy* (1989). See the best beauty makeover ever when furry aliens get done at a trendy L.A. salon called "Curl Up and Dye."

• *Steel Magnolias* (1989). Does she or doesn't she? Your hairdresser knows for sure and so do all her customers at this hair salon.

• *Edward Scissorhands* (1990). That guy sure could cut hair!

Broadway's Mane Musicals

• *Beehive*: Big hair and big voices of all-girl singing groups before the British Invasion.

• *Hair*: The quintessential late 1960s "American Tribal Love Rock Musical" glorified long hair as adornment and political statement. Unlike the first production, now that the show is often in revival, modern players usually need to wear wigs.

• *Sweeney Todd*: Crave a close shave? Go to this guy for a razor cut and you end up as filling in somebody else's pot pie.

Hair-Do Wah Ditties

• *Almost Cut My Hair*—Crosby, Stills, Nash & Young.

• *Are You a Boy or Are You a Girl?*— The Barbarians.

• *The Barber of Seville*—A grand old opera by Gioacchino Rossini, made famous by Alfalfa.

• *Cause I'm a Blonde*—Julie Brown sings it in *Earth Girls Are Easy.*

• *The Boy With the Beatle Hair*—The Swanns. Beatlemania exploitation record ("Look at that boy over there / the one with the Beatle hair / I wish that he would come and dance with me...").

• *Hair*—"*Show it, blow it, long as I can grow it...*" From the Broadway show, but the Cowsills sang it on the charts.

• *I Dream of Jeannie With the Light Brown Hair*—Stephen Foster parented this boffo hit in 1854, satirized a century later by Spike Jones as *I Dream of Brownie in the Light Blue Jeans.*

• *If You're Going to San Francisco* ("*...be sure to wear a flower in your hair*")—Scott MacKenzie penned and sang this flower power anthem.

• *I'm Gonna Wash That Man Right Out of My Hair*—Mary Martin made this song famous in the 1949 musical *South Pacific.*

• *Kookie, Kookie, Lend Me Your Comb*—Edd Byrnes from TV's *77 Sunset Strip*, with Connie Stevens.

• *The Man in the Weird Beard*— written in the 1940s by Milton Drake, who also wrote the immortal *She Broke My Heart in 3 Places* (Seattle, Chicago and New York).

Hawaiian Shirts

No Tiki, No Shirtee

Hawaiian missionaries, scandalized by all the naked Hawaiian flesh, introduced large colorless one-size-fits-all shirts and muu-muus. The natives wanted at least a *little* excitement in their wardrobes, so they took the plain cotton garments and decorated them with bright Polynesian designs.

The first Hawaiian shirt boom came in the 1920s when tourists brought the gaudy, tropical shirts to the mainland as holiday souvenirs. Hawaiian shirts also enjoyed great popularity during World War II, when thousands of American servicemen traveling through Hawaii bought the garish shirts to wear on leave as a cheerful alternative to their drab uniforms.

Hawaiian shirts can sometimes be found second-hand in mint condition, probably owing to the fact that it takes less courage to buy one than to actually wear it. Some collectors will pay hundreds of dollars for genuine rayon shirts with the requisite garishly-colored orchids, hibiscus, palm trees, volcanoes and hula dancers, buttons of coconut shell or wood, and matching pockets that don't interrupt the design. The "Aloha" label fetches top dollar.

Still the garment of choice for vulgar American tourists, the shirt is an acceptable wardrobe item for Hollywood extroverts like Tom Selleck, Ed Begley, Chevy Chase, Bill Cosby, Steven Spielberg and Francis Coppola. You gotta have respect for people who are not too proud to take fashion cues from style-setters like Arthur Godfrey.

Don't Smoke It...Wear It!

Fake grass (plastic) Hula Skirt lets you do fake hula dances.

#9003, $6.95 + 3.00 shipping. Archie McPhee, P.O. Box 30852, Seattle, WA 98103-0852. (206) 547-2467.

Pineapple Computer

Give your computer a festive tropical air. This company sells cool Macintosh-fitted computer cozies in a blue Hawaiian print pattern. Made for your Mac, but there's no reason why they couldn't also be used in a DOS environment.

#D115, monitor cover (also fits Mac Plus, SE), $32.00 + 3.50 shipping. #D119, Mac Plus keyboard cover or #D238, SE keyboard cover, $15.00 + 3.00 shipping. #D122, Imagewriter II, $32.00 + 3.50 shipping. #D124, Laserwriter II, $45.00 + 3.50 shipping. #D118, Mac II monitor (13-in. screen), $40.00 + 3.50 shipping.

Other cozies for other Apple equipment also available. Chicken Boy Future Studio, P.O. Box 292000, Los Angeles, CA 90029. (800) 422-0505.

The Shirt Hits the Sand

The Hawaiian Shirt: Its Art and History by H. Thomas Steele. This is an amazing book. Each is literally cloth-bound: covered with Hawaiian shirt fabric in one of several different styles. The definitive look at the item of clothing that consistently screams bad taste, loaded with color photos of classic patterns guaranteed to make the rest of your world look drab in comparison.

$19.95 + 3.00 shipping. Abbeville Press, 488 Madison Avenue, New York, NY 10022. (800) 227-7210.

The best Hawaiian shirts are on rayon rather than natural fiber because the material holds those bright colors better.

THE PRESIDENT
OF THE UNITED STATES
THE EVOLUTION OF A WARDROBE

Hippies & The Sixties, Man

Flower in Your Hair

When we look back now through a purple haze of memory, the 1960s look pretty good. Back then sex, drugs and rock 'n' roll seemed like not only a viable lifestyle, but a religion and political party as well.

Baby boomers had loudly come of age in the 1960s. Adult society didn't seem to have much to offer: sexual repression, keeping up with the neighbors, conformism, rigid roles, boring music, xenophobic wars, and a slavish pursuit of material goods. You know, sort of like adult society in *our* era.

The word got out that there was something happening in San Francisco—a bunch of kids living a life of voluntary poverty, chemically raised consciousness, wild music and informal sexuality. A pilgrimage began and an entire alternative lifestyle was made up on the spot. The "gentle people with flowers in their hair" didn't last long, but parts of their vision became mainstream.

Fashion took a surrealistic, psychedelic turn, as did arts and politics. Yogurt, whole-grain breads and vegetarianism moved from being way-out hippie food fads in those beef and potato days to good medical advice in ours. The ecology movement, once bitterly decried as a communist plot or worse, is now something even the oil companies pretend to believe in.

Cross Your Heart and Hope to Tie-Dye

You'll need:

- A suitably groovy garment
- Rubber bands or string
- Clothing dye

Two simple techniques:

- Roll the garment tightly into a cylinder and section it off with rubberbands, so it resembles a string of sausages, then immerse all or part of it into the dye bath. This will produce a striped effect.

- Gather a clump of fabric, secure it tightly with a rubberband, then dip it into the dye bath. This will produce a sunburst effect. Clumps of various sizes can be arranged to form patterns, such as spirals. Let the fabric dry thoroughly between different immersions if you want to keep each color distinct; otherwise keep it wet so the dyes blend together for a blurred, watercolor painting look.

The Whole Pop Hippie Film Fest

- *Reefer Madness* (1936)
- *Wild In The Streets* (1968)
- *Easy Rider* (1969)
- *Woodstock* (1969)
- *Revolution* (1969)
- *Joe* (1970)
- *200 Motels* (1971)
- *Rude Awakening* (1989)

AN EARFUL OF AN ERA

Summer of Love. 25 representative tracks from the endless summer of '67, sung by The Byrds, The Monkees, The Turtles, and other '60s creatures.

Scents of the Sixties

Remember when everybody smelled of Patchouli, Sandalwood and Krishna Musk? "Song of India" perfume solids are fragrances distilled from flowers, herbs, spices, woods and resins. They come in one-of-a-kind hand-carved soapstone jars.

"If you can remember the '60s, then you weren't there." —Robin Williams

Street. After living in her San Francisco digs with the band and thirty or forty other people, Joplin, like many of the Dead, moved north to ritzy Marin County, before moving to another place and *really* joining the dead.

• **Airplane House**, 2400 Fulton Street. This mansion bordering the Haight and Golden Gate Park housed most of the Jefferson Airplane at one time or another, later becoming their business office.

• **Charles Manson's San Francisco home**, 636 Cole Street. He currently resides in another part of the Bay Area—Vacaville Prison.

Pilgrimage: One Weird Trip

Haight and Ashbury Streets, San Francisco. If you're going to San Francisco, be sure to wear some flowers in your hair. Honest, you'll fit right in. Really.

Haight Street is now a gentrified tourist attraction where you can buy assorted 1960s artifacts. With a little good karma, you can still pick up those groovy vibes in the Haight-Ashbury:

• **The Dead House**, 710 Ashbury Street. Former residence of the Grateful Dead, "the house band of the Haight."

• **Janis Joplin's House**, 112 Lyon

Flower Power Facts

• The name "hippie" was coined by *San Francisco Examiner* writer Michael Fallon on 9/5/65.

• Gray Line Bus Tours began offering the "Hippie Hop" bus tour through San Francisco's Haight-Ashbury district in 1967, billing it "the only foreign tour within the continental limits of the United States." The hippies responded by holding large mirrors up to the windows of the tour bus.

Paint The Town Phosphorescent

Light Kit. Contains everything you need for a home light show. Three colors of machine-washable, non-toxic glow-in-the-dark paints; a fiber-optics flashlight that sprouts a brush of multi-colored light filaments; and a "Turbo Sparkler" mylar-coated yo-yo that spins a spectrum of colors. Just add Hendrix, switch on a black light, and be the light of every party.

#360206 Set of three $19.95 + 4.50 shipping from The Nature Company, P.O. Box 2310, Berkeley, CA 94702. (800) 227-1114.

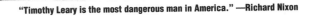

"Timothy Leary is the most dangerous man in America." —Richard Nixon

Dress Like Abbie Hoffman

Heavens to Betsy! It's more than hip 1960s garb, it's probably illegal flag desecration in George Bush's 1990s. Welcome back to the "Amerika" of the 1960s, where you can wear and say what you want, if you don't mind getting beat up and arrested.

#W04 Flag Shorts (M, L, XL) $36 00 + 5.50 shipping. #W05 Peace It Together T-Shirt (M, L, XL) $15.95 + 3.25 shipping. #W06 Flag Shirt (L, XL) $15.00 + 3.25 shipping from The Daily Planet, P.O. Box 1313, New York, NY 10013. (212) 334-0006 / FAX (212) 334-1158.

The First Flash Dance

Let's party! Put on the Airplane or the Dead and liven things up with a strobe light. It pulsates as slow or as fast as you wish, producing that stop-action effect and—rarely—convulsions.

#6536, $39.98 + 5.95 shipping from Johnson Smith Company, 4514 19th Court East, P.O. Box 25500, Bradenton, FL 34206-5500. (813) 747-2356 / FAX (813) 746-7896.

"No Recession!"

"It just goes to show you the flexibility of the human organism that people who would willingly sit in the mud and chant 'no rain' periodically between badly amplified rock groups could suddenly turn out to be the ones to run the U.S. economy."

—Frank Zappa on the Woodstock Generation

Socket to Me

Make your day-glo items "glow in the dark." 75 watt black light bulb fits any standard household lamp or socket.

#6316 Black Light Bulb, $2.98 + 1.35 shipping from Johnson Smith Co., 4514 19th Court East, P.O. Box 25500, Bradenton, FL 34206-5500. (813) 747-2356 / FAX (813) 746-7896.

Counterculture Commodities Catalog

Last Gasp of San Francisco. Not intended for minors, Last Gasp has a catalog of underground comix and books by counterculture heroes such as William S. Burroughs, Timothy Leary, Hunter S. Thompson and J. G. Ballard.

Send $1.00 to 2180 Bryant Street, San Francisco, CA 94110. (415) 824-6636.

Groovy Glasses

Just like the ones John Lennon wore, with mirrored lenses for an even cooler look.

#6590, $6.98 + 2.70 shipping from Johnson Smith Company, 4514 19th Court East, P.O. Box 25500, Bradenton, FL 34206-5500. (813) 747-2356 / FAX (813) 746-7896.

Far-Out Sixties Speak

- *Groovy*: just fine
- *Far out*: great!
- *Out of sight*: terrific!
- *Good vibes*: positive feelings
- *Be-in*: joyous gathering
- *Rap*: discuss
- *Joint*: marijuana cigarette
- *Bread*: money panhandled by flower children
- *Threads*: clothes

Lava Come Back to Me

Like wow, man. It's so psychedelic! It's a Lava Lite! Those pulsating globs are yours to groove to for many hours on end, man. Over 16"—and 8 Miles—high.

#LV102R, large lamp with gold base, yellow liquid and red lava, or #LV102B, large lamp with gold base, blue liquid and white lava. $55.00 + 5.00 shipping for each lamp from The Cat's Pyjamas, 20 Church Street, P.O. Box 1569, Montclair, NJ 07042. (201) 744-3896.

FLASHBACKS

***Only Yesterday: A Quiz on the Sixties* by Paul Cowan.** Flash back to the dawning of the Age of Aquarius. Over 600 questions on song lyrics, fashion trends and politics.

$7.95 + 4.00 shipping from Barnes and Noble, 126 Fifth Avenue, New York, NY 10011. (201) 767-7079.

Lava, or Is It Memorex?

58 minutes of lava lite action, accompanied by generic music. The timeless motion is broken up every *few* minutes—or is it years?—by a torso and hands changing to the next in a series of 15 lamps. Great novelty gift for friends with sleep disorders.

$14.95 + 2.00 shipping from Megapop Production Co., PO Box 124, Hampton Bays, NY 11946. (212) 724-3997.

Boxer Rebellion

They're paisley, man. The fabric is 1960s, even if nobody wore underwear back then.

100% cotton. S, M, L& XL. #18269, Black & White or #18270, Pucci, $12.50 + 2.75 shipping from Wireless, P.O. Box 64422, St. Paul, Minnesota 55164-0422. (800) 669-9999.

The CIA and LSD: A History Etched With Acid

LSD was an extract from a wheat ergot isolated in 1938 by Dr. Albert Hoffman, a Swiss chemist. He unwittingly discovered its hallucinogenic properties when accidentally ingesting a microscopic amount.

What most people don't know is that it was the CIA that unwittingly set the stage for the psychedelic craze, in yet another shameful, still mostly secret, episode in American history (the records were deliberately destroyed in 1973).

It was a program called MKULTRA. Available evidence is that the program cost $25 million and involved more than 185 nongovernmental researchers in 80 institutions in the US, Canada and Europe.

In the 1950s, the agency was researching "truth serums" and ways to incapacitate and demoralize enemies. They gave high doses of LSD and other drugs to unsuspecting people and monitored the results, spreading LSD with a reckless abandon that even acid-crazed hippies would have had second thoughts about, dosing unsuspecting employees, job seekers and mental patients. In a typical "experiment," inmates at the Lexington Narcotics Hospital were given LSD for 75 consecutive days. Another, canceled at the last moment, involved spiking the punch at the CIA's Christmas party to observe the results.

Needless to say, lives were ruined and minds were destroyed. The government has admitted that LSD was given to about 1,000 unsuspecting people from 1955-58, and has paid millions of dollars to settle lawsuits where people became permanently incapacitated or committed suicide.

But not all the CIA experiments were done without participants' consent: some volunteers were also being dosed. Many had negative experiences, but some said "Wow!" and began turning their friends on (LSD was still legal then).

One was writer Ken Kesey, who eventually bought a bus, painted it psychedelic and went around the country presenting "electric Kool-Aid acid tests."

In San Francisco, Kesey met the Grateful Dead and introduced them to counterculture chemist Augustus Owsley Stanley III, giving birth to Acid Rock, with its ecstatic audience participation, light shows, Eastern mysticism and odd new music.

Acid Digestion

"Pursuing the religious life today without using psychedelic drugs is like studying astronomy with the naked eye."

—Timothy Leary

"Lysergic acid hits the spot. Forty million neurons, that's a lot."

—Marshall McLuhan

"My wife and I took a tab of LSD and a birth control pill last night— we wanted to take a trip without the kids."

—Bob Hope

Planet Waves

Alphapacer II+ Brain Machine. Pulsing lights, sounds, magnetic fields and electricity induce Alpha and Theta brain waves, says the manufacturer, so you can travel into deep relaxation and intensified meditation.

$525.00 from Alphapacers, P.O. Box 2385, Eugene, OR 97402. (503) 683-2108.

GOOD GOSH! OPIUM!

OPIUM

HIGH TIMES

Psychedelic CDs

The Best of 60s Psychedelic Rock. A lot of music from the psychedelic era is available again on various labels, too much to recommend here. But here's one CD if what you want is a "greatest hits" sort of package, including one-hit wonders like *Hot Smoke and Sassafras* by the Bubble Puppy, *Pictures of Matchstick Men* by the Status Quo, *Green Tambourine* by the Lemon Pipers, *Journey to the Center of Your Mind* by Ted Nugent's Amboy Dukes and *Pushin' Too Hard* by the Seeds, presented from the master recordings for maximum ear-screeching feedback effect.

Available in record stores. CD, $9.98 or cassette, $4.98. Or contact Priority Records, 6430 Sunset Blvd., Hollywood, CA (213) 467-0151

Mind-Blowing Facts

• Until 1937, marijuana was legal in the U.S.

• Until 1967, LSD was legal in California.

• Timothy Leary ran for governor of California in 1970. Ronald Reagan won instead, despite Leary's having the coolest campaign song: *Come Together*, written for the occasion by John Lennon.

• One of the CIA's tragicomical assassination attempts against Fidel Castro involved a scuba suit filled with itching powder combined with a face mask laced with LSD. The idea was that the Cuban leader would be disoriented by the acid, be driven to an itching frenzy by the powder and end up drowning.

• People you wouldn't expect who took LSD: Claire Booth Luce and husband Henry, Aldous Huxley, Cary Grant, Anais Nin, Groucho Marx and—according to Timothy Leary—Marilyn Monroe and John Kennedy.

Echoes

"Timothy Leary's dead. No, he's outside, looking in." —Moody Blues

"*Take the time to journey to the center of your mind.*" —Amboy Dukes

"*It's so very lonely, you're 2000 light years from home.*" — Rolling Stones

TRIPPY TUNES

• *Good Vibrations*—Beach Boys
• *White Bird*—It's A Beautiful Day
• *White Rabbit*—Jefferson Airplane
• *Strawberry Fields Forever*—Beatles
• *Lucy in the Sky With Diamonds*—Beatles
• *I Am the Walrus*—Beatles
• *Day in the Life*—Beatles
• *Dear Mr. Fantasy*—Traffic
• *Acid Queen*—The Who
• *In a Gadda Da Vida*—Iron Butterfly
• *Purple Haze*—Jimi Hendrix
• *Incense and Peppermints*—Strawberry Alarm Clock
• *Eight Miles High*—The Byrds
• *Timothy Leary*—Moody Blues
• *Journey to the Center of Your Mind*—Amboy Dukes

The Realist

Cross Country Trip

• *The Electric Kool-Aid Acid Test* by Tom Wolfe.

• *On the Bus: The Complete Guide to the Legendary Trip of Ken Kesey and the Merry Pranksters and the Birth of the Counterculture* by Paul Perry with Ken Babbs.

• *The Furthur Inquiry* by Ken Kesey.

Three versions of the merry band on the famous 1937 International Harvester bus "Furthur" which traveled across America in 1964, spreading the psychedelic message. Told from different but complementary viewpoints: The Kesey book is more idiosyncratic; the Wolfe book more dispassionate, and the Perry/Babbs more democratic (their narrative relies on quotes from the fourteen participants and a variety of witnesses).

Wolfe, $5.95. Perry, $21.95. Kesey, $24.95. Add 1.50 shipping per book. Last Gasp of San Francisco, 2180 Bryant Street, San Francisco, CA 94110. (415) 824-6636.

• *The Realist.* For nearly three decades, this underground newsletter has proved that reality is a lot weirder than anything anybody ever made up.

One year (6 issues) $12.00, single issue $2.00. Box 1230, Venice, CA 90294.

• *Mondo 2000.* Equal parts psychedelia and "cyberpunk," this unique publication is the cutting edge of "neuropolitics." Virtual reality, life extension, designer drugs, computer hacking—the message is that the past is the future and the future is now.

Quarterly, $5.95 per issue, or 5 issue subscription for $24.00 from P.O. Box 10171, Berkeley, CA 94709-5171.

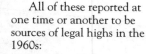

ROCK GRAPHICS:

L'Imagerie. This gallery of psychedelic graphics features a huge selection of original art work, fine art prints and psychedelic concert posters. Features work by artists such as R. Crumb and the late Rick Griffin.

Full-color catalog, $6.00 from 15030 Ventura Blvd., Sherman Oaks, CA 91403. (818) 995-8488.

Pantry Doors of Perception

All of these reported at one time or another to be sources of legal highs in the 1960s:

• *Banana peels*
• *Nutmeg*
• *Chamomile*
• *Kola Nuts*
• *Lettuce hearts*
• *Catnip*
• *Morning Glory seeds*
• *Hydrangea*
• *Heliotrope*
• *California Poppy*
• *Petunia*
• *Wild Cucumber*
• *Wild Lettuce*
• *Hops*

What Would Owsley Say?

Psychedelic Collectibles of the 1960s & 1970s: An Illustrated Price Guide by Susanne White. The pastiche of paisleys, Pop art, op art, fluorescence, and Art Nouveau styles of Psychedelic Art in the mid-1960s has become a hot category for collectors.

$21.95 + 3.00 shipping from Wallace-Homestead Book Co., 201 King of Prussia Road, Radnor, PA 19089. (215) 964-4730.

The Moving Picture is Born

By the late 1800s, British inventor William Friese-Greene had perfected the technology for making celluloid film. About the same time another Englishman, Eadweard Muybridge, was making pictures appear to move with what he called a "zoopraxiscope." In the 1890s scientists at Thomas Edison's laboratory in West Orange, New Jersey began to think about moving pictures: "I am experi-menting upon an instrument which does for the eye what the phonograph does for the ear, which is the recording and reproduction of things in motion..."

So wrote Thomas Edison on October 8, 1888 to the U.S. Patent Office. After less than a year of furious activity at Edison's lab, the first experiments were a success. These early moving pictures even came with sound.

When Edison returned from a jaunt to Europe in 1889, he received the world's first motion picture "Kineto-phonograph" greeting from his assistant, William K.L. Dickson: "Good morning, Mr. Edison," the moving image said. "Glad to see you back. I hope you are satisfied with the Kineto-phonograph."

Despite that initial success, technical difficulties proved insurmountable in using the sound process for longer movies. Silent films reigned for 38 years before "talkies" appeared on the scene.

Thomas A Edison

America's First Film Capital

When Hollywood's productions were still just fruit from fig farms, hundreds of films were being made in Fort Lee, New Jersey— the site of Edison's studios. Before Hollywood stole its thunder, Fort Lee was the place to be. Films made there include:

• D. W. Griffith's first film, *The Adventures of Dolly*

• Mary Pickford's first film, *The Lonely Villa*

• Films starring Dorothy and Lillian Gish, Mae Marsh, Tom Mix, Charlie Chaplin and Will Rogers

• The Keystone Kops' first capers

• Theda Bara's "vamp" films

• The *Perils of Pauline* serials

FILM FIRSTS

• Bless you! The earliest film found in the Library of Congress archives is the sneeze of John Ott, one of Edison's assistants.

• In 1893 Edison built the first movie studio, the "Black Maria" (below), a slang term of the time for a paddy wagon. The Maria was a 50' by 18' tar-paper structure resting on rollers. Because electric lights were not strong enough for the light-hungry film of the time, the filmmakers took the roof off and pushed the entire set around a circular track in order to follow the sun during shooting.

• Edison's first film premiere was on April 23, 1896 in New York. People gathered in a music hall at Herald Square to see movies of boxers, ballet dancers and ocean waves.

• Although Edison was actually the first to produce a "talkie" — a picture in 1913 called *Nursery Favorites* —it took further technological advancements and *The Jazz Singer* in 1927 to end the reign of the silent film.

While Hollywood was still producing figs, over 1000 movies were being made in Fort Lee, NJ.

The Rise of Hollywood

In 1886, Harvey Wilcox, a devout temperance advocate and paraplegic, paid $300 for a 120 acre plot of flatland near the slopes of the Cahuenga mountains. Wilcox and wife Daeida hoped to transform this property — a flourishing fig farm at the time — into a fine community populated by only the best of Christian folk.

Daeida came up with a name for their new spread after falling in love with a friend's Illinois estate that was surrounded by holly trees. Despite the fact that her property was covered with figwood, and that holly wouldn't grow there — even the hardiest species refused to take root — Daeida named their land "Hollywood."

There Goes the Neighborhood. About this time, filmmakers were fleeing New Jersey. Thomas Edison was aggressively pursuing his movie patents with a violent melee complete with lawsuits, raids, camera smashing and professional "enforcers." Other companies decided to get out of town.

Famous Names. Nestor Motion Pictures, in 1911, became the first studio in Hollywood and others quickly followed (Nestor Pictures disappeared in 1912 when Universal sent in an armed group with an offer they couldn't refuse). Leaving their meat and scrap metal company, four brothers named Warner came West to become film producers. Their first, about venereal disease, starred the youngest brother Jack.

Two other Easterners also made the move: Louis Mayer, a junk dealer, and Samuel Goldfisch (later Goldwyn), a glove salesman.

Eventually the Patent War ended, but the movies stayed in Hollywood because the climate allowed year-round filming. By the 1920s, motion pictures were the fourth largest industry in the United States.

Stars or Slaves? Under the old "star system," performers were almost literally "owned" by their film studios, which dictated the parts they got, their public image, even what their names were going to be.

Although many stars were rewarded quite handsomely, management did its best to get their money's worth. The studios demanded that big stars make up to 10 pictures a year and contract players up to 30 or 40. Often even the most intimate aspects of an entertainer's personal life were scripted by the studio execs, from the indignities of the "casting couch" to "romances" manufactured for the fan magazines.

Hollywood Falls

In the late 1940s, the courts dealt one of three decisive blows to Hollywood. They ordered the big studios to divest their very profitable theater chains, ending the monopoly that had quashed independent film production.

And the stars were falling, even the big ones. Lana Turner, Clark Gable and Judy Garland were all cut loose from their contracts because their careers were in the doldrums.

That damn box. Then, like a lightning bolt, television struck the movie industry to its core. Hollywood saw profits drop $500 million from 1948 to 1952.

Meanwhile, the House Un-American Activities Committee descended upon Hollywood in the 1950s hot on the trail of "Communists" and "Tinseltown Pinks." A zealot group published Red Channels, an ever-growing list of "communists" — people mentioned suddenly couldn't find work.

Eager to placate the witch hunters, John Wayne and others formed the Motion Picture Alliance to establish themselves as anti-communists. Some were true believers in the cause; others just wanted to keep working. The filmmaking community was torn apart as friend ratted on friend and people whispered rumors against their rivals.

"The Movie Capital of the World" never fully recovered from these devastating blows.

Ironically the studios that survived did it by creating material for that damned little box, TV.

"Ever since they found out that Lassie was a boy, the public has believed the worst about Hollywood." — Groucho Marx

UNIVERSALSTUDIOS
Hollywood

UNIVERSAL TOURS

When Carl Laemmle founded Universal in 1915, he set up shop on a chicken ranch. Because it was back in the days of the silent movie, he invited visitors to come watch and participate in the filming by booing or applauding the stars. The studio also provided lunch and sold fresh eggs to the audience at the end of the day (not at the beginning — good idea!).

The tradition continues today, with two exceptions— no eggs, and it's rare that you get to see a working film crew when you take the Universal Tours today.

Having learned from Disneyland that having an amusement park that looks like a film set can be more profitable than actually making movies, the Universal grounds are now set up almost exclusively to amuse tourists. Productions made on-site are invariably closed off from tour groups.

Still, the tour's interesting if you want to see the sets of some of your favorite movies, don't know much about movie making, and want to learn a few basics.

Universal Studios, 100 Universal City Plaza, Universal City, CA 91608. (818) 508-9600.

VISIT UNIVERSAL CITY
THE WONDER CITY OF THE WORLD
NEAR LOS ANGELES
THE PLACE WHERE THE FAMOUS
UNIVERSAL MOVING PICTURES ARE MADE

Hollywood — The Orlando of the West?

Family vacation to Hollywood? Taking the kids to see some movie stars and TV and movie sets?

Well, hold on 'cause you're going in the wrong direction. The bright lights and cameras are back thatta way, in Orlando, Florida. While you may still be able to see the stars' foot/nose/thigh prints in front of Mann's (formerly Graumann's) Chinese Theatre, major studios are making tracks to the land of the pink flamingo.

Money, as always, is the bottom line. Florida has less protective labor laws and fewer unions. And tourism, not movies, has become the biggest money-maker for the big studios.

Unlike Hollywood, where the movies came first and the tourists followed, in Orlando, the tourists are already there. New sound stages are now being built with the tourists in mind to defray production costs and create ready-made audiences for game shows and talk shows.

As the mayor of this Florida town, Bill Frederick, has said, "In 50 years, Hollywood is going to be known as the Orlando of the West."

Vintage View

Brilliantly reproduced posters of classic movies.

Framed posters $69.99; unframed $10.95. Add 3.95 shipping. *Casablanca*, #M02785 Framed, #M02947 Unframed. *Citizen Kane*, #M0284X Framed, #M03005 Unframed. *The Philadelphia Story*, #M03102 Framed, #M0317X Unframed. Postings, PO Box 8001, Hilliard, OH 43026. (800) 262-6604.

BOGART BERGMAN HENREID
CASABLANCA

Shower with a Famous Friend

Gable, Grable, Garbo, and Bogie are just a tiny constellation on this shower curtain, showcasing a galaxy of your favorite stars.

#7855, $24.98 + 5.99 shipping from Taylor Gifts, 355 Conestoga Road, P.O. Box 7000, Wayne, PA 19093-7000. (215) 789-7007.

"It's a great place to live — if you're an orange." — Fred Allen

Fallen Stars

"Boulevard of Broken Dreams" pays homage to Edward Hopper's famous painting "Nighthawks." Hopper's anonymous patrons are recast with Bogie, Marilyn, Elvis and James Dean, illuminated by a pink neon tube. 40" x 29" framed print.

#NFBBD997 Neon Classic $239.95 + 6.00 shipping from Markline, P.O. Box 13807, Philadelphia, PA 19101-3807. (800) 992-8600.

Don't Tread On Me

Maybe you can't wait for the Hollywood Chamber of Commerce to install your star on the Walk of Fame. You can order yours, made by the same company, personalized with your own name (up to 15 letters). 12" square plaque in gold-tone frame.

#5844, $24.95 + 4.95 shipping from The Music Stand, 1 Rockdale Plaza, Lebanon, NH 03766. (802) 295-7044.

Filmland Mover & Shaker

Salt & pepper shaker shaped like a camera and clapboard.

#1230, $12.95 + 3.95 The Music Stand, Rockdale Plaza, Lebanon, NH 03766-1585. (802) 295-7044.

Stars Send You?

Now you can send them back with the aid of this handy directory. Filled with over 3,000 addresses of celebrities you'd like to contact. Well, not their home addresses really, but their agent's office, etc.—anyway, the mail gets there.

#4483 Star Guide, $12.98 + 3.50 shipping from The Lighter Side, 4514 19th Street Court East, P.O. Box 25600, Bradenton, FL 34206-5600. (813) 747-2356.

Universal Time

Beveled glass clock keeps you in tempo with its vibrant "Universal Studios, Hollywood" logo.

#1985 Universal Wall Clock, $44.95 + 5.95 shipping from The Music Stand, 1 Rockdale Plaza, Lebanon, NH 03766-1585. (802) 295-7044.

SEAT OF POWER

Shout "Lights! Camera! Action!" from your personalized (up to 10 letters) canvas and wood director's chair. White lettering on black, red, blue, hunter green or teal.

#1757 Director's Chair, $56.00 + 7.50 shipping from John Deere Catalog, 1400 3rd Avenue, Moline, IL 61265. (800) 544-2122.

STAR TRACKS

Ogle the stars' houses without ever leaving your easy chair! One-hour guided video tour lets you follow the route on the souvenir star map (included).

#1767 Stars' Homes Video, $19.98 + 4.20 shipping from Johnson Smith Company, 4514 19th Street Court East, P.O. Box 25500, Bradenton, FL 34206-5500. (813) 747-2356.

What a Dish!

"Walk of Fame" 10 1/4" full color collector plates and 12 oz. steins. Your choice: Burt Reynolds, Jimmy Stewart, Elizabeth Taylor, Joan Collins, Sylvester Stallone or Tom Selleck. "Hand numbered" on back and bottom.

Plates $45.00 each + 2.95 shipping. Steins $24.50 + 2.95. Starlog Press, 475 Park Avenue South, New York, NY 10016. (212) 689-2830.

Pilgrimages

• **The Academy of Motion Picture Arts and Sciences.** The Academy both hands out the Oscars and houses one of the world's largest film libraries with more than 15,000 books, one million still photos, exhibits, costumes and set designs.

8949 Wilshire Boulevard, Los Angeles, CA. (213) 278-4313

• **Graveline Tours.** For the truly morbid (and aren't we all?). Would you find it a rush to see exactly where Janis Joplin or John Belushi overdosed? Would you slit your wrists to see where Lupe Velez and George "Superman" Reeves killed themselves?

Ride in a silver Cadillac hearse with at least six others to LA's "death, sin and scandal sites." Detailed graveyard maps included so you can get a mere 6 feet from many famous people.

PO Box 931694, Hollywood, CA 90093. Tours start daily at noon from the east wall of the Chinese Theatre, Hollywood Blvd. and Orchid. Reservations in advance necessary. For information call (213) 469-3127.

Pocket Projection

Tiny movie viewer (on a key ring) shows continuous loop cassettes of some of your favorite film scenes. Battery included. Trip the light fandango with Fred Astaire.

#C189, $9.00 + 2.50 shipping from Future Studio, P.O. Box 292000, Los Angeles, CA 90029. (800) 422-0505. (Other additional cassettes $4.00 each).

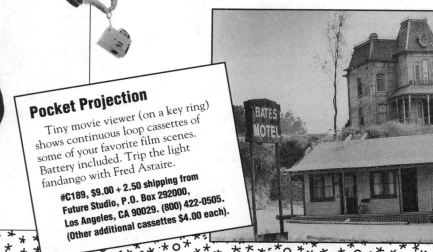

"Hollywood shoots too many pictures and not enough actors."— Walter Winchell

Required Reading

• **Goin' Hollywood**, photographs by **Delmar Watson**, written by **Paul Arnold.** Delmar Watson, himself a former child star who played alongside Shirley Temple in *To the Last Man* in 1932, has put together over 200 Duotone movie star photos chronicling 100 years of Hollywood from 1887 to 1987.

Many taken by Watson and siblings, these are not staged publicity stills, but rare one-of-a-kind shots of stars from Fred Astaire to John

Wayne and Shirley Temple. Choice quotes accompany the visuals.

$19.95 soft cover, $29.95 hard, postpaid. Delmar Watson Publishing, 6762 Hawthorne Ave., Hollywood CA 90028.

• *Hollywood, 50 Great Years* by Jack Lodge, John Russell Taylor, Adrian Turner, Douglas Jarvis & David Castell. Large color and black and white

photographs dominate the pages of this immense book. The five authors break down the history of Hollywood, covering the vast array of the flicks of each decade.

Galahad Books, 166 Fifth Avenue, New York, NY 10010. (212) 679-4200.

• *The Streets Where They Lived* by **Stephen Plumb.** This isn't about the Big Orange, but the Big Apple. Still a lot of Hollywood names show up in this book of celebrity NY homes and hangouts. Researcher Plumb spent five years plumbing significant sites of folks like F. Scott Fitzgerald, Humphrey Bogart, Babe Ruth, Leon Trotsky and the Marx Brothers. Want to know where Brando lived with Wally Cox and his trains? Or see the famous subway vent where Marilyn's skirt got blown skyward?

$12.95 + 2.50 shipping from MarLor Press, 4304 Brigadoon, St. Paul, MN 55126. (612) 484-4600.

• *Who's Had Who* by Simon Bell, Richard Curtis & Helen Field. Features 165 bedtime tales of Hollywood liaisons, some of them pretty darned surprising.

$9.95 + 4.95 shipping from Postings, PO Box 8001, Hilliard, OH 43026. (800) 262-6604.

Movie Magazine

Screen Greats: Hollywood Nostalgia. Deliberately designed to look like fan magazines from the past, this quarterly publication features both old and new stars. Recent issues featured a 1968 Dustin Hoffman interview, Marilyn topless, Elvis' Army physical and fold-out posters of stars ranging from Bette Davis and Greta Garbo to 1990s heartthrob Tom Cruise.

$3.95 per magazine, Starlog Communications Int'l Inc., 475 Park Avenue South, NY, NY 10016. (212) 689-2830.

Movie Memorabilia

The Official Identification And Price Guide to Movie Memorabilia by Richard De Thuin. Unlike most price guides which are based on the author's estimates, this book provides prices that were *actually paid* for movie collectibles like animation art, autographs, toys, costumes, books and posters. Contact information about the dealer who made each sale is also included.

$9.95 + 3.00 shipping from House of Collectibles, 201 E. 50th Street, New York, NY 10022.

Love,
Shirley Temple

"The continental tilt is a phenomenon that has allowed all the loose nuts in the U.S. to slide into Hollywood." — Frank Lloyd Wright

The Reel Thing

• **World Famous Collector's Originals.** Looking for hard-to-find memorabilia and finding it hard to find? Turn the job over to these folks. For $3.00 per search, they'll go through their extensive contacts for you.

PO Box 17522, Memphis, TN 38187. (901) 682-6761.

• **The Cinema City.** Authentic movie ad material, no reproductions. They've got posters, color stills, scripts, autographed items and press kits. Their catalog is constantly being updated.

P.O. Box 1012, Muskegon, MI 49443. (616) 722-7760.

• **Loraine Burdick Movie List.** Send $1 for a current list of movie materials for sale: magazines, posters, sheet music, comics and more.

5 Court Place, Puyallup, WA 98372.

Cue the Fog Machine

For years, airport legend had it that Burbank Airport was the place they filmed the end of *Casablanca* where Bogart fed Ilsa that famous line, "Here's looking at you, Kid."

Well, bad news. Most of the scene was actually filmed on a Warner Brothers sound stage; the rest, at Van Nuys Airport, known at the time as Metropolitan Airport. Unfortunately, Van Nuys doesn't even have passenger flights, so unless you're shipping yourself by Federal Express, there's no way to indulge in your personal *Casablanca* some foggy night.

Oh well. We'll always have Paris.

• **Society of Cinephiles.** Devoted to the history and enjoyment of silent movies, this group of film collectors gathers annually on Labor Day when they hold 24 hour screenings of early films and buy, sell and trade cinemabilia.

2835 North 61st Pl., Scottsdale, AZ 85257.

POSTER NOTES

Reel Art: Great Posters From the Golden Age of the Silver Screen by Stephen Rebello & Richard Allen. This is an impressive, oversized, full-color book of movie posters. Get it!

$49.98 + 4.00 Abbeville Press, 488 Madison Avenue, New York, NY 10022. (212) 888-1969.

Hollywood Sleaze

Sleazy Scandals of the Silver Screen. Books like the notorious *Hollywood Babylon* by Kenneth Anger have been great sources of salacious innuendo, but the comic book is tailor-made for this gossipy genre, showing pictorial reenactments where before we were forced to use our imaginations. The great scandals (Fatty Arbuckle, Monroe, Liberace, and more), with graphic illustration by famous underground cartoonists like Art Spiegelman and Bill Griffith, testify to the cover caption: "Come wallow with us in the muck that was Hollywood."

$2.50 + 1.00 shipping from Kitchen Sink Press, No. 2 Swamp Road, Princeton, WI 54968. (414) 295-6922.

Hollywoodland

The famous Hollywood sign originally read "Hollywoodland." With letters five stories high, it was built on Mount Lee as an advertisement for real estate. The "land" portion of the sign fell in 1939 and it was not until 40 years later that contributors rebuilt the crumbling monument for $249,300 (the original cost only $21,000.)

FEATURED SHORTS (& MORE)

• **A Star Is Worn.** If you can't join the cast, you can at least walk a mile in their shoes, and even get into their pants—literally!

Shop at A Star is Worn, where items such as Victoria Principal's woolen slacks (size 6) have sold for $55, Cher's strapless black bras for $575 and the handkerchiefs of Duran Duran for $25. Some of the proceeds go to charity.

**7303 Melrose, Hollywood, CA.
(213) 939- 4922**

• **Frederick's of Hollywood Bra Museum.** California or bust! Keep abreast of the over-the-shoulder-boulder-holders that tamed and restrained those famous bazooms. Bust shapes and actual bras of Elvira, Madonna, Cher and others.

6608 Hollywood Blvd., Hollywood, CA.

• **Max Factor Museum of Beauty.** Located just around the corner from the Frederick's Bra Museum, this museum showcases makeup through Hollywood film history, from early greasepaint to hairpieces. Two notable exhibits: the Beauty Calibrator, an iron maiden-like head enclosure used to determine which facial features need "corrective makeup"; and the Mechanical Osculator, or Kissing Machine—two sets of rubber lips which press together, designed to test lipsticks' staying power.

**1666 North Highland Ave., Hollywood, CA.
(213) 463-6668.**

Hollywood quotes

"I have no respect for acting. Acting is the expression of the neurotic impulse. It's a bum's life... you get paid for doing nothing and it means nothing. Acting is fundamentally a childish thing to pursue. Quitting acting— that is the mark of maturity."

— **Marlon Brando**

"Brando? Actors like him are good but on the whole I do not enjoy actors who seek to commune with their armpits."

— **Greer Garson**

"So many people attended his funeral because they wanted to make sure he was dead."

— **An anonymous observer at Louis B. Mayer's funeral**

"The most important thing in acting is honesty. Once you've learned to fake that, you're in!"

— **Samuel Goldwyn**

"Hollywood is like Egypt, full of crumbling pyramids. It will never come back. It will just keep crumbling until the wind blows away the last studio props across the street."

— David O. Selznick

Hot Dogs

The Wiener Republic

Boiled, broiled, fried, toasted, grilled or microwaved—no matter how you cook 'em, hot dogs are an American classic.

From picnics to baseball games to carnivals to country fairs to amusement parks to barbecues, hot dogs are an American dietary necessity. Americans eat 50 million franks a day.

A close relative of salami, the frankfurter was invented in Germany during the Middle Ages. A "natural casing" was filled with a sausage mixture and twisted off at equal intervals to form a chain of links. Eventually the frankfurter made it across the ocean with early European immigrants.

Turning the European frankfurter into the all-American hot dog comes from the complementary efforts of two men. Antoine Feuchtwanger, a German immigrant, sold sausages called "red hots" in St. Louis, Missouri. Feuchtwanger supplied his customers with white gloves to protect their hands from heat and grease, but was losing money because his customers would walk off with the gloves. His wife suggested placing his sausages in split buns instead of a glove and the combination was a hit.

But the new gourmet treat wasn't actually named until 1900, when T. A. Dorgan, a sports cartoonist, listened to a vendor at a game yelling "Get your red hots...get your red hot Dachshund dogs." Struck by the imagery, he drew a cartoon of a long talking Dachshund dog sitting in a bun. He made a visual joke out of not being able to spell "Dachshund," and called it a "hot dog." The name caught on.

But sometimes a hot dog is not just a hot dog. There are variations like Bratwurst, Bockwurst, Chorizos, Frankfurters, Coney Islands, Kielbasa, Knockwurst, Kosher Franks, Sausages, Wieners, and Texan Corny Dogs.

Haute Dogge Cuisine

• No franchise, but this hot dog stand is shaped like a hot dog. **311 N. La Cienega, West Hollywood, CA.**

• **First Nathan's Famous Hot Dog store still located at 1310 Surf Avenue, Coney Island, New York.** Nathan and Ida Handwerker took their life savings ($300) and, on the advice of a singing waiter and a piano player, opened up their own food stand on the Coney Island Boardwalk. It was a big success and the one stand grew into a widespread East Coast chain. The waiter and piano player? Eddie Cantor and Jimmy Durante.

Each year, Americans consume 19 billion franks—an average of 87 per person.

"Our Patty loves to rock & roll, a hot dog makes her lose control."

—Theme, *The Patty Duke Show*

Common Fallacy

Although forerunners of today's wieners were popular throughout the ancient world (with regional variations), they were banned by Constantine, first Christian emperor of Rome, because their phallic shape made them an ubiquitous presence at pagan festivals.

RELISH THE THOUGHT

No walkin' the dog for these magnet guys. 3 refrigerator pups with mustard and a cart

#B2333, Hot Dog Magnets, $2.25 + 3.50 shipping from Harriet Carter, North Wales, PA 19455. (215) 361-5151.

"Hotdiggitydogdiggity boom
What you do to me!"

—Perry Como

Curl Your Wienie

If you're ever faced with the problem of placing a long hot dog into an inappropriately round hamburger bun, this gadget will curl your wienie. Cuts at precise intervals halfway through the meat, so that, as you cook, your crimped hot dog will curl into a circle.

#B655555, $5.95 + 2.99 shipping from Colonial Garden Kitchens, P.O. Box 666, Hanover, PA 17333-0066. (800) 752-5552.

A Wiener-Wiener Situation

And buns for both. Hot Diggity Dogger hot dog maker looks like a toaster, cooks two dogs with matching buns simultaneously.

#C738773, $59.95 + 7.50 shipping from Sync, Hanover, PA 17333-0042. (800) 722-9979.

STUPID DOG TRICKS

It looks real. But it's rubber so it can't be eaten...which makes it very similar to the real thing!

#2170, 2 Rubber Hot Dogs, $2.75 + 1.35 shipping from Johnson Smith Company, 4514 19th Court East, P.O. Box 25500, Bradenton, FL 34206-5500. (813) 747-2356 / FAX (813) 746-7896.

I LOVE HOT DOGS 120 FRANK RECIPES

American eat 50 MILLION FRANKS each day!

Cartoons by Dan Youra

by Pat Thompson

¡Kielbasa, Amigo!

I Love Hot Dogs by Pat Thompson. From kebabs to fondue to casseroles, this book has 120 different recipes that are frankly amazing. Includes recipes for homemade sausages, condiments, rolls and buns. So next time you burn a hot dog on the grill, tell 'em it's a Cajun blackened canine.

$4.95 + 2.00 shipping from Still News Press, P.O. Box 353, Port Ludlow, WA 98365.

Alvin the Chipmunk, on his cartoon series, claimed that "Jell-O with a hot dog in it" was his favorite dish.

HULA HOOPS

Take It for a Spin

Before 1958, Elvis' gyrating pelvis was shocking, too lewd to be shown on prime time TV. But during 1958, while Elvis was being all he could be in the Army, the American public conferred respectability on the old burlesque bump-and-grind and made a simple plastic circle a phenomenon. It was the Hula Hoop.

What began as a bamboo exercise ring from Australia became, in the words of Richard Johnson, in *American Fads,* "the undisputed granddaddy of American fads...the one standard against which all national crazes are measured." Children and grownups alike were maneuvering their mid-sections in a Middle Eastern manner.

Endurance contests mushroomed across the nation, many of them televised. Abdominal showmen demonstrated feats of endurance and multiple ringsmanship. At its peak, Wham-O's production was 20,000 hoops a day.

Then one day, the market collapsed. Wham-O had warehouses full of plastic rings that they couldn't give away. A lesser company, having been burned, might have decided never to

deal in the product again. Not Wham-O. A decade later, the company brought them out again, this time with ball-bearings inside to make a shoop-shoop sound. Since then, the Hula Hoop has become a classic toy—no longer a fad, but one that sells predictably and steadily year after year.

Guinness Hoop Records

• Men's record for sustaining the most hoops between shoulders and hips: 81, by William K. "Chico" Johnson in London, 9/19/83.

• Women's record for most hoops: 70, by Luisa Valencia in Las Vegas, Nevada, 5/87.

• Longest single hoop marathon: 90 hours by Roxann Rose of Pullman, Washington, 4/2-4/6, 1987.

Hoops Around the World

• The "Huru Hoopu" was such a hit in Japan that Tokyo police banned them from the streets for obstructing traffic.

• Indonesia also banned Hula Hoops, but their reason was that they "might stimulate passion."

• China's official news agency denounced them as a "nauseating craze."

• The Soviet Union's official view of the hoop was as a symbol of "the emptiness of the American culture."

Hoops A Daisy

• The plastic tubing used for all the Hula Hoops ever made would encircle the Equator more than five times.

• Hula Hoops are not one-size-fits-all: they come in 30, 33, and 36 inch diameters.

• Before settling on plastic as the material to manufacture hoops from, Wham-O founders Arthur "Spud" Melin and Richard Knerr experimented with an ash wood prototype.

• Other names considered for the toy were "Swing-A-Hoop" and "Twirl-A-Hoop."

Chubby Checker admitted that the Hula Hoop craze inspired his dance creation, the Twist.

JEANS

From working class cheeks to leisure class chic, from the gold rush to Gloria Vanderbilt, the history of blue jeans is appropriately patchy.

Tailor Levi Strauss was only 17 when he arrived in San Francisco in the 1850s. Although following the Gold Rush, he quickly realized he could make money selling canvas for tents than by digging in the ground. While canvassing for sales his tailor's eye quickly noticed the beat-up state of the miners' trousers.

Mining was particularly tough on clothes because of continuous squatting, kneeling, and stuffing pockets with ore. Strauss stopped making tents and started stitching his heavy-duty canvas into pants. They were an immediate hit in the gold fields.

Levis, denims, jeans. Although sturdy, the canvas was rough and stiff. This was especially significant to his customers because wearing underwear was a trend that had not yet universally caught on at the time. In the 1860s he replaced canvas with a tough but softer fabric called "serge de Nimes" that was milled in Genoa, Italy, thereby coining two words with one stonewash: "jeans" for the city of origin and "denims" as a corruption of the fabric name.

Mood indigo. He found that the neutral-colored pants sold better if dyed a deep indigo to hide dirt stains. It was about that time that cowboys discovered that you could stretch the jeans to fit by lying down in a horse trough and letting the sun shrink-dry the material.

The pants were strong, but miners complained about the pockets tearing when they filled them with tools and rocks. A tailor Strauss knew suggested copper rivets on the pockets and fly, which solved the problem.

Hot, testy. Rivets were used for years but eventually caused their own problems. As many outdoors people found out, the crotch rivet conducted heat remarkably well when the wearer crouched near a campfire. After many pained campfire howls, these were abandoned. The backpocket rivets also disappeared in the 1930s because of complaints that they gouged wooden furniture. Nowadays, only the hip rivets remain.

Classic Jacket

Blue cotton denim, stone-washed for extra softness. Machine washable.

Sizes XS, S, M, L & XL. #5133E, $56.00 + 5.50 shipping from J. Crew, One Ivy Crescent, Lynchburg, VA 24506-1001.
(800) 562-0258.

Calvin Klein Jeans

LEVI STRAUSS & CO.
SAN FRANCISCO, CAL.

Attempts to market polyester jeans failed because people were disappointed when they wouldn't fade.

Don't Have A Cow…

No cows or leopards died to provide you with these fashionable looks. Jackets are heavy, full-cut denim.

#C06 Cow or #C07 Leopard Jacket (M, L, XL). $69.00 + 7.50 shipping from the Daily Planet, P.O. Box 1313, New York, NY 10013. (212) 334-0006 / FAX (212) 334-1158.

WALL WEAR

These wall-mounted overalls are for organizing your tools, not wearing. 39 pockets make it easy. With brackets and grommets for hanging on doors or walls.

#6985, $29.98 + 5.49 shipping from Taylor Gifts, 355 E. Conestoga Road, Box 206, Wayne, PA 19087. (215) 789-7007.

Seat of Pants Reading

• *Everyone Wears His Name: A Biography of Levi Strauss* by **Sandra Henry and Emily Taitz.** Somewhat by default, the best book we've seen on the life of the man who invented jeans as we know them. With heroic gloss and easy reading, this book is apparently aimed at young adults with the idea that they should emulate the man whose name became synonymous with levis. Especially interesting within the context of San Francisco life after the Gold Rush: did you know that in those Sinophobic times the company advertised for many years that the jeans were "produced by WHITE labor only"?

$11.95 + 2.50 shipping from Dillon Press, 242 Portland Avenue S., Minneapolis, MN 55415.

• *Denim: An American Legend* by **Iain Finlayson.** From its ignominious California debut in 1850 as material for work trousers improvised by Levi Strauss from his cargo of tents, to its current ubiquity, denim is practically synonymous with American style. Iain Finlayson explores the development of jeans as we know them, from durable laborers' uniform for a century, to postwar rebel status reinforced by movie bad boys Marlon Brando and James Dean, to high fashion statement, and back again to its earthy, erotic origins.

$17.95 + 2.50 shipping from Simon & Schuster, Rockefeller Center, 1230 Avenue of the Americas, New York, NY 10020.

"Americans didn't know they had style until the French started wearing blue jeans."—Fran Lebowitz

Jukeboxes

Jukebox Saturday Night

One of America's hallmarks has been the ability to take a good idea and make some bucks out of it. In 1889, twelve years after Edison invented the talking machine, the first coin-operated phonograph began entertaining customers in a San Francisco saloon. The piano player probably wasn't thrilled when this mechanical music maker brought in $15 the first week. But the saloon owner was happy because this new, non-tiring performer didn't make mistakes, drink too much or ask for raises.

It did have some problems, though. It only offered one selection from a cardboard and wax cylinder, and it was awfully hard for more than one person to hear it at a time. Still, the curiosity factor alone was enough to make it a success.

The first "real" jukebox, John Gabel's "Automatic Entertainer," appeared in 1906. It played real discs instead of cardboard cylinders and it offered more than just one selection.

It wasn't until the 1930s that someone coined the term jukebox. "Juke came from "juke house"—slang for a brothel, which eventually got generalized to meaning any sleazy roadside establishment.

Radio then mostly played middle-of-the-road pop and classical music. The jukebox was a way people could hear the latest jazz, blues, hillbilly, and bawdy songs. The fact that radios and phonographs were too expensive for many music fans also played a large part in making jukeboxes the rage.

By 1937 the demand for jukeboxes spawned Seeburg, Mills, AMI (Automated Musical Instruments Co.), Rock-Ola and Wurlitzer. For the next ten years or so, the popularity of the jukebox grew stupendously, and the designs got more and more elaborate.

In the early 1940s, the art deco jukebox of the 1930s made of wood gave way to new, bright styles made of translucent, illuminated plastic.

By 1950, Seeburg was producing machines that could play any of a hundred 45 rpm records. The modern jukebox continued to be a major form of entertainment in those innocent times before TV took over everything.

Jukeboxes fell out of favor in bars, restaurants and maltshops during the 1960s because the vanguard of musical focus became albums, not singles. As they disappeared from the public scene, collectors began discovering their charms.

Jukebox Hits

Juke Box Saturday Night: 36 Number 1 Golden Hits of the '40s and '50s. Includes *Sentimental Journey, Sha-Boom, How High The Moon* and more. Great for your CD jukebox, or for pretending you have one.

#17746, $19.95 + 3.90 shipping from Wireless, P.O. Box 64422, St. Paul, MN 55164-0422. (800) 669-9999.

Celebrity Collectors

- Madonna
- Paul McCartney (has a Wurlitzer 1015 he rented for *Give My Regards To Broad Street* and later bought)
- Dustin Hoffman
- Steven Spielberg
- Elton John
- Huey Lewis (he once recorded a song he first heard on an old jukebox)
- Francis Coppola (has his in his kitchen where it plays old Italian opera recordings)

JUKE FACTS

- Despite what you might think, the Rock-Ola jukebox didn't get its name from rock 'n' roll, but from the actual name of company founder David C. Rockola.
- During the heyday of jukeboxes (roughly 1935-1950) there were more than 700,000 jukeboxes in bars, bowling alleys, soda shops—even gas stations and schools.
- One popular novelty record made especially for jukeboxes was 3 Minutes of Silence, designed so you could pay a nickel and get a little peace and quiet for that amount of time.

Jukeboxes early in the century came with earphones and only one person could listen at a time.

By Any Other Name

Some popular jukebox model names include Singing Towers, the Throne of Music, the Peacock, the Satyr, the Commando, the Mother of Plastic, the Manhattan, Luxury Light-Up, the Rocket and Spectravox.

Reconditioned Jukes & Parts

Wurco carries a complete line of practically everything for jukebox owners and fans. Reconditioned and unrestored jukeboxes, new jukeboxes, wallbox adapters, keys, service manuals, records and more. Call and tell 'em what you're looking for.

Wurco, Inc., Wurlitzer Industrial Park, 908 Niagara Falls Blvd., North Tonawanda, NY 14120. (716) 694-6247.

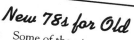

Wurlitzer Music Merchants

I APPRECIATE THE IMPORTANT PART YOU PLAY IN THE DAILY LIVES OF THE AMERICAN PEOPLE

HELP ME SELL NATIONAL DEFENSE BONDS

SHOW YOUR PATRIOTISM. PLACE A RECORDING OF

"Any Bonds Today?"

IN No. 1 POSITION ON EVERY PHONOGRAPH OR WALL BOX YOU OPERATE

DON'T FAIL ME AND I WON'T FAIL YOU

Uncle Sam

Put Another $5,000 In

Nostalgia and the neo-diner restaurant craze have rejuvenated jukebox restoring and collecting to an absurd level. In the 1960s, when jukeboxes began their decline, you could pick one up for as little as $150. Today, these can cost several thousand dollars, and the rarest of the lot can go for as high as $30,000 to $40,000.

One of the most expensive jukeboxes is the Wurlitzer 950, the first to use fluorescent lights. But the most popular was

BUY IT FOR A SONG.

Wurlitzer™ CD Jukebox. This is a reproduction of the original best-selling 1946 "Bubbler," updated with a completely modernized audio system that plays up to 50 of your favorite compact discs. Carved and stained pine cabinet sports period-style chrome and illuminated side pillasters with those ever famous dancing bubbles and alternating colored lights. Six speakers in a 3-way stereo system offer superb digital sound. Use coins or free play.

#17612R, $11,999.00 + 12.50 shipping from Hammacher Schlemmer, 9180 Le Saint Drive, Fairfield, OH 45014. (800) 543-3366.

and is the "Bubbler," manufactured by Wurlitzer. In fact, when the subject of jukeboxes comes up, this is the machine that first comes to practically everyone's mind, the one you see in the background on the TV show *Cheers*. Wurlitzer made nearly 60,000 of these clear-tubed, color-changing, bubbling machines, which makes them relatively common, even comparably inexpensive. A reconditioned one will cost you between $7,500 and $12,000.

You can still buy newly manufactured jukeboxes. One model introduced by Seeburg in 1986 plays CDs and offers up to 1000 songs. Depending on the type of machine you're looking for, a new one can cost between $3,000 and $12,000.

New 78s for Old

Some of the nicest old jukeboxes play only 78 rpm records. That's fine, if you like big bands and Perry Como. But maybe you don't dig that kind of croonin', chum.

Enter ever-helpful Rhino Records. They've released an authorized 78 rpm rock 'n' roll set with 25 records in each deluxe boxed set.

Volumes I and II features 1950s hits by the Everly Brothers, Jerry Lee Lewis, Frankie Avalon, the Dixie Cups, and more.

Volume III gives you great 1960s hits.

**#RNJB 78000, Vol. 1, '50s.
#RNJB 78002, Vol. 2, '50s.
#RNJB 78001, Vol. 3, '60s.
Each $124.98 ppd with title strips from Rhino Records, 2225 Colorado Ave., Santa Monica, CA 90404-3598. (800) 432-0020.**

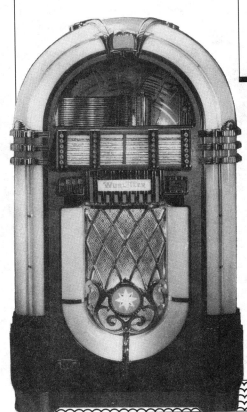

Some old jukeboxes have a reset button on the back. Push it and the current song stops playing.

OFF-THE-WALL BOXES

There was a time when you could sit in a booth in your favorite malt shop and put your nickel into a "Wall-o-Matic" wall box without leaving your table. You know, the ones with those "flipping" music menus. It was sort of like an early remote control.

Did you ever wonder how they work? These wireless wall boxes were speakers that plugged into an ordinary A/C electrical outlet. You chose your tune and electronic impulses were sent to the main jukebox using the establishment's electrical wiring. The impulses made the musical selection and returned it to the speakers in the same manner.

The Wall-o-Matic was marketed because jukebox manufacturers were afraid people might stop using their machines. In the 1920s and '30s, jukeboxes had exposed mechanisms— you could watch them work. People put money in, then gathered around to watch the machinery in action.

But in 1938, the Seeburg Jukebox Co. began enclosing the mechanisms.

Fearing that this might discourage restaurant patrons from popping nickels into their machines, Seeburg came up with a new attraction—the wall units. Now customers didn't have to leave their seats to play music. It was a smash hit.

Other manufacturers joined in, attempting other variations. Until 1941, for example, Wurlitzer made an oversized counter-top jukebox that housed an entire phonograph. Another company put wheels on large wireless units, enabling waitresses to roll jukebox selectors up to their patrons. Neither overtook the Wall-O-Matic, which remains an integral part of diner decor today.

How to tell if that used 45 rpm record was on a jukebox? The "hit" side is almost unplayable from wear, the other side, almost noise-free.

In the Kitchen With Diner

Put this on your kitchen table for an old-time feel. It says "6 Songs For A Quarter" but you need not pay because this jukebox selector is actually a radio/cassette player filled with those modern solid-state electronical things.

It has a 4 in. speaker, lighted radio dial and a set of selection charts that flip.

#C734970 Jukebox AM/FM Radio & Cassette Player, $89.95 + 9.00 shipping from Sync, Hanover, PA 17333-0042.

Rock Around The Watch

Imagine a Wurlitzer jukebox on your wrist. Bright 1950s colors, neon wrist band make this the flashiest watch you'll ever own. Quartz movement, with water resistance.

#5875, $39.95 + 5.95 shipping from The Music Stand, 1 Rockdale Plaza, Lebanon, NH 03766-1585. (802) 295-7044.

Bubble Gum Music

Chew chew, baby with an exciting Jukebox Gumball Machine. It dispenses Good & Plenty, jelly beans, "Mini Malts" and, of course, gumballs. Will accept any coin or can be set for free play.

$19.95 + 3.50 shipping from Golds', 1757 Winthrop Drive, P.O. Box 1968, Des Plaines, IL 60018-1958. (800) 323-8077 ext. 3123.

PORTABLE JUKEBOX

Gee Dad, it's a cassette player! This Wurlitzer 1015 mini "jukebox" has a pulsating light system. Battery-operated or use with an AC adapter (not included).

#7000, $69.00 postpaid from Jukebox Collector, 2545 S.E. 60th Court, Des Moines, IA 50317. (515) 265-8324.

Insert Coin, Select Music

"I know the routine, put another nickel in the machine..."
— One For My Baby (& One For The Road) sung by Frank Sinatra

"Rock the coin right into the slot. The music that's playing is really hot!"
— School Days by Chuck Berry

"Before you punch that number, may I make one request..."
— Don't Rock the Jukebox by Alan Jackson

"...bring your jukebox money."
— Love Shack by the B-52s

There are 20,000 jukebox collectors in the United States.

Required Reading

• **American Jukebox: The Classic Years** by Vincent Lynch. One hundred full-color photographs celebrate the "Golden Days" (1937-1948) of the jukebox. This comprehensive book offers a unique visual history for nostalgia buffs and collectors alike. Also includes a history-tracing introduction and an informative, detailed appendix with dates, descriptions, manufacturers and more. Brilliantly photographed, these jukeboxes, wall boxes, table models and speakers jump right off the page.

$29.95 hardcover, $16.95 paperback + 2.00 shipping from Chronicle Books, 275 Fifth Street, San Francisco, CA 94103. (415) 777-7240.

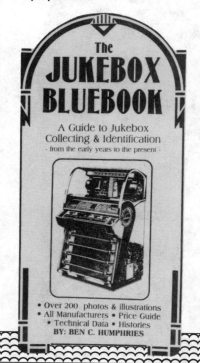

• **Vintage Jukeboxes** by Christopher Pearce. Jukeboxes from the 1940s and '50s come alive in this homage to the music machine. 125 pages with over 100 in full color. Also included are jukebox ads and product literature from the same era.

$14.00 postpaid from Rick Botts, 2545 S.E. 60th Court, Des Moines, IA 50317. (515) 265-8324.

• **The Jukebox Bluebook** by Ben C. Humphries. 96 pages worth of prices, technical info, major (and many smaller) manufacturer histories and, of course, over 200 photos (taken from the original sales literature). Pretty comprehensive and pocket-size, too!

$12.95 postpaid from Jukebox Bluebook, Inc, P.O. Box 1192, Gatlinburg, TN 37738.

Whirlwind Wurlitzer Tour

Wurlitzer Film Video. Original factory films from the Wurlitzer collection. Films produced for Wurlitzer distributors between 1946 and 1948 are included on this one 2 hour videotape. *A Visit To Wurlitzer* shot in 1948 shows how the model 1100 was produced in a "complete start to finish tour of the Wurlitzer factory." *The Power of Advertising* and *How to*

Increase Profits show promotional materials that were used in the national ad campaign. *How To Boost Your Profits with Wurlitzer Engineered Music* shows how the use of remote boxes enhances revenues. Entertaining as well as informative.

$75.00 postpaid from Victory Glass Company, P.O. Box 119, Des Moines, IA 50301. (515) 223-8820.

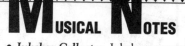

Musical Notes

• **Jukebox Collector**. Jukebox expert Rick Botts oversees this popular magazine, which features a nice mix of people articles, places, shows, prices, auctions and events and classifieds.

One year (10 issues), $30.00 from Rick Botts, 2545 SE 60th Court, Des Moines, IA 50317-5099. (515) 265-8324.

• **Always Jukin'**. This monthly newspaper is jam-packed with jukebox and related info. You'll find a round-up of recent jukebox shows including a listing of jukebox prices, a bit of trivia, hot record ratings, a coming events calendar and a classified section loaded with buy, sell, trade and wanted items.

One year, $21.00 (12 issues) from Silver Age Jukebox Club, 5136 26th Avenue NE, Seattle, WA 98105. (206) 524-5111.

Today there are over 225,000 jukeboxes in use, each week playing 48 million songs for 78 million people.

Kitchens

brightly colored floor coverings.

- 1886: Dishwasher.
- 1890: Electric range.
- 1892: Thermos bottle. First made to store laboratory gases.
- 1903: Aluminum cookware.
- 1910: Toaster.
- 1912: Cellophane.
- 1915: Pyrex.
- 1917: S.O.S. pads. An aluminum cookware salesman hand-made the first ones to give away as a premium, but they took off on their own as a popular product.
- 1921: Whistling teakettle.
- 1928: Vinyl tablecloths.
- 1936: Electric blender.

- 1948: Tupperware.
- 1948: Nylon. Besides replacing silk stockings, it replaced natural bristles in brushes used for kitchen cleaning.
- 1952: Microwave oven. Scientist Percy Spencer accidentally hit on the cooking properties of microwaves in 1946 when they melted a chocolate bar in his pocket, yet he felt no heat.
- 1954: Teflon. Revolutionized cooking without oil or other fats, created a perfect metaphor for the first in a series of obliviously untouched presidents.

Time Line of Kitchen Conveniences

- 1800: Percolating coffeepot.
- 1802: Gas range.
- 1810: Tin can.
- 1858: Can opener. It took almost 50 years before anyone thought to design an opener. Before that, people used a knife or chisel.
- 1860: Linoleum. A mixture of flax and oil, it was durable, cheap, and easy to clean. In the early 1900s, Thomas Armstrong had the idea of using it for

- 1937: Melmac.
- 1938: Styrene drinking glasses and refrigerator egg trays.
- 1938: Formica. Our favorite plastic laminate was perfect for kitchen counters, and matching dinette tabletops too. Bright colors, glitter, and patterns spread to every surface.
- 1947: Aluminum foil.
- 1947: Food processor. A popular appliance in England and France, it didn't catch on in the U.S. until the mid '70s with the Cuisinart.

Long before soaps and detergent cleansers were invented, sand was the preferred scouring powder.

Required Reading

• *Food and Drink Containers and Their Prices* by Al Bergevin. Hundreds of black and white pictures, and 8 pages of color ones, showing antique tins and boxes that once held cocoa, coconut, peanut butter, popcorn, and more. The author tells the approximate dollar worth of these things to collectors. The pictures are interesting, but our main complaint: it's *only* a price list and there's no background information (year, manufacturer, product).

$16.95 + 2.50 shipping. Wallace-Homestead Book Co., 201 King of Prussia Road, Radnor, PA 19089. (215) 964-4730.

• *Fifties Homestyle* by Mark Burns and Louis DiBonis. The authors have decorated a house in Philadelphia with kitschy artifacts of the '50s. Their book is full of color photos and loving descriptions of their collection. It's great fun to look at. The section called "Food — Fast and Flirty" displays the Fifties kitchen in all its gaudy glory.

Harper & Row; out of print but worth tracking down.

• *300 Years of Kitchen Collectibles* by Linda Campbell Franklin. A guide to sausage stuffers, raisin seeders, mayonnaise mixers, sugar nippers, and poppyseed grinders as well as more common kitchen items. Includes nicknames, manufacturers, dates, materials and value estimates. Terrific.

$22.95 + 4.00 shipping. Books Americana Inc., P.O. Box 2326, Florence AL 35630. (205) 757-9966.

Collectors: Everything But the Kitchen Sink

For the many collectors of kitchen implements, there are clubs that provide newsletters and trading opportunities. Send SASE for information about joining.

• **Tin Container Collectors Association.** Hoard tin food and beverage containers? A lot of people do, and many of them are members.

11650 Riverside Drive, North Hollywood, CA 91602.

• *Just For Openers.* A club and newsletter for collectors of bottle openers. It includes new opener discoveries, diagrams of openers, classified ads, the collector of the month, and photos of members. The group holds a yearly convention with plenty of trading and socializing.

6126 McPherson, St. Louis MO 63112. (314) 863-6798.

• *The Milk Route.* A club for collectors of dairy products. Old-fashioned milk bottles and bottle-caps which carried advertising and messages are becoming rarer, so the prices are going up.

4 Ox Bow Road, Westport, CT 06880.

• **American Spoon Collectors.** Offers area clubs, an annual national convention and *Spooners Forum*, a monthly newsletter available only to members with plenty of valuable information for spoon collectors.

4922 State Line, Westwood Hills, KS 66205. (913) 831-0912.

• Are you a victim of planned obsolescence? Need replacement parts for old or discontinued small appliances? That's the specialty of these folks.

Mar-Beck Small Appliance Service Co., 8223 Wornall Road, Kansas City, MO 64114. (816) 523-6931.

"This recipe sure is silly. It says to separate 2 eggs, but it doesn't say how far to separate them." —Gracie Allen

They Might Be Giants

- **Mutant Orange Power Juicer.** Obese plastic orange shape conceals 24 oz. capacity juicer, powered by a heavy-duty 25 watt motor with automatic reverse action to squeeze every drop from your favorite citrus fruit.

#101 Citrus Juicer, $39.95 + 6.00 shipping. The Scope Catalog, 260 Motor Parkway, Hauppauge, NY 11788-5134. (800) 695-4848 / FAX (516) 435-8079.

- **Behemoth Bread-slice Toaster.** The greatest thing since sliced bread! Lexan plastic exterior resembles Texan-sized piece of toast, with wide mouth design to easily accommodate bagels, English muffins and thick frozen waffles. Outside stays cool to touch as electronic micro-chip circuitry ensures consistent browning.

#103-M Toaster, $59.50 + 7.50 shipping. The Scope Catalog, 260 Motor Parkway, Hauppauge, NY 11788-5134. (800) 695-4848 / FAX (516) 435-8079.

- **Enormous Egg.** Egg shell comes apart as a three-container melamine mixing set: a measuring cup plus 2 1/2 qt. and 3 qt. mixing bowls. Also inside the egg (no yolk!): a 5-speed, 130 watt hand mixer, beaters and a measuring spoon.

#102-M Mixing Set, $50.00 + 6.00 shipping from The Scope Catalog, 260 Motor Parkway, Hauppauge, NY 11788-5134. (800) 695-4848 / FAX (516) 435-8079.

- **Titanic Tin Can Opener.** Silver plastic housing looks like a large, unlabeled tin can, but splits in half down the middle to reveal a stainless steel cutting can opener driven by a powerful 60 watt motor. Cord stores inside canister.

#100-M Can Opener, $40.00 + 6.00 shipping from The Scope Catalog, 260 Motor Parkway, Hauppauge, NY 11788-5134. (800) 695-4848 / FAX (516) 435-8079.

NIGHT SHAKES

Ceramic handpainted salt & pepper shakers (left).

#6319A, $15.00 + 3.95 shipping. Post Scripts, P.O. Box 21628, Ft. Lauderdale, FL 33335. (800) 327-3799.

Corny Shakers

#M359 Ceramic Salt & Pepper shakers, $4.95 + 4.00 shipping from Archie McPhee, P.O. Box 30852, Seattle, WA 98103-0852. (206) 547-2467.

Don't Eat The Phone

Place one of these food phones next to the wax fruit on your kitchen table.

Put the Corn Phone (#M727) to your ear and tell corny jokes. Grade A Potato Phone (#M730) also has a-peel.

Each $39.95 + 4.00 shipping from Archie McPhee, P.O. Box 30852, Seattle, WA 98103-0852. (206) 547-2467.

Spudtaneous Fun

How can you tell when it's time to eat? When the Two Potato Clock says so! No batteries required, because this clock actually runs on potato power. But it also works with beer, lemons, apples, even cola.

#11575-2, $14.95 + 3.00 shipping from Schoolmasters, 745 State Circle, P.O. Box 1941, Ann Arbor, MI 48106. (800) 521-2832 / FAX (313) 761-8711.

Socialite Josephine Cochrane, tired of losing fine china to butterfingered servants, invented the dishwasher in 1886.

Dress Up Your Refrigerator

Veggie magnets are hand-made and hand-painted, for your salad days.

#030996, $17.50 + 4.25 shipping from Casual Living USA, 5401 Hangar Court, P.O. Box 31273, Tampa, FL 33631-3273. (800) 843-1881 / FAX (800) 882-4605.

Shark Protection, Gator Aid

Protect your hands, and put on oven-side puppet shows.

#010735, both for $13.95 + 4.25 shipping.Casual Living USA, 5401 Hangar Ct., P.O. Box 31273, Tampa, FL 33631. (800) 843-1881 / FAX (800) 882-4605

Home-Made Food Products

The Velveeta Cookbook. Velveeta, America's favorite "processed cheese food product," can be used for some pretty imaginative things. This cookbook has over 100 "mouthwatering" Velveeta recipes from vegetable cheese soup to Shrimp Milano.

#B2884, $9.98 + 3.50 shipping from Harriet Carter, North Wales, PA 19455. (215) 361-5151.

The Pop Art of Cooking

Wear Pop Art while you fix your Pop Tart. Soup's on!

#B2905 (S), #B2906 (M), #2907 (L), #2908 (XL), each $15.98 + 4.95 shipping from Harriet Carter, North Wales, PA 19455. (215) 361-5151.

Poppin' Fresh Pottery

Now you can have the Pillsbury Dough Boy as your kitchen helper.

#5542 Cookie Jar, $34.98 + 5.49 shipping; #5543 Utensil Holder, $19.98 + 3.99 shipping; #5544 Napkin Holder, $14.98 + 3.99 shipping; #4972 Salt & Pepper Set, $14.98 + 3.99 shipping; #6226 Magnet Set, $8.98 + 3.99 shipping; #6227 Soap Dispenser, $14.98 + 3.99 shipping. Taylor Gifts, 355 E. Conestoga Road, P.O. Box 206, Wayne, PA 19087-0206. (215) 789-7007.

FIFTIES FOOD

The Back of the Box Gourmet by **Michael McLaughlin.** Can't find your recipe for Ritz Crackers Mock Apple Pie? Wracking your brain for Lipton California Dip ingredients? Look no further than this book, containing 75 product-based recipes, actually copied from the backs of boxes.

#F655811, $14.95 + 3.99 shipping from Colonial Garden Kitchens, P.O. Box 66, Hanover, PA 17333-0066. (800) 752-5552.

Kitsch 'n' Ware

Kitchenware that looks like the Jolly Green Giant's helper...Little Sprout!

#6213 Cookie Jar, $34.98 + 5.49 shipping; #6214 Tools & Holder, $19.98 + 3.99 shipping; #6215 Scouring Pad Holder, $14.98 + 3.99 shipping; #6216 Salt & Pepper Set, $14.98 + 3.99 shipping from Taylor Gifts, 355 E. Conestoga Road, P.O. Box 206, Wayne, PA 19087-0206. (215) 789-7007.

Stephen Poplawski invented blenders to whip milk shakes, but bandleader Fred Waring popularized them as cocktail makers.

KITES

It's hard to argue with the staying power of a popular culture item that's been around longer than most of the world's religions. Kites go back over 21 centuries to China, where they were thought to ward off evil spirits.

Yet, in all that long history, no one has yet come up with a convincing explanation of the tree-kite relationship. Are trees hungry? Do kites deliberately aim themselves at trees, like moths to candles? And where do power lines fit in here anyway?

Although kites are ancient, modern design has revolutionized kite flying. Mylar, the plastic which is lighter and more durable than paper, has enabled kite makers to experiment with bold, new designs.

One new design—high-performance stunt kites that are controlled by two or four lines—have taken the world of wind by storm, as it were. The extra lines let you perform a variety of dazzling aerobatic feats—you "drive" the kites around the sky. They're made of light stainless steel, rip-stop nylon, graphlex, and fiberglass, with lines made from the same material as bullet-proof vests.

And yet, although the new kites are designed via space age technology, some people still insist that the best kite is the one you've taped together from the Sunday comics section, attached to a tail of old rags.

Follow the Leader

Blow up a balloon, fasten it to a paper clip by tying with a twist tie, and hook the paper clip onto the kite string. Assisted by the wind, the balloon will climb all the way up to the kite.

KITES AT WORK

Being a kite isn't always a breeze. Some work as stringers, others are still trying to earn their tether:

• Construction workers in ancient Japan used kites to carry baskets of tile and bricks up to workers building towers.

• In India during the Great Mogul period, young men, forbidden by custom to look upon or speak to unwed maidens, sent kites carrying love notes and presents over the palace walls.

• After his voyage to the East, Marco Polo reported on the use of kites there as economic omens. Before a merchant ship left on a voyage, a drunkard or other expendable crew member would be tied to a kite and launched from the ship's deck. If he rose in the air successfully, it would be a good voyage. If he crashed, the sailing date would be delayed.

• In 200 B.C., Han Hsin, a Chinese general, used a kite as a surveying instrument to judge the distance between his army and the walls of a heavily defended city. He used the information to dig an invasion tunnel of the proper length and launch a successful surprise attack.

• In the first century, Roman archers sent dragon-shaped wind socks aloft to sample wind speed and direction.

• During the Civil War, the Union army used kites to drop propaganda leaflets behind Confederate lines.

• Since the 1890s, the U.S. Weather Bureau has used kites to carry instruments to high altitudes.

• In World War I, before the use of airplanes became widespread, kites lifted military observers into the sky for a view of what the enemy was up to.

• During World War II, U.S. warships flew huge box kites to snag enemy planes. Kites designed to look like enemy aircraft were used for artillery target practice. Life rafts carried kites as survival equipment to lift emergency SOS radio antennae.

• In Vietnam, farmers fly predator-shaped kites over rice fields to serve as scarecrows. True in California's Napa Valley, too.

• Natives of the East Indies go fishing with kites woven out of leaves. They fly the kite, its tail sticky with spider web, just over the water. The fish strike at the tail, get their gills caught in the spider web, and it's "reel 'em in" time.

The Japanese have a special term for being fanatical about kites — tako kichi (kite crazy).

Kite Milestones

• In 1752, Benjamin Franklin flew a silk handkerchief kite in a storm to prove that lightning and electricity were the same thing: "And when the Rain has wetted the Kite and Twine, so that it can conduct the Electric Fire freely, you will find it stream out plentifully from the Key on the Approach of your Knuckle." His conclusions led directly to his inventing the lightning rod. But scientists today are still not sure how he managed to survive the experience.

• In 1827, George Pocock, a teacher in Bristol, England, developed kite-powered carriages called Charvolants. Three, each drawn by two 8-foot kites, traveled over a hundred miles of English countryside, at speeds of 25 mph.

• In the 1840s, a small kite-flying boy saved months of time for an engineering team building a suspension bridge over the Niagara River. Winter ice floes made crossing the river impossible and it was feared that work would have to wait until spring.

Young

Homan Walsh, however, labored all day until he flew a kite across the Niagara Gorge. A heavy rope was tied to the kitestring and hauled over, then a larger rope, and finally a heavy wire cable, and work began on the bridge.

• In 1887, English meteorologist E.D. Archibald took the world's first photographs from a kite.

• Buffalo Bill Cody abandoned his Wild West show on a tour of England to take up his son's hobby, kite-flying. A kite he built pulled his boat across the English channel in 1903. After building a kite that lifted a soldier over 2,000 feet, he was appointed chief kite instructor of the British Army.

• The Wright Brothers' experiments with kites paved the way for their Kitty Hawk biplane—essentially a motorized box kite.

JOIN THE CLUB

American Kitefliers Association. The organizational arm of kiting, providing coordination of kite events and activities. Dues include subscription to bimonthly journal, *Kiting*.

One year membership, $15.00. 1559 Rockville Pike, Rockville, MD 20852.

Best Places to Fly
According to *Kite Lines Magazine*

• Shirone, Niigata, Japan
• Sanjo, Niigata, Japan
• Weifang, Shandong, China
• Lincoln City, Oregon
• Chicago, Illinois
• Ocean City, Maryland
• Los Angeles, California
• Long Beach, Washington
• Brussels, Belgium
• Austin, Texas
• Vancouver, British Columbia
• Bandon, Oregon
• Canberra, New South Wales, Australia

Kite Facts

• Flying a kite within 500 feet of a cloud is prohibited, according to federal regulations. (There could be an airplane flying in that cloud.)

• The reason why Charlie Brown has so much trouble with his kite is that the spar or crossbar is down too far on the spine, according to Paul E. Garber, the first curator of the Smithsonian's National Air Museum.

• Kites were banned in modern China by Chairman Mao, who considered them examples of bourgeois decadence.

• Kitefliers have been known to climb into scuba gear and "fly" their kites underwater, towing them behind marine scooters. The kites reportedly behave very much the same in water as in wind, only in slow motion.

NO NEED TO RUN WITH THIS KITE

The "Legs" kite is a parafoil designed as running shorts with a pair of legs which seem to kick for more altitude.

#5873, Legs kite, $175.00 plus 6.50 shipping. Also Available: #536, Realistic seagull or #537, bat kite, $23.00 + 3.90 shipping. #584, Icarus 3-D kite, $210.00 + 6.50 shipping. #586, 3-D Shark, $260.00 + 6.50 shipping and #587, Space Shuttle, $78.00 + 5.20 shipping. Into the Wind, 1408 Pearl Street, Boulder, CO 80302. (800) 541-0314.

Blow Your Own

If you're having a kite party and the wind dies away entirely, don't disappoint your guests. Rent a professional wind machine, just in case. This 60 hp machine can produce winds up to 70 mph, which should just about do it.

Rental cost (per day): $150 for the wind machine plus $250 for the generator operator from John McLeod Special Effects, 332 Jean Street, Mill Valley, CA 94941. (415) 388-0114.

Kite Records

From *Kite Lines Magazine*

- Highest single kite: 12,471 feet.
- Most kites flown on one line: 2,233.
- Highest train of kites: 31,955 feet.
- Fastest kite: 114 mph.
- Largest kite: 5,952 square feet.
- Longest kite tail: 5,560 feet.
- Most figure-eights performed by a stunt kite in one hour: 2,911.

Kites Makes Rites

- **The Smithsonian Institution Kite Festival.** Each spring, hundreds of kiters meet near the Washington Monument. Trophies are awarded for aerodynamics, most beautiful, funniest and more. You have to reel in your kite if a White House helicopter approaches.

For information, write Kite Festival, Smithsonian Institution, 1100 Jefferson Dr. SW, Washington, D.C. 20560. (202) 357-2700.

- **Washington State International Kite Festival.** Held the entire third week of August. Events include a "lighted kite fly" with electrified kites decorating the night sky after dark. While you're visiting Long Beach, you can drop in on the World Kite Museum and Hall of Fame.

For information contact P.O. Box 387, Long Beach, WA 98631. (800) 451-2542.

- **The Great Wall of China.** To fly a kite from the Great Wall is a special goal of many kitefliers. This "China Kites Tour" includes visits to kite shops, Chinese kite festivals, kitemaking, and the Great Wall. Cost is around $2,000 plus international airfare.

Contact Tracy Borders, Roman Associates Inc., 1159 Verdemar Drive, Alameda, CA 94501. (510) 523-4165.

There are about 200 kite-making companies in the U.S. and about 400 full-service specialty kite shops.

Shooting the Breeze:

In times past, kite fliers needed at least a 10 mph wind. These days, though, some of the new lighter kites will fly even in the gentlest of breezes.

Still, different kites perform best in different wind conditions. If you can't find your anemometer, here's a rough guide to estimating windspeed, courtesy of Sir Francis Beaufort, a 19th century British admiral:

• Smoke drifts lazily: 1-3 mph.

• Leaves rustle: 4-7 mph.

• Small flags fly, leaves dance: 8-12 mph.

• Trees toss, dust flies, paper skitters: 13-18 mph.

Required Reading

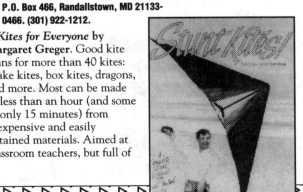

• *The Penguin Book of Kites* by David Pelham. Published in 1976, this book is the kiteflier's bible, including kite history, flying tips, and detailed plans for making more than 100 kites. Demonstrates several ingenious kite gimmicks like the UFO kite made of aluminized Mylar that reflects light from a small flashlight.

$10.95 + 3.00 shipping from Kite Lines, P.O. Box 466, Randallstown, MD 21133-0466. (301) 922-1212.

• *Kites for Everyone* by **Margaret Greger**. Good kite plans for more than 40 kites: snake kites, box kites, dragons, and more. Most can be made in less than an hour (and some in only 15 minutes) from inexpensive and easily obtained materials. Aimed at classroom teachers, but full of helpful advice for all from "the Kite Lady of Richland, Washington."

$13.00 + 1.00 shipping from the author at 1425 Marshall, Richland, WA 99352. (509) 943-3951.

• *Stunt Kites!* by **David Gomberg**. All you need to know when you want to get started flying two-line kites. Tips, safety pointers, techniques. No photos, but nevertheless a sound choice.

$8.95 + 3.00 shipping from Kite Lines, P.O. Box 466, Randallstown, MD 21133-0466. (301) 922-1212.

Kite Magazines

• *Kite Lines*. Features festivals, flying tips, new products, clubs.

$12.00 (4 issues). P.O. Box 466, Randallstown, MD 21133-0466. (301) 922-1212.

• *American Kite*. Features people and events in the kite world.

$10.00 (4 issues). 474 Clentina, San Francisco, CA 94103. (415) 896-3321.

• *Stunt Kite Quarterly*. Everything for the stunt kite enthusiast.

$14.00 (4 issues). 365 River Street, Manistee, MI 49660. (616) 723-6338.

Laurel & Hardy

A Fine Kettle of Fish

Laurel and Hardy, the most popular comic pair in screen history, worked together on 81 shorts and 24 feature films, a partnership which lasted from 1927 to 1952.

Skinny, dithering Stanley and portly, pompous Oliver were masterful slapstick comedians, with Ollie's barking and fuming perfectly setting off Stan's bumbling and squeaking.

Laurel was born Arthur Jefferson in England. Oliver Hardy was born Norvell Hardy in Georgia. Both were successful solo performers before director Leo McCarey brought them together. (He contributed more, too: many of Stan's movie mannerisms were imitations of the hapless McCarey).

Laurel in real life was smart and creatively involved in all aspects of production from his in-studio offices. He was paid more than Hardy and earned it with long working hours while Ollie went to spectator sports and horse races.

Although their active careers ended in the 1940s with competition from newer acts, younger generations discovered them on TV and they continue to be a cultural icon.

Their "pompous fat guy and dim skinny guy" act has been mirrored, perhaps unconsciously, by teams as diverse as Gleason & Carney, Fred & Barney, Bert & Ernie, Belushi & Akroyd and Siskel & Ebert.

> *"This is another fine mess you've gotten us into."*
> —Oliver Hardy

Stone and Ollie

Either 17" stone statue makes an iconic statement, but you really should get both.

#M02122 Laurel. #M02130 Hardy Each $95.00 + 9.95 shipping. #M03099 Both, $175.00 + 19.95 shipping. From Postings, P.O. Box 8001, Hilliard, OH 430226-8001. 800) 262-6604.

Laurel & Hardy Required Reading

Laurel & Hardy: The Magic Behind the Movies by Randy Skretvedt. Critically acclaimed book about Stan and Ollie covers their relationship both onscreen and off. Examines in detail how the perpetually befuddled screen Stan was actually the brains of the act behind the scenes, and the blustering, bullying Ollie was actually a mild-mannered, easy-going guy playing against type as well.

$14.95 + 2.50 shipping from Vestal Press, 320 N. Jensen Road, P.O. Box 97, Vestal, NY 13851-0097. (607) 797-4872.

The Complete Films of Laurel & Hardy by William K. Everson. Exhaustively examines each of the comedy shorts and features made by the duo, including cameo appearances in other films. Plenty of details and photos.

$14.95 + $2.00 shipping from Citadel Press, 120 Enterprise Avenue, Secaucus, NJ 07094. (201) 866-0490 / FAX (201) 866-8159.

Laurel & Hardy's song "Trail of the Lonesome Pine" from *Way Out West* hit #2 on the British pop charts in 1975, long after both had died.

Join the Club

Sons of the Desert. "An organization with scholarly overtones and heavily social undertones devoted to the loving study of the persons and films of Laurel & Hardy," to quote their literature. They also compile statistics, maintain a biographical archives, conduct research programs, and bestow awards. Local groups are called "Tents," and derive their names from Laurel & Hardy films. For example, the Los Angeles Tent is "Way Out West," and the Chicago Tent is "The Bacon Grabbers." They publish *Intra-Tent Journal* quarterly, and *Pratfall* periodically.

For membership info send SASE to: Sons of the Desert, P.O. Box 8341, Universal City, CA 91608. (818) 985-2713.

AURAL & HARDY

Stan and Ollie's best radio routines on cassette.

 # 80139 Laurel and Hardy $3.98 + 1.35 shipping from Johnson Smith Company, 4514 19th Court East, P.O. Box 25500, Bradenton, FL 34206-5500. (813) 747-2356.

Getting Into Laurel & Hardy's Shorts

Available on video, a fine mess of their two-reelers. This is the most complete set we've run across.

Vol. 1: "The Music Box," "The Live Ghost," "County Hospital," "Twice Two." 93 min. #NO4301

Vol. 2: "Blotto," "Brats," "Towed in a Hole," "Hog Wild." 90 min. #NO4302

Vol. 3: "Oliver the 8th," "Their First Mistake," "Busy Bodies," "Dirty Work." 90 min. #NO4303

Vol. 4: "Another Fine Mess," "Laughing Gravy," "Come Clean," "Any Old Port." 90 min. #NO4304

Vol. 5: "Be Big," "Night Owls," "The Perfect Day," "Helpmates." 89 mins. #NO4305

Vol. 6: "The Fixer Uppers," "Our Wife," "Them Thar Hills," "Tit for Tat." 90 min. #NO4306

Vol. 7: "Below Zero," "Thicker Than Water," "Midnight Patrol," "Me and My Pal." 80 min. NO4307

Vol. 8: "Men O' War," "Scram," "Laurel and Hardy Murder Case," "One Good Turn." 89 min. #NO4308

Vol. 9: "Beau Hunks," "Chickens Come Home," "Going Bye Bye," "Berth Marks." 108 min. #NO4309

$14.95 each or entire 9 cassette collection #XNOX1 for $99.99 + $3.95 shipping from: Blackhawk Films 5959 Triumph Street Commerce, CA 90040-1688 (800) 826-2295

Pilgrimage

A few of the sites where Laurel & Hardy had some of their finest hours still exist in the real world.

• The 131 stairs where the boys struggled with a piano (and lost) in **The Music Box** (1932), between 923 and 925 Vendome Street in Culver City, California.

• The house the boys almost wrecked when its owner refused to order a Christmas tree in July (**Big Business**, 1928) at 10281 Dunleer Drive in Los Angeles. After filming, the window panes and a doorpost had to be replaced and the entire front of the house repainted.

Lawn & Yard

Getting Down to Grass Facts

• Our lawns reflect our pride in ownership, our overly optimistic sense that we can actually triumph over the forces of nature. With lawn and garden displays we turn our yards into showcases for our inner psyches, which in many cases seem to be populated with the animae of flamingos, sheep and gnomes. Our yards even serve as a barometer of national climate during times of war, election campaigns and other national crises.

• Modern Americans relate best to grasses when they've been puffed, flaked, shot from guns, and drowned in sugar and milk; or, in the case of Kentucky Blue and Creeping Fescue, mowed down, treated with over a million tons of toxic chemicals a year, and drowned in nearly one hundred gallons of water per day per yard.

• Our passion for a totally unnatural carpet of solid green is a relatively recent phenomenon—the manicured, weed-free expanse became the rage in England during the 1840s, partly as a result of the burgeoning interest there in golf and bowling. At the same time "the natural look" lawn, liberally sprinkled with a variety of weeds, nettles and wild flowers growing tall, was the vogue in America.

• Scything was the most popular method for clearing a patch of grasses until the invention of the lawn mower in England in 1830. Letting a flock of sheep or other ruminants loose on the grounds was another effective method of controlling lawn growth, though the divots from their hooves and their droppings made the lawn unsuitable for sport or play.

• The first gasoline-powered rotary mower was an American invention, developed in 1919. This affordable mower along with the rubber garden hose, invented in 1871 by B.F. Goodrich, helped manicured lawns become fashionable among the American middle class in the 1920s. Around this same time Orlando Mumford Scott developed the first weed-free grass seed, followed by Turf Builder fertilizer in 1928. Since then, Scott's name has become synonymous with the lawn on which we stage the American dream.

• In the other industrialized nations of the world, grass is for real cows, soccer, golf and parks. The Japanese wouldn't think of planting their yards wit⌐   ⌐ couldn't ea⌐

Don't It Make Your Brown Lawn Green

Drought turned your verdant playland lawn into a field of shredded wheat? Don Wyatt of Landscape Services in Santa Barbara will wave his magic wand and turn it green again.

The secret is a non-toxic, permanent green pigment called "Green-It." It's advertised as being rain and sprinkler proof, but Don warned us not to sit down for a picnic in our white shorts just to be on the safe side.

It only costs about 20¢ a square foot to apply. Without knowing it, you've seen this stuff before—professional sports stadium groundskeepers have been painting the bald spots and the team colors in the end zones for years. Because it comes in a variety of colors, you don't have to stick with green—how about a pink camouflage habitat for your lawn flamingos?

Don doesn't make house calls far out of the Santa Barbara area, but will give advice if you want to do it yourself.

Don Wyatt, Proprietor, Landscape Services, 807 W. Mission, Santa Barbara, CA 93101. (805) 682-5296.

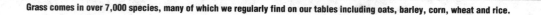

Grass comes in over 7,000 species, many of which we regularly find on our tables including oats, barley, corn, wheat and rice.

Because They Don't Know The Words!

That's why hummingbirds hum? Okay, not funny. But these whirligigs are sure to raise a smile. You'll get either a Velvet Purple Coronet or a Blue-Tufted Starthroat or the famous Ruby-Throated hummingbird. Each comes with steel 8-way mounting rod for lawn, garden or patio.

#A514513, $4.99 + 2.99 shipping from Hanover House, Hanover, PA 17333-0002. (717) 633-3333.

MOO MAIL

Cow mailbox meets all U.S. Post Office specs. But what will your neighbors say?

#17612, $35.00 + 4.95 shipping from Wireless, P.O. Box 64422, St. Paul, MN 55164-0422. (800) 669-9999.

Arachnophobics Beware!

Giant eleven foot spider won't trash your lawn. In fact, he's a trash bag and actually holds leaves, paper and other assorted stuff. The manufacturer says he's degradable, recylable and compostable, too.

#B3561, Stuff-A-Spider, $7.98 + 3.98 shipping from Harriet Carter, North Wales, PA 19455. (215) 361-5151.

11-FEET WIDE!

"Eight percent of the flamingos are purchased by people who think of them as a joke. I've seen them in the front yards in the snow with ribbons and scarves around their necks and little woolen caps on their heads."

—Don Featherstone, designer of the first pink lawn flamingo and Vice President of Union Products, world's largest manufacturer of plastic flamingos (see our special flamingo section).

Jockeying for Bad Taste

As the 1990s dawn, those offensive, stereotypical caricatures of black jockeys (holding one arm out, often with a ring clenched in his fist for tying up the horses) have almost passed into the realm of suburban legend.

Though they were still found in some insular parts of the country decades after the civil rights movement began (see above), most of the once ubiquitous jockeys have apparently disappeared forever. Only a few found their way into collectibles shops; fewer still remain where they've always stood, invariably with their hands and face painted white, probably done furtively at night by flashlight.

The jockey has been largely replaced by equally unlikely characters, none of whom have managed to form strong lobbying groups to make their political voices heard. The "height-impaired" (formerly called dwarfs), our elders (old folks with their fannies in the air), tropical birds and various farm animals are now the butts of open-air indignities.

It's not that racism has disappeared, it's just more covert these days. As for the hope of driving bad taste underground? Not a chance.

24% of all Iowans have pink flamingos or some sort of ornament on their lawns.

Mail Chauvinists

RFD Country! Mailboxes and Post Offices of Rural America by Bill and Sarah Thornbrook. Homemade, creative RFD (Rural Free Delivery) mailboxes—designed to look like farmhouses, flags, farm implements, animals, cowboys, trucks, even people—can be found along many a cornfield and cow pasture across the rural South and Midwest. The art form even has developed its own visual cliche, seen over and over again in every rural county in the nation—an auxiliary box set ten feet off the ground, labeled "AIR MAIL."

Like any true artform, post-box expressionism must deal with the threat of governmental censure. To quote the book's foreword by Postmaster General Preston R. Tisch: "Whereas earliest man could draw a buffalo on the wall of a cave he called 'home,' modern man has to cope with a Postal Service providing guidelines within which his imagination must work. Today's RFD customer must first request permission to stray from the conventional, then meet specific size and placement rules...It is all the more remarkable, then, that we still find the time and the ability to be creative, to add that very personal touch to that most routine of everyday services—the rural mail box."

RFD Country, $14.95 + 2.00 shipping from Schiffer Publishing, Ltd., 1469 Morstein Road, West Chester, PA 19380.

The "IN" Yard:

- hammocks
- grottoes
- lily ponds
- wildflower meadows
- horseshoe pits
- porch and tree swings
- flamingos

The "OUT" Yard:

- black plastic
- bug zappers
- barbecue pits
- bird baths
- gnomes
- aluminum furniture
- flamingos

Blowin' in the Wind

Shelburne Museum. Lobsters whir and twirl. Lumberjacks chop. Ducks flap their wings. Whirligigs are more common sights in the Northeast than anywhere else, set in motion by the Atlantic winds. There have even been X-rated variations on the theme—passionate couples rocking together faster and faster as the wind velocity increases.

The best place to buy interesting ones are in little roadside curio shops in the Northeast. This example of American folk art is alive and well and on display in yards across the country, and, more formally, at the Shelburne Museum, which has the largest known collection of amazing and one-of-a-kind whirligigs.

Shelburne Museum, Shelburne, VT 05482. (802) 985-3344.

In lawn ornaments, the wealthy go for lions and pineapples; the middle class favors cherubs, water fowl, and, if they have a sense of humor, flamingos.

Pest? Aside!

Large garden pests? Here are a couple of ingenious ideas. We make no claims as to their effectiveness, but both sound like a whale of a good time.

Go-Pher It. "No more traps, gas or poison," says the manufacturer. Just pound this battery-operated 12 in. electronic vibrating stake into the ground where gophers hang out and the ultrasonic vibes will send 'em running—into your neighbor's garden.

#2712, $49.95 + 5.95 shipping from Johnson Smith Co., 4514 19th Court East, P.O. Box 25500, Bradenton, FL 34206-5500. (813) 747-2356 / FAX (813) 746-7896.

Squirrel-A-Whirl. This 3-armed contraption is advertised to keep squirrels away from bird feeders, but whether you have a bird feeder or not, it's a laugh riot to see the little critters spinning around and around as they go for the ears of corn.

#9752, $18.95 + 4.20 shipping from Johnson Smith Co., 4514 19th Court East, P.O. Box 25500, Bradenton, FL 34206-5500. (813) 747-2356 / FAX (813) 746-7896.

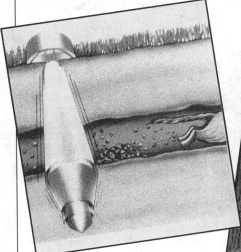

Croc O' the Walk

Some skeptics wonder whether plastic owls or inflatable snakes have ever actually prevented the neighborhood vermin from pilfering anyone's garden. Probably not. And neither will this authentically detailed 30 in. solid rubber crocodile (above), unless you're plagued by stupid, tropical pests. But what the hay, plant it in the shrubbery alongside your house and give the meter reader a good scare. Good for pool and bathtub fun, too.

$19.95 + 4.50 shipping from The Nature Company, P.O. Box 2310, Berkeley, CA 94702. (800) 227-1114 / FAX (606) 342-5630.

BETTER GNOMES IN GARDENS

Three Jolly Gnomes are caught in the act of doing what they like to do best. Goin' fishing, drinking beer and contemplating butterflies.

#E9016, $26.98 + 6.50 shipping from Harriet Carter, North Wales, PA 19455. (215) 361-5151.

The Prodigal Gnome

The English in particular, with their love of formal display, are mad for lawn ornaments. They are especially fond of gnomes, an ornament not nearly as popular in the United States.

This past decade saw a spate of lawn gnome kidnappings in England, perpetrated with rather an unusual British flair. Plaster gnomes disappeared into the dead of night, and no trace would be seen until one day a photograph would turn up in the morning post: The abductors had taken the gnomes (sometimes implying that they had run away of their own free will) to all corners of the globe, photographed them "wish you were here" style and mailed cards and letters back to the baffled owners.

Some of the gnomes were never heard from again, and some returned as mysteriously as they had left, sometimes years later.

Garden decorations are direct descendants of the sculptures that once graced the gardens of ancient Roman villas.

These Go Together Like Love & Marriage

Horse and Carriage Whirl-A-Gig gallops in the breeze. The horse's head bobs up and down and the legs move, too! And the propeller even shoos away unwanted garden guests of the insect variety. Includes metal stake for mounting, not eating!

B3495, Horse & Buggy, $7.98 + 3.98 shipping from Harriet Carter, North Wales, PA 19455. (215) 361-5151.

Mold Your Melons

"Grow a garden elf out of an eggplant, or raise a pickle puss from a cucumber." Put a Vegiform mold around a growing round fruit or veggie, and they'll be squeezed into unique shapes as they grow. They used to make an Elvis until his estate objected. Too bad.

#17607, Garden Elf or #17608, Pickle Puss. Each $12.95 + 2.75 shipping. Wireless, P.O. Box 64422, St. Paul, Minnesota 55164-0422. (800) 669-9999.

PIG OUT!

The Earl of Hamlet stands outside and is hand-painted and ready to cook practically anything but pork.

#45032, $65.00 + 8.95 shipping. W.M. Green & Company, P.O. Box 278 / Highway 64 East, Robersonville, NC 27871. (800) 482-5050.

Put Your Assets in Arrears

Grandpa And Grannie Fannie In All Their Glory. For some reason these things have replaced flamingos as a tacky way to annoy your neighbors. Join the vanguard—or is it the rear guard?—of the lawn desecration. You'll get a rearful of fun with these full-color, all-weather gardeners.

#G9048, $19.98 + 4.95 shipping from Harriet Carter, North Wales, PA 19455. (215) 361-5151.

Lawn Ornament Headquarters

Does your lawn want sheep, cows, giant butterflies, cute "animal crossing" signs, sundials or windmills? This is the best source we've run across if what you're looking for is the classic cute motif.

Send for a full-color catalog from Holst, Inc., 1118 West Lake, P.O. Box 370, Tawas City, MI 48764. (517) 362-5664.

Wacky Pool Signs

You don't even necessarily need a pool to enjoy these—just hang 'em up around your patio, garage or rec room—or so advises the catalog we found them in. These are your classics (see above). Loads of yucks. Buy one for Uncle Melvin, he'll laugh.

Each sign $3.95 + 1.35 shipping from Johnson Smith Company, 4514 19th Court East, Box 25500, Bradenton, FL 34206-5500. (813) 747-2356 / FAX (813) 746-7896.

The Patio

The front yard may be the showcase for the owner's individuality, but the back yard's where all the action is.

It hasn't changed all that much from our youth—it's still where the grownups hang out, swilling cold drinks, swatting at mosquitoes in the flickering light of those citronella candles in pineapple-shaped glass holders. Remember how the June Bugs went "thwak" as they dive-bombed the mildewed umbrella that shaded the round, white, metal table?

The summer patio took on special importance as a remote kitchen when the sweltering weather made cooking in the real one impossibly sticky. If the patio remains the focal point of the yard, the heart and hearth of the patio still has to be the barbecue.

Back Yard Humor

What's Irish and hangs around your barbecue? Paddy O'Furniture.

A typical "lawn" in Austria is planted with cabbages and kohlrabi. The Swiss like onions in their front yards.

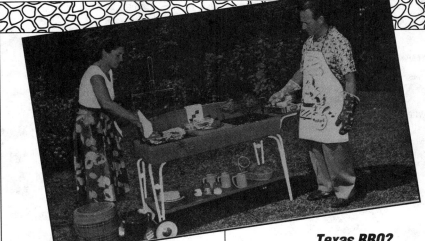

THE GRILL OF IT ALL

Barbecue has been elevated from humble hamburgers and hot dogs to haute cuisine involving grilled exotics like swordfish steaks, eggplant and zucchini. The act of outdoor cooking is still mostly a man's thing—it may be because of all the accessories and gadgets that are available to enhance the experience.

• In recent years, women have gained more equality in the outdoor kitchen, but men still do 59% of all the grilling chores.

• Even though true barbecue fiends feel gas grills are wimpy, they're rapidly gaining in popularity. Charcoal grills are still the most popular, and the Weber Kettle (first sold in 1952) is the most commonly purchased brand.

• Don't get your bag of charcoal wet and then store it indoors for the winter. It can react with the air as it dries and generate enough heat to spontaneously combust.

• Just what IS "Liquid Smoke?" Right out of the bottle, it tastes like licking out an ashtray. Sources at the manufacturer won't tell, urging us to read the label again and it will tell us all we need to know. We did, and found: Water, natural hickory smoke flavor, vinegar, flavoring, and brown sugar...the ingredients provoke more questions than they answer.

Texas BBQ?

It's a place you might expect folks to know good barbecue and have the good sense to leave well enough alone. Instead, we've found that in a misguided attempt to compete with other regional trends, Texas restaurants have spawned a number of gastronomic oddities in the name of the grill:

• **Flaming Pyramid of Meat**—Papaguayo's, Houston

• **Blackened Chicken Omelette**—Bay Street, Dallas

• **Nacho Oysters with Guacamole**—Bayou City Oyster Company, Houston

• **Barbecued Bologna Sandwich**—Texas State Fair, Dallas

Grill of My Dreams

Weber Kettle grills are great and can be picked up anywhere, the small model starting around $20. But if you want cream-of-the-coals barbecue, call Charles Eisendrath and order one of his patented "Grillery" grills.

It's made of stainless steel v-shaped bars that channel juices into a basting pan, and the grill rises and lowers easily.

It costs around $750, but it'll last forever. Eisendrath's only sold about 500, partly because he isn't too easy to reach. He prefers it this way because it keeps him from wasting time with people who really just want a Weber.

Eisendrath lives in Ann Arbor, Michigan, and just might answer this number: (313) 995-2164.

BBQ BOOKS

• *Barbeque'n with Bobby* by Bobby Seale. "Barbecue information floating around reflects an oniony and garlicky misunderstanding," he writes. "This commercialized misunderstanding has insulted our taste buds." Despite his fondness for gallons of liquid smoke, his recipes are "Right on!"—as he might've said in his Panther days.

$12.95 + 1.25 shipping. Ten Speed Press, P.O. Box 7123, Berkeley, CA 94707. (800) 841-2665.

• *The Complete Book of Outdoor Cookery* by James Beard and Helen Evans Brown. This is a reprint of the classic 1955 barbecue bible. Most of the advice works as well now as it did then, but some of the recipes are showing their age like cubes of "Spam" and bananas on a skewer, and the huge steaks dripping with real butter.

$9.95 + 3.50 shipping from Harper Collins, Downsville Pike, Rte. 3, Box 20-B, Hagerstown, MD 21740. (800) 331-3761.

• *Char-Broil's Grill Lovers Grill Book.* This catalog contains everything for the grilling gourmet.

Free, P.O. Box 1300, Columbus, GA 31993-2499. (800) 241-8981.

Seeing is BBQing

The Official Barbecue Guide video takes you on a tantalizing trip through BBQland. Learn the techniques, recipes, side dishes and all important sauces. 60 minute video gives you a regional taste of eleven different recipes that can be prepared at home. Tour the country's finest restaurants including K.C. Masterpiece and Arthur Bryant's in Kansas City, and the Rendezous and Leonard's restaurants in Memphis.

#37445H, $19.95 + 4.00 from Hammacher Schlemmer, 9180 Le Saint Drive, Fairfield, OH 45014. (800) 543-3366.

The word barbecue comes from the Mayan word *barbacoa*, for a lattice of thin, green sticks, over which they grilled fish and game.

LUNCH BOXES

Box Populi: You Are What You Carry

Long before we grew up to strive for the right car, clothes and house, the lunch box was the identifying status symbol that declared who we were—Barbie boxes were toted by grammar school glamour girls, *Laugh-In* boxes were carried by class clowns, and the standard issue red plaid boxes were packed by the social untouchables.

The first lunch boxes were actually biscuit, cookie and tobacco tins from the 1800s that kids appropriated as a suitable container for carrying the midday meal, much classier than the utilitarian lunch pails carried by their parents. In 1902, a lithographed picnic basket shaped box depicting children at play was manufactured as the first true American kids' lunch box.

Mickey Mouse became the first licensed lunch box character in 1935; his box sold for a buck.

In 1950, TV cowboy Hopalong

Cassidy's wildly successful box (600,000 sold in its first year) launched a box fad. The principle manufacturers, Aladdin, American Thermos (later called King Seeley Thermos) and Ohio Art were in constant furious competition over licensing rights to TV characters.

Aladdin is still embarrassed about passing up the opportunity to do the Peanuts and Barbie lunch boxes, figuring they were "too adult" for the lunch box crowd. "We thought *Hogan's Heroes* was a better bet," admitted a company representative. King Seeley Thermos raked in the millions instead. On the other hand, KST inadvertently returned the favor by turning down *Batman*, which then made millions for Aladdin.

Vinyl boxes emerged in 1959. At first just plastic-covered cardboard, they were followed in 1972 with durable injection-molded plastic boxes. They were clearly inferior to the metal masterpieces, yet they eventually took over the market. Why? Because of legislation and fear of lawsuits. Kids were using metal lunch boxes as martial arts weapons, according to a crusading mother whose son was conked on the head with one.

They were banned in Florida. Safety legislation spread to other states, and plastic lunch boxes and thermoses took over.

Because of technical limitations, the plastic lunch boxes could never come close to the visually (or physically) stunning metal boxes. Fittingly, the last potentially lethal metal lunch box, manufactured in 1987, depicted that well-known headbasher, Rambo.

Hail the Conking Hero...

Portrait of the Artist as a Lunch Box Designer

Lunch box artists didn't have it easy. The box often had to be designed before the TV program or movie was filmed. The *Get Smart* box, for instance, was designed using 8x10 in. black and white glossies of the stars and ten minutes of rough film footage. Some designers didn't even get that much. For *Batman*, there was no footage available, and the designers had no idea the show was going to be "camp." That's why the lunch box looks more like the comics than the TV show, with straight violence and nary a POW! BIFF! or BAM!

Then you had to deal with temperamental stars. Rex Harrison rejected art for the *Dr. Doolittle* box five times. Diahann Carroll, according to designer Nick LoBianco, was "a real bitch" about her *Julia* box art.

Worst of all was the pay: usually a flat fee of $500-700 per kit (box, thermos, etc.). After the box was manufactured, the artists' tempura twice-as-large renderings were usually tossed in the garbage.

Plastic Menagerie

Mingle with a menagerie of aquatic, jungle and folk art animals, silk-screened on plastic lunch boxes of assorted colors.

Each $9.00 + 2.00 shipping from Traffic Works Inc. of L.A., 2417 E. 54th St., Los Angeles, CA 90058. (213) 582-0616.

Lunch Money

Aside from a *Jetson's* box once going for an unbelievable $3000 during an overheated auction, the most expensive boxes are as follows, according to the only price guide on the subject. Prices given are for mint condition; most with normal wear will sell for significantly less. Some collectors say these prices are way above reality, so don't pay without first checking out the market.

- *Mickey Mouse*, 1935, $1000
- *Beatles*, $350-600
- *Star Trek*, 1968-9, $250
- *Bullwinkle*, 1963, $200.
- *Lost in Space*, 1967-8, $145
- *Beany & Cecil*, 1963, $150

Prices from: *The Official Price Guide to Lunch Box Collectibles* by Scott Bruce.

$11.95 postpaid. The House of Collectibles, 201 East 50th Street, New York, NY 10022.

Lunch to Go

Plastic reusable boxes resembling Chinese restaurant "to go" cartons come in white, black or red.

Small ($1.15, below), medium ($1.30) and large ($1.50) Add 2.00 shipping from Traffic Works (see above).

Secret Notes Have a Peel

Hey, everybody loves invisible spy messages. Save an old inkless ballpoint pen and use it to write on the peel of the banana you're packing into a lunch. The message is invisible at first, but hours later, (sooner, if the box sits near a radiator) your covert message will be magically revealed in brown lettering as the banana ripens.

...And the Ricky Ricardo Box Was Really Glorifying Che Guevara

"By the mid-'70s the TV series *Kung Fu*, which had a lunch box in 1974, basically was a tacit recognition of America's defeat by the Viet Cong. You had the *Kung Fu* character, basically a Ho Chi Minh stand-in, dispensing wisdom and tough love to rednecks on the frontier."

—Scott Bruce, author of *The Fifties and Sixties Lunch Box*, who likes to call himself "Mr. Lunch Box"

Roy Rogers and Dale Evans hold the record for inspiring the most lunch box versions of their characters—ten.

LUNCH BOX

For Collectors Only

***The Fifties and Sixties Lunch Box* by Scott Bruce.** Bruce tells the story of lunch boxes in their heyday, profiling the artists behind the boxes, outlining the tension between the major manufacturers and their battles over licensing images. Anecdotal and opinionated, Bruce brings back the musty smell of childhood lunch boxes, accompanied by gorgeous color photos of almost mint-condition boxes from his own collection.

$16.45 postpaid from JO-D Books, 81 Willard Terrace, Stamford, CT 06903. (203) 322-0568.

New Box, Ancient Design

Dine with dinosaurs. Matching dino-designed, spill-proof 15 oz. thermos has a built-in straw.

#353417 Lunch box, $10.95 + 2.95 shipping; #337956 Thermos, $8.95 + 2.95 shipping from The Nature Company, P.O. Box 2310, Berkeley, CA 94702. (800) 227-1114.

Ultra Box

An unusual, insulated lunch non-box is made in Japan by Nissan. Essentially a vertical plastic cylinder lined with stainless steel that holds two removable containers, one for hot, the other for cold foods, it also comes with a stainless spoon in an attachable red plastic case.

At a cool $52.95, this box will keep your tempura separate from your sushi. Kitchen Arts, 161 Newbury St., Boston, MA 02116. (617) 266-8701.

Pilgrimage: The Box-O-Rama

The only collectibles show devoted entirely to boxers and their acquisitions, Box-O-Rama is open to serious collectors, dealers and curiosity seekers. Lunch box artists are on hand to autograph their designs.

The annual show offers seminars on how to start a lunch box collection and how to gauge the value of rare boxes. A giant lunch box auction closes the event.

For more information, send SASE with query to event organizer Bill Henry, 104 Davidson Lane, Oak Ridge, TN 37830. (615) 483-0769.

Paileontology: Where to Dig Up Old Boxes

Scooby's Toys and Collectibles. This is a great store for anything from your childhood, but especially lunch boxes. Scooby's has a rotating stock of 150 boxes available at any given time and will tell you prices and availability by phone. Their toy collectibles, mostly from the 1960s and 1970s, are usually well below "list" prices.

2750 Adeline St., Berkeley, CA 94703. (510) 548-5349.

9 million of the Walt Disney domed school bus design boxes were sold from 1961 to 1973, making it the all-time best-seller.

NAKED LUNCH

• A 1954 *Howdy Doody* box with Princess SummerFallWinterSpring was pulled off the shelves in 1957. The makers felt that actress Judy Tyler, who portrayed the chaste Indian royal on TV, compromised her virginal image by starring in an Elvis Presley vehicle, *Jail House Rock*.

• A 1959 *Gunsmoke* lunch box somehow made it past the proofreader with Marshal Matt Dillon misspelled "Marshall."

• A 1963 lunch box featuring U.S. astronauts was yanked when *National Geographic* magazine claimed the artwork was lifted from its pages.

• On the lunch box inspired by the 1966-68 TV series *Flipper*, the likeness of the cetacean star is rumored to have been modeled on Bob Hope. Flipper was unavailable to confirm or deny this vicious piece of gossip.

• John Lennon uttered his infamous "Beatles are bigger than Jesus Christ" remark the same month Aladdin came out with the first Beatles lunch box. Well, J.C. still doesn't have a box, but Beatles lunch kits fetch top dollar at auction.

• First the Rockefeller Center and now this: the Thermos Co., maker of all those lunch boxes and vacuum bottles, was bought in 1989, by Nippon Sanso, a Japanese manufacturer of industrial gas.

Collector's Newsletters

• *Hot Boxing: The Quarterly of Lunch Box Collecting.* Another Scott ("Call Me Mr. Lunch Box") Bruce publication with tips on trading, up-to-date price listings and features.

One year subscription, $12.00. P.O. Box 87, Somerville, MA 02143.

• *Snot Boxing* by Steve Bob. Obviously irked by Mr. Lunch Box, Steve Bob, a.k.a. "Mr. Pailhead," has published his own one-man boxer's rebellion, a "once-only issue parody of lunch pail collecting." Perfect for those who resent anyone with the coldeyed foresight to corner a dubious collectible market, drive prices up sky high, then sell at an inflated cost to buy a house, as Bruce has bragged to the press about having done. An angry, sometimes funny, parody.

List price is $23.00 (but you can negotiate way down...unless, of course, "Mr. Pailhead" is trying to buy a house, too. Try sending $2.00). 11379 Kelowna Road, San Diego, CA 92126.

The thermoses from collectible lunch boxes are also valuable—as much as $60-$90 in certain cases.

Magic

EGYPTIAN HALL PICCADILLY
ENGLAND'S HOME OF MYSTERY
THE BIRTH OF FLORA PRODUCED BY DAVID DEVANT Daily at 3 & 8.
A MARVELLOUS & BEAUTIFUL DEVELOPMENT

Quicker Than the Eye

It's magic! The magician's art is still alive and flourishing in spite of a jaded public assaulted with fastbreaking scientific and technological achievements. Superconductivity, microsurgery, artificial intelligence and designer genes are all well and good, but the rabbit pulled out of the hat can hold its own.

Magician David Copperfield, who knocks himself out to create spectacular stage illusions, says that as often as not the audience goes away amazed about a trick done with no more than a pencil and a borrowed bill. That's because it is the sense of wonder created by magicians that is the essence of magic, not the props, techniques and spectacle that they use.

Behind the Veil

• An early magic reference was to Dedi, a wizard of ancient Egypt who performed 5,000 years ago for the Pharaoh Cheops, builder of the Great Pyramid. His big trick was beheading animals (birds, a bull calf), then restoring their heads and lives.

• Moses, the Bible says, went to the Pharaoh in Egypt to release the Jews from bondage. Pharaoh didn't believe the first "signs and wonders" Moses performed—a staff into a snake, water running with blood and a plague of frogs—because the court magicians were able to duplicate them.

• One of the oldest tricks is the Cups and Balls. (The trick is sometimes used by street hustlers in the "old shell game," as in "Which walnut shell is hiding the pea?"). Skill at the trick is still a standard measure of a magician's skill.

• "It's all done with mirrors!" Mirrors do have a long association with magic—we know that the silvered mirror was used as a conjuror's tool by wizards in ancient Egypt, Chaldea, Babylon, and, according to legend, the lost continents of Atlantis and Mu.

• Tough audience! In the 1400s, a girl in Cologne, Germany, was charged with practicing because she tore a handkerchief into pieces, then restored it.

NOT SO HAPPY MEDIUMS

In 1986, magician **James Randi** ("The Amazing Randi") won a prestigious MacArthur Foundation "genius" grant, winning a five-year, tax-free stipend of $272,000. He won the award because, like Houdini, he uses his skills as a professional magician to uncover fraudulent mystics and psychics who use magicians' techniques for evil.

> "In any quest for magic, in any search for sorcery, witchery, legerdemain, first check the human heart."
> —**Rod Serling, *The Twilight Zone***

"Abracadabra!" The word came from the name of a god once worshipped by the Syrians.

Magical Notes

- ***Do You Believe in Magic?*** (1965) by John Sebastian. A big hit for the Lovin' Spoonful.

- ***Abracadabra*** (1944). Words and music by Cole Porter. Introduced in a musical, *Mexican Hayride*.

- ***Magic Moments*** (1957) by Hal David and Burt Bacharach. Best-selling record by Perry Como.

- ***That Old Black Magic*** (1942) by Johnny Mercer and Harold Arlen. Sung by Bing Crosby, Frank Sinatra—even Marilyn Monroe, in the 1956 film *Bus Stop*.

Pop Poetry

"When I am stripped and manacled, nailed securely within a weighted packing case and thrown into the sea, or when I am buried alive under six feet of earth, it is necessary to preserve absolute serenity of spirit."

—Harry Houdini

"Magic as entertainment is all fraud and deception. The magician is a swindler, a liar, and a cheat. What he offers is not true magic but mere illusion based on the tricks of the theater and the confidence man. And yet, at his best, the skilled magician can show us things so astonishing, so utterly impossible and without explanation that our senses reel, and for a brief moment the trick we're watching becomes real magic."

—Allan Zola Kronzek

Magic Books

The Klutz Book of Magic by John Cassidy and Michael Stroud. Make a successful magical debut with this friendly and reassuring introductory book, "your klutz-proof step-by-step guide to personal amazing-ness." You are tutored by experts as you learn to perform 31 simple tricks. Clear, easy-to-follow instructions, color illustrations showing exactly how to make the moves. The book even comes with a few simple props. Astound your friends, confound your enemies.

$12.95 + 3.00 shipping from Klutz, 2121 Staunton Court, Palo Alto, CA 94306. (415) 424-0739.

Magic: A Pictorial History of Conjurors in the Theatre by David Price. This fat volume may be the best way to trace the history of magicians in the theatre up to the time of World War II. Over 500 pages about the lives of magicians like Cagliostro, Robert-Houdin, Blackstone, the Great Raymond, and, of course, Houdini.

$60.00 + 2.30 shipping from Cornwall Books, 440 Forsgate Drive, Cranbury, NJ 08512. (609) 655-4770.

Folding Money

Sure, you can fold your paper money, but how about folding this quarter? Hairline cuts are undetectable. Fold the coin and slip it through the neck of a bottle. Don't tell your friends how you did it—just let them admire you. The powers are to be used for magic and joke use only, of course—not for evil.

#5970, $7.98 + 2.70 shipping from Johnson Smith Company, 4514 19th Court East, P.O. Box 25500, Bradenton, FL 34206-5500. (813) 747-2356 / FAX (813) 746-7896.

HOUDINI

T he name has become synonymous with "magic." He became famous for walking through brick walls, for making full-size elephants disappear, and for escapes from ropes, handcuffs, leg irons, milk cans, straitjackets, sealed coffins, trunks thrown into rivers and even Chinese Water Torture Cells.

Harry Houdini was an ingenious technician, writer, collector, lecturer, movie star, and an adventurer (in 1910, he became the first person ever to make a sustained plane flight on the Australian continent). Most of all he was one of the greatest showmen the world has seen: a gifted escape artist and magician who hypnotized crowds with his feats, and whose talents in advertising and promotion helped him to create his own legend.

Houdini was born Erich Weiss in Budapest, Hungary, on March 24, 1874. The son of a rabbi, he was brought as an infant to Appleton, Wisconsin, the town he later claimed as his birthplace as "a true American" in later life. (Beware of magicians' accounts of their pasts—deception and illusion are not confined to the stage!)

Even as a toddler, the Weiss and future Houdini was interested in locks. It's said that when he was very young his mother once put a freshly baked apple pie in a cupboard with a padlock, and—well, you know the rest. He was remembered by townsfolk later as a high-spirited, troublesome little boy who one night unlocked the stores of all the merchants on the street.

At 13, working as an assistant necktie-lining cutter, he read a biography of Robert-Houdin, France's great magician. He borrowed the name, egotistically adding an "i."

He challenged all comers—police departments, ironwelders, rival magicians—for a device from which he could not escape. He sued those who publicly questioned his claims and won his court cases by performing escapes in front of a startled judge and a courtroom full of onlookers. He liked to walk into cities and challenge the police to lock him in their most inescapable cell. In one such challenge, he not only got free but switched all the other prisoners around as well.

Houdini loved to accept challenges where death was the price of failure. In England, he allowed four Royal Navy petty officers to tie him to the muzzle of a loaded cannon, with a twenty-minute fuse. In Germany, he was lashed to the railroad tracks exactly fifteen minutes before the Berlin-Dresden Express train was due. He had gotten his hands untied, and was starting to work on his feet, when the Express came around the bend—*early*. In the last seconds he managed to gain a little slack, and the train missed him by inches, cutting the ropes instead.

Intensely devoted to his mother, he was greatly affected by her death, and tried to contact her in "the other world" through mediums. First disappointed and then outraged with the "evidence" they presented, he became a leading debunker of fraudulent spiritualist claims.

Houdini died on Halloween night in 1926. He had pledged that, if it were possible, he would contact his wife and friends after death with a prearranged phrase. The message never came. Still, it's a tradition for fellow magicians and admirers to hold a yearly seance in his honor. Houdini, phone home.

HOUDINI
LE MAÎTRE DU MYSTÈRE

HOUDINI'S

In a tragic misunderstanding, Houdini died from getting punched in the stomach by an admirer.

Now You See It...

Historic films of Houdini, the man who showed us that nothing is impossible.

#1765, $16.98 + 4.20 shipping from: Johnson Smith Co., 4514 19th Court East, P.O. Box 25500, Bradenton, FL 34206-5500. (813) 747-2356 / FAX (813) 746-7896.

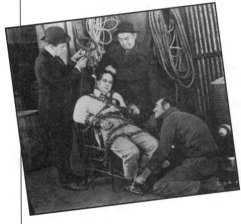

Magician's Memento

Reproduction of 1925 Houdini performance program.

#1383, $6.98 + 2.70 shipping. Johnson Smith Co., 4514 19th Court East, P.O. Box 25500, Bradenton, FL 34206-5500. (813) 747-2356 / FAX (813) 746-7896.

HAT TRICK

Rabbit-In-The-Hat Costume fits all waist sizes up to 42 in.

#T2626, $39.98 + 5.75 shipping. Funny Side Up, 425 Stump Rd., North Wales, PA 19454. (215) 361-5130.

PILGRIMAGE SITES

• **Houdini's Hall on a Hill.** Not far from the site of the spectacular waterfall rescue scene in Houdini's first self-produced film, *The Man from Beyond,* this museum displays the $100,000 Houdini Handcuff Collection, a Steel Trunk used by Houdini in a dangerous underwater escape, and the equipment used for cutting a woman into eight pieces! Also the 3 ft. by 5 ft. Chinese Water Torture Cell Escape, an underwater effect a handcuffed Houdini did for years.

The Houdini Magical Hall of Fame, Atop Clifton Hill, Niagara Falls, Ontario, Canada. (416) 356-4869.

• **Houdini Historical Center.** Appleton, Wisconsin was Houdini's hometown (locals knew him as little Erich Weiss). This exhibit contains the world's largest collection of Houdini memorabilia, including the oversized milk can used in one of his most famous escapes. While in Appleton (a city that has a statue, a school, and a plaza in honor of the magician), you can enjoy the 16-stop Houdini walking tour.

Outagamie Museum, 350 East College Avenue, Appleton, WI 54911. (414) 733-8445.

• **The Magic Castle** (Private Club). Located in the heart of Hollywood just north of the Chinese Theatre, and operated by a non-profit organization, the Magic Castle is a magic enthusiast's dream: a classic 1909 Gothic-Victorian mansion, that has been transformed into an enchanting, magical world. From the moment guests enter the reception room and whisper "Open Sesame" to the golden, blinking owl, it's time to be amazed. You can hear "Invisible Irma," the ghost, musically answer questions on the piano, watch real magicians performing, and take a look at a museum of old and rare magical equipment and antique pinball machines. You can enjoy an Old English dinner served by butlers in white tie, tails, and gloves in the club's dining room.

The Academy of Magical Arts, Inc., 7001 Franklin Avenue, Hollywood, CA 90028. (213) 851-3313. (Okay, so how the heck do you get in, given that it's a private club? Assuming that you don't have any friends who are club members, try pro magicians in your own home town. Many magicians are clubby types, and know others who are members. Ask around and do some magic of your own.)

Bag of Tricks

It used to be that only magicians collected "magicana"—the books, films, tapes, tricks, posters, letters, and other memorabilia related to past eras of magic. The number of magic enthusiasts has grown to include more and more "just plain folks" who not only have never sawed a woman in two, but need both hands to shuffle a deck of cards.

Most popular are artifacts from the late 19th and early 20th century, especially ones associated with famous vaudeville stage magicians like Houdini (top of the list), Keller, Thurston, and Blackstone. Large, brilliantly colored advertising posters with illustrations of magicians preparing to perform

dangerous and wondrous feats are much sought after.

The Magic Collectors Association. If the historical side of magic interests you, you'll find plenty of company in this organization. A number are current or past performers of magic, but you don't have to be. The association publishes *Magicol*, a quarterly journal with articles of historical interest and news about magic collecting.

One year membership is $10.00. MCA c/o Walter J. Gydesen, Executive Secretary, 19 Logan Street, New Britain, CT 06051

Conundrum Fits

These eight mysterious linking rings come apart and join together in countless combinations. An oldie but a goody.

#4570 Linking Rings, $9.98+ 2.70 shipping from Johnson Smith Company, 4514 19th Court East, P.O. Box 25500, Bradenton, FL 34206-5500. (813) 747-2356 / FAX (813) 746-7896.

Collapsible Top Hat

What's more magical than a top hat? Made of black flocked plastic, this collapses from 5 1/2 inches tall to less than 2 when collapsed. Great for producing rabbits, which you'll have to order from somewhere else.

$21.50 + 2.95 shipping from Hank Lee's Magic Factory, 125 Lincoln Street, Boston, MA 02111. (617) 482-8749.

No Time for Levity?

Who says you don't understand the gravity of the situation? Cause objects to float in mid-air without any visible means of support. Suspend everything, even your disbelief, and order today.

#3648, $4.98 + 1.35 shipping from Johnson Smith Company, 4514 19th Court East, P.O. Box 25500, Bradenton, FL 34206-5500. (813) 747-2356 / FAX (813) 746-7896.

Power Stick

No mere cheap prop, this wand wields the power of wizardry! Void where prohibited.

#3248 Magic Wand, $2.49 + 1.35 shipping from Johnson Smith Company, 4514 19th Court East, P.O. Box 25500, Bradenton, FL 34206-5500. (813) 747-2356 / FAX (813) 746-7896.

"Nothing I do can't be done by a 10-year-old boy—with 15 years of practice." — Harry Blackstone, Jr.

Torture Your Friends

***Penn & Teller's Cruel Tricks for Dear Friends* Videotape** (1988). Penn Jillette and Teller (born Raymond Joseph Teller, but now just "Teller," even on his bank checks) are definitely magicians, but then they're also something else entirely.

Penn is the tall (6'6") articulate one and Teller is the smaller, silent partner. Audiences love what turns other professional magicians apopleptic: in their act they routinely reveal the secrets of their tricks to their audience. In this videotape, they demonstrate seven scams, each using the specially designed clips on the tape itself. Our favorite is where the newscaster on TV tells your friend which card was chosen.

#40-1367, $20.00 + 4.50 shipping. Movies Unlimited, 6736 Castor Ave., Philadelphia, PA 19149. (800) 523-0823.

Mind Bending Techniques

Uri Geller made a career of "psychically" bending everyday metal objects—now you too can fold flatware with the same secret method. You can even give Indiana a south bend!

#3277, $7.49 + 2.70 shipping from Johnson Smith Company, 4514 19th Court East, P.O. Box 25500, Bradenton, FL 34206-5500. (813) 747-2356 / FAX (813) 746-7896.

Join the Club

International Brotherhood of Magicians (I.B.M.)
Same initials as the large computer firm you know about, but the International Brotherhood of Magicians isn't listed on the stock exchange. This is the world's largest magic organization, with chapters (called "rings") in over 80 countries, including most large U.S. cities. Members receive *The Linking Ring*, a monthly magazine of information on new and old tricks, book reviews, and news of the magic world. You don't have to be a professional magician, but you need to have an interest in magic to join.

Fees and yearly dues, $30.00. Junior memberships for persons 14-18, $20.00. Marilyn Edwards, International Executive Secretary, P.O. Box 89, Bluffton, OH 45817.

Society of American Magicians. S.A.M. is the major magic organization exclusively oriented toward the United States magic scene. It was formed in 1902 by thirteen magicians who met in the back room of a New York magic shop. Harry Houdini once served as president of the Society. S.A.M publishes *M-U-M*, a monthly journal of magic news and features.

One year membership $25.00 to Richard Blowers, Administrator P.O. Box 290068, St. Louis, MO 63129.

Funny Money

Use this coin to fool your friends. It looks solid enough, but this quarter conceals an opening that you can pass a pencil or cigarette through.

#3361, $19.98 + 4.20 shipping. Johnson Smith Co., 4514 19th Court East, P.O. Box 25500, Bradenton, FL 34206-5500. (813) 747-2356.

The Cape for a Weekend

Swirl onto the scene wearing this cape and your audience is already half won over. (And you can use it for playing Dracula at Halloween). "Heavy black knit fabric with red lining and stunning stand-up collar. 56 inch length."

$59.99 + 7.95 shipping from Abracadabra Magic Shop, P.O. Box 711, Middlesex, NJ 08846-0711. (201) 805-0200.

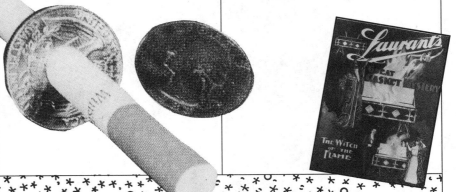

THE MARX BROTHERS

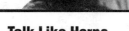

Marxist Analysis

Groucho's cigar and eyebrows. Chico's Italian accent and handgun piano technique. Harpo's angelic harp and devilish behavior. Long after you forget the plot and dialog, these images remain.

Their anarchy grew out of brotherly rapport, slapstick instincts, ad-libbing genius, and a strong aversion to rehearsal. Before movies they had honed their personalities in vaudeville, aided by stage mother, Minnie.

Groucho always played a fast-talking con artist (even his mustache was a grease-paint phony). Harpo's honks, harping, pantomime and angelic demeanor hid a mischievous devil. His trench coat would suddenly reveal silverware or a steaming cup of coffee. If he liked you, he'd swing his leg over your arm or eat your buttons (he also had a taste for flowers and ink).

Chico murdered the English language, since silent partner Harpo couldn't correct him. An "Italian" vendor of peanuts, candy, ice cream, and dirty postcards, Chico was a virtuoso at the piano, his trademark style punctuated by his technique of "shooting the keys."

The brothers made 14 films together (five with Zeppo, nine without). Solo, Harpo made two movies. Groucho made five and TV show *You Bet Your Life*.

> *"Why, you're one of the most beautiful women I've ever seen, and that's not saying much for you."*
>
> —Groucho to Margaret Dumont

Talk Like Harpo

With a genuine brass Bombay Taxi Horn, you can sound like Harpo. A squeeze of the black rubber bulb causes the horn to blast like a rude tuba.

How They Got Their Names

Art Fisher thought up Hollywood nicknames as a sideline. From oldest to youngest, here are the monickers he hung on the Marxes:

• Chico (real name Leonard) got his name from his romantic proclivities, which is also why his name is always pronounced Chick-o.

• Harpo (Adolph), from the harp.

• Groucho (Julius), from his morose expression.

• Gummo (Milton), before leaving the act to join the garment industry, because of his preference for gum-soled shoes.

• Youngest brother Zeppo (Herbert) replaced Gummo, and his nickname signifies nothing—zip. Zeppo later became a successful agent, and Gummo joined him to manage the other three brothers.

> *"Go, and never darken my office towels again!"*
>
> —Groucho

"The world would not be in such a snarl, if Marx had been Groucho instead of Karl." Irving Berlin

Marxist Manifestos

The Marx Brothers Scrapbook by Groucho Marx and Richard J. Anobile. Groucho is the author of many books, some dealing with his take on the family act, but this one made him mad—he sued co-author Richard Anobile for $15 million in an attempt to stop publication. Obviously, Groucho failed, and his much-publicized lawsuit actually increased sales. Very personal glimpses by Groucho, his family, and friends, with photos.

HarperCollins Publishers. Out of print, but worth tracking down.

Groucho, Chico, Harpo and Sometimes Zeppo by Joe Adamson. The book's subtitle is "A Celebration of the Marx Brothers and a Satire on the Rest of the World." Witty, anecdotal, informative, and chock-full of pictures, this book is often referred to as the Marxist bible. Snippets of funny film dialogue compete with insightful comments from family and friends.

Simon & Schuster, Inc. Out of print, but worth tracking down.

Flywheel, Shyster and Flywheel—The Marx Brothers' Lost Radio Show. Edited by Michael Barson. Never-before-available transcripts from the Marx Brothers' (minus Zeppo and Harpo and his honker) first radio show, broadcast by NBC in 1932-33. Groucho played a malpracticing lawyer, and Chico his not-so-trusty assistant. Includes publicity stills.

$9.95 + 2.00 shipping. Pantheon Books, 201 East Fiftieth Street, New York, NY 10022. (800) 726-0600.

MARX TOYS

Groucho Glasses

Become the wisecracking spokesman for the Brothers Marx. Horn-rimmed frames with "realistic" nose, bushy eyebrows and mustache make you 30% funnier in seconds.

4384, $2.98 + 1.35 shipping from Johnson Smith Company, 4514 19th Court East, P.O. Box 25500, Bradenton, FL 34206-5500. (813) 747-2356.

Mannikin Depressive

Make Groucho "say the secret woid" as he sits on your lap! 30" tall, nattily dressed ventriloquist "figure" (Who are ya calling a dummy?) comes complete with trademark cigar, raised eyebrows and sneer, daring you to put words in his mouth. Padded seat and shoulders and a safety lock on the head to keep it from rolling away.

6279 Deluxe Groucho $84.00 + 7.95 shipping from Johnson Smith Company (see above).

Marx Facts

• The brothers were adept at impersonating one another, as we saw in the *Duck Soup* pantomime mirror scene with two Grouchos (and a third lurking in the shadows). In the stage version of *Animal Crackers*, Zeppo actually took over for Groucho while he recuperated from an appendectomy.

• The Marx Brothers once mock-threatened to sue the Warner Brothers over the name "Brothers," which the Marxes insisted they owned because they were older.

• How much did they ad-lib? Playwright George S. Kaufman, backstage during a Marx Brothers performance of his comedy *The Cocoanuts*, was heard to silence a friend with "Shush! I think I just heard one of my lines!"

• Caught kissing a chorus girl by his furious wife, Chico blithely denied any adulterous act, explaining that he was "just whispering in her mouth."

• Harpo, enchanted with a little blonde moppet, offered to buy her for $50,000. The parents declined to sell their child, Shirley Temple.

• Hello, Dali! Surrealists considered the brothers kindred souls, and artist Salvador Dali wrote a script for them called *The Marx Brothers on Horseback Salad.* It never made it to the screen.

• When filming *A Night in Casablanca* United Artists offered Harpo $50,000 if he would say one word on-screen— "Murder!"—so they could advertise "Harpo Speaks!" He refused. He spoke in performance only once—when he announced his retirement from the stage at the end of his last performance.

• One story has it that Oprah Winfrey was named after Harpo by her Marx-loving mom. (Oprah spelled backward is…)

"Soup" From Nuts

Duck Soup (1933). The Brothers spread their Marxist political propaganda in this hilarious satire about the usefulness of declaring war to boost national image. Co-starring Margaret Dumont.

#VHS 880407 $19.95 + 4.95 shipping from Postings, P.O. Box 8001, Hilliard, OH 430226-8001. (800) 262-6604 / FAX (614) 777-1470.

Other Great Marx Videos

A Night at the Opera (1935)

A Day at the Races (1937)

Room Service (1938)

At the Circus (1939)

Go West (1940)

Copacabana (1947)

Love Happy (1949)

$19.95 each + 3.95 shipping from Blackhawk Films, 5959 Triumph Street, Commerce, CA 90040-1688. (800) 826-2295

You Bet Your Life. Groucho proves he's the fastest wit in the west in these excerpts from the classic TV show.

VHS #1572239 $7.95 + $4.00 shipping from: Barnes & Noble, 126 Fifth Avenue, New York, NY 10011. (201) 767-7079.

EAR MARX

• *Three Hours…Fifty-Nine Minutes…Fifty-One Seconds with The Marx Bros.* This 4 record set is a great collection of original radio broadcasts from the 1930s and '40s. **From now-defunct Murray Hill Records. Out of print, but worth tracking down.**

• Vintage cassette recording of a Marx Brothers radio routine "Hollywood Agents" from 1939.

#80118, $3.98 plus 1.35 shipping. Johnson Smith Company 4514 19th Court East P.O. Box 25500 Bradenton, FL 34206-5500 (813) 747-2356

Join a Marxist Party

Marx Brothers Study Unit. The Marx Brothers wouldn't approve of the academic name, but members are privy to research services plus a library of over 100 volumes, 31,000 magazine and newspaper articles, 2000 photos and 200 posters. Since 1978, the club's stated purpose has been to assist "authors, actors, producers, and other artists interested in accurately depicting the Marx Brothers." Members receive the semi-annual "Freedonia Gazette."

For membership info, send SASE to Marx Brothers Study Unit, Paul G. Wesolowski, Director Darien 28 New Hope, PA 18938 (215) 862-9734

"There ain't no Sanity Clause."
—Chico

On the Wall

Animal Crackers full color poster from one of their best movies ever. Measures 22" x 30".

M02866 Framed $69.99 + 8.95 shipping
M03021 Unframed $10.95 + 3.95 shipping
Postings, P.O. Box 8001, Hilliard, OH 430226-8001. (800) 262-6604 / FAX (614) 777-1470.

Norman Cousins credits laughing at Marx Brothers movies with curing his cancer.

PLAYER PIANOS

Look Ma, No Hands!

From the 1890s to the Great Depression, America's entertainment center was likely to be the player piano in the front parlor, bringing "live" music to its audience. Commonly called pianolas after an early mechanical piano player that was rolled up to a keyboard to play it, player pianos underwent further improvements that brought the actual playing mechanism inside the piano. Foot-pumped bellows operated the instrument, producing sound pneumatically.

Coin-operated nickelodeons were the next development, driven by an electric motor and designed for entertainment in public places. They were decorated with colorful inlaid stained glass, electrically illuminated from inside the instrument to create a crude visual forerunner of Wurlitzer jukeboxes, light shows and MTV. Other instruments were often added besides piano, including organ pipes, drums, tambourines, xylophones, and a stringed mandolin effect.

Reproducing machines allowed people to hear exact copies of great musicians' keyboard artistry. An artist would play a live performance on a master piano, which used carbon rods dipped in mercury beneath each key to mark the note's duration on a moving paper roll. Simultaneously, another musician would listen carefully to the performance to capture characteristic pedaling, dynamics, phrasing, shading and other nuances by noting them on a copy of the score. From this a master roll was created, consisting of a long roll of paper with holes punched to correspond to the notes as they were played. Copies of these rolls, when run through a player, sounded just like Scott Joplin, W.C. Handy or Fats Waller performing in your living room.

Ragtime piano music, its rapid-fire staccato style too difficult for most people to play, was a natural choice for player pianos since the machines couldn't make errors and speed was no obstacle to them. But much as people enjoyed the spectacle of "no hands" playing fast rhythms, the Depression put a damper on this popular but costly entertainment vehicle. Radio's static-crackling, canned music became the economical alternative to what was once heard "live" in the parlor.

Still, the idea never completely died. You can still buy piano rolls (many offer contemporary songs) if you have anything to play them on. And a new generation of computer disc-driven player pianos is captivating a small but significant segment of the home audience.

Nine Instrument Nickelodeon

Besides a piano, the Muzelle™ is a cymbal, bass drum, tambourine, snare drum, timpani, woodblock, mandolin and glockenspiel. Comes with two 45 minute music rolls (over 150 others are available from manufacturer), and can also be played manually. Mahogany piano is ebony-finished, and features a stained-glass, rock 'n' roll jukebox design. Can be easily converted to coin-operated.

#17620W, $13,000.00 from Hammacher Schlemmer, 9180 Le Saint Drive, Fairfield, OH 45014. (800) 543-3366.

Famous musicians who have made piano rolls: Scott Joplin, Jelly Roll Morton, Fats Waller and George Gershwin.

PILGRIMAGES

• **Antique Music and Wheels Museum**. A large variety of various mechanical music machines on display. Bring plenty of coins.

Daniel Boone Antique Village No. 60,

Route I-85 Exit 164 (12 miles west of Durham), Hillsborough, NC 27278.

• **The Musical Museum**. Family collection of mechanical musical machines is large and varied.

The Sanders Family, State Route 12-B, Deansboro, NY 13328.

• **Museum of the Musical Box Society International**. Varied collection with emphasis on music boxes, and a reference library of literature on mechanical musical machines.

295 West Avenue at the Lockwood Mathews Mansion, Norwalk, CT 06856.

Reading Music

• *Encyclopedia of Automatic Musical Instruments* by Q. David Bowers. This outstanding reference book was written for everyone who has ever considered buying player pianos, orchestrions, music boxes and all the many manifestations of music machines produced in the U.S. and Europe over the years. Filled with useful, money-saving information and loaded with photos.

$59.95 + 2.50 shipping from Vestal Press, Ltd., 320 North Jensen Road, P.O. Box 97, Vestal, NY 13851-009. (607) 797-4872 / FAX (607) 797-4898.

• *Rebuilding the Player Piano* by Larry Givens. This comprehensive book tells you everything you need to know to refurbish old player pianos. Not that it's easy since player pianos have roughly 16,000 pieces to remove, restore, then return.

Even seemingly simple tasks like replacing all of the cloth, rubber and felt, are complicated and time-consuming. On a brighter note, instruments restored to mint condition have been appreciating in value approximately 25% a year, making this pastime a possible lucrative sideline.

$9.50 + 2.50 shipping from The Vestal Press, Ltd., 320 North Jensen Road, Vestal, NY 13851. (607) 797-4872 / FAX (607) 797-4898.

Organizations

Automatic Musical Instruments Collector's Association. Membership includes a subscription to the AMICA News Bulletin, which contains articles, classified ads, valuable do-it-yourself advice for restoring instruments, and information about chapter meetings and conventions. Excellent source for buying piano rolls, antique instruments and their parts.

To become a new member, send $27.00 ($22.00 annual membership plus $5.00 one-time processing fee) to AMICA International, P.O. Box 172, Columbia, SC 29202-0172.

Music for the '90s

(1890s, That Is)

These are recordings from restored automated antique musical instruments, once housed in the museum of the Gay 90s Village. These instruments toured the country, appearing at the New York World's Fair, numerous state fairs, even the *Today Show* and *I've Got a Secret*. The collection was disbanded in 1970, and 14 truck loads of machines were sold to private collectors, Disneyland, Disney World and King's Island.

Before they were sold, music for the various machines was recorded for sale. Here are some cassettes we liked:

• **5162-85 The Emperor Speaks, a Mortier Organ** (*Dixie, Sweet Georgia Brown, Won't You Come Home Bill Bailey*, and 22 other selections).

• **5176-77 Queen of King's Island, a #157 Wurlitzer** (*Skater's Waltz, Blue Danube Waltz, Ben Hur Chariot Race*, and 18 other selections).

• **5180-94 Yaller Dawg Saloon, a Seeburg "E"** (*Beer Barrel Polka, Oh, You Beautiful Doll, Bronco Bill Rag*, and 17 other selections).

• **5181-99 Fair Time With Loud Mouth Sadie Mae, a Gavioli Organ** (*In My Merry Oldsmobile, My Wild Irish Rose, Oh, My Darling Clementine*, and 23 other selections).

All above cassette tapes $12.95 each + 1.50 shipping from Gay 90s Village, Inc., P.O. Box 569, Sikeston, MO 63801. (314) 471-1347.

Each player piano has 16,000 pieces, roughly 4,000 more than a regular piano.

Piano's Forte

- **Prelude & Fugue.** The "Sextrola," a player piano patented in 1908, was specifically designed to provide appropriate musical entertainment for the parlors of your classier whore houses. What kind of music? Ragtime was most popular, but an occasional romantic or even sentimental number was occasionally thrown in for a change of mood.

- **Grateful Dead.** Funeral parlors had special self-players to choose from as well, such as the Seeburg Mortuary Organ Model H-O, which played a lot of hymns and other sad music in minor keys.

- **Eh, Luigi!** Mussolini attempted to recall hand-cranked street pianos to prevent Italians from operating them in other countries because he thought the stereotype was an affront to Italian dignity. In 1944, when Il Duce was down at the heels, but not yet hanging by them, a fellow countryman greeted the arriving victorious Allied troops in Naples with a rousing Neapolitan rendition of *The Star-Spangled Banner* cranked out of a street piano.

Punch, punch, punch with care. Composer Conlon Nancarrow, known as the "father of electronic music," writes his complex scores not on paper in standard musical notation, but on piano rolls by manually punching the holes. Since his composing skills are much better than his piano playing skills, his singular technique allows him to play as masterfully as he'd like. His difficult scores are admired by fellow musicians as diverse as Frank Zappa, who employs a similar, though updated, composing technique on the synclavier—the floppy disc has replaced the paper roll, so no punching allowed.

Rollin' Along

Q-R-S. Write Q-R-S for a catalogue of their wonderful music rolls and accessories. This is an old company from the heyday of player pianos that has remained in business by offering a variety of products and providing good customer service. Cost of each piano roll? About $3.50.

Q-R-S, 1026 Niagara Street, Buffalo, NY 14213.

- **BluesTone Music Rolls.** BluesTone features never-before available ragtime, blues and jazz piano rolls. Their specialty is reissuing "hot" rolls by such artists as Jelly Roll Morton, Luckey Roberts and Fats Waller. Write to Rob DeLand for an ever-changing list of titles and prices.

Rob DeLand, 240 N. Ashland, Palatine, IL 60067.

- *Punching a Hole, Playing a Roll,* is a fascinating tour of the Q-R-S piano roll factory in Buffalo, New York. This video pilgrimage takes you on a trip from the recording to the end result of manufacturing a piano roll. You'll get to see and hear the product played on vintage instruments.

VHS or Beta (56 min.), $39.95 + 2.50 shipping from Vestal Press Ltd., 320 North Jensen Road, P.O. Box 97, Vestal, NY 13851 (607) 797-4872 / FAX (607) 797-4898.

Briefcase Full Of Blues

Or jazz or rock 'n' roll if you want. Sturdy rayon briefcase includes four pockets to carry your piano rolls.

#8753, Keyboard Briefcase, $15.98 + 3.99 shipping from Taylor Gifts, 355 E. Conestoga Road, P.O. Box 206, Wayne, PA 19087-0206. (215) 789-7007.

DIAL IT AGAIN SAM

Wood crafted Player Piano Phone has a keyboard for dialing. And instead of ringing, its "stained glass look" panel lights up as it plays *When The Saints Go Marching In*.

#8669, $79.98 + 8.99 shipping from Taylor Gifts, 355 E. Conestoga Road, P.O. Box 206, Wayne, PA 19087-0206. (215) 789-7007.

For Cool Piano Players

They'll want to tickle your ivories when you show up in these cozy acrylic keyboard clothes.

#T9092, Keyboard Hat and Scarf, $15.98 + 4.95 shipping from Funny Side Up, 425 Stump Road, North Wales. PA 19454. (215) 361-5130.

Music Box Memories

Recordings of antique, metal disc-driven musical devices from bygone days.

• **The Glorious Regina.** The "Glorious Regina" was an outstanding American manufactured model produced between 1880 and 1920.

—Vol. 1: Waltzes and Vaudeville Songs (*Der Fledermaus, My Old Kentucky Home, Yankee Doodle Dandy* and more). #E171

—Vol. 2: Cakewalks, Rags and Marches (*That College Rag, Stars and Stripes Forever, Washington Post March*

Put Another Nickel In

• **Cliff House Mechanical Museum.** This collection of nostalgic, coin-operated arcade machines includes nickelodeons, orchestrions, and music boxes. They also have other antique coin-operated machines like games, flip-card viewers, and fortune tellers.

Historic Cliff House, 1090 Point Lobos Avenue, San Francisco, CA 94121.

• **Tower of Beauty at San Sylmar.** This collection belonging to J. B. Nethercut, head of Merle Norman Cosmetics, contains all sorts of mechanical musical keyboard instruments, as well as player string instruments. Tours by appointment only. No jeans, shorts, halters or thongs.

Tower of Beauty, 15180 Bledsoe Street, Sylmar, CA. (818) 367-2251.

• These amusement parks display the bulk of the mechanical music machines from the late great Gay 90s Village collection:

—*Disneyland*

—*Disney World*

—*King's Island, Cincinnati, Ohio*

and more). #E172.

• *Music of the 3 Disc Symphonion Music Box.* An excellent German music box known for its clear, bell-like tones. Full, orchestral sound recordings of operatic works, including *Aida, Tales of Hoffmann, Cavalleria Rusticana,* and *The Wedding March.* #E105X.

Each audiocassette above: $8.95 + 2.50 shipping. from Vestal Press, Ltd., 320 North Jensen Road, P.O. Box 97, Vestal, NY 13851. (607) 797-4872 / FAX (607) 797-4898.

Mechanical Music for a Song

Can't afford a player piano? How about a music box? Many shapes and sizes are available to fit all musical tastes and pocketbooks.

• **Gazebo Music Box** is an exquisitely detailed touch of nostalgic Victoriana, delicately decorated with floral garlands and electric lanterns that cast a romantic light on a miniature couple waltzing to *True Love.* 7 1/4 in. tall, takes two AA batteries.

#2756 Gazebo Music Box $59.95 + 6.95 shipping.

• **Chopin Nutcracker Music Box** depicts the composer *as a nutcracker* (how Suite!) in powdered wig seated at a piano. The nutcracker's mouth, arms and legs are hinged for flexible movement, including swiveling on its bench. The wooden piano conceals fine Swiss Reuge movement which plays an Etude by the composer. Comes with candle stand and candle to illuminate the concert. Unusual collectible is 11 1/2 in. tall.

#1248 Chopin Nutcracker $149.95 + 8.95 shipping.

These and a score of other music boxes available from: The Music Stand, 1 Rockdale Plaza, Lebanon, NH 03766-1585. (802) 295-7044 / FAX (802) 295-5080.

Early computer punch cards were derived from player piano punched-hole note-reading technology.

Player Piano Scenes

- **Horsefeathers** (1932). This Marx Brothers classic features a speakeasy where a malfunctioning nickelodeon offers perpetual music.

- **Algiers** (1938). Don't shoot me, I'm only the player piano. In a twist on an old gangster movie cliche, a stool pigeon fleeing a mobster falls against a nickelodeon, which starts playing. Facing the music, both stoolie and nickelodeon are shot.

NEW PLAYER PIANOS FOR YOUR PARLOR

Prices for new player pianos run between $2,500 — $4,500, compared to regular nonplayers that sell for between $800 — $3,000 on average. For catalogs and information, contact the companies directly:

- *Aeolian Company, 2718 Pershing Avenue, Memphis, TN 38112.*

- *Kimball International Company, 1549 Royal Street, Jasper, IN 47546.*

- *Universal Piano Company, Suite 311, 1000 Santa Monica Boulevard, Los Angeles, CA 90067.*

- *Wurlitzer Company, Box 388, DeKalb, IL 60115.*

- *Yamaha Corporation of America, Piano Department, Keyboard Division, P.O. Box 6600, Buena Park, CA 90622.*

Player Piano Lit 101

"Since some of the passengers were leaving the ship the next day at Pago-Pago they had a little dance that evening and in his ears hammered still the harsh notes of the mechanical piano."

— **Somerset Maugham, *Rain***

"All I know about him is that…he played Liszt on an old pianola for half an hour every morning after breakfast, not because he liked music but because the action of pedalling was stimulating to his intestines."

—**Beverley Nichols, *Laughter On The Stairs***

"The musical box of his nursery days…had always made him miserable when his mother set it going on Sunday afternoons. Here it was again, the same thing, only larger, more expensive, and now it played The Wild, Wild Women and The Policeman's Holiday, and he was no longer in black velvet with a sky blue collar."

—**John Galsworthy, *The Forsyte Saga***

Tickling the Floppies

The Yamaha Disklavier is a new breed of player piano, where modern computer technology replaces wind as the force which triggers the hammers to play the strings. It uses 3.5 in. floppy discs that hold up to 90 minutes of music. This electronic marvel eliminates the noise, distortion, and tonal irregularities of paper rolls.

It's not just a player piano, but a sophisticated tool for composers and musicians as well. Using MIDI (musical

instrument digital interface) capabilities, sound can be manipulated as easily as a word processor handles copy. Rhythm machines can be added and musical passages can be edited, overdubbed, transposed and stored. Tempo and timbre can be altered, and tones blended to resemble a harmony usually produced by a number of other instruments.

Besides its sophisticated digital features, the Yamaha Disklavier can be played and enjoyed as an acoustic

grand. (Although the average price for a Yamaha Disklavier Grand Piano is a steep $20,000, uprights start at $8500.) There is a lot of musical "software"

available for it, including discs that pianist and Gershwin scholar Artis

Wodehouse has lovingly converted from over 100 recently discovered piano rolls cut by George Gershwin himself.

For more information and brochures, contact Yamaha Corporation of America, Piano Department, Keyboard Division, P.O. Box 6600, Buena Park, CA 90622.

"Put another nickel in, in the nickelodeon. All I want is loving you and music, music, music."
—sung by Teresa Brewer

EXPENSIVE FUN

Play Treble & Bass-Ackwards. You can pretend to be Edgar Varese with a Yamaha Disklavier. Take any arrangement of music on disc, and program your Disklavier to play it backwards (an easy thing to do). Do some musical tastetesting by telling unsuspecting friends they're listening to an original composition.

Player pianos are primitive computers, using a digital language input to produce a music output.

MILITARY CHIC

What *is* Pop War, Anyway?

Pop war is marching in formation, medals, drums and bugles, G.I. Joe and John Wayne. Pop war has people leading charges into certain death with a brave quip. In pop war, most casualties are scowling enemies; the only one who gets it on our side is a babyfaced guy with a nickname like "Kid" who has a mom, a girl and a pet goat back home on the farm. Pop war is what keeps up morale during wartime and keeps kids entertained at matinees and on TV for years afterward.

Pop war is our noble side fighting a dastardly enemy. Pop war is exciting.

Real war is a failure of foreign or domestic policy, often consisting of civilian casualties, and lower middle class kids sacrificed for dubious goals. Real war is a bunch of scared 19-year-olds looking at each other in different uniforms, wondering what the hell they're doing there, many of whom (military studies have determined) never even get up the courage to fire their guns. Real war is mind-freezing, immobilizing terror.

Unfortunately, pop war is what makes it easy to convince kids to enlist in the armed forces, to slaughter and be slaughtered in real war, and to convince their parents and loved ones that it's okay, even noble.

Sometimes pop culture can be hell, too.

Bureaucracy's Funniest Home Videos

Federal Follies Videos. Entertainment Tonight says it's "Comedy at its best!"

Made as training films for U.S. government agencies from 1934-1973, these unintentionally hilarious shorts cover some unusual topics from the famous "Duck and Cover" atomic blast survival film to how to avoid hookworm. Four volumes to choose from, each with 50 minutes of 2-5 short subjects. Our favorite is Vol. 4, which includes *Jap Zero* with Ronald Reagan (Army Air Force).

VHS $19.95 each + 3.90 shipping, or all four $79.00 + 7.75 shipping from Wireless, P.O. Box 64422, St. Paul, MN 55164-0422. (800) 669-9999.

War's Dirtiest Dozen Movies

- To Hell and Back
- Apocalypse Now
- Bridge On The River Kwai
- Dirty Dozen
- Full Metal Jacket
- Green Berets
- Best Defense
- Patton
- Platoon
- Top Gun
- Stalag 17
- M*A*S*H

The Empire Strikes Back!

The First Empire Dragoons, that is, bearing the flag of Napoleon's 17th regiment. Set of four, 3¹/₂" tall, hand-cast from original molds and hand-painted by C.B.G. Mignot of France.

#6733, $95.00 + 3.90 shipping from The Smithsonian Institution, Washington, D.C. 20073-0006. (703) 455-1700 / FAX (703) 455-4843.

Shell Shocked

Looking for a dummy of your own caliber? These non-explosive casings have holes drilled in them so you can wear them as a necklace or use them on the Xmas tree.

50 mm caliber dummy shell, $2.50 + 4.00 shipping; 20 mm caliber shell, $2.75 + 4.00 shipping. Jerryco Science Center, 601 Linden Place, Evanston, IL 60202. (708) 475-8440. Ask for their disarmingly honest catalog.

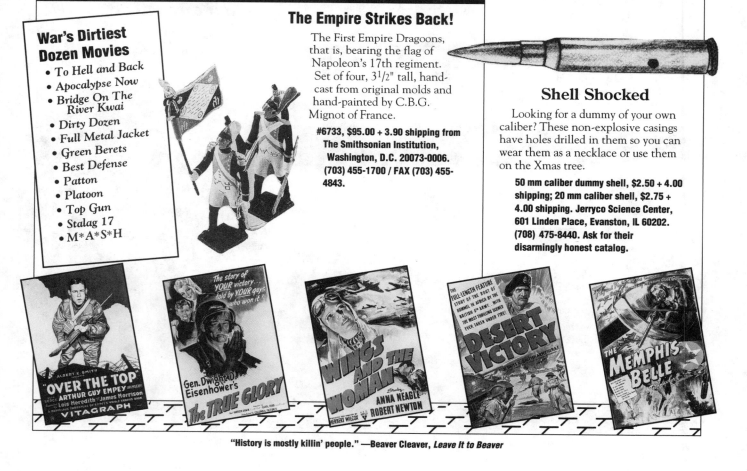

"History is mostly killin' people." —Beaver Cleaver, *Leave It to Beaver*

HEAVY METAL

Medieval Suits of Armour. Also available are replica weapons: cannons, old-west guns, swords, including samurai swords, sabers and cutlasses.

For complete information, contact Collector's Armory, Inc., 800 Slaters Lane, P.O. Box 59, Alexandria, VA 22313-0059. (800) 544-3456 Ext. 515

War 6 Times a Year

Priding itself on accuracy, **Military History** brings to life not just one war, but the entire history of armed conflict. It goes beyond the dates, facts and figures to the study of warfare and takes you right to the front lines, except you don't bleed. As their copywriter put it: "The fighting men. The battles they fought. The weapons they used. The tactics they employed. The results they obtained."

One year subscription (6 issues) $11.97 from Empire Press, P.O. Box 8, 105 Loudon Street S.W., Leesburg, VA 22075. (703) 771-9400.

Dressed to Kill: Uniform & Artifact Collectors

Association of American Military Uniform Collectors. These folks have been studying and preserving 20th Century military uniforms since 1977. Dues entitle you to four issues of the *Footlocker* newsletter and the right to publish up to four ads each year. Members also receive a detailed membership list coded to indicate each member's specific collecting interest.

One year membership, $12.50. AAMUC, P.O. Box 1876, Elyria, OH 44036. (216) 365-5321.

The American Society of Military Insignia Collectors. Devoted to collecting and preserving military insignia of all types. Its quarterly for members, *Trading Post*, features informative articles covering medals, patches, buttons and the like. They also publish an annual membership directory.

One year membership, $20.00. ASMIC, 526 Lafayette Avenue, Palmerton, PA 18071.

Pineapple Grenade

A replica of the famous forbidden fruit, the pineapple grenade used in the 1940s and 1950s. It sports a two piece removable fuse that unscrews from the body. Makes a wonderful paperweight that no one will touch.

#X-310, $6.95 + 3.95 shipping from Kaufman's West LTD., 1660 Eubank NE, Albuquerque, NM 87112. (505) 293-2300 / (800) 545-0933.

Toy Soldiers Will Follow If Lead

Collecting Toy Soldiers: An Identification And Value Guide by **Richard O'Brien.** Billed as "The most comprehensive book on toy soldiers ever published," and this is no exaggeration. Covers toy soldiers made of every material from lead to plastic to zinc, including a special section on G.I. Joe. Also lists notable dealers, collectors and publications. If you're pricing toy soldiers and accessories, this book is a "must have."

$19.95 + 2.50 shipping. Books Americana, Inc., P.O. Box 2326, Florence, AL 35630. (800) 239-9966.

"Individuality is fine. As long as we do it together." —Major Frank Burns, *M*A*S*H*

G.I JOE

FREEDOM FIGHTER

Scenarios of a War Doll

VINCENT SANTELMO

The Continuing Saga of G.I. Joe

No son of mine is gonna play with dolls! Ah, but an "action soldier" is an altogether different thing. And so begin the adventures of G.I. Joe.

What does it say about our culture that the most popular boy toy is a professional killer and the most popular girl toy, a conspicuous consumer?

Designed, the company says, from a composite of the faces of 23 Congressional Medal Honorees, G.I. Joe also sports a scar to make him look more masculine. But that's not all—Joe has a birth defect: a misplaced thumbnail.

Joe was born in a brainstorming session at Hasbro Toy, Inc. Seeing the success of Barbie, they were trying to figure out how to sell similar accessory-laden dolls to boys, without calling them dolls.

Joe has changed a lot over the years. At first there were only four G.I. Joes—Army, Navy, Air Force and Marine. But as times changed, the force has grown to more than 230 variations.

In 1986, wrestler "Sgt. Slaughter" become the first "real-life" person to join the G.I. Joe

corps, the same year that *Toy & Hobby World* named Joe the best-selling toy in America. In 1987, Chicago Bear William "The Refrigerator" Perry also joined the team.

Joe has been everything from a Green Beret (when the Vietnam war was popular) to a "Kung Fu" figure (during the martial arts craze) to a near-civilian adventurer recovering buried treasure (when the Vietnam war became unpopular).

It's not always easy to know who next week's enemy is going to be. Hasbro doesn't even try keeping up with the twists and turns of America's foreign policy any more—now all of Joe's battles are against **Cobra**, a paramilitary organization with undefined political goals and an evil heart.

Joe's **Army Task Force,** of course, is a paramilitary organization with undefined political goals and a *good* heart.

G.I. Joe collectors will pay over $1,000 for some of the dolls, $3,000 for some accessories.

Reading G.I. Joe

• **G.I. Joe, Freedom Fighter: Scenarios of a War Doll** by **Vincent Santelmo**. This fact-filled, definitive history of G.I. Joe is illustrated with photographs of the collectible action figures and accessories from 1964 through 1978. Everything you wanted to know, Joe, but were afraid to ask.

$29.95 + 3.00 shipping from Hobby House Press, Inc., 900 Frederick St., Cumberland, MD 21502. (301) 759-3770 / FAX (301) 759-4940.

• **G.I. Joe Value Guide** by **Carol Moody**. If you want to know how much your G.I. Joe or accessory is worth, this is the guide. Lots of photos, some in color; even sketches of hard to find gear. Contains values for dolls and accessories from 1964-1978.

$9.95 + 3.00 shipping from Hobby House Press, Inc., 900 Frederick St., Cumberland, MD 21502. (301) 759-3770 / FAX (301) 759-4940.

G.I Joe on Video

G.I. Joe cartoon shows, for kids who need help in making up their own fantasy plots. Twelve volumes have been released on video.

Each volume $9.95 + 5.00 shipping from Family Home Entertainment, 2030 E. University Dr., Rancho Dominguez, CA 90220. (800) 765-5005 / (800) 423-7455, ext.3368.

21 MOVABLE PARTS!

ALMOST A FOOT TALL!

AUTHENTIC EQUIPMENT FROM HEAD TO TOE

PAINTBALL

Paintball, the grown-up version of childhood's "Capture The Flag," lets teams of combatants shoot paint-filled spheres at each other with realistic-looking air guns. If you get splattered with the (washable) paint, you're out of action. Players of the sport have uniforms, guns and elaborate combat settings.

• *Paintball Sports*. As the sport grows by leaps and bounds, *Paintball Sports* keeps track of it. Articles cover rules and changes, new products, strategy, technical tips, a calendar of events and more.

One year subscription $24.75. Paintball Publications, Inc., 295 Main Street, Mt. Kisco, NY 10549. (914) 241-0020.

SPLAT 'EM!

SplatMaster Rapide Semi-Automatic Paint Pistol. Get an edge in your next paintball battle. 20-shot magazine.

Rapide Paint Pistol, $109.95 + 8.95 shipping. Extra Rapide Magazine, $13.95 + 4.95 shipping. U.S. Cavalry, 2855 Centennial Avenue, Radcliff, KY 40160-9000. (800) 777-7732 / FAX (502) 352-0266.

Paintball Tourney

War CAN be healthy for children and other living things! Proceeds from this Paintball tournament and trade show go to the National Kidney Foundation. All types of paint guns are allowed.

For information, contact the National Kidney Foundation, 61-B South Main St., Dayton, OH 45458. (513) 438-9594.

Camouflage Ties

#T9752 Camo Tie or #T9753 Camo Bow Tie, $14.98 + 3.95 shipping from Funny Side Up, 425 Stump Road, North Wales, PA 19454. (215) 361-5130.

If You Only Like To Watch

This reenactment of the Battle of Gettysburg is historically accurate except that it doesn't take place at Gettysburg National Military Park but on private farmland about five miles Southeast of the town. It's sponsored by the American Civil War Commemorative Committee and managed by Napoleonic Tactics, Inc., a firm that specializes in reenactments.

For more information about the next battle call (717) 334-0631, or contact the Gettysburg Travel Council, 35 Carlisle St., Gettysburg, PA 17325. (717) 334-6274.

I Want You... To Buy These Posters!

Remember the woman rolling up her shirt sleeve to show her muscle with the words "We Can Do It!" written underneath? Or Uncle Sam saying, "I Want You"? How about "Buy War Bonds" posters? The National Archives in Washington D.C. has them all and is selling high quality reproductions. Ah, but that's not all. Get your favorite posters imprinted on magnets, signs, shirts, sweatshirts, too.

Twenty assorted 20 x 28" posters, $50.00 + 2.50 shipping from National Archives Trust Fund, NEPS Dept. 721, P.O. Box 100793, Atlanta, GA 30384.

BETTER LEAD THAN DEAD

Historically authentic Union Artillery set. Each piece is hand cast in lead, hand painted in documented detail and signed by artist James Mann. Four miniatures include "Napoleon" 12-pound cannon, pull-cord private, a rammer and mounted color bearer on prancing steed.

Civil War Lead Collectibles, $99.00 + 8.50 shipping from Wireless, P.O. Box 64422, St. Paul, MN 55164-0422. (800) 669-9999.

Stylish Toilet Paper

Camouflage toilet paper is the perfect gift for your soldier friend, hunter or military groupie.

#T1582, $3.98 + 3.50 shipping from Funny Side Up, 425 Stump Road, North Wales. PA 19454. (215) 361-5130.

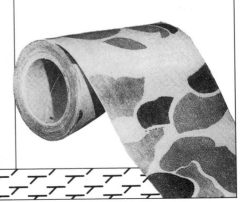

"In time of war, the devil makes more room in hell." —German Proverb

miniatures

Small Game

Self-effacing small-game hunters can display these trophies with humility. Handpainted and mounted on walnut plaques, looking just like the big ones that got away. Moose, bear, mountain goat, boar, deer, and fish—average size 2 1/2 ".

Each head, $50.00 + 6.00 shipping from The Lawbre Company 888 Tower Road, Unit J Mundelein, IL 60060 (708) 949-0031 Catalog $4.00 (refundable with purchase)

It's a Small World After All

While people have created miniature scenes and dollhouses for eons, the hobby of making and collecting miniatures as it is practiced in the United States today had its beginnings only a few decades ago, with a small group of handcrafters who built everything from scratch.

Today, there is a vast network of clubs reaching around the world, and a thriving miniatures industry. Besides the approximately 2,500 miniature specialty shops in the United States, larger chain stores have begun featuring limited miniature lines, making this tiny realm as accessible as if Club Med had opened a resort in Lilliput.

Just what is it that makes miniature enthusiasts so, well, enthusiastic about their craft? Tiny worlds are fun. The scale transports us back to our childhoods and brings out the omnipotent god in us at the same time. Who doesn't want to create a more perfect, more manageable world?

Miniature nails, just 3/32 of an inch long, little bricks, functioning double-hung windows just three inches high, microscopic carved moldings, itty-bitty door knobs — an entire universe can fit on a tabletop.

Hot Tub Kit

Build this tiny spa (11 x 14 x 8 in.) for your decadent hamsters and they'll think they're in California. All-wood kit has everything needed for deck, tub, and privacy screens.

$69.95 ppd. from Betty's Wooden Miniatures, 6150 Northwest Hwy, Chicago, IL 60631. (312) 774-8848.

Small Yard

Not just generic green astroturf and lumpy bushes, but: spring and summer grass, summer and fall leaves, assorted flowers and shrubs, evergreens, palms, wood chips, snow, stones, mulch, even tiny weeds (to add that irritating touch of realism to your tiny yard).

Send $1.00 for price list to: Holliday & Associates 1518 5th Ave. Canyon, TX 79015

"The delight is in the detail."—Vladimir Nabokov

Pilgrimages

- **Miniature Kingdom.** Arthur Thuijs created these 50 tiny structures over a decade. It's the ultimate city planning nightmare. Buildings range from castles to villages to modern main streets, all on the same densely developed "site." But at least there's no traffic problem: while there are 300 working street lamps, 1,000 trees and 2,000 people, there are only 150 cars in the entire burg.

  Miniature Kingdom, 350 Rte. 31 S., Washington, NJ 07882. (201) 689-6866.

- **Bird's Eye View Museum.** Local landmarks from Wakarusa and nearby Bonneville Mill, Illinois, lovingly crafted from toothpicks and popsicle sticks. Evokes the prefranchised feel of an American town before McDonald's and Fotomat moved in.

  Bird's Eye View Museum, 325 S. Elkhart St., Wakarusa, IN 46573. (219) 862-2367.

BOOKS

- ***The Complete Book of Making Miniatures* by Thelma R. Newman and Virginia Merrill.** A good general overview of how to make, assemble or purchase all you need for a miniature dream house. A chapter on improvising shows how to make a Louis XIV clock out of an old earring and beads, and a Tiffany lamp shade from an eggshell.

  $16.95 + 2.00 shipping from Random House, 400 Hahn Road, Westminster, MD 21157. (800) 733-3000.

- ***How to Make Miniature Furniture* by John Davenport.** Curator of London's Victoria and Albert Museum's miniatures collection, Davenport's is an expert's guide to fine woodworking. Not for beginners, but if you're ready for a challenge, Davenport gives all the information needed—on tools, materials, suppliers, woods, veneers and techniques for crafting amazing furniture in 1/12th scale.

  $14.95 + 1.25 shipping. Wynwood Press, 935 Industrial Park Road, Iowa Falls, IA 50126.

Tiny Scale on the Small Screen

- Where but in the *Twilight Zone* would you find a dollhouse in which the dolls are alive? And a miniaturist just obsessive enough to slip into the *Zone* and find himself, at last, inside a little diorama with the doll of his dreams.

- It happened in Fernwood, too — that's where Mary Hartman found her tiny, perfect dollhouse world come alive as she experienced a nervous breakdown. The contrast between the perfect world in front of her and the anarchy of her own real life was the final straw in a memorable episode of *Mary Hartman, Mary Hartman.*

"He that despiseth small things will perish by little and little."—Ralph Waldo Emerson

Mini Magazines

• *Miniatures Showcase.* Each issue is devoted to a specific theme or historical period. Articles are geared toward the hobbyist rather than the collector or the craftsman. We found ourselves looking at the "big" world through different eyes after reading some of the helpful hints, thinking "Hey, those buttons would make terrific miniature fruit compotes if you just glued a little metal eyelet on the back…"

Quarterly, $12.95 per year from Kalmbach Publishing Co., 21027 Crossroads Circle, PO Box 1612, Waukesha, WI 53187.

• *Nutshell News.* "Have you ever noticed those tiny punchings that fall from the center of sequins?" *Nutshell News* says use them as pocket change for your dollhouse dwellers. Features product innovations, miniaturist news, interviews with artisans, plus show and exhibit information.

Monthly, $29.00 per year from Kalmbach Publishing, 21027 Crossroads Circle, PO Box 1612, Waukesha, WI 53187.

JOIN THE CLUB

The National Association of Miniature Enthusiasts. How about this oxymoron—NAME is the largest miniature organization in the world. Functions mainly as a miniaturists' networking club, with officers, by-laws, local chartered groups — everything but a secret handshake. 12,000 Americans and Canadians are card-carrying NAME members.

$20.00 per year (includes 4 issues of *The Miniature Gazette*) to NAME, PO Box 1178, Brea, CA 92622. (714) 529-0900.

A Big Little Catalog

The Miniatures Catalog, published annually by Kalmbach Miniatures. This is like a Sears-Roebuck catalog of the miniature dimension. Nearly 400 pages of beautifully crafted tiny things that can be ordered directly. Includes a shop and museum guide and a show calendar.

$16.95 + 2.50 shipping from Miniatures Bookshelf, PO Box 465, Lawrenceburg, IN 47025.

Small Businesses

The Guide to American Miniaturists. Craftspersons, stores and shows described in detail, listed geographically and fully indexed. This is the directory we'd use if we were looking for something tiny. Updated every two years.

$5.00 + 1.50 shipping from Jane Haskell, 56 Harkness Drive, Madison, CT 06443. (203) 421-4183.

Wanna Play House?

This dollhouse kit captures the romance and charm of the Victorian era. Highly detailed with thirteen rooms, including baths and hallways, stairways and clapboard siding. If this were a full-size home, it would cost a couple of million bucks. Size is 37L x 26D x 43H".

Made by a highly respected company that offers over 50 houses ranging in price from $69 to $900. Send for their catalog ($4.00).

#NC-3205 *Hawthorne*, $569.00 + 20.00 shipping. Real Good Toys, 10 Quarry Hill, Barre, VT 05641. (802) 479-2217 / FAX (802) 479-2591.

Mr. Potato Head

This Spud's for You

Like so many of us, Mr. Potato Head's hitting middle age. Sprouted by Hasbro on April 30, 1952, he was the first toy ever advertised on TV.

Mrs. Potato Head's still around, but the Potato Head Kids were not so lucky. A few years ago, their Saturday morning cartoon was cancelled and they likewise disappeared, perhaps having joined the French fryin' legion.

Mr. Potato Head was originally a real potato. His eyes, mouth, etc. came with sharp points to make them easy to jab into a real potato. Later, sharp points on kid toys became unfashionable; the real potato was replaced with plastic and the toy's sharp edges were smoothed. Sort of a metaphor for our times.

Although safer, not everybody was happy. Stephen Viccio, a philosophy professor at the College of Notre Dame in Maryland, criticized the changes in the *NY Times*. "One of the most wonderful things used to be that the child could place the eyes, ears, nose and mouth anywhere, creating potatoes like Salvador Dali might have made if he were God," he said and also objected to the unnatural longevity of the plastic Potato Head. it taught kids an important lesson: "the rotting potato skin began to act as a metaphor for the way of all flesh."

> "Only two things in this world are too serious to be jested on—potatoes and matrimony."
> —Irish Aphorism

The Three Faces of Mr. Potato Head

In the old days there were only a small number of Sybil-like multiple personalities which the tuber could manifest. But now there are thousands.

• The basic. The standard limited assortment of body parts.

• Mr. Potato Head and His Bucket of Parts. Sounds like a slasher film, but the Bucket of Parts is a storage case with 27 pieces.

• Super Silly Mr. Potato Head. Lots of silliness, designed to take Mr. Potato Head right over the edge with 38 pieces ranging from beehive hairdos to arrows through hats.

When it first came out, Mr. Potato Head didn't come with a body and any fruit or veggie would work.

Call Me Mr. Potato Head (& Other Near-Mrs.)

Highlights from the official Hasbro/Playskool biography of Mr. Potato Head:

• Born in Rhode Island in 1952. Began as a boxed set of eyes, ears, mouths, noses, but no body—you provide the vegetable.

• "A year later, Mr. Potato Head met Mrs. Potato Head and, after a whirlwind courtship and a brief honeymoon in Boise, Idaho, they became conspicuous consumers, acquiring their own convertible boat, trailer, airplane and locomotive, as well as a variety of household items." (Editor's Note: Playskool's publicist told us that Mrs. Potato Head's maiden name was—Mrs. Potato Head.)

• "In 1964, the Potato Heads took shape in the form of molded bodies."

• "In 1966, there was a 'whole lot of shakin' goin' on,' and Mr. Potato Head became 'Jumpin' Mr. Potato Head.' To keep up with the Joneses, Mr. Potato Head now jumped, played with his jackhammer

and flew kites. Mrs. Potato Head, not yet liberated, acquired a feather duster, floor polisher, dinner bell and vacuum cleaner."

• "But life in the fast lane caught up with him in 1974. Mr. Potato Head recognized the onslaught of middle age when he doubled in size...Facelifts, bendable arms and a trap door to store their spare parts followed in 1983."

Pilgrimage

The Unknown Museum. On display are over 200 Mr. Potato Heads, detailing the history and evolution of the famous potatomorph, from healthful spud to oversized plastic potato. "He's put on weight," explains curator Mickey McGowan. "Now he looks more like a kidney bean" (perhaps the result of giving up smoking?).

PO Box 1551
Mill Valley, CA 94942
(415) 383-2726
Open by appointment only.

Potato Head Politics

• In a bitter primary race for California attorney general in 1990, Ira Reiner called his baldheaded rival Arlo Smith "Mr. Potato Head." Reiner apparently miscalculated the potato's appeal: Smith won.

• The eyes have it? In the 1985 mayoral election in Boise, Idaho, Mr. Potato Head received four write-in votes.

Potatoes Gone Bad

It has long bugged health militants that Mr. Potato Head smoked a pipe. "Not only is it dangerous to his health, it gives the message to kids around the country that smoking is not a bad thing to do," complained Surgeon General C. Everett Koop in 1987.

Finally, at age 35 Mr. Potato Head surrendered. So now, instead of the pipe, Mr. Potato Head comes with a hypodermic needle—just kidding, he is officially drug-free. Next, Mr. Potato Head goes organic?

• A shareware computer game called Mr. Potato Head spread a computer virus called "Peace" across the world. 20 copies of the purposely infected game were passed out at a Macintosh users' meeting, sufficient to infect thousands of computers worldwide.

Who You Calling "Potato Head"?

Louis Armstrong had a hit with "Potato Head Blues" back in the 1930s. Uncanny psychic premonition? No, Satchmo was using the phrase in its original meaning denoting somebody of low intelligence.

Mr. Potato Head was appointed "Official Spokespud" of the Great American Smokeout in 1987 after surrendering his pipe.

MONOPOLY

Monopoly is like baseball: each game seems to last forever, yielding five parts of boredom for each brief moment of excitement. Still, the game remains popular over the years, a testimony to how well its underlying message matches the national psyche.

What is the message of Monopoly? That people get rich by ruthless acquisition and selfishness. Interestingly, the message is such that you can get comfort no matter what your station: if you're already well-off, or striving to be, it helps justify heartlessness; if you're poor, it shows that you're better off than the wealthy who have no friends, no family, just competitors to beat and renters to exploit. Not surprisingly, the game became most popular during the Great Depression.

The long-term popularity of Monopoly is indisputable: witness the laughably anachronistic 1930s prices of property, intact in even the computer versions of the game. What is in question are the

origins and early history of Monopoly. First, the longtime legend:

Charles Darrow, an out-of-work heating engineer, invented the game during the Depression to amuse his

children. He borrowed the street names from Atlantic City, New Jersey, of which he had fond memories from trips in happier times. At first he was turned down by Parker Brothers, which identi-

fied 52 fatal flaws in the game which made it unsalable (concept too dull, rules too complicated, games went on too long, players circle around the board instead of heading for a defined destination, etc.). Later Darrow marketed it himself and it was such a hit that Parker Brothers reconsidered and the rest is history.

More recently, this legend has come to be discredited during a long and

bloody series of legal skirmishes between Parker Brothers and Ralph Anspach over Anspach's "Anti-Monopoly" game, and other stories have emerged.

A Chicago woman named Elizabeth Magie-Phillips invented a very similar game, although lacking houses and hotels, to illustrate Henry George's single tax principles in 1904. She called it "The Landlord Game." And there were at least eight widely separated groups which played Monopoly-like games before Darrow, including one at Harvard Law School and another at a utopian community in Arden, Delaware.

There's evidence Darrow learned the game from a group of Quakers in Atlantic City, possibly adding only Chance Cards and the Railroads as original contributions.

After Parker Brothers bought the game they bought up all known public domain copies they could find as well and spread the story of Darrow's "invention."

TITLE DEED
MEDITERRANEAN AVE.

RENT $2.

With 1 House	$ 10.
With 2 Houses	30.
With 3 Houses	90.
With 4 Houses	160.
With HOTEL $250.	

Mortgage Value $30.
Houses cost $50. each
Hotels, $50. plus 4 houses

If a player owns ALL the Lots of any Color-Group, the rent is Doubled on Unimproved Lots in that group.

If it weren't for the wild success of Monopoly, the Parker Brothers company wouldn't have survived the Depression.

Pass Go, Collect 200 Rubles

Monopoly is translated into twenty-three languages and marketed in eighty countries. In most international editions, currency and street names are taken from local equivalents. The Russian language edition, introduced in 1988 and featuring a Russian bear as one of the tokens, replaces Boardwalk with "Arbat" a pedestrian mall where Reagan and Gorbachev once walked. Here are some other examples:

Country, "Boardwalk," Currency:

- *United Kingdom*, Mayfair, Pound sterling
- *Germany*, Schlossallee, Deutsch mark
- *France*, Rue de la Paix, Franc
- *Spain*, Paseo del Prado, Peseta
- *Japan*, Ginza, American dollar (?!)

Foreign Language Monopoly. Russian (#15080), British (#16759), Spanish (#16761) or French (#16760). Each $3 + 4.95 shipping from Signals Catalog, 274 Fillmore Avenue East, St. Paul, MN 55107. (800) 669-9696.

Life Imitates Art

In 1974, Alfred Dunhill of London, the exclusive gift company, offered a special edition of Monopoly, featuring a gold-tooled leather board, 9K gold hotels, gold and silver tokens and "Georgian style" houses. Retail cost? £1675, or about $5,000. Nieman-Marcus offered an all-chocolate version of the game in the 1970s for $600.

Roll Dice, Collect Real Money

So you think you're pretty good at Monopoly? Parker Brothers sponsored a grueling set of local and national elimination tournaments leading up to the World Monopoly Championship, held every three years. The prize for being world champion? A top hat full of real money—$15,140 (the amount of play money that comes in a new Monopoly set).

For information write: Monopoly Tournament Director, Parker Brothers, 50 Dunham Road, Beverly, MA 01915.

You Can Never Go Home Again

Atlantic City, New Jersey. For the Monopoly fanatic thinking of visiting the idyllic streets which match their favorite Monopoly properties, we have one piece of advice: don't. Here's what you'll find, according to Nathan Cobb, a *Boston Globe* writer who made the pilgrimage a few years ago:

- You can't take a ride on the Reading. The only railroad left is Conrail, which doesn't take passengers.
- Advance to St. Charles Place? Wiped out by a casino parking lot.
- Of the 22 Monopoly streets which still exist, many are lined with buildings that are boarded up and run down (what do you expect with rents as low as $8?). One wine-guzzling derelict sitting on Oriental Avenue, when told it could be had for $100 on the Monopoly board, declared, "Damn, it ain't worth that much."
- Kentucky Avenue is a string of burger huts and seedy bars.
- Pacific Avenue is alive with hookers. New York Avenue is nearly as shabby.
- Marven Gardens, misspelled on the board, isn't even in Atlantic City; it's nearer to Margate, two towns to the west.
- There's no longer a Community Chest or the old Water Works. Free Parking is nearly impossible.

In 1972, a city official, mindful of the low-rent image presented by the Monopoly board, proposed changing the names of the real Baltic and Mediterranean Avenues to Fairmont and Melrose. An international storm of protest ensued.

TIME FOR MONOPOLY?

The official Monopoly watch. #17123, $26.95 + 4.95 shipping. Signals, 274 Fillmore Avenue East, St. Paul, MN 55107. (800) 669-9696.

Official World Monopoly Records

• *Longest game (substitution players allowed)* — 1,680 hours (70 days).

• *Longest game in moving elevator* — 384 hours (16 days).

• *Longest game in bathtub* (minimum 6 in. of water) — 99 hours.

• *Longest game played underwater* — 1200 hours (50 days). 1500 divers in wetsuits played in shifts.

• *Largest outdoor game* — 938 feet by 765 feet (larger than a city block, so players were informed of their moves by bicycle messengers equipped with walkie-talkies).

• *Smallest game* — 1 inch square (participants in the 30 hour game looked through magnifying glasses).

• *Longest "anti-gravitational" game* — 36 hours (played upside down on a ceiling).

The Monopoly Decade

"There is something peculiarly 1980s about Monopoly. It has an enduring and broad appeal—and not a little influence on the real world. This is evidenced by the lifestyles of the first generation of Monopoly devotees—the stock market players, the IRA and money market investors, and those who live from one credit card bill to the next. One assumes that the few who are satisfied with interest on savings accounts and who pay the bills on time did not bother to learn Monopoly's lessons about free enterprise and financial juggling..."

—Editorial, *Boston Globe*, 1985

Go Directly to...

Parker Brothers Headquarters. This is the place where they actually manufacture the game. Each year they print over $40 billion dollars worth of Monopoly currency on this site (this compares favorably with the $70 billion generated annually by the U.S. Bureau of Engraving and Printing). Right here they've also put over 3,200,000 little green houses into boxes.

Unfortunately, Parker Brothers stopped giving tours a few years ago, so Monopoly fans have to content themselves with loitering outside and wistfully pressing their faces against the windows.

190 Bridge Street, Salem, MA, (508) 927-7600.

Variations on a Theme

For most people there is just one Monopoly game, which is the standard-issue modern day plastic and cardboard variety. However, there are other choices, even for those unable to afford the $5000 version.

• **Deluxe Anniversary Edition.** Issued for Monopoly's Fiftieth Anniversary in 1985. Last time we looked, this was still on the toy shelves. It features special tokens and specially designed money and title trays.

• **Commemorative Edition.** Also issued in 1985, this is a replica of the original board game, with the 1935 tokens, wooden houses and hotels, and a square tin box.

Blind Ambition

Braille Edition Monopoly. Large type, raised ridges separating properties on the board, braille-embossed cards and money.

$52.00 + 6.00 shipping from the American Foundation for the Blind, Consumer Products, 15 West 16th St., New York, NY 10011 (212) 620-2171.

The squares most frequently landed on are Illinois Avenue, GO and the B & O Railroad.

Required Reading

The Monopoly Companion, **by Rich Uncle Pennybags as told to Philip Orbanes.** Rich Uncle Pennybags, the dapper Monopoly cartoon character logo, reveals all in this Parker Brothers sanctioned romp through Monopoly's history, rules and world championship tournaments. Filled with tips or winning strategies like:

• There are only 32 houses available with each game. If you have only low-rent sets, quickly build up 4 houses on each property to confront your opponents with a building shortage.

• Try to keep track of the order of Chance and Community Chest Cards played. The rules do not allow for shuffling when you've cycled through them, so the second time through you'll know what's coming up and when.

• Know when to stay in jail. Get out as soon as possible early in the game, but later when things get dangerous on the board, jail becomes a sanctuary.

$5.95 + 1.50 shipping from Bob Adams Publishing, Inc., 840 Summer St, Boston, MA 02127.

Monopoly on Computer

It isn't the same, playing Monopoly without the rattle of dice against the board, the feel of curled currency in hand. Still, if Monopoly must join the 21st Century transformed into a video game, this isn't a bad way to go. The computer acts as banker and automatically calculates the rent, mortgages and taxes. One to eight players can play against each other and/or against computer-generated opponents. The graphics are quite good and you even get a musical score as you play. Unfortunately, the cybernetic players don't embezzle, cheat, sulk, taunt, gloat, bicker, try to take advantage of younger players, throw tantrums, "accidentally" tip the board, or otherwise act like real players, thereby ruining a lot of the fun of the game.

$39.99 postpaid for Commodore, IBM and Atari. Virgin Mastertronic International, 18001 Cowan, Suite A, Irvine, CA 92714. (714) 833-8710.

Status Thimbles

Monopoly's Original Tokens in 1935:

• *Flat Iron*

• *Cannon*

• *Pocketbook*

• *Lantern*

• *Race Car*

• *Thimble* (with "For a Good Girl" engraved on it, later dropped)

• *Baby Shoe*

• *Top Hat*

• *Racehorse*

• *Battleship*

• The hotels, incidentally, were made of wood and had "GRAND HOTEL" written on each.

After England's 1967 "great train robbery," the hijackers played Monopoly with real money.

Marilyn Monroe

A Star Is Born

She was born Norma Jean Mortenson on June 1, 1926 in Los Angeles. Her mother, Gladys Pearl Baker, was a negative cutter in a Hollywood film studio and was not married to her child's father Edward Mortenson, a baker.

At age three, little Norma Jean was left in the home of her Aunt Grace when her mother entered a sanitarium. Several years later, her aunt dropped Norma off at the Los Angeles Orphanage where she was neglected and sexually abused. Four foster homes later, Norma Jean, age 16, rushed into marriage with an aircraft worker to avoid placement in yet another temporary home.

Discovered. While working at a defense plant, Marilyn was discovered by an Army photographer whose boss had told him "to take some morale-building shots of pretty girls for *Yank* and *Stars and Stripes*." The photographer's boss, a captain who spent World War II supervising such morale-building from a desk in Hollywood, was Ronald Reagan.

China Doll

You'll clean your limited edition, fine china collector's plate to get a look at Marilyn in *The Seven Year Itch.* 8 1/2 inches.

#3861, $24.75 + 2.89 shipping.
The Bradford Exchange
9333 Milwaukee Avenue
Niles Chicago, IL 60648
(800) 541-8811

Cheap Shots. In desperate financial straits, Marilyn Monroe agreed to pose for the now famous nude calender shots. Over a million of the photos were sold, making $750,000 in profits, from which Monroe received only her original modeling fee of $50.

Something Gives. After three husbands (including Joe DiMaggio and Arthur Miller), two miscarriages, one reported abortion, affairs with two Kennedys and 29 movies, Norma Jean Mortenson threw in the towel. Fired from Cukor's *Something's Got to Give,* she died of an overdose of barbiturates while listening to a Frank Sinatra record. Like every celebrity death, revisionism is rife — murder by the Kennedys? Assassination by Kennedy enemies to embarrass them? The theories are titillating — if only they were a little more plausible.

Monroeabilia

More than 30 years after her death, Marilyn Monroe is still big business. She remains, in the words of Norman Mailer, "every man's love affair with America" and many are prepared to pay dearly for Monroeabilia.

A letter from Marilyn Monroe to her guardian written on the day before she met her father for the first time sold for $11,000. Andy Warhol's "Red Marilyn" 1964 painting brought a record-breaking $4 million at auction in 1989. And recently, a black cotton polka-dot swimsuit worn by Monroe in 1954 went for $22,400.

Monroe Pilgrimage

The northwest corner of Lexington Avenue and East 52nd Street, New York City. On a chilly September night in 1954, a large crowd had gathered to watch the most notorious panty peek of the century — the shot of Marilyn Monroe's skirt rising sky high as the starlet stood over a subway vent for *The Seven Year Itch.*

Photos of the event were to become one of the best selling posters of all time.

According to friend Ultra Violet, Andy Warhol's goal was to be "the male Marilyn Monroe."

Join the Club

Marilyn Monroe International Fan Club. This 2,000 member club appreciates Monroe and exchanges Monroeabilia.

Send SASE for membership information. 836 Linden Avenue, Long Beach, CA 90813.

Sex Goddess or Grubby Nazi Zombie Dentist?

Although many of the American public adored, drooled on and dreamed of Marilyn Monroe, those who worked with her were less impressed. Anne Baxter described her as "a grubby sort of thing, very frightened." Clark Gable said that working with Monroe in *The Misfits* almost gave him a heart attack and that he had "never been happier when a film ended."

To Nunnally Johnson, conversing with Marilyn Monroe was something like talking to an "underwater zombie." And Tony Curtis, her co-star in the 1959 film, *Some Like it Hot!* said that smooching Marilyn Monroe was "like kissing Hitler."

Billy Wilder gave her somewhat better marks when he compared making a picture with Monroe to going to the dentist. "It was hell at the time," he said, "but after it was all over it was wonderful."

SOME LIKE IT

Turn Me On

How's this for a switch. Turn Marilyn on with this hand-painted, ceramic switch plate that fits all standard lights. A lovely thing to look at before you turn off the light at bedtime.

#1619, $17.00 + 3.50 shipping. Clay Art, 1320 Potrero Avenue, San Francisco, CA 94110. (800) 252-9555 / FAX (415) 285-3017.

Watch Her Shake

Hand-painted, hand-glazed salt and pepper shakers. Betcha didn't know Marilyn had holes in her head!

#H1618, $18.00 + 3.50 shipping from Clay Art (see above).

Take A Powder

Hand-painted, ceramic powder box is perfect for the makeup table. Or use it to store paperclips.

#H1604, $37.00 + 5.50 shipping from Clay Art (see above).

Life According to Norma Jean

On Intelligence
"A smart girl is one who knows how to play tennis, golf and piano — and dumb."

On Wearing Clothes
"I think I wanted them to see me naked because I was ashamed of the clothes I wore...What do I wear to bed? Why Chanel No. 5, of course."

On Promptness
"It makes something in me happy to be late.

People are waiting for me. People are eager to see me."

Metaphysical Attraction
"They'll pay you $10,000 for a kiss and 50 cents for your soul."

On Women
"Women exist for men. Any woman who tells you different is a liar."

These and other quotes from *Marilyn Monroe: In Her Own Words*, collected by Guus Luijters. $14.95 + 3.00 shipping from Music Sales Corporation, 225 Park Avenue South, New York, NY 10003. (212) 254-2100.

"I never understood it, this sex symbol — I always thought symbols were those things you clash together!"—Marilyn Monroe

Beautiful Bust

Marilyn at her beautiful best, dressed to kill in her famous subway scene dress from *The Seven Year Itch*. Hand-painted, ceramic bust.

#1501, $100.00 + 7.50 shipping from Clay Art, 1320 Potrero Avenue, San Francisco, CA 94110. (800) 252-9555 / FAX (415) 285-3017.

Marilyn Merlot

You've seen the movies and read the books. Now drink the wine! That's right. Marilyn Merlot is a wine, and a pretty good one at that. Merlot has a deep red color, a velvety texture, and a sweet and herbal taste. It's a bit drier than a Cabernet Sauvignon and very drinkable when it's young. The 1985 vintage is from Napa Valley. The 1987 vintage is from France.

Look for it at your local wine outlet or contact Nova Partners, P.O. Box 1014, St. Helena, CA 94574. (707) 579-0357.

Lifesize Lovely

Never be lonely again. Sturdy die-cut image of Marilyn about to jump into the swim of things will stand for just about anything with attached easel. James Dean also available.

#4251M, $29.95 + 5.25 shipping from Enticements, PO Box 4040, New Rochelle, NY 10802-4020.(800) 243-4300 / FAX (800) 244-4591.

Paper Mates

A lot has been penned about the romantic interludes between Marilyn and President John F. Kennedy. Now you can create scenes of your own by mixing and matching from these paper doll sets. Just don't let the Jackie doll find out!

• *Marilyn Monroe Paper Dolls* by Tom Tierney includes 31 full-color designs on heavy stock. Comes with costumes from *The Asphalt Jungle*, *Gentleman Prefer Blondes* and 22 other films. One doll with 16 color plates. #23769-9 Pa. $3.95 + 3.50 shipping (see below).

• *John F. Kennedy and His Family Paper Dolls* by Tom Tierney. Set includes six dolls (including kids) and 34 authentic costumes both formal and casual. #26331-2 Pa. $3.95 + 3.50 shipping. Dover Publications, 31 E. 2nd St., Mineola, N.Y. 11501-3582.

Required Reading

The Complete Films of Marilyn Monroe by Mark Ricci & Michael Conway. A complete retrospective of Marilyn's movie career.

#5-1016-1, $12.95 + 2.00 shipping from Citadel Film Books, 120 Enterprise Avenue, Secaucus, N.J. 07094. (800) 477-BOOK.

Marilyn left much of her estate to her acting coach.

A Horror Story

What? No blood? Today's young horror hounds probably think that the subtler horror films of the '30s and '40s are pretty boring. They find the ultra-graphic images and special effects that surround their heroes Freddy Krueger, Leatherface, Jason and Michael Meyers much more appealing. Fanatical fans of Frankenstein, Dracula and the Wolf Man, on the other hand, are apt to show a lot of disdain for the special effects that dominate the genre today.

True, motion picture techniques have changed in the eighty or so years since movies were invented. So too have the audiences. But the studios haven't. They're still out to capture the largest audience they can. After all, it means bucks. And if film-goers want gore, Hollywood is not going to disappoint. In fact, it seems that today's filmmakers spend more money on make-up than they do on the script.

It's to television that the original movie monsters of the '30s and '40s owe a huge debt. In 1957, Universal Pictures put their long dead and buried monster films into TV where a whole new generation discovered them, late at night on the local station's creature feature, most often hosted by a badly made-up, waggish weatherman. If you were a smart marketer in the '60s, you manufactured a monster product with the hopes of creating a monster profit, knowing that when kids see something on TV, they immediately want one.

The renewed interest in those old horror pictures became directly responsible for the success of today's grizzly epics, because it's mostly the kids who were watching TV in the '60s who are producing and directing them now. You can see where they've borrowed many of the basic ideas that were first created in the '30s and '40s.

Only Have Eyes for You!

Keep your eye on your keys with this key ring attached to an authentic, hand-painted, very realistic eyeball—the same kind that special effects wizards use.

- **Motion Picture Eye (blue or brown)**, $30.00
- **Eye with Blood Vessels (blue, brown or green)**, $17.00
- **Fire Eye (red), $30.00**

Add $4.50 shipping, Starlog Press, 475 Park Avenue South, New York, NY 10016.

Three Ways to Kill a Vampire

1) Expose him to sunlight.

2) Throw a bucket of holy water on him a la the Wicked Witch in the *Wizard of Oz*. It acts like acid.

3) It's not enough to drive a stake through his heart, you also have to chop off his head and stuff garlic in his mouth.

Favorite Fright Flicks of the '30s and '40s

- *Dracula* (1931)
- *Frankenstein* (1931)
- *Dr. Jekyll and Mr. Hyde* (1931)
- *King Kong* (1933)
- *Bride of Frankenstein* (1935)
- *Dracula's Daughter* (1936)
- *Son of Frankenstein* (1939)
- *The Wolf Man* (1941)
- *Cat People* (1942)
- *Son of Dracula* (1943)
- *Phantom of the Opera* (1943)
- *Frankenstein Meets the Wolf Man* (1943)

"You can't kill me...because I am already dead." —Barnabas Collins, *Dark Shadows*

Timeline Of Terror

In the beginning most of the good horror flicks came to us from places like Germany—most notably *The Cabinet of Dr. Caligari* and *Nosferatu*.

The first King Of Fright was Lon Chaney—the "Man of 1000 Faces"—who gave us the Hunchback of Notre Dame and the Phantom of the Opera.

In 1930, when Universal bought the screen rights to Bram Stoker's *Dracula* for $40,000, it was already a hit play in London and New York. Chaney was slated for the role of the vampire but he wasn't available due to a death in the family—his own.

So a hammy Hungarian who starred in the stage production was brought in. *Dracula* was released in 1931 and Bela Lugosi became a star.

Today, if a movie is a hit it spawns a sequel. In the 1930s, Universal did make more *Dracula* films but not immediately. To cash in on the success of *Dracula*, they stayed in the horror genre and created *Frankenstein*.

Lugosi was supposed to be the Monster in this movie version of Mary Shelley's 1816 novel. But he was a star now and was unwilling to play a role where he didn't speak. And, since he was fond of his new-found fame, he didn't relish having to wear so much makeup that people wouldn't recognize him. So the part went to unknown actor William Henry Pratt—also known as Boris Karloff.

Karloff's acting ability brought both horror and sympathy to the Monster. Sure, he was scary looking. But Karloff made us actually "feel" for the Monster. *Frankenstein* became an even bigger hit than *Dracula*.

Paramount rushed *Dr. Jekyll and Mr Hyde* to the screen and the monster movie race was on. Every studio tried to out-shock each other. Eventually RKO got in on the fad, creating numerous pictures that added another dimension to the horror format. Due to smaller budgets, RKO's entries required the audience to use its imagination more often than other thrillers of the era. *King Kong* was an exception, costing $650,000 to make, an incredible amount of money for a film of the 1930s, but it was worth it because the big ape saved RKO from bankruptcy.

The content of horror movies came to a head when, in Great Britain, they began designating films with "H" ratings (much like today's "X") if they were deemed too terrifying. But once an audience's blood appetite was whetted, it had to be satisfied. And in 1938, the second wave of the horror craze was on the roll again. In 1941, Lon Chaney, Jr. skulked out from his father's shadow as the star of *The Wolf Man*.

As World War II drew to a close, horror in the cinema died a quick death. Writer (*The Wolf Man*) and director (*Bride of the Gorilla*) Curt Siodmak theorizes that it was the need for escapism that allowed the movies to flourish during the war and, once over, weren't necessary. Others think that it was because Hollywood had over-saturated the audience with too many poorly made films. Still others think the writers and directors simply ran out of gas and had exhausted all the possibilities at hand. Whatever the reason, by the time Abbott & Costello met Frankenstein, the monsters were only good for laughs, not terror.

"Whoever fights monsters should see to it that in the process he does not become a monster." —Nietzsche

PERFECTLY FRANKENSTEIN

The poet Percy Bysshe Shelley, his wife, Mary, Lord Byron, and Dr. John Polidori were sitting around one stormy night in Switzerland reading ghost stories when they decided that it would be fun if each wrote one of their own for reading at their next gathering.

Mary came up with one about a scientist who created life in a laboratory. It was so good she decided to extend it to book length. Mary's monster was named Monster; Frankenstein, first name Victor, was the Genevan university student who had figured out a way to "bestow animation upon lifeless matter."

The first film to feature the *Frankenstein* story

was an Edison silent released in 1910 starring Charles Ogle as the Monster. But it was the "Big Three" who gave popular life to the Monster in the 1930s and '40s: Boris Karloff, Lon Chaney, Jr. and eventually Bela Lugosi. Glenn Strange also played the role in several sequels and a host of other actors followed in his very large footsteps.

The Hollywood movie, like most, took tremendous liberties with the book—even changing Victor's name to Henry. But, to Hollywood's credit, the Monster still comes off, like in the book, as a well-meaning though clumsy creature who is misunderstood and more pitiful than feared.

Read All About It

- *Dracula* by Bram Stoker and *Frankenstein* by Mary Shelley. Read the original Gothic stories back to back in this single volume...but not when you're home alone!

  #1572866, $7.95 + 4.00 shipping from Barnes & Noble, 126 Fifth Avenue, New York, NY 10011-5666. (201) 767-7079.

- *The Frankenstein Catalog* by Donald F. Glut. You can bet there's a glut of products out there featuring Frank. The subtitle on this comprehensive catalog is: "Being a Comprehensive Listing of Novels, Translations, Adaptations, Stories, Critical Works, Popular Articles, Series, Fumetti, Verse, Stage Plays, Films, Cartoons, Puppetry, Radio & Television Programs, Comics, Satire & Humor, Spoken & Musical Recordings, Tapes, and Sheet Music Featuring Frankenstein's Monster and/or Descended from Mary Shelley's novel." That about says it.

  #0984 (540 page hardcover), $45.00 + 2.00 shipping. AMOK, P.O. Box 861867, Terminal Annex, Los Angeles, CA 90086-1867. (213) 665-0956.

No White Jacket Required

Mad Scientist Monster Lab. A Graveyard Smash! Now you too can say, "I've created a monster!" Assemble the skeleton bones of your monster, then smear them all over with sickly-looking liquid green monster flesh, choosing your favorite ears, claws, fangs...the works.

When you're done, you can sizzle the flesh off your Monster's bones. Great fun for twisted little minds, ages 7 and older.

Is there any irony in the fact that this has been safety tested?

#M503, $24.95 + 4.00 shipping. Archie McPhee, P.O. Box 30852, Seattle, WA 98103. (206) 547-2467 / FAX (206) 547-6319.

Picture This...Your Favorite Horror Scene!

Charlie and Bob Smith began collecting movie posters, lobby cards and stills way back in 1910. Send your want list (up to ten titles) plus a SASE and they'll check their files and make a high quality, glossy photographic print. TV titles available, too.

8 x 10", $3.00; 11 x 14", $6.00. Contact Film Favorites, P.O. Box 133, Canton, OK 73234. (405) 886-3358.

Scripts To Scare You Stiff

Original shooting scripts and more! Production notes, interviews, behind-the-scene looks at some of your favorites, including *Dracula, Frankenstein Meets the Wolf Man, The Ghost of Frankenstein* and a hearse-load of others. Includes complete pressbook, too.

Each $19.95 + 3.00 shipping from MagicImage Filmbooks, 740 S. Sixth Avenue, Absecon, NJ 08201. (609) 652-6500.

As Frankenstein, Boris Karloff wore 62 pounds of makeup and costume, and size 24 boots.

Dinner? Uh, Thanks, Vlad, But, Uh, Something Came Up

Dracula: Prince of Many Faces, by Radu R. Florescu and Raymond T. McNally. Forget Hollywood. You want to know about the real person Dracula was modeled after? He was a helluva lot scarier than those depicted in the Lugosi pictures. Nicknamed Vlad the Impaler, because he regularly skewered people on spiked poles and kept them hanging around his castle. Oh yeah, and he skinned and boiled people alive, and even forced mothers to eat their own children roasted.

Vlad was a hero in Romania for driving out the Turks. During battles he was so reckless and brave that he won the designation "dracula" ("the dragon" or "the devil"). But he had a dark side. Once he invited his servants over for Christmas dinner and proceeded to burn them all to death because he thought they were insufficiently grateful. Another time he hosted a feast for a visiting dignitary. When the honored guest complained about the stench created by all those people suspended from poles, guess who was also impaled—but on a taller pole so he would be above the smell? This is one great source book for the historically minded who also like a little raw meat.

#1698489, $10.95 + 4.00 shipping from Barnes & Noble, 126 Fifth Avenue, New York, NY 10011-5666. (201) 767-7079.

Hit the Road, Drac

He's neither living nor dead and has been around since the beginning of time. And boy does he get around. You'll find vampire stories in all civilizations and in every country throughout the world. You'll even find your cereal aisle shelves vamped with sweet Count Chocula.

There have been hundreds of vampires in literature. It's believed that Dr. John Polidori came up with his version, *The Vampyre*, with the Shelleys and Lord Byron back in Switzerland. Another version of the vampire legend, *Varney the Vampire*, was authored by Thomas Prest in 1847.

But it was Bram Stoker's truly horrific and atmospheric *Dracula*, published in 1897, that Universal bought in 1930. Stoker based his vampire not only on Polidori's Lord Ruthven and Prest's evil-doer but on historical sources as well.

For the past fifty years, Dracula has been pretty much stereotyped to look and act like Bela Lugosi. He's a wealthy, suave Count with a charming, hypnotic personality who always dresses in a tux with a cape and lives in a cobwebbed, crumbling castle in Transylvania. And he must drink blood! Some of the historic legends of the vampires vary somewhat from this image. Recently, in fact, science has theorized that vampirism may even be an actual mental disorder or even a rare disease.

Dish The Dirt With Dracula

Dracula Soil Pendant contains authentic dirt from the Transylvania castle of Vlad the Impaler! Comes in a coffin shaped pendant with a cheap gold chain.

$9.95 + 4.00 shipping from Fantaco, 21 Central Avenue, Albany, NY 12210-1391. (518) 463-3667.

Not A Blood Bank

Put a coin in Drac's backpack and he'll climb the ladder to claim his victim. The ladder tips and the coin disappears into the tree. Drac's victim is saved and so is the coin!

#2174, $6.98 + 2.70 shipping. Johnson Smith Co., 4514 19th St. Court East, P.O. Box 25500, Bradenton, FL 34206-5500. (813) 747-2356 / FAX (813) 746-7896.

When Bela Lugosi died, he was actually buried in the cape he wore as Dracula.

The '50s: Monsters Turn Ugly

Something changed with the advent of the atom bomb. The sympathetic monsters from the '30s and '40s were born out of literature and folklore and in most cases weren't willing participants to the horror they struck in the minds and hearts of humankind. They were victims themselves. Frankenstein didn't ask to be reborn. The Wolf Man didn't ask to be cursed. And when the monsters from the '30s and '40s killed their victims, for the most part they did it out of ignorance or self-protection.

The horror films of the '50s, however, were different. This time around, the films were more shocking and more graphic than ever before, predecessors to the splatter films to come.

Out of the rubble of the atomic age (duck 'n' cover, kids) came creatures like *The Creature, Godzilla, The Tarantula, The Fly, The Thing,* and the unforgettable *Them*—nameless, and sometimes faceless, monsters that were as much science fiction as fantasy. They were mutants, often because of radiation. And, on top of everything else, they were hideous, oversized, angry...and out for blood, more often than not a metaphor for the Communist Menace.

F ifties Facts

• The opening minutes of the 1975 film, *Jaws,* is almost an exact copy (even the music) of the scene in which the Creature From The Black Lagoon follows Kay in the aquarium tank at the oceanic institute.

• Even though the *Creature* was filmed in black and white, the monster's costume came in two different colors. Green for the land scenes, yellow for the underwater scenes (it photographed better against dark backgrounds).

• Before **James Clavell** turned his attention to Japanese warlords in the novel *Shogun,* he wrote the screenplay for *The Fly.*

• **Raymond Burr** was in the movie Godzilla, but only when in America. His scenes were added to the original movie for its American release two years after its premiere in Japan.

The Fifties' Finest Fearsome Favorites

Godzilla (1956)

• *Them (1954)*

• *The Fly (1958)*

• *The Thing (From Another World) (1951)*

• *The Creature From The Black Lagoon (1954)*

• *The Tarantula (1955)*

• *Curse of the Demon (1958)*

• *Horror of Dracula (1958)*

Books of the Dead

• *Horrors* by Drake Douglas. Acclaimed as the definitive work on the history of horror movies and their creators. An in-depth look at the literature and folklore that sparked Hollywood's romanticized horror heroes since the early thirties. Also includes profiles of writers like Machen, Lovecraft and Poe. Over 75 vintage film stills, too!

$22.50 hardcover + 2.95 shipping. The Overlook Press, RR #1, Box 496, Woodstock, NY 12498. (914) 679-6838.

• *Classics of The Horror Film* by **William K. Everson.** Takes the reader from the "days of the silent film to the Exorcist." Highlights the historic backgrounds of the stories, and the stars that scared us out of our wits. Interesting backstage tidbits and over 250 still photos.

$15.95 + 2.00 shipping. Starlog Press, 475 Park Avenue South, New York, NY 10016. (212) 869-2830.

• *The Encyclopedia of Monsters* by **Jeff Rovin.** One of the best organized, most fun sources on the subject. For some reason Dracula and Phantom of the Opera are left out, but otherwise, this book will give you all the fiend facts you need.

$19.95 postpaid. Facts On File, 460 Park Avenue, New York, NY 10016. (800) 322-8755 / FAX (800) 678-3633.

Scenes cut out of the original *King Kong:* a native gets squished flat, and Kong "peels" Fay Wray from her clothes like a banana.

Creature Charisma

• *Creature From The Black Lagoon*— Said to be modeled after the Oscar statue given at the Academy Awards, the Gill Man, as he was affectionately called, was six feet, three inches tall and was covered with green scales. Shot in 3D, the creature was played by two different actors: Number one if by land, two if by sea.

• *Godzilla*—He was a 400 foot tall, fire-breathing prehistoric amphibian awakened by H-bomb testing in the Pacific Ocean. Angry, he flattened everything he stepped on and scorched everything else with his radiation-loaded breath.

• *The Fly*—Andre´ Delambre tinkered around a tad too much with his teleporter and turned himself into a tiny housefly with a human head. The best scene comes at the end of the movie when Andre´ the Fly Guy gets trapped in a spider's web and cries, "Help meeeeee!"

• *Mothra*—Mothra wreaked havoc first as a 200 foot long caterpillar, then as a moth with a wingspan of between 400 and 800 feet. Its menacing mission in life was to reclaim a pair of foot-tall priestesses from kidnappers.

• *The Blob*—It slithered, it slinked, it oozed, it ate everything in sight. Steve McQueen figured out how to stop it.

• *Them*—The first of the giant mutated insects genre (8 ft. tall, 25 ft. long ants). It was in this film that Walt Disney spotted Fess Parker and turned him into Davy Crockett. Also featured in the film were James Arness (one year away from becoming Marshal Dillon) and Leonard Nimoy (before he was Vulcanized).

• *The Thing*—Featured 6 ft. 5 in. James Arness (*Gunsmoke*) wearing 4 in. lifts making him nearly 7 ft. tall. His on-screen appearance lasted a total of 3 minutes.

• *The Tarantula*—Giant Spider (60 ft. tall, 50 ft. wide).

• *It*—200 foot long octopus from *It Came from Beneath the Sea.*

This Godzilla model is almost 2 feet tall, fully assembled, painted, and comes with flexible limbs.

THREE AMIGOS!

3 windup, walking, sparking monsters, together at last. It's Godzilla joined by the Swampmonster (who bears a strong resemblance to the Creature from the Black Lagoon) and King Kong. Each stands 3" tall.

"Are You Just Roaring Glad to See Me, or...?"

Monster In My Pocket Game is a combination of strategy, chance and the monsters' beastly ability to survive.

"Now, now, Eddie, sensitive intelligent creatures such as we do not stomp on one another." —Herman Munster, *The Munsters.*

You'll Laugh to Death

Plan 9 From Outer Space. Possibly the worst movie ever made. Audiences love laughing at its ineptness. It featured Bela Lugosi, who died halfway through, so half his scenes are played by somebody a lot taller than him. Great fun! Count the mistakes!

"Mesmerizingly awful...actually improves with each viewing," says Leonard Maltin, and we agree.

Available on video (B&W, 78 mins.) #FHV 3908 B-V, $19.95 + 3.00 shipping from Dickens Videos By Mail, 5323-A Elkhorn Blvd., Sacramento, CA 95842. (800) 228-4246.

• *Plan 9 From Outer Space: The Original Uncensored Screenplay.* This book lets you see how bad it really was, and includes some equally awful bonus scenes that were never filmed. Once you've seen the film, relive these great scenes. How about this surrealistic exchange? "What happened, Jeff?" "I saw a flying saucer." "A saucer? You mean the kind from—up there?" "Yeah. Or its counterpart." Huh? Or this observation: "We are all interested in the future because that is where you and I are going to spend the rest of our lives..." Also available from the same source: *Plan 9 From Outer Space: the Graphic Novel* (comic art adaptation).

Script, $9.95 + 3.00 shipping; Graphic Novel, $4.95 + 1.50 shipping. Malibu Graphics, 5321 Sterling Center Dr., West Lake Village, CA 91361. (818) 889-9800.

They Walk Among Us!

• **Vampire Research Center.** Do vampires suck? Not according to Stephen Kaplan, a vampirologist and parapsychology teacher, who operates the center. He's dead serious about it, and estimates from questionnaire results that there are as many as 200 vampires living in the U.S. (20 in California alone) and perhaps 500 worldwide. They don't have fangs or turn into bats, but they do have a taste for blood. Other interesting vamp-facts: Many are monogamous, fearing the AIDS virus; all vampires look younger than their real age; most vampires are tall men with brown hair and blue eyes. Women vampires often have blond hair and green eyes. Of course, they all love Halloween! The V.R.C. maintains a speakers' bureau and a Vampire Hall of Fame.

You can become a VRC member by ordering a T-shirt, $7.95 + 3.50 shipping, or sweatshirt, $14.95 + 3.50 shipping, bearing the slogan "The World Famous Vampire Research Center," from Learning Source, Dept. VRC, 344 Cypress Road, Ocala, FL 32672. (904) 687-2202 / FAX (904) 687-4961.

Kaplan has also written a book titled *Vampires Are.*

#2744 Vampires Are, $6.95 + 2.00 shipping from AMOK, P.O. Box 861867, Terminal Annex, Los Angeles, CA 90086-1867. (213) 665-0956.

TERROR TIMES

• Both of these marvelous mags are great for appreciators of monster movies. The premier publications for today's fans of the fantastic.

Fangoria: $24.47 (10 issue subscription), $3.95 single issue

Gore Zone: $11.99 (4 issue subscription), $3.95 single issue

Both from Starlog Communications International, Inc., 475 Park Avenue South, New York, NY 10016. (212) 869-2830.

• *Filmfax: The Magazine of Unusual Film and Television.* Pretty much as the subtitle says. They cover the gambit, but they do such a great job that you might just become interested in something other than this deranged horror stuff you're obsessed with!

$25.00 (6 issue subscription) from Filmfax, P.O. Box 1900, Evanston, IL 60204. (708) 866-7155.

• *Psychotronic Video.* Psychotronic? They're those movies that are "traditionally ignored by or ridiculed by mainstream critics at the time of their release—horror, exploitation, action, science fiction and movies that used to play at drive-ins or inner-city grind houses." Contains reviews, interviews and assorted weirdness.

$20.00 (6 issues), $3.00 single issue from Michael J. Weldon, 151 First Avenue, New York, NY 10003. (212) 673-3823 / FAX (212) 925-6073.

"What a picture of domestic tranquility...hemlock on the hearth and my wife feeding the piranha." —Gomez Addams, *The Addams Family*

Monster Parodies on Video

• *Fearless Vampire Killers, Or, Pardon Me But Your Teeth Are In My Neck* (1967)—Splendid spoof finds Professor (Jack McGowran) and assistant (Roman Polanski) in Transylvania tracking vampires who ride coffin-shaped toboggans. Features the late Sharon Tate.

#VHS 950324, $19.95 + 4.95 shipping. Postings, P.O. Box 8001, Hilliard, OH 43026. (800) 262-6604 / FAX (614) 777-1470.

• *The Rocky Horror Picture Show.* (1973)—Starring Tim Curry, Susan Sarandon and Barry Bostwick.

—So bad it's fun. Cult classic introduces the viewer to a campy, comedic, kinky, rock 'n' roll mad-scientist turned transvestite who sings and dances! Best to see it at the cinema at midnight with lots of silly people, but the video is almost as good.

#VHS V08117, $89.95 + 4.95 shipping. Postings, P.O. Box 8001, Hilliard, OH 43026. (800) 262-6604 / FAX (614) 777-1470.

—*Rocky Horror Boxed Set.* Not a coffin but the definitive 15th anniversary celebration collection on CD. Features movie soundtrack, a disc of rarities including original movie trailer and out-take *Rocky* songs. Booklet, photos and other stuff.

#D00995 4-CD Set w/ Booklet, $39.95 + 4.95 shipping from Postings, P.O. Box 8001, Hilliard, OH 43026. (800) 262-6604 / FAX (614) 777-1470.

• *Young Frankenstein* (1974)—Mel Brooks' satirical and hysterical movie knocks every classic horror film convention. Not only a must-see, but a must-have.

#KV1103, $19.95 + 3.95 shipping. Blackhawk Films, 5959 Triumph St., Commerce, CA 90040-1688. (800) 826-2295.

Little Shop of Horrors (1960 & 1986)—"Feed Me!" Buy Me! 1986 musical remake of the 1960 Roger Corman classic that featured a very young Jack Nicholson. This one's got Rick Moranis and Steve Martin. (114 mins.)

#VHS 2775, $19.98 + 3.95 shipping from Waldenvideo, P.O. Box 305188, Nashville, TN 37230-5188. (800) 322-2000

Tapes of Classic Terror

• *The Horror Of It All.* **Jose Ferrer** narrates this very comprehensive overview of the horror genre. #BR9197.

• *Frankenstein - The restored version (B&W, 71 mins.),* #MC55004.

• *Dracula (B&W, 75 mins.),* #MC55003.

• *King Kong (B&W, 100 mins.),* #THE6010.

• *The Mummy (B&W, 72 mins.),* #MC80030.

Each video $19.95 + 3.95 shipping from Blackhawk Films, 5959 Triumph Street, Commerce, CA 90040-1688. (800) 826-2295.

MONSTER HITS

Elvira Presents Haunted Hits.
• *Monster Mash* by Bobby Pickett
• *Haunted House* by Jumping Jean Simmons
• *The Creature from the Black Lagoon* by Dave Edmonds
• *I Put a Spell on You* by Screamin' Jay Hawkins
• *Dead Man's Party* by Oingo Boingo
• *Addams Family Theme* by Vic Mizzy
• *The Purple People Eater* by Sheb Wooley

And many more. Available on LP, CD or cassette.

#R12P71492, LP, $14.98; #R42P71492, cassette, $14.98; or #R21S71492, CD, $13.48. Add 2.00 shipping. Rhino Records, 2225 Colorado Avenue, Santa Monica, CA 90404-3598. (800) 432-0020.

Attack of the Killer Tomatoes

The classic spoof of '50s horror films.

$19.98 + 4.20 shipping. Johnson Smith Co., 4514 19th St. Court East, P.O. Box 25500, Bradenton, FL 34206-5500. (813) 747-2356 / FAX (813) 746-7896.

Attack of the Killer Tomatillos

Mexican monsters were an integral part of the film industry of Mexico from the 1950s to the 1970s. All your dastardly demons from mythology show up and some of 'em even have a decidedly Aztec bent. English dubbed, so bad they're good, many quite entertaining.

For a list of videos, contact Discount Video Tapes, Inc., P.O. Box 7122, Burbank, CA 91510. (818) 843-3366 / FAX (818) 843-3821.

It took five hours each day to apply the yak hair that transformed Lon Chaney, Jr. into the Wolf Man.

GORILLA MY DREAMS

Run for your lives! It's a miniature King Kong. Only 8 inches high, but rubber, completely hollow and highly pliable.

#9387, $7.50 + 4.00 shipping from Archie McPhee, P.O. Box 30852, Seattle, WA 98103. (206) 547-2467 / FAX (206) 547-6319.

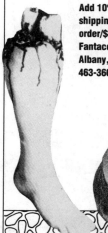

BODY SHOP

Many of your favorite body parts, in bloody splendor.

- *Liquid Latex Rubber "Skin Effects" 2 oz. (4071), $4.75*
- *Stage Blood. 16 oz. (DA34), $12.50*
- *Vampire Kit. Professional quality (DE40), $10.50*
- *#FA92 Nail In Face, $1.95.*
- *#FA76 Cut Off Finger, $2.50.*
- *#FA75 Cut Off Ear—great for Van Gogh wanna-bes or Blue Velvet fans, $5.50.*
  - *#FA13, Cut Off Arm, $17.00*
  - *#FA111 Cut Off Leg, $22.70*
  - *#VA04 Realistic Rotting Skull, $21.95*
    - *#VA114, Cut Off Head, $70.00*

Add 10% of total purchase for shipping ($20.00 minimum order/$4.00 minimum shipping). Fantaco, 21 Central Ave., Albany, NY 12210-1391. (518) 463-3667.

Change Your Image

Masks of high quality, comparable to those used in the movies. They totally cover the head and will allow you to terrorize your hamlet at will.

- *Werewolf, $95.00.*
- *Upside-Down Head, $55.00.*
- *Mr. Hyde, $65.00.*

Add 3.50 shipping. Death Studios, 431 Pine Lake Ave., LaPorte, IN 46350. (219) 362-4321.

Ya Big Ape!

King Kong tells the tale of 50 foot tall Kong, taken from his jungle home to New York by a movie producer who puts him on display as "The Eighth Wonder of the World." Obviously camera shy, Kong breaks his chains when photographers take flash pictures of him on opening night and he takes to the streets looking for Ann (Fay Wray), his little woman.

After leveling several buildings, he finds Ann, a lady with a big monkey on her back, and carries her away to the top of the Empire State building where he finally realizes that, even though he's the proverbial 20-ton ape sitting on the tallest building on earth, people still don't look up to him.

Resigned to the fact that he's only the king of the jungle and not New York (he couldn't make it there which means he couldn't make it anywhere), he puts Ann down and commits suicide by jumping to his death. A cop standing over the dead Kong thinks that the airplanes got him but movie producer Carl Denham knows the truth, "Oh no. It was beauty killed the beast."

Trade You a Kong For a Fly

These trading cards feature the greatest horror flicks of all time.

#6-NT88-08, 90 Card Set, $19.95 + 3.50 shipping from Pacific Trading Cards, 18424 Highway 99, Lynnwood, WA 98037. (800) 551-2002.

Guess What's Coming To Dinner

Spice up your meals with King Kong (with airplane in hand) salt and pepper set.

#2632, $13.98 + 3.50 shipping. The Lighter Side, 4514 19th St. Court East, P.O. Box 25600, Bradenton, FL 34206-5600. (813) 747-2356 / FAX (813) 746-7896.

The King Kong you saw climbing the Empire State Building was only 18 inches tall.

TV Terror and Takeoffs

• *The Night Stalker* (1971)—A plausible script, about a vampire that terrorizes Las Vegas, and Darren McGavin make this one of TV's few good serious efforts.

• *It* (1991)—Another good serious flick from a story by Stephen King. Would have been better if two hours of hugging was edited out so it could be shown on one evening instead of two.

• *SCTV's Count Floyd*—Nobody has done a better spoof of local late night creature features than Joe Flaherty's host of *Monster Chiller Horror Theater*. Oooo, scary kids!

• *The Addams Family*—TV's most fiendish, but fun family was headed by Gomez and Morticia. Then there was Cousin It, Pugsley, Wednesday (who never smiled,) Kitty Kat (the lion) and, of course, Thing. The best TV horror spoof, based on Charles Addams' cartoons from *The New Yorker* magazine. The full-length movie stars Anjelica Houston as Morticia and Raoul Julia as Gomez.

• *The Munsters*—An immensely popular take-off about Herman Munster (a funeral director for Gateman, Goodbury and Graves) his frightful family (including Lily, Grandpa, Eddie, and the "abnormal" niece Marilyn) plus pet dragon Spot, all of whom resided at 1313 Mockingbird Lane.

—You probably didn't know that there were three pilots to this silly show. This is the first one that aired, with half the cast made up of different actors (31 minutes).

$19.95 + 3.00 shipping. Dennis Atkinson, P.O. Box 25, Frankenmuth, MI 48734. (517) 652-9699.

—*The Munsters: Television's First Family of Fright* by Stephen Cox. More than 170 never-before-seen photos of the Munster family, plus interviews with cast members and backstage anecdotes.

#1781, $9.95 + 2.00 shipping from AMOK, P.O. Box 861867, Terminal Annex, Los Angeles, CA 90086-1867. (213) 665-0956.

Dark Shadows
Volumes 1-44

Frightened of Frid? Think Hall is horrible? Watch the 175+ year old vampire continue his reign of repulsive vampire villainy. Each 4 tape set offers 16 episodes of the daytime soap. Buy them all and get 24 hours of suspense and terror.

#VHS-5217 is the first set—call for information on the next 11 sets in the sequence. Each is $79.98 + 3.95 shipping. WaldenVideo By Mail, Dept. 678, P.O. Box 305188, Nashville, TN 37230-5188. (800) 322-2000.

RICH THING

It's creepy and it's kooky, mysterious and spooky, it's Thing from TV's *Addams Family*. Rock a coin right into the slot and the box begins to shake. Suddenly the lid raises and Thing reaches out ever so slowly and before you know it, he snatches the coin and the lid snaps shut.

#14208, $14.95 + 2.75 shipping from Wireless, P.O. Box 64422, St. Paul, MN 55164-0422. (800) 669-9999.

Dismembership Organization

The Munsters/Addams Family **Fan Club.** Send SASE to M/AFFC, c/o Louis Wendruck, P.O. Box 69A04, West Hollywood, CA 90069.

Dark Shadows
Collector Newsletter

Memorabilia and more about this, TV's only vampire soap opera.

Contact Steven Hall, 11634 Sagepark Lane, Houston, TX 77089.

Shadow Stuff

• *Dark Shadows Tribute* by Edward Gross and James Van Hise. Scared of your own shadow? Gruesome guide to the shocking *Shadows* shows. Photos, interviews and synopses of all 600 daytime soap shows.

#044692, $14.95 + 4.95 shipping from Postings, P.O. Box 8001, Hilliard, OH 43026. (800) 262-6604 / FAX (614) 777-1470.

MOTORCYCLES

Born to be Wild

Can you really tell how happy motorcyclists are by counting the bugs in their teeth? We don't know, but there are plenty of bikers who say the best they ever feel is when they're riding: the wind blowing against your face, the motor throbbing beneath you, the road skidding beneath you.

Most motorcyclists view themselves as an oppressed minority with an unjustified bad rep. They say they're

not reckless outlaws in search of cheap thrills, but decent, law-abiding folks who just like to ride. They say that automobile drivers routinely give them too little clearance, turn left in front of them, and generally ignore their presence—this behavior (at best) enrages them, and (at worst) sometimes sends them to the hospital or an early grave.

A Kickstart History of Motorcycling

In 1885, Gottlieb Daimler of Kannstatt, Germany developed the first known motorized two-wheeler. Ten years later, the brothers Hildebrand and Alois Wolfmuller started building motorcycles for sale to the public.

In Milwaukee a few years later ,William S. Harley, age 21, and boyhood chum Arthur Davidson

attached a small engine to a bike. They liked it, built three more in 1903, and incorporated as a company in 1909. They must have done something right: of more than 150 American companies that subsequently came to produce motorcycles (with names like Ace, Excelsior, Henderson, Sunbeam, Humber, and Scott Flying Squirrel), only Harley-Davidson remains today.

The first "motordrome," a wooden oval race track with steep, banked turns, opened in Paterson, New Jersey in 1908. Many others followed in

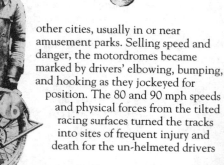

other cities, usually in or near amusement parks. Selling speed and danger, the motordromes became marked by drivers' elbowing, bumping, and hooking as they jockeyed for position. The 80 and 90 mph speeds and physical forces from the tilted racing surfaces turned the tracks into sites of frequent injury and death for the un-helmeted drivers

and unlucky onlookers. Great sport!

The madness of the "murder-dromes," as they came to be called, was eventually ended by governments. In the meantime, however, motorcyclists had earned a reputation for daredevil antics and unthinking enthusiasm.

In 1912, kickstarters appear for the first time. Before that, motorcyclists push-started their machines, popping the clutch and jumping on.

Soichiro Honda produced his first true motorcycle, a small 90cc B-type, in 1948. In post-war Japan it took over a decade before Hondas were exported to America. They were initially sold as a safe, non-threatening, non-"biker"

little bike for students and young professionals, using pictures of wholesome looking people with the slogan, "You meet the nicest people on a Honda."

In 1989, sales of new motorcycles in America totaled 293,726 bikes. The leading manufacturers were Honda with 26% of the market, Yamaha 22%, and Harley 19%.

A 1000 cc Indian brand motorcycle first broke the 100 mph land speed barrier in 1921.

Black Leather Facts

- **Steve McQueen's** 102 motorcycles were appraised at $500,000 for the entire group, and brought in $852,250 when auctioned off in Las Vegas. The bikes seemed to have been touched by the magic of a man who grew up tough, was demoted seven times by the Marine Corps, and had loved to race fast motorcycles. One of them, a 1909 four-cylinder Pierce, fetched $25,000, apparently a record price for a single motorcycle.

- **Elvis**, Biker King? Presley may have looked like a biker, but he only wore black leather on stage once (during his 1968 NBC-TV comeback special) and once again for the cover photo shoot for the May, 1956 issue of Harley-Davidson magazine, *The Enthusiast*.

- In the fall of 1983, **Kermit the Frog** turned up in black leather on the cover of the *The Muppet Magazine*.

- Mandatory helmet laws? They continue to be highly controversial in the motorcycle community. According to the National Highway Traffic Safety Administration, on a per-mile basis, cyclists are 20 times as likely to be killed as auto drivers or passengers. The relative chances of injury are even higher (motorcyclists send more than their share to the hospital's "vegetable garden," the ward for people with bad head injuries). But the right to choose whether or not to wear a helmet is jealously guarded by some. Dennis Hoffman, a member of American Brothers Aimed Toward Education (ABATE), a group that has worked against helmet laws, says that the best way to stay out of the hospital is to know how to ride. "The only difference a helmet will make if going over 30 mph…is whether the person has an open casket or a closed one."

Headless Hogman

"Forget the helmet—I don't have a head." Bikers have several times reported seeing a ghostly headless hogman riding a 1940s motorcycle on a popular cycle route near Ojai, California. He appears to take great pleasure in joining them for a romp up and down Old Creek Road.

Now you can scare the hell out of the Hell's Angels by pretending to be him. Just don this Headless Cape costume, grab your wheels and head (no pun intended) for Ojai! If you really wanna have some fun, carry a cut-off head with you and toss it at terrified travelers.

"Motorcycle Poet"

"There's no other motorcycle that's as close to a horse. It's made the old way, a lot of history in it. It's rider-friendly in a way that's like a horse. It bucks. It stinks, it backfires… [Harleys] are built for riding the range. I feel like I can get up in the morning and whistle and my bike will come."

—Martin Jack Rosenblum

Rosenblum, a college administrator and obvious Harley enthusiast (he subscribed to the Harley-Davidson newsletter when he was in the third grade!), has published two books of motorcycle poems, after obtaining permission from Harley-Davidson to use the company name in the titles.

The second book, *The Holy Ranger: Harley-Davidson Poems*, is actually sold as Part #99310-89V in the Harley-Davidson parts and accessories catalog.

"Harley-Davidson is the only company that I know of where its customers are so loyal that some of them tattoo its logo on their body."
—**Jerry Wilke, V.P. of Sales and Marketing, Harley-Davidson**

MILWAUKEE 1987
MOTOR
HARLEY-DAVIDSON
CYCLES
HEAVY BEER
Wisconsin brewed in limited quantity using only the finest ingredients available to provide a most satisfying taste

Magazines

• *Harley Women*. More and more women are riding Hawgs. This new glossy publication is geared toward women who are moving from the back seat to the front. Offers articles on bike repair and maintenance. One of the few outlets that regularly publishes motorcycle poetry.

One year subscription $10.00 (6 issues, plus *HW* bumpersticker), from Asphalt Angels Publications, P.O. Box 374, Streamwood, IL 60107. (708) 888-2645.

• *Easyriders: Entertainment for Adult Bikers*. Articles on motorcycles old and new, plus features about races and other biker events should appeal to all ages and sexes, but the barebreasted beauties astride bikes are why they call this magazine adult entertainment.

One year subscription $24.95, single issue $3.95 from Box 553, Mt. Morris, IL 61054. (818) 889-8740.

Black Leather on the Big Screen

• *The Wild One* (1954). Directed by Laslo Benedek, starring Marlon Brando and Lee Marvin. This is THE original motorcycle film, and still a classic. Brando plays Johnny, the sullen leader of a motorcycle gang that terrorizes a small town. (The film was based on a real-life incident that happened in Hollister, California, in 1947.) Brando's supercharged performance created strong feelings about motorcyclists among the viewing public, and bikers blame the film for transforming the image of motorcyclists into a highly negative one and subjecting bikers forever after to all manner of social criticism.

Observant viewers will note that Brando didn't ride in on a Harley, but on a British-made Triumph Speed Twin. One of the movie's nicely written exchanges occurred when Kathy (played by actress Mary Murphy) asked Johnny, "What are you rebelling against?" Brando replied "Whadda ya got?"

• *Lawrence of Arabia* (1962). Directed by David Lean, starring a young Peter O'Toole as Lawrence. The opening minutes of the film feature a dramatic re-enactment of the motorcycle accident that killed T.E. Lawrence. The motorcycle's a British Brough Superior, considered the "Rolls Royce of motorbikes."

• *The Great Escape* (1963). Directed by John Sturges, starring Steve McQueen, James Garner, Richard Attenborough, and Charles Bronson. An all-around exciting World War II movie. The unforgettable motorcycle scene comes when Steve McQueen escapes from the German prison camp and tries to ride a bike to freedom.

• *Easy Rider* (1969). Directed by Dennis Hopper, starring himself, Peter Fonda, Karen Black, and Jack Nicholson. A motorcycle tale of the emerging counterculture in a film made for $370,000 that took in more than $40 million at the box office. Fonda and Hopper ride their choppers across America. Nicholson's role as a boozy ACLU lawyer made him a star.

Biker Songs

• Black Denim Trousers and Motorcycle Boots (1955)
— **The Cheers and Les Baxter Orchestra**
• Motorpsycho Nightmare (1964)
— **Bob Dylan**
• The Motorcycle Song (1967)
— **Arlo Guthrie**
• Born to Be Wild (1968)
— **Steppenwolf**
• Motorcycle Mama (1972)
— **Sailcat**
• Bad Motor Scooter (1973)
— **Montrose**

Cycle Stuff

American Motorcycles Poster. In 1987, the Smithsonian in Washington, D.C. presented "American Motorcycles and Motorcyclists, 1900-1940." This is the poster from the exhibit featuring five historic bikes including a 1902 Indian, a 1914 Harley racer, a 1918 Cleveland touring cycle, a 1923 Indian Chief with a Princess sidecar, and a 1937 world speed record bike used at Daytona.

$8.00 from Smithsonian Institution, National Museum of American History, Publications Office, Room BB53, Washington, DC 20560.

Parking Signs. Want to protect parking places for your Harley and those of your friends? These three signs, followed by your own brand of gentle enforcement, ought to do the job. The 12 x 18" signs are:

- *"Hawg Parking Only—All Others Will Be Crushed," black on orange*
- *"Harley Parking Only—All Others Will Be Crushed," black on white*
- *"Never Mind the Dog— Beware of Owner," black on white*

$3.95 each, or all three for $10.00. Add 4.95 shipping. Mr. B's Accessories, 12 Northfield Drive, Fort Salonga, NY 11768.

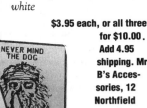

Tattoo You

Temporary Tattoos. Be part of the gang without pain or needles. Looks bright, lasts several days, and can be removed at any time with cold cream. Carry a few with you at all times, in case you find yourself drunk and alone in a strange city.

$2.00 to $25.00 each + 1.00 shipping, or $3.00 for sample and color brochure from Creative Alternatives, 2904 South Barnes, Springfield, MO 65804. (417) 887-8961.

Cycling Handbooks

- *Hell's Angels: Three Can Keep a Secret if Two Are Dead* by Yves Lavigne. "Hell's Angels go out of their way to appear like law-abiding citizens. The Manhattan chapter in New York City has a strict rule that when a car full of rival bikers or other enemies pulls up in front of the East Village clubhouse for a hit, you shoot everyone but the driver. He must be allowed to escape with the bodies so the Angels are not implicated in a shooting." There isn't much doubt that journalist-author Yves Lavigne does not consider the Hell's Angels a group of misunderstood folk heroes. According to Lavigne, the Hell's Angels are now one of the most powerful crime organizations in North America, rivaling even the Mafia, and they're trading in their switchblades and leather for Jaguars, Uzis, and pinstripe suits. Lavigne gives you a close-up look at the Angels and other motorcycle clubs like the Pagans, the Bandidos, and the Outlaws—with information on where they operate, how members make money, and what the chapter rules are. The book is full of crude language and graphic descriptions of grisly scenes—an account that's definitely not for the delicate.

$9.95 + 2.00 shipping from Lyle Stuart, 120 Enterprise Ave., Secaucus, NJ 07094. (201) 866-0490.

- *The Big Book of Harley-Davidson* by Thomas C. Bolfert.

This is a big book all right—nearly 500 pages packed with over 2,000 photos, hundreds in color. Every model through the year 1990, and reprints of ads and brochures. As much information as just about anybody would want.

$39.95 plus 4.50 shipping from Motorbooks International, P.O. Box 1, Osceola, WI 54020. (800) 826-6600.

"Bikers are the closest thing we have to the primitive warrior of ancient times."—Suzanne Forster

Organizations

• **Antique Motorcycle Club of America.** These folks who love old motorcycles have been organized since 1954, with about 4,000 members (comedian Jay Leno is a member). The focus is on both restored and unrestored antique motorcycles.

One year membership, $20.00 (includes *Antique Motorcycle* quarterly). AMC, Dick Winger, Membership Chairman, P.O. Box 333, Sweetser, IN 46987.

• **American Motorcycle Association.** The AMA lobbies in behalf of motorcyclists, monitoring laws and attending hearings, representing members in over 1,000 clubs throughout the country. Membership benefits include organized riding tours and events, motorcycle shows and a toll-free hotline that links you to over 8,000 riders and dealers who help other riders in distress.

One year membership, $20.00 (includes subscription to *American Motorcyclist*). AMA, 33 Collegeview Ave., P.O. Box 6114, Westerville, OH 43081. (800) AMA-JOIN.

Harley Wallet

#7328, $12.98 + 4.20 shipping. Johnson Smith Co., 4514 19th Court East, P.O. Box 25500, Bradenton, FL 34206-5500. (813) 747-2356.

Upscale Bikers

• **Rolex Warriors.** The motorcycle market is going upscale. This isn't too surprising, since most motorcycles cost in the $4,000 to $13,000 range. Most buyers are men who enjoy the life of the "weekend biker," when they get to put on their leather jackets and fingerless gloves and ride that machine. One observer wistfully recalled that bikers used to recognize each other on the road through a hand signal: a clenched fist raised in salute that meant power or solidarity or something. Now, bikers just put up their left hand and wave. Maybe in a few years the official biker salute will be an exchange of business cards.

KICKSTART YOUR VCR

Interested in spectacular footage of the Black Water '91 enduro race through the bayous, where the object is to become completely covered in slime? How about seeing the Daytona '91, or the entire '91 World-Wide Road Grand Prix racing series?

For a free catalog of these and other exciting motorcycling thrills on video, contact On 2 Wheels Entertainment, 31672 Pacific Coast Highway, S. Laguna Beach, CA 92677. (800) 688-6686.

Hog Horn

Shaped like the classic tear-shaped gas tank.

#99405-91V, $54.00 + 5.00 shipping from Harley-Davidson, P.O. Box 3044, Milwaukee, WI 53201-3044. (414) 935-4958.

Biker Bears

It's your choice! Biker Widow or Biker Chick.

Each $19.95 + 3.95 shipping from K.V., 19 E. Main St., Smithtown, NY 11787.

And Not Sidesaddle

"*I Am Woman. Hear Me Roar.*" From an ad in a motorcycle magazine, showing a woman on a Harley.

In 1960, only 1% of cycle owners were women. Now, female ownership is over 8%. No longer content to sit behind men as just passengers, more and more women are buying their own. Some join clubs with names like The Zodiac Angels, Leather Ladies, The Iron Maidens, Leather and Lace, and even the Dykes on Bikes.

> "*Sitting over a thumping engine is like the first time you feel your baby kick.*"
> —**Kathy Cat-Lou, mom and Harley Sportster rider**

Women are the fastest growing segment of the motorcycle market.

PILGRIMAGES

- **The Black Hills Motor Classic.** Held each year in early August, the Classic has been attracting bikers to the tiny town of Sturgis, South Dakota, for decades. Begun in the 1930s by the local dealer for Indian motorcycles (J.C. "Pappy" Hoel), it's become South Dakota's largest tourism event.

Everybody agrees that the 50th anniversary of the event, held in August, 1990, will be talked about for a long time. About 300,000 cyclists invaded Sturgis, which is normally home to only about 6,000 residents (in fact, normally the *whole state* has only about 600,000 residents). The bikers spent about $100 million in their week-long celebration, which may explain why the locals don't get too upset about it.

A lot of what bikers do at Sturgis is "profile," the motorcycle equivalent of cruising. There are also races, concerts, rodeos and

day-trip motorcycle tours of South Dakota and neighboring states. Hotels fill to capacity within 200 miles of Sturgis. Temporary campgrounds spring up over thousands of acres, but they fill up rapidly, too, so if you're thinking of going, make sure you make some arrangements beforehand.

Black Hills Motor Classic, P.O Box 504, Sturgis, SD 57765. (605) 347-2556.

- *Sturgis—Motorcycle Mecca* by **Martin Garfinkel**. Too busy or scared to make Sturgis this year? Get this picture book of celebrations past, a fascinating collection of black and white photographs of the biker subculture. Everything here is about what you'd expect, with all kinds of customized motorcycles and their riders—

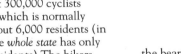

the bearded, the tattooed, tough-looking moms with babies, and even 80 year-olds who still think that a ride in the morning is the way to start the day.

$29.95 hardcover, $19.95 paper. Add 2.00 shipping. ZG Publishing, Box 670, Carbondale, CO 81623. (303) 963-3823.

- **The Harley Davidson Museum.** See the old and the new—when you visit the Harley-Davidson Museum in York, you can also tour the plant that produces new Harleys as well. Take the combination museum-and-plant tour at 10 a.m. or 2 p.m., Monday through Friday, or the museum tour alone at 12:30 each day. The museum features motorcycles and memorabilia from 1903 to present.

1425 Eden Road, York, PA 17402. (717) 848-1177, Ext. 5900. Free admission. No kids under 12. No cameras allowed.

Holy Rollers

Christian motorcycle clubs? Yup. Many are just guys who love both Jesus and Harleys, but some are folks who've seen the light and crossed over from a life on the dark side. The members of "Christ's Sons," a motorcycle ministry connected to Set Free by Christ, a church in Anaheim, California, think of themselves as "Heaven's Angels." One of the charter members referred to his life before he got involved with Christ's Sons: "Three or four felonies before noon was natural," he said. "It also meant I probably overslept." The largest group is the Christian Motorcyclists of America (CMA), which counts 33,000 members in more than 300 chapters in the U.S. and Canada.

"Our bikers are your average 9-to-5 guy, with the two kids at home and the picket fence, who loves his wife and country and rides his bike for Jesus."

—Russ Cooper, of the Christian Motorcyclists of America

MUSIC

Do-It-Yourself Music: Everybody is a Star

How do you get to Carnegie Hall? Practice, practice, practice. There is something within all of us that makes us want to be musical, which whispers despite all evidence to the contrary that we too could be a famous musician. From singing in the shower to the sing-alongs in the local bars, we play this impulse out, sometimes with tragic results.

Years ago all music was home-made music. There were no "professionals"— everyone who could played or sang a part when, somewhere in the dawn of time, people started to distinguish mere noisemaking from music.

The first musical instruments were sticks and bones played percussively for rhythm, but eventually the Egyptians came up with harps and flutes sometime before 4000 B.C. From these developed the myriad varieties of string and wind instruments we have today, and skill started becoming a prerequisite for playing.

The French horn was invented in the 1660s. The musical comedy in the 1710s. Moveable type was first used for musical notation in 1750 and the first how-to-play guitar manual in English was published shortly after, in 1758.

Not all musical inventions were unambiguously good things. Benjamin Franklin invented an improved harmonica in 1762, making it a practical but not necessarily desirable musical instrument for the first time. The concertina was patented in 1829, paving the way for Lawrence Welk and endless renditions of *Lady of Spain*. Steinway started making pianos in 1853, leading to kids banging endless versions of *Heart & Soul* and *Chopsticks*. Electric

Hammond organs became a home music craze in 1935, just in time for *The Beer Barrel Polka* in 1939. And then there was the electric guitar…

The 20th century, besides engendering the greatest emergence of new musical styles from ragtime to rock to rap, has also put a spin on traditional instruments with synthesizers, enabling novice musicians to sound as good or bad as what's on MTV.

Still, you have to admire the people who make music solely for their own pleasure. Unfortunately, these people are few—most, regrettably, try to share the pleasure with the rest of us. As Oscar Wilde so admirably put it: "Musical people always want one to be perfectly dumb at the very moment when one is longing to be absolutely deaf."

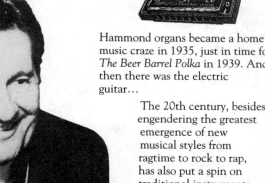

POP POETRY

- "Music is the magic that makes everything sunshiny."

  —Ira Gershwin, *I Can't Be Bothered Now*, 1937

- "The song is ended, but as the songwriter wrote, the melody lingers on."

  —Ira Gershwin, *They Can't Take That Away From Me*, 1937

- "Some like a bop type refrain… I'm sure that if I heard even one riff that would bore me terrifically too."

  —Cole Porter, *I Get a Kick Out of You*, 1934

- "You're a melody from a symphony by Strauss."

  —Cole Porter, *You're the Top*, 1934

- "Over the piano was printed a notice: 'Please do not shoot the pianist. He is doing his best'."

  —Oscar Wilde, *Impressions of America*

- "The Fiddle: An instrument to tickle human ears by friction of a horse's tail on the entrails of a cat."

  —Ambrose Bierce, *The Devil's Dictionary*

- "Music has charms to soothe a savage breast."

  —William Congreve

Buy It For a Song

• **Cheap Backup.** Pocket Songs are sound-alike versions of hundreds of hit musical arrangements on cassette tape. Side one contains a performance with band and singer to help you get your musical bearings. Turning down the right channel of your tape player will remove the vocals. Side two contains the same performance in stereo, but without the vocal track so you can fly solo! For just $12.98 per tune, only $22.98 for a complete Broadway show, you can sing the hits.

$1.00 for a catalog. Pocket Songs, P.O. Box 229, 50 South Buckhout Street, Irvington, NY 10533. (800) NOW-SING.

• **Cheap Backup With Amplifier.** Be a very loud life of the party with a portable "karaoke" machine—a handheld cassette player with microphone and built-in speaker. Added features let you hook it up to stereo speakers for a really big sound, and use such enhancements as echo and an electronic fade.

#1965 Starmaker, $79.95 + 7.95 shipping from The Music Stand, 1 Rockdale Plaza, Lebanon, NH 03766-1585. (802) 295-7044 / FAX (802) 295-5080.

Like a Balalaika...

The Music Maker is a solid-wood string instrument modeled on the traditional Russian balalaika, but new and improved because it's easier to play. Just slip one of the twelve music sheets included behind the strings and start strumming! Additional sheet music available for $4.95 a set.

#M102 Music Maker, $49.95 + 4.00 shipping from What on Earth, 25801 Richmond Road, Cleveland, OH 44146-1486. (216) 831-5588.

Old Fashioned Glove Songs

Tap your fingers and make music. Colorful electronic gloves give the effect of tickling the ivories without a keyboard! Each fingertip has a built-in piezo-electric chip that plays a distinct tone when depressed on a hard surface. Built-in speakers on the back of each glove transmit the tones. Included are an instructional booklet containing six children's songs and batteries.

#36847W Musical Gloves, $24.95 + 3.50 shipping from Hammacher Schlemmer, 9180 Le Saint Drive, Fairfield, OH 45014. (800) 543-3366.

Musical Notes Are Our Forte

• Some researchers think Top 40 tunes can be reliable economic indicators. They claim that when the public is buying sad songs over bouncy, upbeat melodies, the forecast for the nation's pocketbook is grim.

• *Yesterday*, the 1965 John Lennon-Paul McCartney tune, is the most-played song of the past 50 years, having been performed over 5 million times. *Never My Love*, written by Richard and Donald Addrisi, is the second most-played song.

• World record: Rory Blackwell once played an astonishing 314 instruments in 1 minute, 23.07 seconds in a single rendition on May 27, 1985 in Devon, England. He can play 24 instruments simultaneously in a single tune.

2,200,000 Americans play the accordion. Run for your life!

Escape the Humdrum...

Play a thumbdrum, an ancient African percussion instrument. Made from an "acoustic gourd" (as opposed to an electric gourd?), this easy-play instrument sounds like a marimba. Instructions included.

#M260 Thumbdrum, $39.95 + 4.00 shipping. What on Earth, 25801 Richmond Road, Cleveland, OH 44146-1486. (216) 831-5588.

Techniques for Tickling the Ivories

Learn how to play a melody during your first lesson with Richard Bradley's easy videotape teaching method.

• **Vol. 1**: Introduces the keyboard and reading music. (56 min.)

#DC001 $39.95 + 4.95 shipping.

• **Vol. 2**: Shows how to sight read, major and minor chords, improvisation techniques. (49 min.)

#DC002 $39.95 + 4.95 shipping.

• **Vol. 3**: Demonstrates advanced techniques and more. (59 min.)

#DC003 $39.95 + 4.95 shipping.

Buy all 3 VHS tapes and save $10.00. #DC100 $109.85 + 6.95 shipping. Special Interest Video, 100 Enterprise Place, P.O. Box 7022, Dover, DE 19903-7022. (800) 522-0502.

Harmonic Convergence

• *Country and Blues Harmonica for the Musically Hopeless* by Jon Gindick. Illustrated by Barry Geller. All it takes is two lips, a little wind and a whole lotta soul to transform your inner groove into recognizable harmonies.

This classic book is the best-selling "harmonica how-to" ever written, and it's good. It starts with the utter basics, like which side of the instrument to mouth. Our reviewer, a white bread & mayo type from the suburbs of the Midwest, was sounding like he'd come from the suburbs of the Mississippi Delta in just a few short lessons. Book is accompanied by instructional cassette and a Hohner harmonica. Play something soulful, and help save the wails.

$12.95 + 3.00 shipping for paperback, instructional cassette and Hohner harmonica from Klutz Press, 2121 Staunton Court, Palo Alto, CA 94306. (415) 857-0888.

Play *'S Not Unusual* or *Nobody Nose the Trouble I've Seen*

Playing a humanitone is as easy as blowing your nose, because it's a "snoot flute." You blow through your nose and move your mouth to change tones. Unless you have a cold, you can make music with every little breath you take.

#1281, $1.49 + 1.35 shipping from Johnson Smith Co., 4514 19th Court East, P.O. Box 25500, Bradenton, FL 34206-5500. (813) 747-2356 / FAX (813) 746-7896.

"Wagner's music is better than it sounds." —Bill Nye

"Music is the refuge of souls ulcerated by happiness."—E. M. Cioran

Music Between the Sheets

• *Sheet Music Magazine.* Sheet music is getting more expensive all the time, but with a year's subscription to *Sheet Music Magazine*, you can get music for about 25¢ a song, or what sheet music cost in 1910. Great way to build a pop music collection, from golden oldies to love ballads to Broadway show tunes. Available in three editions: Easy Play, Standard Piano/Guitar, and Organ.

One year subscription (6 issues) , $15.97 from Sheet Music Magazine, P.O. Box 58629, Boulder, CO 80322-8629.

• **Bagaduce Music Lending Library.** With over half a million pieces of vocal, choral, instrumental and keyboard sheet music valued at $1.6 million, the Bagaduce collection is a one-of-a-kind resource for scholars seeking rare old works and for music groups seeking multiple copies for performances. Membership and a modest rental fee required for borrowing from the library. Surplus sheet music is also for sale.

One year membership $5.00 from Bagaduce Music Lending Library, Greene's Hill, Blue Hill, ME 04614.

Sheet Music Clubs

Collect, trade and treasure sheet music? Send SASE for membership information.

• **Remember That Song Club, 5623 North 64th Avenue, Glendale, AZ 85301.**

• **National Sheet Music Society, 1597 Fairpark Avenue, Los Angeles, CA 90041.**

Bagpipes & Stuff

• **Andy's Front Hall.** This traditional and acoustic music store is a terrific mail source for song books, recordings, instructional videos and instruments like banjos, bagpipes and dulcimers.

Free catalog. Andy's Front Hall, P.O. Box 307, Voorheesville, NY 12186. (800) 759-1775.

• **The Music Stand** offers great gifts inspired by the performing arts from piano keys on clothes to music boxes and salt & pepper shakers. Great stuff, whether you're a music lover or not.

Free catalog. The Music Stand, 1 Rockdale Plaza, Lebanon, NH 03766-1585. (802) 295-7044 / FAX (802) 295-5080.

Read the Dots

The Basic Guide To How To Read Music by Helen Cooper. Make your minor musical knowledge major. Learn the principles of reading music (it's easier than you think). Also covers pitch, rhythm, and other aspects of theory.

#DG19, $7.95 + variable shipping. Publisher's Choice, P.O. Box 4263, Huntington Station, NY 11746-9273. (800) 282-8086.

New Age

Age of Aquarius

The New Age may have first dawned at the fringes of the continent, but now it shines squarely on the heartland, thanks to the proliferation of small innovative publishers, tabloid-TV and even the funny pages, where cartoonist Garry Trudeau has spoofed the spirit-possession industry with his character Boopsie, Hollywood ingenue and channeler of the entity Hunk-Ra.

The 1960s brought many controversial topics to the public's awareness, including civil rights, sexual liberation and the notion of expanded consciousness through chemical and non-chemical means. It also brought the reemergence of beliefs and superstitions that many people thought had been laid to rest in the time of Copernicus or Voltaire.

While many New Agers do rely on astrology and channeled spirit guides to help them navigate our complex world, not all do, nor does everyone's Auntie who follows the stars consider herself a proponent of the New Age. The overlap is as ambiguous as some of the claims and results promised by these modern metaphysicians.

Get Behind It

Magic 8-Ball. This classic seems to be enjoying a revival in some toy and variety stores, so check local sources, too. Ask it a yes or no question, turn it over and your answer is magically revealed. Spirit channeler, or some kind of UFO-guided computer? The manufacturer isn't saying, but you can stop making those difficult choices alone!

$7.50 + 4.00 shipping from Archie McPhee, P.O. Box 30852, Seattle , WA 98103. (206) 547-2467 / FAX (206) 547-6319.

Other-Worldly Sources

• **The New Age Catalogue** by the editors of **Body Mind Spirit Magazine.** The authors reassure the reader that they have not only personally examined the products and services they list in this comprehensive catalog of New Age resources, but also that they *felt good* about them, from channeling to Zen, through rebirthing, acupuncture, New Age music and Gaia-consciousness. Book reviews, product reviews and short essays transform the reader into an informed New Age consumer. Why not take a full curriculum of New Age? Not that it will get you a high-paying job at IBM, but you might be able to move up a few chakras or straighten out some of that bad Karmic energy from that time you insulted the king in 13th century Persia...

$17.45 postpaid from Doubleday Books, P.O. Box 5071, Des Plaines, IL 60017. (800) 223-6834, Ext. 9479.

• **The Llewellyn New Times.** "Since 1901, the Americas' oldest and leading publisher of esoteric sciences and technologies for consciousness growth and planetary awareness." Besides offering personal astrological services, the catalog contains articles on Paganism, Celtic and Norse mythology, Egyptian mysteries, Wicca, erotic mysticism, crystal healing and more.

One year subscription (6 issues) $2.00 c/o Llewellyn Publications, P.O. Box 64383, St. Paul, MN 55164-0383. (800) THE-MOON.

Tea for the Talisman

"Have You the Courage to be Lucky, Loved and Rich? Get Everything You Want with THE MOST POWERFUL TALISMANS IN THE WORLD!" We've received our lucky talismans, not by their own esoteric powers, strangely enough, but by the ESOTERIC POWERS OF THE US POSTAL SERVICE (could it be that the Cosmic Powers, like UPS, can't deliver to a P.O. Box?). Here are some available options:

• **Pentacle of Venus**—gain and keep love.

• **Medieval Luck Talisman**—win whenever gambling.

• **King Soloman Pentagram**—ward off evil.

• **King Soloman Hexagram**—get peace and a happy home.

• **Medieval Agia Talisman**—brings wealth.

• **Pentacle of Mars**—ensures good health.

$6.00 each, postpaid. Neck chain, add $1.00. From House of Talismans, Box 11392-R, St. Paul, MN 55111.

Paranormal Periodicals

FATE Magazine. "True reports of the strange and unknown," reported by real, down-home folks, from conversations with departed loved ones to premonitions of a pet's death, *FATE* is full of poignant tales, but our favorite feature is "Strange Coincidences." Here's a sample: "In 1974, an employee at a Pepperidge Farm plant in Downington, Pennsylvania, was killed when he fell into a vat of chocolate. His name was Robert C. Hershey." Great reading, full of unbelievable items you'll want to post on either side of your refrigerator door.

One year subscription (12 issues) $22.95 from 170 Future Way, Marion, OH 43305.

Gallons of Quartz

Buy your crystals direct.

• Coleman's Quartz Mine, Rt. 1, Box 160, Jessieville, AR 71949.

• Wegner Quartz Crystal Mine, Rt. 1, Box 528, Norman, AR 71960.

Magical Blend. A mystical mixture of visionary art and poetry, spirituality, channeling, and other signposts along the transformative journey.

One year subscription (4 issues) $14.00, single issue $3.95 from P.O. Box 11303, San Francisco, CA 94101-7303.

Ghost TV Reception

• *My Mother the Car.* The first TV show about reincarnation.

• *Bewitched.* Sympathetic portrayal of paganists and Satan-worshippers.

• *The Ghost and Mrs. Muir.* Love between a crusty old sea captain's ghost and a young widow. Not a ghost of a chance.

• *I Dream of Jeannie.* Bottled beauty from the Arabian nights is decanted by an astronaut who falls victim to her ancient spells.

• *Topper.* The poltergeists were mischievous, but friendly. Neil the dog is our favorite otherworldly St. Bernard drunk.

• *Casper the Benevolent Disembodied Entity.* The children all loved him so.

Cleveland resident Coyote Powhatan channels a vegetable entity named Produce.

Fly By Night

Herbal Flying Ointment. Applied topically, these legal, mildly psychotropic herbs promote a relaxed, trancelike state to facilitate astral projection. Don't leave your body without it.

Send SASE for information to Briar Rose, P.O. Box 22332, Long Beach, CA 90801-5332.

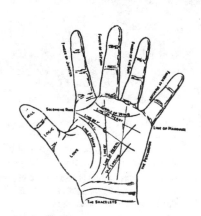

See Me, Feel Me, Touch Me, Heal Me

Spiritual Emergence Network. Having a spiritual crisis? According to some transpersonal psychotherapists, a spiritual awakening can sometimes mimic the symptoms of mental illness, including hallucinations, anxiety and confusion. We suppose the reverse may also be true. This international referral network of psychiatrists, therapists, parapsychologists, and spiritual teachers will be happy to provide assistance for people having spiritual experiences they can't handle. They also publish a newsletter and provide training and workshops.

Institute of Transpersonal Psychology, 250 Oak Grove Ave., Menlo Park, CA 94025. (415) 327-2776.

Bully Crystals

Once relegated to dusty old storefronts in bad parts of town, rock shops used to cater mainly to geologists, lapidaries and amateur rock hounds.

In the 1980s a resurgence of interest in stones and crystals as meditative and healing tools among New Agers dramatically changed the rock business. Shops moved uptown to cater to a clientele whose modern crystal healing techniques involve laying stones on the body in patterns.

Stones are believed by some to emit emanations that influence the body and mind. They have been used by shamans and healers for medicinal purposes since ancient times, which may help explain the brutally short lifespans of the times.

• *The Crystal Sourcebook* by John Milewski. Explains how crystals are used for personal development and healing and lists sources for getting magic rocks.

$26.95 postpaid from Mystic Crystal Publications, 1439 W. Highway 39, Sedona, AZ 86336.

'C' axis — Pyramid face — Truncated pyramid face — Prism Face — TERMINATIO

Faces of crystals

The Silicon Astrologer

Astro-Pro. How often do you get a chance to meld the cutting edge of modern technology to superstitions that were getting threadbare centuries ago? No more mistakes when you calculate natal horoscopes, transits , progressions, compatibility charts, biorhythm charts and numerology charts.

IBM and Macintosh. Get a free demo from AstroResearch, 1500 Massachusetts Ave. NW, #764, Washington, D.C. 20005. (202) 775-9423.

Fast Forward Into the Future

Tarot Video gives you instructions on how to conduct readings. Learn "how to develop a bond with your cards so you can confidently interpret the present and carefully predict the future." Includes bonus Tarot deck.

#6437, $29.98 + 4.95 shipping from Johnson Smith Co., 4514 19th Court East, P.O. Box 25500, Bradenton, FL 34206-5500. (813) 747-2356 / FAX (813) 746-7896.

Paranormal Phenomena

• Astrology as practiced today was originally developed in 2,000 BC. by Ptolemy, the same guy who erroneously told us that the universe revolves around the earth.

• One in six Americans believes that they have been in touch with someone who has died.

• More than half believe in the devil, and one in 10 claim to have talked to him personally.

Solar Plexus

Magic Golden Solar Energy Chamber.
Place this new, experimental unit in
sunlight, and it operates by solar power.
Add crystals and run it on solar and
crystal power. Includes instructions,
special Hot Pink Focus Sheet, Special
Multi-PYRAMID-POWER Focus
Sheet plus four additional colors,
special "research report" on how to use
colors to solve "specific problems and
needs." If it doesn't increase your
energy, grow hair or bring you material
wealth, it could probably be adapted
for drying fruit, or maybe for freeze-
drying dead pets.

**Complete Kit, $15.00 + 1.50 shipping from
Aries Productions, P.O. Box 29396,
Sappington, MO 63126. (Other kits
available. Send SASE for catalog).**

The Transcendental Tourist

• **Salem Witch Museum.** More a
performance venue than a museum,
their "powerful half-hour multi-sensory
presentation" is housed in a scary old
church more befitting Count Dracula
than those unfortunate victims of
persecution presented here a la Disney.
Don't miss the witch-kitsch giftshop on
the way out.

**19 1/2 Washington Square N., Salem, MA
01970. (508) 744-1692 (Coincidentally,
1692 was the year witch-hunt hysteria
was at its peak).**

• **Deja Vu Tours.** Visit some of the
Earth's most exotic sacred spots with
sensitive guides. Partake of the healing
energies and then relax at a tropical
resort where you may find snorkeling,
scuba diving and sun bathing useful
adjuncts to your spirituality.

**Gail Halloran, General Manager, 95
Belvedere Street, San Rafael, CA 94901.
(415) 459-3551.**

• **Rosicrucian
Egyptian Museum.**
Run by the Rosicrucian
Order, AMORC. Claiming to be the
world's oldest fraternal group (ancient
Egypt, circa 1400 B.C.), the
Rosicrucians offer its members a system
of studies in metaphysics, philosophy,
psychology, science and
parapsychology. The Rosicrucian
Egyptian Museum is the only Egyptian
museum in the world located in
authentic Egyptian-style architecture in
very serene surroundings. It draws
approximately 200,000 visitors a year
and houses the largest collection of
Egyptian, Babylonian and Assyrian
artifacts and replicas on the West
Coast. And, it's not far from the
Winchester Mystery House, another
genuinely spooky place.

**1342 Naglee Avenue, San Jose, CA 95191.
(408) 287-9171.**

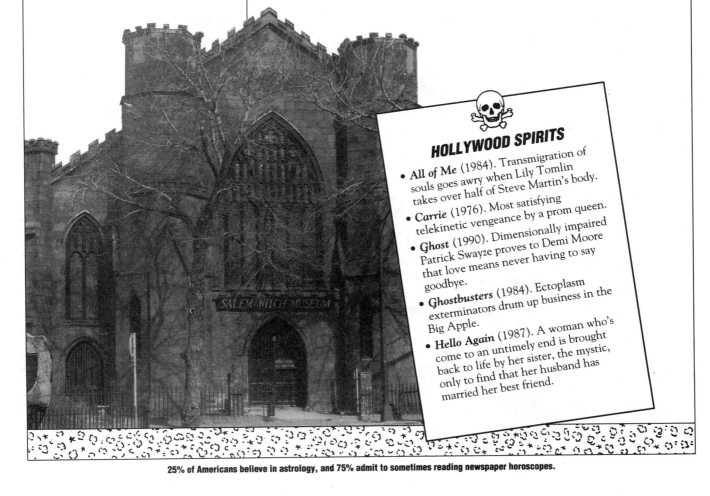

HOLLYWOOD SPIRITS

• *All of Me* (1984). Transmigration of
souls goes awry when Lily Tomlin
takes over half of Steve Martin's body.

• *Carrie* (1976). Most satisfying
telekinetic vengeance by a prom queen.

• *Ghost* (1990). Dimensionally impaired
Patrick Swayze proves to Demi Moore
that love means never having to say
goodbye.

• *Ghostbusters* (1984). Ectoplasm
exterminators drum up business in the
Big Apple.

• *Hello Again* (1987). A woman who's
come to an untimely end is brought
back to life by her sister, the mystic,
only to find that her husband has
married her best friend.

That You Do So Well

Voodoo Doll. Great for long-distance acupuncture. 5" tall, bright red. Comes with 5 white and 5 black pins.

> $4.50 + 4.00 shipping. Archie McPhee, P.O. Box 30852, Seattle WA 98103. (206) 547-2467 / FAX (206) 547-6319.

NOT GIBBERISH

Beyond Words by Paula B. Slater and Barbara Sinor. Are you confused when you overhear people talking about "synchronicity" and "power spots?" *Beyond Words* is the Fodor's Guide for making your way through the New Age. It's an annotated dictionary of New Age words, which also includes a recommended reading list at the end of each section. The commentary lists literary, psychological and historical origins of over 100 "new language" terms, such as: "Aura—An AURA is the energizing halo or life-force which surrounds animate and inanimate objects. This glowing energy has been called a 'non-physical matrix,' or 'electric blue print.' The Aura's spiraling vibrational field can be seen, felt and interpreted." Easier than a Berlitz course, and more fun, too.

> $16.95 postpaid from Harbin Springs Publishing, P.O. Box 1132, Middletown, CA 95461. (707) 987-0477.

THE RIDER TAROT DECK

INSTRUCTIONS

THE MAGICIAN.

U.S. GAMES SYSTEMS, Inc.
38 EAST 32nd STREET • NEW YORK, N.Y. 10016

WHEEL of FORTUNE.

Read 'Em & Weep

Tarot cards are thought to have evolved from the Hermetica of ancient Egypt and Greece. Modern Tarot uses 78 cards, the symbolism of which embodies Western esoteric tradition.

> Ask for a catalog of decks from U.S. Games Systems, Inc., 179 Ludlow St., Stamford, CT 06909. (800) 544-2637 / FAX (203) 353-8431.

Smells Like a Pisces in Here!

Personal Power Oils. Potent oil blends that perfectly capture your astrological essence and say "Smell my sign." Send sun, moon and rising sign information, or, if unknown, birth date and time.

> $19.95 postpaid from Astrological Blends, 12439 Magnolia Blvd., Suite 191, North Hollywood, CA 91607.

Cosmic Catalog

The Gaia Catalogue Company.
"Ecological and Spiritual Resources
for an Awakening World." At Gaia
you'll find books on the Earth and
ecological living, cross-cultural mythology and personal growth, women's
spirituality and men's transformation.
Gaia also offers a large selection of
goddess images, great ethnic drums and
sacred art.

**Gaia, 1400 Shattuck Avenue #9, Berkeley,
CA 94709. (800) 543-8431 / (510) 548-
4172.**

What's on the Other Channel?

• *Metapsychology,* edited by **Tam
Mossman.** A variety of spirit entities
discuss a wide range of topics in this
elegantly produced periodical. This
magazine devoted entirely to
channeling gives new meaning to the
term "ghost-written."

**One year (4 issues), $20.00, single issue
$5.00 from Box 3295, Charlottesville, VA
22903.**

• *Spirit Speaks,* edited by **Molli
Nickell.** A lively flow of channeled
material primarily from Southern
California mediums ("media"?).

**One year (6 issues), $24.00, single issue
$4.95 from Box 84304, Los Angeles, CA
90073.**

Strike a Happy Medium

Channeling is the
New Age term for an
old shtick. Spirit
speaking has been
practiced by oracles,
prophets, shamans
and frauds in many
cultures since the dawn of
organized religion. In the late 1900s,
spiritualists had large, loyal followings.

Today's channelers no longer need
to resort to the obvious parlor tricks of
the past, like floating a glowing
trumpet on a wire or materializing

fingerprints of the dead by pressing
their toes to inked pads beneath the
table. Usually, a heavy accent and
change in timbre is all that's needed to
convince the susceptible—some
channelers even speak in their usual
voices. Hundreds of mediums lucra-
tively channel spirits all over the
world, thanks in part to publicity
surrounding Shirley MacLaine's
1983 *Out on a Limb.*

Some famous channelers
and their cosmic side-kicks:

• J.Z. (Judy Zebra) Knight
manifests Ramtha, a
35,000-year-old warrior
from Atlantis. She first
encountered him, Knight
told *L.A. Weekly,* when she
put a pyramid on her head
and in barged "the Ram."

**Ramtha books, tapes and videos
can be ordered from: Sovereignty,
Box 926, Eastsound, WA 98245.**

• Jack Pursel, a retired Florida
insurance salesman, has rivaled
Knight as the champion of
the channels with his
entity Lazaris, who has as
many fans among
movie and television
celebrities as "the

Ram" has.

**Lazaris books, audio and video tapes can
be ordered from Concept: Synergy, 279 S.
Beverly Dr., Suite 604, Los Angeles, CA
90212.**

• Dozens of mediums are channeling a
spirit called Seth, first channeled
through the late Jane Roberts. The
best known channeler bringing Seth to
the airwaves today is Jean Loomis.

**Contact her at 116 Montowese St.,
Bradford, CT 06405.**

• Penny Torres, a Los Angeles
housewife, channels Mafu, a 2,000-
year-old man.

• David Swetland channels Mates, a
35,000-year-old black female spice
trader.

• Jessica Lansing channels Michael, a
"recombinant entity" who consists of
more than a thousand souls.

• Scores of channelers—Virginia
Essene, Elwood
Babbit, and Annie
Stebbins,
among
others—
channel
Jesus.

The Office

The elegant efficiency of the modern office ("This is the voice message system. Please leave a message.") was built on the achievements of our ancestors, who probably never dreamed that we would make huge strides in making what was once a dehumanizing institution even more so. Here are short histories of some of our more notable

instruments of daily torture:

• **Keyboard** (1870s). The first typewriter was built by Christopher L. Sholes of Milwaukee in 1873. His Remington No. 1 Type-Writer had 44 keys arranged in a keyboard much like modern ones and sold for $125. Mark Twain bought one of the new machines and became the first author to submit a typed manuscript to a publisher (*Life on the Mississippi*).

The strange and awkward "QWERTYUIOP" letter arrangement? It was designed to slow typists down, because they were jamming the mechanisms of the prototype machines as they picked up speed. People have come up with more efficient arrangements (putting the e, t, and other common letters in a less awkward place, for instance) which would dramatically increase typing speed and decrease effort and strain, but they've never been generally adopted.

• **Carbon paper** (1806). English inventor Ralph Wedgewood soaked paper in ink and dried it. It gave two impressions, a good readable one on the front of the copy and a "negative" one on the back of the original.

• **Rubber bands** (1845). London inventor Stephen Perry stretched his imagination and came up with bands for holding things, made from the wonder material of the time, vulcanized rubber.

• **Ballpoint pen** (1938). Two Hungarian brothers, George and Lazlo Biro, patented the first ballpoint pen in 1938. The pen became popular with bomber crews in 1944 when they found that it didn't blot or leak at high altitudes. The new pens premiered in 1945 at Gimbel's, where they quickly sold out for $12.50 each.

• **Photocopying** (1937). In 1937, Chester Carlson, a New York law student was rewarded for his years of research when he discovered the process of "xerography," electrostatic dry copying (the Greek word *xeros* means dry). The Haloid Company of Rochester, New York, bought the rights to the process in 1946, and began placing Xerox machines in offices in 1950.

• **Calendar** (34,000 B.C.). Some of our ancestors were keeping track of the phases of the moon on antlers, bones, and stone during the Ice Age.

• **Paper clip** (1899). The Norwegian Johann Vaaler discovered this use for bent wire. During the Nazi occupation of Norway, the paper clip became a symbol of Norwegian patriotism and people wore paper clips on their jacket lapels, which irritated the Germans and even led to arrests.

• **Cellophane tape** (1930). "Scotch tape"— cellulose film coated with rubber glue—was invented by the Minnesota Mining and Manufacturing Corporation. 3M also came up with masking tape (1925) and Post-it notes (1980).

• **Stapler** (1868). The stapler was patented by G. H. Gould of Birmingham, England. We don't know whether or not he stapled together the pages of his patent application.

WHITE COLLAR BLUES

Hail to the office, and the old "9 to 5." With the work on farms and in industry disappearing, the office has become the American workplace for more and more folks. On Monday morning, you can almost hear the wave of groans travel across the country's time zones as workers slug down strong coffee and crawl to the office to struggle with those unfinished projects waiting on their desks from Friday afternoon.

Wastebasketball

Mini basketball hoop clips onto wastebasket so you can do some lay-ups before you're laid off. Crumble up your boss' memos and go for a three-pointer, or use the included foam ball. Special sensor cheers when you make the shot!

#5630, $24.98 + 4.95 shipping Johnson Smith Company, 4514 19th Court East, P.O. Box 25500, Bradenton, FL 34206-5500. (813) 747-2356 / FAX (813) 746-7896.

"Lizzie Borden took a fax And sent her father forty stacks Of pointless paper, just for fun, Then sent her mother forty-one."

—David English, who earned "Honorable Mention" in a *New York Magazine* bad verse competition.

The Fine Art Of Rubber Band Shooting

Elevate rubber band shooting to its rightful place in office warfare with this solid walnut gun.

#4376, $27.95 + 5.25 shipping from Enticements, P.O. Box 4040, New Rochelle, NY 10802-4040. (800) 243-4300 / FAX (800) 244-4591.

If Only It Were Really This Exciting

"A fledgling tyrannosaurus peers uncertainly into the strange new jungle, alive with the hostile stares of alien lizards. Briefcase tucked under her foreleg, she begins to hack her way alone through the tangled grapevines. Will she take the wrong turn? Will she be ambushed and barbecued by the other dinosaurs? Won't anybody show her the way?"

—Albert J. Bernstein and Sydney Craft Rozen from *Dinosaur Brains: Dealing with All Those Impossible People at Work.*

LIGHTEN UP

Remember this old flex arm metal desk lamp? There was a time when you could find it in practically every office. This is not a reproduction—it's made by the same company that introduced it in 1938 and it hasn't changed, even sporting the same pencil grooves. And it still comes in one basic color —gloomy grey. Two standard 15 watt fluorescent tubes included.

#18415, $125.00 + variable shipping. The Vermont Country Store, P.O. Box 3000, Manchester Center, VT 05255-3000. (802) 362-2400.

Decisions, Decisions

Successful business executives are said to be always on the ball. But their big secret is that they've been relying on the **Magic 8-Ball** all these years. No wonder American business decisions have consistently been right on all these years.

#M371, $8.50 + 4.00 shipping from Archie McPhee, P.O. Box 30852, Seattle, WA 98103-0852. (206) 547-2467.

The reason paper cuts hurt fingers so much is that hands contain the most surface nerve endings.

Business Cards

"Here's my card. Give me a call." It's the way we do business now, and it's been done that way since about 1620 in England.

They were called "tradesmen's cards" back then, later shortened to "trade cards" and then, around 1880, "business cards." In the beginning, tradesmen's cards were often 3 x 5" or larger, and included name, product, service, and some form of decoration. The cards were aimed at the upper class—about the only people who could afford to be customers.

According to business card expert Avery Pitzak, business cards of past centuries often displayed imaginative illustrations and elaborate type styles. Paul Revere, hero of the revolution and metalsmith, handed out ornate trade cards embellished with bells, cannons, tools, and an eagle to advertise his foundry. America's Great Depression forced businesspeople to rein in their creativity, and established a standard 2 x 3 1/2" white card, printed simply in black.

Since the late 1960s, there has been a

growing trend back to creative business card designs—cards in a variety of colors and forms (cards shaped, for example, like light bulbs, garbage trucks, steers, and pretzels). There are die-cut cards, cards that fold and unfold (one ventriloquist's business card unfolds into a dummy whose mouth can be made to move), and cards printed on plastic, wood, and even metal.

Cards With A Calling

Turn business cards into a sculpture in a bottle. It's the most unique, personal gift you can give to someone who's all business. Send 15 cards and 6 or 7 weeks later they'll return fashioned into a ship, bi-plane, skier or other distinctive design. Each sculpture is cut and constructed by hand, then sealed in a clear glass bottle set on a solid oak base.

#T32 Clipper Ship; #T33 Golfer; #T31 Bi-Plane: #T60 Scale of Justice; #T54 Antique Auto; #T13 Police Car; #T17 Skier; #T14 Fire Engine. Each $39.98 + 3.50 shipping. The Lighter Side, 4514 19th St. Court East, P.O. Box 25600, Bradenton, FL 34206-5600. (813) 747-2356 / FAX: (813) 746-7896.

Pick a Card, Any Card

• **American Business Card Club.** These folks collect and trade antique, unusual (strange shapes or colors) and celebrity business cards. Some members have amassed hundreds of thousands of 'em. Send SASE for information, and (of course) enclose your business card if you have one.

Membership $8.00 per year + 2.00 registration fee. ABCC, P.O. Box 460297, Aurora, CO 80046-0297. (303) 690-6496.

• *Make Your Business Card Incredibly Effective* by Avery N. Pitzak. "Most business cards are poorly designed or not designed at all...They're among the most frequently overlooked, underexploited, and misunderstood promotional pieces in existence," says ABCC President Pitzak, who has collected business cards since he was six. Your goal should be a successful business card that will make an immediate impression on the viewer, be saved for future reference, and be memorable.

$15.00 postpaid from Avery N. Pitzak, P.O. Box 460297, Aurora, CO 80046-0297. (303) 690-6496.

C. Y. A.

It's no surprise that the penalty was steep at a firm when an employee was caught Xeroxing her derriere. After all, "cover your ass" has always been the watchword of corporate life. In this topsy turvey world, when corporate felons keep their jobs and chiselers and psychopaths get promotions, the multicopy mooner was fired.

> *"People who work sitting down get paid more than people who work standing up."*
>
> —Ogden Nash

No More Teeth-Marked Pencils

Instead of chewing on your pencil or eraser, alleviate stress and teeth marks by sucking on this benippled pencil.

#T1962, Stress Pencil, $2.98 + 3.50 shipping from Funny Side Up, 425 Stump Rd., North Wales, PA 19454. (215) 361-5130.

Don't Play House...Play Office!

With so many women working now the kids' pretend game of "playing house" is really outdated. Kids should be "playing office" instead. And this activity center gets them off on the right foot. Includes ringing phone, drawers, clock, pencil caddy, writing surface, telephone/address book, calendar and memo pad, too! If your child is late coming home, don't worry! Maybe he or she is putting in a little overtime!

#243295, My Office Activity Center, $65.00 + 8.80 shipping from FAO Schwarz, P.O. Box 182225, Chattanooga, TN 37422-7225. (800) 426-TOYS.

Reproductive Freedom

• *Xerolage*. "Makin' copies?" If you get tired of copying, collating and stapling excerpts from the latest procedures manual, this publication may help you to view the copy machine in a totally new way. Artist Miekal And coined the word "xerolage" to suggest the new world of art propagated with Xerox technology.

Each issue of *Xerolage* contains the copy art-work of a single artist. Mainstream, it's not—it's one of the fun, slap-in-the-face underground things. After a few issues, you may be tempted to put your body parts up against your office machine.

One year subscription (4 issues, sent out once a year) $14.00 + 2.90 shipping from Xeroxial Endarchy, Ltd., 1341 Williamson St., Madison, WI 53703. (608) 258-1305.

• *Ginny's Annual Copy Art Competition.* "When a copy machine meets a creative mind, you have a powerful recipe for new artforms." That's the idea behind the annual Copy Art Competition of Ginny's Copying in Austin, Texas, first held in 1976.

Artwork must be "processed or modified by a copy machine," and be no larger than 24 x 36" (or 24 x 24 x 24", if it's a 3-D piece). 1st place award is $100 plus $100 in copying services. A recent winner dumped the entire contents of her purse onto the copy machine.

Send SASE for entry guidelines to Ginny's Printing and Copying, c/o Patricia Cochran, 5417 N. Lamar, Austin, TX 78751. (512) 454-6874.

"The trouble with the rat race is that even if you win, you're still a rat." —Lily Tomlin

Money **O**inks

Okay, Capitalist Pig, why not make a distinctive statement through your business checks? Each book of these checks contains four alternating, full-color pictures of great porkers. In addition to the checks, you get 100 "Pig Talk" stickers with such messages as "Hogs and Kisses," "Hogwash!" and "Boaring!"

200 checks, $12.95 + 3.00 shipping. Novel Check Corporation, P.O. Box 218557, Houston, TX 77218-8557. (800) 443-1666.

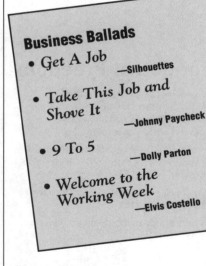

Back to the Future

This 5½" diameter Backward Clock ("The Original Nurdanian Clock") runs in reverse. The numbers are reversed, too. It gives the office clockwatchers something to figure out.

#T-939, $14.98 + 3.95 shipping from Funny Side Up, 425 Stump Road, North Wales, PA 19454. (215) 361-5130.

Fax A Go-Go

Lost and lonely without your fax machine?

Now you can fax from the beach, fax from your car phone, fax between acts when you're at the theatre. This Mitsubishi Portable Fax is a cordless contraption that easily connects to a cellular phone, pay phone...any phone.

Feel important and oh so indispensable no matter where you go.

#0129, Portable Fax, $1,299.00.
#0129A, Battery Pack, $139.00
#0129B, Car Adapter, $95.00.
#0129C, Carrying Case, $59.00.
Shipping varies. Attitudes, 1213 Elko Drive, Sunnyvale, CA 94089. (800) 525-2468 / FAX (408) 734-8004.

"Just the Fax"

Liven up those dull and impersonal faxes with some silliness in your cover sheets and messages. "Just the Fax" lets you choose from 75 pieces of clip-art (or make your own), 20 templates, 16 type styles, and 10 borders. "Rise above the clutter of ordinary, everyday faxes." Runs on the IBM and compatibles.

$24.95 + 3.00 shipping from Britannica Software Inc., 345 Fourth Street, San Francisco, CA 94107. (800) 572-2272 / FAX (415) 546-1887.

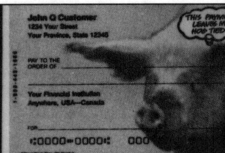

Business Ballads

- Get A Job
  —Silhouettes

- Take This Job and Shove It
  —Johnny Paycheck

- 9 To 5
  —Dolly Parton

- Welcome to the Working Week
  —Elvis Costello

"Who first invented work and bound the free / And holiday-rejoicing spirit down?" —Charles Lamb

GLOAT GLOBE

Got friends who still live where it snows? Rub in the fact that you're where it's warm! Whether you've moved to a sunny climate or are just vacationing, send a reminder that shows you miss 'em.

#449, Florida Snowman or #450, California Snowman. Each $3.98 + 2.50 shipping from The Lighter Side, 4514 19th St. Court East, P.O. Box 25600, Bradenton, FL 34206-5600. (813) 747-2356 ext. 5 / FAX (813) 746-7896.

Shaker Colony

Six strange snowdome styles to choose from: Bathing Beauty & Sea Monster; Beach Walker; Pink Flamingos; VW Convertible in a Blizzard; Waving Water Skier; and good ol' Hollywood.

Each $5.95 + 4.00 shipping from Ruby Montana's Pinto Pony Catalog, 603 Second Avenue, Seattle, WA 98104. (206) 621-PONY.

Welcome to the Pleasure Domes

• *Snowdomes* by Nancy McMichael. Snowdomes—those smooth, round, liquid-filled, "snow"-swirling baubles—have long served as desktop paperweights. Now, they're sought-after collectibles as well. Author Nancy McMichael has compiled the world's first book on the subject. It's a clear and thorough account of the many different kinds of snow globes.

There have been snowdomes depicting Jesse James' Hideout, Jiminy Cricket, Paul Bunyan, and products such as Jell-O, Mountain Dew, and Solid Olsonite toilet seats ("Tops for Bottoms").

$19.95 + 2.00 shipping from Abbeville Press, 488 Madison Ave., New York, NY 10022. (800) 227-7210.

• *Snow Biz, The Newsletter for Snowdome Collectors.* This quarterly newsletter of the snowdome collector's club includes articles on history, collectors, and buy/sell/trade information.

One year subscription (4 issues) $10.00 from Snow Biz, P.O. Box 52362, Washington, D.C. 20009.

PAPERWEIGHTS

Collectors' Paperweights Price Guide and Catalogue by Lawrence H. Selman. This is a bright guide to over 400 antique and contemporary glass paperweights, with color photos and descriptions. Includes information on the history of manufacturing techniques, and artists. L.H. Selman Ltd. (a quality paperweight manufacturer) sends several updates a year to purchasers of the catalog.

$15.00 postpaid. L.H. Selman Ltd., 761 Chestnut Street, Santa Cruz, CA 95060. (800) 538-0766.

Keep From Getting Blown Away

Paperweight Collectors' Association. Founded in 1953, the PCA is a group of over 1400 members who are interested in the origin, history, and quality of paperweights.

Send SASE to PCA, 150 Fulton Ave., P.O. Box 468, Garden City Park, NY 11040. (516) 741-3090.

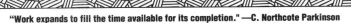

"Work expands to fill the time available for its completion." —C. Northcote Parkinson

MIGHTIER THAN SWORDS

"Men often get married to their pen, and it is well that they do. A certain pen action and that one only will suit them. But pens are as different as individuals, and just as there is a wife for every man, if he will patiently look for her, so, only with no trouble at all in the finding, there is a Waterman Ideal Fountain Pen that will suit every taste and every habit in pen action."

—from a Waterman company correspondence course in salesmanship, 1902

What You Need to Know about Collecting Fountain Pens by **Judson Bell**. A 96-page guide to collecting fountain pens—how to identify interesting pens, where to find them, how to estimate their value, and how to bargain for them.

$12.95 + 2.00 shipping from World Publications, 2240 North Park Drive, Kingwood, TX 77339. (713) 359-4363.

Stylish Scribbler

The Canetti fountain pen is encased in brass, then nickel-plated to take on a lustrous "gunmetal" color. The iridium tip accepts ink cartridges (two included), or choose a look-alike ball point pen (with one Parker refill).

#46706, Fountain Pen, $79.95 + 6.50 shipping or #46708, Ball Point Pen, $39.95 + 5.00 shipping from Hammacher Schlemmer, 9180 Le Saint Drive, Fairfield, OH 45014. (800) 543-3366

"As through this life you travel, You'll meet some funny men: Some'll rob you with a 6-gun, And some with a fountain pen."

—Woody Guthrie, *Pretty Boy Floyd*

The Quill Pen Is Alive & Ink Well

Authentic Handcut Quill Pen and Inkwell. Instead of whipping out a cheap ballpoint, pick up your quill pen, lovingly dip it into your octagonal ceramic limited edition floral motif inkwell, and lazily inscribe your John Hancock at the bottom of the page with the flourishes that'll give your signature distinction. Be sure to specify whether you write right or left handed (yes, it matters).

Quill pen, $4.95 + 1.50 shipping. Inkwell $30.00 + 1.50 shipping. Society of Inkwell Collectors, 5136 Thomas Ave. South, Minneapolis, MN 55410.

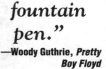

"The pen is the tongue of the hand." —Henry Ward Beecher

Cross Your I's, Strip Your T's

Pick up ballpoint pen to write and clothes disappear. Tilt pen the other way and clothes magically reappear. Naughty!

#T833, Female. #T834, Male. Each $2.98 + 3.50 shipping from Funny Side Up, 425 Stump Rd., North Wales, PA 19454. (215) 361-5130.

INK STAINED WRETCHES

Pen World. This magazine for the pen lover has news pieces, interviews, histories, photographs and columns (including "Dear Miss Inkly..."). It also operates a repair facility called "The Fountain Pen Hospital."

One year subscription (6 issues), $42.00 from World Publications, 2240 Northpark Drive, Kingwood, TX 77339. (713) 359-PENS.

A Pen For "His Nibs"

A custom-made fountain pen with a nib created to match your writing style. All you do is answer a brief questionnaire and provide a sample of your writing style. A specially crafted nib is then fashioned to complement your unique writing manner. Three styles to choose from...all made from water buffalo horn. Allow 3-4 months for delivery.

#2030, $495.00 + variable shipping from Attitudes, 1213 Elko Drive, Sunnyvale, CA 94089. (800) 525-2468 / FAX (408) 734-8004.

Write-On Clubs for Collectors of the Implements

• **The Pen Fancier's Club.** Formed in the late 1970s. Before word got out about the value of vintage pens, "it was a universally accepted practice among antique dealers to routinely pull all solid gold nibs from quality old pens for their scrap value and toss the remains into the trash! This abysmal ignorance caused millions of beautiful writing instruments to be lost forever to those of us who would have treasured them." *The Pen Fancier's Magazine* keeps collectors in touch with news of all the old pens—Parker, Sheaffer, Wahl-Eversharp, Montblanc, A.T. Cross, A.A. Waterman, and others.

One year membership $45.00 (includes subscription to the monthly *Pen Fancier's Magazine*). PFC, 1169 Overcash Drive, Dunedin, FL 34698. (813) 734-4742.

• **The Society of Inkwell Collectors.** Founded in 1981 and dedicated to the art of collecting inkwells, SIC has recently broadened to include blotters, quill cutters, nibs and other writing instruments and accessories. Members share information in *The Stained Finger* newsletter and attend the Society's International Convention.

One year membership $22.50. 5136 Thomas Ave. South, Minneapolis, MN 55410. (612) 922-2792.

• **American Pencil Collectors Society.** Contact other people who are attached to old golden Dixon Ticonderoga #2s.

Send SASE to APCS, c/o Henry T. Kamphuis, 4601 W. 101st Street, Oak Lawn, IL 60453.

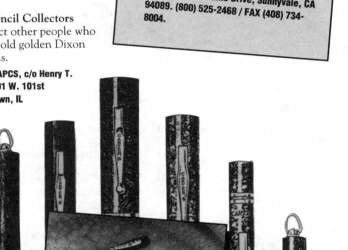

Tiny, 1¹/₂" long Waterman promotional fountain pens from the early 1900s can be worth $800-$1200.

Our Gang

Alfalfa's Greatest Hits

- *I'm in the Mood for Love*
- *She'll Be Comin' Around the Mountain When She Comes*
- *I'm the Barber of Seville*

Little Rascals

Enterprising Spanky, bowler-hatted Stymie, lisping Porky, insecure Alfalfa, coquettish Darla...director Hal Roach cast these Depression-era kids in his comedy film shorts to play themselves. The humor came out of the characters as much as it did their situations. For instance, picture love-lorn Alfalfa singing to his elusive sweetie, Darla. Singing very badly and nasally, but in earnest (he believed at the time that he really was a great singer), scrunching up his freckled face in the effort. Maybe that was a tension cowlick jumping out of his hair.

Part of the charm of *Our Gang* is their lack of self-consciousness, and their ingenuity in creating something out of nothing, like their makeshift, pedal-powered wooden fire engine. Hal Roach made his Little Rascals typical kids living during the Depression who dressed shabbily and had few toys, but never wanted for imagination. And in spite of the rivalries between the Gang and rich nerd Waldo or between the gang girls and the He-Man Woman Haters club, perhaps the most interesting aspect in this series of short comedies is that they were unself-consciously racially integrated.

Alfalfa, real name Carl Switzer, died after pulling a switchblade during a drunken argument with a neighbor about a lost hunting dog.

PEANUT BUTTER

Creature from a Beige Legume

Chunky, creamy, with jelly, spread on bread or rice cakes or baked into cookies, scores of us would agree peanut butter is a gift of the gods.

Although a 100,000-year-old fossilized peanut was recently found in China, its history as a dietary staple actually began in what's now Brazil and Bolivia. Peanuts were so much a part of the Inca diet that they were buried with the dead for afterlife snacks.

Pizarro's Conquistadores took the "ynchic" back to Spain and traded it to Africans, who cultivated the legume extensively. African slaves brought the peanut full circle by reintroducing it to the Americas (the term "goober" comes from "nguba," the Congolese name for a peanut).

Botanist George Washington Carver saw great potential in the peanut and came up with hundreds of products from it including ink, lipstick, shaving cream, cooking oil, ice cream, paper, flour, shampoo, even explosives. But not peanut butter.

Actually a legume, not a nut, its debut as peanut butter is attributed to an unknown St. Louis doctor who in March of 1890 used a meat grinder to make a protein supplement for elderly patients who couldn't chew meat. Later, John Kellogg of cereal fame received a patent for his process of preparing it at his Battle Creek Sanitarium.

The biggest butter boom came during World War II when the U.S. government fed it to soldiers. Upon their return, they fed it to their kids. Pretty soon this high energy, protein rich food became a $1 billion industry and an American classic.

So, whether it's proletariat Jif, Peter Pan, Skippy, Smuckers, or upscale spreads like Freshly Ground or Krema Natural, peanut butter will probably stick around for a very long time.

Sticky Explanations...

So why does peanut butter stick to the roof of your mouth? Actually, the culprit is the high level of protein. The substance in peanut butter absorbs and holds moisture—it actually sucks your saliva dry. Before you know it your tongue is velcroed to the roof of your mouth.

Some people even have a phobia about this. The condition is called *arachibrityaphobia* (which, when pronounced correctly, sounds as if your tongue was stuck to the roof of your mouth.)

Peanut Butter Meets Its Match

> *"You got your chocolate in my peanut butter!"*
> *"You got your peanut butter in my chocolate!"*

The biggest marriage of the century? Chocolate and peanut butter in any combination you can imagine. Peanut butter is the biggest thing to hit the candy industry since nougat. Reese's Peanut Butter Cups are among the most popular products around, threatening to overtake Snickers as the candy king. A newish candy bar called PB Maxx has a higher peanut butter to chocolate ratio than Reese's Cups, and M&M's and others have come up with copycat peanut butter candies to rival Reese's Pieces, E.T.'s favorite.

> ## *"I know that I shall never see,*
>
> *A poem as lovely as Skippy Peanut Butter."*
>
> —William F. Buckley

No joke—don't let kids eat chunks of peanut butter. Some die every year from choking; it's so sticky even the Heimlich Maneuver dœsn't work.

Won't Stick To The Roof Of Your Mouth

But this Peter Pan Peanut Butter magnet will stick to the door of your refrigerator or anything else that's steel. Set of three magnets, each 2" long.

#M591, 3 Magnets, $3.95 + 4.00 shipping from Archie McPhee, P.O. Box 30852, Seattle, WA 98103-0852. (206) 547-2467.

Notorious Nut Junkies

Jimmy Carter's farm and **Annette Funicello's** "choosy mothers choose JIF" ads aren't the only celebrity peanut connections. How about these?

- **Elvis Presley's** favorite meal was a sandwich of peanut butter and bananas, grilled in butter.
- Tennis star **Chris Everett** eats a peanut butter sandwich before matches.
- Political writer **George Will** eats a peanut butter and sweet pickle sandwich at least twice a week.

THE HOUSE OF A MILLION NUTS

Nutty Info Nuggets

- An acre of peanuts can produce 30,000 peanut butter sandwiches.

- Peanut Butter uses 52% of the annual U.S. peanut crop, currently figured at 4 billion pounds of peanuts a year.

- It takes about 548 peanuts to make a 12 oz jar of the stuff.

- Americans are expected to eat 800 million pounds of peanut butter this year. That's an average of 3.3 pounds per person and enough to smoothly coat the entire floor of the Grand Canyon.

MR. PEANUT

"A *sandwich a day, keeps your children at play."*

—inscription from a 1910 peanut butter can (that empty can is today a collectible item which could sell for up to $250.)

The peanut plant's flowers are above the ground, but its fruits (the peanuts) are underground.

PETS

Fresh Poop on Pets

• Pets act as our best friends, family members, and substitute children. We treat them better than the people we live with.

• But that's always been true. Egyptians worshipped cats as gods. If one died, it was mummified and the people in its household shaved their eyebrows in mourning.

• Cats are the only domesticated animal never mentioned in the Bible.

• The most popular name for dogs is Lady. For cats, Baby.

• 58% of American households have pets. Of the 170 million pets, 58 million are dogs, followed by 49 million cats. Fish and birds account for 8% and 5%, respectively.

• 65% of cat and dog owners give their pets Christmas presents. 25% also celebrate their pet's birthday.

"The problem of the cat vs. the bird is as old as time…In my opinion, the State of Illinois and its local governing bodies already have enough to do without trying to control feline delinquency."

—Gov. Adlai Stevenson, leash law veto, 4/23/49

You Think *Your* Dog's Spoiled?

• An estate worth $4.3 million was left to the 150 mongrels of Eleanor Ritchey, an oil heiress who died in 1968. At last report, only one dog, Musketeer, remained, and his human attendant earned $17,000 per year looking after him.

• There's a ritzy apartment building just for dogs in Osaka, Japan, with apartments available by the day, week, month or year. Not a mere kennel, dogs get a chance for a taste of the good life while their guilty owners are away.

• In swank Palm Beach, Poodle Paradise acts as the doggy equivalent of Elizabeth Arden. A complete beauty makeover costs hundreds of dollars. The store sells $125 doggy overcoats and $1800 deluxe dog beds from India (a country where, coincidentally, $1800 is the average yearly income for a family of seven).

"Rats greet you, they interact, they try to please. They are as close to a dog as you're going to get in a rodent."

—Elizabeth Fucci, president of the Northeast Rat and Mouse Club, quoted in *Newsweek*

Persistent Urban Pet Myths

• *If you leave a cat alone with a sleeping baby, it will perform reverse CPR by sucking out the baby's breath until it suffocates.*

• *A wet poodle was placed in a microwave to dry and exploded.*

• *Given a choice of food, mice and rats prefer cheese (actually most choosy mice choose peanut butter.)*

• *The correct way to pick up rabbits (or beagles, if you're like the late LBJ) is by their ears.*

• *Baby alligators and turtles that people have flushed down the toilet are flourishing and mutating in our sewer systems.*

His Master's Voice?

• "Hey, bulldog!" John Lennon asked George Martin to edit in a high-pitched tone to end *Sgt. Pepper's* A Day in the Life to excite any dog listening. Listen to test how good your hearing is in the 15 kilocycle range.

• And speaking of hi-fi pet annoyance, the Beach Boys' **Pet Sounds** CD ends with the sound of Brian Wilson's dogs barking.

• The dogs got the last laugh on the Fab Four, at least. On *Beatle Barkers*, dogs barked out Beatle hits, augmented by chickens, sheep, pigs and cats.

Our Favorite Pet Films

Sure, we could recommend *Old Yeller*, *All Dogs Go to Heaven* or *Lady & the Tramp*, but everyone already knows about them. Here are two you maybe haven't seen.

• *Devil Dog: The Hound of Hell.* Satanists pick the prize bitch of the kennel to worship as their dark lord's incarnation. Stars Richard Crenna and Yvette Mimieux.

$69.95 + 4.00 shipping from Mr. Dickens Videos by Mail, 5323-A Ekhorn Blvd., Sacramento, CA 95842. (800) 228-4246.

• *Gates of Heaven.* A documentary about pet cemeteries and their owners is really about the big issues: immortality, success and failure, the American dream. With this movie, laughter is always one frame away from a poignant tear; out of dozens of favorite scenes, ours has to be the last—a long shot of Bubbling Wells Pet Cemetery's fork lift trundling by a grave site with a collie-sized coffin held aloft.

$69.95 + 4.00 shipping from Mr. Dickens Videos by Mail, 5323-A Ekhorn Blvd., Sacramento, CA 95842. (800) 228-4246.

FOR YOUR FELINE'S CANINES

Petrodex Dental Kit. Fight Fido's bad breath and prevent Pussycat's plaque. Complete dental care for dogs and cats includes one tube of special no-rinse toothpaste, soft toothbrush, treated dental gauze pads for polishing, and, before those big dates, breath spray.

#H2260, $15.00 from Animail Pet Care Products, 2515 East 43rd Street, Box 23547, Chattanooga, TN 37422-3547. (800) 255-3723.

Couch Potato Pet Videos

• For a homemade video your house-bound cat will watch over and over again: set your video camera next to a busy birdfeeder and let the tape run.

• **Aquarium TV.** This video of an aquarium makes a perfect gift for Couch Potato cats or even people. Just as attractive as a real tank of tropical fish, but no need to feed or clean, and no fishy smell. The soundtrack even gurgles.

$19.95 + 3.00 shipping from Relax Video, 419 W. 119th St., Suite 8-L, New York, NY 10027. (212) 496-4400.

• **The Doggie Adventure Tape.** Shot from the perspective of a dog (about two feet off the ground), it includes an exciting duck chase and a ride in the car. Three-and-an-arf stars!

$19.95 + 3.90 shipping from Signals, PO Box 64428, St. Paul, MN 55164. (800) 669-9696.

D oggie Style

• **Doggie-Sox.** Protect paws with deerskin booties sewn to knitted leggings with attached suspenders. Size S, M, L. #H1817, $25.95.

• **Denims.** Pre-washed blue or stone-washed black denim jacket for casual outings. Sizes 10" to 30". #H1810 , $35.00.

• **Raining Cats & Dogs.** Protect your precious pet with a hooded yellow rain slicker. Sizes 10" to 30". #H1804, $20.00.

• **For Chilly Dogs.** Machine-washable acrylic sweater in a classic black-and-white "houndstooth" check. Sizes 10" to 20". #H1826, $20.00.

• **Hydrant Hygiene.** Dogs will salute to the rear when they see this ceramic, fire-engine red replica of their favorite urban fixture. #H7435, $15.00.

Animail Pet Care Products, 2515 East 43rd St., Box 23547, Chattanooga, TN 37422. (800) 255-3723.

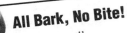

All Bark, No Bite!

• Burglars will envision a huge, vicious Doberman nipping at their heels when they encounter the electronic dog guard — a crime prevention system that detects intruders and chases them away by "barking" loudly like an English bulldog. Lasts 50 seconds, then resets.

#IQBB3, $59.95 + 3.50 shipping. Markline, PO Box 13807, Philadelphia, PA 19101-3807. (800) 992-8600.

• Or protect yourself from your *food* with this magnetically attached Diet Dog which growls whenever your refrigerator door is opened.

$24.95 + 3.25 shipping from Enticements, PO Box 4040, New Rochelle, NY 10802-4020. (800) 243-4300 / FAX (800) 244-4591.

"If man could be crossed with the cat, it would improve man, but it would deteriorate the cat."—Mark Twain

Pet Psychology:
Off the Couch!

• **No Bad Dogs the Woodhouse Way** by **Barbara Woodhouse.** Woodhouse maintains there are "no bad dogs, just inexperienced owners." In *No Bad Dogs*, Woodhouse tells a lot about everything, even how to detect dog schizophrenia. Woodhouse, listed in the *Guinness Book of World Records* for having trained over 17,000 dogs, has been known to grab dogs in the street away from their startled owners to administer proper training.

$7.95 + 1.00 shipping from Simon & Schuster, 1230 Avenue of the Americas, New York, NY 10010. (800) 223-2348.

• **How to Get Your Cat to Do What You Want** by **Warren Eckstein** with **Fay Eckstein.** Less authoritarian than Woodhouse's approach for dogs, Eckstein says it's not hard to convince your cat to be your best friend and refrain from scratching and spraying your furniture. The key is learning how and what cats think. We hope their cognitive process isn't too complicated for mere humans to master.

$17.95 + 2.00 shipping from Random House, Inc., 400 Hahn Rd., Westminster, MD 21157. (800) 733-3000.

• **The Four Footed Therapist: How Your Pet Can Help You Solve Your Problems** by **Janet Ruckert.** It's not your anima or animus, but your *animal* that's the key to your inner self. Pets can mediate conflict between couples and guide humans in their search for self-worth.

$8.95 postpaid from Ten Speed Press, PO Box 7123, Berkeley, CA 94707.

• **What Sign Is Your Pet?** by **Dr. Donald Wolf.** Does your dog race around in circles when excited? Relax. He's just a Gemini. Looking for a pet that you can dominate? Better not get a Leo! Is a Pisces cat compatible with a Leo fish? This book reveals all!

$8.95 + 2.00 shipping from Taylor Publishing, 1550 W. Mockingbird Lane, Dallas, TX 75235. (800) 677-2800.

Putting on the Dog

Your pet wouldn't be caught playing dead in off-the-rack duds? How about some "haute dog" couture designers, so exclusive they don't want their addresses listed?

• **Silk-'N'-Satin Designs** by **Patricia Henderson.** Liz Taylor's Lhasa Apsos dress up here. Prices range from $39.95 to thousands of dollars. Yes, she does weddings.

• **Alma Ballard** has appeared on *David Letterman* with parrots modeling her custom wedding dresses and a Napoleon outfit. Reach her at (516) 271-6953.

• Some feel clothes on real animals are a little cruel. For them, there's the *Victorian Cat Family* paper doll book.

$4.95 + 2.50 shipping from Dover Publications, 31 East 2nd St., Mineola, NY 11501.

BONE APPETIT!

• **For Paws** pet store hosts a buffet brunch for fifty dogs the first Sunday of every month featuring Kibble Quiche.

1017 Larkspur Landing Cr., Larkspur, CA 94939. (415) 461-2820.

• **Famous Fido's Doggie Deli** features meat and poultry tarts, carob chip cookies and velvety liver mousse cake. Also delivers Fido-grams of birthday wishes.

Famous Fido's Doggie Deli, 1533 West Devon St., Chicago, IL 60660. (312) 761-6028.

• **Nat's Country Pets,** named after proprietor Shira Barkon's Alaskan husky Natasha, carries home-baked goods and other sundries. Barkon (her real name) even offers bagels.

Great Valley Farmer's Market, Rte. 30 & 401, Malvern, PA. (215) 251-9465.

• **The Doggery.** After all that gourmet food takes its toll, Fido may need this dog spa which offers nutritional consultation, aerobics classes, a treadmill, sauna and Jacuzzi. It's where Zsa Zsa's pooch gets pumped up.

Charmaine's Doggery Animal Center, 3455 Overland, W. Los Angeles, CA. (213) 204-1331.

"No favor can win gratitude from a cat." —La Fontaine

Dogs in High Places

• Millie, the Bush dog who "wrote" a best seller, isn't the first or last animal willing to use its position to personal advantage.

• After he returned from a Pacific trip in 1944, Franklin Roosevelt realized his beloved Scottish terrier, Fala, had been accidentally left behind. He promptly sent a destroyer to retrieve the pooch. Fala now lies buried at the foot of FDR's grave in Hyde Park, NY.

• "We did get something—a gift— after the election . . .It was a little cocker spaniel dog in a crate that had been sent all the way from Texas…Trisha, the six-year-old, named it Checkers. And you know the kids love the dog, and I just want to say this right now, that regardless of what they say about it, we're going to keep it." —Richard Nixon, the "Checkers Speech "

• Nancy Reagan adopted a new dog, Rex, from the William F. Buckleys, displacing Lucky, who was banished to the Reagan's California ranch.

• Dog Save the Queen. A London newspaper reported that Queen Elizabeth's corgis have been treated by Roger Mugford, an animal psychologist. The corgis have nipped members of the royal family (Ouch! There goes the dynasty…).

Choker Collar

Popular three-strand faux pearl adjustable necklace gives your pets a new leash on lifestyle elegance.

#4235, $24.95 + 3.25 shipping from: Enticements, P.O. Box 4040, New Rochelle, NY 10802-4040. (800) 243-4300.

Snakes Alive

East Bay Vivarium. This store is great to browse in, or they'll sell you animals and supplies by mail order. They have a wide variety of reptiles, amphibians and arachnids, most of which are bred on site. This vivarium doesn't stock anything highly venomous, just creepy and crawly like giant 2' coconut crabs, or 20' long pythons. Contact for mail order information.

1827 Fifth Street, Berkeley, CA 94710 (510) 841-1400.

Yuppie Puppies

Le Beastro of Berkeley, California is a wonderful shop for Bowser to browse through with decidedly yup-scale merchandise like cat condos and bathrobes for dogs.

They specialize in health-conscious foods like "Bowser Brittle" with trendy rainforest nuts, "Pupcorn," and "Poocheezies," dog biscuits made from real mozzarella and garlic (keeps fleas away, for starters).

Good place for traditional, high-quality British grooming products and pet-oriented gifts for people. Visit if you're in the area, or contact them for their mail order catalog.

Le Beastro 1600 Shattuck Ave. Berkeley, CA 94709 (510) 644-0860.

MAGAZINES

• *Bird Talk.* Did you know that all parrots love Italian food, particularly spaghetti, ravioli and tortellini? You would if you read the ever-amusing *Bird Talk.* Covers the world of exotic birds and the avian brains who love them.

$23.97 (12 issues), PO Box 57347, Boulder, CO 80322. (303) 447-9330.

• *Cat Fancy.*

• *Dog Fancy.*

Articles on care, health, grooming, breeds, activities, events. Not as amusing as *Bird Talk,* but just as informative.

$21.97, 12 issues for either. PO Box 52864, Boulder, CO 80322. (303) 447-9330.

Hopping for the Best

House Rabbit Society. Rabbits make soft and affectionate pets. This bunny-loving organization is for people who live with floppy-eared friends. Also available from them: *The House Rabbit Handbook* ($8.95 + 1.05 shipping), loaded with what you need to know before becoming rabidly rabbitty.

Membership: $12.00, 1615 Encinal Ave., Alameda, CA 94501. (510) 528-8141.

Your Next Dog May Be a Pig

• Miniature pot-bellied pigs make a non-shedding, flea-resistant alternative to dogs. First mentioned in Chinese literature around 4000 B.C., pot-bellied pigs have been bred in the U.S. for just a half-dozen years, but breeders are having difficulty keeping up with the demand.

• They measure 14-20 inches in length, and normally weigh 40-70 lbs. (but they can balloon to 150 lbs. if you let them make pigs of themselves). Like dogs, they live 12-20 people years, but are smarter and cleaner (except for uncastrated males who, like uncastrated males everywhere, periodically stink and foam at the mouth).

• Males cost between $1000 and $1500; a pregnant sow can fetch up to $3500.

For more information contact *Pig Tale Times*. It's the porcophile's newsletter and it has articles on how to train, register, feed and care for these little piggies.

$16 per year (6 issues), *Pig Tale Times*, PO Box 227, Pescadero, CA 94060. (415) 879-0605.

Don't be a Paleface!

Good Ads Tell a Tail

• *The Dog Made Me Buy It!*
• *The Cat Made Me Buy It!*
• *The Black Cat Made Me Buy It!* by Alice L. Muncaster & Ellen Sawyer. Beautiful color reproductions of classic old advertisements featuring either dogs or cats selling everything from shoes to coal oil. Great for lovers of animals or old commercial art.

Each book: $12.95 + 2.50. Crown Publishers, 201 East 50th St., New York NY 10022. (212) 254-1600.

2 Things You Can Do With a Dead Cat

• **Pet Haven Pet Cemetery.** Over 32,000 pets rest in peace on this 3 1/2 acre "happy hunting ground." Many celebrities' pets are here, including Tina Turner's Great Dane, Michael Landon's beloved horse "Lady," and dogs owned by Jaclyn Smith, Rhonda Fleming, Groucho Marx and Jerry Lewis.

18300 S. Figueroa St., Gardena, CA 90248. (213) 321-0191.

Joe Kulis Freeze-Dry Systems. For owners who can't bear to part with expired pets, freeze-drying is one alternative to traditional taxidermy. They'll freeze your dead pet and slowly extract the water so it will "keep" indefinitely at room temperature. It's the same process that's used with "just add hot water" camping food.

There are over 400 entrepreneurs practicing pet freeze-drying nationwide, but if there isn't one near you, Joe Kulis will take care of your defunct best friend through the mail. Services run anywhere from $350 for small critters in a "sleep" pose to $1500 for a large dog frozen in an attack stance. The process can take from two months to one year, depending on the size of the pet. Pets can be sent via Federal Express, Air Freight or (no joke here) Greyhound, but call first for information and instructions.

Joe Kulis Freeze-Dry Systems, 725 Broadway, Bedford, OH 44146. (216) 232-8352.

Want a good food for your reptile? Try Purina Monkey Chow (made *for*, not *of*, monkeys).

Phonographs/Records

A Matter of Record

Well, kids, hard to believe, but before cassettes, DATs and CDs, people listened to music on what was called a "record." And even before that, there was another obsolete format. No, not the 8-track, that came later—it was the cylinder.

French scientist and poet Charles Cros first thought of what would later be known as the cylinder phonograph. But it was Thomas Edison who, in December 1877, actually came up with the real thing. The first sound recording? Edison himself reciting *Mary Had a Little Lamb*.

Edison thought his invention was going to be used primarily as an office machine for taking dictation, not as a means of entertainment. In the phonograph's earliest form, Edison recorded sound on a low-fi tinfoil cylinder. He experimented with other materials, including wax, before settling on celluloid.

In 1887, Emile Berliner took a different tack with the same idea and patented the "gramaphone," which played a flat disc. He started the Gramaphone Company in 1885. Edison a year later founded the National Phonograph Company (later known as Thomas A. Edison, Inc.) to compete with Berliner's company. Both companies began manufacturing talking machines and issuing recordings of bands, recitals, operas, small orchestras, comedians and sound recreations of historic and current events.

The difference between the recording methods of each company was dramatic. With Berliner's flat disc, it was easy to make a master recording from which copies could be stamped out. Edison's process, however, required individual recording of each cylinder. So while Berliner's artists just needed one good take into a single sound horn (this was before microphones), Edison's would have to do it over and over again, projecting loudly to the dozens of recording devices laid out to capture multiple copies of each performance.

In 1902, Edison figured out a way to mass-produce the cylinders, using a material that shrank free of

the mold, and the competition continued. Berliner teamed up with one Eldridge Johnson to create The Victor Talking Machine Company.

Edison's recordings had better sound fidelity, but Victor was winning in the marketplace because flat records were easier to store, not as breakable and allowed a song on each side. Edison finally saw the light and in 1912 issued his first flat disc.

In 1926, just three years before he retired from the phonograph business, Edison developed an early version of the LP. It was 12 inches in diameter, one-half-inch thick and weighed two pounds.

PHONO PILGRIMAGES

• **Edison Winter Home and Museum.** Believe it or not, you'll find a larger collection of phonographs and cylinders here than at the Edison National Historic Site and Laboratory in New Jersey. Plus you'll also get to tour Edison's winter home, garden and laboratory.

> **2350 McGregor Blvd., Ft. Myers, FL.**

• **Music Library and Sound Recordings Archives.** It's the largest academic library of recorded popular music with more than 400,000 popular recordings and print documentation for public perusal.

> **Bowling Green State University, Bowling Green, OH 43403-0179. (419) 372-2307.**

Required Reading

• *The Illustrated History of Phonographs* by Daniel Marty. Over 200 pages and 200 illustrations of early phonographs. Plus an enlightening look at phonographic history by one of the world's foremost authorities on the subject.

> **Available for $19.95 + 2.50 shipping from Vestal Press Ltd., 320 N. Jensen Road, P.O. Box 97, Vestal, NY 13851-0097. (607) 797-4872.**

• *Official Price Guide to Music Collectibles.* A great overview of many related subjects including old phonographs and recordings, giving a concise summary of the historical aspects of a variety of items and how to get a collection started. Also a terrific source for societies, newsletters, museums, etc.

> **Available for $11.95 + 1.50 shipping from House of Collectibles, 201 East 50th Street, New York, NY 10022. (800) 733-3000.**

• *American Premium Record Guide* by L.R. Docks. Record historian Docks has put together a definitive work listing 60,000 collectible 78s, 45s and LP records from Aardell to Zynn. The first 45 pages feature a terrific selection of photos of antique record labels.

> **Available for $16.65 postpaid from Books Americana, Inc., P.O. Box 2326, Florence, AL 35630.**

Get To The Point

500 steel needles (loud and/or soft tone) for your vintage Talking Machine. Why would anyone want 500 steel needles? Because you should use each needle only once before recycling it. Use it twice and you could ruin your valuable 78s. Also available: antique phonographs, motor parts (from springs to nuts), sound boxes and horns, cabinet parts, books, and accessories. This supply shop has it all:

> **Package of 500 steel needles, $13.50 postpaid. The Antique Phonograph Supply Co., Route 23, P.O. Box 123, Davenport Center, NY 13751-0123. (607) 278-6218.**

Shake It Up, Baby

Phonograph and Record Stack salt & pepper shakers.

> **#1243, $15.95 + 3.95 shipping from The Music Stand, 1 Rockdale Plaza, Lebanon, NH 03766-1585. (800) 295-7044 / FAX (802) 295-5080.**

"Genius is one percent inspiration and ninety-nine percent perspiration." —Thomas Alva Edison

RECORD ROUNDUP

69, 1990 Number Three

45s and 33s 86ed

Cassettes and CDs have taken over and it won't be long until vinyl records have gone the way of 8-track tapes, so get 'em while you can. Here are some great mail-order sources that still have interesting music on vinyl (as well as on those new-fangled formats).

• **Down Home Music.** Carries over 25,000 different titles in practically every category, covering especially well acoustical, historic, blues, folk, rhythm & blues, international and other things you won't hear on top 40 radio. They also handle the renowned Arhoolie Records catalog of Zydeco, Cajun, Tex-Mex, South American and more.

6 catalogs per year, $4.00 from 6921 Stockton Avenue, El Cerrito, CA 94530. (510) 525-1494 / FAX (510) 525-2904.

• **Roundup Records.** Lots of independent labels along with "the majors." All types of music especially folk, World Beat, African, Reggae, Political, Andean and Klezmer and much more.

Catalog: Roundup Records, P.O. Box 154, North Cambridge, MA 02140. (617) 661-6308.

• **Good Music Record Company.** The good thing about Good is the number of collections they carry that you can't find in most stores. For example: *The Fabulous Big Bands* (60 selections); *The Wacky World of Spike Jones*; *Stage Door Canteen* (44 WWII hits); *Golden Classics* (36 selections from the world's greatest composers); *Amazing Grace* ("60 stirring songs of faith..."); *Unforgettable Fifties* (50 biggest hits of the '50s); *55 Original Country Classics*; *The Bing Crosby Collection* (48 hit songs); *50 Mario Lanza songs*; *Mairzy Doats* (plus 43 more wacky hits); and, of course, the unforgettable magic of Zamfir.

Catalog: Good Music, 352 Evelyn Street, P.O. Box 909, Paramus, NJ 07653-0909. (800) 538-4200.

Needle Your Friends

Bet your friends...win big money! Pose the question, "*Which has more grooves: a 45 RPM single or a 33 RPM album?*"

The answer, of course is neither: they both have exactly two grooves, one on each side.

Sort It Out

Album Trax. Get your records organized via this database written specifically to keep music collections organized. Requires MS-DOS computer.

$25.00 postpaid. Saugatuck Software Inc., P.O. Box 2238, Westport, CT 06880.

One for the Nipper

English artist **Francis Barraud** thought he had a great idea to make some money. He painted a dog listening quizzically to an Edison phonograph and gave it the name "His Master's Voice." He figured that as soon as Edison saw this tribute to the high fidelity of his recordings, he would want to buy the painting and use it as a trademark. But Edison turned him down flat.

So Barraud went to work. He painted over the Edison phonograph and replaced it with a Victor gramaphone. Victor owners Berliner and Johnson loved it and "Little Nipper" the dog soon became world-famous. And he still is, as evidenced by these products:

• **Tin for the Price of One.** A storage device with the dog & phono (left).

#8012-5, $6.49 + 1.95 shipping from Miles Kimball, 41 West Eighth Avenue, Oshkosh, WI 54906.

• **Your Mug Looks Like A Dog.** 10 oz. ceramic mug (right).

#1174, $6.95 + 2.95 shipping from The Music Stand, 1 Rockdale Plaza, Lebanon, NH 03766-1585. (800) 295-7044 / FAX (802) 295-5080.

• **You'll Howl At This.** Ceramic Nipper music box spins around as it plays *Oh Where, Oh Where Has My Little Dog Gone.* 5-1/2" tall (right).

#1915, $44.95 + 5.95 shipping from The Music Stand, 1 Rockdale Plaza, Lebanon, NH 03766-1585. (800) 295-7044 / FAX (802) 295-5080.

• **Old Dog Tray.** Nipper helps you serve your guests.

#M-49X, $4.95 + 2.50 shipping from Vestal Press Ltd., 320 N. Jensen Road, P.O. Box 97, Vestal, NY 13851-0097. (607) 797-4872.

• **Shake, Rattle and Growl.** Nipper & Victrola ceramic salt & pepper shakers (above). 3" high.

#2413, $12.98 shipping from The Lighter Side, 4514 19th St. Court East, P.O. Box 25600, Bradenton, FL 34206-5600. (813) 747-2356 ext. 5 / FAX (813) 746-7896.

Speed Kills

It's great to listen to those old 78s. Or Edison's 80 rpm and Berliner's 70 rpm records. But the problem is you can't find those speeds any more, except on antique phonographs. They're expensive, don't plug into your modern sound system and their heavy arms cause unnecessary wear on your records. Esoteric Sound has the answer. Its excellent Vintage Turntable plays 33·1/3, 45, 71.29, 76.59, 78.26 and 80 rpm—each with a variable pitch of +/- 8%.

Vintage Turntable, $229.00 + variable shipping from Esoteric Sound, 4813 Wallbank Avenue, Downers Grove, IL 60515. (708) 960-9137.

Join the 21st Century

Okay, let's say you're ready to stop sniveling and admit it: the record is dead, and good riddance to its surface noise, ticks and skipping. If you're willing to surrender to the inevitability of progress and come along peacefully, we'll share our favorite sources for making sure you won't waste the extra money those darned CDs cost.

• **CD Review**. Our favorite monthly CD magazine. Just the right blend of reader interaction, music reviews of wide range, from classical to pop to quirky as hell, plain-talk technical news, and some healthy skepticism.

$24.94 for 12 issues, P.O. Box 58835, Boulder, CO 80322-8835. (800) 274-6754.

• **CD Review Digest**. Not affiliated with *CD Review* magazine, the *Digest* is a quarterly compilation of excerpts of reviews from thirty-some diverse music publications such as *Musician, Rolling Stone, Beatlefan, JazzTimes, Stereo Review* and even *Modern Drummer*. Especially good if you're trying to build up a definitive collection for a library, radio station—or to really impress your friends.

Classical, $29 year (4 issues), Jazz, Popular, Etc. $18 year (4 issues), from The Peri Press, Hemlock Ridge, P.O. Box 348, Voorheesville, NY 12186-0348.

No Cracks, Please

Got any any broken 78s or cylinders or old phonographs you want to have repaired? It's not easy, but this is a good source of information and help.

Contact: Lany Donley, Seven Acres Antique Village and Museum, 8512 S. Union Road, Union, IL 60180. (815) 923-2214.

Phonography By Mail

Antique Phonograph Collector's Club. This organization for collectors and appreciators gives an opportunity for sharing information and buying books and reprints of old phono manuals, etc. The membership magazine, *Antique Phonograph Monthly* features informative articles on phonographs and records and great classified ads.

Membership $14.00, c/o Allen Koenigsberg, 650 Ocean Avenue, Brooklyn, NY 11226.

Small Sound

5" reproduction of turn-of-the-century gramaphone actually plays miniature 2" records (6 included). Hear tunes like *Turkey in the Straw* and *Old Grey Mare*. Requires 2 AA batteries.

#711, $16.98 + 3.50 shipping from The Lighter Side, 4514 19th St. Court East, P.O. Box 25600, Bradenton, FL 34206-5600. (813) 747-2356 ext. 5 / FAX (813) 746-7896.

RECORD TIME

Marbled white watch face features 1 RPM record spinning on turntable.

#5856 Turntable Watch, $39.95 + 5.95 shipping from The Music Stand, 1 Rockdale Plaza, Lebanon, NH 03766-1585. (800) 295-7044 / FAX (802) 295-5080.

"Let no one imagine that in owning a recording he has the music. The very practice of music is a celebration that we own nothing."—John Cage

Phonographic Memories

As in everything, rarity, demand and condition determine the value of an old cylinder or disc machine. These are some typical prices for some of the classics, in excellent shape:

- *Berliner "Standard" Gram-O-Phone Type A (disc)*, up to $2600.
- *Berliner "Bijou" Type E (disc)*, $1200.
- *1902 Columbia Type AO (cylinder)*, up to $450.
- *Columbia "Baby Grand" Phonograph (disc)*, up to $2800.
- *1911 Edison Amerola Model 1B (cylinder)*, up to $2500.
- *1912 Edison Amerola Model III (cylinder)*, up to $1500.
- *A 1904 two-horn Victrola Model 5 (disc)*, up to $2,500.

Two For The Records

- *Goldmine Magazine*. The dealer and collector ads in *Goldmine* are a great source for old records of all speeds. The tremendous classified ad section covers practically every musical taste, from polkas to punk. Each issue spotlights a musical talent including a discography and price listing.

  Single copy $2.50 / $35 a year (26 issues), Krause Publications, 700 E. State Street, Iola, WI 54990, (715) 445-2214 / FAX (715) 445-4087.

- Pre-1940 Records & Cylinders. A free auction list of great old music.

  Tom Hawthorne, 4731 Melvin Dr., Carmichael, CA 95608. (916) 973-1106.

Record Prices

Cylinders. Although only in production for about 30 years, millions of cylinders were produced. So if you find some lying around the attic, they're of sentimental, not financial, value unless especially unusual and in good condition. Run-of-the-mill cylinders are worth as little as $3, but a few command high-end prices:

- *Admiral's Favorite March* (Columbia #51544), up to $22.
- *Darky's Tickle* (Columbia #515519), up to $35.
- *Down on the Suwanee River* (Columbia #515064), up to $42.
- *Liberty Bell March* (Oxford #500), up to $22.
- *Roosevelt's Inaugural Parade* (Oxford #32749), up to $40.

- *Early Caruso cylinders, as much as* $1000.

78 RPM Records. The old discs are still sometimes found in varying conditions at flea markets, resale shops and garage sales for as little as 50¢ each. Depending upon condition and rarity, some are highly valued. Some of these in the blues and jazz category:

- *I'm Gonna Gitcha*, Louis Armstrong (Okeh 8343) up to $50.
- *Frog Tongue Stomp*, Louie Austin and her Serenaders (Paramount 12361) up to $100.
- *Mistreatin' Mama*, Rabbits Foot Williams (Black Patti 8052) up to $250.
- *Cho Cho*, The Washingtonians (Blu Disc 1002) up to $300.
- *London Blues*, Fred (Jelly Roll) Morton (Rialto) up to $500.

"Get out those old records, the ones that Granny used to play..." —Georgia Gibbs

PINBALL

only 4% of the annual seven billion dollars spent on "coin-operated entertainment" in 1984, up to a respectable 35% in 1989. That's a lot of quarters (just under 10 billion, or $2,368,080,000).

Once upon a time pinball was the premiere way to satisfactorily squander a few minutes and a few quarters. Diners, student unions, bowling alleys, bus terminals, airports, billiard parlors, even laundromats sported the flashing, buzzing, clanging machines. Flipper stroking and machine nudging were skills accorded great respect, and the delivery of a new game was accorded great notice and large crowds

of players, spectators and kibbitzers. But then along came the novelty of video games. Pinball went into a fast, many thought terminal, decline.

Still, after a decade of losing ground, pinball's popularity rebounded, from

Pinball's comeback is due in part to the novelty of coin-operated video games wearing off, and partly because pinball designers have struck back. If you haven't played the game lately, you'll be pleasantly surprised.

The new games are whimsical, with elaborate story lines, digital sound and hyper playing fields. For instance, there's Earthshaker, which actually shakes and simulates a California earthquake. There's Whirlwind, which creates a tornado (even down to spinning disks to "blow" the ball in strange directions and a "windmaker" fan to blow air in your face). Or Elvira & the Party Monsters, featuring dancing ghouls

and the lady's digitalized voice. Or Taxi, in which the goal is to pick up various celebrity riders, including Marilyn Monroe, Santa Claus and Dracula, each with appropriate voices.

Pinball's main strength against video games is that it's concrete: real balls,

real bounces, real mechanical actions. Lucky (and unlucky) rebounds, randomness, spin, body english and even machine malfunctions are an integral part of the game. You can eventually figure out and master a video game, but a pinball machine, even one you know well, will continually surprise you.

Pinball and the Law

Did you know that many cities still have anti-pinball statutes on the books?

On one notorious day, January 21, 1942, the city of New York confiscated 1800 of the 11,800 pinball machines operating in the city. Within three weeks they had found and destroyed 3252 of them. They used the machines' wooden legs to make nightsticks for the police and turned over five tons of scrap metal to the war effort, including 3,000 pounds of steel balls.

Ironically, Chicago—home of Gottlieb, Bally and Williams, the big three manufacturers of pinball machines—is one of the cities which had a long-term ban on the game.

First commercially successful pinball machine was Baffle Ball by Gottlieb, made in 1931.

P

inball Facts

- Pinball got its name because the first games were bumperless, flipperless playing areas with holes you tried to get the balls into. The holes were protected by "pins"—configurations of nails to make it hard to get the ball in. In those pre-tilt days, players were supposed to shake, rattle and roll the game to effect the movement of the balls.

- Pinball designers work toward this ideal: the game should be easy enough to keep novices from getting discouraged, yet challenging enough to keep "wizards" interested. The average game should last from 2 1/2 to 3 minutes, or roughly 47 seconds a ball, and the player should get a free game for every four played.

- The "tilt," which penalizes players who shake, bump and abuse machines, was originally called "The Stool Pigeon" by its inventor, Harry Williams (sometimes called "the Thomas Edison of Pinball"). He didn't particularly like the name but hadn't come up with anything better. He was watching people play the prototype machine set up in a drugstore. One activated the "stool pigeon" and exclaimed, "Damn! I tilted it!" A buzzword was born.

- Advances in pinball bumper technology led to the first typewriter for persons with cerebral palsy and similar handicaps. If the person had control of a single body movement—a shoulder twitch, for instance—the solenoid mechanisms amplified that into specific strokes on a keyboard.

- In 1931, you got seven balls for a penny. Then ten balls for a nickel. In 1933, when steel balls replaced glass marbles, it became five balls per nickel. By the late 1960s, the cost had become three five-ball games for a quarter. 1970s inflation whittled that down to two five-ball games a quarter, then one five-ball game a quarter, then one three-ball for a quarter. Now fifty cent three-ball games are the norm.

PINBALL PILGRIMAGES

- **Broadway Arcade.** Maybe the best pinball arcade anywhere. Who says so? Pinball experts like Henny Youngman, Roberta Flack, Paul Simon, Matthew Broderick and Lou Reed, all of whom have been seen hanging around this NYC institution. Reed even wrote a song about it—*Down at the Arcade*, on his **New Sensations** album.

The Broadway has been at this location since 1930, and its clientele is so respected in the industry that pinball companies have been known to test prototype machines there.

1659 Broadway (at W. 52nd Street), New York, NY 10019. (212) 247-3725.

- **Pinball Expo / Flip-out Pinball Tournament.** Every Autumn Robert Berk hosts this three-day event in the Chicago area, the home of pinball manufacturing. Registration for the entire marathon of seminars, banquets and a tour of a pinball factory is $60, although for $5 you can attend the exhibits or enter the Pinball Tournament (grand prize: a new pinball machine).

For information about the Pinball Expo and Tournament, call (800) 323-FLIP.

> *"Pinball feeds on vast sums siphoned from the worn pockets of those least able to afford the sucker's game of rigged odds. If allowed to get out of hand, it can wreck the civic enterprise and economic well-being of any village, town, or city."*
>
> **—James Connor, St. Louis Crime Commission, 1950s**

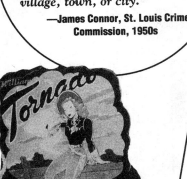

Pinball Firsts

- *Tilt mechanism: Advance, Bally, 1932*
- *Electric game, and game with sounds: Contact, Pacific Amusement, 1933*
- *"Backglass" (the decorated vertical scoreboard area): Stoner Manufacturing Company, 1933*
- *Spring bumpers: Bumper, Bally, 1937*
- *Solenoid "thumper bumpers," 1946*
- *Free game mechanism, 1941*
- *Flippers: Humpty Dumpty, Gottlieb, 1947*
- *Talking machine: Gorgar, Williams, 1979*

It wasn't until 1976 that pinball was finally legalized in its own hometown, Chicago.

The Classic Antique Pinball Games (pre-1975)

According to **Harry McKeown**, pinball expert and author of *Pinball Portfolio* (currently-out-of print, alas), these are the classic machines issued before 1978.

• *Fireball* (1972, Bally). "Possibly the finest machine produced." Features a spinning rubber disk directly above the flippers which hurtles the ball unexpectedly in odd directions. Also, ball traps and releases that allow the synapse-bursting possibility of up to three madly-careening balls on the field at a time.

• *Wizard* (1975, Bally). Inspired by Tommy, it features scenes from the film. "It's not a machine that can be mastered without intensive play. It demands tight nerves and extreme concentration. Provides some wonderful games."

• *Gigi* (1963, Gottlieb). Features a colorful circus motif. "An extremely tricky machine."

• *Magic City* (1967, Williams). "A simple machine that packs lots of enthralling play onto an uncluttered exciting field, it's not difficult to understand why this machine has captured the hearts of many, many players."

• *Cowpoke* (1965, Gottlieb). A Wild West motif featuring wholesome looking cowgals. "A dazzling game to play. Great opportunities for some real skill shots."

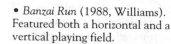

Classic Contemporary Pinball Machines (Since 1975)

These are the classics from more recent times, according to **Roger Sharpe**, author of *Pinball!* (another out-of-print-gem):

• *Sharpshooter* (1979, Game Plan). True, Sharpe designed this one and that's his portrait on the backglass. Still, he swears it's a classic, even allowing for prejudice. The Smithsonian Institution, no less, agrees—they have a Sharpshooter on display.

• *Caveman* (1982, Gottlieb). The first hybrid pinball/video machine.

• *Banzai Run* (1988, Williams). Featured both a horizontal and a vertical playing field.

• *Cyclone* (1988, Williams). Winner of "The Most Played Game" award from the Amusement and Music Operators Association in both 1988 and 1989. One of the new hyper-designed machines with chutes and bumpers everywhere, Cyclone features a carnival motif, digitalized barkers and unusual features like a "ferris wheel" for balls.

• *Cleopatra* (1977, Gottlieb). Gottlieb's first solid state pinball machine featured a bank of colored drop targets all over the field. "Simple, but wonderful," says Sharpe.

• *Mata Hari* (1977, Bally). A beautiful machine from what is considered the golden age of artwork from Bally.

• *Orbiter I* (1982, Stern). Stern Electronics' last game before biting the dust featured a moonscape playing field pitted with craters and other lunar obstacles.

It takes a team of six designers about nine months to invent and debug a pinball game.

Recommended Reading

Pinball: The Lure of the Silver Ball by Gary Flower and Bill Curtz. A profusely illustrated look at the history and art of the pinball machine and examples of the promotions and advertisements that launched them. Check out the comprehensive list of every pinball machine made in the U.S. since 1939.

$12.98 + 3.00 shipping from Chartwell Books, 110 Enterprise Avenue, Secaucus, NJ 07094. (201) 864-6341.

Getting the Full Tilt on Pinball

Here are our favorite pinball publications:

• *Pinball Player.*

One year, $30.00. The Pinball Owners' Association, P.O. Box 2, Haslemere, Surrey, England GU27 2EQ.

• *Pinball Trader.* Buying and selling.

One year (12 issues), $24.00. P.O. Box 440922, Brentwood, MO 63144. (314) 962-4750.

• *Pinball Collector Newsletter.* Extensive service tips, machine lore and classified ads.

One year (6 issues), $45.00. 200 S. Semoran Blvd., Orlando, FL 32807. (407) 249-1022.

• *Gameroom Magazine.* Not just pinball, also features jukeboxes, slot machines, arcade machines, Coke machines or other coin-operated antiques.

One year, $24.00. 1014 Mt. Tabor Road, New Albany, IN 47150. (800) 462-4263.

Pinball Prose

Who can explain author **William Saroyan's** fascination with pinball? In two of his works he featured the game prominently.

Not surprisingly, he saw deeper meaning in those bumpers and balls: "The game itself needs expert explaining of course, but what it is is a head-on confrontation to acquire signs, symbols, messages, [and] instructions that are satisfying and useful..."

In the stage directions of his 1939 play *The Time of Your Life*, Saroyan describes a confrontation between a character named Willie and the on-stage pinball machine:

"He pushes down the lever, placing one marble in position. Takes a very deep breath, excited at the beginning of great drama. Stands straight and pious before the contest. Himself vs. the machine. Willie versus Destiny. His skill and daring vs. the cunning and trickery of the novelty industry of America. He is the last of the American pioneers, with nothing more to fight than the machine..."

> "If I won on every try, there'd be no fun to this game; losing every time would make me quit, too. It's like chasing a woman. There's always the chance you'll catch her. But if you knew for certain, the chase would hardly be worth it."
>
> —Player, quoted by author Julius Segal, *Harpers Magazine*

Kids, Try These at Home!

Just like the real things, only they're a tad smaller and a lot cheaper.

• **Astro Shooter II.** Lightning-fast pinball action complete with flashing lights, arcade sound effects, automatic scoring and three (count 'em three) flippers.

#FTM707, $119.95 + 8.50 shipping. The Sharper Image, P.O. Box 7031, San Francisco, CA 94120-7031. (800) 344-4444.

• **Atom Pinball.** Bells ring, lights flash and you get special effects and "laser" sounds. And it's plastic, so it's the most affordable pinball game you can get with all the action you want!

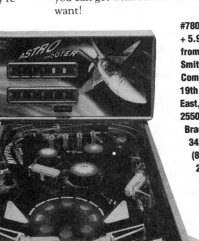

#7804, $39.98 + 5.95 shipping from Johnson Smith Company, 4514 19th St. Court East, P.O. Box 25500, Bradenton, FL 34206-5500. (813) 747-2356 / FAX (813) 746-7896.

Pinball is called *Les Flippers* in France.

Pinball-Besotted Art

• *Tommy* by the Who (1969). The first full-length "Rock Opera" describes a deaf, dumb and blind boy who "plays by intuition" and becomes the spiritual leader to thousands by virtue of his pinball wizardry. *Tommy* became a ballet and a movie starring Ann-Margret and Tina Turner.

• *TILT* (1978). Brooke Shields is a young pinball champion named Tilt who enters a competition to help her boyfriend become a rock star. "The dialogue is laughable and the performances are generally putrid" wrote one critic. If only Saroyan had done the screenplay.

• *Amarillo*, a song by Emmylou Harris: "...He saw the lights and had to hear them ring / And he was never the same after he won his first free game / I lost him to the jukebox and a pinball machine."

Scientific Pinballogy

" A ball hit with the end portion of a flipper leaves more quickly than one hit near the pivot. It is obvious that the further a point on the flipper is from the pivot the further it moves during a flip.

The flipper is simply a lever rotating about an axis through a restricted part of a circle. Let 'a' be the angle in range between the flipper's up and down positions, and 'r' be the distance of a point from the axis of rotation. Then during a flip the point moves a distance of 'ar'. This establishes that a ball hit further out on the flipper is in contact for a greater distance. It is also true that such a ball is pushed at greater speed while on the flipper..."

—From *Pinball Wizardry* by Robert Polin and Michael Rain.

Buying Your Own Machine

There comes a time in every pinballer's life when he or she wants to own a machine. While there are some home versions—and some aren't bad—true aficionados set sights on the real thing.

• Check your local Yellow Pages, flea markets, or the want ads. Roger Sharpe of Williams Electronics Games, Inc.

suggests an even more direct route: if you have a favorite machine you play somewhere, ask the proprietor when they expect to get rid of it and whether they plan to sell it.

• Sharpe says prices for a used machine in decent working order are generally

$2000 and up for anything less than two years old, $800-1500 for one two to five years old; and for "a solid, wonderful game from the past" $750 or even less.

• He suggests buying a machine only if you've had a chance to try it, for two reasons: make sure it works and make sure you'll want to keep playing the game for the coming weeks, months, even years.

"I tell people not to buy a machine they can beat now, because they'll get bored with it," says Sharpe. "Buy something that's going to keep being a challenge."

Used Pinballs for Your Extra Quarters

For Amusement Only. Our favorite source for completely reconditioned machines (and repairs

on sick ones). Proprietor Jim Tolbert, author of the out-of-print classic on ownership and repair, *Tilt, the Pinball Book*, sells used machines and parts worldwide. In his warehouse he has hundreds of old machines.

The price? $600 to $1500, including reconditioning, for most machines, going as high as $3000 for especially old or unusual machines. Expect to pay another $100-200 for shipping.

For a pinball interior decorating motif, Tolbert also sells extra "backglass" (the profusely decorated vertical surface displaying score and number of games left) from selected machines, suitable for lighting and

displaying on a wall—or maybe as a stained glass window.

For Amusement Only, 1853 Ashby St., Berkeley, CA 94703. (510) 548-2300.

Some pinball pros wear steel-toed shoes so they can wedge their toes under the machines to slow the ball down.

Puzzle

'TIS A PUZZLEMENT

- What do Hulk Hogan, Popeye, John Wayne, Bart Simpson, Faberge eggs, teddy bears, baseball cards, fields of tulips, Barbie, maps and Escher prints all have in common? Their pictures have all been cut up into cardboard pieces, boxed and sealed, and sold to the unsuspecting public, whose task it has been to painstakingly recreate the pictures.

- The first known jigsaw puzzles were the creation of a London printmaker by the name of John Spilsbury. Sometime in the 1760s he took some maps, mounted them on wooden boards and cut them along country boundary lines. It then took twenty years before anyone came up with the idea of using something other than a map—next came Biblical scene puzzles.

- Interlocking border pieces came next. The late 1800s saw the invention of the jigsaw and plywood, making it possible to make more difficult puzzles. By the turn of the century, puzzles for adults became a hit. Even though they didn't contain all that many pieces (75-100), they were pretty difficult, because there was no helpful picture on the box and cuts were made along color boundaries, causing adjacent pieces to be of different hues.

- Puzzlemania continued through the Depression as an inexpensive form of entertainment for young and old. From 1932-33, advertising puzzles were a big thing, given away for free. Listerine, TipTop Bread, Standard Oil, A&P, Chevrolet, Procter & Gamble, and 20 Mule Team Borax and many others gave away puzzles with the purchase of their products. Dairies would even deliver them with the morning milk.

Exchanging a Few Crosswords

- December 21, 1913, a day that will live in...a six-letter word ending in y. Enmity? No. Infamy? Yeah, that's it. That's the day the first crossword puzzle appeared, thanks to the *New York World* and Arthur Wynne, the first crossword creator.

- "Attention Crossword Puzzle Fans! The First Book of Crossword Puzzles — $1.35. Your Money Back If Not *100% Satisfied!*"That was the wording of the first ad for the first crossword puzzle book, published in 1924 by Simon & Schuster.

- $1.35 in 1924 wasn't cheap, even allowing for the fact that a freshly sharpened pencil was attached to each copy of the book. The fledgling publishing company sold 40,000 copies in three months launching it toward the media giant it has since become. The Simon, in Simon & Schuster? He was singer Carly Simon's father.

"What is mathematics, after all, except the solving of puzzles?" —Martin Gardner

Get the Picture?

The National Jigsaw Puzzle Championship. Held every August in Athens, Ohio. There are both singles and doubles events. For information contact:

P.O. Box 747, Athens, OH 45701. (614) 592-4981.

Putting It All Together

Jigsaw Puzzles: An Illustrated History and Price Guide by Anne D. Williams. A concise history of jigsaw puzzles, including a study of major manufacturers, concentrating on U.S. puzzles produced after 1850. Williams is a puzzle collector with over 1,800 puzzles of her own. Her book is a visual feast of illustrations with descriptions and prices of puzzles categorized into topical chapters.

$27.45 postpaid from Wallace-Homestead Book Co., One Chilton Way, Radnor, PA 19089-0230. (800) 345-1214, Ext. 4730.

Maddening Upwardly Mobile Mosaics

• **Stave Puzzles, Inc.** Since 1974, Stave has earned the nickname "Rolls-Royce of Jigsaw Puzzles" for hand-cut, custom-made wooden puzzles, costing from $95-$7,000. The richest woman in the world, Queen Elizabeth, has one, and so do other well-heeled fans with names like du Pont, Mellon and Roosevelt. Stave's goal is to make the very best to "drive you all nuts."

The puzzles have irregular edges, hidden designs, split corners and silhouette pieces (the clown is founder Steve Richardson's signature piece). Each puzzle contains an extra trick like a rebus which when solved earns redeemable prize points, and sometimes

the company throws in a few extra pieces that won't fit anywhere. Of course there are no pictures on the boxes to give any clues. Sadistic, yes? Sadism sells.

Stave Puzzles, Inc., P.O. Box 329, Norwich, VT 05055. (802) 295-5200.

• **Elms Puzzles** are made of mahogany and are usually reproductions of art classics: Botticellis, Currier & Ives, Van Goghs, Renoirs, etc. No pictures on these boxes either, but Elms does give you a title which is a clue to the finished puzzle. Elms offers a "Puzzlers" club with a $50 lifetime household membership fee. Members can rent puzzles (which sell for $30-$1,000) and receive discounts on orders.

Elms Puzzles, Inc., P.O. Box 537, Harrison, ME 04040. (207) 583-6262.

• *Sunday Afternoon on the Island of La Grande Jatte.* The Art Institute of Chicago has the world's best collection of Impressionist paintings, and offers puzzles of them, like a deluxe limited edition of 500 picturing George Seurat's famous painting.

$250.00 + 9.50 shipping, or $32.00 + 4.50 shipping for the same in a smaller, unlimited edition. Art Institute of Chicago's Museum Store, Michigan Avenue at Adams Street, Chicago, IL 60603. (800) 621-9337 (send $1.00 for a 32-page catalog of collectible and gift items).

Free Personality Test

Jigsaw puzzlers usually fall into one of four categories: edge people, picture people, shape people and color people. Expert puzzlers are usually not edge people and many are ambidextrous.

Jigsaw jargon: the "nubs" are the outies, and the "voids" are the innies. Successfully hooking a nub and void together is called a "lock."

Crosswords at the Crossroads

- **Railroad crossing.** The crossword fad caught on so quickly that by 1925 the B & O Railroad put dictionaries on all its mainline trains for its many crossword solving passengers.

- **Cross-dressing.** The crossword craze also affected fashion during the Roaring Twenties, when black and white checked fabric became all the rage.

- **Cross to Bear.** In 1924, a woman in Cleveland was granted a divorce from a puzzle addict. Testifying in court, she described his obsession. "Morning, noon and night, it is crossword puzzles."

- **Cross fire.** In December, 1925, Theodore Koerner, 27-year-old employee of the New York Telephone Co., shot and wounded his wife because she refused to help him solve a crossword puzzle. He then killed himself.

- **Doublecross.** In 1925, three men in a New York restaurant refused to leave at closing, so engrossed were they in a crossword puzzle. By 3 A.M. the police arrived and arrested the ringleader. He was given 10 down— days in jail.

- **"3 across: farewell…"** In 1926, a Budapest waiter, Julius Antar, committed suicide. He left a note behind explaining why, but it was incorporated into a crossword puzzle. The police were unable to solve it.

A Club With Members Who Are Cross and Down

American Crossword Federation. While most people do the newspaper crossword puzzle now and again, there are still some fanatics around. The ACF publishes a newsletter full of membership information and tips on mastering the crossword experience.

One year membership $14.97 from ACF, P.O. Box 69, Massapequa Park, NY 11762. (800) 729-1999.

Nubbed & Voided

- **Marriage in pieces.** Big news in Zurich, Switzerland several years ago centered on a puzzling divorce case. The wife, addicted to jigsaw puzzles, left only a corridor free of puzzles from the front door to the bed, and completed puzzles piled twelve deep in every room. Banned from his own living room, the husband complained he couldn't even find a piece of bread to eat since the housekeeping money was spent on more puzzles. The divorce went uncontested by the wife, who remarked, "For years I had to put up with the stench of his cigars."

- **Piece at home.** How many jigsaw puzzle pieces does it take to cover almost every square inch of space in a six room house? About a million. Charley Lang, a true puzzlemaniac, put together and glued (with 16 gallons of special glue) 1,135 puzzles in a novel home-decorating scheme—walls, ceilings, doors and even some floors are covered with a world tour of scenes. Charley figures that if the average puzzle piece is one inch wide, his puzzle pieces laid end to end would measure 15.8 miles.

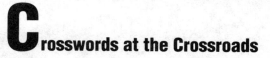

P.C. Puzzlers

Never worry about losing another jigsaw puzzle piece. Put it together on your computer. "Jigsaw!" **is** designed for IBM, Amiga and Apple II personal computers and contains 20 images of landscapes, animals, art masterpieces, and world-famous sites.

$40.00 + 4.00 shipping from Britannica Software, 345 Fourth Street, San Francisco, CA 94107. (800) 572-2272 / FAX (415) 546-1887.

CROSS YOUR OWN WORDS

If you own an IBM or Apple II p.c., Disney Software can help you create your own crossword puzzles using word and / or even picture clues! "Mickey's Crossword Puzzle Maker" also includes ready-made crossword puzzles.

$38.99 + 5.00 shipping from Egghead Discount Software, 22011 SE 51st Street, Issaquah, WA 98027-7004. (800) EGGHEAD / FAX (206) 391-0880.

Where to Get Old Puzzles

Old puzzle values are determined by age, rarity, graphic appeal, quality, number of pieces and condition. Most are priced in the $5 to $100 range, making puzzle collecting still affordable. An original Spilsbury puzzle (not an easy find) could be worth up to $3,000, varieties from the 1800s hover in the $50-$400 area and cardboard puzzles for adults made in the 1930s can be purchased for less than $10. The best source we've found for buying or selling old puzzles (and other old toys and games as well) is *The Toy Shop*.

One year subscription (12 issues) $18.95 from *The Toy Shop*, 700 East State St., Iola, WI 54990.

I'm In Pieces, Bits & Pieces

Our favorite source for puzzles of all sorts is the Bits & Pieces catalog. Here are three of theirs we especially like:

• **The World's Smallest Jigsaw Puzzles** (left). 99 tiny wooden pieces will form a 2¹/2" square picture (tweezers are suggested to put these together). Set of three mini-puzzles.

#05-J4074, $19.95 + 3.95 shipping. Available from Bits & Pieces, 1 Puzzle Place, B8016, Stevens Point, WI 54481-7199. (800) JIGSAWS / FAX (715) 341-5958.

• **One Tough Puzzle.** Nine solid color pieces which form a 7 inch square (300,000 incorrect combinations possible).

#04-J5516, $6.95 + 3.95 shipping from Bits & Pieces (see above).

• **The World's Longest Puzzle.** Metamorphosis, an ever-changing Escher design, makes a great puzzle of 3,000 pieces which, when assembled, form a cardboard runner measuring 8¹/2" wide x 153" long (nearly 13 feet).

#03- J1110, $39.95 + 5.95 shipping from Bits & Pieces (see above).

What's a 14-letter word for a crossword maniac? CRUCIVERBALIST.

Tuning in to Radio

"Dot dot dot." Radio officially began in 1895, when Italian physicist Guglielmo Marconi, the father of wireless telegraphy, developed a way to transmit and receive signals by Hertzian waves. On December 11, 1901, he sent a wireless message across the world: Morse code for the letter "S" from England to Canada.

On Jan. 18, 1903 the development of the vacuum tube allowed a transmission of spoken good-will messages between President Theodore Roosevelt and King Edward VII. Seventeen years later, on Nov. 2, 1920, a radio station in Pittsburgh (KDKA) announced the results of the Harding / Cox presidential election, scooping the newspapers on a big story for the first time.

At first, radios could be listened to only with earphones and a great deal of patience. Tuning in to a favorite station often meant fiddling with as many as 27 different dials and knobs.

But by 1921, radios started featuring loudspeakers powered by vacuum-tube amplifiers. A few years later, tuning in to the limited number of stations available became the simple one-dial operation it is today. The Radio Corporation of America (RCA) began

Radio Days

In our time, when radio is just talk or a jukebox, it's hard to imagine the variety of programming that used to be.

Here's a way to get a clue. On September 21, 1939, Washington DC radio station WJSV recorded its entire broadcast day from sign-on to sign-off. It's now available in a cassette set.

Starting with the early morning farm reports, you'll hear 18 hours of music, conversation, comedy, drama, sports, news and commercials. Highlights include *Sundial with Arthur Godfrey*, a special

selling radios and broadcasting from some of the nation's first radio stations. In 1926, RCA created the National Broadcasting Company (NBC), headed by David Sarnoff, to handle its broadcast operations. 1928 brought forth a second network, United Independent Broadcasters, which eventually became CBS. Not long after came the Mutual Broadcasting System.

With the advent of these three networks, the "golden age" of radio was born and continued until television ended radio's reign in the late 1940s. How was it the "golden age?" It had stars like W.C. Fields, Abbott &

Congressional address by President Roosevelt, and Louis Prima and His Orchestra. Highly recommended.

#11875 (12 cassettes in a bookshelf album), $29.95 + 3.90 shipping. Wireless, P.O. Box 64422, St. Paul, MN 55164-0422. (800) 669-999. (Ask for their catalog—a great source of various radio-related stuff).

Costello, George Burns and Gracie Allen, Fred Allen, Eve Arden, Jimmy Durante, Edgar Bergen and Charlie McCarthy, as well as all the best bands. And how about these continuing series?

- *Jack Armstrong, the All-American Boy*
- *Sergeant Preston of the Yukon*
- *Fibber McGee and Molly*
- *Tom Mix*
- *Sky King*
- *The Lone Ranger*
- *The Shadow*
- *The Bickersons*
- *The Green Hornet*
- *Ted Mack's Original Amateur Hour*
- *Lum and Abner*
- *Hopalong Cassidy*
- *Lux Radio Theater*
- *Mercury Theater of the Air*

"Radio has no future." —William Thomson, Lord Kelvin, president of the Royal Society, 1890-95

The Conspiracy Against FM Radio

In 1940, technological advances allowed radio receivers to expand from the standard AM band into the higher-quality FM band. But it took more than 20 years before FM found mass acceptance. Corporate greed, political maneuverings, sabotage, dirty tricks, and senseless suffering all played a role in the story.

Edwin Armstrong had been granted a patent for the superior-sounding FM format in 1933. He knew that FM's quality was better than AM and went out to convince anyone he could.

General Electric began mass-producing FM radios. Unfortunately, the war effort quickly put a damper on this and every other commercial venture. During the war, Armstrong allowed the government to use his patent for free, and FM became the standard of battlefield communication.

When World War II ended, FM found itself on a different kind of battlefield. FM had been assigned the frequencies between 42 and 50, but AM radio industry execs convinced the FCC to change them to 88 to 108, effectively knocking FM out of the range of existing radios (it later backfired because the new frequencies actually offered superior reception).

To further inhibit Armstrong's FM from gaining any ground, the AM companies fired a volley of lawsuits. One by one, they sued him, keeping him in court every day for the next 18 years, with their lawyers grilling him and calling him a liar and cheat.

The strategy worked. FM was stalled for many years, and poor Armstrong finally gave up. Broke and profoundly discouraged, he jumped out of his New York apartment window at age 65.

Later, once FM finally looked inevitable, most FM licenses were bought up by AM interests. They merely simulcast their AM shows on it, squelching any public enthusiasm for the new medium.

FM finally got a chance in the mid-1960s. Automakers started putting FM receivers in new cars, and consumers got used to FM's stereo, more varied programming and better sound. And in 1965 the FCC began requiring AM stations to break simulcast at least half the day.

Ironically, it was the initial lack of success that set the stage for FM's sudden popularity. FM stations sold fewer commercials, so DJs had more uninterrupted time to run longer and more diverse music like jazz, classical and underground rock. By the late 1970s, FM surpassed AM in popularity.

Crystal Memories: Collecting Old Radios

To most collectors, the Golden Age of Radio didn't end with the advent of TV in the late '40s, but somewhere between the late 1950s and early '60s, when solid-state circuitry was introduced.

Hot on the collectors' market are plastic radios molded into whimsical shapes and sizes including baseballs, Peter Pan, bottles of beer and hamburgers.

Most early ones were made of either brown Bakelite or the marbled, more colorful Catalin. Manufacturers created new models which, like autos, were introduced yearly.

Collectors these days pay dearly for old models, even if they don't work. Here are going rates for mint quality, working models—

• Air King "Skyscraper"—$10,000.

• Emerson's Snow White and the Seven Dwarfs, 1938—up to $800.

• Mickey Mouse radio, 1934—$900.

• Radio showing the Dionne quintuplets—about $135.

Yes, it is possible to pick up audible radio transmissions with the fillings in your teeth. Same principle that works in crystal radios.

Radiology 101

Want more information about radio collecting? Check these out.

• *The Radio Collector's Directory and Price Guide* by Robert E. Grinder and George H. Fathauer. This guide lists all types of old radios, along with their manufacturers, model numbers, years from which they date, styles, etc. Lots of pictures.

$17.95 postpaid from Ironwood Press, P.O. Box 8464, Scottsdale, AZ 85252.

• *Radios: The Golden Age* by Philip Collins. A beautiful view of all radio eras with over 100 color photos. An affectionate and whimsical look back.

$14.95 softbound / $25.00 hardbound. Add 3.00 shipping from Chronicle Books, 275 Fifth Street, San Francisco, CA 94103. (800) 722-6657.

Buy Gone Days

Crystal Radio Kit. Batteries aren't included, because you don't need any—crystal radios run on the energy from the radio waves.

No tubes or tools required either. Once you get it together, it costs nothing to operate, and it plays indefinitely! Comes complete with tuning coil, antennas & earphone.

#6127, $10.98 + 4.20 shipping. Johnson Smith Co., 4514 19th Court East, P.O. Box 25500, Bradenton, FL 34206-5500. (813) 747-2356.

Crosley Classic

It's an authentic, romantic replica of a 1938 Zenith radio. Brown cabinet in a sleek, chic Art Deco design. You can almost hear the Big Bands playing.

Actually, you CAN hear the Big Band sounds if you've got the cassette tapes (it plays them as well as tuning in AM/FM radio).

#15182, $69.95 + 7.75 shipping from Wireless, P.O. Box 64422, St. Paul, MN 55164-0422. (800) 669-9999.

'40s Style…'90s Sound!

Curvy corners, camel-back top, classic elegance describes this 1940 replica radio. No tubes or cloth speakers…it's got solid-state electronics for superior sound and reception. Metallic red finish and illuminated station indicator dial. Runs on four D batteries (included!).

#45212W, $39.95 + 3.00 shipping from Hammacher Schlemmer, 9180 Le Saint Drive, Fairfield, OH 45014. (800) 543-3366.

SPARTAN SPECIAL

A reproduction of the 506 Spartan "Bluebird" Radio, introduced in 1935. This art-deco styled radio has been updated by Sony and features all the hi-tech AM/FM essentials to give it a clear '90s sound. Front of radio is a thick cobalt blue mirror trimmed in chrome and sports an illuminated rotary station dial.

#45213W, $249.95 + 12.50 shipping from Hammacher Schlemmer, Midwest Operations Center, 9180 Le Saint Drive, Fairfield, OH 45014. (800) 543-3366.

"When [humanity] ceased any longer to heed the words of the seers and prophets, Science lovingly brought forth the Radio Commentator." —Jean Giraudoux, 1933

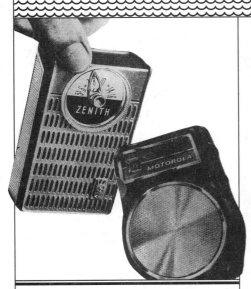

REMEMBER YOUR BUDDY FROM THE '30s?

Say, don't you remember this authentically styled, classic Crosley Buddy console radio. 1990s version has AM/FM with hi-tech conveniences, a side-loading cassette player and a wide-range speaker. Plus a full 10 year warranty.

#C738468, $129.95 + 9.00 shipping from Sync, Hanover, PA 17333-0042. (800) 722-9979.

Radio Traders

The Antique Radio Classified. Want to buy or sell an old radio, parts, supplies? The best source we've found, in addition to the radio collectors' organizations, is this chock-filled tabloid.

P.O. Box 2, Carlisle, MA 01741. (508) 371-0512.

I'm Looking Through You

Hear crystal clear sound on this transparent AM/FM radio. The antenna is threaded through a set of spectacular LED wheels, for a multi-colored combo of sound and light.

#C739151, $39.95 + 7.50 shipping from Sync, Hanover, PA 17333-0042. (800) 722-9979.

Up-To-Date Technology of the '30s!

• *Fun With Radio* pamphlet explains dozens of radio tricks such as the famous "Talking Newspaper" and "Hearing Radio Through Your Teeth." Great cover.

#9370, Fun, $2.00.

• *Beginner's Radio Dictionary* takes the angst out of words like "capacitative reactance" and "biasing potential." 1938 reprint is a hoot!

#9364, $2.00.

Add $4.00 shipping for total order. Archie McPhee, P.O. Box 30852, Seattle, WA 98103-0852. (206) 547-2467.

RADIO'S NOT DEAD YET

There are several shows on radio that buck the trend, presenting drama, humor and variety on the "obsolete" medium. Here are a few of our favorites, available on your local

stations or on cassette.

• **ZBS** creates funny and mysterious serials. One of our favorites features a futuristic detective, Ruby; another an accidental cosmic tourist, Jack Flanders, who reluctantly finds the strange and metaphysical in jukeboxes, shopping malls, and a suffocatingly comfortable green chair. Our favorite Flanders is *Moon Over Morocco*.

—*Ruby* (3-1/2 hours on 4 cassettes), $25.00 + 3.00 shipping.
—*Moon Over Morocco* (8 hours on 6 cassettes), $40.00 + 3.00 shipping.
ZBS Foundation, RR #1 Box 1201, Fort Edward, NY 12828. (800) 662-3345.

• **Garrison Keillor.** *A Prairie Home Companion* borrowed the format from the *Grand Ole Opry* show and gave it a good shake. Garrison Keillor was at his peak in these:

—*Prairie Home Comedy Radio Songs And Sketches* (#10800 2 cassettes), $16.95 + 3.90 shipping.

—*A Prairie Home Companion Final Performance* (#12809 video), $29.95 + 3.90 shipping.

Wireless, P.O. Box 64422, Saint Paul, MN 55164-0422. (800) 669-9999.

1 More Time

• Old-time radio shows from *The Bickersons* to *The Whistler*…*The Life of Riley* to *Lum And Abner*. Comedy, westerns, drama, suspense. Even World War II newscasts and early commercials. Only $3.98 per show (buy 5 and get 1 free!). Call for a complete list of over fifty fabulous memories.

Johnson Smith Company, 4514 19th Court East, P.O. Box 25500, Bradenton, FL 34206-5500. (813) 747-2356 / FAX (813) 746-7896.

• More old radio programs. Sports, Big Band sounds, air checks & singers—all this and World War Too! Roosevelt, Churchill and Hitler's greatest hits!

Send SASE for large list or send in your requests. The Can Corner, Box AC1173, Linwood, PA 19061.

• A terrific source of vintage radio programming information. Plenty of different shows available—contact for a complete list.

Send SASE to Friends of Old Time Radio, P.O. Box 4321, Hamden, CT 06514.

Classic Bladio Roopers

Radio Bloopers. The slightly scandalous on-air slurs and Freudian slips. These original broadcasts by well-known newscasters and radio personalities will have you rolling in the aisles. Two hours of rip-roaring, riotous, raucous recordings on two cassette tapes.

#2186, $8.98 + 2.70 shipping from Johnson Smith Company, 4514 19th Court East, P.O. Box 25500, Bradenton, FL 34206-5500. (813) 747-2356 / FAX (813) 746-7896.

Yo Ho, a Pirate's Life for Me

• *The Complete Manual of Pirate Radio* by **Zeke Teflon**. Detailed pamphlet tells you all you need to know in order to build your own illegal, secret radio station: transmitters, antennas, mobile operation, even studios. Also offers a rationale on the necessity of keeping communications free. When the commies, Trilateralists or the Top 40 Conspiracy take over, you'll trade your BMW for information like this. 20 pages with illustrations.

#0506, $2.00.

• *Clandestine Confidential* by **Gerry L. Dexter**. They're out there. Secret stations, rebel shortwave, foreign broadcasts even government intelligence stations. Find out what's really going on in the world. Tune in, turn it up and watch out! 84 pages includes illustrations.

#0454, 8.95.
Add $4.00 shipping *per order*. AMOK, P.O. Box 861867, Terminal Annex, Los Angeles, CA 90086-1867. (213) 665-0956.

Radio Pilgrimage

Museum of Broadcast Communications. A 14,000-square-foot museum that offers an unique blend of nostalgia and modern technology. Highlights include the more than 57,000 radio programs, TV shows and commercials available for public viewing and/or listening; an exhibit of memorabilia that includes Edgar Bergen's original Charlie McCarthy, Mortimer Snerd and Effie Klinker puppets; and a recreation of Fibber McGee's closet full o' junk.

River City, 800 S. Wells Street, Chicago, IL (312) 987-1500.

SECRET PEN

Write On! This FM radio is disguised to look like a pen.

#4942, $18.98 + 4.20 shipping from Johnson Smith Company, 4514 19th Court East, P.O. Box 25500, Bradenton, FL 34206-5500. (813) 747-2356 / FAX (813) 746-7896.

Tie One On

Philco's 1928 radio was the inspiration for this terrific navy blue tie. Should get you a good reception where ever you go.

#17004, $18.00 + $3.90 shipping from Wireless, P.O. Box 64422, Saint Paul, MN 55164-0422. (800) 669-9999.

Join the Network

Antique Radio Club of America. There are about 30 antique radio clubs scattered around the world and approximately 10,000 antique or historical radio collectors. The Antique Radio Club of America is a national organization with a number of regional clubs. Contact them about joining the national group, as well as to see if there's a local chapter in your area. Membership includes a subscription to the *Antique Radio Gazette*.

ARCA, c/o Jim and Barbara Rankin, 3445 Adaline Drive, Stow, OH 44224.

Off the Beam

A man brought a suit against the State of New Jersey for broadcasting a voice into his brain. The case was dismissed by the U. S. District Court on the grounds that "unlicensed radio communication comes under the sole jurisdiction of the FCC."

The court helpfully suggested that the man could stop receiving the broadcast by grounding himself: "A short chain of paperclips pinned to the back of a trouser leg to touch the ground could prevent anyone from talking to him inside his brain."

ROCK AND ROLL

1956 is the year rock had its first "mainstream" hits with *Don't Be Cruel/Hound Dog, Heartbreak Hotel, Blue Suede Shoes,* even Kay Starr's *The Rock and Roll Waltz*. Before this, the music was considered disreputable and repugnant to the great majority—like punk or rap more recently. Most American teens didn't even listen to it.

Bill Haley deserves some credit as one of the first artists to have a rock 'n' roll song on the pop charts with his 1953 tune, *Crazy Man Crazy*.

But that date doesn't mark the actual beginning. Rock was a creature that evolved mostly from rhythm and blues, from people playing uptempo tunes in the 1940s and early 1950s:

• **Louis Jordan** was doing great rhythm and blues in the 1940s.

• **Little Richard**, the brilliant showman, had great songs like *Long Tall Sally, Good Golly Miss Molly, Tutti Frutti*.

• **Chuck Berry** came up with *Maybellene, Roll Over Beethoven, School Days, Sweet Little Sixteen, Johnny B. Goode*. Even now, old enough for Social Security, he's still goin' strong.

• **Bo Diddley**, the riff king, brought a modernized African beat to pop music. Bo himself says it, "I opened the door and everyone ran through. I was left holding the door knob."

• **Fats Domino** scored a big transitional hit (*Blueberry Hill*) and showed up on the charts throughout the 1950s.

"It's only rock and roll (but I like it)."
—the Rolling Stones

"Sha Na Na Na Sha Na Na Na Na...Yip Yip Yip Yip Yip Yip Yip Yip Boom Boom Boom Boom Boom, Get a job!" —Silhouettes

Dig These Rhythm & Blues

- *Atlantic Rhythm & Blues: Vol. I—1947-52, and Vol. II—1952-55.* If you're looking for a good introduction or sampler, this isn't a bad place to begin. Atlantic records was a great source of the music with songs like *Mama, He Treats Your Daughter Mean* and *Drinkin' Wine Spo-Dee-O-Dee.* Both of these CDs are great jumpin' collections of music.

  Each CD available for $15.50 + 2.00 shipping from Round-up Records, P.O. Box 154, North Cambridge, MA 02140. (617) 661-6308.

- *Joel Whitburn's Top R & B Singles 1942-1988, Compiled Exclusively From Billboard* by Joel Whitburn.

  This is a good reference book of who did what on 45s and even 78s in the world of rhythm & blues.

  $50.00 + 3.00 shipping from Record Research, Inc., P.O. Box 200, Menominee Falls, WI 53051. (414) 251-5408.

Motown Reading

Heat Wave: The Motown Fact Book by David Bianco. The book starts way before Motown was founded and provides a detailed biography of Berry Gordy, Jr., his family and finally the corporate dealings. Next comes a definitive chronology of all the important (and some not so important) events. Then there are the discographies of every artist on Motown and its sister labels. It's complete, comprehensive and coherent—all the information you'll ever want to know about one of the most successful record companies ever, and the personalities that made it become so.

$45.00 + 4.00 shipping from Popular Culture, Ink., P.O. Box 1839, Ann Arbor, MI 48106. (800) 678-8828.

We've Got Sunshine on a Cloudy Day

20 Motown Classics, Vols. 1 & 2. Berry Gordy was the mastermind behind Motown and its related labels. A perfectionist who started Motown in 1958 on $800 of borrowed money, he initiated a "hits only" policy, and his artists didn't let him down. Check them out on this two-volume CD set.

$11.98 each vol. + 3.65 shipping from Bose Express Music, 50 West 17th St., New York, NY 10011. (800) 233-6357.

> "Rock and roll is a means of pulling the white man down to the level of the Negro. It is part of a plot to undermine the morals of the youth of our nation."
> —Secretary of the North Alabama White Citizens Council

"Rock 'n' roll is just rhythm and blues up-tempo"—Little Richard

Let's All Sing Like the Bird Groups Sing

• **The Doo-Wop Sing-Along Songbook** by John Javna. Subtitled *The Classic Rock & Roll Songs and Syllables You've Always Wanted to Sing*, this look at nonsense syllable-laden group sound provides a nice overview of this musical style, its structure and the groups that made it popular. But the fun comes from singing along with the songs and this doo-wop devotee. Also includes Doo-Wop Duds (as in clothes), Doo-Wop Sign Language and a great glossary of syllables.

$5.95 + 2.00 shipping from **Publishers Book and Audio Mailing Service, P.O. Box 120159, Staten Island, NY 10312. (800) 288-2131.**

• **The Best of Doo-Wop: Ballads Vol. I and II. The Best of Doo-Wop: Up-Tempo Vol. I and II**. In no time you'll be putting the bomp in the bomp-sha-bomp along with Mr. Bassman, and going "whoot-whoo" with the high voices. Snap those fingers and polish up those moves.

Each volume: cassette, $8.98 postpaid; CD, $13.48 postpaid. **Rhino Records, 2225 Colorado Ave. Santa Monica, CA 90494-3598 (800) 432-0020.**

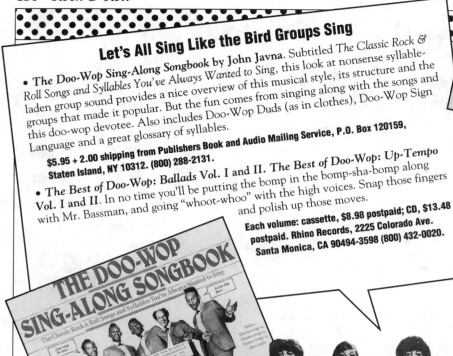

Washed Up Rock Star

Ever notice how you sing much better in the shower? Well, this soap on a rope looks like a microphone to better enhance the total effect.

#2793, $10.95 + 2.95 shipping from The Music Stand, 1 Rockdale Plaza, Lebanon, NH 03766-1585. (802) 295-7044.

Rock 'n' Write

Realistic looking brushed chrome microphone desk set lets you sing while you slave.

#4451, $19.95 + 3.95 shipping from The Music Stand, 1 Rockdale Plaza, Lebanon, NH 03766-1585. (802) 295-7044.

Doo Lang Doo Lang Doo Lang

• *Wonder Women: The History of the Girl Group Sound, Vols. 1 and 2*. In the early 1960s, "Girl Groups" were in full flower, reviving a type of doo-wop sound that the guys had explored and abandoned a few years earlier. This great compilation gives you nearly every well-known and significant contribution to the genre. Features *Leader of the Pack* and more by the Shangri-Las, *One Fine Day* and *He's So Fine* by the Chiffons, *Chapel of Love* and *People Say* by the Dixie Cups, *Baby, It's You* and *Will You Still Love Me Tomorrow* by the Shirelles and much more.

Each volume: cassette $8.95, postpaid; CD, $13.45 postpaid, from Rhino Records, 2225 Colorado Ave. Santa Monica, CA 90494-3598. (800) 432-0020.

• *Girl Groups—Story of a Sound*. This is the video you want if you see what you hear. The Ronettes, Shangri-Las, Supremes, Shirelles, Dixie Cups and more—25 different songs.

$19.95 from Warner Video, available through special order from your local video store.

> *"Rock and roll is phony and false, and it's sung, written, and played for the most part by cretinous goons."*
>
> —Frank Sinatra 1957

The British Are Coming!

• *The History of British Rock.* The Beatles arrived in America in 1964, and opened the floodgates for the Dave Clark Five, Gerry and the Pacemakers, the Hollies, Herman's Hermits, the Kinks, the Who, the Rolling Stones, the Animals, the Yardbirds and many more. Want a great compilation of British Invasion tracks? Most of your fab faves are here, even Freddie and the Dreamers. Four volume CD, 80 songs.

#D29276, $49.95 + 4.95 shipping (4 CDs). Postings, P.O. Box 8001, Hilliard, OH 43026. (800) 262-6604 / FAX (800) 777-1470.

• *Ready Steady Go.* A series of videos from the British TV rock show during the 1960s when the bands started flexing their musical muscles. You'll see people like the Beatles, Rolling Stones, Gerry and the Pacemakers, Dave Clark Five, the Animals, Dusty Springfield and the Who captured in their prime. Great performances in black and white.

Thorn / EMI. Available by special order from local video store.

"*So you want to be a rock 'n' roll star. Then listen now to what I say. Just get an electric guitar and take some time and learn how to play.*"

—The Byrds (making fun of the Monkees, actually) 1966

Rock 'n' Radio

You can hear the music playing but you don't know where it's coming from. Well, if it's rock music it's gotta be coming from a rock, right? This realistic-looking fiberglass boulder is actually a weather-proof wireless speaker. Just plug the included transmitter into your stereo or TV and it will deliver crisp, clear sound up to 150 feet away.

#FDW800, $149.95 + 6.00 shipping. The Sharper Image, P.O. Box 7031, San Francisco, CA 94120-7031, (800) 344-4444.

The first bootleg album was Bob Dylan's *Great White Wonder* (1969).

Take Rock for Granite?

Never! This rock and (kaiser) roll move to the beat with dancing feet!

#T2101, $4.98 + 3.25 shipping from Funny Side Up, 425 Stump Rd., North Wales, PA 19454. (215) 361-5130.

Extra, Extra, Read All About It...Extra!

Rock & Roll Confidential. This is a good source for insider information about rock's business and politics. It has clout beyond its smallish circulation, because it's considered both a good tip sheet as well as the conscience of the industry.

12 issues, $27.00. P.O. Box 341305, Los Angeles, CA 90034. (213) 204-0827.

Goldmine: The Collector's Record & Compact Disc Marketplace. News, reviews and feature articles on music industry personalities. Also a convention schedule, comprehensive classified section and a collector's showcase that spotlights rare and collectible record dealers and their wares. Plus pages upon pages of ads advertising everything from World War I 78s to those new-fangled digital things.

One year (26 issues), $35.00 from Krause Publications, 700 E. State Street, Iola, WI 54990. (715) 445-2214 / FAX (715) 445-4087.

Jump on the Bandstand

Rock, Roll & Remember by Dick Clark and Richard Robinson. In 1957 *American Bandstand* became the first network series ever devoted to rock. Dick Clark actually "fell into" the job of MC in 1956. He admits he knew very little about rock 'n' roll then.

Return to those thrilling days of yesteryear—a simpler time when rock was as young as Dick Clark will always look. Relive the beginnings of rock 'n' roll on TV (every afternoon!), how the changes in the music changed the show and our lives, how the kids on the show rated the Beatles' *She Loves You* at only a 73.

Out of print, worth tracking down anyway.

1950s American Bandstand Fan Club. Dedicated to the memories of the 1950s and 1960s—Dick Clark, the music, the Bandstand dancers and performers, and more. Members receive oldies record, issues of *Bandstand Boogie*, classic pix and an opportunity to place free ads (for life!) in the club newsletter. If this club is good enough for Bobby Vee (he's a member), it's good enough for you.

$10 lifetime membership, c/o Dave "Pop Frosty" Frees, P.O. Box 131, Adamstown, PA 19501. (717) 738-2513.

Nowhere to Run

• **Rock 'n' Roll Hall Of Fame.** Go to Cleveland and look around. See it? Nope! The officially sanctioned R&R Hall of Fame is yet to be built. Still, it's an idea, not yet a place, which means you can visit it no matter where you are—thinking, as the Moody Blues put it, being the best way to travel.

• **Altamont Speedway.** Four months after Woodstock, the dream was over. As the Stones played on-stage, a member of the Hell's Angels (who were—foolishly, in hindsight—hired as security guards for the concert) beat people with pool cues and stabbed 18-year-old Meredith Hunter to death.

Altamont's gone now. Where? The answer my friend is blowing in the wind: there are windmills standing on the site, just off Interstate 580 between Livermore and Tracy in Northern California.

Rock Zaniness

• *The Best of Louie, Louie Vols. 1 and 2*. Rock'n' Roll's #1 party song is rendered (in some case literally) by 20 disparate, even desperate, groups from the Rice University Marching Band to the Sandpipers to Pete Fountain to Black Flag. Great for reaching a strange type of transcendental state, but for us—whoa, baby now, we gotta go.

Each volume: record or cassette, $6.98 postpaid; CD, $9.98 postpaid from Rhino Records, 2225 Colorado Ave. Santa Monica, CA 90494-3598. (800) 432-0020.

• *Teenage Tragedy.* Morbidity was rampant in the early 1960s Top 40. Songs about tragic deaths involving stalled cars on railroad tracks, suicides, crashes, and a mom who "the angels took… for their friend" are filled with funny bathos now. *Teen Angel, Tell Laura I Love Her, Leader of the Pack, Last Kiss, Dead Man's Curve* are a few of the "serious" songs with two parodies added for sick fun: *The Homecoming Queen's Got a Gun* and the necrophiliac *I Want My Baby Back*.

$8.98 postpaid from Rhino Records (see above)

Don't Know Much About History...

• *Behind The Hits* by Bob Shannon and John Javna. A back-stage look at how some favorite songs were written and recorded, what those songs really mean, whose voice is really on that record, what transpired during the recording session…and more! Did you know that *Mony Mony* was written about a major financial institution? It's factual, fascinating and fun.

$10.95 + 2.00 shipping from Warner Books, Inc., 666 Fifth Avenue, New York, NY 10103. (212) 484-3191.

Fast & Lewis

Gary Lewis & The Playboys International Fan Club. Forget Jerry Lee Lewis. Never mind Ramsey Lewis. Who needs Huey Lewis? There's really only one rock 'n' roll Lewis that counts. That's right! Gary…comedian Jerry's son.

Betcha didn't know that Al Kooper (of Blood, Sweat & Tears fame) co-wrote *This Diamond Ring* which hit #1 in 1964. Betcha didn't know that Leon Russell arranged it and played piano. Betcha there's lots you didn't know about the group that had seven (yes, seven) Top 10 hits. Gary Lewis, wherever you are, you are a rock god.

P.O. Box 16428, Rochester, NY 14616.

• *Rock 'n' Roll Reference Resource*. Don't see it here? For a book, magazine or even a rock comic, check out Last Gasp. They have practically everything from AC/DC to Zeppelin.

Last Gasp, 2180 Bryant St., San Francisco, CA 94110. (415) 824-6636 / FAX (415) 824-1836.

• *Rock Movers & Shakers* edited by Barry Lazell. If it's rock and roll you wanna know, Billboard's book gives you a good look (in a timeline setup) with all the dates and places intact.

$16.95 from Billboard Publications, 1515 Broadway, New York, NY 10036.

Shake, Rattle & Oink!

#1284, Rockin' Pig Salt & Pepper Shakers, $15.95 + 3.95 shipping. The Music Stand, 1 Rockdale Plaza, Lebanon, NH 03766-1585. (802) 295-7044.

Legendary Rock 'N' Roll Hits

Runaway (Del Shannon), *Wild Thing* (The Troggs), *Hang On Sloopy* (The McCoys), *The Great Pretender* (The Platters), *Lucille* (Little Richard), *Blueberry Hill* (Fats Domino), *Ferry 'Cross The Mersey* (Gerry & the Pacemakers), *Under The Boardwalk* (The Drifters) plus the Beach Boys, The Penguins, even Percy Sledge! 220 hits of the 1950s and 1960s by the original artists—all on 22 CDs. If you only have one collection of rock 'n' roll's most influential songs, this is it. And what a bargain!

#1692268 (22 CDs), $89.95 + 4.00 shipping from Barnes & Noble, 126 Fifth Avenue, New York, NY 10011. (201) 767-7079.

Rocky & Bullwinkle

"Allow Me to Introduce Myself..."

The creative team of producer Jay Ward and writer/animator/vocal talent Bill Scott, according to the PBS special *Of Moose and Men*, "...assembled a creative team that became famous for its social satire, outright silliness and world-class puns."

Bullwinkle J. Moose, Rocket J. Squirrel, Dudley Do-Right, and the rest were brainchildren of Alex Anderson, former partner of Jay Ward when they worked on the first cartoon developed for TV, *Crusader Rabbit*. Bullwinkle and crew were bit players on the show. Anderson sold half his rights to them when Ward teamed up with Scott.

It was Scott who gave Bullwinkle his distinctively moronic voice, Mr. Peabody his smug tone and Dudley Do-Right his bray. June Foray spoke for Rocky, Sherman, Natasha and Nell, Hans Conreid, for Snidely Whiplash, and Edward Everett Horton delivered the gently cultured narration for *Fractured Fairy Tales*. Paul Frees and Walter Tetley added their vocal characterizations to round out the huge cast of supporting players.

From the Isle of Lucy to the shores of Veronica Lake, from the Wayback Machine to Whatsamatta U., from Moosylvania to Potsylvania, from Frostbite Falls, Minnesota to the Great White North, there's never been a more fearless leader, er, irreverent animated offering in the annals of network television.

"We've corrupted a new generation!" —Bill Scott

HOKEY SMOKES!

The Adventures Of Rocky And Bullwinkle. You don't have to set your Wayback Machine to watch six volumes of the original shows. Each features three Rocky and Bullwinkle cartoons, *Bullwinkle's Corner*, *Fractured Fairy Tales*, Mr. Know-It-All, *Dudley Do-Right*, and Mr. *Peabody and his boy Sherman.* 40 minutes each.

Each tape is $12.99 + 3.99 shipping from The Dudley Do-Right Emporium, 8200 Sunset Boulevard, Hollywood, CA 90046. (213) 656-6550.

Pilgrimage: Jay Ward Ho!

The Dudley Do-Right Emporium. If you're ever in the Hollywood area, you've gotta stop at this place. First of all, there's the 15' statue of Bullwinkle holding Rocky for the obligatory celebrity photo opportunity. And if you're lucky enough to be there when the place is open, the most amazing collection of R & B material awaits you.

8200 Sunset Boulevard, Hollywood, CA 90046. (213) 656-6550.

Buying and Celling

The whole gang is available on full-color, hand-painted and hand-inked cels. Not actually used in productions (those were all recycled to reuse the acetate years ago and were in black & white besides), these were all drawn by the same Jay Ward team that did the originals. All are a tad bigger than 6" x 8".

#6, Rocky, Bullwinkle, Boris & Natasha, $285.00
#5, Sherman, Peabody & the Wayback Machine, $325.00
#3, Dudley Do-Right, Nell & Snidely Whiplash , $285.00
#12, Rocky & Bullwinkle (see top of page), $175.00

Add 9.49 shipping. From The Dudley Do-Right Emporium, 8200 Sunset Boulevard, Hollywood, CA 90046. (213) 656-6550.

Badenov to be Good?

The *Dudley Do-Right* ditty, the *Fractured Fairy Tales* tune, the Moosylvania U song, even "If I could be anyone in the world, I'd be happy to be Bullwinkle." All these on one cassette tape. Added bonus: *George of the Jungle* and *Super Chicken*!

$12.95 + 3.99 shipping. The Dudley Do-Right Emporium, 8200 Sunset Boulevard, Hollywood, CA 90046. (213) 656-6550 or (213) 654-3050.

"My name is Peabody. I suppose you know yours."— Mr. Peabody

Amazing Facts:

• The Moose's moniker came from the days Ward lived in Berkeley, California. He often passed a car dealership named Bullwinkel Autos and imagined what somebody named that would look like.

• Heard that voice before? William Conrad, the Fatman of *Jake and the…*, was narrator for the show.

• No-goodniks Boris Bad-enov and Natasha Fatale were *not* Russian spies, as is popularly believed, they were *Potsylvanian* spies.

• Square-jawed Bullwinkle publicist Howard Brandy was the model for Dudley Do-Right.

• Some Canadians were offended by Dudley Do-Right. The Canadian Broadcasting Company felt that the satire of Mounties was harmful to their image, and refused to show it.

• TV personality Durward Kirby was likewise offended by the "Kirwood Derby" (the ultimate weapon, causing the wearer to be the smartest person in the world). When he threatened to sue, Jay Ward encouraged him, saying "we need the publicity."

• Disney was satirized as a prince in *Fractured Fairy Tales'* Sleeping Beauty. Rather than kiss the princess to break her spell, the prince envisions "Sleeping Beautyland," a theme park with perfect traffic flow.

• The network once refused to allow a story line where Rocky and Bullwinkle were to be eaten by Indians because they couldn't allow cannibalism on TV. Arguments that the two weren't human fell on deaf ears.

• Bay of Moose: Jay Ward and company toured the country promoting statehood for Moosylvania. They were turned away at the White House by a guard brandishing a gun. Only later did they find out the reason for the pistol-packing paranoia: it was the day of the Cuban Missile Crisis, so nobody was taking any chances.

COUNTER CLOCKWISE

Bullwinkle Clock really runs backwards! Precision quartz movement. Battery-operated by 1 AA battery that's actually included.

$31.98 + 5.99 shipping. The Dudley Do-Right Emporium, 8200 Sunset Boulevard, Hollywood, CA 90046. (213) 656-6550.

"If it wasn't for progress, where would we be today? On radio, that's where."
—Bullwinkle J. Moose

Moose For A Day

The Bullwinkle & Rocky Role Playing Party Game. Journey to Frostbite Falls or enroll at Whatsa-matta U as Boris or Bullwinkle! This game is actually three games in one.

$15.00 + 3.99 shipping from The Dudley Do-Right Emporium, 8200 Sunset Boulevard, Hollywood, CA 90046. (213) 656-6550.

Funny-Looking Feet

Cover the ugliest part of your body with Bullwinkle, Rocky, Natasha or Boris socks.

80% acrylic/20% nylon. One size fits all…humans, not moose.

$10.00 + 3.99 shipping from the Dudley Do-Right Emporium, 8200 Sunset Boulevard, Hollywood, CA 90046. (213) 656-6550.

Hey, It COULD Say "Bullwinkel Auto"

License Plate Frame. Red lettering on white plastic frame reads "Member Bullwinkle Fan Club."

$3.50 + 2.99 shipping from the Dudley Do-Right Emporium, 8200 Sunset Boulevard, Hollywood, CA 90046. (213) 656-6550.

HOW ABOUT SOME SCRIPTS, HOWARD?

Bullwinkle Shows #1 and #2. Copies of the scripts used in the show.

$8.00 + 2.99 shipping. The Dudley Do-Right Emporium, 8200 Sunset Boulevard, Hollywood, CA 90046. (213) 656-6550.

Romance Novels

Their glossy, heavily embossed "clinch covers," featuring buffed, bare-chested men and bosomy, bare-shouldered women in passionate poses, seize your attention from across a crowded Kmart. They've got titles like *Love's Tender Passion* and *Till Dawn Tames the Night*. Their prose is often laughably turgid, and the same plot has been used over and over again. Likewise, the endings are always happy. On the other hand, happily-ever-after romance novels account for 40% of the paperback book market. Lots of people make fun of them, but millions more read them.

I BET I COULD BE RICH! THEN ALL THE MEN WOULD TAKE ME OUT...YES, BUT HOW... HOW?

FILM FUN WITH ROMANTIC FICTION

• **Misery.** A deranged romance novel fanatic (Kathy Bates) holds her favorite author (James Caan) prisoner to force him to continue writing the pap he's grown to despise. When she says "Break a leg!" she means it.

• **Romancing the Stone.** An introverted romance writer (Kathleen Turner) awakens her passions when she teams up with a roguish adventurer (Michael Douglas) on a dangerous quest through the Amazon jungle.

• **She-Devil.** A frumpy but saintly housewife (Roseanne Barr Arnold) devilishly transforms herself after a glamorous romance author (Meryl Streep) who tries to "only think beautiful thoughts" steals her selfish husband (Ed Begley, Jr.).

QUEEN OF ROMANCE

The nonogenarian queen of the pink dresses and purple prose is the most prolific writer in the world. Barbara Cartland has produced over 500 romances, a Guinness world record. Reclining on a velvet sofa, she dictates her stories to a secretary at a rate of approximately 6,500 words a day—a completed novel every two weeks!

The secret of her success is giving her readers what they want. "My readers think the old-fashioned 'Me Tarzan, You Jane' way is the best." The only difference being that her Tarzans tend to favor military uniforms, and her Janes are Victorian virgins.

British-born Cartland's romance novels may have provided inspiration for the fairytale match between Diana Spencer and Prince Charles. Lady Di is a fan of Cartland's books, and incidentally is the author's step-granddaughter.

Cartland's fiction may have provided solid advice on winning a Prince. Unfortunately, her happy endings tend to culminate in festive nuptials, with no indication of how to proceed once the honeymoon's over.

"Harlequins are ready-made daydreams... Women who read romances are fantasizing about freedom." —Margaret Ann Jensen, *The Harlequin Story*

MULTI-MEDIA LOVE

• **Romantic Interludes.** For those who find reading a novel too taxing or who simply want to give their eyes a rest, why not try a romantic audio- or videocassette? **Interludes** audiocassettes offer "intimate stories of affairs of the heart... filled with intense love, burning desire and gripping emotion that will enflame the most tender regions of your soul." Yow! Titles include *Stolen Desire, Can This Be Forever?* and *Out of the Shadows.*

Each tape $7.95 from Brown Multimedia Enterprises, P.O. Box 2949, Richmond, CA 94802.

• Lorimar Home Video has taken a stab at low-budget romance titles, producing made-for-video-only movies. They include *Moonlight Flight*, starring *Knot's Landing*'s Peter Reckell, *Lilac Dream* with *Dallas'* Dack Rambo, *Indigo Autumn* with Marc Singer, and *Champagne for Two*, with no one you've ever heard of before.

Check your local video store. Each contains two movies for the price of one and retails at $79.95.

• In 1978, Harlequin Romances actually produced its own feature-length movie, *Leopard in the Snow*, starring Keir Dullea and the unforgettable Susan Penhalgion. The film was not well-received. Harlequin ditched its plans to be, as one executive put it, "to women in the romantic field as Disney is to children." But *Leopard in the Snow* lives on, perhaps, at your local video rental store.

• ***Teen Angst, A Treasury of '50s Romance*, edited by Tom Mason.** Before the Comics Code Authority set strict standards for the industry, romance was a popular comics genre. The romances selected for this anthology date from pre-Code 1950-53, and bear such sensational titles as *Our Love Was Battle-Scarred, I Was A Love Gypsy*, and *Make-Believe Marriage*. Jim Korkis' introduction nicely sums up the genre's appeal: "While sappy and melodramatic, the stories provided hope each month for a nation of insecure, acne-ridden teens that true love was just around the corner."

$15.00 postpaid. Malibu Graphics, Inc., 5321 Sterling Center Drive, Westlake Village, CA 91361. (818) 889-9800.

Hate Love?

Members of the **People Outraged at Romance Novels** objected to romance novels because they treat men as objects. "Romance novels are just as unrealistic and destructive to real-life relationships as pornography is," reads one PORN manifesto. "They create a distorted and exploitative image of what men are and should be."

Unfortunately, the club is defunct.

ROMANCE • COMICS
$14.95
$17.95 in Canada

THE HOUSE OF HARLEQUIN

Hear the phrase "romance novel" and the next word you think of is probably "Harlequin."

Launched in 1949 in Winnipeg, Manitoba, Harlequin Books started out by reprinting romance novels from the British publisher Mills & Boon. In 1958, Richard and Mary Bonnycastle bought the company, rechristened it Harlequin Enterprises and set up headquarters in Toronto. Their product really took off in the 1970s, with sales soaring from 3 million in 1970 to 206 million in 1986.

Today, Harlequin publishes books in at least 17 languages, distributing them to over 100 countries, with Asia as the fastest-growing market. It is estimated that the company sells six copies of its wares per second.

For a good overview of the history of Harlequin Enterprises, as well as an insightful critique of the societal ramifications of romance fiction, read ***Love's Sweet Return: The Harlequin Story*** by Margaret Ann Jensen.

$20.95 + 2.00 shipping. Popular Press, Bowling Green University, Bowling Green, OH 43404. (419) 372-7865.

SOMETHING FOR THE GUYS

According to *Silhouette* editor Leslie Wainger, the few men who read romance novels are "men in prison, on oil platforms, in nursing homes." But don't feel left out, fellas. There are series of virtually indistinguishable novels tailored for you, too. Action-adventure fiction is the male counterpart of romance fiction, and it's a booming enterprise. Along with series like *The Executioner, The Destroyer* and *The Avenger*, publishers are cranking out, at one count, 66 different series filled with violence, patriotism and unbeatable heroes.

Readers range between 22 and 50 years old. The books contain, on average, 192 pages. Organized crime figures used to be the villains of choice. Last we checked, evil scientists seemed to be more popular.

CATEGORIES WITHIN CATEGORIES

There are more sub-categories of romance novels than the uninitiated might first suspect. Herewith, a handy guide:

• **Basic.** "Sweet and gentle," as opposed to "sensuous and sophisticated." Simple plots, heroine holds "traditional" moral values. Sex kept to the barest minimum. Hugs and kisses okay.

• **Temptations.** Because they allegedly "mirror the lives of contemporary women," realistic depictions of sex are encouraged. The couple, however, must be in love before they become intimate.

• **Super Romance.** Leans more towards the mainstream. Characters at least make an attempt at being multidimensional, and there are a number of subplots. Love scenes may be "explicit."

• **Intrigue.** More action-oriented and can include whodunits, spy thrillers and psychological suspense.

• **Historical Romances.** Usually set before the beginning of the Twentieth Century and sarcastically called "bodice rippers." Often involve women kidnapped by Native Americans, pirates of the Caribbean and/or Civil War soldiers.

• **Regency Romances.** Set in England during the Regency period (1811-20). Usually light-hearted, with rakish heroes, intrigue and skullduggery. Truly amazing how nine years' worth of history can provide fodder for so many novels.

• **Futuristic Romances.** Use the trappings of sci-fi—psychics, galactic empires, time travel, etc.—as backgrounds for tales of all-consuming passion. Very definitely a mutant strain of romance novel.

HEARTS OF STEEL

She's the reigning heroine of the romantic bestseller. Millions of readers breathlessly await her next glitzy offering. She's Danielle Steel, super-author, super-mom, super-commodity, the person responsible for *Daddy, Zoya, Changes, Palomino, To Love Again* and many, many more. Steel has published dozens of books, with more than 150 million sold.

By racking up eleven consecutive number one bestsellers between 1983 and 1989, she earned herself a spot in the *Guinness Book of World Records*.

The book that broke the streak was *Message from Nam*, deemed a downer by many members of the reading public. Still, she's made a significant transition from the "pink ghetto" of paperback originals, the traditional domain of Cartland, to the mainstream big leagues in hardcover.

Thrice-married and lately the spouse of executive John Traina, Steel has nine children: five with Traina, his two sons from a previous marriage, and her son and daughter from her previous marriages. Somehow, Steel typically writes ten hours a day, sleeps four a night and spends the rest of the time with her family. She refuses to try computers, preferring to write on her 1947 Olympia manual typewriter. She wears a beeper for child-related emergencies.

Steel's first big seller was *The Promise*, a novelization of a 1979 movie starring Kathleen Quinlan and Stephen Collins. In his *TV Movies and Video Guide*, Leonard Maltin dubs the movie a "BOMB" and gives this synopsis: "Boy loves girl. Girl loses face in car accident. Boy thinks girl is dead. Girl gets new face from plastic surgeon. Boy falls for old girl's new face. Viewer runs screaming from room."

READ ALL ABOUT IT

Romantic Times. For some folks, the books themselves aren't enough. They crave the inside scoop on the romance novel business. That's why there's this monthly magazine published by Kathryn Falk. Readers get over 100 reviews of current releases, full-length profiles of various authors, previews, market reports, gossip tidbits and classified ads.

Admittedly, *Romantic Times* does not have an especially critical perspective on its subject. The book reviews feature ratings of three to six hearts, from "fair/acceptable" to "classic." Apparently, no real dogs are ever critiqued. Four hearts ("excellent") seems to be the average rating.

If you're itching to initiate a correspondence with your favorite romance writer, **Romantic Times** is a great place to start. Most of the author profiles end with something like: "If you enjoyed *Sunswept Desire*, write to me at P.O. Box..."

One year subscription (12 issues) $36.00, single issue $3.50. *Romantic Times*, 55 Bergen Street, Brooklyn, NY 11201. (718) 237-1097 / FAX (718) 624-4231.

There Are a Lot of Good Men Around ...At Least on Paper

Romantic Heroes of Fiction by John Axe. If you want a paper tiger you can call your own, one the other women cannot steal, here's a book of heroic men with "dashing costumes." Included are such fictional hunks as Heathcliff (not the cartoon cat), Hamlet and Sinbad the Sailor. #3690, $4.95 + 2.75 shipping from Hobby House Press, 900 Frederick Street, Cumberland, MD 21502. (301) 759-3770 / FAX (301) 759-4940.

**BILL...
DON'T...**

"W̲E HAD HARDLY REACHED A SECLUDED SPOT IN THE GARDEN BEFORE BILL GRABBED ME ROUGHLY, PULLED ME TO HIM AND KISSED ME. UNTIL THAT MOMENT, I HAD WONDERED WHY HE HADN'T KISSED ME BEFORE. NOW THAT IT HAD HAPPENED, I DIDN'T WANT IT...OR BILL TO BE THE SAME AS THE REST..."

> *"It used to be that he was 36 and the hard-driving head of a conglomerate, and she was 18 and a governess. Now he's still 36 and the head of a conglomerate, but she's 32 and the director of personnel for a rival firm."*
>
> —Leslie Wainger, a senior editor for Silhouette Books

LEARN TO ROMANCE, YOURSELF

• Tired of reading other people's fantasies? Think you've got what it takes to pen prose powerful enough to promote palpitations? Want to try your hand at writing a romance novel? Here's what you do:

Send for guidelines. If you ask them nicely and enclose a self-addressed, stamped envelope, most publishers will send you guidelines on how to write the kinds of books they want. Not that they have formulas, mind you. It's just that they're very particular about certain details. Harlequin prides itself on being "the publisher that reads every manuscript," (as opposed, one guesses, to those companies that never read the manuscripts they publish), so you'll be given a fair shake should you submit a novel.

For a copy of Harlequin's guidelines, write to Harlequin Enterprises, Limited, 225 Duncan Mill Road, Don Mills, Ontario, Canada M3B 3K9. (416) 445-5860 / FAX (416) 445-8655.

• **The Romance Writers of America.** Established in 1981, this organization now boasts over 4800 members, including published authors, aspiring authors, agents, editors and booksellers. They publish *Romance Writers' Report*, a bimonthly magazine full to the brim with market reports, author profiles, letters to the editor, conference listings and announcements of recent releases. RWA also organizes an annual conference and sponsors two contests, Golden Heart for unpublished writers and Golden Medallion for published ones.

For more information, write to RWA, 13700 Veterans Memorial Dr., Suite 315, Houston, TX 77014. (713) 440-6885.

• If you want something a little more structured, you might try the International Romance Writers' Institute. Founded by Lynn Erickson, author of "26 successful novels," the Institute allows students to study the craft in their own home, at their own pace.

For a free, no obligation writing appraisal (we bet you pass!), contact the International Romance Writers' Institute, P.O. Box 7916, Aspen, CO 81612. (800) 882-8148.

• Writing the great American romance novel? A note of caution: don't quit your day job. Publishers receive up to 1000 unsolicited manuscripts every month. For the few books they buy, they pay advances between $1,000 and $15,000, with royalties of seven or eight percent. Most writers can't expect to make a living until after their third or fourth sale.

W- WHAT DO YOU MEAN, BILL? I DON'T UNDERSTAND.

OH, YOU DON'T? LISTEN-- YOU'RE KNOWN AROUND SCHOOL AS THE "EASY MARK"! FOR THE LIFE OF ME, I CAN'T UNDERSTAND WHY YOU'RE THAT WAY! MAYBE YOU HAVE YOUR REASONS, BUT I JUST DON'T GET IT!

RUBBER STAMPS

Making a Good Impression

Rubber stamps first made an impression sometime in the 1860s, about 20 years after Charles Goodyear discovered how to vulcanize rubber. Before that, people used less effective, less flexible materials like metal, stone and hand-carved wood.

Government and industry quickly recognized how useful the new invention was, and started using them everywhere. Artists took much longer  to catch on. In the 1920s, the Dada Movement finally figured out that rubber stamps could be used for more than POSTAGE DUE, 2ND WARNING and PAID and designed their own stamps as art statements.

Soon after, though, stamps as art  went into a hiatus again, not surfacing again until the 1960s when, inspired by McLuhan, artists started looking for new media to massage. *Be Here Now*, Baba Ram Dass' counterculture meditation classic, was probably the first book illustrated completely by rubber stamps.

Kids and artists like  the flexibility and dependability of stamp images. You can even buy food-safe inks. Bologna, eggs, fruit rolls, hard-crusted breads and hot dogs are especially satisfying surfaces to stamp on, proving once again that the art is in the stamping, not the stamp.

> "Rubber stamping doesn't make people compulsive, but compulsive people are definitely drawn to rubber stamping."
> —Cathy Endfield, rubber stamp artist from Sherman Oaks, California

STAMP FACTS

• Owner of the world's largest collection of rubber stamps? The U.S. Postal Service, of course.

• Former U.S. Senator Chauncey M. Depew was the first person on record to call spineless legislators "rubber stamps." This occurred during a Fourth of July speech in 1914.

• "Serious" artists who have used rubber stamps in their work: Kurt Schwitters, Saul Steinberg, Andy Warhol and Sister Corita Kent.

• In parts of Africa, they carve stamps from thick animal hide. Plant juices are used for ink.

• Some small rubber stamp manufacturers' names are as delightfully strange as the images they make. Here are some of our favorites:

Alice in Rubberland

Kinky Ink

The Lady & the Stamp

The Rubber Room

See Spot Run

Get Your Hand Stamped at the Door

The Original Rubber Stamp Convention. Manufacturers and stamp fanatics from all over gather under one roof for these annual stamp-monger conventions. You'll get to see all the latest designs and products. What other reasons do you need to attend? Write for upcoming locations and dates.

Send a STAMPED self-addressed envelope to: The Original Rubber Stamp Convention, PO Box 5160, Long Beach, CA 90805.

There are more than 100,000 images currently available on rubber stamps.

STAMPEDE

Stampa Barbara. This is our mecca for rubber stamp worship, because they are said to be the largest stamp store in the world, carrying the stamps from more than 200 companies. Even the best catalog can't compare to the feeling you'll get standing in the aura of the 80,000 stamps on display in their Santa Barbara store.

The L. A. store has a smaller stock, but it's still said to be the Los Angeles area's best rubber stamp selection.

Because they have so many stamps they don't publish a catalog. But you can still order from a distance. Call them and tell them the category you want like "cats" or "skeletons," and they'll track down what you want.

- **Stampa Barbara, Studios 15, 16 & 20, El Paseo, 813 Anacapa St., Santa Barbara, CA 93101. (805) 962-4077.**
- **Stampa Barbara on Melrose, 6903 Melrose Ave., Los Angeles, CA 90038. (213) 931-7808.**

America's Rubber Stamp Paradise

See You Latex

Inka-Dinka-Do, Inc. If your creative juices start to flow when you get a whiff of hot rubber, a visit to this rubber stamp factory and store will be an inspiration. They welcome individuals and groups for a tour of the plant, where you'll see how they turn a black and white drawing into a rubber stamp. After you've seen them made, you can buy 'em in their attached retail store.

Faneuil Hall Market Place
Boston, MA
(617) 426-3458

Our Favorite Stamp Catalogs

Because there is such a wide variety in stamp images, ranging from fuzzy-head rabbit cute to buzzard-head rabid punk, we recommend a lot of diverse sources. If you can't find what you want here, get out the eraser and X-Acto blade and start carving.

- **All Night Media.** These folks began marketing rubber stamps in the mid-1970s. Now their catalog is thick and slick and the artwork is superb—check out their *Winnie the Pooh* and *Wizard of Oz* sets. Their images? Pretty tame, with lots of bunnies, bears, dinosaurs, cats, unicorns and Santas.

  PO Box 10607, San Rafael, CA 94901. (415) 459-3013.

- *Kidstamps.* This kids' catalog we almost passed over, but younger heads prevailed, and we're glad. The stamps are reproductions of great kid book illustrations like Maurice Sendak's *Wild Things*, James Marshall's very funny *The Stupids*, Edward Gorey's *Doubtful Guest*, and many more. The stamps are reinforced to survive even preschoolers' high-impact techniques.

  PO Box 18699, Cleveland Hts., OH 18699. (800) 727-5437.

- **RubberStampede.** *Rocky &*

Bullwinkle, Looney Tunes, The Flintstones, The Jetsons, Betty Boop, and unusual alphabet and number stamps.

  PO Box 246, Berkeley, CA 94701. (800) NEAT-FUN.

- **100 Proof Press.** Full of 1890s style advertising cuts, public domain art, dingbats and other great and weird stuff.

  Catalog $2, refundable with order over $10. RR 1 Box 136, Eaton, NY 13334. (315) 684-3547.

- *Rubber Stamps of America / Ken Brown Stamps.* Contemporary ad look—1950s appliances, lava lites, TV dinners, etc. Same company really, but RSA features animals, foods and other things; KB has mostly people images.

  Catalogs free. PO Box 567, Saxtons River, VT 05154. (802) 869-2622.

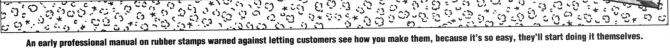

An early professional manual on rubber stamps warned against letting customers see how you make them, because it's so easy, they'll start doing it themselves.

Stamp Your Salami

Food-grade meat branding stamp ink to decorate your meat products (your guests will say they never sausage a thing…). Comes in red or violet, FDA approved.

Quart, $19.15 + 2.70 shipping. Pride Industries (ask for Roxanne Hale) 300 Berry St., Roseville CA 95678. (916) 783-5266 / FAX (916) 783-8234.

STAMP COLLECTORS

Enthusiastic Stamp Collectors Correspondence Club Network. This "stamp-pals" network will fill your mailbox with stamp-art postcards and letters from all over the country. An SASE and 50¢ gets you a list of stamp fans' names and addresses (including special areas of interest) and gets your name added to the next list.

ESCCCN, c/o Marian Valli, PO Box 1209, Fremont, CA 94538-0120.

Stamp Books

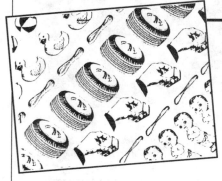

• *Rubber Art, a Guide to Rubber Stamping* by Jeanne Borofsky, Laurie Indenbaum and Andy Toepfer. This is the perfect book for people who have not yet achieved the blinding revelation that there's more than one way to use even the most mundane stamp. Good for beginners: the authors teach good stamping techniques and how to care for and repair stamps and supplies. There's a special section of projects to do with kids.

$7.95 + 2.50 shipping from Rubber Stamps of America, PO Box 567-WP, Saxtons River, VT 05154. (800) 553-5031.

• *Imaginative Stamping*. This is a good sourcebook for inspiration: ideas on using stamps to make stationery, greeting cards, wrapping paper and announcements, and stamping on clothing to make personalized t-shirts and scarves.

$5.99 + 1.50 shipping from Co-Motion Rubber Stamps, 820 E. 47th St., Suite B-9, Tucson, AZ 85713. (800) 225-4894.

Keep 'Em in their Place

Get your stamps out of your sock drawer. These oak or walnut finish cabinets are specially designed to display rubber stamps. 10 drawers, each measuring 17 x 16 x 1 3/4" inside, with brass label holders and felt lining.

$225 00 + 33.00 shipping. Vector, Inc., 70451 Scott Road, White Pigeon, MI 49099. (616) 483-2007.

Ink Stained Wretches

• *Rubberstampmadness*. This is a cool tabloid; 56 pages of idea-stimulating articles and news about stamp art outrageously illustrated with—what else?—rubber stamped images. If you're new to stamping, your first issue may compel you to blow the baby's shoe money on stamps and accessories. If you're a seasoned stamper and haven't subscribed, put this book down and go do it now. We'll wait for you.

$18 per year (6 issues), sample copy $4. PO Box 6585, Ithaca, NY 14851.

• *National Stampagraphic*. 36 pages of how-to articles, artist profiles, mail-order sources and other good stamp stuff. Not quite as "mad" as *Rubberstampmadness*, but is a good read. It's full of creative stamped images and articles on the creative potential of rubber stamps.

$14 per year (quarterly). 1952 Everett St., N. Valley Stream, NY 11580.

STAMP AWAY!

Stamp-A-Story

33 rubber stamps—people, animals, trees, cars, toys, etc. Complete with non-toxic ink pad and idea booklet.

#6023X, $19.00 + 3.95 shipping from Post Scripts, P.O. Box 21628, Ft. Lauderdale, FL 33335-1628. (800) 327-3799.

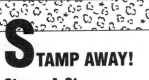

The Paws That Refreshes

It's a cat's paw track. Or several of them if you want. Perfect for letters, notes, cards. Our favorite place to leave the mark is on a piece of toast at the morning meal. It's a laugh riot!

#456, $5.98 + 2.50 shipping from The Lighter Side, 4514 19th St. Court East, P.O. Box 25600, Bradenton, FL 34206-5600. (813) 747-2356 ext. 5 / FAX (813) 746-7896.

Stamp Out Communism

Zdravstvoyte, comrades! Perestroika to all. These Russian political stamps will either open doors, or get you visited by plainclothes feds.

#R17, Gorby (with ink pad), $10.00 + 3.25 shipping; #R18, Lenin (with ink pad), $11.00 + 3.25 shipping; #R19, Peace With USSR (w/ pad), $10.50 + 3.25 shipping. Or #R20, Set of all three stamps with three different color pads, $28.50 + 4.50 shipping from The Daily Planet, P.O. Box 1313, New York, NY 10013. (800) 334-0006 / FAX (212) 334-1158.

The National Bird

Express yourself. 1 inch image of America's Favorite Gesture leaves no doubt of your true feelings.

#T1105, $4.98 + 3.50 shipping from Funny Side Up, 425 Stump Rd., North Wales, PA 19454. (215) 361-5130.

Stamp Out 3-D Images

Make your own 3-D comics. Here's how: First, stamp an image in light blue ink. Then stamp the same image in red ink, offset just a little to either side from the blue image (to the left side to make your image look like it's *protruding from* the page; to the right, to to look like it's *receding into* the page) Find a pair of 3-D glasses (see our *3-D* chapter for sources) and admire your creation.

Stamps **H**appen

You take a lot...so give some back. Pass along that document with a stamp that tells it like it is, complete with the thrill of using a forbidden word!

#T1770, *Important* Stamp. #T1870, *Happens* Stamp. Each $4.98 + 3.25 shipping. #T223, *Bull* Stamp, $3.98 +3.25 shipping from Funny Side Up, 425 Stump Rd., North Wales, PA 19454. (215) 361-5130.

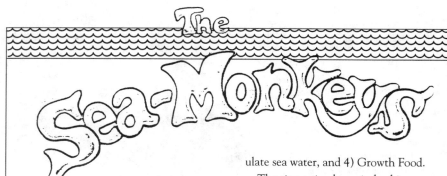

The Sea-Monkeys

Monkey Sea, Monkey Don't

Sea-Monkeys. How many of us have seen those little ads in comic books and pulp magazines promising little families of remarkably human-like playmates? If you ever sent away for them, you found that the Sea-Monkeys were a little different from the pictures in the ads. Still fascinating in a way, but not quite what you expected.

Here's what you get if you buy the standard Sea-Monkey kit, costing about $4: A little plastic aquarium containing the *Official Sea-Monkey Handbook,* and four packets: 1) Water Purifier 2) "Instant Life," the Sea-Monkeys themselves in suspended animation, 3) Plasma II, containing salt and other elements to sim-

ulate sea water, and 4) Growth Food.

The tiny animals are indeed in suspended animation, not in eggs, so they come alive as soon as they hit water ("Sea-Monkeys are real TIME-TRAVELLERS asleep in biological time-capsules for their strange journey into the future!" says the manual). They're actually a type of brine shrimp developed in the laboratory, a hybrid species, the company says. Sea-Monkey crystals grow into 1/2 to 3/4 inch aquatic animals with a small "monkey" tail.

And it is amazing. You follow the directions and the little crystals turn into tiny swimming specks that over weeks eventually turn into insect-like little crustaceans. Little crustaceans that mostly swim around randomly in their plastic sea, but that can be induced into doing simple "tricks" based on their attraction to light and anything that looks like it might be food.

But the real genius is in the

marketing of these little sea creatures. The company has taken a creature whose main function in the order of things seems to be protein for larger species, and given it a lovable and salable persona.

Hey, Hey, We're the Sea-Monkeys. As we write this, the company's making plans for a Sea-Monkey TV show (a combination of animation and live-action, with actors dressed in Sea-Monkey costumes), as well as Sea-Monkey-shaped toys, so be on the lookout.

The Man Behind the Monkey

Sea-Monkeys were invented in 1960 by Harold von Braunhut, president of Transcience Corporation (now a division of the Philadelphia toy company Larami Corporation).

Braunhut, who now runs the company's animal research station, is an enthusiastic inventor and marketer extraordinaire. He has brought America other scientific and biological novelties as well, including the famous gag "X-Ray Glasses." In 1975, he introduced "Crazy Crab," the pet land hermit crab that crawls around your shoulder ("It's getting popular again," says Braunhut). The latest Transcience concept is a laboratory-developed, long-living, cobalt blue, miniature pet lobster. Braunhut believes that his product-pets, hype and all, turn kids on to the wonders of the world of nature.

Scientists usually refer to Sea Monkeys, or brine shrimp, as plankton.

Monkeying With the Copy

The fact that you can create "Instant-Life" by adding water to the crystals can be considered something of a miracle. Is the real miracle, though, the copywriting and the cartoony graphics showing cheerful little pink creatures with antennae and wide smiles? Consider this passage from the *Official Sea-Monkey Handbook*:

"Fighting Sea-Monkeys...Because they are equipped with graspers, only male Sea-Monkeys fight. Using their graspers like wild stags use their horns, they lock together in head-to-head combat. Thrashing and fumbling wildly like a pair of maddened alligators, each fighting Sea-Monkey seeks to get the better grip on his opponent. Once joined, the battle stubbornly continues—sometimes for hours—until one of the combatants surrenders."

Reading those words, it's easy to forget that we're talking about 1/2 inch long brine shrimp here. But the *Handbook's* seemingly outrageous claims (such as "...we found a way to train Sea-Monkeys to actually play REAL GAMES ...with PEOPLE!") turn out to be colorful ways to show off various natural brine shrimp behaviors.

> *"They didn't look like pets to me. They looked more like intestinal parasites, the sort of things you might find wriggling around in a glass from the Nile River."*
>
> —James Gorman

Sea-Monkeys for Corporate Flunkies

The Executive Sea-Monkeys for Grown-ups. While it's true that the kids' plastic Sea-Monkey Kit is cheaper, why not go for the deluxe gold and ebony colored model? Listen to this description: "The greatest Sea-Monkey Kit EVER MADE for your favorite GROWN-UPS! Many psychologists believe that the presence of fish and other live pets in a hectic office produces a calmer, LOWER STRESS ATMOSPHERE which creates a happier, healthier, LIFE PRESERVING environment for busy adults." We wouldn't even try to say it better.

Comes with everything you need to bring your Sea-Monkeys to life. (The tiny creatures are guaranteed to grow, and there's even a Sea-Monkey Life Insurance Policy.)

$6.00 + 1.50 shipping from:
Transcience Corporation
PO Box 809
Bryans Road, MD 20616

Sea-Monkey Accessories

• **Super Sea-Monkey Race Course.** Brine shrimp swim against any current, so this has a little manual pump at the finish line. As you pump away, up to six sea-monkeys can compete. Place your bets, boys and girls. $5.00 + 1.50 shipping.

• **Amazing Live Sea-Monkeys Sea-Bubble**, a pendant on a gold necklace that is actually a mini-aquarium fashion statement holding up to 6 Sea-Monkeys. $2.00 + 75¢ shipping.

• **"Cupid's Arrow" Mating Powder** ("For those shy bachelor Sea-Monkeys who fear marriage, this fabulous formula puts them 'in the mood for love.'") $1.00 + 50¢ shipping.

• **Sea-Monkey Pocket Aquarium Pen**. Comes with steel pocket clip, leakproof cap and official Sea-Monkey Club Emblem, for taking your pets on walks. $1.50 + 75¢ shipping.

• **Sea Diamonds**. Tiny little sparkly toys for your pets to "juggle...even ride around like underwater surf boards." $1.00 + 50¢ shipping.

All of the above from:
Transcience Corporation
PO Box 809
Bryans Road, MD 20616

IT'S FUN TO RAISE PET Sea Monkeys

OFFICIAL SEA-MONKEY® HANDBOOK

the END

Sea Monkeys can live in brine six times saltier than seawater.

SHIPS

Floating Alone

Ships! They represent travel, adventure, romance. And as any boat owner can tell you, they also represent washing, oiling, fixing, sanding, painting, caulking, and—worst of all—scrubbing (there's a nasty, slimy, foul matter that somehow attaches itself to the bottom). But ships are great for getting you across the water, because they float. Even the metal ones. It's incredible, but it's true.

The evolutionary biologists tell us that we crawled out of the sea millions of years ago. That's why members of the human species can be forgiven for skipping work occasionally to follow a primal call to float and fish.

People have been building boats since the Stone Age. The impulse to "get to the other side" inspired the best minds of that time. They found a number of solutions—in fact, marine craft invented during the Stone Age are still in use today in some parts of the world. These include the reed boat, the raft, the dugout, the bark boat and the skin boat (hides inflated or stretched over a wooden framework).

As time went by, creativity and experience enhanced the sailor's art. The early ships gained sophistication, going far beyond the primary requirement of merely being able to float. Wood plank boats were invented by (perhaps) 4,000 B.C. in the Middle East; they appeared later around (we think) 2,500 B.C. in northern Europe. The most crucial event in the history of ships, the invention of the sail, came some time before 3,500 B.C.

Basically, the challenges of ancient seamanship, like now, were figuring out where you are, where you're trying to get, and how to make your vessel get there. But modern seamanship presents additional problems. Sailors can generally make the ship go where they want, and finding the way has become less difficult. But now, a major concern is avoiding other ships. Although the wide open seas still offer plenty of elbow room, all the nautical traffic around harbors and other heavily traveled areas can drive a captain dingy.

Out of the Bottle

Model Ship Builder. As the "world's largest model ships & boats magazine," *Model Ship Builder* covers the craft of craft-building. There's news of model shows and competitions, and features on nautical history and culture, with lots of black and white photographs throughout.

One year (6 issues), $23.00 from Phoenix Publications, Inc., P.O. Box 128, Cedarburg, WI 53012.

Nautical, Yet Nice

• Blazers, those dark blue jackets decorated with metal buttons long associated with things nautical, were first issued by the British Royal Navy in the 1820s.

• Why are the right and left sides of a ship called starboard and port, besides to confuse landlubbers? In ancient times, ships had their rudder on the right side of the ship. The Anglo-Saxon word "steorbord" meant "steer side." When ships came into port, the left side of the ship was used to avoid damage to the rudder, so it got to be known by that name.

• How dangerous is it to christen a ship, with all that flying glass in the bubbly? It can be, if you don't know this trick—professionals cover the bottle with metal mesh to protect the bottle-basher and on-lookers.

• The four gourmet restaurants on the luxury passenger ship Queen Elizabeth 2 require the services of about 140 kitchen personnel and more than 200 waiters.

• The most beautiful ships ever gone to sea were the wind-powered clipper ships, dating from the 1840s. Constructed of the finest wood, and carrying more sail than any ship before, clippers were as fast as the steamships of their time. They were used extensively for carrying goods and gold-seekers from the East Coast around Cape Horn to California. Some companies advertised "Ninety days to 'Frisco!"—at the time unbelievably fast for a sea voyage of 12,000 miles.

What's It All Aboat?

Royce's Sailing Illustrated by Patrick M. Royce. *Royce's* has been a bible for beginning sailors since it first came out in 1956 (it's been updated many times since). Packed with useful knowledge, trivia, and plenty of advice. Many illustrations by the author, who exhibits a fine sense of humor.

$11.95 + 2.50 shipping from Running Press, 125 South 22nd Street, Philadelphia, PA 19103. (800) 345-5359 / (215) 567-5080.

Just Want to Be Alone

One popular fantasy is to buy a boat and sail away from it all, around the world. (Ah, think of the gently lapping water in the tropical bay in the moonlight, as you slowly sip your drink…) Turning the fantasy into reality is no easy trick. Says one boater: "You wouldn't believe how many people dream of doing great things and have never been in a gale or practiced a man-overboard drill. You have to plan and save and practice."

The grueling demands of shipboard life in an isolated, enclosed environment put relationships to the test as well. Best friends don't always stay that way, and couples who go off on extended cruises together often find out more about each other than they would have liked. The evidence often shows up at cruise "change points" like Honolulu, Tahiti, and the Panama Canal: that's where you see boats on the block with "For Sale—Cheap" signs, and where disgusted boaters and crew who "have had it up to here" head for the airport.

BOTTLED BOAT

If you've ever wracked your brains trying to figure out how to fit a ship through a bottleneck, this kit will solve the mystery. You'll get a one liter bottle, instructions, modeling clay, masts and a pre-carved hull.

#K5429, $29.95 + 4.39 shipping from Mason & Sullivan Classics in the Making, 586 Higgins Crowell Rd., West Yarmouth, MA 02673. (800) 933-3010.

Explore the New World...

In this 21¼" long, 1/65 scale model of the Santa Maria. Kit features die-cut wood parts, plank on frame construction, metal fittings, cloth sails and detailed instructions (base not included).

#K5651, $139.00 + 7.00 shipping from Mason & Sullivan Classics in the Making, 586 Higgins Crowell Rd., West Yarmouth, MA 02673. (800) 933-3010.

Famous Ships in History

• *Beagle.* It set off in 1831 on a round-the-world voyage that lasted almost five years. On board was a 22-year-old unpaid naturalist with only a little scientific training—Charles Darwin.

• *Bismarck.* After sinking Britain's largest warship (the Hood) on May 24, 1941, this World War II German battleship became the target of a massive "Sink the Bismarck" campaign conducted by over 40 British warships. Tracked down and hit by three torpedoes, the Bismarck went to the bottom on May 26.

• *Bounty.* Skippered by brutal Capt. William Bligh, the Bounty was the scene of a famous mutiny in 1788. Acting lieutenant Fletcher Christian and most of the crew took over the ship to try for a quieter life on Tahiti.

• *Kon-Tiki.* This 45 x 18" balsa log raft was built by Norwegian explorer Thor Heyerdahl to prove that the ancients could have made great ocean cruises. Named for an Inca sun king, it sailed from Peru to Polynesia in 1947.

• *Mayflower.* She carried the Pilgrims to the New World in 1620. The Mayflower's intended destination was the Virginia Colony, but storms blew her off course and she made her way to Plymouth Rock on the Massachusetts coast. Close enough.

• *Monitor and Merrimac.* The world's first contest between ironclad warships took place during the Civil War on March 9, 1862. The Union Monitor and the Confederate Merrimac fought for several hours, but nobody won.

• *Nina, Pinta, and Santa Maria.* In 1492, Columbus sailed the ocean blue. All of the ships made it to the Americas, but one didn't make it back home. No, the Pinta didn't burst into flames after being rammed in the rear—it was the Santa Maria, wrecked on a reef shortly after Columbus Day (December 5, 1492).

• *Titanic.* With its double bottom the Titanic was trumpeted by press agents as unsinkable. It hit an iceberg on its maiden voyage in the north Atlantic shortly before midnight on April 14, 1912. Over 1,500 passengers and crew died in one of the greatest disasters at sea.

Time in a Bottle

The Ships in Bottles Association of America. The techniques for building ships in bottles were developed during the early 1800s when off-watch sailors kept themselves entertained during voyages that lasted months or even years. Today's building and collecting members of the Association are carrying on the traditions of this nautical art form, which require the hands of a surgeon and the patience of a saint.

One year membership $15.00 (includes quarterly newsletter *Bottle Shipwright*). Don Hubbard, Membership Chairman, P.O. Box 550, Coronado, CA 92118.

ME SKIPPER...

U-Boat! Build the pride of the German Navy that skims the water and even dives. 18", motorized plastic model requires 3 "C" batteries.

#4186 Motorized U-Boat, $23.98 + 4.75 shipping from Johnson Smith Co., 4514 19th Court East, P.O. Box 25500, Bradenton, FL 34206-5500. (813) 747-2356 / FAX (813) 746-7896.

Squeeze Me & Finger Me, Sailor

Concertina & Squeezebox. Got those memorable sea chanteys in your blood? Remember Popeye sweetly bellowing out a tune, accompanying himself on a concertina which he later used for smacking Bluto? *Concertina & Squeezebox* magazine fills you in on the musical instruments used by sailors to pass the time on long sea voyages (and still played by enthusiasts today). There are historical articles, news of festivals like "The Squeeze-In," held yearly in western Massachusetts, interviews with musicians, and more.

One year (4 issues), $15.00 from P.O. Box 6706, Ithaca, NY 14851.

Sea Rations

Nautical Brass—For the Nautical Enthusiast. Articles cover shipwrecks, navigational instruments, naval battles and marine art.

One year (6 issues), $36.00. P.O. Box 3966, N. Ft. Myers, FL 33918-3966.

Join the Club

U.S. Lighthouse Society. Lighthouses—they conjure up thoughts of adventure, isolation, romance, and mystery. (Remember the 1936 movie *Captain January*, where the kindly lighthouse keeper rescued Shirley Temple after her parents drowned at sea?) The U.S. Lighthouse Society keeps lighthouse lovers informed about which lighthouses are open for public tours, what's happening in preservation efforts, and the rich contributions of the lighthouse in the nation's nautical history.

One year, $25.00 (includes subscription to quarterly *The Keeper's Log*). 244 Kearny St., 5th Floor, San Francisco, CA 94108. (415) 362-7255.

Reef Madness

Tropical Shipwrecks: A Vacationing Diver's Guide to the Bahamas and Caribbean by Daniel and Denise Berg. "Wreck dives are like a short visit into history," say the authors, both experienced scuba divers. They take you under the waves for a look at 135 shipwrecks throughout the Caribbean—background about the history and present condition of the wreck; information about depth, visibility, currents and bottom composition; tips on taking pictures of the wreck; and a preview on what aquatic life you can expect to see. There are lots of excellent and tantalizing photographs that convey the excitement of exploring shipwrecks.

$9.95 + 2.50 shipping from Aqua Explorers Inc., P.O. Box 116, East Rockaway, NY 11518. (800) 695-7585 / (516) 868-2658.

What's Collectible?

Martifacts, Inc. Before the 1940s, almost nothing was saved from a ship being retired. Any practical, portable items were taken for use on other vessels, and just about everything else was scrapped for the metal. The idea that "old stuff" from ships should have "collectible" value would have been good for a laugh from the crew. The resulting scarcity of collector items today only adds to the romance, and the expense.

Martifacts sells all manner of old nautical things. Many are hard-to-get items, and so are subject to availability, but here are some recent offerings from their inventory:

- *Navigation lights: $100 and up*
- *Ships' bells (authentic, from 7 to 112 lbs, many with the ship's name on them): $190-1,100*
- *Hatch covers: $60*
- *Wooden wheels: $380-500*
- *Stateroom blankets: $65.*
- *Tablecloths: $20.*
- *Compartment name plates used for crew and working spaces: $10.*

For current stock, call or send $1 for their catalog.

Martifacts, Inc., P.O. Box 8604, Jacksonville, FL 32239-0604. (904) 645-0150.

The Whole Pop Floating Film Fest

The Black Pirate (1926). Douglas Fairbanks, Sr. is the cheerful swashbuckler out to get the dastardly crew who blew up his father's ship.

Mutiny on the Bounty (1935). Stars Charles Laughton and Clark Gable. "Casting me adrift 3,500 miles from a port of call! You're sending me to my doom, eh? Well, you're wrong, Christian. I'll take this boat, as she floats, to England if I must. I'll live to see you—all of you—hanging from the highest yardarm in the British fleet..."

The Sea Hawk (1940). Errol Flynn in the days of piracy. Exciting dueling and battle scenes.

The African Queen (1951). Humphrey Bogart as a boozy river trader and Katharine Hepburn, a prim missionary, on a trip down a dangerous African river. A lot can happen on a boat.

Francis in the Navy (1955). Donald O'Connor, Martha Hyer, and Jim Backus. Francis the talking army mule (forerunner to TV's *Mister Ed*) takes to the sea.

Moby Dick (1956). Gregory Peck as Captain Ahab, obsessed with a great white whale in the days before Greenpeace.

Run Silent, Run Deep (1958). Starring Clark Gable and Burt Lancaster, this one focuses in on underwater tension between submarine officers. *Time* said, "Mostly good sea fights. Otherwise it's damn the torpedoes, half speed ahead."

Ship of Fools (1965). "My name is Karl Glocken, and this is a ship of fools. I'm a fool. You'll meet more fools as we go along. This tub is packed with them. Emancipated ladies and ballplayers. Lovers. Dog lovers. Ladies of joy. Tolerant Jews, Dwarfs. All kinds. And who knows—if you look closely enough, you may even find yourself on board!"

Fitzcarraldo (1982). A movie about madness and obsession, based on a true story. Best boat scenes: transporting a real steamboat over a mountain and seeing it smashed in the rapids while Caruso sings on the Victrola.

Fit for the Tide

Tide Watch. This state-of-the-art digital wrist watch tells the tide's status and height, for any time up to 364 days ahead, in any tidal location on the East or West Coast.

#K5294, $59.00 + 3.24 shipping from Mason & Sullivan Classics in the Making, 586 Higgins Crowell Rd., West Yarmouth, MA 02673. (800) 933-3010.

VIDEOS

The Annapolis Book of Seamanship Videos. Based on a widely respected reference work for sailors by journalist John Rousmaniere, these instructional video tapes (written and hosted by the author) help you get more fun out of sailing. A handy "quick reference feature" allows the viewer to find topics quickly through section numbers displayed on the screen.

- **Volume I:** *Cruising Under Sail (basic seamanship)*
- **Volume 2:** *Heavy Weather Sailing*
- **Volume 3:** *Safety at Sea*
- **Volume 4:** *Sailboat Navigation*
- **Volume 5:** *Daysailers—Sailing & Racing*

Each tape is $49.95 + 4.50 shipping from Creative Programming, 447 Battery St., Suite 300, San Francisco, CA 94111. (800) 426-4962.

Life on the Mississippi

Recreate the bygone riverboat days with this 23¹/₂" long, 1/150 scale paddlewheeler, the Robert E. Lee, once the fastest vessel on the Big Muddy. Kit includes blueprints, instructions, pre-carved wood hull, die-cut wooden parts, turned wooden smokestacks, and etched brass details (base not included).

#K5652, $379.00 + 7.00 shipping from Mason & Sullivan Classics in the Making, 586 Higgins Crowell Rd., West Yarmouth, MA 02673. (800) 933-3010.

Sunken Living Room?

The Complete Live Aboard Book **by Katy Burke.** Why not get out from under those ridiculous monthly housing payments? Sell your house or tell your landlord goodbye, because naval architect Katy Burke tells you how to get your own money-saving floating accommodations. It's 343 pages of information on what you need to know to set up permanent housekeeping aboard a boat. The best part is you don't have to mow the lawn and if your neighbors start to get on your nerves, you can drift off to somewhere else.

$34.95 + 3.50 shipping from Sailors Bookshelf, 623 Ramsey Ave., P.O. Box 643, Hillside, NJ 07205.

ROCK THE BOAT

"Thanks for the Wake! You Jerk" **Flag.** Give the word to uncouth boaters who disregard basic rules of boating etiquette. Express yourself, and maybe relive ancient naval battles, with this long-lasting nylon flag. 22 x 20" in blue, black, red, or orange.

$10.00 + 3.00 shipping from Mayabay Yachting Stuff, 170 Butler Rd., Quincy, MA 02169. (617) 479-6465.

What to Do With Your Empties

Ships-in-Bottles: A Step-by-Step Guide to a Venerable Nautical Craft by Commander Donald Hubbard, USN (Ret.). *"How do they get that big ship into that little bottle anyway?"* Commander Hubbard answers all your questions as he teaches you how to do it from scratch yourself. The book tells you how to get the tools you need (including ten-inch long tweezers and electric drill bits), selecting suitable bottles, and carving a crew from toothpicks. Lots of illustrations and photographs to help you.

$14.95 + 1.50 shipping from Sea Eagle Publishing Co., P.O.Box 550, Coronado, CA 92118.

Silent Comedies

Sound of Silents

Silent films have no language barrier, pantomime being a sort of physical Esperanto. As Gloria Swanson said in *Sunset Boulevard*, "We had faces," meaning that silent film stars could do more with a look than contemporary stars can do with lines of dialogue.

BUSTER KEATON— General Madness

No longer as famous as Charlie Chaplin, Keaton was actually funnier and just as popular in his time. The man who defined deadpan, Keaton grew up in a vaudeville family. His father used to literally throw him around the stage during acrobatic performances, and Keaton perfected his poker face to mask the very real physical pain he felt during pratfalls in front of the audience. His stony countenance was the key to his comedy, the everyman who never flinched while all about him was chaos.

An introduction to Roscoe "Fatty" Arbuckle launched Keaton from the stage to films in 1917. After making over a hundred film shorts for Mack Sennett's Keystone Company, Arbuckle left to form the Comique Film Company, and asked Keaton to appear in his new two-reeler productions.

Keaton often mentioned that he learned everything about film technique from Arbuckle, who gave him his first opportunities to direct. Eventually, Keaton wore all the production hats: actor, director, screenwriter, gag-man and editor.

He was funny amd inventive. His trademark was incredible stunts, done without camera trickery. For instance, the two-ton building front that fell around him in *Steamboat Bill, Jr.* Keaton survived only because he knew exactly where the opening of a small second story window would be as the building collapsed around him. Had he stood even six inches off center in any direction, he would have been killed.

Unfortunately, his business instincts were not as good as his stunt and comedic ones. Poor business judgment forced him to give up his production independence to join MGM, but his films suffered in the factory atmosphere of the large, impersonal studio. Although his career slid downward, he was able to earn a living at other studios as an uncredited gag-man, after a time returning to MGM.

A TV guest shot in 1950 on *The Ed Wynn Show* led Garry Moore to offer Keaton a contract to appear as a regular on his variety show. Instead, Keaton got his own show, *Life With Buster.*

He appeared in a *Twilight Zone* episode in which he played an unwitting time traveler who journeys from 1890 to 1962. Parts were done in "Silents" style. It's quintessential Keaton.

The Keaton family act was banned in many cities by child-protection agencies because his father threw Buster around so much.

KEATON FACTS

• From the tender age of six, Keaton received top billing in the family act, and at nine, the entertainment trades listed him as "Buster Keaton, Acknowledged to be the Best Comedian of his Age and Inches on the Stage!"

• The nickname Buster was given him as a child by the magician Houdini.

• Keaton only laughed twice onscreen: once in *Fatty at Coney Island* (1917), and at the end of a French film, *Le Roi des Champs-Elysees* (1934) as he was about to finally embrace the woman he loved.

• Keaton explained in a 1926 **Ladies Home Journal** article that the reason he never smiled had to do with his realization as a child performer that the audience was laughing at him, not with him.

• Playwright Samuel Beckett wrote a 22 minute film for Keaton called *Film—Esse Est Percipi* (To be is to be looked at). Keaton, seen only from behind, plays a man wearing a cloth to hide his face, who enters his home, puts the dog and cats out, barricades the door, draws the curtains, covers the bird cage and fish tank, tears up photographs, and in the final frames, lifts his veil and confronts his own face in a mirror with a horrified expression. Not funny, but probably "Art." Keaton thought the film would have been much better if Beckett had listened to his gag ideas—and had cut out about 17 minutes of footage.

Buster Keaton on Video

• *Buster Keaton: A Hard Act To Follow* (1989). Rare footage of the deadpan acrobat who was one of the brightest stars of the silent era. A masterful account about a brilliant comedian. Three video cassettes totalling 156 mins. in color and B&W.

• *Buster Keaton Comedy Classics Collection.* Some of Keaton's most hilarious work, with stunts that were spectacular and unfaked. For instance, in *The General*, that really is a steam train falling through the burning bridge, not a miniature. Then in *Steamboat Bill, Jr.* there's the amazing scene where he escapes death only because of a small but well-placed window! Save your pennies and buy the whole collection.

In several movies Keaton was nearly a victim of his stunts. In one, he nearly drowned when the rope that was keeping him from hurtling uncontrolled down rapids *snapped*.

Hanging's Not Too Good for This Kid

Poster depicts Chaplin as the little tramp holding the hand of the orphan, played by Jackie Coogan (later Uncle Fester in the *Addams Family*), in *The Kid*, one of Chaplin's best–loved

sentimental favorite films.

#M02823 framed (22" x 30"), $69.99 + 8.95 shipping. #M0298X unframed, 10.95 + $3.95 shipping. Postings, P.O. Box 8001, Hilliard, OH 43026-8001.
(800) 262-6604.

Chaplin Lost & Found

Unknown Chaplin. Daughter Geraldine Chaplin introduces and James Mason narrates this three video set of home movies and lost studio film footage found after a period of 70 years. Great documentary capturing the legendary comedy genius as he lived and worked. We get to see him improvising some of his best bits.

#VHS 8533, *Unknown Chaplin* (3 cassettes, 55 min. each) $39.99 + 3.95 shipping from WaldenVideo By Mail, P.O. Box 305188, Nashville, TN 37230-5188. (800) 322-2000.

"*America, I am coming to conquer you! Every man, woman and child shall have my name on their lips — Charles Spencer Chaplin!*"

—Witnessed by Stan Laurel upon their ship's arrival to the U.S. in September, 1910.

Charlie Chaplin: The Gentleman is a Tramp

Charlie Chaplin was once the biggest star in the world. His wistful yet very funny figure of the Little Tramp continues to be an immediately recognizable pop icon generations after the fact.

Almost everyone could identify with the waifish but well-mannered underdog, always dignified, even in the worst of situations. Picture him in his dapper little mustache, shabby swallowtail coat, bowler hat, and down-at-heel shoes, twirling his walking stick as he waddles toward the horizon to another adventure.

He was unusual at the time in that he managed to painlessly make the transition to sound film. Besides the Little Tramp character, he may be best remembered for his dual role in *The Great Dictator*, playing both a mild Jewish barber and his doppelganger, Adenoid Hynkel, a strutting dictator who bore a close resemblance to a certain Austrian painter turned politician.

The ambitious Cockney slum boy grew up to socialize on an equal footing with such notables as Albert Einstein, Winston Churchill, George Bernard Shaw, Pablo Picasso, Aldous Huxley, Arturo Toscanini, Jean-Paul Sartre, and Gandhi. On January 2, 1975, he received a knighthood from Queen Elizabeth II.

In the famous shoe-eating scene in *The Goldrush*, the leather was made of black licorice.

AROUND THE FILM WORLD

Our Favorite Chaplins

- *City Lights* (1931)
- *The Gold Rush* (1925)
- *The Great Dictator* (1940)
- *Limelight* (1952)
- *Modern Times* (1936)
- *Monsieur Verdoux* (1947)
- *The Tramp* (1915)

Each $19.98 + 3.60 shipping or ask for VHS videotape rental information from Home Film Festival, P.O. Box 2032, Scranton, PA 18501. (800) 258-FILM.

- *A Burlesque on Carmen* (1916). Chaplin plays lover Don Jose to Edna Purviance's Carmen in this silent spoof of the opera which also features wall-eyed, walrus-mustached Ben Turpin.

VHS: 1639558 $14.95 + 4.00 shipping from Barnes & Noble, 126 Fifth Avenue, New York, NY 10011-5666. (201) 767-7079.

> *"Comedy is life viewed from a distance; tragedy, life in a close-up."*
> —Charlie Chaplin

Tell It to the Chaplin

- Chaplin started out his career in London music halls, playing drunken swells in contrast to his later incarnation as the humble Little Tramp.
- Chaplin teamed himself with Buster Keaton, who played a piano accompanist, in a comedy sketch in the film *Limelight*.
- Stan Laurel was acknowledged to impersonate Chaplin almost better than the original, a fact which disturbed the widely-imitated, egotistical star.
- Chaplin was a good mimic, too. At a dinner he stood up and stunned everybody with a very good impromptu operatic aria. "I didn't know you could sing," said a friend. "I can't," replied Charlie, "I was just imitating Caruso."
- Laurel and Chaplin arrived as unknown comedians to America on the same ship from England.
- Although his screen persona was a shy, shabby, mincing tramp, the offscreen Chaplin was a Lothario with a reputation for being generously endowed. His last marriage, to Oona O'Neill (playwright Eugene's daughter), 36 years his junior, produced a litter of eight children.

HEAD SHOTS

Chaplin Mask and Magnets. Decorate your walls and appliances with Charlie Chaplin's poignant face. Same design on both, but mask is about twelve times bigger than the magnets. Hand-painted and glazed.

#H1070 Charlie Chaplin Mask $50.00 (gift boxed) + 7.50 shipping and #1758 Charlie Chaplin Magnets (6 per set) $36.00 + 3.50 shipping from Clay Art, 1320 Potrero Avenue, San Francisco, CA 94110. (800) 252-9555 / FAX (415) 285-3017.

"In the end, everything is a gag."—Charlie Chaplin

Silly Putty®

I'VE NEVER SEEN ANYTHING LIKE IT.

From Silicone to Silly Putty

Like so many technological discoveries which changed the world—the Slinky and LSD come to mind—Silly Putty was discovered while trying to do something else completely.

During World War II, the government was looking for an inexpensive rubber substitute. At General Electric's New Haven laboratory, chemical engineer James Wright was working on that problem when he combined silicone oil and boric acid in a test tube. They polymerized into a gooey pink substance. Excited, he tossed some down on the counter.

Boing! To his surprise it bounced right back at him. With high hopes, GE sent glops of the substance to scientists around the world, challenging them to find practical uses for it.

They couldn't come up with any.

Not that they didn't try. One scientist, noting that it retained its strange properties down to -70° F., tested to see if it might work as an insulating or caulking material in Arctic climes. No such luck.

Wild science. "Bouncing putty," as GE dubbed it, languished in limbo. Still, fun-loving GE scientists took to mixing up small batches for parties. At one such affair in Connecticut in 1949 a chunk was passed to Peter Hodgson, Sr., high school drop-out, advertising consultant and bon vivant. As he fingered and massaged the chunk, the phrase "silly putty" suddenly came to him. Although already $12,000 in debt, he borrowed $147 and bought 21 pounds of it from GE at $7 a pound, which he packed into little plastic eggs and began selling as an adult toy at an incredible markup ($2 per half ounce).

He was doing pretty well, selling as many as 300 eggs a day at a few outlets, when the *New Yorker* featured the putty in a small story. Within days, he received orders for 230,000 eggs. Silly Putty, "the toy with one moving part," was on its way to becoming a national mania.

Soft Marketing. Originally, adults were the target market. Hodgson believed that kids wouldn't appreciate its richness and subtlety: "It appeals to people of superior intellect," he told a reporter. "The inherent ridiculousness of the material acts as an emotional release to hard-pressed adults."

That marketing strategy worked for about five years until the initial "80% adults-20% children" ratio inverted.

Sticky problem. Kids loved the stuff. So much that the manufacturer had to go back to the labs to reformulate. The problem was a stack of complaints from parents about Silly Putty getting permanently into hair, clothing, upholstery and carpeting. So the Silly Putty of today is less sticky than that made 40 years ago.

NO MORE EASY PICK-UP

One of the joys of Silly Putty has been that you can "pick up" reverse images from newspapers. Unfortunately, new inks and a better grade of paper mean many newspapers won't work any more.

NEA, Please Note

Silly Putty is more than an object of play, it can be an *objet d'art*.

• Artist Cherie Doyle of Minneapolis makes "linear laminated sculptures" from huge chunks of it.

• "Even though I work with Silly Putty, I consider myself a serious artist," notes New York artist George Horner, whose works, addressing issues like homelessness and AIDS inside Silly Putty-filled frames, have sold for up to $5,000.

An eggful of Silly Putty (13.3 grams) costs about exactly the same as 13.3 grams of silver.

Stretching the Truth

"Silly Putty really is what it says it is: a liquid solid," says Peter Hodgson, Jr., son of the man who brought us that strange pink substance. "It's just a paradox, a kind of puzzle, an enigma you can hold in your hand."

That enigma has been more successful than most: over 200 million plastic eggs have sold filled with 3,000 tons of the non-biodegradable stuff—enough to fill a Goodyear blimp.

But besides being a potential solid-waste problem, Silly Putty can be:

• Rolled into a ball and bounced higher than a rubber ball (albeit less accurately).

• Stretched like taffy if pulled slowly.

• Snapped if pulled quickly.

• Shattered when struck by a hammer, yet easily reassembled.

• Left to ooze into a puddle.

Silly Putty Readings

101 Uses for Silly Putty by Linda Sunshine and Libby Reid. Trying hard to be funny, and sometimes it shows. Still, it's hard to hate a book with an egg of Silly Putty attached and that's printed on cheap paper so the pictures'll pick up easily.

$8.95 + 2.00 shipping. Andrews & McMeel, 80 East 11th St., New York, NY 10003.

Feed Your Head

In 1990, with the country in the middle of a 1960s nostalgia binge, Binney and Smith brought out Silly Putty in fluorescent blue, green, yellow and magenta. Get out your black light and groove with it, baby.

REAL LIFE USES

• By Apollo 8 astronauts to keep tools from floating away.

• For preparing patients for CAT scans because it has the specific gravity of human flesh.

• In creating geological simulations, because its characteristics mimic those of the Earth's crust.

• As a lint and cat hair remover.

• As a typewriter key cleaner.

• To lift dirt from car seats.

• To stabilize wobbly chair legs.

• To plug leaks of various types.

• In therapy, to reduce stress, and in stop-smoking clinics, as something to do instead of lighting up.

• In physical therapy, to squeeze when recovering from hand or wrist injuries.

• By the Cincinnati Zoo, to make casts of gorilla hands and feet.

VISIT SILLY-CON VALLEY

See more Silly Putty in one day than most people will see in their next ten reincarnations—take a guided tour of Binney & Smith's Silly Putty plant in Easton, Pennsylvania. Here's what you'll see:

• 225 pound blobs of hot silicone rubber being swirled in mortar vats.

• The oozing liquid being cooled and then cut up into bread-sized loaves.

• The loaves being fed into a taffy-cutting machine, creating little chunks which humans stuff into plastic eggs (about 12,000 a day).

• Special bonus: a tour of the Crayola crayon production line is included.

Reservations are necessary, preferably months in advance. Contact: Binney & Smith Product Tours, 1100 Church Lane, PO Box 431, Easton, PA 18044-0431. (215) 559-2632.

Skateboards

Sidewalk Surfin'

"Skate or die, dude." Sounds like outlaw talk. And the general impression held by the public is that skateboarders lean toward the outside of the law. So prime skateboarding districts, even entire cities, have been legislated out of bounds to protect decent citizenry from these rebels without a skate key.

But look, where do you want them to "ollie their sticks"? "No Skateboarding Allowed" signs are the main problem for the enthusiast, whose average age is 13.8 and whose political clout is "little or none." The skateboarders respond, mostly to an indifferent or hostile world: treat skateboarders the same as ballplayers, bicyclists, and shuffleboard players and give us special recreation areas—or pull those "No Skateboarding" signs down and let us take our chances on the streets and sidewalks.

"There's new cement being poured every day."

—Kevin Thatcher, Editor, *Thrasher* magazine.

SKATE SOURCE

One of many sources for all things skateboard is California Cheap Skates. They carry practically everything for the sport: decks, wheels, trucks, board bags, protective gear (including helmets, elbow & knee pads, etc.), accessories and videos. They've also got a huge array of fashionable attire like T-shirts, caps, shoes, jackets, pants and patches. Ask for their catalog.

California Cheap Skates, 4035 S. Higuera St., San Luis Obispo, CA 93401. (800) 477-9283 / FAX (805) 546-0330.

Skateboard Jargon

- *Air*: Any maneuver where rider and board take flight.
- *Bail*: To get out of a bad situation before the consequences.
- *Bizotic*: Bizarre and exotic.
- *Deck*: The board itself, the surface you stand on.
- *Faceplant*: Total facial contact with the skating surface.
- *Half-pipe*: A U-shaped skating ramp.
- *Shredder*: A skateboarder.
- *Stick*: Your skateboard.
- *Wheelies, impossibles, kickflips, hurricanes, rock 'n' rolls, air handplants, slappies, disasters, handrails, stalefishes, shove-its, fingerflips, reverts, no-complys, McTwists*: Various moves, tricks.

Required Reading

The Ultimate Skateboard Book by Albert Cassorla. There's plenty of information about skateboarding here—history, equipment and maintenance, building a ramp, and lots of tricks. Excellent resource section listing manufacturers, retailers, magazines, and more.

Author Cassorla (who also wrote *The Skateboarder's Bible* in the 1970s) fills the book with his enthusiasm for the sport: "Give yourself a treat. Skating a new neighborhood can get you stoked. Do some ripping while you wait at the bus stop. And don't forget the shredder's transit advantage: a skateboard is always an available seat while waiting for the bus."

$9.95 + 2.50 shipping from Running Press, 125 South 22nd Street, Philadelphia, PA 19103. (800) 345-5359 / (215) 567-5080.

There are about 10 million active skateboarders in the United States.

A "STICK" IN TIME

Scooters? Well... The first skateboard-type contraptions were seen decades ago, in the 1930s and 40s—they were "scooters" built out of something like an orange crate with metal roller skate wheels tacked on. You stood on them and they rolled, but it wasn't until the development of smoother-riding clay wheels and flexing axles ("trucks") that the modern skateboard became possible.

First Wave. In 1958, Bill Richards and son Mark of the Val Surf Shop in Dana Point, California, ordered skate parts from the Chicago Roller Skate Company and mounted them on square, wooden boards. They sold for about $8.

The new devices became popular with surfers and the hobby began to be called "terra-surfing." In 1963, with the advent of a new double-action axle which turned the wheels when you leaned, skateboarding took off. More manufacturers entered the field, clubs started organizing competitions and skateboarding began to capture the national imagination. But it didn't last long.

Concrete problems. Basically, the fad ended at emergency rooms all over the country. Broken bones and other injuries to young skateboarders, generally riding without protective equipment, caused parents to put the lid on the new hobby—pronto. By 1966, the first wave of skateboarding had hit its first big wipeout.

Second Wave. In 1973, Frank Nasworthy introduced the polyurethane skate wheel and singlehandedly brought the sport back to life. Manufacturers tooled up again and began mounting Fiberglass boards on the softer, more maneuverable wheels.

The wheels made a world of difference. Unlike metal or clay, the poly wheels didn't slide sideways on tight turns, making it possible to do amazing turns and stops never before possible. Skateboards were no longer something that went mostly in a straight line, pulled by gravity down a hill—skateboarders could now move with a self-propelling zigzag. The wheels were also much quieter, making them less annoying—but also more dangerous—to pedestrians.

Ramp Arts. This next wave of skateboarders strutted their stuff at skateparks—specially designed, ramp-filled play areas. At the peak, there were about 200 of these around the country. Once again, however, accidents put an end to the quickly growing fad. This time, it was the skateparks' insurance liability problems that brought skateboarding to an end. In one year, 1979, over three-fourths of the parks closed.

But, hey. They couldn't keep the skateboard down for too long. By 1983, skateboarding's third wave had begun. Though skateboarders continued to have to fight for public acceptance and the use of public spaces, skateboard sales mushroomed through the 1980s, not so much as a fad this time, but as a separate subculture. Skateboarding moved from the coasts into the center of the country.

Like most subcultures composed of the politically dispossessed, the mainstream world did its best to stomp this thing out, nip it in the bud. Through legal prohibitions, skateboarders continue to be treated as a menace to be stamped out instead of a constituency that could be reasoned with, regulated and worked with. Pretty bizotic, dude.

Snowboarding is a winter off-shoot of skateboarding, just as skateboarding was a spin-off of surfing.

Sidewalk Surfing Facts

• While you can get a "toy" for $30 or less, serious skateboards run for $100 or more, often made of tough laminated maple. Dedicated skateboarders assemble their boards (suited to their personal taste) by component—the "deck" (the board itself), "trucks" (the axles), and the wheels themselves.

to be—today's models are usually about 10 by 30 inches, with concave shaping and precision bearings.

• The skateboard industry rolls up more than $300 million in equipment sales annually. Add another couple of hundred million if you want to throw in accessories and clothing as well.

• The art on the board is an important part of the sport, too—mostly things like skulls and skeletons, dragons, snakes, screaming faces, and barbed wire. Surreal designs are popular too.

• Some street skaters use almost anything to skate on—drainage ditches, empty swimming pools, hand railings, and even the tops of dumpsters. Fueled by the development of a move called the "ollie" (an off-the-tail leap of the board which launches rider and board up onto benches and even over cars), skaters are exploring previously unskateable territory. Some get going so fast that they shoot up as high as ten feet above the top edge of the vertical surface they're skating on.

• Recommended safety equipment includes $95 kneepads and $40 elbow pads, as well as helmets (usually $35 to $45) and special high top sneakers.

• Serious boards are bigger than they used

Shredding Light at the Whole Pop Double Feature

Gleaming the Cube (1989). A spiky-haired, rebellious, southern California skateboarder with an attitude has his life disrupted when his brother is murdered. He then sets out to track down the killer. But when the young anti-hero trades in his outlaw skater image for a "Mr. Clean-Cut" look, believability may have, as the shredders say, "bailed."

Nevertheless, the skateboarding action rings true. Skateboard pro Stacy Peralta was a consultant and there's plenty of skateboarding wizardry and a final chaotic chase scene in this one. (The film's title, by the way, refers to a mystical state of exalted feeling achieved by skateboarders at the top of their form.)

Back to the Future II (1989). This comedy featured Michael J. Fox riding on a futuristic hoverboard. Takes the idea of "air" maneuvers to new heights.

HANG NAILS

Give your fingers the ride of their lifetime. Better yet, maybe your gerbils want to go shreddin' on these tiny skateboards that double as keychains.

$3.95 + 5.00 shipping from California Cheap Skates, 4035 S. Higuera St., San Luis Obispo, CA 93401. (800) 477-9283 / FAX (805) 546-0330.

Sidewalk Surfin' by Jan & Dean was the first known skateboarding recording. It included metal-wheels-on-pavement sound effects.

Magazines

Thrasher. Great photos and product information. But what's surprising is the amount of peripheral skateboard culture: movies, music, product reviews, snow-boarding—even food!

$10.00 per year, 12 issues. High Speed Productions, P.O. Box 884570, San Francisco, CA 944188. (415) 822-3083.

Poweredge. Skateboard lifestyle magazine, lots of photos and product information.

$17.70 per year, 12 issues. 20930 South Bonita, Suite T, Carson, CA 90746. (800) 435-0715.

OFF THE WALL

Wall Ride Poster shows an elaborate stunt. Kids, don't try this at home!

$4.95 + 1.00 shipping from Thrasher Magazine, P.O. Box 884570, San Francisco, CA 94188-4570. (415) 822-3083.

Key to a Good Skate

License to Skate Video. Learning how to skateboard can be a bruising education. You can take some of the pain out of the process through these videos. You'll still fall, but you won't be a dweeb who doesn't know why.

• *Fundamentals* teaches such basics as how to start, stop, turn, and how to fall.

• *Freestylin'* shows such tricks as wheelies, walking the dog, spacewalking, pogos, and finger flips.

• *Street Master* takes you through speed riding, rail slides, grinds, ollies, and airwalks.

• *Ramp Riding* shows how to go airborne with elevator drops, fakies, and axle drops.

$9.95 + 2.50 shipping for each video tape, from: Pantheon Home Video, 6325 N. Invergordon Rd., Scottsdale, AZ 85253. (602) 948-5883.

SKATING SUMMER

Summer Skateboard Camp. A skateboard summer camp? Radical! For more information, contact:

Woodward Training Center, P.O. Box 93, Route 45, Woodward, PA 16882. (814) 349-5633.

The average skater spends about $200 for a board, hardware, protective pads and shoes.

Shreddin' & Hackin'

Skate Or Die, the "first simulation of America's fastest growing sport." features high-speed skating through various levels of difficulty.

IBM 384K RAM; CGA, EGA, $31.99 + 4.00 shipping. Apple IIGS 768K; color only; 3 1/2 in. disks, $32.99 + 4.00 shipping. Egghead Software, 22011 SE 51st Street, Issaquah, WA 98027-7004. (800) EGGHEAD / FAX (206) 391-0880.

VOX POP

"They're not going to stop kids from skateboarding. Skateboarders have an attitude. It's a freedom thing."

—Kevin Thatcher, Editor, Thrasher.

"It's a freedom sport. Gliding on concrete, you feel like rolling thunder. It's a very ultimate feeling."

—Doug Boyce, professional skater, and creator and exhibitor of "skateboard art"

"That kid's going to break his neck someday. It makes my blood run cold."

—Retired schoolteacher, observing Boyce on his board.

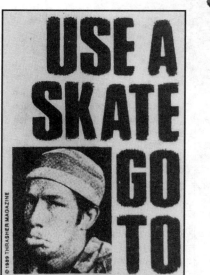

GIVE 'EM A LITTLE SHIRT

T-shirts for skaters from *Thrasher Magazine*. Your choice:

- *"Give Blood—Skateboard!"*
- *"Use a Skate, Go to Prison"*
- *"Save a Skater's Life…Drain Your Pool!"*

Sizes: S, M, L, XL. $11.95 ea. + 1.50 shipping from *Thrasher*, P.O. Box 884570, San Francisco, CA 94188-4570. (415) 822-3083.

Full-Color Design

Join the Club

National Skateboard Association. Support skateboarding through a membership and you will get a membership card, NSA newsletters (including contest information), a packet of stickers, and spectator discounts at NSA events.

Membership, $10.00 per year. 7755 Red Bud Rd., Granite Bay, CA 95661. (916) 791-3720.

GIVE BLOOD. SKATEBOARD

Thrasher

Slinky® Brand

Slinky Springs Eternally

The Slinky has been with us for nearly half a century, and a more unlikely toy is hard to imagine—a torsion spring which happens to be addictive. It doesn't do much, but what it does, it does well.

The exact number sold over the years is unreported by the family-owned company, but others estimate total sales figures of about fourteen million. All the company will reveal is this mystery: while Slinky's appeal is fairly stable, its popularity inexplicably goes through a cycle of "spring fever" peaking every seven years. "We don't know why," a company representative admits.

There's something hypnotic about that slink-slink sound and the rubber-legged gait it affects coming down the stairs, like Mickey Mouse used to walk when he was still an anarchist and not yet a corporate symbol.

Buoys and Coils. During World War II, 26 year old marine engineer Richard James was experimenting with fast-responding springs in a Philadelphia shipyard, looking for ways to keep nautical instruments stable in rough seas. One day while working aboard a ship, rough seas knocked a large torsion spring off a shelf. James watched in amazement as it crawled down the shelves, onto a stack of books, then a table top and finally onto the floor, where it landed upright.

Further experimentation showed that the spring was even more impressive when crawling down stairs. He smuggled one of the springs home to show his wife Betty. They agreed it would make a great toy. Richard started working on prototypes.

Betty, meanwhile, spent two days leafing through the pages of a dictionary, looking for the right name. When she happened on the word "slinky," the proverbial light bulb lit.

Sprung forth. A little test marketing with kids around the neighborhood convinced them they had a potential hit. During the Christmas season of 1945 they convinced Gimbels in Philadelphia to let them introduce Slinky to the public. Richard James went alone, carrying a small demonstration stairway with him. Betty decided to go a little later with a friend to cheer him up if there were no buyers, each carrying a dollar bill so at least he would have two sales.

"When we got there we could barely see him," she remembered. "He was surrounded by an enormous crowd of people, all waving dollar bills. In an hour and a half, he sold 400 Slinkies."

From that came James Industries, which started small—Betty used to take the day's production home at night and hand-wrap the Slinkies in yellow paper—but grew fast. Betty took control of the company in 1960 when Richard dramatically lost interest and abandoned both business and family to join a religious cult in Bolivia (he died there in 1974).

Slinky Variations

Besides the classic metal Slinky, there are the variations on the theme:

- **Plastic Slinky**—brilliant colors, doesn't bend out of shape as easily.
- **Slinky, Jr.**—smaller versions of the metal and plastic Slinkies. Cute, but they don't make it down stairs.
- **Crazy Eyes**—eye-popping fun.
- **Slinky Pull Toys**—dogs, trains, "cater-pullers" and more. For the younger set.

Pop Poetry

"It walks downstairs
Alone or in pairs
It makes a Slinkety sound;
A spring, a spring
A marvelous thing
Everyone knows it's Slinky.

"It makes a big lift
When wrapped as a gift
A very likable toy
Its falling in place
Brings smiles to your face
Something that kids can enjoy.

"It's Slinky, It's Slinky
For fun it's a wonderful toy
It's Slinky, It's Slinky
It's fun for a girl or a boy...."

The Slinky Song by Tom Cureton available on *TV Tunes: The Commercials*.

$8.98 for LP or cassette, $14.98 for CD. Add 3.50 shipping. TVT, 59 W. 19th St., New York, NY 10011. (212) 929-0570.

The worst part of Slinky is that if it gets tangled, it takes a genius to untangle it.

Slinky Facts

• Each Slinky starts as 87 feet of flat wire. When coiled into three inch loops it makes a cylinder less than two inches high when stacked.

• Slinky has made cameo appearances on many TV shows including *Happy Days*, *LA Law* and *St. Elsewhere*. Surprisingly, it has never appeared on *Remington Steele*, *Fall Guy*, *Upstairs Downstairs*, heavy metal segments of MTV or any shows starring Spring Byington.

• Watch for the Slinky commercial in John Waters' *Hairspray* during the beatnik scene.

• All the Slinkies ever made could slink end to end down a stairway from the moon. Well, maybe not, since Slinkies don't slink too well in space (see below).

Practical Uses of Slinky

There's no evidence that Slinky ever solved the nautical problem which inadvertently gave birth to it, but the company reports that it's been used for other real-life purposes. For instance:

• Slinkies are used in pecan picking devices in Texas and Alabama.

• They were mounted on lighting fixtures in Harrah's Casino in Las Vegas because of the fascinating shadows they cast.

• They're prescribed by physical therapists for coordination development.

• During the Vietnam War, they were sometimes called into service as makeshift two-way radio antennas. Troops found they could sling one end over trees for a fast signal boost.

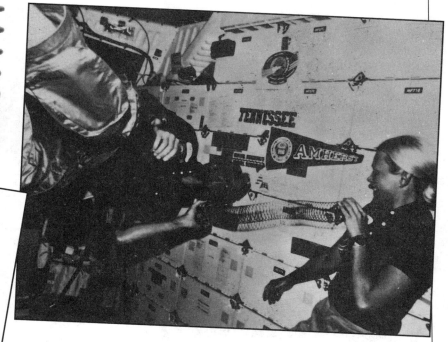

Slinkies in Space

In 1985, the astronauts of the Discovery Space Shuttle distinguished themselves by playing with toys in zero gravity as part of an education project sponsored by the Houston Museum of Natural Science. The intention was to demonstrate principles of physics to children, using familiar objects. Shown above, Mission Specialists Margaret Rhea Seddon and Jeffrey Hoffman wrestle with a Slinky. In space, it acted almost as if alive, pulsing and throbbing in a "continuously propagating wave" motion, suspended in mid-air. But, as Seddon noted, "It won't slink. It sort of droops over."

Snack Foods

Recreational eating has gotten a bad name in the land of the fiber, home of the lo-cal diet. The puritans among us would have us believe that snacks are not just bad for us, but like any pleasurable activity, sinful as well.

In moderation, of course, snack foods have little effect either way on anything. Now, if only we could learn to take them in moderation…

But to paraphrase the NRA, snacks don't consume people, people consume snacks. We eat them because we like to, and what's wrong with that?

The Twinkie Tale

Continental Baking Co. has baked close to 40 billion Hostess Twinkies since they were first baked in 1930. That's over *two million tons* of the little yellow loaves.

Twinkies were invented by James Dewar in 1930. When he was still trying to decide on a name, he spotted a sign advertising "Twinkle Toe Shoes." He liked the name, and called the cakes "Twinkies."

At first they were filled with banana cream but in the '40s banana was replaced by vanilla. He called them the "cream puff of the proletariat." Twinkies caught on immediately.

Some say that the Twinkie cake will outlast the wrapper, but that's not true. True, the Twinkie's shelf life is much longer than many baked goods. That's because its air-tight packaging and low water content make it hard for microorganisms to grow, and the artificial creme moistens the cake and keeps it from going stale. Still, Continental Baking removes all unsold Twinkies from the shelves after only ten days.

Are they bad for you? Continental claims that one man lived solely on a diet of Twinkies and Cutty Sark for years. Dewar himself, as well as his children and grandchildren, ate Twinkies as a regular part of their diet. Apparently many others have followed suit, since Twinkies have been selling at a rate of 1 billion per year.

Twinkie Trivia

• The Midwest eats more Twinkies per capita than any other part of the country.

• "Twinkie" is sometimes used as a derogatory slang term for blonde women and sometimes gays.

• The "Twinkie Defense" of Dan White, who murdered two San Francisco city officials, was one of the most notorious ever. White successfully claimed in court that he was mentally unstable from a diet too high in sugar.

• Legend has it that during Jimmy Carter's presidency a Twinkie vending machine was installed in the White House.

• If you laid all the Hostess Twinkies that were sold in the '80s end to end in a straight line, they would go completely around the earth ten times.

Twinkie's Impact on Culture

Song writer **Larry Groce** wrote *The Ballad of the Junk Food Junkie* in 1974, a hit tune which mentioned Twinkies favorably.

In Cleveland, part of West 20th Street was renamed Twinkie Lane after a Hostess bakery was built there.

Twinkies were a staple of Archie Bunker's diet on the series *All in the Family*. He referred to them as "WASP Soul Food."

"Old people shouldn't eat health foods. They need all the preservatives they can get." —Robert Orben

Fritos

Cream-Filled Colossus

The World's largest Twinkie was made in 1981 in Boston and was 10 feet long, filled with 75 gallons of creme and was created in honor of Twinkies' 50th anniversary. It had to be transported in a 40 foot trailer from the bakery and took 500 pounds of flour, 200 dozen whole eggs, which took three days to crack, and 250 quarts of milk.

What's In a Name?

Munchos, Korkers, Diggers, Onyums, Funyons, Fluffernutters, Snackadoos, Doo Dads, Fiddle Faddle, Fandangos, Hanky Panky, Piffles, Chipniks, Zooper Dooper, Kanga-Moo, Sesame Sillys, Salty Surfers, Bugles, Cornets, Cheez-Its, Devil Dogs, Dreamsicles, Fritos, Doritos, Tostitos, Oreos, Ovaltine, Rocket Push Ups, Pringles, Slim Jims, Yoo Hoos, Jell-O, S'mores, Screaming Yellow Zonkers…

Aerosol Flavorings

When you crave a rich dessert, but swear you'll settle for "just a taste," spray a one-calorie blast of Sweet Ones in your mouth and savor sweet victory.

#2155 Chocolate Mousse Spray, $3.49 + 1.35 shipping; #2156 Banana Split Spray, $3.49 + 1.35 shipping; Any two or more, $2.98 each + 1.35 shipping from Johnson Smith Company, 4514 19th Court East, P.O. Box 25500, Bradenton, FL 34206-5500. (813) 747-2356 / FAX (813) 746-7896.

World Pig-Out Capitals

Largest Consumption of:

- *Cheez Whiz: Puerto Rico*
- *Fritos: Dallas*
- *Twinkies: Chicago*
- *Spam: Hawaii*

Makes You Think, Donut?

Sure, they look, even smell real, but they'll last forever because they're fiendish fakes, so plastic their name should be spelled "do-nots." Two per package, in wrappers evocative of those of Dunkin' Donuts.

#M728, $2.95 + 4.00 shipping from Archie McPhee, Box 30852, Seattle, WA 98103-0852. (206) 547-2467 / FAX (206) 547-6319.

Little Debbie

POPPING CULTURE

North American Indians raised popcorn, and it may have appeared at the Pilgrim's Thanksgiving table. Americans munch on 56 quarts per person every year; sales topped one billion dollars last year.

Why does corn pop? Moisture inside the kernel vaporizes from the heat, but can't escape because of the kernel's hard shell. The pressure builds until the corn explodes.

Flavored popcorns are an alarming trend, with varieties like caramel, nacho, sour cream 'n' onion, watermelon, even hot pepper.

Puttin' Up the Ritz

Metal sign reproductions of famous Nabisco product packages.

#31093, Animal Crackers, $22.99 + 5.00 shipping. #31092, Ritz Crackers, $24.99 + 5.00 shipping. #31090, Triscuit Crackers, $18.99 + 3.50 shipping. Sturbridge Yankee Workshop, P.O. Box 4000, Westbrook, ME 04098-1596. (800) 343-1144 / FAX (207) 774-2561.

Movie Theater Popcorn

Popcorn always tastes best at the movies, and that's because commercial poppers cook hotter than electric home poppers. This popper is built like the commercial ones, but on a smaller scale to fit your stove top or barbecue grill. A through-the-handle stirring mechanism keeps kernels moving and works with or without oil. Recipes included.

#B642579 Detonator Popcorn Popper, $29.95 + 6.99 shipping from Colonial Garden Kitchens, P.O. Box 66, Hanover, PA 17333-0066. (800) 752-5552.

Origins of Famous Fruity Faves

Kool-Aid. This classic non-juice got its start in 1927 when Edwin Perkins stirred up a summertime concoction for his family. By 1931, he had a Chicago factory and in 1953 General Foods acquired the business. There are fifteen flavors, the most popular of which is Lemonade, followed by Fruit Punch, Cherry and Grape.

The Popsicle: This was the creation of a careless 11-year-old boy named Frank Epperson who left his glass of fruit drink on the porch during a cold night back in 1905, and the next day found his drink frozen solid with a wooden stirring stick firmly frozen in place. When he got older he did it on purpose. His "Eppsicles" didn't take off, but when he changed the name to Popsicle, consumers quickly thawed. It wasn't until the Depression that Popsicles were made with two sticks so that they could be split and shared.

Cherry is the favorite flavor of all Popsicles.

The Potato Chip Chronicle

In 1853, when Commodore Cornelius Vanderbilt sent back his plate of potatoes because they were "too thick," the cook, George Crum, whimsically sliced up the next batch paper-thin, fried them crisp, heavily salted them and sent them back. The joke was wasted, however, since Vanderbilt and his friends loved the new creation and "crunch-sliced potatoes" were born.

The plain chip still outsells all other types of snack chips. Potato chips form a $10.2 billion annual market. Last year Americans consumed 698 million pounds of regular chips, 512 million pounds of ridged chips, 171 million pounds of "fabricated" chips (e.g., Pringles) and 99 million pounds of kettle-cooked.

Have You Got A Chip On Your Shoulder?

If not, we can arrange it! This rippled chip with eyes that move is really a pin.

Get Nutty, Self-Serving, Corny & Twisted

- **The Nut Museum** is famous for the collection of nuts housed there, most notably the 35 pound coconut.

  303 Ferry Road, Old Lyme, CT 06371.

- **The Pink Palace Museum** is a replica of the first self-service supermarket, a Piggly Wiggly store, established in 1916. There are antique cash registers, cracker barrels and produce bins, and the goods are marked with their original prices.

  3050 Central Ave, Memphis, TN 38111.

- The **Corn Palace** is decorated with murals made from three thousand bushels of corn every year, decorated with huge mosaic panels made of kernels individually glued in place. It attracts thousands of hungry crows, and tourists. A-maizing!

  Smack in the middle of Mitchell, South Dakota (the birthplace, incidentally, of George McGovern).

- **Sturgis Pretzel Co. Museum.** The pretzel had a humble start in a monastery in the fifth century and was shaped to resemble a child whose hands are folded in prayer.

  You can visit the home where the first commercial hard pretzel was made in 1784. You'll get a tour and even get to twist your own pretzel.

  219-221 E. Main St., Lititz, Pennsylvania.

Soda Pop

SODA POP CULTURE

"Impregnated Water." In the early 1800s, the closest thing to the modern day soft drink was a corked bottle of plain carbonated water ("impregnated water," the inventor called it), marketed and sold for its apparent medicinal magic. For years it was claimed as a cure for fever, nausea, dehydration, indigestion—and nearly any other common sickness they could think of.

By the 1850s, farmhouse cooks, pharmacists, and random experimenters started adding various flavors—birchbark, dandelion, sassafras, ribwort, any root they could find for these first peculiar sodas. "Root beer" and "ginger beer" were just that—nonalcoholic, flavored by roots and ginger by farmhouse cooks.

Staying a Float. Because of its supposed medicinal value, soda water soon moved to the drugstore in the form of a soda "fountain." The druggists experimented with their own flavors and colorings, quickly learning to artificially recreate nearly any natural fruit flavor. The new flavorings were very popular, and the druggists sold their concoctions in the form of syrup which was squirted individually

into each glass of soda water. Soon, inventors and businessmen worked on ways to bottle the popular soft drinks in order to make them portable and convenient.

Soda Pop. The first attempts to portabalize soda, around 1860 or 1870, met with mixed success. The pressure in the bottles tended to explode or blow the cork suddenly out of the bottle (metal caps hadn't been

invented yet, and home recipes usually warned "tie cork securely to bottle"). These bottles made the familiar "pop" sound as the cork left the pressurized neck—hence the name we still use today. Eventually, glass manufacturing quality improved, flavors became regulated and patented, and by 1892, the "crown cap" was in widespread use. The soda business was under way.

> *"No less than five persons, during the forenoon, inquired for ginger beer or root beer or any kind of similar beverage, and obtaining nothing of the kind, went off in exceedingly bad humor."*
>
> **—Nathaniel Hawthorne**
> *The House of the Seven Gables*

What We Call It

Soda · Pop · Tonic · Soft Drink · Soda

> *"Coca-Cola has tried to associate itself with motherhood, the flag, and 'country sunshine.' Pepsi has tried to tie itself to feistiness, youthfulness, and California girls."*
>
> **—Richard S. Tedlow,** *New and Improved*

Classic Recipe

Genuine 1861 Root Beer

INGREDIENTS: 2-1/2 lbs. loaf sugar, 1-1/2 oz. bruised ginger, 1 oz. cream of tartar, rind and juice of 2 lemons, 3 gallons boiling water, 2 large tablespoons thick and fresh brewer's yeast.

Peel lemons, squeeze and strain juice. Put peel and juice into large earthen pan with bruised ginger, cream of tartar, and loaf sugar. Pour over these ingredients 3 gallons of boiling water; let stand until just warm, add yeast. Stir contents well and let remain near the fire all night, covering with a cloth. The next day skim off yeast, and pour the liquor into another vessel, leaving the sediment; bottle immediately, and tie corks down. In three days the ginger beer will be fit for use. Sufficient to fill 4 dozen ginger-beer bottles. This should be made during the summer months.

From *Soda Poppery* by Stephen Tchudi.

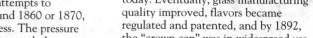

SODA POP FACTS

- Despite widespread popular belief, a glass of Coke will not dissolve a tooth placed in it. On the other hand, another rumor is true: Coke kills spermatozoa (so much for "Coke Adds Life").

- In 1900, Americans were drinking an average of twelve bottles and glasses of soft drinks per year. By the year 1980, the number had risen to 359 bottles per person, nearly a bottle a day.

- Strange coincidence: Coca-Cola, Pepsi Cola, Dr. Pepper and Moxie were all invented by Civil War veterans.

- Diet soda facts: Saccharin is about 500 times sweeter than sugar, and aspartame ("Nutra-Sweet") is about 200 times sweeter than sugar.

- Some prohibitionists wanted to ban soft drinks as well as alcohol, believing carbonated water to be a mild intoxicant. This belief got incorporated into blue laws in some parts of the country making it illegal to sell anything carbonated on Sunday. Soda fountains responded with ice cream, fruit, nut and chocolate concoctions so they could stay in business that day— that's how they got the name "sundaes."

- The truth about caffeine: Only about five percent of all soft drink caffeine comes from cola nuts. The other 95% is added during the manufacturing. Where does the caffeine come from? Usually the left-overs from the processing of decaffeinated coffee.

- Most caffeine in a soft drink per 12 oz serving? Jolt is #1, with 72 milligrams, followed by Mountain Dew (54), Coke (46), Dr. Pepper (40) and Pepsi (38). A cup of coffee contains 50-200 milligrams.

- Some 950,000 Americans drink Coca-Cola for breakfast. Maybe that's why, in 1989, Pepsi briefly considered a campaign to sell their soda as a new morning drink: "Pepsi A.M."

Pop Book

Soda Poppery: The History of Soft Drinks in America by Stephen N. Tchudi. We loved this book. It's an entertaining and informative history of soft drinks and their inventors, their packaging, and even their ad campaigns.

And if you're feeling adventurous, the book includes recipes for inventing your own professional-tasting sodas. Get good at it and your name may be plastered on walls, windows and signs.

RESTORE LOST MANHOOD

The Pure Food and Drug Laws at the beginning of this century made soft drinks quit claiming to be medicines. Before that though, rather than simply being a "pause that refreshes," sodas had startling, even miraculous medical properties:

Dr. Pepper: "Brightens the mind and clears the brain," cures hangovers, nervousness, sleeplessness and is the antidote to excessive cigarette smoking. "Alone on the bridge defending your children against an army of caffeine doped beverages" (since then, caffeine has been added).

Moxie: Feeds the nerves, cures "nervous exhaustion, loss of manhood, imbecility, helplessness, paralysis, softening of the brain, locomotor ataxia, insanity (when caused by nervous exhaustion). It gives a durable solid strength, makes you eat voraciously, removes fatigue from physical and mental overwork, will not interfere with the action of vegetable medicines."

Hires: "Soothing to the nerves, vitalizing to the blood, refreshing to the brain, beneficial in every way."

Coca-Cola: "Relieves tiredness, cures dyspepsia."

7-Up: "For Home & Hospital Use," this elixer "Cures 7 Hangovers."

THE REAL THING

The archetype of sodas, Coca-Cola is the most famous and most consumed soft drink worldwide, with over 1,500 bottling plants in 150 countries worldwide. This "Coca-Colonization" has been so successful that it's said that its name is the first English word spoken by many people.

How did such a product come into being? Actually, like many others, it was originally mixed in the 1880s as a kind of medicine; the syrup was supposed to relieve tiredness, give a lift to the spirits, and cure upset stomach. Inventor John Pemberton's first attempt was French Wine Cola, made with wine and coca leaves (like then, the process today uses coca for flavoring, but unlike then, the drink now has only traces of cocaine in it).

Teetotalers objected to the wine in his syrup, so Pemberton added cola nuts to give the brew a caffeine kick. The first druggist who carried it is said to have accidentally mixed it with carbonated water; another story has it that a customer asked for the mix to help his nervous stomach. Regardless, the magic combination of tonic and bubbly water came together, never again to be torn asunder.

The name was coined by Frank Robinson, Pemberton's bookkeeper, who even took out his pen and roughed out the flowing script signature which is still the company's trademark.

The recipe has always been a source of great secrecy, and even today the formula is maintained in a vault in Georgia. Only a handful of people actually know the full recipe from beginning to end. The icon of Coke permeates America, and their advertising through the years has become nearly as important as the drink itself.

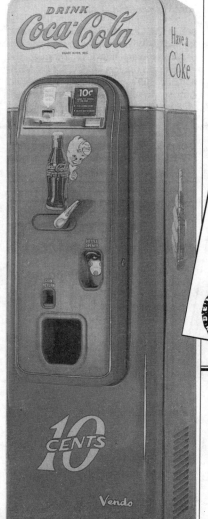

Coke in Little Bottles

There are those that swear that Coke tastes best in the little machine-size, 6 1/2 oz. bottles. You can find the bottles, but it's not easy—only some of the Coca-Cola bottlers handle them. One bottler we called had them available, but would only give them up on a one to one exchange of empties "because people from out of town were buying them and not returning them and we can't get the bottles any more." She suggested going to garage sales and antique stores to buy the empties in order to exchange them for full bottles!

Still, they're worth tracking down, and if you have an antique machine, they're the only size that works. How to find a bottler in your area that has them? Check your phone book, or enlist the help of Coca-Cola's Consumer Affairs Department at (800) 438-2653.

Coke has played a role in several movies as a symbol of cultural imperialism, including *The Gods Must Be Crazy* and *The Coca-Cola Kid*.

BITING THE WORLD'S TADPOLE

Despite the success of America's colas in the world, the international marketing road has not always been without bumps:

• When Coke first arrived in countries, it was often to an antagonistic reception from politicos and newspapers. In Italy, one paper said Coke had "the taste of a damp rag for cleaning floors," while another said it was like "sucking the leg of a recently massaged athlete." Belgians were led to believe that it was really a laxative, and some Muslims believed that American infidels had flavored it with pigs' blood.

• Coca-Cola pronounced phonetically in Chinese means (depending on the intonation) either: "Female horse stuffed with wax" or "Bite the wax tadpole."

• "Come Alive!", Pepsi's slogan in the 1960s, ran into trouble when translated into German as "Arise From the Grave!"

• In a similar bit of unintentional false advertising, "Coke Adds Life!" was translated into Chinese as "Coke Brings Your Ancestors Back From the Dead."

Coke Fiend?

If you can't get enough of the stuff, The Cola Clan is for you.

Membership: $12 per year. The Cola Clan, c/o A. Fisher, 2084 Continental Drive NE, Atlanta, GA 30345.

NOW YOU'RE COKIN'

Free cookbooks from the Coca-Cola Company. *Cooking With Coke* has classics like "Family Pop Pot Roast" (below). Or how about something more exotic? Try *Cooking With Coke International*, sharing recipes from Coke-guzzling chefs the world over (but alas, no "Coke au Vin").

Contact: The Coca-Cola Company, Industry and Consumer Affairs, P.O. Drawer 1734, Atlanta, GA 30301. (800) 438-2653.

Classic Recipe

Family Pop Pot Roast

Coca-Cola and spaghetti sauce mix give a unique flavor to the saucy meat gravy.

3 lbs. chuck roast, any cut
2 tbsps. oil
1 can tomatoes
1 cup Coca-Cola
1 cup finely cut onion

1 pkg. spaghetti sauce mix
3/4 cup finely cut celery
1 1/2 tsps. salt
1/2 tsp. garlic salt

Brown meat in oil for 10 minutes on each side. Drain fat. Break up tomatoes in their juice; add remaining ingredients, stirring until spaghetti sauce mix is dissolved. Pour over meat. Cover; simmer 2 1/2 hours or until meat is tender. Thicken gravy and serve over sliced meat. Makes 6 to 8 servings (about 3 cups sauce).

Coca-Collectibles

Price Guide to Coca-Cola Collectibles by Deborah Goldstein Hill. From blotters to watch fobs, from bottle openers to playing cards, this book tells the going price and places to find every imaginable kind of Coke memorabilia. If you had no idea of the sheer quantity and variety of Coke-related products, you'll find this a reason to be amazed.

$15.95 + 2.50 shipping from Wallace-Homestead Book Co., 201 King of Prussia Road, Radnor, PA 19089. (800) 695-1214.

PILGRIMAGES

The World of Coca-Cola. In Atlanta, birthplace of Coke, the company has opened a $15 million Coca-Cola museum, containing 1000 pieces of advertising gimmickry and other Coke history. The price of admission ($2.50 for adults) includes all the Coke you can drink, plus 18 flavors Coke sells only outside North America, like honey-lemon "Mone" (Japan), quinine-flavored "Beverly" (Italy), "Fanta Mango" (Germany), and fruity "Guarana Tai" (Brazil).

55 Martin Luther King Drive, Atlanta, GA 30303-3505. (404) 676-5151.

![PEPSI bottle cap logo]

Pepsi-Cola: It's the Real Imitation

The history of Pepsi-Cola is pretty much a copy of Coca-Cola, which is as it should be, since the drink began as a copy in the first place.

The original logo was even similar to that of Coke's. The two colas have been fierce competitors for decades now, both in the market and in the courtroom, with Coke suing for patent

"...a mystical, dark compound of magical ingredients with indeterminant powers."
—**Richard S. Tedlow**, *New and Improved*

and trademark infringement several times.

Still, the sweeter tasting copy continues to gain on the original, to a point that some believe it may actually achieve its goal of the last near-century: to outsell Coke worldwide.

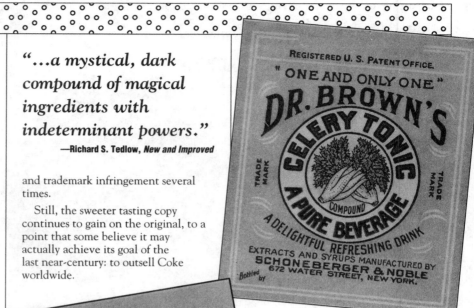

The Other Dr.

Although it once had to compete with Celery-Cola and Celro-Zola, Dr. Brown's Cel-Ray celery tonic has outlasted them to become a kind of cult carbonated beverage available in better delicatessens. Its cool, crisp taste provides a nice counterpoint to spicy pastrami on rye sandwiches.

Nobody seems to know whether or not there ever was an actual Dr. Brown, but the beverage company so named has been around since 1869 in New York City. Besides originating celery-flavored soda, its other claim to fame is the much-copied cream soda.

Hits the Spot

***Pepsi-Cola Collectibles* by Bill Vehling and Michael Hunt.** From the earliest days, soft drink manufacturers offered all sorts of giveaways and gimmicks to entice the public to buy their product. Pepsi premiums included playing cards, serving trays, tin signs, and records. This invaluable guide to collecting Pepsi sodabelia lists prices along with cataloguing the wide variety of nostalgia items.

$14.95 + 2.00 shipping from Vestal Press, 320 N. Jensen Rd., PO Box 97, Vestal, NY 13851. (607) 797-4872.

Lost Pepsi Generation

14" metal reproduction of a classic Pepsi serving tray.

$5.00 + 2.00 shipping. Vestal Press, 320 N. Jensen Rd., PO Box 97, Vestal, NY 13851. (607) 797-4872.

Hires Root Beer

Root beer goes back to colonial days. But most people had little patience with the whole process of collecting and boiling roots and herbs, so a few pharmacists in the 1800s started selling premixed root packets for home brewing.

HIRES
ROOT BEER
THE GREAT HEALTH DRINK
Package makes 5 gallons.
Delicious, sparkling, and appetizing. Sold by all dealers. *FREE* a beautiful Picture Book and cards sent to any one addressing
C. E. HIRES & CO..
Philadelphia.

One such pharmacist, Charles F. Hires, spent his honeymoon in 1870 experimenting with root beer recipes (what his new wife did during this time is not recorded). He came up with a 16-ingredient mixture that was especially tasty and started selling it around Philadelphia as "Hires Root Tea." A friend who liked the tea suggested that the name was too wimpy and suggested the more-robust "Hires Root Beer."

Hires' packets sold for 25¢ and needed to be brewed up with yeast, water and sugar to make 5 gallons of root beer. While the homebrew packets were selling well enough through magazine ads, it became clear to Hires that bottled soft drinks were going to be the wave of the future. He switched over in 1882 and by 1885 was selling 3 million bottles a year (still, the company offered the homebrew version until 1983 when the market evaporated into nothing).

YOO-HOO!

Cursed with one of the more ridiculous brand names, Yoo-Hoo chocolate-flavored drink has never been a big seller outside New Jersey and New York, but it continues to hang in there after nearly seven decades.

In the 1920s, soft drink manufacturer Natale Olivieri got the idea for a chocolate soda pop but had a heck of a time bottling it, unable to find preservatives that wouldn't ruin the taste. Inspired by the sight of his wife canning tomato sauce, Olivieri decided to try heat processing, and history was made. Because his competitors' products featured such dopey names as Whoopie and Vigor, Olivieri fell right in line and dubbed the concoction "Yoo-Hoo."

In the Fifties, Yoo-Hoo somehow became associated with the New York Yankees. During the team's winning seasons, stars like Yogi Berra, Mickey Mantle, Bill Skowron, Elston Howard and Clete Boyer all endorsed the product.

Can't buy Yoo-Hoo where you live? Canfield's makes a chocolate fudge soda pop (that also comes in a diet version), and soda fountains that make old-fashioned cherry Cokes by adding cherry syrup to cola can make *chocolate* Cokes by adding chocolate syrup to cola. Or you can make your own chocolate "Egg Cremes," so-called despite a lack of either egg or cream.

Pour about a tablespoon's worth of Fox's-U-Bet chocolate fountain syrup (it's less viscous for smoother mixing) into a glass. Add a slightly greater amount of milk and stir thoroughly. Spritz in some seltzer. Stir gently to avoid decarbonating, and drink. Ahh!

In *She-Devil*, Meryl Streep's glamorous image is blown when her butler vengefully offers Yoo-Hoo to a visiting journalist.

Wouldn't You Like to Be a Pepper Too?

Dr. Pepper's story is similar to the others. But how it got its name could've been made into a romance novel or made-for-TV miniseries.

In the early 1880s Wade Morrison worked at a pharmacy in Rural Retreat, Virginia and developed a crush on his boss's daughter. His boss didn't look too kindly on the idea of romance between the two and encouraged Wade to "go west, young man" to prove himself worthy.

Eventually Morrison settled down in Waco, Texas and eventually became owner of his own drug store. One of his clerks was experimenting at the soda fountain and came up with a combination of flavors he liked. Morrison, remembering his lost love, suggested naming it after her father, Dr. Kenneth Pepper.

VIM
VIGOR
VITALITY
SATISFACTION
IN EVERY GLASS

5 CENTS AT FOUNTAINS

DRINK

Dr. Pepper
—TRADE MARK—
KING OF BEVERAGES
FREE FROM CAFFEINE

Y es, You Can

National Pop Can Collectors. These folks collect soda pop cans and other soda related items (*"sodabelia"*), and put out a monthly newsletter containing historical information, collector profiles, soda-related items for sale, and other assorted articles.

> **Membership $18 year.**
> **NPCC, 1124 Tyler Street**
> **Fairfield, CA, 94533**
> **(707) 426-5553.**

The TV mini-series ending would be that Morrison went back to Virginia with soft drink in hand and won his beloved's father's approval and her hand in marriage (in fact, a legend around the soda runs exactly that way). But the reality is less romantic. Morrison never went back, never saw her again and eventually married a lady he met in Texas.

THE UN-COLA

Invented in 1928 by one C.L. Grigg, 7-Up was originally known as *Bib-Label Lithiated Lemon-Lime Soda.* Sounds yummy, doesn't it?

Containing a certain amount of the anti-depressant lithium, the drink was advertised as a cure for upset stomach and hangover. "Takes the Ouch Out of a Grouch" its advertising suggested.

In the 1970s, 7-Up marketed itself as the Un-Cola, an exciting alternative to Coke. The company even brought out upside-down, Coke-style soda-fountain glasses to drive the point home.

In the uptight Eighties, when folks started getting riled over the allegedly unhealthy effects of caffeine, 7-Up trumpeted the news that it was totally caffeine-free. (They neglected to mention that the lemon-lime taste is artificial.) A skittish public bought the "Never had it. Never will." campaign, and sales soared.

Cola Clones...
that tried to ride Coca-Cola's coat tails.
- **Afri-Cola**
- **Cafa Cola**
- **Carbo-Cola**
- **Caro-Cola**
- **Chero-Kola**
- **Klu-Ko-Kola**
- **Sola Cola**
- **Taka-Kola**

7up

AMERICA NEEDS MORE MOXIE

Moxie? What's that?

Almost everybody has heard the expression that came from the drink ("She has plenty of Moxie"), but almost nobody has heard of the drink itself. And yet, it's still made and has a cult following in pockets of New England, accounting for a full 1/100 of one percent of the U.S. soda market. It stays afloat somehow with devoted and dedicated drinkers who track it down in dusty corners of local markets. "If you want Moxie, you drink Moxie," says author David Bowers. "There is no Almost-Moxie."

The problem is not that, like Coke, Pepsi and Dr. Pepper, it started out as a medicine; the problem is that, unlike the others, it *tastes* like a medicine. Its very bitter aftertaste comes from gentian root, said to be good for hangovers and stomach problems. It deserves to be mentioned because it paved the way: it was the first still-existing soft drink to be manufactured (developed by Augustine Thompson in 1876). And it was the first to be merchandised in a big way, proving the power of hype and hoopla to overcome the shortcomings of a product.

The Moxie company had been seeing their market shrink each year as the 1920s approached. They decided to pull out all stops, and they did so brilliantly, creating a novelty campaign featuring The Moxie Man, The Moxie Girl, The Moxie Kid and even The Moxie Dog. There were Moxie china settings, Moxie cigarette lighters, Moxie candy, Moxie ash trays, even a Moxie record featuring the first two recorded singing commercials ever, sung by popular recording star Irving Kaufman. Touring the country were a fleet of Moxie horsemobiles, each a full-size dummy horse mounted on an automobile

chassis, rigged so the driver could steer from the saddle.

The brilliant merchandising worked. Moxie became so well-known that it actually outsold Coca-Cola in 1920. Unfortunately, that success didn't last long. Now finding Moxie is difficult even in New England.

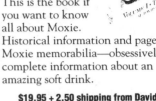

MOXIE PILGRIMAGE

Clark's Trading Post. Visit the largest publicly displayed collection of Moxie memorabilia, including the only known surviving Moxie Horsemobile. Clark's Trading Post also sponsors "Moxie Day" every year. And while you're there, get an ice-cold Moxie right on the premises.

Clark's Trading Post, Rt. 3, Lincoln, NH 03251. (603) 745-8913.

Book With Moxie

The Moxie Encyclopedia by David Bowers. This is the book if you want to know all about Moxie. Historical information and pages of Moxie memorabilia—obsessively complete information about an amazing soft drink.

$19.95 + 2.50 shipping from David Bowers, PO Box 1224, Wolfeborough, NH 03894.

SODA SIGN

"Ted Williams Says Make Mine Moxie" vintage sign. Photo lithograph on metal in full color. 13 x 11".

$18.00 + 7.50 shipping from Kitchen Sink Press, 2 Swamp Road, Princeton, WI 54968. (414) 295-6922 / FAX (414) 295-6878.

Moxie's taste? At first gulp, a little like Dr. Pepper, pleasant and sweet. Then, WHAM, a bitter, medicinal aftertaste.

SPACE

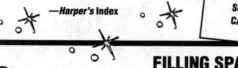

5, 4, 3, 2, 1 BLAST OFF!

Stop the world, we want to get off. We've had it with this planet—the traffic, lousy jobs, the injustice and poverty, the Cubs always losing. As the T-shirt says, "Beam me up, Scotty. There's no intelligent life down here."

Ah, space. Remember the dreams of drinking Tang with the astronauts? Goose flesh at the countdown, rockets blasting off, the triumph of the space walk? That excitement is mostly gone these days as NASA exploration budgets get slashed, as space becomes less a frontier to be explored than just another natural resource to be exploited.

Still, the excitement of space calls, if you listen. It's out there waiting for us, past layers of smog, ever-widening holes in the ozone layer, and the toxic levels of political expediency. We'll blast off, start new civilizations out there, and this time we won't screw it up. Honest!

In the Stars

Number of astronomy columns appearing in newspapers in the U.S.: Fewer than 10.

Number of astrology columns: Over 1,200.

—*Harper's* Index

FILLING SPACE

• The tax-supported galactic money grab has begun—it's predicted that commercial space operations will generate at least $50 billion annually by the year 2000. (Of special interest: your departed loved ones can float in space forever. "Burial" launch services are scheduled for the year 1995.)

• You probably know that the first American to orbit the earth was astronaut John Glenn, who traveled 83,450 miles in three orbits on February 20, 1962. You may not know that Glenn, a Marine Corps lieutenant colonel at the time, earned $245 in flight pay for the trip—less than one third of a penny per mile traveled.

• Humans first set foot on the moon on July 20, 1969. Back on earth, TV viewers were thrilled to see the first pictures of the moon's surface. Our excitement about space faded however—within a few years, TV stations routinely received complaints whenever live coverage interfered with the game shows and soap operas.

• In the early 1960s Turkish farmers marched on the Soviet and American embassies to demand compensation for flood damage to their crops which was caused, they said, by the spaceships which had torn "holes in the sky."

• A study by NASA in 1982 revealed the ideal physique for space travel. Physically fit, taut-bodied, young? No—middle-aged, drooping and slightly paunchy, the better for flexibility during multi-G acceleration.

• Fasten your seat belt. Right now, you're not sitting still at all—you're hurtling at speeds of just under 1,000 mph around the earth's axis, about 66,000 mph around the sun, about 43,000 mph (along with the sun) toward the bright star Vega in the constellation of Lyra and about 660,000 mph around the center of our galaxy. Barf bag, anyone?

Space traveler: If the sky is pink, you're on Mars. It's that way because of red dust particles suspended in its atmosphere.

Pigs in Space

Astronauts in space start looking worse and worse. If you already don't look that great in the morning, consider these body changes from time without any gravity:

• Your skin becomes chronically dry.

• Your face becomes puffy and your eyes bloodshot.

• You get bags under your eyes.

• Veins in your neck and forehead swell up.

• You become taller (because the fluid between your spinal column discs is no longer compressed by gravity).

• Your waist gets smaller and strangely proportioned because your internal organs shift upward.

Budget Space Tour

Take a space trip without leaving the country. Visit these actual cities and towns.

• *Sun City, Arizona*
  • *Star City, Arkansas*
  • *Earth, Texas*
  • *Mars, Pennsylvania*
  • *Mercury, Texas*
  • *Jupiter, Florida*
  • *Pluto, Texas*
  • *Saturn, Indiana*
  • *Neptune, Ohio*
  • *Venus, Pennsylvania*
  • *Valley of the Moon, California*

GUM WRAPPER SPACE JOKE

1st astronaut: I sure hope we get to visit the Sun.

2nd astronaut: I dunno. I heard the Sun's pretty hot—like thousands of degrees.

1st astronaut: No problem—we'll land at night!

Space Bulletins

• *Sky and Telescope.* Lots of news and features for star-struck amateur astronomers.

$24 per year, 12 issues from Sky Publishing, P.O. Box 9111, Belmont, MA 02178-9918. (617) 864-7360.

• *Model Rocket News.* Frustrated by NASA delays? Launch your own rockets according to your personal schedule. Send $1.00 for catalog of rocketry supplies, buy something, and receive the quarterly *Model Rocket News* for free.

Estes Industries, P.O. Box 227, 1295 H Street, Penrose, CO 81240. (719) 372-6565.

Meteorites by Air Express

Why is the cosmos throwing rocks at us? Actually, don't call meteorites just rocks anymore, they're authentic space collectibles from other worlds.

Robert "The Meteorite Man" Haag hunts, buys and sells meteorites. His catalog is a friendly and newsy trip through his collection. It features color photos of the debris from outer space, shots of Haag at sites around the world, even tips on how to tell whether that rock in your backyard came from "out there."

Haag's prices are by weight, and he has them from pebble to bowling ball size. Or you can buy them in finished form, like a set of meteors set in silver earrings for $65 postpaid. Send $5 (refundable on first order) for his color catalog.

**Robert A. Haag—Meteorites
Box 27527
Tucson, AZ 85726
(602) 882-8804**

Anti-Gravity Game

No Nintendo necessary. This hands-on game is a great combination and test of hand-eye coordination, quick thinking and the ability to deliver under pressure. Launched "satellite" actually floats on a cushion of air—defying gravity—as you maneuver it through hoops while a timer records your flight time.

#6753, $34.98 + 3.50 shipping from The Lighter Side, 4514 19th St. Court East, P.O. Box 25600, Bradenton, FL 34206-5600. (813) 747-2356.

Big & Bright

Sleep under the stars every night! Paint an accurate, glow-in-the-dark sky full of stars on your bedroom ceiling. Kit includes 8-foot stencil, special non-toxic, phosphorescent "ceiling wax" paint, and brush. Your choice: summer sky or winter sky. It's a lot easier than going camping.

#91301, summer sky or #91301, winter sky, $27.50 + 4.25 shipping from Discovery Corner, Lawrence Hall of Science, University of California, Berkeley, CA 94720. (510) 642-1016.

Flash Gordon Would Be Proud

Especially if he saw you wearing this pin that reminds us of his spaceship. 2 1/2 in. long, silver colored

#D244, $10.00 + 2.50 shipping from Chicken Boy Future Studio, P.O. Box 292000, Los Angeles, CA 90029. (800) 422-0505.

The Whole Pop Space Film Festival

- Spaceballs
- Alien
- Star Wars Trilogy
- 2001: A Space Odyssey
- Star Trek (all but the disappointing #1 and annoying #4)
- Flash Gordon Conquers the Universe

Private Space

The first rule about going to the bathroom in space: be sure you're wearing your seat belt so you don't float off the seat (a few escaped messes in Skylab were very unpleasant).

You strap yourself on the toilet, fit your boots into the foot restraints, and grab the handholds. An air fan blows the solid wastes and gasses into a special compartment, and a unique urine collection device takes care of liquids (it's unisex, basically a suction funnel with a hose).

The best part is the hatch window: while you're downloading, enjoy a spectacular view of the earth below.

Journey to the Center of Space

Space Center. Located "at the top of New Mexico Highway 2001," the Space Center gets you thinking galactic. See the space show in the "Omnimax" dome theater, moon rocks, the Little Joe Rocket, the Sonic Wind Rocket Sled, and lots more space stuff in this four-story museum. Don't leave the site without paying your respects to Ham, the world's first astrochimp, whose remains are buried in the front lawn.

**P.O. Box 533
Alamogordo, NM 88311
(800) 545-4021 or (800) 634-6438**

JOIN THE CLUB

National Space Society. The Society is a non-profit, publicly-supported organization "dedicated to the creation of a space-faring civilization which will establish communities beyond the Earth." Runs the "Dial-A-Shuttle" hotline and conducts annual space conferences. Members get the opportunity to take tours of the space shuttle.

Dues: $30 per year. Includes subscription to monthly *Ad Astra*. 922 Pennsylvania Ave. SE, Washington, DC 20003. (202) 543-1900.

Astronomical Society of the Pacific. The Society, "bringing the stars down to Earth for 100 years," is ready to help beginners with information on subjects like selecting a first telescope or astronomy software. Membership includes a monthly Sky Calendar and Star Map to help you get oriented to the galactic neighborhood.

Dues: $29.50 per year. Includes subscription to monthly *Mercury*. 390 Ashton Avenue, San Francisco, CA 94112. (415) 337-1100.

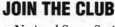

Space Talk

"Can You Talk the Language of the Age of Space?"—Title of Air Force recruiting brochure, late 1950s.

The space effort spurred on a lot of scientific advancements. But best of all, it spawned a lot of great jargon:

- **"A-Okay"** - Fine; the best.
- **"Chicken switch"** - An abort switch or other control that stops the mission.
- **"Mark one eyeball"** - Human sight;

the phrase came into play during the moon landings.

- **"Spaghetti suit"** - The long underwear worn by astronauts, which is composed in part of tubes that carry cool water.
- **"Tinman"** - Aluminum space suit.
- **"Unobtanium"** - A substance or piece of hardware that is desired but not obtainable.

—from *SLANG!* by Paul Dickson, Pocket Books.

Sex, Space & Rock 'n' Roll

In 1977, a group of fundamentalist Christians protested the launching of the Voyager spacecraft. They weren't worried that the craft was going to crash into heaven and disturb the angels—they were upset because it was spreading the twin scourges of rock 'n' roll and taxpayer-subsidized pornography into space.

The Voyager had been designed to cruise past certain planets and then out into the cosmos. Scientists decided that there was an infinitesimal chance that some alien life out there might come in contact with it sometime in the next zillion years. Out of whimsical species egotism, if nothing else, they decided to send a friendly greeting along with it.

To show where we live, they sent diagrams of our position in the universe. To show what we look like, they included tasteful line drawings of a standing nude man and woman. It was the nudity that upset the evangelists. So did the 90 minute digital recording of "the world's greatest music," because it included—along with nature sounds, classical music and greetings in over 50 languages (including whale)—Chuck Berry singing *Roll Over Beethoven*.

> *"I see nothing in space as promising as the view from a Ferris wheel."*
> —E.B. White

Pennies For Heaven

Name your own star in the sky. As Carl Sagan says, there are "billions and billions" of 'em out there, and not all of them have been named. Your star name is registered in "a government archive in Washington D.C.," possibly the copyright office, so it's sort of official, kind of. You get a certificate, two sky charts, star coordinates and directions for locating your star with any small telescope.

#8323X, $45.00 + 7.45 shipping from Post Scripts, P.O. Box 21628, Ft. Lauderdale, FL 33335-1628. (800) 327-3799.

SATURNALIA

> *"The scientific theory I like best is that the rings of Saturn are composed entirely of lost airline luggage."*
> —Mark Russell

A Real Earth Shaker

Earth salt shaker sits in easy chair peppered with stars and planets.

#M729, $14.95 + 2.00 shipping. What On Earth, 25801 Richmond Road, Cleveland, OH 44146. (216) 831-5588.

SOUNDS OF SPACE

Eavesdrop on Space Shuttle conversations with Mission Control by calling the National Space Society's "Dial-A-Shuttle" hotline. Activated two hours before launch, the hotline lets you listen in as the astronauts talk spacetalk live with NASA's Johnson Space Center in Houston.

Dial-A-Shuttle: (900) 909-NASA.

$2.00 for first minute, 45¢ each additional minute.

Now Boarding at Gate 2001

Over 93,000 people signed up for Pan Am's official waiting list for the first commercial passenger flight to the moon—which means you should get to the spaceport early to avoid bumping.

In 1964, an Austrian journalist named Gerhard Pistor whimsically asked a Vienna travel agency to book him on a flight to the moon. The agent sent the request to both Aeroflot, the Soviet airline, and Pan Am. The Soviets laughed off the request, but Pan Am accepted his name and started a waiting list. When he wrote about it, applications started coming in from all over the world.

After the moon-circling Apollo 8 mission and the Apollo 11 lunar landing, applications really took off. The airline issued numbered membership cards and enrolled applicants in a "First Moon Flights" club. When the company closed the list to new applicants on March 3, 1971, it contained names from every state in the U.S. and more than 90 countries around the world.

Space Out Music

- *Venus & Mars* —Paul McCartney and Wings
- *Fly Me to the Moon*—Frank Sinatra
- *When You Wish Upon a Star*—Cliff Edwards
- *The Martian Hop*—The Ran-dels
- *X-M* and *Starship* —Jefferson Starship
- *Third Stone from the Sun* —Jimi Hendrix
- *Kahoutek* —Journey
- *2000 Light Years from Home* — Rolling Stones
- *Telstar*—Tornadoes
- *Rocket Man*—Elton John
- *Major Tom*—David Bowie
- *Eclipse* —Pink Floyd

Perfect Landing Every Time

This Hungarian-made toy Space Rocket reminds us of our old metal toys of the 1950s. The rocket runs along the floor (no batteries necessary) until it hits something. It immediately hoists itself up vertically as it unfolds its staircase where a smiling cosmonaut waits to disembark.

#R56, $24.00 + 4.50 shipping from The Daily Planet, P.O. Box 1313, New York, NY 10013. (800) 334-0006 / FAX (212) 334-1158.

To The Moon Alice!

Moonbase. Our choice among the plethora of space computer games out there. You get to create your own civilization, and what could be more fun than that? Allocate resources, deal with unbalanced budgets, doomsayers and destructive forces—just like being the mayor of a large city in the U.S.! Will you create a utopian world or a moon colony hell?

$44.99 + 5.00 shipping. Egghead Software, 22011 SE 51st St., Issaquah, WA 98027-7004. (800) EGGHEAD.

THE WRITE STUFF

This pen, developed for use by astronauts in outer space (for writing post cards home?), will do it all, in any position, and at temperatures from -50° to +400° F. Even writes under water, so doodling in the hot tub is no sweat. Two refills included.

#91710, $8.95 + 3.25 shipping from Discovery Corner, Lawrence Hall of Science, University of California, Berkeley, CA 94720. (510) 642-1016.

"Put three grains of sand inside a vast cathedral, and the cathedral will be more closely packed with sand than space is with stars." —Sir James Jeans

Suborbital

Real 12 in. rocket reaches heights up to 1000 ft. and floats back to earth with a recovery parachute. Includes electrical ignition/launch system, 3 solid fuel rocket engines and orange and white parachute.

#7096, $21.98 + 4.95 shipping from Johnson Smith Company, 4514 19th Court East, P.O. Box 25500, Bradenton, FL 34206-5500. (813) 747-2356 / FAX (813) 746-7896.

Up & Away, Space Cadets

U.S. Space Academy. This three-day, hands-on program is offered at the U.S. Space & Rocket Center where NASA develops space vehicles. You get to perform astronaut training activities—get dizzy in the Multi-Axis Simulator, get heavy in the triple-gravity Centrifuge, and shed pounds in the one-sixth gravity simulated moon walk.

The program is straight out of NASA. Some of the equipment has actually been in space, and a working astronaut talks to the group. Tuition is $450, which includes meals and dormitory accommodations. They also offer the very popular Space Camp for kids age 10 and above. For information, contact:

US Space Academy
U.S. Space & Rocket Center
One Tranquility Base
Huntsville, AL 35807
(800) 63-SPACE

SPACE AGE SPIN-OFFS

Here are a few things that owe their existence to the technological impact of the Space Age:

- Heat-resistant paint
- Scratch-resistant sunglasses (from NASA research on the visors of space helmets)
- Sensors for smoke alarms
- Cooling sportswear containing heat-absorbing gel packets
- Solar collectors
- Cordless tools
- Pocket calculators
- Live TV from other countries
- Satellite TV weather photos
- HBO, CNN and MTV
- Spy satellites
- Reliable five-year flashlights
- Corningware
- Bras for female athletes
- Intercontinental ballistic missiles
- Freeze-dried food
- Tang, the breakfast drink

World's Fastest Food

These meals will really take off with the younger set. Space Shuttle place setting includes compartmentalized tray, tumbler, spoon and fork. The payload bay door converts to a salad plate and the red tail section is removable.

#91305, $23.00 + $4.25 shipping from Discovery Center, Lawrence Hall of Science, University of California, Berkeley, CA 94720. (510) 642-1016.

Astronaut Ice Cream

As eaten by astronauts in space, you can feast on real neapolitan ice cream (strawberry, chocolate, and vanilla) that has been frozen to -40° F, vacuum dried, and sealed in a mylar foil pouch.

This stuff tastes just like ice cream, except it isn't cold when you eat it, it looks and feels like plastic foam, and it's semi-crunchy like candy. Like many great experiences, it's awfully weird the first time, but gets addictive quickly.

$1.95 each, 3/4 oz. pouch. Shipping for any amount up to $20 total is $3.25. Discovery Corner, Lawrence Hall of Science, University of California, Berkeley, CA 94720. (510) 642-1016.

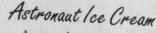

"Space is merely an escape, because it is easier to go to Mars or the moon than it is to penetrate one's own being." —Carl Jung

The Original *Star Trek* Shows

Columbia House's Star Trek Collector's Edition Videos. Trekkies are everywhere, following the adventures of the Starship Enterprise through two generations. The original episodes, unedited and without commercials, are available from this Klingon-of-the-month subscription service. They send you a two episode tape every five weeks or so. First one is $4.95 plus shipping; after that, $19.95 plus shipping. No obligation, you can cancel any time.

For information about subscribing, contact Columbia House Video, P. O. Box 1112, Terre Haute, IN 47811. (800) 538-7766.

SCI-FI TV FUN

40 Years of Sci-Fi TV. Documentary video retrospective looks at *Outer Limits, Night Stalker, Lost In Space, Superman* and *Star Trek*, including some infamous *Star Trek* bloopers. 30 minutes.

#1776, $13.98 + 4.20 shipping. Johnson Smith Company, 4514 19th Court East, P.O. Box 25500, Bradenton, FL 34206-5500. (813) 747-2356 / FAX (813) 746-7896.

Not So Logical

Golden Throats: The Great Celebrity Sing-Off! William Shatner sings...make that butchers...*Lucy In The Sky With Diamonds* and *Mr. Tambourine Man!* Leonard Nimoy ruins *Proud Mary* but is actually pretty decent warbling *If I Had A Hammer.* Trekkies can hear them both, along with other singing celebrities like Jack Webb, Andy Griffith, Mae West and more on this strange novelty collection.

#R11G 70187 LP, $8.98 + 2.00 shipping. #R41G 70187 cassette, $8.98 + 2.00 shipping. #R21S 70187 CD, $13.98 + 2.00 shipping from Rhino Records, 2225 Colorado Avenue, Santa Monica, CA 90404-3598.

(800) 432-0020.

Vulcanized Rubber

Rubberized? No, rubber eared. Pointy, rubber ears just like Mr. Spock's. Includes elastic band to hold 'em in place. Two pair, in case you need to lend an ear to a friend.

#8283, 2 sets., $2.95 + 4.00 shipping from Archie McPhee, P.O. Box 30852, Seattle, WA 98103-0852. (206) 547-2467.

For Enterprising Model Builders

Put together any of three different replicas of the U.S.S. Enterprise. Each comes with a display stand or can be suspended from the ceiling.

• Original Enterprise from the TV show.

#6993, 8 1/2". $9.98 + 2.70 shipping.

• The Enterprise from the movies.

#6991, 22", $14.98 + 4.20 shipping.

• *The Next Generation* wessel (as Chekhov would say) with detachable saucer.

#6992, 18", $14.98 + 4.20 shipping.

All from Johnson Smith Company, 4514 19th Court East, P.O. Box 25500, Bradenton, Florida 34206-5500. (813) 747-2356 / FAX (813) 746-7896.

Does anybody still remember the *Star Trek* Saturday morning cartoon series?

SPACE ADVENTURE COLLECTIBLES

by T. N. Tumbusch

FREE WILL

Humanity has the choice for good or evil. And so do you. Kirk or Klingon, you decide.

#5201, Kirk Mask or #5202, Klingon Mask, each $21.98 + 4.95 shipping from Johnson Smith Company, 4514 19th Court East, P.O. Box 25500, Bradenton, FL 34206-5500. (813) 747-2356 / FAX (813) 746-7896.

Lost in Storage Space

• *Space Adventure Collectibles* by **T.N. Tumbusch.** *Buck Rogers, Flash Gordon, Space Patrol,* and on through the whole gang in *Star Trek* and *Star Wars*—it's a reference guide with price list, tips for beginning collectors, and info on your favorite space heroes.

$19.95 + 2.50 shipping from Wallace-Homestead Book Co., 1 Chilton Way, Radnor, PA 19089. (800) 695-1214.

• *An Encyclopedia of Trekkie Memorabilia: Identification and Value Guide* by **Chris Gentry and Sally Gibson-Downs.** *Star Trek* fans have got it all here in one place— games, clothing, art, animation cels, videos, buttons, patches, and much more.

$16.95 + $2.00 shipping from Books Americana, P.O. Box 2326, Florence, AL 35630. (800) 239-9966.

• *The Official Price Guide to Star Trek / Star Wars Collectibles.* Find out how valuable your favorite space merchandise is. Includes advice on building and storing your collection.

$8.95 + 2.70 shipping. House of Collectibles, 201 East 50th St., New York, NY 10022. (800) 733-3000.

"Man on the moon. The poor magnificent bungler! He can't even get to the office without undergoing the agonies of the damned, but give him a little metal, a few chemicals, some wire and 30 or 40 billion dollars and, vroom! There he is, up on a rock a quarter of a million miles up in the sky."

—*Russell Baker, July 21, 1969.*

JABBA WACKY

Our favorite character from *Star Wars* is over 4" tall, 9 1/2" long and has moveable arms. And, if you twist the last four inches of his tail, his head turns! Other than that, this slime ball does nothing. Buy several and have a slug fest!

#9013, $2.95 each + 4.00 shipping from Archie McPhee, P.O. Box 30852, Seattle, WA 98103-0852. (206) 547-2467.

Our Favorite TV Space Shows

Star Trek
The Jetsons
Hitchhiker's Guide to the Galaxy
Captain Video
Lost in Space
Fireball XL-5
Space Patrol
Tom Corbett, Space Cadet

Meet
George Jetson

Need more space in your house? The Cricket Gallery sells *Jetsons* animation cels and artwork at prices in the $400 - 800 range guaranteed to get you all the space you can afford. One recent offering we liked was a limited edition called *The Jetsons' Sunday Drive* that shows the spaceship with the whole gang: George, Jane, Judy, and Elroy, their dog Astro and Rosie the Robot too.

#HB-210289, $400.00 + 8.00 shipping from The Cricket Gallery, 529 Covington Place, Wyckoff, NJ 07481. (800) BUY-CELS.

CREW SHIRTS

Look like a member of the Enterprise crew with 100% polyester replica uniforms from the TV show.

#98903, Executive gold or #98904, Science blue, each $26.98 + 4.95 shipping from Johnson Smith Company, 4514 19th Court East, P.O. Box 25500, Bradenton, FL 34206-5500. (813) 747-2356 / FAX (813) 746-7896.

SPACE FOR YOU IN THESE CLUBS

• *Lost in Space* Fannish Alliance, 7331 Terri Robyn Road, St. Louis, MO 63129.

• **Battlestar One** (*Battlestar Galactica*), P. O. Box 988, Astor Station, Boston, MA 02123.

• *Star Trek* Welcommittee (publishes a guide to all the myriad *Star Trek* organizations), P. O. Box 12, Saranac, MI 48881.

• *Space 1999* Barbara Bain / Martin Landau Fan Club, c/o Terry Bowers, 603 N. Clark St., River Falls, WI 54022-1404.

Technical Reading

The Star Trek Manual. The Star Fleet handbook guides you through the academy, fleet organization, codes, interstellar space/warp technology and, of course, the Articles of Federation.

#1207, $10.95 + 2.70 shipping from Johnson Smith Company, 4514 19th Court East, P.O. Box 25500, Bradenton, FL 34206-5500. (813) 747-2356 / FAX (813) 746-7896.

Bid-by-Mail Space Collectibles

Like the excitement of an auction? Subscribe to Hake's auction catalogs—you get 4 catalogs for $20—and let the bidding begin. See something you like in the catalog, make a written bid by the cut-off date, and you might be the lucky purchaser. Hake sells a little bit of everything, but here are some typical recent space-related offerings:

• Moon landing commemorative button with pendant.

• *TV Guide* issue of July 19, 1969, week of the first moon landing.

• "Men Walk on the Moon" newspaper mug featuring a replica of the *New York Times* front page coverage of the first moon walk.

• *Captain Video and his Video Rangers*, an RCA Victor record album including three punch-out figures (Captain Video, a Video Ranger, and enemy Octavio), two 78 r.p.m. records, and one book.

Hake's Americana and Collectibles, P.O. Box 1444, York, PA 17405. (717) 848-1333 / FAX (717) 848-4977.

SPIES

Nest of Spies

As long as there have been societies, there have been spies. For centuries, to be a spy was nothing to brag about—a profession considered repugnant even by those who engaged in it. As recently as World War II, a high governmental official sniffed, "Gentlemen don't open each other's mail."

It wasn't until the 1960s that the Cold War brought the dubious profession out from undercover and made it "glamorous." It was a time

when America gave up on the idea of maintaining moral or ethical superiority in tactical means—the justification being that we had to be just as ruthless, bloodthirsty and deceitful as we thought our enemies would be.

Spies didn't usually reveal their profession, even after they retired. But former British spy Ian Fleming decided to come out of the spook closet and capitalize on his career by glamorizing it in a series of novels.

Unlike real spies who try to blend into the background, his suave hero, James Bond, wore a tux and drove a flashy Aston Martin. A positive public remark by John Kennedy boosted Fleming's sales in America and spawned a host of pop culture spies.

The revelations in the 1970s of real-life dirty tricks, assassinations and even incompetence removed the gloss from "good guy" spies. The 1970s and '80s presented a grittier, more sinister look at espionage, evident in *The Prisoner, Three Days of the Condor* and the British TV miniseries *Tinker, Tailor, Soldier, Spy*, with decidedly unglamorous George Smiley.

Male Bonding

"He certainly looks like 007, and I don't know who could have done it better."

—**Ian Fleming on the casting of Sean Connery to play James Bond**

"For now, I'm reasonably content. After all, I can kill any s.o.b. in the world and get away with it; I've got the powers of the greatest governments in the world behind me; I eat and drink nothing but the best; and I also get the loveliest ladies in the world. What could be better?"

—**Sean Connery, on playing James Bond**.

Destroy After Reading

SpyGame: Winning Through Super Technology **by Scott French and Lee Lapin.** How super sleuths capitalize on the latest technologies, constructing and using starlight scopes, remote laser beam listening devices and more.

"Spies are of no use these days. Their profession is over. The newspapers do their work nowadays."—Oscar Wilde

Whole Pop Spy Paranoia Film Festival

- *Little Nikita*: A kid with a security secret becomes the pawn of the FBI and the KGB.

- *Three Days of the Condor*: CIA-induced murders and cover-ups prompt an employee who knows too much to flee the pursuing Agency.

- *The Spy Who Came in from the Cold*: Realistic depiction of embittered Cold War spy's unglamorous life. Not for Bond lovers.

- *The Manchurian Candidate*: Brainwashing by commies turns a war hero into a time bomb in this thriller par excellence. Withdrawn by Frank Sinatra for two decades after Kennedy's assassination.

- *The Fourth Protocol*: A British agent tries to stop a plot to detonate a nuclear bomb.

- *The Third Solution*: Red Commies and the Vatican's Red Cardinals are in cahoots to rule the world.

- *Topaz*: Hitchcock spins a spy yarn about ferreting out Russia's involvement in Cuba.

007? No, Never

From *Dr. No* to *Never Say Never*, get your 007's worth on video. Yes, all of Sean Connery and Roger Moore's best. And George Lazenby's worst. 16-movie set includes *The Living Daylights* with Timothy Dalton, but not *Casino Royale* with Woody Allen.

#MM310, set of 16 movies, $299.20 + 6.95 shipping from Special Interest Video, 100 Enterprise Place, P.O. Box 7022, Dover, DE 19903-7022. (800) 522-0502 / FAX (302) 678-9200.

"The name is Bond, James Bond."

CANDID CAMERA

Just like the ones the big boys use! Even takes photos in near darkness! Auto focus from 3 ft. to infinity. Use standard daylight or infrared film in Minox-style 8mm cartridges. No winding necessary for quick in and out spy sessions.

#C739045, $350.00 + 12.50 shipping from Sync, Hanover, PA 17333-0042. (800) 722-9979.

Our Favorite Cartoon Spies

- *Lancelot Link, Secret Chimp and Mata Hairy*

- *Secret Squirrel*

- *Boris Badenov and Natasha Fatale*

Undercover Underwear

Mata Hari would have loved this lace-lavished nylon tricot lingerie that's designed to discreetly hide a woman's valuables. Her money, too. The camisole has a 4" zippered compartment on the bodice, tap pants have a zippered pouch below the waist in back, half-slip has 4" deep zippered pocket around the hemline.

**#3380 Camisole, $32.50 + 1.75 shipping.
#3281 Tap pants, $32.50 + 1.75 shipping.
#3258 Secure Slip, $25.00 + 1.95 shipping.
Life Force Technologies LTD, P.O. Box 755, Basalt, CO 81621. (800) 922-3545.**

Captive Audience

The Official Prisoner Companion by Matthew White and Jaffer Ali. Behind-the-scenes stories, rare photos and information about the cult TV series starring Patrick McGoohan. Enter the sinister storybook world of The Village, within which there is no freedom, and from which there is no escape.

#ET5094, $9.95 + 2.75 shipping
Laissez Faire Books
942 Howard Street
San Francisco, CA 94103
(800) 326-0996 / FAX (415) 541-0597

Not a Shred of Evidence

If Oliver North can purposely destroy evidence and government property and get off scot-free, why not you? With a touch of a button, tempered steel blades will destroy 4 sheets of paper at a time—the entire Constitution in a few seconds! Plus it's portable, so you can do your shredding anywhere. Heck, maybe the president will call you a hero and you can do speeches for $20,000 a pop.

#3311 Cross-cut Shredder, $229.50 + 4.00 shipping from Hammacher Schlemmer, 9180 Le Saint Drive, Fairfield, OH 45014. (800) 543-3366.

EYE SPY

No need to look over your shoulder with see-behind sunglasses. Tiny mirrors let you ogle with deniability.

#1292, $7.98 + 2.70 shipping. Johnson Smith Co., 4514 19th Court East, P.O. Box 25500, Bradenton, FL 34206-5500. (813) 747-2356 / FAX (813) 746-7896.

'Scopes Trial

A precise, quality periscope that magnifies your target up to 4.7 times with fast focus. Plus it's lightweight for easy carrying. Perfect for golf tournaments, parades, and harassing giraffes.

#DPS918, $99.95 + 7.25 shipping. Life-style Fascination, 345 W. County Line Rd., Jackson, NY 08527-2003. (800) 669-0987 / FAX (908) 928-1812.

INSIDE INFO

Inside the CIA. This video set lets you take a look inside one of the world's most powerful secret organizations. Part 1 traces the history of the Central Intelligence Agency. Part 2 exposes the assassination plots against world leaders. Part 3 uncovers CIA subversion—its attempts to "destabilize" or overthrow foreign governments. 174 mins. on three VHS cassettes.

#17559, $59.95 + 6.60 shipping from Signals, P.O. Box 64428, St. Paul, MN 55164-0428. (800) 669-9696.

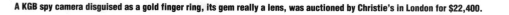

A KGB spy camera disguised as a gold finger ring, its gem really a lens, was auctioned by Christie's in London for $22,400.

SECRET CLUBS

- **James Bond 007 Fan Club.** Founded in 1974, the club offers pen pal correspondence, photos, free offers, and Bond merchandise and memorabilia to its 2500 members. The club magazine is called *Bondage*.

   Send SASE c/o Richard Schenkman, President, P.O. Box 414, Bronxville, NY 10708.

- **UNCLE HQ.** This club for fans of the *Man* and *Girl from UNCLE* offers information, pen pals, memorabilia, updates on stars, and re-run support groups. Quarterly *HQ Newsletter* and annual convention.

   c/o Darlene Kepner, Secretary, 234 Washo Drive, Lake Zurich, IL 60047.

- **The McCallum Observer.** Some people don't know when to cry UNCLE. Since 1985, this 250 member fan club has followed the ups and downs of Illya Kuryakin, er, David McCallum's career. Their newsletter features photos and classified information.

   c/o Lynda Mendoza, P.O. Box 165, Downers Grove, IL 60515.

- **Six of One Club: The Prisoner Appreciation Society.** For fans of the 17-episode allegorical series *The Prisoner*, the maddeningly enigmatic show about a struggle for freedom in a sham paradise. Publishes *Number 6 Magazine*, holds an annual meeting at the Portmeirion, Wales site where much of the series was filmed.

   c/o Bruce A. Clark, P.O. Box 172, Hatfield, PA 19440.

Secret Spy Spots

The Ian Fleming Thriller Map. A blueprint to all of James Bond's adventures with over 100 international locales where 007 saved the Free World time and again. Profusely illustrated with lots of Bond iconography.

$5.75 postpaid from Aaron Blake Publications, 1800 S. Robertson, Ste. 130, Los Angeles, CA 90035.

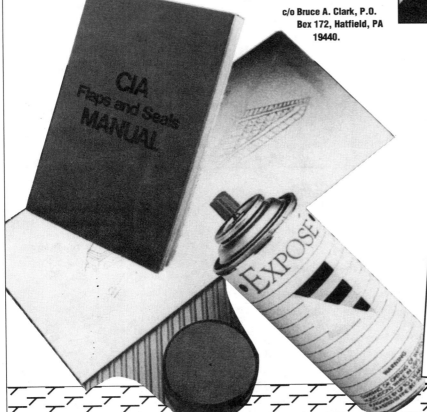

Invade Privacy, Go to Jail

A spritz of Exposé turns opaque paper translucent for 30 to 60 seconds. Read through one or two sheets of paper (even brown kraft paper) before the envelope returns it to its original state with no markings, discoloration or odor.

Comes with CIA manual full of info and tips on invading privacy. And speaking of tips, remember this: tampering with written communication in United States Postal Service channels is punishable by up to 5 years in jail and/or a $2,000 fine (REF SEC 1702, TITLE 18, USC).

#3284, Exposé with manual, $30.00 + 2.00 shipping, Life Force Technologies LTD., P.O. Box 755, Basalt, CO 81621. (800) 922-3545.

> "I am not a number,
> I am a free man!"
> —**Number 6**, *The Prisoner*

Ace Of Spies

That's *Reilly, Ace of Spies*, the sexy superspy from the popular, reality-based PBS mini-series. This is the premiere episode and it's available on tape.

#16742, $29.95 + 3.90 shipping from Signals, P.O. Box 64428, St. Paul, MN 55164-0428. (800) 669-9696.

Left in the Dark?

The Night Penetrator lets you conduct after-dark surveillance anywhere, anytime. Hand-held night vision viewer is the smallest professional scope available. Use it for map-reading, maritime and astononomical observation, viewing nocturnal wild life, or reading under the covers.

Can be attached to 35mm SLR camera or CCTV system. 75mm objective lens and 10X eyepiece for an effective range of 700 meters and 136 degree field of vision. Lots more technical jargon, incomprehensible acronyms and accessories to justify its steep price tag. Batteries included!

#3280, $7,995.00 + 12.50 shipping from Life Force Technologies LTD, P.O. Box 755 Basalt, CO 81621 (800) 922-3545

Spook Images on the TV

- *Man From UNCLE.* After Bond, the television networks fell all over themselves trying to copy the guy. One could boast the involvement of Ian Fleming himself. Fleming named the lead character Napoleon Solo and helped lay the groundwork for the series before a heart attack caused him to leave the production.

- *Mission: Impossible.* Its expert crew in tactics and disguises consistently succeeded at over-elaborate scenarios.

- *Get Smart.* Mel Brooks and Buck

Henry created this sitcom spy spoof. Maxwell Smart and Agent 99 fought against KAOS each week.

- *I Spy.* Bill Cosby's first series, with Robert Culp, featured two spies who pretended they were pro tennis players.

- *The Avengers* featured Diana Rigg as martial artist Emma Peel.

- *Secret Agent* gave us that great Johnny Rivers song and served as Act I for *The Prisoner*.

Expensive Spy Fantasies

Garrison Keillor used to do a funny series of ads for a store whose motto was "Serving All Your Phobia Needs." If you believe there are enemies around every corner, check out this slick catalog, a great source for upscale paranoiacs.

**Life Force Technologies LTD.
P.O. Box 755
Basalt, CO 81621
(800) 922-3545**

BUGGED?

Phone Guard checks for simple taps or off-hook extensions. Scans radio range to detect hidden wireless microphones in and near your phone. Also "jams" any missed bugs with interfering white noise.

#Q9154, $299.95 + 8.95 shipping from U.S. Cavalry, 2855 Centennial Avenue, Radcliff, KY 40160-9000. (800) 777-7732 / FAX (502) 352-0266.

Ian Fleming named his spy after ornithologist James Bond, the author of his favorite birdwatching guide.

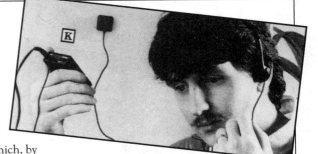

GO DOWN ON THIS!

The Sea Urchin is a one-person, one-atmosphere sub capable of diving 300 feet and operating underwater for 6-8 hours without recharging the batteries (which, by the way, are included).

The hull is certified by ABS (American Bureau of Shipping), equipped with a 72 hour oxygen life support and CO_2 scrubber system. Weighs 1700 lbs., with a displacement weight of 1900 lbs. and a payload capacity of 300 lbs.

#3270 The Sea Urchin (FOB Vancouver, B.C.), $40,000.00
Optional accessories:
Navigational compass, $220.00
Sonar, $1500.00
Manipulator Arm, $600.00
Transport Trailer, $4500.00
Delivery time is 6 months from order date and a down payment of 25% is required.
Life Force Technologies LTD.
P.O. Box 755
Basalt, CO 81621
(800) 922-3545

Ears for Walls

Don't let a simple concrete, metal or any other kind of 12" wall come between you and the secrets that are being spoken on the other side. "Ear" amplifies sound, even whispers, up to 25,000 times, while audio limiter stops louder noises from blowing your ear drums. Special micro-chip to amplify whispers. Range: 300-3000 Hz. Stick-on putty and battery included.

#Q9152, $199.95 + 8.95 shipping from, U.S. Cavalry, 2855 Centennial Avenue, Radcliff, KY 40160-9000. (800) 777-7732 / FAX (502) 352-0266.

"Sorry about that, Chief."

—Maxwell Smart

I Spy...
TV Collectibles

• Send $1.50 for a catalog of TV spy show products, plus James Bond products. *TV Guide* catalog spanning the years 1951—1990 also available for $2.00.

Howard Rogofsky, Box GZ107, Glen Oaks, NY 11004.

• *Hake's Guide to TV Collectibles* by **Ted Hake** gives you the goods on all those TV spy collectibles.

$14.95 + 3.50 shipping from Americana and Collectibles, PO Box 1444, York, PA 17405.

SUPERMAN

How Superman Came to Be

During a sleepless summer night in 1934, Jerry Siegel came up with the idea of Superman. At dawn he ran 12 blocks to wake up his artist pal Joe Shuster, who caught Siegel's excitement. Together, the two friends from Cleveland, Ohio developed the ultimate superhero. They were both 17 years old.

Siegel and Shuster's proposed comic strip of an alien strong-man from a faraway planet was turned down by almost every newspaper comic strip editor in the country. "A rather immature piece of work," read one typical response. DC Comics finally took the risk, paying the young team $130 for 98 panels which were then pasted up in comic book page layout.

Superman's first appearance was in the June, 1938 *Action Comics No. 1.* Readers loved him, sales figures climbed, Supe was a winner, and it was up, up and away.

Although fast when he first came on the scene, Superman couldn't outrace a speeding bullet. And he couldn't actually fly, though he could leap high in the sky and hop swiftly about a city. Eventually, he acquired more fantastic powers, until he was able to push whole planets around.

Other Kryptonian characters were added to the cast, such as Super-girl, Superboy (Supe as a boy), Superhorse, and Krypto the Superdog.

In 1986, DC Comics gave Superman a makeover. Clark became an upwardly mobile, career-minded columnist, who worked on a novel in his spare time (so did Lois Lane). He used Nautilus weight-training equipment to explain his fantastic physique. The Man of Steel also became a "sensitive guy," open about his feelings, vulnerable to more than just Kryptonite.

Up, Up and Oy Vey!

Two notable ethnic superheroes inspired by Superman:

Brotherman is a rock-jawed, black superhero who works a day job as an assistant district attorney, and at night takes vigilante action to wipe the "slime of society" from Big City's streets. Created by actual brothers David, Guy, and Jason Sims, who are black. The street-smart comic debuted in April, 1990, and sold out its first issue of 10,000 copies.

The world's second Jewish comic book superhero (the first was SuperJew), Shaloman is a muscle-bound, curly-haired supermensch, who lives in a rock (he's the Man of Stone) atop "Mount Israel." He is activated by the Yiddish cry of distress, "Oy vey!" Created by retired Philadelphia hairstylist Al Wiesner, Shaloman (Shalom is the Hebrew word for peace) fights evil. What else?

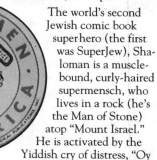

SUPERMAN, FIRST APPEARANCES

- Comic book: 1938
- Newspaper comic strip: 1939
- Radio: 1940
- Feature-length cartoons: 1941
- Novel: 1942
- Movie serials: 1948-50

- Feature films: 1951-1987
- TV series: 1951-57
- Musical on Broadway: 1966 (**"It's a Bird...It's a Plane...It's Superman!"**)
- TV cartoons: 1966-68
- Display in the Smithsonian Institution: 1988 (50th anniversary)

Superman is 6'2", but Clark Kent is only 5'11". (He slouches.)

SUPERMAN FACTS

• That was some amazing disguise Superman used: he put on a suit and a pair of glasses. Yet somehow it worked and for years he fooled all his friends and coworkers, even those hard-eyed investigative reporters.

• Originally 10¢, Superman's debut in *Action Comics #1*, in "very fine" to "near mint" condition, would likely sell for over $50,000 today.

• Those memorable words— "Look! Up in the sky! It's a bird! It's a plane! It's Superman!"—were first heard on the radio on February 12, 1940. The star of the show was Budd Collyer, later host of TV's *Beat the Clock*. He used a tenor voice for Clark Kent, a bass for Superman.

• George Reeves, who played Superman in the 1950s TV series, had a small part in the 1939 classic *Gone with the Wind* (he played Brent Tarleton, one of a set of twins courting Scarlett O'Hara early in the film). Reeves died in 1959, an apparent suicide.

• It has been reported that in spite of the Man of Steel's intense comic book battles against the Japanese and other World War II axis powers, Emperor Hirohito of Japan considered Superman his favorite fictional character.

• Supermensch? Nazi Propaganda Minister Joseph Goebbels once leapt to his feet during a Reichstag meeting, waving an American comic book about, and denounced Superman as a Jew.

"If Jesus and Superman had a fight, who would win?"
—Universal grade-school theological question.

The Whole Pop Superman Film Fest

• *Superman and The Mole Men* (1951). Drilling the world's deepest oil well invades the underground world of the Mole Men, who come stumbling out onto the earth's surface. Superman gets involved when the townspeople try to kill them. Launched the career of George Reeves, who went on to star in the television series.

• *Superman* (1978). Wonderfully entertaining film traces the life of Superman (Christopher Reeve) from Krypton to Smallville to Metropolis.

• *Superman II* (1980). Superman goes up against three super-powered villains from his home planet.

• *Superman III* (1983). Richard Pryor's a computer tech who unwittingly paves the way for the villain to get at our hero.

• *Superman IV* (1987). Supe goes warhead to warhead with Nuclear Man for peace's sake.

Man and Superman

Did Jerry Siegel or Joe Shuster resemble their creation? According to one description, they were "two small, shy, nervous, myopic lads." Kinda like Clark Kent.

Siegel and Shuster say that their model for Superman was Douglas Fairbanks, Sr., swashbuckling star of films like *The Mark of Zorro, Robin Hood*, and *The Black Pirate*.

There's no evidence that either had ever read or even heard of Nietzsche's *Man and Superman*.

Creators Siegel and Shuster signed over rights to Superman when they became employees of DC Comics in 1938. They became stunned witnesses to Superman's wild popularity, but did not receive any significant monies for all the movies, TV shows, cartoons, and marketing activities that were a part of the Superman phenomenon.

Fired in a dispute in 1948, the two originators waged various legal battles without success. Finally, after they tangled with the company again in the late 1970s when *Superman, the Movie* was a blockbuster, DC granted them a small pension and medical coverage, and restored their names as creators.

Superman artist Joel Shuster eventually married the model he had many years earlier hired for the first sketches of Lois Lane.

Books

• *Superman at Fifty: The Persistence of a Legend*, edited by Dennis Dooley and Gary Engle. A super book of fascinating essays. Dooley and Engle have put together an imaginative, entertaining book that gets right to the crux of things, like what accounts for the superhero's astounding and enduring appeal. Lots of Superman lore, and serious answers to questions like "Why didn't Lois Lane write to Ann Landers?"

#SMN50HC, $9.95 + 2.00 shipping from Bud Plant Comic Art, P.O. Box 1686, Grass Valley, CA 95945. (800) 242-6642/ (916) 273-2166.

• *Superman Archives No.1*, by Jerry Siegel and Joe Shuster. Here's a full-color volume (272 pages) of the first four Superman comic books (Superman Nos. 1-4), reprinted in a high-quality hardcover edition, with all covers and advertisements included. Nice introduction by Jim Steranko, comic artist and author of *Steranko's History of Comics.*

#SMARC01, $39.95 + 3.00 shipping from Bud Plant Comic Art, P.O. Box 1686, Grass Valley, CA 95945. (800) 242-6642 / (916) 273-2166.

Quotes of Steel

"Clark Kent grew not only out of my private life, but also out of Joe's. As a high school student, I thought that some day I might become a reporter, and I had crushes on several attractive girls who either didn't know I existed or didn't care I existed...It occurred to me: What if I had something special going for me, like jumping over buildings or throwing cars around or something like that?"

—**Jerry Siegel**

"Superman had only to wake up in the morning to be Superman. In his case, Clark Kent was the put-on. The fellow with the eyeglasses and the acne and the walk girls laughed at wasn't real, didn't exist, was a sacrificial disguise, an act of discreet martyrdom. Had they but known!"

—**Jules Feiffer**

"There are only five fictional creations known to every man, woman and child on the planet—Mickey Mouse, Sherlock Holmes, Tarzan, Robin Hood and Superman."

—**Harlan Ellison**

Bend Cardboard In Your Bare Hands

1979 Superman trading card set. 99 color cards from the 1978 movie.

#6-NM79-01, $19.50 + 3.00 shipping from Pacific Trading Cards, 18424 Highway 99, Lynnwood, WA 98037. (800) 551-2002.

A Few Things That Superman Can't Do

Having an invincible body—including impenetrable skin—can make it tough on a guy. Superman observer Arvydas Berkopec has come up with some disadvantages to being the Man of Steel. For example, Superman can't:

• Get a tattoo.

• Get a vaccination. This places restrictions on the countries where he can travel. Superman's first comic book words ever were "Try again, Doc!" as a physician was trying to give him a shot.

• Get a tan.

• Experience a surprise birthday party. With his X-ray vision and super hearing, who can sneak up on him? (In a wartime Sunday comic strip, Superman flunked a pre-induction physical when he inadvertently read the wrong eye chart. His X-ray vision was directed at the one in the adjoining room.)

• Carry loose change. You've seen his leotard—no pockets.

Super Vision

- **The Adventures of Superman Videos, Vols. 1-3.** The original animated adventures of the Man of Steel, produced by the Fleischer studios in 1941. The cartoons were heralded by a heavy promotional campaign, and even included "coming attraction" trailers, very unusual for cartoon shorts. The public was

pleased—the cinematically sophisticated cartoons were exciting dramatic adventure stories, filled with lots of special effects. Three full-color tape volumes, each approximately 50 mins., with 6 full-length cartoons on each.

$14.99 each, $44.97 for 3-volume set. Add 3.00 shipping from The Funny Papers, 7253 Geary Blvd., San Francisco, CA 94121. (415) 752-1914.

- **Rare Superman Video.** Contrary to popular belief, Superman didn't have Wheaties for breakfast. This video shows Superman (George Reeves) hawk Kelloggs cereals in a test commercial shot in his bedroom (where Reeves later shot and killed himself).

In other Kelloggs spots, Perry White and Jimmy Olson need Superman's help to secure more corn flakes. Includes screen tests of actresses trying for the part of Lana Lang, *Stamp Day For Superman*, made for the Treasury Department, and more.

60 min. VHS. The Superman Archives Collectors Edition: Vol. 3, $24.95 + 3.95 shipping from Video Resources New York, Inc., 220 W 71st St., New York, NY, 10023. (212) 724-7055.

POSTERIFFIC!

Super 1-sheets (27 x 41 inches).

#WB-1978, Superman, $45.00 + 1.10 shipping; #TS-1985, Supergirl, $20.00 + 50¢ shipping from Cinema City, P.O. Box 1012, Muskegon, MI 49443. (616) 722-7760.

Songs Which Pay Homage to Superman

- *Sunshine Superman* (1966)—Donovan
- *You Don't Mess Around With Jim* (1972)—Jim Croce
- *(Wish I Could Fly Like) Superman* (1979)—The Kinks
- *I'm Your Superman* (1981)—Rick Springfield
- *Theme from Superman* (1983)—Barbra Streisand
- *Land of Confusion* (1987)—Genesis

Superman: Word For Word

The shooting script for the 1978 *Superman* starring Christopher Reeve.

$50.00 + 1.10 shipping from Cinema City, P.O. Box 1012, Muskegon, MI 49443. (616) 722-7760.

Pop Poetry

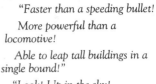

"Faster than a speeding bullet!

More powerful than a locomotive!

Able to leap tall buildings in a single bound!"

"Look! Up in the sky!

It's a bird!

It's a plane!

It's SUPERMAN!"

"Yes, it's Superman, strange visitor from another planet, who came to Earth with powers and abilities far beyond those of mortal men; Superman, who can change the course of mighty rivers, bend steel in his bare hands; and who, disguised as Clark Kent, mild-mannered reporter for a great metropolitan newspaper, fights a never-ending battle for truth, justice, and the American way!"

—from the 1940 *Adventures of Superman* Mutual Network radio show.

SUPERMAN ON THE RECORD

- **The Adventures of Superman** has four radio shows from 1945-47. Batman is missing and Robin enlists Supe to help find him. Plus a Radiosound Portrait of Bud Collyer, the voice of Superman.

#150, $7.95 + 2.50 shipping from Filmfax Products, P.O. Box 1900, Evanston, IL 60204.

Surfing

NEW WAVE, OLD WAVE, GNARLY WAVE

Surfin' thru history. Many people think surfing's a young sport that sprang from California with the Surfaris and Frankie & Annette in the early 1960s. But it's actually ancient, going back many centuries in Polynesian history. Hawaiian chants from the 16th Century sang its pleasures, and Captain James Cook described it in detail from his travels in 1777.

Evil pleasures. The best surfing was in November (called *Ikuwa* in Hawaiian, or "deafening winds").

A 19th Century scholar wrote: "*It is a month of rough seas and high surf that lure men to the sea coast. The wife may go hungry, the children, the whole family, but the head of the house does not care. He is all for sport, that is his food. All day there is fine sport; then from innocent pleasure they turn to evil pleasures.*" Cowabunga! Just like now!

Wipe-out. Surfing almost died during the 1800s when Europeans arrived. Foreign diseases ravaged the native population, which declined from about 300,000 at the time of Captain Cook to 40,000 in 1893. Besides, the missionaries frowned on surfing's frivolity and the accompanying sex, drinking and gambling.

Call of the wild. Few people know that it was author Jack London who helped save the sport by introducing it to the rest of the world in 1907. While in Waikiki he wrote about his surfing teacher, George Freeth, who was then invited to give surfing demonstrations on the mainland. Freeth became the first person to ever surf in California.

Surfing spread along the California coast, and so did the "beach boy" lifestyle of partying and otherwise scandalizing the rest of the world.

Flotsom. In 1926 Tom Blake revolutionized the sport by inventing the hollow surfboard, allowing it to be smaller, lighter and faster. Within a few years, the average weight of a board dropped from about 135 pounds to 85. Blake later added the dorsal fin, improving stability.

Further experiments in the early 1950s with styrofoam sandwiched between wood and covered with plastic resin created even lighter and more maneuverable boards.

"*He is flying through the air, flying forward, flying fast as the surge on which he stands. He is a Mercury— a brown Mercury. His heels are winged, and in them is the swiftness of the sea…*"

—Jack London
A Royal Sport: Surfing at Waikiki

WATCH, WATCH, WATCH THE WILD SURF MOVIES

Gidget (1959). The film, starring Sandra Dee, was the first surf culture to get national exposure.

• Pale, dark-haired, non-surfing Frankie and Annette were supposed to represent the tanned, tousled and tawny-haired Southern California teen ideal. Still, their six beach movies starting with *Beach Party* (1964) have a certain campy charm.

• *Ride the Wild Surf* (1964) actually focused more on the actual sport than the partying highlighted by most other surf flicks. Starred Fabian and Tab Hunter and a host of top-quality surfers.

• *The Endless Summer* (1970). Real surfers scoffed at Hollywood surf films. But they liked this follow-the-sun trek to find the perfect wave. Breath-taking photography of exotic beaches around the world.

"I tried surf-bathing once…The board struck the shore, without any cargo, and I struck the bottom about the same time."—Mark Twain, *Roughing It*

SURFING FACTS

- Much less than 1% of the population has ever surfed.
- "Real" surfers rarely drove woodies, despite popular conception—most drove panel trucks.
- Real surfers never much liked the surfing boom in the 1960s—it crowded the beaches with pretenders and poseurs.
- Surfers around LA were pretty much regarded as derelicts. It was only away from home that surf champions were treated with any respect.
- Most unlikely surfer? President Richard Nixon, who was given a board by his daughters for Father's Day, 1969. "I rode a surfboard 30 years ago," he was quoted as saying. Still, there's no evidence that he ever actually used his daughters' gift, blue with his name inscribed in yellow.

REQUIRED READING

Surfing: The Ultimate Pleasure
by Leonard Lueras, Workman Publishing, $12.95.
Out of print, but worth tracking down.

Perhaps the most complete book ever written about surfing, tracing its development from its Polynesian roots to its emergence as a unique subculture in the twentieth century. Lueras uses vivid detail, action photos and quotes to describe why this sport creates a romantic obsession between surfer and surf.

We meet figures like Hawaiian Duke Kahanamoku, a 1912 Olympic gold medalist for swimming who gave

SMOKE THAT RADICAL ZIPPER

- Eskimos are said to have 600 words for snow. Surfers come a close second in their vocabulary about the waves.

- *Nouns*: *ankle-snapper, bombora, creamer, dumper, foamie, grinder, heavy, looper, mushburger, peeler, roller, screamer, tunnel, widow-maker, zipper.*

- *Verbs*: *blast, curl, dribble, feather, gutter, heave, jack, kick, lob, pinwheel, slam, smoke, spin, spit, steamroll, thunder, warp.*

- *Adjectives*: *awesome, brutal, classic, filthy, gnarly, hideous, insane, juicy, lumpy, mindless, outrageous, pissweak, radical, spooky, tasty, unreal, wimpy.*

Surfing Periodically

Surfing Magazine
P.O. Box 565, Mt Morris, IL 61054
(800) 545-9364.
$18.95 / 12 issues.

Good magazine, whether you're a surfer or a mere gremmie wannabe. First-person travel pieces by aficionados on surfing location, interviews and photos, new products, bikinis and beefcake, lots of colorful ads, and information on competitions held all over the world.

surfing demonstrations which popularized the sport across the world.

Lueras includes lists of discs, films, and books to document surfing's impact on popular culture. Ancient Hawaiian engravings, modern surfboard art and even vintage postcards celebrate the never-ending quest for the perfect wave.

SURFIN' FIELD TRIP

Santa Cruz Surfing Museum
Santa Cruz, CA 95060
(408) 429-3429

All the classic California surfing beaches are in the LA Metro area except one: Santa Cruz. Surfers have been riding the waves here for most of this century and the Surfing Museum covers it all. The Evolution of Surfboards display shows the transition from old-fashioned redwood plank to fiberglass "stick." Other displays feature wetsuits, archival photographs, surfing videos, and—out the window—awesome views of Monterey Bay.

I'd Rather be Surfing

Surf Boards By Mail

New York's a lonely town when you're the only surfer boy. But that doesn't mean you can't get all your surfing accessory needs taken care of (excluding, of course, a beach and pounding waves). The Innerlight Store offers everything from surfboards new ($269-800) and used ($39-399) to wetsuits and bitchin' clothes.

For more information and catalog contact:
Yancy Spencer's Innerlight
1020 N. 9th Avenue
Pensacola, FL 32501
(904) 932-5134.

SURF SOUNDS

• *"If everybody had an ocean across the USA, then everybody'd be surfin' like Californi-ay…"* Surf music exploded across the US in the early 1960s, painting a tantalizing picture of sand and endless summer. Hundreds of teenage garage bands who had never even seen the ocean copied the sound.

• **Who started it?** Dick Dale, leader of the Del-Tones. A real surfer himself, Dale tried to imitate crashing waves in his instrumental songs. His innovation? The heavy back-beat and guitar vibrato from a new gadget, the "reverb."

• **The Beach Boys** added the falsetto voices singing in unexpectedly complex harmonies. Beating out their neighbors Jan & Dean, they became the most popular surf group around.

• **Friendly rivalry**: the two groups from Hawthorne, CA helped out on each other's songs. Brian Wilson wrote

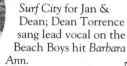

Surf City for Jan & Dean; Dean Torrence sang lead vocal on the Beach Boys hit *Barbara Ann*.

JUMPIN' OFF THE WOODIE
From surf band to distinguished career:
• *The Crossfires became the Turtles.*
• *"Ned & Nelda" (Frank Zappa and Ray Collins) formed the Mothers of Invention.*
• *The Jesters' Jim Messina went on to the Buffalo Springfield, then Loggins and Messina.*
• *Mike Curb left music completely and became Lt. Governor of California.*

BOOK SURFIN'

The Illustrated Discography of Surf Music: 1961-1965, by John Blair. Popular Culture Ink, PO Box 1839, Ann Arbor, MI 48106. (800) 678-8828, hardcover, $32 postpaid.

From the Aquanauts to the Zitts, Blair documents every known group in the history of this short-lived but potent genre. Lots of photos.

Of related interest: *Surf's Up!* by Brad Elliott listing every Beach Boys recording and release from 1961 to 1981 (hardcover, $35 postpaid).

Top Surf Hits

"Surf City"
Jan & Dean (1963)

"Wipe Out"
Surfaris (1963)

"Surfin' U.S.A."
Beach Boys (1963)

"Pipeline"
Chantays (1963)

"Surfin' Bird"
Trashmen (1963)

"Surfer Girl"
Beach Boys (1963)

"Let's Go"
The Routers (1962)

"Surfer's Stomp"
The Marketts (1962)

"California Sun"
The Rivieras (1963)

"Penetration"
The Pyramids (1964)

PAPA OOMA MOW MOW

Bitchin' surf retrospectives are showing up on CD, including greatest hits packages from the Surfaris, the Ventures, Jan & Dean, Dick Dale, and the Beach Boys. But for a quick sampler of what it was all about, start with these three anthologies:

• *Surfin' Hits*
• *History of Surf Music, Vol. I* (Instrumentals) and **Vol. II** (Vocals).

Each available for $13.48 (CD) or $8.98 (record or tape) from: Rhino Records, 2225 Colorado Ave., Santa Monica, CA 90494, (800) 432-0200.

"New Wave" Surf Music. The Surf Punks are more surf nazi than beach boy. No lilting harmonies or Chuck Berry guitars—these are ear-ramming songs like *No Fat Chix* and *The Dummies*, about things like wave-hoggers and beach-trespassers.

Available from your local record store, or contact: Surf Punks Fan Club, PO Box 374, Malibu, CA 90265.

Dennis Wilson was the only Beach Boy who'd ever actually surfed. He also once wrote a song with Charles Manson *(Never Learn Not to Love)*.

Teddy Bears

Forebears of the Modern Teddy

Some people never get over teddy bears. And why should they? Teddy bears are about security, comfort and non-judgmental friendship.

The teddy bear began in 1902 with President Theodore Roosevelt travelling to Mississippi where he organized a hunting party. An advance team came upon an old bear (in alternate versions, a cub). They tied it to a tree for Roosevelt to come and kill, but the president refused to shoot the helpless creature.

At the time, that was apparently an unusually kind act. Word of it spread around the country and gave Brooklynite Morris Michtom an idea for marketing some toy bears his wife had sewn.

Michtom got the president's permission to call the stuffed toys Teddy's Bears, and they began selling out as fast as Mrs. Michtom could make them. By 1907, Morris and his wife were overseeing the manufacture of one million bears a year under the name Ideal Novelty Company. That later became the Ideal Toy Company.

"If you go down in the woods today

You're sure of a big surprise

If you go down in the woods today

You'd better go in disguise.

For every bear that ever there was

Will gather there for certain because

Today's the day the teddy bears have their picnic."

—From *Teddy Bears' Picnic* by Arthur Pryor & Jimmie Kennedy, 1907

Picnic Time for Teddy Bears

The Teddy Bears' Picnic by Jimmie Kennedy; illustrations by Alexandra Day. A colorful picture book interpretation of the old song, beautifully drawn and reproduced. Includes a cassette with two renditions of the old favorite, one new by the "The Bearcats," the other, by Bing Crosby.

$19.95 + 3.00 shipping
Green Tiger Press
435 East Carmel St.
San Marcos, CA 92069-4362

Bear-ly Huggable

Big bear is so big kids can hardly get both arms around it.

#355727, $79.00 + 9.80 shipping from FAO Schwarz, P.O. Box 182225, Chattanooga, TN 37422-7225. (800) 426-TOYS.

TEDDY, BARE

The Chippendale mascot comes complete with bow tie, shirt cuffs and cuff links, streaked forelock and "padded" satin pants.

#5936A, Chippendale Teddy, $32.00 + 6.45 shipping from Post Scripts, PO Box 21628, Ft. Lauderdale, FL 33335-1628. (800) 327-3799.

BEAR FACTS

• Russ Barrie, gift magnate and owner of Miami's Gold Coast Suns (Senior Professional Baseball League) gave the White Haven Super Sox a payment of 500 teddy bears to obtain the rights to Luis Tiant, one time Cleveland Indians pitcher. The bears were given away in a Christmas promotion. How Tiant felt about the arrangement was not reported.

• Winnie the Pooh, the world's most famous teddy bear, first hit bookstores in 1924. The probably second best-loved fictional bear, Zen Master Tim, the serene mohair companion of the elementary reader's Dick, Jane, and Sally, first appeared in the 1940 edition of *Scott, Foresman's Basic Readers*.

• Now that real fur is considered morally and environmentally retrograde, fashion designers have been killing teddies for their coats. Jean-Charles de Castelbajac created a $4000 jacket of 39 teddy bears sewn together (over $100 per teddy!). And the October, 1986 cover of *Vogue* featured a shoulder-baring evening dress, designed by Franco Moschino, also made of teddy bears.

Bear Market

Stuff It! Basic Brown Bears Factory & Store. "Stuffing it yourself" at this small, friendly bear factory is, according to their literature, "a BEARY fun thing to do." Designer Merrilee Woods (her real name, she claims) has created thirty different styles which visitors can see

designed, cut, sewn and stuffed. Kids and grownups are invited to stuff their own basic brown bear to take home at the end of the tour. They also do mail order on a variety of cute bears and accessories. Send or call for a catalog and tour information.

444 De Haro St., San Francisco, CA 94107. (415) 626-0781.

These Magazines Bear Watching

• **Teddy Bear and Friends.** This bi-monthly features photos, advice on the care of collectibles, bear projects to make, and even some short fiction with a Teddy theme.

$24.95 per year (6 issues) from Hobby House Press, 900 Frederick Street, Cumberland, MD 21502. (301) 759-3770.

• **Teddy Bear Review.** In addition to the usual adorable photos, book reviews, stories and ads, this has "The Furry Astrologer," and "KimBEARlee's Kitchen," a recipe column.

$17.97 per year (6 issues) from Collector Communications Corporation, PO Box 1948, 8 Honeywell Lane, Marion, OH 43305.

No Stinkin' Badgers

Bear desperado in camouflage headband, with bandoleer filled with 24 Tootsie Rolls.

#T2189, $9.98 + 3.50 shipping. Funny Side Up, 425 Stump Rd., North Wales, PA 19454. (215) 361-5130.

Not Yet Dead Earnest

His name is Ernest and he's a bear. You're supposed to string him up and watch as he attempts death-defying acrobatics on his unicycle.

#5406, $16.98 + 3.50 shipping from The Lighter Side, 4514 19th St. Court East, P.O. Box 25600, Bradenton, FL 34206-5600. (813) 747-2356 / FAX (813) 746-7896.

"Isn't it funny / How a bear likes honey? / Buzz! Buzz! Buzz! / I wonder why he does?"—A. A. Milne, *Winnie the Pooh*

PLEASE!

SMOKEY

Only you can prevent forest fires

The Story of Smokey the Bear

In 1943, the Foote, Cone & Belding advertising agency took over the US Forest Service account and began an aggressive forest fire prevention campaign. With slogans like "Careless Matches Aid the Axis," patriotic Americans were encouraged to keep America green.

As the war ended, it became clear that the old approach wouldn't work any more. They tried to get the rights to use Walt Disney's Bambi as spokes-animal, but that didn't work out. Squirrels were the first animal they tried and even produced one poster, but that didn't quite do it. Finally, the agency convinced the client that a bear would best represent the authoritative yet loveable image the Service wanted to promote.

The first Smokey the Bear poster came out in 1945 from an illustration by New York artist Albert Staehle. In 1947, copywriters penned the slogan "Remember, only YOU can prevent forest fires." Not long after, announcer Jack Weaver put his head into a barrel and gave voice to Smokey in his first radio spots.

Smokey the Bear actually became flesh, fur and blood in 1950, when a scorched bear cub was rescued from a New Mexico forest fire by a state game protector. The Forest Service quickly named the cub Smokey, created an after-the-fact story which claimed that the little charred cub was the inspiration for the Smokey ad campaign, instead of vice versa, and transferred the cub to the National Zoological Park in Washington, DC.

Ben Michtom, Chairman of the Board of the Ideal Toy Company and son of the original creators of the teddy bear, won permission to market a toy Smokey in 1952. Millions of the ranger-hatted bears were produced, and a certificate was included with each, which children could fill out and send to the Service to become Junior Forest Rangers. More than 5 million kids enlisted.

A 26-foot wooden Smokey the Bear was erected in 1954 by the "Koochi-ching County Keep Minnesota Green Committee," in Inter-national Falls, Minnesota.

Smokey was given his own zip code number in 1964, in recognition of the large volume of mail he receives. Smokey's zip: Washington, DC 20252.

In 1969, Smokey the Bear appeared in his own weekly half-hour animated comedy adventure. The show ran for two years on the ABC Network.

The original living Smokey the Bear mascot died in 1967. Smokey II died in 1990.

Remember — Only you can
PREVENT FOREST FIRES

SMOKEY SAYS —
Hold 'til it's cold...
prevent forest fires

Bears Ride With "Smokey"

In many cities across the country, teddy bears ride shotgun in police cars and ambulances to soothe children involved in accidents, traumas and other emergencies. "When we go in wearing our uniforms and a gun, we look nine feet tall to children, and mean," said one policeman. "But the child's attention is drawn to the teddy bear. They grab it, hug it and pull it to them. As a result, a child who might have gone into shock or hysterics is more likely to stay in control and communication."

One bear success story: a toddler had crawled out onto a third floor ledge. An officer was able to coax him back into the apartment with a department-issued bear.

"Some children can't communicate because of language barriers," noted another police officer. "But a teddy bear speaks all languages."

THANKS, FOLKS,

SMOKEY

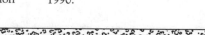

The Teddy's favorite hymn? *Gladly, the Cross-Eyed Bear.*

BINGO BEAR

Brings you luck at church. Dressed for the part, too!

#2478, $15.98 + 3.50 shipping from The Lighter Side, 4514 19th St. Court East, P.O. Box 25600, Bradenton, FL 34206-5600. (813) 747-2356 / FAX (813) 746-7896.

A Big Cheese Bear— Not a Common Bear

• *Teddy Bears and Steiff Animals* by Margaret Fox Mandel. Margarete Steiff produced a stuffed toy bear in Germany the same year the Michtoms hit the US market with "Teddy's Bears." Steiff's dolls and toys were innovative for their time because they embodied lifelike features and poses rather than the insipid demeanor of other factory-made toys. The popular "button in the ear" animals have long exhibited unusually high levels of craftsmanship, and are valued by fans and collectors. This is a full-color book featuring the Steiff animals. It also includes care and feeding instructions to keep these valuable antiques looking as new as possible.

$11.95 postpaid from Collector Books, PO Box 3009, Paducah, KY 42001.

• *Bears* by Geneviève and Gerard Picot. The Picots feature bears from their own collection in this pictorial tribute to the world's best loved toy. 82 color and 43 black and white illustrations make this a good "coffee table" gift book for any bear fan.

$36.50 postpaid from Crown Publishers, 201 East 50th St., New York, NY 10022. (800) 733-3000.

Bear Museums

"Everybody loves teddy bears, so why aren't there more bear museums?" we wondered.

The reason, we discovered, is that plush toys are highly perishable and difficult to store properly. Atmospheric pollution, ultraviolet light, moisture and insects are the bane of all bear conservationists. These bear museums are ambitious labors of love, with special care taken to restore and display delicate older specimens.

• **Frannie's Teddy Bear Museum, 114 Mooring Park Dr., #810, Naples, FL 33942. (813) 598-2711.**
• **McCurdy Historical Doll & Bear Museum 246 North 100 East, Provo, UT 84601. (801) 377-9935.**

Creature Comforts

1000 piece puzzle depicts teddy bear at a bed & breakfast inn with homey surroundings.

#02-J0481, $12.95 + 3.95 shipping from Bits & Pieces, 1 Puzzle Place, Box 8016, Stevens Point, WI 54481-7199. (800) JIGSAWS.

BEAR DIP

This shampoo is specially formulated to safely clean stuffed animals without alcohol or chemical solvents.

$7.99 + 2.75 shipping from The Bear Care Company, 279 S. Beverly Dr., Suite 957-F, Beverly Hills, CA 90212. (213) 397-4082.

The Right to Arm Bears

Cute and cuddly bears trained to kill. Dressed in full military regalia, even bear tags, these 22 inch bears will drop in anywhere and leave no survivors.

#Q8762, Drill Inst.; #Q4128, Soldier; #Q3426, Ranger; #Q7225 Navy; #Q3424, Special Forces; #Q3425 Airborne; #Q7224, Marine. Each $39.95 + 5.95 shipping from U.S. Cavalry, 2855 Centennial Ave., Radcliff, KY 40160-9000. (800) 777-7732 / FAX (502) 352-0266.

Throw in the Tao

The Tao of Pooh by **Benjamin Hoff.** Anybody who has read Pooh stories knows that the bear of very little brain is in fact a very modest creature of mystical abilities. According to this book, that's because A.A. Milne's effortlessly calm Winnie the Pooh is the perfect embodiment of the essence of Tao (a 6th century B.C. Chinese philosophy based on the teachings of Lao-tse, advocating simplicity and selflessness). This clever integration of Taoist principles and Pooh stories reveals the serene bear as the exemplar of "Wei Wu Wei," which literally means "to do without doing."

$8.45 postpaid from:
Penguin USA, 120 Woodbine St.
Bergenfield, NJ 07621. (201) 387-0600.

Music From the Heart

Light-Up Melody Bear plays 16 tunes your child will love. His heart blinks to the beat of songs such as *Old MacDonald, London Bridge, Rock-A-Bye Baby* and 13 others.

#B2366, Blue Bear, or #B2379, Pink Bear, each $12.98 + 3.95 shipping from Harriet Carter, North Wales, PA 19455.

A Teddy Orgy

Store up to 20 stuffed animals, dolls, or toys in this flexible hammock that installs easily on the wall in a corner, or on the ceiling. Made of blue or pink nylon.

#3658, Blue Teddy Bed, or #3659, Pink, $24.98 + 3.50 shipping from The Lighter Side, 4514 19th St. Court East, P.O. Box 25600, Bradenton, FL 34206-5600. (813) 747-2356 / FAX (813) 746-7896.

> *"Teddy bears are close enough in their general configuration to a human—outstretched arms, a gentle gleam in their eyes—to have an obvious potential to be a comforter, like a mother. These objects are potent stuff."*
>
> —Dr. Paul Horton, Psychiatrist

Roll Playing

Tootsie isn't ready to go out in public yet. Not until you remove her curlers and EAT THEM! Plush teddy sweetheart in slippers has 24 real Tootsie Roll rollers.

#B2354, Tootsie Bear, $9.98 + 3.50 shipping from Harriet Carter, North Wales, PA 19455. (215) 361-5151.

Bear from the Womb

Rock-A-Bye Bear. Cuddly, cute and able to put most babies right to sleep with actual intrauterine sounds recorded by a physician.

$49.95 + 3.00 shipping from Right Start Catalog 5334 Sterling Center Drive Westlake Village, CA 91361 (800) 548-8531

BEAR BAITING

Women who have had it with men and would rather cuddle alone with a hairy friend will love this fun book: *Teddy Bears Are Better Than Men Because…*

#T2179, $3.98 + 3.25 shipping from Funny Side Up, 425 Stump Rd., North Wales, PA 19454. (215) 361-5130.

Telephones

Alex Bell, Phone Home

Some inventions languish for years before they become part of our culture, but it didn't take long after Alexander Graham Bell invented the telephone for the gadget to catch on. The advantages were obvious to almost everybody, and as soon as you could afford one, you got one.

Graham invented the phone in 1876 and the first commercial telephone service began the very next year, the first and last time that the Bell System ever worked so fast.

It was only two years later on Aug. 13, 1889 that the first pay phone was patented by William Gray. The idea came to him at work one day when his foreman wouldn't let him use the company telephone to check on his sick wife.

The automatic switchboard was introduced in 1892.

The first transcontinental telephone call between Alexander Graham Bell in New York and Dr. Thomas Watson in San Francisco took place in 1915. It was such a momentous occasion that a popular song was written about it: *Hello, Frisco, Hello.* Actually, like most new technological marvels from the subway to the airplane, scores of songs were written about the telephone, including the World War I tearjerker, *Hello, Central, Give Me No Man's Land.* By the end of WWI the telephone had become a common household item.

In 1956, Bell telephone began development of a "visual telephone" and transatlantic cable telephone service was inaugurated. One caught on, the other didn't. But that makes sense—do you always want to be dressed and groomed for visitors every time the phone rings? On the other hand, picture phones might make 900-sex-talk calls much more interesting.

Since then, lots of things have changed. Since the breakup of the one true phone system, the old dog telephone has learned a lot of new tricks: we've got car phones, answering machines, computer modems, faxes and a bunch of other things on the horizon.

On the other hand, not all changes are improvements. We wish we'd been around for four digit numbers, the really cool old telephones, the chance to shout into the phone "Hello Central..." and the cheap entertainment of listening to the neighbors' conversations on the party line.

> "If the phone doesn't ring, it's me."
>
> **—Jimmy Buffett**

Phone Antiques

Here are typical estimates of what some antique phones and paraphernalia are worth, according to the **American Telephone Collectors Association:**

- *1908 Vought-Berger wall phone (with cherry crank). $140*
- *1908 Western Electric wall phone (white oak). $195*
- *1914 Stromberg-Carlson walnut phone booth with velvet seat. $1200*
- *1920s Candlestick desk phone (black enamel). $60 - $125*
- *A.E. Strowger 11 digit wall phone (good condition). $425*
- *New York Phone Book (circa 1920s). $25*
- *Brown leather briefcase issued to Bell supervisors. $25*
- *Bell System lineman's voltmeter with leather case. $40*
- *Western Electric pole climbing spurs. $15*

Obsolete Phone Terms Still in Use

- *"Dial."*
- *"Off the hook"* and *"hang up."* (Decades ago, phone receivers used to hang from an actual hook on the wall.)
- *"Give me a ring."* (Only a few phones ring any more; most chirp.)
- *"AT&T"* (American Telephone and Telegraph has nothing directly to do with either telephones or telegraphs—they control only the connecting lines between regional phone companies.)

Old Phones for Sale

The problem with modern phones, with a few exceptions, is that they have no character, no soul. They're plastic. They sound like crickets on steroids when they ring. They're too light. And they don't last very long.

The old Bell Western Electric phones were heavy, hefty and sturdy. How sturdy? In the old days operators told people to throw their phones through a windowpane if trapped in a fire emergency. These days, it's the phone that would shatter.

You want a phone with character? Phoneco is the best source we've found for reconditioned old phones. Contact them for availability and current prices. Here are some typical prices:

- All-nickeled "candlestick" telephone, reconditioned for today's lines (candlesticks are those tall, thin ones you see in old movies, with mouthpiece on the phone and receiver on the cord): $190
- Same as above, but brass: $95
- Pay phones: $59 and up
- Phones from the 1920s: $42 and up

Call them for more information and availability. Phoneco, P.O. Box 70, Galesville, WI 54630. (608) 582-4124.

Reach Out & Touch the Past

Before the breakup there was only Ma Bell. You couldn't even legally buy a phone, you had to rent it through her. Now there are plenty of phone manufacturers, which is where we started in the first place. Back before Bell was the mother of us all, practically everyone tried their hand at building a better phone.

When Alexander Graham Bell's basic patents (transmitter and receiver) expired in 1893 and 1894, hundreds of companies began manufacturing and selling telephones.

Today there are at least 2,000 active antique phone collectors in

the United States, searching for the Wilhelm telephone, the Roycroft, the San Francisco "potbelly," Strowger "candlesticks," and the ever elusive Ness Automatic (not a machine gun but a) Telephone.

If you have an antique phone that dates back to between 1877 and 1894, you're among the select few who have a treasured part of history. Phones made during this period are among the hardest to obtain and therefore some of the most valuable.

TELEPHONE BOOK
Old Telephones Scrapbook Vols. 1, 2 & 3 by Ron Knappen. Considered one of the best books on the identification of antique telephones, with lots of photos, esoteric information and descriptions.

All 3 volumes available for $50 from: Phoneco, P.O. Box 70, Galesville, WI 54630. (608) 582-4124.

Candlestick phones were also known as "daffies." We don't know why.

Gorgeous Gotham Phone

Exquisite Art Deco recreation of a 1930s phone offers push button touchpads in an immovable dial for antique elegance with modern convenience. Body is made by the same plastic injection mold process used in the 1930s and hand painted with a high-gloss enamel finish. Available in Red or Black.

#17083, Red or #17084, Black, each $79.95 + 7.75 shipping from Signals, P.O. Box 64428, St. Paul, MN 55164-0428. (800) 669-9696.

JOIN THE CLUB

• **The Antique Telephone Collectors Association's** purpose is to raise the awareness of "the historical importance of old telephones" and to provide "a means of communication between telephone collectors." Members receive 10 newsletters a year with price lists, articles on collecting, letters from members, vintage phone exhibit news, classified advertising section and more. Send SASE for information.

ATCA, 614 Main Street, LaCrosse, KS 67548. (Ironically, no phone number available.)

• **Telephone Collectors International, Inc.** Organized as a not-for-profit corporation in 1986, the organization now boasts about 400 members. Members receive the monthly newsletter *Singing Wires* which contains articles on telephone history, ads for old telephones and telephone books, even an occasional wiring diagram. TCI holds an annual show for buyers and sellers of phones, technical literature, catalogs, pole hardware and old telephone company stock certificates.

Dues: $26.00. TCI, 19 North Cherry Drive, Oswego, IL 60543. (708) 554-8154.

Ancient Walking Fingers

The first phone book was issued by the Telephone Dispatch Company in 1878. The Boston company's "book" was a single page and listed 97 telephones... not numbers, just names. (There was no such thing as direct dial then; you picked up your receiver and said, "Martha, please give me Mrs. Thompson.")

We've found a company that has old phone books from 1910 to 1927— thousands of them from all over the country. Choose a city and a date, and they can tell you if they have it. The price is unbeatable: $9.90 each, postpaid.

But that's just the beginning. The company stocks a huge amount of phone parts and supplies from antique phones. If you need a part, send your want list and they'll find it for you. Or send $1.00 for their catalog.

**Billard's Old Telephones and Parts
21710 Regnart Road
Cupertino, CA 95014
(408) 252-2104**

Phony Car Phone

Let 'em think you're somebody who thinks a car phone is a big deal. It actually rings and makes dialing noises. Or drop the pretense at the press of a button, and produce bomb, police siren or machine gun sounds.

#8260 Phony Car Phone, $19.98 + 3.99 shipping from Taylor Gifts, 355 E. Conestoga Road, P.O. Box 206, Wayne, PA 19087-0206. (215) 789-7007.

Phonetasia

Phonies: Telephone Answering Machine Messages. If you feel compelled to have a creative phone message because of the clever crowd you hang around with, but can't think of anything that fits the bill, Phonies has a variety of funny messages. Or, if you have a one-person office and want a professional sound, they've got messages spoken by polished-sounding receptionists with office ambiance in the background.

• **Rich Little.** 8 volumes of the impressionist's voices from Nixon to W.C. Fields. $9.95 each.

• **Everyday Phonies: Office Messages**—makes your home office sound like a bustling beige saltmine. $7.95.

Add $1.25 shipping from Phonies, 4275 34th St. S., Suite 330, St. Petersburg, FL 33711. (813) 864-0490.

FLASH FONE

You can see 'em ringing! Neon phones will brighten any room. They light up on incoming calls and feature an electronic tone ringer, auto-release line hold complete with music, last number redial and more.

#NE-587P, Pink Neon Phone, $99.95 + 7.50 shipping, or #NE-587B, Blue Neon Phone, $99.95 + 7.50 shipping. The Scope Catalog, 260 Motor Parkway, Hauppauge, NY 11788-5134. (800) 695-4848 / FAX (516) 435-8079.

Songs About Phones

- **Ring My Bell** (1978)—Anita Ward
- **Telephone Line** (1977)—Electric Light Orchestra
- **Call Me** (1980)—Blondie
- **Call Me** (1965)—Chris Montez
- **Hello It's Me** (1974)—Todd Rundgren
- **Operator** (1970)—Jim Croce
- **You Know My Name, Look Up My Number** (1967)—The Beatles
- **Pennsylvania 6-5000** (1940)—Glenn Miller
- **Telephone (Long Distance Love Affair)** (1983)—Sheena Easton
- **Telephone Man** (1977)—Meri Wilson

ROBO PHONE

Kids can dial like adults with three programmable one-touch automatic dialing memories. All they have to do is remember circle, square or triangle. Program it to dial Grandpa or Mom with just a touch, or even 911 for emergencies. Cover is removable to reveal 10-key touch-tone pad.

#359729, $100.00 + 9.80 shipping from FAO Schwarz, P.O. Box 182225, Chattanooga, TN 37422-7225. (800) 426-TOYS.

Lighten Up

The phone is ringing and it's clearly for you! This see-through phone lights up every time it rings. The inner workings are visible and are housed in a shatterproof case. Last number redial, lighted fingerpad and all the usual features found on most phones today. Table top or wall mount.

#6314A, See-Thru Phone, $35.00 + 6.45 shipping from Post Scripts, P.O. Box 21628, Ft. Lauderdale, FL 33335-1628. (800) 327-3799.

When Superman's In London...

Dr. Who would love this one! A real, honest-to-goodness, 1930s cast iron phone booth, imported from England. Measures 8 1/2 feet tall by 3 feet square.

$1,600.00 from Rick Koudys, #94 First St. South, St. Catharines, Ontario, Canada L2R-6P9. (416) 687-6581.

Alexander Graham Bell insisted there was only one correct way to answer the phone. Not hello, but "Ahoy!" or "Hoy! Hoy!"

TELEVISION

What better a name for an inventor than "Philo T. Farnsworth"? In fact, the name of Donald Duck's inventor friend, Gyro Gearloose, is suspiciously similar. Yet, while it sounds almost like somebody made it up, Philo Farnsworth really was his name, and he invented the first practical electronic television.

While he was growing up on a farm in Idaho, Farnsworth received a lot of his science education from stacks of *Popular Science* magazines left behind by a previous occupant. It was there that he read about the potential of television, and the problems inventors were having bringing it to fruition.

One day, while plowing the fields, inspiration struck 14 year old Farnsworth. The rows of the plowed earth became a TV screen for young Philo, and the idea of electrons plowing back and forth across the screen seemed like the answer to television's technical difficulties.

Farnsworth's idea became an obsession. He sketched it out on the blackboard for his physics teacher, who admitted that Philo was way ahead of him and encouraged him on.

On his wedding night, working on his invention kept him away from his new wife for hours. When he finally returned, he announced, "You know, there is another woman in my life. Her name is television."

During the early years of their marriage the two of them worked together in their home, first in Los Angeles and then Berkeley, to develop the idea. In the days of Prohibition, neighbors and policemen interpreted the constantly drawn shades to mean one thing only — they were making homemade liquor. One day they were even raided by the cops.

Finally, on September 7, 1927, Philo T. Farnsworth demonstrated the first all-electronic television transmitter and receiver at his Green Street laboratory in San Francisco.

For many years, Farnsworth didn't get much credit —his glory was stolen, along with his ideas, by Vladimir Zwyorkin from RCA. Zwyorkin had visited Farnsworth's home in 1930 to see Philo's work, exclaiming, "Beautiful. I wish I had invented it myself." Not long after, he did.

Although court decisions eventually established that Farnsworth was indeed the inventor of the all-electronic TV, Zwyorkin, through years of backing by RCA's publicity department, is still often mistakenly cited as the "Father of Television." In 1984, the US Postal Service issued a stamp honoring Farnsworth.

Required Viewing

The Story of TV. If you want a quick history of television, on video yet, this one gives you old film shorts and newsreels about the early history of TV and its development.

$24.95 + 3.95 shipping from:
Video Resources New York, Inc.
220 W 71st St.
New York, NY 10023
(212) 724-7055.

Clumsy Poet Wrecks 18th Century TV Set

"...This cabinet is form'd of Gold
And Pearl and Crystal shining bright
And with it opens into a World
And a little lovely Moony Night…

"I strove to seize the inmost Form
With ardor fierce and hands of flame
But burst the Crystal Cabinet
And like a Weeping Babe became."

—**William Blake (1757-1827)**

Antique TV Shows on Video

• **Video Resources** has an amazingly varied and complete selection of videos, including commercials, *Abbott and Costello* outtakes, the *Lost in Space* original pilot that was never aired, and hundreds of old TV shows both well-known and obscure.

Video Resources New York, Inc., 220 W 71st St., New York, NY 10023. (212) 724-7055.

• **Shokus Video** is another great source we like for classic old TV shows. Tapes cost between $19.95 and $24.95, which generally include 3 or 4 shows on each. Their catalogue is available for $2.00. Our

favorite listings: *Bosko the Speed King*, Nixon speeches, and *Rootie Kazootie*.

Shokus Video, P.O. Box 8434, Van Nuys, CA 91409. (800) 541-6219 / (818) 704-0400.

• **Videos Every Month.** Sign up with the **Columbia House Video Library** and get a tape of your favorite series every five weeks. Very clear prints, unedited, with many series available, like *Taxi, Beverly Hillbillies, Gunsmoke, Star Trek, The Life of Riley, Burns & Allen, Outer Limits, Rich Man, Poor Man* and that long series that was on all the channels and wouldn't end, *The Vietnam War*.

$4.95 for the introductory tape, then $19.95 from then on (cancel any time). Add 3.19 shipping. Columbia House Video Library, 1400 North Fruitridge Avenue, Terre Haute, IN 47811. (800) 457-0866.

TV Earitations

The tunes are catchy and they always seem to stick in your mind—that's the genius of the music that permeates TV. On these collections are your favorite TV theme songs and even the most annoyingly memorable TV commercial jingles, ("Charlie says, love that Good & Plenty…").

• *The Top 50 Commercial Jingles of All Time.*

Cassette, $8.95; CD, $14.95 postpaid.

• *TV Theme Songs from the '50s and '60s Vol. 1 and Vol. 2. TV Theme Songs from the '70s and '80s Vol. 3.*

Each cassette, $16.95; CD, $19.95 postpaid.

TVT Records 59th St., 5B New York, NY 10011. (212) 929-0570.

Required Reading

• **Classic TV** is great if you're TV obsessed: they'll take a classic series and give you titles, episode numbers, original air dates, synopses, and guest stars. "If you're a true TV fan, you won't want to miss an issue," they say, and we agree. Great ads, too.

$30.00 for one year (12 issues) or $3.00 for a single issue. 2980 College Ave., Suite 2, Box 25, Berkeley, CA 94705. (510) 548-4237.

• **Reruns Magazine**: "The Magazine of Television History" gives you articles, quizzes, complete listings of old shows. This is a magazine for dyed in the wool TV fans of all types.

Published 6 times a year for $12.00 a year or $2.50 an issue. P.O. Box 832, Santa Monica CA 90406-0832.

Sing Along With Yogi

The TV Theme Song Sing-Along Song Book Vols. 1 & 2 collected by **John Javna**. You want to know melody, chords and all the words for TV theme songs? These'll give you almost any theme you can think of, including some commercials. Best of all, you get unknown lyrics to themes from *The Munsters, Hogan's Heroes, The Andy Griffith Show* (*The Fishin' Hole*) and all 20 verses of *Davy Crockett!*

$6.95 each + 1.50 shipping for 1 book, add 50¢ for each additional book, from St. Martin's Press, 175 Fifth Avenue, New York, NY 10010. (800) 221-7945, ext. 661.

TV in Black & White

Journal Graphics transcribes most of the TV news and talk shows and makes copies available to the public at a reasonable rate. So if you want to have in black and white something you saw in color, get in touch with these people. Cost? Most transcripts are $3-5.

Which shows? *Phil, Oprah* and *Geraldo, CNN, 20/20, 60 Minutes, Good Morning America, MacNeil-Lehrer* and scores of others. An annual index, with over 30,000 listings arranged by subject, is available for $14.95 (includes $10 coupon).

**Journal Graphics Office
267 Broadway
New York, NY 10007
(212) 227-7323**

TV FANATICS

There are hundreds of fan clubs for most of the long-running TV shows (and some of the short-running ones). A complete list would be impossible, but if you want information on a club for your own favorite, try *Rerun Magazine* (see **Required Reading**). Here are a few clubs to get you started—send SASE if you want information.

• **The TV Terror Society**. These people are interested in keeping alive old TV horror and science fiction.

515 O'Farrell St. Suite 74, San Francisco, CA 94102.

• **UNCLE HQ**. For fans of *The Man From UNCLE* and *The Girl From UNCLE*.

c/o Susan Cole, 2710 Rohlwing Road, Rolling Meadows, IL 60008.

• **National Association for the Advancement of Perry Mason**. They put out a monthly newsletter about the heroic lawyer as he appears in any and all

media, including (but not exclusively) TV.

2735 Benvenue #3, Berkeley CA 94705. (510) 548-4237.

• **The *Howdy Doody* Club**. Say, kids. What time is it?

Jeff Judson, RD 2, Box 87, Flemington NJ 08822.

• *Beany and Cecil* **Collectors Fan Club**. Enclose $1 and a stamped long envelope for a list of collectible items.

c/o Jeff and Maria Falasca, 340 S. Mary St., Coal City, IL 60416. (815) 634-4614.

• **Mr. *Ed* Fan Club**. These fans get their information straight from the horse's mouth!

P. O. Box 1009, Cedar Hill, TX 75104.

• **Betty White Fan Club**. Who could hate Betty White?

c/o Kay Daly, 3552 Federal Ave., Los Angeles, CA 90066.

Real Simulated Life

Wanna make your TV room a little more romantic but don't have a fireplace? Like to have an aquarium but you don't want the hassle of taking care of the fish? Or maybe you want to go to the beach, but it's -20° outside? These 60 minute, full-color videos let you experience the sights, sounds and relaxing effects of the real thing, without the drawbacks.

#3574, Video Fireplace. #3572, Video Aquarium. #3573, Video Ocean. Each $19.98 + 4.20 shipping from Johnson Smith Company, 4514 19th Court East, P.O. Box 25500, Bradenton, FL 34206-5500. (813) 747-2356 / FAX (813) 746-7896.

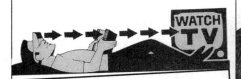

Don't Leave The Sack...
Watch On Your Back

Right Angle Viewer. Couch Potatoism is its own reward. This lightweight device lets you view all your favorites while lying flat on your back. Even fits over glasses.

#4456, $9.98 + 2.70 shipping from Johnson Smith Company, 4514 19th Court East, P.O. Box 25500, Bradenton, FL 34206-5500. (813) 747-2356 / FAX (813) 746-7896.

Some Dish!

Have you got the type of neighbors who would object to the esthetic blight of a satellite dish in your backyard? Probably just jealous, but some communities have outlawed them because of their out-and-out ugliness.

If you want to be a good neighbor (or surreptitious scofflaw), get yourself one of these satellite dishes that looks like a patio umbrella and table. In fact, it can be used for that purpose—the kids can have a picnic beneath it while you watch hundreds of channels from space.

Cost ranges from $3495-3995, including receiver. For more information contact: Schudel Associates, 199 N. El Camino Real Suite 303, Encinitas, CA 92024. (619) 942-1609.

WISDOM FROM THE TUBE

Primetime Proverbs, selected by Jack Mingo and John Javna. Thousands of great quotes from fictional TV characters, collected into hundreds of categories. We think it's ten times more fun than *Bartlett's*, but we might be prejudiced. Still, check out these from the category of **Television.**

• *"The only fathers that don't yell at their kids are on television."*

—Wally Cleaver, *Leave It to Beaver*

• *"You know something, if you couldn't read, you couldn't look up what was on television."*

—Beaver Cleaver, Ibid

• *"Any schedule without Buddy Ebsen sucks eggs."*

—George Utley, *Newhart*

• *"You know the really great thing about television? If something important happens, anywhere in the world, night or day…you can always change the channel."*

—Reverend Jim Ignatowski, *Taxi*

$9.95 + 2.00 shipping from
Harmony / Crown Publishers
400 Hahn Road
Westminister, MD 21157
(800) 733-3000

Primetime Proverbs
The Book of TV Quotes

Confused? Perplexed? Lost in Space? Here is the collected wisdom of the Electronic Oracle…TV Guidance on vitally important issues in your life, like…

MARRIAGE: "Stay clear of weddings, because one of them is liable to be your own." Pappy Beauregard Maverick, *Maverick*

AGING: "You don't need any brains to grow up, it just happens to ya." Whitey, *Leave It to Beaver*

RELIGION: "God don't make no mistakes. That's how He got to be God." Archie Bunker, *All in the Family*

Plus more than 1,000 other gems…

BY JACK MINGO AND JOHN JAVNA

"As you can see, crime does not pay, even on television. You must have a sponsor."

—Alfred Hitchcock

Hey Kids…Tell Him What Time It Is!

Howdy Doody Wall Clock. It's 10 inches, round and runs on one AA battery that even Finnias T. Bluster could figure out how to install. So what time is it? Every second of the day, it's Howdy Doody time!

#VA587, $35.00 + 5.00 from The Cat's Pyjamas, 20 Church Street, P.O. Box 1569, Montclair, NJ 07042. (201) 744-3896.

TV VIEWER

It's a fabulous fifties TV set. This tiny TV (2 inches high) shows you what life was like in the good ol' days. Look through the peep hole in the back of the set, press the button at the base and see 8 different color scenes.

#8684, $2.25 + 4.00 shipping *per order* from Archie McPhee, P.O. Box 30852, Seattle, WA 98103-0852. (206) 547-2467.

The first TV Dinner, shipped in January, 1952, contained turkey with cornbread stuffing and gravy, peas, and sweet potatoes in butter and orange sauce.

TV Facts

- If all the TV sets in the United States were placed end to end, they would stretch around the world more than twice.

- When children aged 4-6 were asked in a survey, "Which do you like better, TV or your daddy?" 54% said "TV."

- The word "television" is a bastardization of the Greek *tele*, "far" and the Latin *videre*, "to see."

- 70% of all VCR owners have never used its timer.

- A few minutes after the last episode of M*A*S*H was broadcast, the New York City sewer flow rate suddenly jumped 320 million gallons, equivalent to one million toilets flushing at the same time.

- You burn 1 to 2 calories per minute watching TV—50% more than while sleeping.

- A 1979 Roper Poll of 3001 couples showed that a leading cause of marital disputes was disagreement about which TV shows to watch.

- In West Germany, zookeepers put a TV near the gorilla cages in hopes of increasing their sexual activity. The tactic didn't work—the gorillas decided they'd rather watch TV. Their preferences? Love scenes, weight lifting, and auto racing.

- Why is there no Channel 1 on the television set? Because the frequency was taken away from the TV broadcasters back in 1948 by the FCC and given to the US military.

- 4.4 % of all TV shows videotaped by Americans are episodes of *All My Children*.

- Watching TV is the activity Americans spend the most leisure time doing (even more than eating and shopping, which placed second and third, respectively).

"Television is a medium which permits millions of people to listen to the same joke at the same time, and yet remain lonesome." —T. S. Eliot

The Lucy Show

> "Since we said, 'I do,' there are so many things we don't."
> —Lucy on marriage

I Love Lucy

Many couples weren't doing much on Monday nights in the '50s. Almost everybody was tuned to *I Love Lucy*.

When Lucille Ball was first offered a show of her own, she insisted that her real husband, Desi Arnaz, be her TV husband, too. CBS rejected the idea, saying that no one would believe or accept the combination. To prove them wrong, Lucy and Desi toured the country doing live performances to great reaction. CBS finally gave in.

In the pilot episode, Lucy and Desi played themselves—a Hollywood actress and a famous bandleader. The sponsor suggested they make their characters less upscale, so they became a sometimes struggling middle class couple in New York City. This was just the right touch, and the show was an instant success.

Current sitcoms owe a lot to *I Love Lucy*: the format, the style, the characterizations, the humor and the 3 camera filming process they developed to capture the live performance. Instead of doing the show live on air, or filming it like a movie and adding a laugh track later, Desi came up with a hybrid of the two. They performed the show live in front of an audience and filmed the whole thing from three perspectives, making the show easy to edit and eventually syndicate (*Lucy* has been the most broadcast show worldwide).

The show's instant popularity touched people's lives across America: PTA leaders demanded that the show be broadcast earlier so school children could get to bed. Department stores, doctors and dentists in many cities changed their evening hours.

Why was it so popular? The pacing of the show, Lucille Ball's comedic skills, and the balance among the four characters—these are some of the reasons experts suggest. But there's also one more—Lucy struck a chord with the millions of women dissatisfied with being stuck in the role of a 1950s housewife. It may have been the first feminist sitcom.

Comics

- *I Love Lucy: A Comic Retrospective*
- *I Love Lucy in Color*

Back in the 1950s and '60s, comic books looked to TV to provide grist for their pulp mills. Nearly every popular TV show had a corresponding comic book, from *Dobie Gillis* to *Rawhide*.

I Love Lucy was no exception. These two books from Malibu Graphics are reprints of old *Lucy* comic books, originally published between 1954 and 1959. The comics captured a lot of the manic energy from the TV show and actually allowed more elaborate setups since it's easier to draw something than go on location, build the props and rehearse the actors.

For many years there was not a minute in the day when *Lucy* was not being broadcast somewhere on the globe.

Trivia

- Ricky's favorite meal: arroz con pollo (chicken and rice).
- What kind of car the Ricardos and the Mertzes drove to California in 1955: a new green Pontiac convertible.
- Lucy Ricardo's middle name: Esmerelda or Frimel, depending on which episode you believe. Her maiden name was McGillicuddy.
- Fred Mertz's middle name: Hobart.
- The famous "Uh-oh" from the audience comes from Dede Ball, Lucy's mom, who never missed a show. They always placed her near a microphone.

WHAT A DOLL!

"Lucy" doll, 14" tall, immortalizes the queen of comedy. Vinyl doll has movable arms so she can get a job in a candy factory.

#4459, $39.98 + 3.50 shipping. The Lighter Side, 4514 19th St. Court East, P.O. Box 25600, Bradenton, FL 34206-5600. (813) 747-2356.

Board By Lucy?

I Love Lucy **Game.** Relive some of the show's magical moments. Object is to find Fred & Ethel's apartment. Along the way you may be forced to give your impression of Ricky's rendering of *Babalu* or your improv interpretation of Lucy stomping grapes.

#6551, $17.98 + 3.50 shipping from The Lighter Side, 4514 19th St. Court East, P.O. Box 25600, Bradenton, FL 34206-5600. (813) 747-2356.

Required Reading

The I Love Lucy Book by Bart Andrews. The final say on the show by an expert and fan. Andrews provides the reader with plot summaries, important facts and things to watch for on each individual episode.

$12.95 + 2.50 shipping from: Doubleday 666 Fifth Avenue New York, NY 10103. (212) 765-6500.

Universal Lucy

The Lucy Museum at Universal Studios in Hollywood. Plenty of memorabilia—Emmys, scripts, costumes and everything else you'd expect—in a heart-shaped building.

Universal Studios, 100 Universal City Plaza, Universal City, CA 91608. (818) 508-9600.

Playing Fast and Lucy With the Facts

- 27 million people watched the first televised presidential inauguration—Eisenhower's on January 20, 1953. But the historic event was upstaged in ratings the night before when 44 million people tuned in for the birth of Little Ricky.
- They weren't allowed to use the word "pregnant" on TV at the time. The word they used to describe her condition? "Expectant."
- William Frawley and Vivian Vance (Fred and Ethel Mertz) in real life were not on the best of terms. Vance, who was in reality a year younger than Lucille Ball, couldn't see why anyone would believe she was married to "that old man." Frawley, for his part, referred to Vance as "that sack of doorknobs."
- *I Love Lucy* was so popular in some African nations that the name Lucy has been edging out traditional tribal names for girls.
- Lucille Ball was accused of being a communist and was nearly blacklisted in those lovely McCarthy days. Had she not been so popular, she probably would've been banned from the air.

I Love Lucy **was banned for many years in certain Moslem countries because Lucy "dominated" Ricky.**

The Twilight Zone

"You're travelling through another dimension, a dimension not only of sight and sound, but of mind; a journey into a wondrous land whose boundaries are that of the imagination. That's the signpost up ahead! Your next stop…*The Twilight Zone*."

Anything could happen on the *Twilight Zone*, and often did. In one of the best-known episodes, a passenger on a plane spies a creature merrily ripping away part of a wing. Nobody else can see it. With his masterful touch, writer Rod Serling made this man a recently released mental patient, and the tale became an exploration into the nature of madness and reality. *Twilight Zone* was never renowned for its special effects—if you look, you can see human shoes on the feet of the creature—but to the devout, that's evidence of its emphasis on good writing and plot development more than visual trickery.

The show lasted five seasons, from 1959 to the end of 1964. The final program won an Emmy, but was ironically a French film that had won first prize at the 1962 Cannes Film Festival, *An Occurrence at Owl Creek Bridge*.

The *Twilight Zone* lives on in the minds and bad dreams of many, with Rod Serling's haunting voice narrating the journey for us.

A Show of Serling Silver

Rod Serling not only introduced the *Zone* each week, but wrote many of the episodes as well. Born December 25, 1924, he became a successful writer of TV dramas, including the award-winning *Requiem for a Heavyweight*.

But he got tired of sponsors and directors messing with his carefully crafted scripts, so he worked toward developing his own show. One where he could make some social commentary, even if he had to disguise it as science fiction.

He was a strangely discomforting narrator, talking in a tight-lipped monotone. It turns out, Serling was as unsettled as he was unsettling. He was a nervous wreck in front of the camera, sometimes soaking through several shirts just getting through the few minutes of on-screen time. It was his idea to introduce and close the episodes himself (the producers wanted Orson Welles), but he remained an uneasy, shaking mess right through the last show.

The title was Serling's creation, or so he thought. As he said, "I've heard since that there is an Air Force term relating to a moment when a plane is coming down on approach and it cannot see the horizon, it's called the twilight zone, but it's an obscure term which I had not heard before."

Rod Serling was an insomniac, and a lot of his scary stories came from sleepless nights.

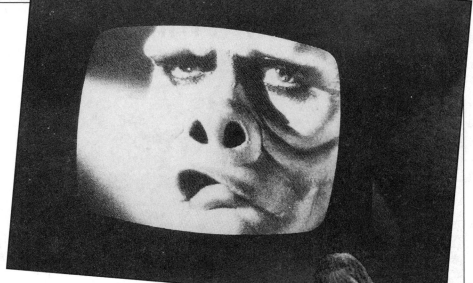

Nightmares on the Nightstand

Visions from the Twilight Zone by **Arlen Schumer**. Submitted for your approval, a wonderfully disturbing oversized, black-and-white, sleek collage of surrealism. This art book is filled with original photography shot from video masters of actual shows combined with evocative phrases from the soundtrack. It's an eerie recreation of the program's feel; it stays away from the ordinary format of TV books—no trivia, anecdotes or episode info. Highly recommended.

$19.95 + 2.00 shipping from Chronicle Books; 275 Fifth St., San Francisco, CA 94103. (800) 722-6657.

Zone Out Monthly

The *Twilight Zone* **Collector's Edition.** Sign up for this service and you'll receive a videocassette of three classic *Twilight Zone* episodes every four to six weeks. Uncut, painstakingly restored and cleaned up from best possible prints.

$4.95 for the introductory tape, then $19.95 from then on until you cancel. Add 3.19 shipping. Columbia House Video Library, 1400 North Fruitridge Avenue, Terre Haute, IN 47811. (800) 457-0866.

Setside Reading

The Twilight Zone Companion by Marc Scott Zicree. A more typical TV book with complete rundowns on every episode, excellent commentary and backstage facts. Also highly recommended.

$9.95 + 2.50 shipping from Bantam Books, 666 Fifth Avenue, New York, NY 10103. (212) 765-6500.

"BOURGEOIS LSD"?

"*Twilight Zone fantasy was one of America's few means for thinking about the unthinkable.*"

—**J. Hoberman.**

"*The Twilight Zone not only inspired a new wave of anthologies of the supernatural, but created a context for the fantastic sitcoms and 'kitchen magician' commercials which were dosing America's living rooms like bourgeois LSD.*"

—**J Hoberman.**

"*How in God's name can you sustain a theatrical mood when every twelve minutes the thrust of the drama is stopped and onto the screen gallop twelve dancing rabbits with toilet paper?*"

— **Rod Serling, on commercials.**

"*The Twilight Zone was an embodiment of great storytelling. Back when we all had animal skins for clothing, there were great stories told around campfires, and these same principles are at work in The Twilight Zone.*"

—**Earl Hamner, Jr.**

Buster Keaton, Robert Redford, and Burgess Meredith all showed up in the *Zone*.

The Honeymooners

Ralph Kramden (Jackie Gleason) drove a bus through the grimy streets of New York, and shared a two-room walk-up with his wife Alice. He couldn't handle the smallest of life's frustrations, so he took that anger out on the one person with whom he was never angry—his wife Alice. But Ralph was no wife-beater, and Alice gave as good as she got. When push came to shove, she'd turn him into a mewing kitten because she was the best thing in his life and he knew it.

Ralph's other asset was his best friend, Ed Norton, who loved Ralph almost as much as Alice did (and who gave and took an equal amount of abuse). Somehow this was *The Honeymooners'* secret. On the surface, the show was about lower class tension, yelling and hostility, but on a deeper level, it was a tribute to the values of friendship and marital unselfishness. At the end of the show, nearly every time, Ralph and Alice would end up in the kitchen in an embrace.

The Beast. Jackie Gleason had fared poorly as the star of NBC's *Life of Riley* in the 1949-1950 season. But as host of Dumont's *Cavalcade of Stars*, he was an instant smash. He attracted a large audience and got rave reviews, and for the third show, he wanted to come up with something special. He proposed a domestic sketch based on his childhood environment.

His writers wanted to call the skit "The Beast," but Gleason didn't like it. "The Lovers" was their next suggestion, but this still wasn't quite right. Finally, it was Gleason himself who thought of "The Honeymooners." The sketch was on only for a few minutes, but it elicited an enormous response from viewers. It became a regular feature. In 1955, *The Honeymooners* briefly became a series.

Thereafter, it periodically resurfaced on Gleason's variety shows.

For syndication they pieced together 39 of these episodes and these ran repeated for years. A few years ago, an additional 75 episodes ("the Lost Episodes") came to light, filmed between 1952 and 1956, which now appear on cable TV channels and videotape.

Live Lunacy

During those days of "live" television, Gleason amazed and sometimes terrified his cast by never actually memorizing or rehearsing his scripts, instead simply looking at them for an hour or two before going on the air. The rest of the cast would have to work around him if he messed up. When he forgot his lines, he would pat his stomach as a signal for help.

In one episode, Gleason missed a cue, leaving Art Carney alone on stage. Carney didn't flinch. He calmly walked to the icebox, pulled out an orange, and calmly ad-libbed a hilarious skit about peeling it. But it worked both ways—another time, Art Carney showed up fully inebriated. Gleason did the whole show by asking a sitting, incoherent Carney yes and no questions.

During a live *Honeymooners* episode, the door stuck. Art Carney solved the problem by climbing through the window.

WISDOM FROM ED NORTON

"As we say in the sewer, if you're not prepared to go all the way, don't put your boots on in the first place."

"As we say in the sewer, time and tide wait for no man."

"As we say in the sewer, here's mud in your eye."

I Once Was Lost

The best of the "lost episodes." This company has over thirty volumes of *Honeymooner* material available on video.

Each volume is $29.98 + 3.95. MPI Home Video, 15825 Rob Roy Drive, Oak Forest, IL 60452. (708) 687-7881. Their catalog is $5, deducted from first order.

"Down in the sewer, we got a slogan. Keep your mouth shut."

—Ed Norton

Join the Club

The Royal Association for the Longevity and Preservation of the Honeymooners (RALPH). The club to join if you're nuts about *The Honeymooners.*

Send SASE for membership information. RALPH c/o C.W. Post Center, Greenvale, NY 11548.

Honeymooners By the Book

The Official *Honeymooners Treasury* by Peter Crescenti and Bob Columbe. This book is the last word in "Honeymooners" lore with trivia, dialogue, skit synopses, black-and-white photos, and many little-known facts.

$13.95 + 2.00 shipping from Perigree Books, 200 Madison Ave., New York, NY 10016. (800) 631-8571.

Our Favorites of Ralph's Get-Rich-Quick Schemes

1. Pills that turn water into gasoline
2. Plastic shoehorns
3. Furniture shampoo
4. Goat gland vitamins
5. Glow-in-the-dark shoe polish
6. A campaign to make Secaucus, New Jersey, a honeymooner's paradise

" One of these days, Alice. One of these days—POW! Right in the kisser."

3 DIMENSION

Comin' at Ya

You gotta feel sorry for 3-D. It keeps trying to be a great fad in one medium or another.

For about fifteen minutes there, it was the hottest thing in movies. You put on those silly-looking blue & red glasses and things started jumping out of the screen.

Movie studios introduced it in the early 1950s as a way to fight the new medium, television. It was a desperate time for the studios and they were throwing themselves headlong into developing new filming and projection processes: big screens, wide screens, curved screens—any crowd pleaser that TV wouldn't be able to duplicate.

Audiences loved the gimmicks and the first 3-D movies were big successes. Yet while some of the wide-screen applications continued for years in good favor, by 1954 the 3-D boom had gone bust.

Why did 3-D end up as a flash in the pan (just as would, six years later, "Smell-O-Vision—The Process to End All Processes")? First of all, the glasses were annoying. And theater managers didn't like the hassle and expense.

But ultimately, the gimmickry ran thin after a while. Arrows, hatchets, avalanches, stampedes, trains and even Jane Russell's bust didn't make up for the flimsy plots and characters.

Despite the movies' crash, 3-D never actually went away. 3-D View-Masters, computer games, comic books and holograms continue to be popular. Add lasers, computers, and other high-tech hotshot stuff, and it looks like just a matter of time before animated holographic images will become part of our everyday lives. 3-D is on the verge of becoming the next big thing.

Maybe.

3-D FACTS

• *Bwana Devil*, the first commercial 3-D film, premiered in 1952. Its success spurred a rash of 3-D movies, the majority of which were reviewed in terms like "amazing trash."

• Alfred Hitchcock's 1954 film *Dial M for Murder* was filmed in 3-D. Unfortunately, by the time the film was ready, 3-D was box office poison, so the stereoscopic version wasn't released (three decades later, the studio allowed a few rep theaters to finally show the 3-D version. Not surprisingly, Hitchcock used the process with subtlety and style).

• The first 3-D comic book was the October, 1953 *Mighty Mouse*. It had a printing of one and a half million copies, and though it sold for a whopping 25 cents (2.5 times the normal comic book price at the time), the issue was an immediate sell-out.

How 3-D Movies Work

To take 3-D pictures, photographers use cameras with twin lenses separated by the "interocular" distance (the space between your eyes).

• In a black & white 3-D movie projection, one lens view passes through a red filter, and the other through blue. 3-D glasses give you the (mostly) correct view for each eye, and your brain is fooled into seeing depth.

• Color 3-D movies are filmed the same way, but projected through two polarizing filters, each of which allows only light vibrating in the right direction to pass through and appear on the screen. The image for the left eye is vibrated one direction; for the right eye, a different direction. The glasses you wear let only the correct polarized light reach each eye, providing the 3-D illusion.

"Do You Want a Good Movie—Or a Lion in Your Lap?"—An ad for a traditional "flat" film, pooh-poohing 3-D.

See 3-D Video

Right Now!

This low tech video 3-D method has been used for a Superbowl half-time show and a Rolling Stones concert special. You can do it any time you're watching TV and about 25% of the time you'll see 3-D.

Look through a sunglass lens with only your left eye, and leave your other eye clear. Now everything moving right across your screen will appear in the foreground, everything moving left will be in background, and everything else stays in-between. Switch to the other eye and everything is reversed.

How it works: the darkened eye takes a split second longer to see, so it registers moving images a little to the left or right of where the undarkened eye sees them. This simulates "interocular distance."

Try this at home, switching from eye to eye, and you won't have to wait for some expensive future 3-D process.

PILGRIMAGE

3-D is alive in Disneyland and Disney World.

Captain EO, starring Michael Jackson and produced by *Star Wars* creator George Lucas, is a 17-minute, three-dimensional space fantasy movie using the polarized light method and various other effects in the theater.

Known by some as "Captain Ego," it offers Michael Jackson doing his same old music video schtick, this time dressed unconvincingly in a space suit; Lucas does his *Star Wars* thing. The 3-D effects are fun, so see it before the Disney corporation realizes what a dated mid-1980s artifact it is and retires it.

Cheap 3-D Glasses

Your plain, old, everyday, traditional 3-D workhorse glasses, red and blue cellophane in a cardboard frame. They're only 85¢ each, but since this place requires a $10 minimum order, why not buy 12!

#D231, 12 pairs 3-D glasses, $10.20 + 4.00 shipping from Archie McPhee, P.O. Box 30852, Seattle, WA 98103-0852. (206) 547-2467.

3-D Films From 1952-55

- *Bwana Devil*
- *It Came From Outer Space*
- *Creature From the Black Lagoon*
- *Murders in the Rue Morgue*
- *The French Line*
- *Kiss Me Kate*
- *House of Wax*
- *Fort Ti*
- *Hondo*

3-D CARTOONS

- *Popeye the Sailor Meets Sinbad the Sailor*
- *Hypnotic Hick* (Woody Woodpecker)
- *Popeye, The Ace of Space*
- *Boo Moon* (Casper)
- *Lumber Jack Rabbit* (Bugs Bunny)

Wham Bam! 1970s 3-D Revival

- *Andy Warhol's Frankenstein*
- *Kiss My Analyst*
- *The Stewardesses*

"*I first saw 3-D when I looked into the pages of three-dimensional comics starring Mighty Mouse in 1953. I was six at the time and it was really my first religious experience.*"

—**Ray Zone**

Deluxe 3-D Glasses

Are your cardboard red-blue 3-D glasses torn and out of shape? Be first on your block to have these durable permanent 3-D glasses. Lots of other 3-D items available too: 3-D comic books , 3-D T-shirts, 3-D paper dolls, and more.

$3.95 + 2.00 shipping from The 3-D Zone, P.O. Box 741159, Los Angeles, CA 90004. (213) 662-3830.

A total of 38 3-D feature films were released between 1953 and 1954.

(16). Dixon crossing Niagara below the Great Cantilever Bridge, U.S.A.

19th Century 3-D

At the turn of the century, many Americans got their first look at the Pyramids, London Bridge and the Leaning Tower of Pisa from 3-D stereoscopes, developed by author-physician Oliver Wendell Holmes in the 1850s.

Two companies dominated the market—Keystone View and Under & Underwood. The companies' traveling salesmen toured the country on bicycles or on horseback to sell the instruments and the double-imaged, postcard-sized stereographs.

Families spent evenings passing around the stereoscope. As time went by, the picture cards expanded their content beyond cultural and educational views to include stories and funny vignettes.

Today, these millions of 3-D negatives and picture cards constitute a valuable archive of photographs of the time. For instance, some of the best photos of the Wright brothers' early flight attempts are preserved in stereographic pictures.

A NEW Gift IDEA!

PICTURES that "Come to Life"

Civil War photographer Matthew Brady took most of his shots in 3-D, including portraits of Abraham Lincoln.

View-Master —Out of a Cave

In 1938 Harold Graves was visiting the "Oregon Caves" tourist attraction. He learned that another visitor, William Gruber, was photographing in stereo—taking two pictures at once—with a special camera that Gruber had invented himself.

Graves was the president of a photographic services company in Portland, Oregon and so was professionally as well as personally intrigued. The two men talked, and soon decided to develop stereo products together. By Christmas, 1939, the new partners' View-Master 3-D viewers and picture reels were on the market.

And they still are. Those 4" cardboard reels, unchanged through the years, each provide seven 3-D views.

View-Master only made scenic reels until the 1950s, when they added cartoon characters and top TV shows.

They'll Have You Reeling

If you're depressed because you can't find View-Master reels of *Snoopy and the Red Baron* or *Royal Wedding—Prince Charles & Lady Diana* at your neighborhood toy store, cheer up. Worldwide Slides of Minneapolis, Minnesota, carries a full line of View-Master 3-D reels (landmarks, national parks, TV shows, cartoons, etc.), available by mail order.

View-Master Catalog: $1.00 from Worldwide Slides, View-Master Division, 7427 Washburn Ave. S., Minneapolis, MN 55423. (612) 869-6482.

View-Master-Pieces

Fine art on your View-Master? The works of three serious 3-D photographers (Pat Whitehouse, Jacobus G. Ferwerda, and Stan White) are available on View-Master reels. Each set includes 3 reels and a small booklet about the photographer.

Each 3 reel set, $16.95 + 1.70 shipping; all 3 sets, $48.95 + 4.90 shipping. Worldwide Slides, View-Master Division, 7427 Washburn Ave. S., Minneapolis, MN 55423. (612) 869-6482.

REQUIRED READING

• *3-D Past and Present,* by Wim van Krulen. Here's a look into three dimensions, the story of 3-D from daguerreotypes through albumen prints, View-Master reels, 3-D comic books, 3-D movies and 3-D aerial photography. Includes three View-Master picture reels that go with the text.

$21.95 + 2.20 shipping from Worldwide Slides, View-Master Division, 7427 Washburn Avenue S., Minneapolis, MN 55423. (612) 869-6482.

• *Fantastic 3-D,* edited by David Hutchison. Lots of art and 3-D photos in this one. Covers the history and future of 3-D, comic books, movies, making 3-D photos (even with a regular camera), 3-D clubs, and more.

$12.95 + 4.00 shipping from Reel 3-D Enterprises, P.O. Box 2368, Culver City, CA 90231. (213) 837-2368.

"Don't Know Much About Holography..."

Take a class and learn how to make holograms yourself! Holography has every sign of being a great adventure—shooting off lasers, fooling around with lenses and mirrors, and creating 3-D art! There are lots of commercial applications (it's a growing multi-million dollar industry), so maybe you'll be developing valuable job skills at the same time.

The bad news is that we couldn't find any holography correspondence schools. You have to take classes in person.

• **The Holography Institute.** Short courses teach how to create every kind of hologram, build your own studio, equip your darkroom, and display and market your holograms. Classroom lectures and laboratory workshops. Four hour make-a-hologram class is $160.

Holography Institute, P.O. Box 446, Petaluma, CA 94953. (707) 778-1497.

• **Holography Workshops.** Learn how holograms are made, and make one to take home for your mom's refrigerator in a 2¹/₂ hour introductory workshop. Instruction is personal—there's a two student maximum. The $45 tuition includes workbook, studio time, hologram, and certificate. Other workshops and programs available too. Instructor Frank DeFreitas is the editor and publisher of *The Holo-Gram*, holography's widest circulated newsletter.

Frank DeFreitas Laser Studio, P.O. Box 9035, Allentown, PA 18105. (215) 434-8236.

Magazines

• *The Holo-Gram.* This well-designed quarterly will keep you current on what's happening on the international holography scene. Best of all, it's free.

Frank DeFreitas, Editor, P.O. Box 9035, Allentown, PA 18105. (215) 434-8236.

• *L.A.S.E.R. News.* Published by the nonprofit Laser Arts Society for Education & Research, this journal features articles on making holograms and interviews with holographers. For the experienced and those just getting ready to (ahem!) add depth to their art.

$20 per year, 4 issues. Patty Pink, Editor, P.O. Box 42083, San Francisco, CA 94101. (415) 822-1326.

SHRINES

Inventor Dr. Dennis Gabor won a Nobel prize in 1971 for his holographic process. You can see what all the fuss was about at either of these museums.

• **Museum of Holography**
11 Mercer St.
New York, NY 10013
(212) 925-0581

• **Museum of Holography, Chicago**
1134 W. Washington Blvd.
Chicago, IL 60606
(312) 226-1007

Half a Gram? Hologram!

A hi-tech laser light created these 3-D images you can wear.

#91106, Satellite Stud Earrings, $22.00; #91107, Dolphins Bolo, $35.00; #91110, Crystal Pin, $26.50. Add 4.25 shipping. Discovery Corner, Lawrence Hall of Science, U.C., Berkeley, CA 94720-0001. (510) 642-1016.

4-D in 3-D

You've got your choice of a 3-D cat or a 3-D eye on the face of this hologram watch. We prefer the eye—you can have your watch watching you as you're watching your watch. When the image disappears, you see the five-function digital readout.

$13.98 + 3.50 shipping from The Lighter Side, 4514 19th St. Court East, P.O. Box 25600, Bradenton, FL 34206-5600. (813) 747-2356.

Join the Club

- **National Stereoscopic Association.** P.O. Box 14801, Columbus, OH 43214. Dues: $30/yr., includes subscription to *Stereo World* (6 issues/yr).

- **Photographic Society of America, Stereo Division.** Pauline Sweezy, Membership Director, 4594 Las Lindas Way, Carmichael, CA 95608.

Hollywood Or Bust

Be careful when you turn the pages of Hollywood 3-D because you could get stars in your eyes! 32 page full-color book features 3-D photos of movie greats Jayne Mansfield, Zsa Zsa Gabor, Jane Russell, Maureen O'Hara, Yvonne DeCarlo and...Art Linkletter! Also includes two full-length 3-D comic book stories about Hollywood. Free glasses included.

Hollywood 3-D book, $2.50 + 2.00 shipping from The 3-D Zone, P.O. Box 741159, Los Angeles, CA 90004.

Hollywood Babes All Dolled Up

3-D paper dolls are in full color! Comic book artist Trina Robbins created simply gorgeous costumes and fashion accessories for both of her glamorous Hollywood starlets, Rita and Jayne. 8 color pages on deluxe stock. Free glasses included.

$2.95 + 2.00 shipping from from The 3-D Zone, P.O. Box 741159, Los Angeles, CA 90004.

THIS IS 3 DIMENSION!

NATURAL VISION

First Class 3-D

"Sometimes, there are certain things you want to say to someone that just won't work on a regular postcard, no matter how ugly it is." Trust us, each postcard is tackier than the next. We love them.

6 different assorted cards, $5.00 + 2.00 shipping from Klutz, 2121 Staunton Court, Palo Alto, CA 94306. (415) 424-0739.

Fly Me to the Moon

With these 3-D glow-in-the-dark boxer shorts, there'll be no dark side to your moon! Be the hit of every party and set off UFO sightings all over town. The design? Little spaceships on a background of shooting stars. 100% cotton. Includes one pair 3-D glasses.

$15.00 + 3.00 shipping from Klutz, 2121 Staunton Court, Palo Alto, CA 94306. (415) 424-0739.

The 1988 yearbook of Hollywood High School was in 3-D.

The Three Stooges

Stooge Story

One of the all-time greatest unsolved mysteries of the world is why the Three Stooges ever became so popular. There are funnier comedy teams and more developed characters. But Larry, Moe and Curly (or Joe or Curly-Joe or Shemp) have endured for nearly sixty years, through 24 features and an incredible 191 shorts.

Yep, sixty years of head banging, face slapping, eye poking, hair pulling, stomach punching, nose twisting, ear ripping, knee kicking and foot stomping. How did slapstick keep the Stooges alive all these years (though technically dead)? The answer is as obvious as a blow to the head—TV.

Local TV stations in the 1950s showed cartoons, Little Rascals, and a whole bunch of 3 Stooges.

Why more Three Stooges than anything else? For one, kids love seeing adults acting stupid and hurting each other. But mostly because stations had lots of material available. Screen Gems released 80 Stooge shorts in 1958, followed a year later by another 40.

Very Faux & Curly

Need a Curly impersonator? SOITENLY you do! Dave Knight—"the man who would be Curly"—looks and sounds like the most beloved of all Stooges. He'll come and shmooze in character at your next business or social gathering. Give a call for more information and a free "WOOB woop woop woop!"

Dave Knight, 4068 Electronics Road, Marion, NY 14505. (315) 589-3029.

Sights For Sore Eyes

These videos are a whole lot better than a poke in the eye! Before Kung Fu there was Moe, and these tapes'll qualify you for a black and blue belt in the ancient occidental arts.

The Making of the 3 Stooges. Comedian Steve Allen narrates this back-stage look at the humorous history of the three zanies. Rare footage

makes it something Stooge fans couldn't possibly live without. VHS only, 45 minutes. Color & B&W.

#WA063, $19.95 + $3.95 shipping from:
Blackhawk Films
5959 Triumph Street
Commerce, CA 90040-1688
(800) 826-2295

3 Stooges Comedy Classics. Watch Larry, Moe, Curly and Shemp suffer the comic consequences in five of their back-breaking best. Chaotic comedies include "Hollywood on Parade," "Disorder in the Court," "Malice in the Palace," "Brideless Groom," and "Sing a Song of Six Pants." 70 minutes, B&W. (VHS)

#RP7835, $19.95 + $3.95 shipping from Blackhawk Films (see above).

Stoogeaholics Collection. Have a mayhem marathon with a set of six tapes featuring 18 of the Stooges' best comedy shorts from 1935 through 1951. B&W, 55 minutes each.

X3SC4 (6 cassette set) $84.88+ $3.95 shipping. Blackhawk Films (see above).

The Stoogephile Trivia Movie. 55 minutes of Stooge history. Never-before-released footage of personal appearances and looks behind the scenes. For true fans. (VHS)

#3908 Stooge Video $19.98 +$4.20 shipping from:
Johnson Smith Co.
4514 19th Court East
P.O. Box 25500
Bradenton, Florida 34206-5500
FAX (813) 746-7896.

"The Stooges weren't worth a damn without Larry."—Ed Bernds, Three Stooges Film Director.

STOOGES OF HISTORY

In 1922, Moe and Shemp Howard stopped in to heckle the vaudeville act of childhood friend Ted Healy. The audience roared, so Healy brought the pair on stage. For the next ten years, the brothers worked with Healy when not busy with their own acts.

In 1928, Shemp booked himself into another show. Healy needed a replacement fast, so Shemp suggested Larry Feinberg (later shortened to "Fine"), a violinist turned comedian. A year later, Healy decided he wanted 3 "stooges" to kick around in a new act, so Shemp and Moe re-joined.

They were in rehearsal one day when Larry Fine arrived late with wet hair. Jake Shubert, the show's producer, scolded him, roughed up his hair and shoved him on stage. His new hairstyle contrasted nicely with Moe's bowl cut and, with this distinctive new look, the act took off.

Things went well for a while, but Shemp got tired of working with Healy and quit in 1932. Moe offered up his younger brother Jerry as a replacement. His brother, chunky with wavy hair and handlebar mustache wasn't funny-looking enough, said Healy. Intent on getting Jerry into the act, Moe taught him the routines and shaved his head—much to Jerry's objection that the girls "won't come near me!"

Assuring Jerry that not even their mom would recognize him, Moe again introduced him to Healy, this time as a hot, new comic. While delivering the newly-taught routine, Moe called Jerry "Curly" and Larry ad-libbed along. Healy hired him on the spot.

Their success on stage led Healy & His Stooges to Hollywood in 1933, where they appeared in several film shorts. A year later, the Stooges split from Healy and signed with Columbia where they made nearly 200 films over the next 24 years.

Curly had a stroke in 1946 while filming their 97th short. Shemp came back to replace him, but he died in 1955 and was replaced by former vaudevillian Joe Besser, who was in turn replaced by Joe DiRita, dubbed "Curly-Joe."

In 1958, Screen Gems began releasing their film shorts for television viewing. Parents, clergy and civic leaders began expressing concern over the effect of Stooge violence on children. Despite that, their increasing TV popularity led to seven new feature films in the early 1960s.

In 1970, Larry suffered a stroke. He died in 1975. Moe followed five months later.

In 1983, the Stooges received a star on the Hollywood Walk of Fame.

"The only thing I learned from the Three Stooges was how to duck!"—Lucille Ball

BUY THIS, YA KNUCKLEHEAD!

Stooge Shirts

• "Outta The Way, Ya Knuckleheads" t-shirt lets 'em know you're coming. #27-5.

• "Just Say Moe!" with angry portrait, black background with red lettering. #27-3.

  100% cotton. Adult sizes M, L, XL. $16 ppd from: Stoogestore 10220 Calera Road, Philadelphia, PA 19114. (215) 637-5744.

Joystick Slapstick

The Stooges on your computer? Take an abuser-friendly journey full of flying pies and poke-you-in-the-eye graphics. Digital sound brings to life every "nyuck, nyuck, nyuck" and "bonk." (IBM).

  $39.99 + $4.00 shipping from: Egghead Software 22011 SE 51st Street Issaquah, WA 98027-7004 (800) EGGHEAD / FAX (206) 391-0880.

Pleasant Dreams

"Hey, wake up and go to sleep!"— Moe. Sleep easier on this restful pillowcase.

  $12 each or 2 for $22 (postpaid) from: Stoogestore, 10220 Calera Road, Philadelphia, PA 19114. (215) 637-5744.

Three? Fore!

When they're not swinging at each other, they're swinging at a golf ball. This 11" x 14" poster on textured stock is perfect for your favorite golfer.

  #210-005, $5.95 + $3.95 shipping from Golf Day, 395 Beecham Street, Chelsea, MA 02150 (800) 669-8600

Watch It!

Quartz watch with black leather band and a very silly face.

  #18384, $39.95 + 4.95 shipping from Wireless, P.O. Box 64422, Saint Paul, Minnesota 55164-0422. (800) 669-9999

"Shake? SPEAR!"

You may be surprised that what looked liked random mayhem was actually *carefully scripted* mayhem. Here are actual stage directions from Stooge movie scripts:

• "Double cheek slap"
• "Poke in the eyes"
• "Triple slap"
• "Forehead slap"

STOOGE LIT 101

Larry—The Stooge In The Middle by Morris "Moe" Feinberg. Written by Larry's brother, this bang-up biography shows us the Stooges through Larry's eyes. We witness the birth of the "poke-in-the-eye" routine, find out how Al Jolson played a role in Larry's rise to Stooge-dom, and more. Includes an appendix by Jack Kerouac. Yes, THAT Jack Kerouac.

$13 postpaid from Stoogestore, 10220 Calera Road, Philadelphia, PA 19114. (215) 637-5744.

Moe Howard & The 3 Stooges by Moe Howard. Get Moe's side of the story: a bone-crunching chronology of knee-slapping stories, mad-cap memories, magic MOEments and more! Over 200 photos.

$18 postpaid from Stoogestore, 10220 Calera Road, Philadelphia, PA 19114. (215) 637-5744.

Curly: An Illustrated Biography of the Superstooge by Joan Howard Maurer. The youngest Howard was the first to go but left loads of nyuks. Written by his niece (Moe's daughter), it contains over 100 rare photos from the family album. The foreword was written by Michael Jackson. Yes, THAT Michael Jackson.

$18 postpaid from Stoogestore, 10220 Calera Road, Philadelphia, PA 19114. (215) 637-5744.

The 3 Stooges Scrapbook by Jeff Lenburg, Joan Howard

Maurer, Greg Lenburg. A side-spliting synopsis of the head-bashing burlesque boys. Includes a complete filmography plus amusing anecdotes of backstage antics. Over 100 rare photos.

#T1401, $12.95 + $3.95 shipping from Funny Side Up, 425 Stump Road, North Wales, PA 19454. (215) 361-5130.

The Three Stooges Book of Scripts by Joan Howard Maurer. Three of their most brilliant screenplays: "You Natzy Spy," "Three Little Pigskins," and their Oscar nominated "Men In Black." Also bios and a backstage look at the goings-on during filming. Lots of film frame blow-ups.

#635987, $9.95 + $3.00 shipping from Edward R. Hamilton, Falls Village, CT 06031-5000.

Finger Puppets

3 Stooges finger puppets let you play out your Stooge fantasies without any danger of being poked in the eye. Each puppet is 4 inches high.

Stoogestore is a great source for everything Stooges, by the way. They have virtually all authorized merchandise plus some collectibles. Where else could you get 3 Stooges beach towels, Christmas ornaments, air fresheners, window wavers and laundry bags? Send $1 for their catalog.

Puppets—set of 3 for $10 postpaid
Stoogestore
10220 Calera Road
Philadelphia, PA 19114
(215) 637-5744.

Stooge Stats

- No other comedy team has appeared in more films than the Three Stooges.

- They were nominated for an Academy Award...just one...for their comedy short, *Men in Black*, a satire of a popular medical drama called *Men in White*.

- Despite the lack of critical acclaim, theater owners loved 'em. They won the Motion Picture Exhibitors' Laurel Award for top-grossing shorts in 1950, '51, '53, '54, and '55.

- The Stooges rehearsed their on-stage act constantly and never got seriously hurt. But movies didn't allow that level of rehearsal and demanded ever-changing tricks. Once, Moe broke Larry's nose with a rubber hammer. In another stunt Moe broke three ribs (his own).

Which Stooge Are You?

Ivan Stang of the Church of the Sub-Genius says each of us is one of three different types personified in the Three Stooges. Most of us are Larrys. A few of us are Moes. And almost none are Curlys.

- **The Moe Personality**. At best, a leader and planner. But watch out if those plans go awry, because all Larrys and Curlys will suffer. Still, Larrys and Curlys seem to need a Moe.

- **The Larry Personality**. A born follower. Reacts rather than initiates action. If you had to hire one of the Stooges, it would be Larry because he would best follow your orders. When Moe's abuse finally does make Larry

mad, does he lash back? No. He takes it out on Curly.

- **The Curly Personality**. Divine Fool. Not good at the scheming required by a Moe-dominated society. In society,

Curlys are branded as crazy, or just plain stupid. In reality it is only Curly who understands the truth.

Co-existence. Curly and Moe are drawn together by some inexplicable balance of nature. The Larrys are the go-betweeners, caught in a crossfire of cosmic dualities. All three personality types need each other to survive.

Norman Maurer went from drawing these comics to marrying Moe's daughter Joan, to writing and directing Stooges' films.

$14.95 + $3.00 shipping from Malibu Graphics,1355 Lawrence Drive #212, Newbury Park, CA 91320. (805) 499-3015

- **The 3 Stooges in 3-D**. We were afraid to open this one with the glasses on, figuring Moe might reach out of the page and poke us in the eyes. But no, the guys stay safely inside their little boxed frames in these reprints from 1963-66 comic books. Successfully rebuts the argument that the Stooges lack depth. 32 page 2-color comic book includes 3-D glasses.

Available for $3.95 + 1.50 shipping from Malibu Graphics (see above).

Drawn & Quartered

The Knuckleheads Return! In the 1950s a lot of comedians appeared as comic characters in their own comic books. *Knuckleheads* is a collection of stories from the 3 Stooges' comic books.

N-YUK! N-YUK! N-YUK!

The End

"A wiseguy, eh?" (POW!) "Hey, what's the big idea?"

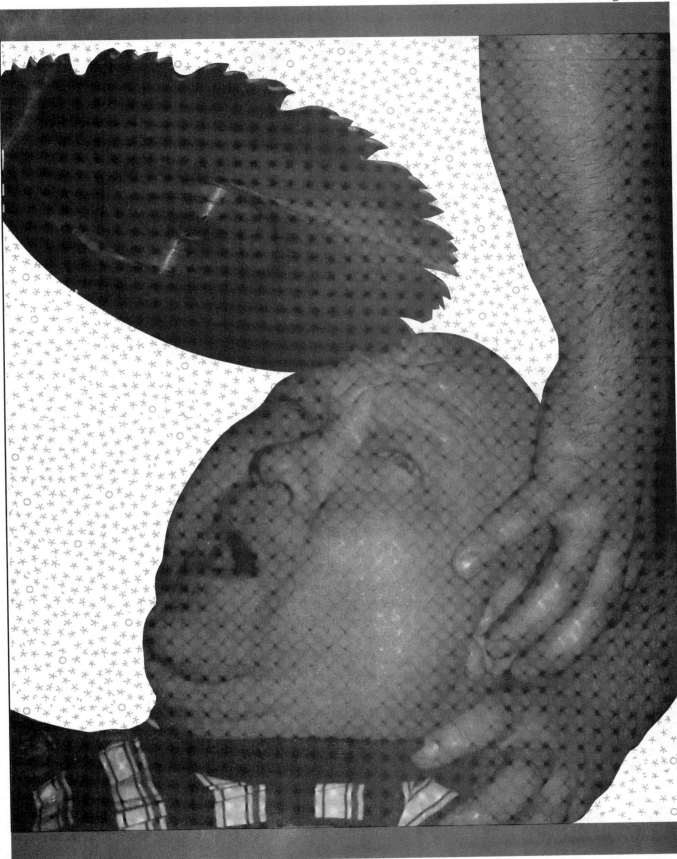

Trains

Tunnel Vision, One Track Minds

Long ago a train engineer had a job that everyone thought was the height of romance and excitement. People stopped to watch a train go by and hung around train stations for close-up looks.

Today's train buffs keep alive that sense of wonder. There are millions of them lurking about with their railroad caps, timetables, pocket watches, and basements full of elaborate but tiny towns, tracks and tunnels.

The first American railroad, the Baltimore and Ohio, started in 1830. Later the transcontinental routes became, as Jessamyn West put it, "a big iron needle stitching the country together."

Never mind that the railroad companies were among the most corrupt ever. You could hop a train and be on the other side of the continent in a week instead of six months 'round the Horn. Train travel was fast. And it was (and is) exciting.

Model trains got underway in a big way after the 1933-34 Chicago World's Fair featured an impressive electric layout seen by 100 million visitors. The National Model Railroad Association formed a year later.

The heavy train travel of World War II added interest to anything having to do with trains (1944 was America's peak year of train travel ever). Postwar economic and baby booms suddenly gave fathers both the money and the excuse to invest in train sets. Lionel and American Flyer were the big names at the time. HO scale, first designed in the 1920s, started coming into its own in the late 1950s.

Railroad enthusiasts come in three major subgroups, with many straddling the line into more than one category:

- Model railroaders.
- Train memorabilia collectors, hoarding old tickets and timetables.
- Preservationists and "railfans." These folks obsessively ride the rails that still exist and try to keep railroads alive.

Tracks & Facts

- The "little red caboose" was also sometimes brown, green, blue, or yellow. It was also called the cabin car, crummy, buggy, hack, snake-wagon, zoo, ape cage, throne room, monkey house, shanty, office, and bedbug haven. Whatever you call them, they're no longer being manufactured and are rapidly disappearing from active trains.

- Chicago is a big name in railroad history. In 1890, 40 railroads had the name Chicago in them. It was the main hub where all the major rail lines met—you could take a train from a majority of U.S. cities to Chicago with only one stop or fewer.

- It was the power of the railroads that caused America to adopt standard time zones. Before that, "noon" in each town was whenever the sun was directly overhead. It drove railroad schedulers crazy, since moving across the country required keeping track of each town's idiosyncratic "time zone."

- Top management in action: At the ceremony to finish the Transcontinental Railway on May 10, 1869, rail baron Leland Stanford took hammer in hand to take a swing at the Golden Spike. He missed it completely.

- Marklin toy trains from the golden age of German toys (1885-1914) have sold for as much as $100,000. Ironically, they're so valuable that collectors don't dare use them, fearing derailments, collisions and even exploding miniature steam engines.

- Young comedian Wally Cox was a model train nut in the 1950s when he shared a two-bedroom apartment in New York City's 57th Street with a roommate who was into Zen Buddhism, fencing, yoga, and bongo playing. The trains eventually crowded out his roommate—Marlon Brando.

Allied Model Trains in Culver City, CA, the world's largest toy train store, is designed to look like Union Station.

Train Quotes

"You know what the most exciting sound in the world is, Uncle Billy? That's it—a train whistle!"

—James Stewart as George Bailey in
It's A Wonderful Life

"Think, boys, how useful the knowledge will be to you when you grow to manhood, the electrical and mechanical knowledge that you will gain while playing with your Lionel Outfit; the problems in transportation that you will be able to solve and the many other advantages you will have when you are ready to fight life's battle."

—Joshua Lionel Cowen,
1923 Lionel Catalog

"The relaxing moments in beautiful lounge cars, the leisurely enjoyment of the trip and the thoughtful service all add up to my being such an enthusiastic Domeliner fan."

—Actor Ronald Reagan in an ad for
Union Pacific, 1959. (In 1985, he
tried to remove all funds for Amtrak.)

"They go and they come with such regularity and precision, and their whistles can be heard so far, that the farmers set their clocks by them, and thus one well-conducted institution regulates a whole country."

—Henry David Thoreau

Hobbyists Gone Amok

There's abundant evidence that train nuts just don't know when to stop.

• In Southern California, camera-laden railfans sneak into train yards to get shots of their favorite locomotives. Special agents are continually throwing them off the property for their own safety.

• Model railroaders get hooked on collecting trains and gradually begin to gobble up more and more space for their layouts. "Pray for me," reads one bumper sticker, "my husband's a train collector."

• Hobbyists often buy a particular house because it has a good "railroad basement"— lots of space, no outside entrance, steps in the middle, and little else to interfere with a track layout.

• Michael Burgett, a 10-year-old from Sebewaing, Michigan, sent a letter to a railroad company in Florida asking for a real train car. The company said okay—if you pay shipping. Michael's community rallied behind him, and now he has a bright yellow 1937 Chessie caboose in his backyard.

• You want an old-fashioned steam locomotive? They're no longer made here— you have to go to China, which still makes them from a 1918 American model they copied. China uses steam trains because they require only coal and human labor—two commodities China has plenty of. They've recently sold three to Americans. Cost? About $300,000 plus shipping.

Just Whistle

Your own train whistle? Vestal Press sells plans for making one, which sounds just like the real thing. Great for your home layout, or for scaring people as they cross railroad tracks. But remember the right whistle for the right occasion:

• **One long blast**—The train is coming to the station.

• **Three short blasts**—The train is backing up.

• **Two long blasts, one short, one long** (TOOOT! TOOOT! TA TOOOT!)—The train is coming to a crossing.

• **Short repeated blasts**—Get off the tracks, idiot!

#R-46X, *Build Your Own Locomotive Whistle*, $7.50 + 2.50 shipping from Vestal Press, 320 N. Jensen Road, P.O. Box 97, Vestal, NY 13851-0097. (607) 797-4872.

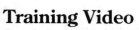

B_{ig} N_{ame} in Little Trains

Joshua Lionel Cowen, an inventive college dropout, founded the Lionel Manufacturing Company to make electric motors and novelties. In 1901, he put one of his electric motors in a model railroad car for fun. When Cowen persuaded store owners to put the new trains in their display windows to attract customers, people responded

enthusiastically—but instead of looking at the store's merchandise, they wanted to buy the trains. The Lionel company was on its way.

Cowen capitalized on some brilliant marketing techniques. One was tying the idea of playing with toy trains to father-son bonding. "This father never knew his own son!" screamed the guilt-inducing Lionel ads. The solution: buy a Lionel toy train set, and spend time with your son building train layouts.

Another smart move was linking the toy train to Christmas. It was common at the time for people to build a nativity scene at the base of the Christmas tree, often including miniature streets and houses too. Lionel's ads and displays started showing trains threading through the buildings, and after constant repetition, trains became associated with the holiday season.

Lionel produced all sorts of auxiliary products to complement their basic cars and track. Cowen realized that the designing and building of entire train layouts got the child involved, and was critical to continued enjoyment of the hobby.

As he put it: "A few minutes of that (just running a train in circles) and the little nippers will wander off and squeeze out some toothpaste or set fire to the curtains. They've got to be in on it!"

Training Video

Toy Trains in Action. This 60-minute video takes you back into the world of old Lionel and American Flyer television ads and promotional films. Includes a wildly funny Joe McDoakes short comedy (1940s) about a man obsessed with his trains.

Working for Scale

When railroaders say their layout is to scale, they mean it.

• **Living miniature plants** that look like bigger plants or trees. Modelers buy these from special nurseries that specialize in "small."

• **Miniature Metal Mammals.** How about a dog biting a postman? Or a hobo, telephone lineman, dog spraying a hydrant, fat man eating?

Blood on the Tracks

In the modeling world, there's a great divide, even name-calling, between those who take pleasure in simply running toy trains and those who obsessively work so their models will be exact scale duplicates of actual trains.

Scale modelers call toy train operators "tinplaters" (most toy train track is coated with tin to prevent rust and corrosion) and "junkmen." The tinplaters strike back at the scale modelers as "rivet counters" (wanting their model train to exactly match the real thing, down to the last rivet).

One of the latest gizmos is a miniaturized video camera that you can mount on the cab of your model train for an engineer's eye view of the track ahead.

Pilgrimage: Strasburg, Pennsylvania

You'll have a hard time finding a more railroad-crazy place than Strasburg, Pennsylvania.

• **The Strasburg Railroad.** This is America's oldest short-line railroad, originally chartered in 1832. Enjoy a Victorian depot, refurbished parlor and observation cars, and a half-dozen steam locomotives.

• **The Railroad Museum of Pennsylvania.** A fine museum with railroad memorabilia. Lots of gleaming locomotives, mostly steam engines.

• **Red Caboose Motel and Age of Steam Museum.** The largest private collection of railroad memorabilia anywhere, and caboose suites. The restaurant is two 80-ton dining cars that shimmy to give the effect of riding on the rails. Reservations: call (717) 687-6646.

• **Choo-Choo Barn—Traintown USA.** This barn-size electric train layout is a miniature representation of Lancaster County with farms, homes, tiny animated figures, a three-ring circus, and a house on fire.

• **The Toy Train Museum.** Operated by the Train Collectors Association, with lots of model trains in all sorts of sizes and layouts.

For more information on all Strasburg attractions, contact the Visitor's Bureau at (717) 299-8901.

For Model Train Fans

• *The Train Collectors Association.* About 20,000 "tinplaters" belong to the TCA, which operates the Toy Train Museum in Strasburg, Pennsylvania. They meet twice a year in nearby York, filling 7 buildings with trains.

Dues: $20 per year. P.O Box 248, Strasburg, PA 17579. (717) 687-8623.

• *National Model Railroad Association.* Founded in 1935 during model railroading's infancy, the NMRA has 24,000 "rivet-counting" members.

Dues: $24 per year. 4121 Cromwell Rd., Chattanooga, TN 37421. (615) 892-2846.

JOIN THE CLUB
Fans of Full-Size Trains

National Railway Historical Society. These folks work for the preservation of train equipment and railroad cars. Help arrange train car rentals. They have 19,000 members, many of them on any given weekend riding the rails.

Dues: $13 per year, includes *The National Railway Bulletin* (6 issues). P.O. Box 58153, Philadelphia, PA 19102. (215) 557-6606.

Rhythm of the Rails

Great American Train Songs, Vols.1 & 2 (audiocassettes). Hear Johnny Cash, Steve Goodman, Roy Acuff and others sing classics like *Wabash Cannonball, City of New Orleans, Casey Jones*, and more. Includes a 6-minute testimonial about Casey Jones' famous wreck by Casey's actual fireman.

**$9.95 each + 2.00 shipping
Roundhouse Records, Inc.
P.O. Box 210-314
Nashville, TN 37221-0314
(800) 242-1171
(615) 646-5661**

Train Memorabilia Collectors

Railroad Collectors Association. The 1200 members collect artifacts of train travel from all time periods: tickets, timetables, dining room china, bells, engine pieces, uniforms, track nails, lanterns and almost anything else.

**Dues: $15 per year
Railroad Collectors Association
795 Aspen
Buffalo Grove, IL 60089
(708) 537-0891**

Gary Coleman reportedly blew much of his $70,000 weekly salary from *Diff'rent Strokes* on model trains.

Train-o-Saurus Wrecks

If, like Walt Disney and Pugsley Addams, you're a fan of train wrecks, these are books for you.

• *Train Wrecks: A Pictorial History of Accidents on the Main Line* by Robert C. Reed. Even an "iron horse" sometimes stumbles. In 1875 alone, there were 8,216 reported rail accidents (roughly 22 a day). This book features sobering pictures from 150 years of train history illustrating what happens when tons of steel get off on the wrong track at high speed.

Hardcover, $10.99 + 2.00 shipping from Random House, 400 Hahn Road, Westminster, MD 21157. (800) 733-3000.

• *Train Wrecks For Fun and Profit* by F. A. Schmitt. The story of a Midwestern farmer named Joe Connolly who staged locomotive collisions at state fairs in the early 1900s. What a way to make a living! Still, while not a career guide per se, this could suggest an easy lateral shift for people in similar fields like corporate raiders, munitions manufacturers, savings and loan executives.

Paperback, $6.95 + 2.50 shipping from Vestal Press, 320 N. Jensen Road, P.O. Box 97, Vestal, NY 13851-0097. (607) 797-4872.

On the Right Track

• *Model Railroader*. "How-to" projects, great layouts, new products, workshop hints.

$27.95, 12 issues. Kalmbach Publishing, Box 1612, Waukesha, WI 53187. (800) 446-5489.

• *Garden Railways*. Specialty magazine for the *outdoor* model railroader.

$18.00, 6 issues. Sample copy $4.50. P.O. Box 61461, Denver, CO 80206. (303) 733-4779.

• *Trains*. All aboard for the romance of real railroading (or "1:1 scale" in the joke of the hobbyists). Explores the world's railroads, past and present.

$27.95, 12 issues. Kalmbach Publishing, P.O. Box 1612, Waukesha, WI 53187-1612. (800) 446-5489.

Catch the Reading Railroad

Greenberg's Model Railroading with Lionel Trains by Roland E. LaVoie. One of a series of *dozens* of train books from Greenberg Publishing, a great one-stop source for model train information (get their catalog!). This clear and friendly beginner's guide tells you how to begin collecting and operating the country's most popular brand of trains. Lots of photographs and illustrations.

$19.95 + 2.50 shipping. Greenberg Publishing, 7566 Main Street, Sykesville, MD 21784. (301) 795-7447.

TINY TRAIN

Instant, too! Ready-to-run (after you run to the store and pick up an AA battery) this train has snap-together track for easy set-up. Measures 9 in. and includes authentically-detailed steam locomotive, tender car and caboose.

#9132, $6.98 + 1.35 shipping from Johnson Smith Company, 4514 19th Court East, P.O. Box 25500, Bradenton, FL 34206-5500. (813) 747-2356 / FAX (813) 746-7896.

"Pardon me, boy—is that the Chattanooga Choo Choo?...
Dinner in the diner, nothing could be finer Than to have your ham and eggs in Carolina."
—Glenn Miller & his Orchestra

"Rail travel at high speed is not possible, because passengers, unable to breathe, would die of asphyxia." —Dr. Dionysus Lardner (1793-1859)

Moveable Feast

Dinner in the Diner: 300 Recipes from America's Era of Great Trains by Will C. Hollister. Unlike their cousins, the airlines, railroad companies took pride in excellent cuisine, and served it in shining dining cars with sparkling clean table linen. Hollister collected recipes from the Northern Pacific, Illinois Central, the Atchison, Topeka and Santa Fe, and other railroads known for outstanding meal service. Includes photographs of dining cars and trains.

Hardcover, $21.95 + 3.50 shipping. Trans-Anglo Books, P.O. Box 6444, Glendale, CA 91205. (818) 240-9130.

HO What Fun

Most toy trains now are plastic. This one isn't. It's a working HO scale model kit of locomotive and tender, which takes about 10 hours to assemble and hooks up with any HO cars. All parts metal, including some brass. Track not included.

#K5319, $99.00 + 4.39 shipping from Mason & Sullivan's Classics In The Making, 586 Higgins Crowell Rd., West Yarmouth, MA 02673. (800) 933-3010 / FAX (508) 775-5581.

Run Your Train on a Deficit

2-6-0 Mogul Locomotive. The 2-6-0 was the workhorse of the Colorado & Southern Railroad. This is a hand-painted, extra-large (1:25 scale) G-gauge replica in brass and stainless steel. Comes with transformer, controls, track, station lamp, and 12 lifelike figures. Even puffs smoke!

#0001, $1,285.00 + 50.00 shipping from Attitudes, 1213 Elko Dr., Sunnyvale, CA 94089. (800) 525-2468 / FAX (408) 734-8004.

Makes Good Time

Not only is it *fast*, but Tyco's Turbo Train is ready to play with in minutes. 42 section track snaps together easily. Includes turbo locomotive, coach and caboose.

#DTT371, $69.95 + 7.25 shipping. Lifestyle Fascination, 345 W. County Line Road, Jackson, NJ 08527. (800) 669-0987 / FAX (201) 928-1812.

This year model railroaders in the U.S. will spend more than $200 million on their hobby.

Railroad Ties

Wear locomotives around your neck. That's what's embroidered on this classic navy blue striped tie.

#14453, $16.50 + 3.90 from Wireless, P.O. Box 64422, St. Paul, MN 55164-0422. (800) 669-9999.

THOMAS
The Tank Train Toy

Ringo Starr's favorite train is choo-chooing into the hearts of kid train lovers everywhere.

• Read All About Him: The first four *Thomas The Tank Railway* series classics by the Rev. W. Awdry. Also included is a 40 min. video narrated by the former Beatle drummer.

#359562, $35.00 + 6.80 shipping.

• Thomas makes tracks without tracks. You tell him where to go with battery-operated remote control.

#307355, $25.00 + 5.80 shipping. Both items from FAO Schwarz, P.O. Box 182225, Chattanooga, TN 37422-7225. (800) 426-TOYS.

ADJUST YOUR TRACKING

• **Love Those Trains.** National Geographic video takes you on a 60 minute railway journey with the world's most famous trains, both present and past.

#VS078, $29.95 + 4.95 shipping. Special Interest Video, 100 Enterprise Place, P.O. Box 7022, Dover, DE 19903-7022. (800) 522-0502.

• **The Illinois Central.** "Good mornin' America, how are ya." This is a 145 minute video of the railroad that the late Steve Goodman wrote about in his song, *City of New Orleans.*

#GFP003, $79.95 + 5.95 shipping. Special Interest Video, 100 Enterprise Place, PO Box 7022, Dover, DE 19903-7022. (800) 522-0502.

Amtrak is the source of most rail travel in the US. You can rent an entire Amtrak railroad car, in case you like to travel in the company of a lot of friends.

Amtrak charges $1.00 to $2.60 per mile, depending on the length of the trip. Fees for switching cars from one train to another are extra, and it costs $75 to park a rail car when it's not being hauled. Average cost for a 3,155 mile trip from New York to Los Angeles? In most cases, about $4,100, including everything.

Private cars are usually put at the end of the train, and owners can go anywhere they want on 10 days' notice.

For more information, call (800) 872-7245.

Pilgrimage: Casey Jones Museum

Casey Jones Museum. Everybody knows the song about Casey Jones. But not everybody knows the true story. On April 30, 1900, 37-year-old John Luther Jones, nicknamed Casey after his hometown of Cayce, Kentucky, was the engineer of the Cannonball Express. He was behind schedule and speeding to make up for lost time.

This was nothing new for him: he was well known on the line as a "rounder" who went too fast. He had been suspended a total of 145 days over his eight-year career for nine different incidents ranging from missing flagmen's signals to rear-ending other trains.

On this foggy night, as he approached the town of Vaughan, he again missed signals, this time for a lumber train that was stalled. When Jones suddenly saw the train ahead, he hit the brakes and managed to slow the train from 75 to about 45 MPH before impact. His passengers were shaken but uninjured, but Jones died from a giant splinter of wood through his head.

A friend and coworker, Wallace Saunders, wrote a song about him, which spread rapidly across the country. While there were more than 100 train wrecks that year, many worse, only Casey's is still remembered—because of that song. Legend has it that

Saunders sold the rights to it for a bottle of whiskey.

Tourists from as far away as Japan, Australia and England now come to the museum at Casey Jones' death site. By the way, despite the Grateful Dead song, the museum assures us there is no reason to believe Jones was "high on cocaine" or anything else that night.

The Casey Jones Museum, off Interstate 55 about 30 minutes north of Jackson, MS. For information call (601) 673-9864.

> *"A private railroad car is not an acquired taste. One takes to it immediately."*
> —Eleanor Belmont

Tupperware®

SEALED UP TIGHT

Been to a Tupperware party lately? If not, why not? Tupperware parties are a peculiarly successful social institution—and are so square they're hip. If you need proof, look at the imitation by dozens of other products—clothes, makeup, books, toys, even "marital aids." The story behind the parties and much-imitated "burping" storage containers is one of ingenuity and perseverence.

From the Slag Heap. Earl S. Tupper began working with plastics at DuPont in the 1930s. When he and the company parted, he was determined to develop his own line of products.

Synthetic polymer polyethylene appeared in 1942. It was softer, more pliant and durable than its forerunners. To Tupper it looked like the wave of the future, but because of the war he couldn't buy the raw materials, so he started scrounging Dupont's leftovers. One day, he took home a black slag heap of discarded petroleum waste and managed to turn it into prototypes of the plastic food containers that bear his name.

Burp. First he came out with 7-ounce bathroom tumblers in novelty pastel colors, followed shortly afterward with bowls with the trademark "burping" lids. The 1947 issue of *House Beautiful* featured Tupperware in a story titled "Fine Art for 39¢."

Other plastics manufacturers were decorating their products with boomerangs and atomic-age designs, but Tupper kept his objects simple, depending on that special patented Tupper lid-seal for product differentiation.

The seal was modeled after paint can lids, only inverted. This kept the contents of the bowl fresher than other types of covered containers, and if a full Tupperware bowl was dropped, it was less likely to spew forth all over the floor.

Join the Party. Although his "Poly-T Wonder Bowls" got good press, they still weren't selling particularly well in retail stores. Tupper figured that consumers needed to see the bowls in action so he pulled Tupperware from store shelves and devised his home party system. He bypassed the stigma of door to door sales by having local distributors sell bowls in the homes of "Tupperware Hostesses" who got a free bowl for the trouble. It was a brilliant ploy and by his third year in business, he'd topped $25 million in sales.

In a few decades, the Tupperware ladies were annually selling over $900 million worth of items by sales booster rituals which have also been emulated in hundreds of other sales organizations.

Worldwide? Yup. While the Tupperware Wonderleir® bowl (the classic everybody recognizes) is popular the whole world over, some specialty items have appeared in other countries. Our favorites are the "kimono keeper," a big seller in Japan, and the "tortilla keeper," which sells like hot churros in Mexico.

"Even stupid people have a point of view." —Earl S. Tupper

Pilgrimage

Tupperware World Headquarters. The Tupperware Gallery, just a hop, skip and burp from Disney World in Florida, features over 150 historic food containers, but not everything on display here is plastic—some items go back 6,000 years including Phoenician baskets, clay pots and Grecian urns.

The piéce de résistance is the "Tupperware Home," the most exciting part of which is, of course, the kitchen.

Live models demonstrate the latest in Tupperware. Every counter, cupboard, table and refrigerator shelf is covered with

Tupper products filled with impeccably detailed plastic model food.

There's a separate play area for the kids (filled, of course, with Tuppertoys.)

You get a free sample at the end of the tour. Yet, strangely enough, you can't buy Tupperware here. The company is so firmly committed to the home party model that they refuse to exploit even this perfect selling opportunity.

3175 S. Orange Blossom Trail (near US 192), Orlando, FL 32802. See map above. Admission: free.

> *I've got that Tupper feeling deep in my heart*
>
> *Deep in my heart*
>
> *Deep in my heart*
>
> *I've got that Tupper feeling deep in my heart*
>
> *Deep in my heart to stay.*
>
> **—Tupperware Official Song**

Parties to a Great Success

While the home party was not Tupper's invention—it had been around since the 1930s, with clothing and jewelry parties—Tupper honed it to a science with the help of one of Tupperware's first dealers, Brownie Wise.

In the early days of Tuppermania, critics denounced the parties as aggressive merchandising thinly disguised as socializing. What took the sting out of the critics' words was the Tupper company's complete agreement—selling their product was the purpose of the parties. It was the suburban housewives who willingly attended the parties who made Tupperware a success.

Why did the parties succeed so well? Suburbia was a strange, new and isolated place in the 1950s. If you were a homemaker, what better way to meet your neighbors than a Tupperware party? The whole proposition was one of low risk for everybody. Turning down an invitation was as easy as saying "no thanks, I really don't need any right now." If you went and didn't like the other guests, focusing on the games and products made any real socializing unnecessary.

Also, unlike a cocktail party or a barbecue, you didn't have to reciprocate a Tupperware party. An attendee could fulfill any sense of obligation by buying an inexpensive butter dish or measuring spoon set. And even if the hostess had a disastrous time, at least she got some Tupperware out of it, plus the electric frying pan or cake mixer she received as her special hostess gift.

How to Host Your Own Party

Feeling the need for Tupperware, and can't get anybody to invite you to a party? Try hosting your own.

• Check your white pages under Tupperware. If nobody's listed there, call the Tupperware Headquarters at (800) 858-7221. They'll be glad to connect you with representatives in your area.

• You can host a party just about anywhere: At home, at work (after hours or during lunch, of course), at a bridal shower, local club, or anywhere that will donate or rent you a room for a couple of hours.

• This *is* the 1990s: men are even encouraged to participate. Mixed, even all-male parties are not uncommon.

• The traditional party takes about two hours of friendly, frenetic fun and games to get everyone into that Tupper Feeling. Don't have time? You can sign up for what Time magazine calls a "Yupperwear Party"—a 20 minute pitch for lunch breaks and the like. New products offered along with the traditional egg trays and Jello molds? Tuppertoys, desk accessories, even plastic portable desks.

• Our favorite party sales trick isn't the Tupperware spoon race—it's a sly one. They provide the pencils for filling out the order forms—but none of them have erasers attached, making it all the more difficult to change your mind later.

Every 2.7 seconds, a Tupperware party begins somewhere in the world.

UFOS

UFOs Through Space & Time

We're not alone—folks have been filing UFO reports for centuries.

• One of the first written accounts, recorded on Egyptian papyrus over 3,400 years old, describes foul-smelling circles of fire about 16' in diameter. "These things became more numerous in the skies than ever. They shone more than the brightness of the sun, and extended to the limits of the four supports of the heavens."

• Over 700 years before the term "flying saucer" was coined, Japanese described an object spotted on the night of October 27, 1180, as a flying "earthenware vessel."

• In the year 1235, a Japanese general called for an investigation of mysterious lights seen by his troops. He relaxed when he received the report: "It is ...only the wind making the stars sway." Scientific debunking or governmental whitewash? You decide.

• A rash of UFO sightings—dozens of them—took place in 1896 and 1897. Most reports were of airships, generally "cigar-shaped" and "metallic." 10,000 Kansas City residents saw a great black airship, and in Everest, Kansas, people described an object resembling a 25- to 30-foot long Indian canoe with "a searchlight of varying colors." One California man reported hearing a "mysterious airship" crew singing "Nearer, My God, to Thee."

• In 1961 Joe Simonton, a plumber in Eagle River, Wisconsin, filled a water jug for a UFO that hovered over his yard. In return he received four cookies. Northwestern University's analysis of the cookie content was "flour, sugar and grease."

UFO Sightings of the Rich & Famous

• Jimmy Carter, when governor of Georgia, reported seeing a UFO on January 6, 1969. "It was the darndest thing I've ever seen. It was big; it was very bright; it changed colors; and it was about the size of the moon."

• Muhammad Ali says he saw a cigar-shaped UFO over the New Jersey Turnpike and one "like a huge electric light bulb" in Central Park.

• Professional courtesy? William Shatner, Capt. Kirk of *Star Trek*, saw a silvery spacecraft above him as he pushed his stalled motorcycle through the Mojave Desert. He reported that it advised him, through an unspoken message, about which way to go for help.

• Dick Gregory saw two green lights and one red light darting about the sky for 40 minutes.

• Jamie Farr, Klinger on *M*A*S*H*, saw a zigzagging light that stopped and hovered over his car near Yuma, Arizona.

• Jackie Gleason saw UFOs in London and Florida. About one-third of the Great One's 3,700-volume library dealt with UFOs, the occult, and parapsychology.

TRUE FACTS

• Spoil-sport psychiatrist Carl Jung considered UFOs merely a psychological projection of people's hopes and fears in an uncertain world.

• The usually stuffy Soviet Tass news agency reported a UFO landing in Voronezh in October, 1989. Out from the "banana-shaped" ship came tiny-headed, three-eyed, humanoid creatures, nine or ten feet tall, and a small robot. They made a short promenade into the bushes, said not a word about borscht or perestroika, strolled back into the ship, and departed.

• "Reach Out and Touch...Something?" In November, 1988, AT&T offered New Yorkers a chance to send messages into outer space toll-free. Using "space phones" set up at their headquarters and satellite dishes, AT&T beamed messages "out there" in a straight line where they'll hit something decades hence. Probably "Hi, we're not here right now, please leave a message..."

• Over half of all Americans believe UFOs are real objects that come from other worlds.

How *"Flying Saucers"* Got Their Name

On June 24, 1947, Kenneth Arnold, a businessman and pilot, was flying a small plane over Washington's Cascade Mountains. He claimed he saw nine circular objects flying in formation at high speed, several times faster than any jet he'd ever seen. Later that day, he told reporters that the mysterious objects "flew like a saucer would if you skipped it across the water." They picked up on the phrase and the "flying saucer" era began.

UFO QUOTES

"The Air Force is not hiding any UFO information. And I do not qualify this in any way." **—Richard E. Horner, Asst. Secy. of the Air Force, 1958**

"I've often wondered what if all of us in the world discovered that we were threatened by…a power from outer space, from another planet? Wouldn't we all of a sudden find that we didn't have any differences between us at all…and wouldn't we come together to fight that particular threat?"

—Ronald Reagan, May, 1988

In Case You Wondered

• **Close Encounter of the First Kind:** A UFO is spotted at close range, but doesn't interact with the environment.

• **Close Encounter of the Second Kind:** A UFO interacts with the environment, causing physical effects like scorched grass, stalled auto engines or appliances, or scared animals. Humans may experience minor burns or cloudy thinking.

• **Close Encounter of the Third Kind:** Contact with alien beings in or near a UFO, up to and including giving a ride in a space ship or human abduction.

Radio Active: Waves of Panic

"We take you now to the Meridian Room in the Hotel Park Plaza in downtown New York, where you will be entertained by the music of Ramon Raquello and his orchestra...Ladies and gentlemen, we interrupt our program of dance music to bring you a special bulletin...at 8:50 p.m. a huge, flaming object, believed to be a meteorite, fell on a farm in the neighborhood of Grovers Mill, New Jersey...Just a minute! Something's happening! Ladies and gentlemen, this is terrific!...It's coming this way. About 20 yards to my right..."

(Crash of microphone, silence.)

It was October 30, 1938, the night Americans got the Halloween eve scare of their lives.

The Mercury Theatre of the Air began its broadcast on 100 CBS stations with an announcement that the following program was a dramatization of H.G. Wells' *War of the Worlds*. Six million heard the broadcast. Unfortunately, many didn't tune in till Charlie McCarthy's opening skit on another channel had ended, missing Orson Welles' opening disclaimer.

The show was produced as if it were a series of news bulletins breaking into regular radio programming. Despite announcements at the end of each commercial and station break, tens of thousands of people took the invasion from Mars as real.

• Thousands phoned local newspapers, but couldn't get through because the lines were jammed.

• Mistaken for a Martian spaceship, Grovers Mill's water tower became pockmarked with bullet holes.

• People in and around New York City hid in their basements. Hundreds of others ran to the nearest police station, screaming and seeking shelter.

• Residents of Grovers Mill packed themselves into cars. Some drove to Trenton, some to the next state, some just drove.

• In some places, traffic was at a standstill. Folks jammed the streets looking at the sky.

• One hospital in Newark, N.J. treated 15 for shock and hysteria.

Why did people react so weirdly? With Naziism rising and war just over the horizon, people were inclined to take invasion news of any sort very seriously. And a lot of it had to do with how well the production was written and performed. If you haven't heard it, get a copy (below) and listen to it with the lights out.

The original broadcast that shook the world, parts I & II (two cassettes). #80250 / #80251, $7.96 + 2.50 shipping from Johnson Smith Co., 4514 19th St. Court East, P.O. Box 25600, Bradenton, FL 34206-5600. (813) 747-2356.

"In a time of nuclear threat, it is not surprising that people should look to the stars for salvation." —John W. White

Where Do They Come From?

Ufologists have widely differing theories about what brings ETs to Earth.

• Ufologist Thomas Stults believes that "we are being investigated by seven to nine alien races" who kidnap humans to conduct scientific experiments on them, in part to improve gene pools so that we'll be better-equipped for space travel. He also maintains that President Nixon's resignation was forced because Nixon planned to tell America the truth about UFOs. To stop him, powers in the government fed damaging information to Woodward and Bernstein.

• Jose Arguelles, in his 1987 book *The Mayan Factor*, claimed the Mayans were extraterrestrials who left instructions for the Harmonic Convergence to guide our troubled planet. By 2012, we'll make great evolutionary progress and become fit company for other life forms in our galaxy.

UFOs Turn Into IFOs

90% of UFOs are eventually found to be of this world. Some common Identified Flying Objects:

• *Aircraft*
• *Birds*
• *Falling satellites and other space debris*
• *Kites*
• *Unusual atmospheric conditions (ball lightning, for example)*
• *Weather balloons*
• *Meteors*
• *Planets (Jupiter, Mars, Saturn, and especially Venus)*
• *Deliberate hoaxes*
• *Swarms of migrating insects (Electrical fields from storm fronts cause insects' antennae to glow).*

You a Friend, or UFO?

Westerns are old hat, claims *Alien Nation* director John Carpenter, because "alien invaders, with their tremendous power for good and evil, have come to represent our new myths."

School of Cosmology

The Unarius Academy of Science. Have you ever wondered about the meaning of life? Life on other planets? In 1954, cosmic couple Dr. Ernest L. and Ruth E. Norman co-founded UNARIUS (Universal Articulate Interdimensional Understanding of Space) to advance the understanding of these big questions. We give their videotape library (over 100 titles) four stars for inspiration, production values and other-worldly entertainment even for (especially for?) non-believers. These are tapes you'll watch again and again.

And for something you don't get at Harvard—students in their on-site classes are personally inspired and telepathically guided in their studies by Uriel, an Advanced Spiritual Being incarnate on this plane in the body of Ruth E. Norman herself. She drives a pink Cadillac with a flying saucer welded on the top.

Unarius Publications Catalog is $2.00, with 60 pages of fascinating stories like:

• *Have You Lived on Other Worlds Before?*

• *My 2000 Year Psychic Memory as Mary of Bethany, 13th Disciple to Jesus of Nazareth*

• *Underground Cities of Mars*—a video documentary (!)

145 S. Magnolia Ave., El Cajon, CA 92020. (619) 447-4170.

Out of This World Books

• *Communion* by Whitley Strieber. Details the author's abduction by aliens from a cabin in upstate New York, on 12/26/85. He describes two types of beings: some 3 1/2 feet tall, and others "about five feet tall, very slender and delicate, with extremely prominent and mesmerizing black slanted eyes... and almost vestigial mouth and nose."

$17.45 + 1.50 shipping from William Morrow Publishing, 39 Plymouth St., Fairfield, NJ 07004. (800) 843-9389.

• *Intruders: The Incredible Visitations at Copley Woods* by Budd Hopkins. Tells the story of "Kathie Davis," who recalled a "dream" of aliens removing her fetus. The next day she suffered what doctors called an unexplained lost pregnancy. Includes reports about aliens displaying babies that abducted women thought were their own half-human, half-alien children.

$4.95 + 2.00 shipping from Random House, 400 Hahn Rd., Westminster, MD 21157. (800) 733-3000.

• *UFO—Abductions: A Dangerous Game* by Philip J. Klass. A leading UFO debunker, Klass takes a skeptical look at the sudden rash of abduction claims. "Are extraterrestrials abducting human beings and subjecting them to terrifying physical examinations? Have UFOnauts invaded the bedrooms of teenage girls to impregnate them and later return to remove their unborn babies?" He thinks not.

$16.95 + 3.00 shipping from Prometheus Books, 59 John Glenn Dr., Amherst NY 14228. (800) 421-0351.

"It Was Sorta Cigar Shaped, Officer!"

Now you can create a stir in your city with this Giant Solar UFO. It can hover hundreds of feet in the sky. Powered by the sun, it needs no motor, helium or batteries. Thin plastic film, comes with a 65 ft. nylon cord. 10 x 2'.

#7572, $4.98 + 1.35 shipping. Johnson Smith Co., 4514 19th Court East, P.O. Box 25500, Bradenton, FL 34206-5500. (813) 747-2356.

"Hey, Mr. Spaceman
Won't you please take me along
I won't do anything wrong
Hey, Mr. Spaceman
Won't you please take me along for a ride..."
—The Byrds

Our Favorite TV Martians

• V's purple people eaters
• Uncle Martin, *My Favorite Martian*
• Mork from Planet Ork
• Space guide Ford Prefect, *The Hitchhiker's Guide to the Galaxy*
• *Star Trek's* Spock
• Cally from Planet Auron, *Blake's 7*
• *SNL's* Coneheads

Close Encounter Of The Toy Kind

Out of this world UFO is out of control! Watch it bounce off walls as it blinks colored lights. Two AA batteries not included.

#3964-1, $7.98 + 1.95 shipping from Miles Kimball, 41 West Eighth Avenue, Oshkosh, WI 54906.

Our Favorite Bad Aliens

• *The Thing* (1951). Starring James Arness in the title role, it was called "the ultimate hostile alien invaders film of the 1950s." This one serves up that memorable line, "Keep watching the skies." Remade in color in 1982.

• *Invaders from Mars* (1953). In this film of the early flying saucer era, the whole invasion is seen through the eyes of a young boy. Remade in 1986.

• *War of the Worlds* (1953). Martians lay waste to Los Angeles, which is almost enough to consider them for the "Good Aliens" category.

• *Plan 9 From Outer Space* (1959). Weird and wonderfully bad combination space alien/walking dead story.

• *Adventures of Buckaroo Banzai Across the Eighth Dimension* (1984). The underlying premise is that the famous Orson Welles *War of the Worlds* radio broadcast was true.

FAVORITE GOOD ALIENS

• *The Day the Earth Stood Still* (1951). A highly refined spaceman climbs out of his flying saucer with a warning to Earthlings about mending our dangerous nuclear ways. "Klaatu Barada Nikto!"

• *Close Encounters of the Third Kind* (1977). Setting the stage for *E.T.* (1982), these were the first of the cute 'n' cuddly childlike space aliens.

• *Earth Girls Are Easy* (1989). Can a goofy alien find love with an equally goofy manicurist?

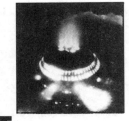

E.T.—Phone Home

The "UFO Contact News Line" was formed by Paul Shepherd to spread the word that aliens are visiting Earth. A recent message revealed that the US government has secretly established underground bases for otherworlders (we *thought* they were illegal aliens).

(213) 976-UFOS. $2 / first minute, then $1 per min., plus long distance charges to Los Angeles.

Unidentified Buying Object

This 11-inch, aerodynamic, high-impact flying saucer disk has battery-powered light-emitting diodes set into the rim. When it's flying, you see lots of weird multi-colored optical illusions—the lights seem to stop spinning, hover, reverse—which make you feel you're watching a UFO with portholes.

$16.98 + 3.50 shipping from The Lighter Side, 4514 19th St. Court East, P.O. Box 25600, Bradenton, FL 34206-5600. (813) 747-2356.

Great UFO Book Titles

We never read these, but from the titles alone, we wish we had. We found them in the **Books in Print** listings.

• *UFO Connections of Jesus Christ*
• *Nazi UFO Secrets & Bases Exposed*
• *UFO Contact from Undersea*
• *UFO Contact from the Pleiades: A Preliminary Investigation Report*
• *UFO Contact from Planet UMMO, Vol. I: The Mystery of UMMO*
• *UFO Contact from Planet Acart, from Utopia to Reality*
• *UFOs, Space Brothers & the Aquarian Age*
• *My Friend From Beyond the Earth*
• *UFOs: What on Earth is Happening?*
• *Saucerama*

What to Do If You See a UFO

The Center for UFO Studies (CUFOS) advises the following procedures if the Martians come:

• Get witnesses to watch the thing with you. Sightings by one person just don't carry much weight.

• Take pictures if you can. Try to get background and foreground details in the pictures.

• As soon as you can, write down details such as how long you saw the UFO, the color, estimated size, direction, and behavior. Get names and addresses of the other witnesses.

• If the UFO touches down on the ground, don't disturb the area. Take pictures from outside the area.

• Contact CUFOS to report a UFO sighting by calling their 24-hour phone line: (206) 722-3000.

"It Looked Like Something You'd See In The Movies...Or On TV!"

• Jupiter 2 from *Lost In Space*. 6 in. model, $15.95.

• *War Of The Worlds'* Martian War Machine. 8 in. model, $19.95.

Add 3.75 shipping to each. Rocketships & Accessories, 625 S. 4th St., Philadelphia, PA 19147. (215) 923-7465.

"And It Made These Weird Sounds!"

It does everything but fly. This UFO Radio Cassette even puts on a galactic light show.

#C739094, $149.00 + 9.00 shipping. Sync, Hanover, PA 17333-0042. (800) 722-9979.

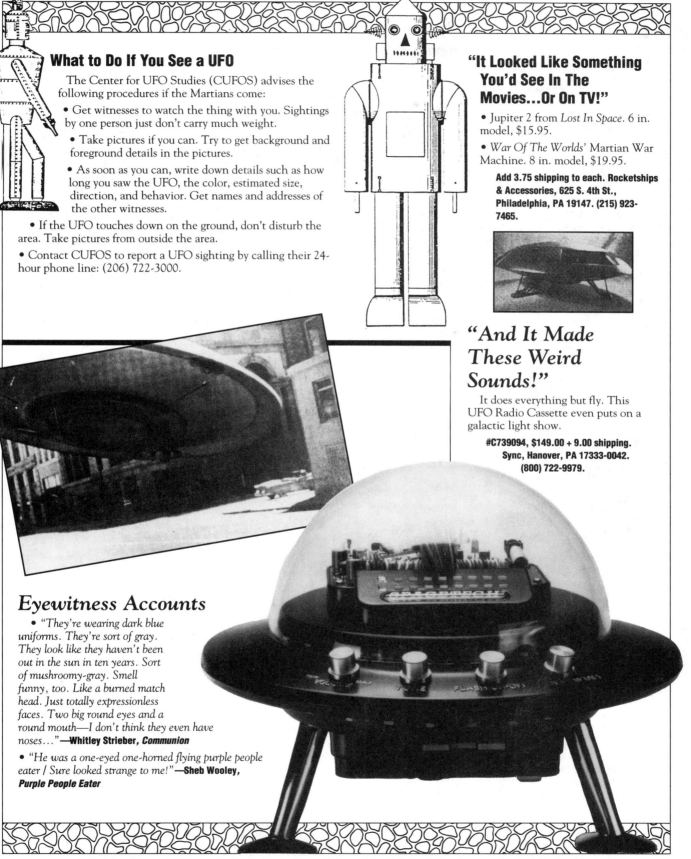

Eyewitness Accounts

• *"They're wearing dark blue uniforms. They're sort of gray. They look like they haven't been out in the sun in ten years. Sort of mushroomy-gray. Smell funny, too. Like a burned match head. Just totally expressionless faces. Two big round eyes and a round mouth—I don't think they even have noses..."* —**Whitley Strieber,** *Communion*

• *"He was a one-eyed one-horned flying purple people eater / Sure looked strange to me!"* —**Sheb Wooley,** *Purple People Eater*

The town of Elmwood, WI (pop. 990) plowed a UFO landing pad into a soybean field shaped like a human and an ET shaking hands.

Invade Someone's Space

• *Cut & Assemble UFOs That Fly: 8 Full-Color Models* by David Kawami.

• *Cut & Fold Extraterrestrial Invaders That Fly* by M. Grater.

Assemble your own paper UFOs that you can fly around your own personal space. Each craft comes with a cut-out alien, suitable for abduction and examination.

$2.95 each + 2.50 shipping per order, Dover Publications, 11 East 2nd Street, Mineola, NY 11501.

I Was a Communist Martian for the FBI

The Flying Saucer. The first UFO movie ever! Features Denver Pyle in this tale of special agents, UFOs and Communist scientists in Alaska.

#RNDV 1422, $14.95 + 2.00 shipping from Rhino Video, 2225 Colorado Avenue, Santa Monica, CA 90404-3598 (800) 432-3670.

Join the Interstellar Club

• **J. Allen Hynek Center for UFO Studies (CUFOS).** Founded by the late J. Allen Hynek, who was the chief scientific advisor for the Air Force's Project Blue Book program of UFO study. He became a spokesman, advocating the serious continued collection and analysis of UFO reports. CUFOS has an extensive library of UFO information. A major contributor to the organization has been movie director Steven Spielberg, who consulted with Dr. Hynek while making *Close Encounters of the Third Kind* (the title is Hynek's and he even made a cameo appearance in the film).

2457 W. Peterson Ave., Chicago, IL 60659. (312) 271-3611. Subscription to *The International UFO Reporter* is $25 per year.

• **Committee for the Scientific Investigation of Claims of the Paranormal (CSICOP).** This is an investigative organization of skeptical scientists, educators, journalists, and others who maintain that "extraordinary claims require extraordinary evidence." Conducts educational seminars to counter unsubstantiated claims about UFOs and other paranormal phenomena. Publishes a quarterly, *The Skeptical Inquirer.*

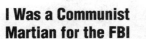

Dues: $25 per year (includes subscription to quarterly) to Box 229, Buffalo, NY 14215-0229. (716) 834-3222.

• **Mutual UFO Network (MUFON).** Founded in 1969, investigates UFO sightings, sponsors an Annual International UFO Symposium, and publishes the *MUFON UFO Journal,* a 24-page monthly that reports on significant UFO incidents, research and topical issues (sample copy available for $2.50).

Dues: $25 per year (includes subscription to journal) to 103 Oldtowne Road Sequin, TX 78155-4099. (512) 379-9216.

GO WEST, YOUNG MAN!

The Old West. It's a part of the American spirit: prospectors, homesteaders, Indians, cowboys and outlaws. And land, lots of land.

What we think of as "the West" was defined in the last half of the 19th century. Before that "the West" was whatever land was just beyond European settlements (earlier, when the editorialist exhorted "Go west, young man!" he was talking about Ohio and Michigan).

While some adventurers arrived much earlier, it wasn't until after 1850 that large waves of white settlers began to arrive west of the Mississippi.

Free real estate was one incentive: in 1862 Congress passed The Homestead Act, which provided 160 acres of free land to any person who would live on

YIP···EE!

THE WEST

it and "improve" it for five years. The government also gave enormous tracts of land to the railroads, which extended their lines westward to develop new markets. By 1890, the settlers had engulfed the region at such a rate that the Census Bureau reported that no frontiers remained in the United States.

It was the cowboys who became the most famous symbols of the West. Their reputation for bravery and hard work turned them into heroes, at least from a great distance back East. (In Western towns they were treated with all the respect modern itinerant farm workers get).

Much of what we think about the West is only a myth—so many of our cherished beliefs were dreamed up by an entertainment industry unconcerned with historical accuracy.

What many people don't realize is that there were never more than a total of 100,000 cowboys in U.S. history, and their heyday was really only about 20 years, from the mid-1860s to the mid-1880s. That was the time when cowboys tended great herds of cattle on the open range and took them on trail drives to railway stations for shipment east. Just a minor part of American history, but our myth-making has been so successful that some international visitors are surprised to find that nobody wears cowboy garb any more.

That the West was fertile land for stories was discovered early. *Malaeska: The Indian Wife of the White Hunter*, published in 1860, established the popular long-lived genre of the "dime novel."

Then, starting with *The Great Train Robbery* in 1903, Hollywood got on that horse and rode it until it could run no more.

JUST SAY WHOA

Round-Up Time

ROUNDUP OF WESTERN FACTS

• Between 1860 and 1880, more than $300 million worth of silver and gold came out of Nevada's Comstock Lode. In 1876, Virginia City, in the heart of the mining area, had a population of 23,000, which was served by 20 laundries, 54 dry-good stores, 6 churches, and 150 saloons.

• Usual pay for a cowboy was food, a place to sleep in the bunkhouse (when he was within riding distance of the ranch), and a dollar a day.

• Beside the cowboys, two other men were crucial for a trail drive. One was the horse wrangler, often low man on the social scale, who looked after the "remuda," the herd of extra horses needed since each cowboy might go through several mounts in a day. The other was the cook, who managed all the provisions, acted as doctor, and drove the balky oxen that pulled the chuck wagon.

• Cowboys were also called cowpokes or cowpunchers because they poked cows with sticks to get them onto loading ramps.

• A trail drive covered up to 1,000 miles and often took some two or three months (the herd traveling typically about fifteen miles a day). The drives started in Texas and followed the Chisholm Trail north to where the railroad lines ended in boisterous new Kansas towns like Abilene, Newton, Wichita, Hays City, Caldwell, Ellsworth, and (the wildest of all) Dodge City.

Long Little Doggy

Saddle up your pet dachshund or cat. #D252, $9.50 + 2.50 shipping. Chicken Boy, PO Box 292000, Los Angeles, CA 90029. (800) 422-0505.

Shake, Pardner!

German-made western scenario snow dome. Hours of simpleminded fun!

$7.95 + 4.00 shipping from Ruby Montana's Pinto Pony Catalog, 603 Second Avenue, Seattle, WA 98104. (206) 621-PONY.

Ghost Writers in the Sky

Ghost Town Quarterly. No kidding! This is a magazine about ghost towns! It's for anyone "interested in the colorful traditions, history, and heritage, past and present, of ghost towns all over the United States, Canada, and Mexico." Articles, poetry, photographs. Close your eyes and— there now! — you can shore nuff see the creaky saloon door hanging on one hinge, and hear the tumbleweeds blowing through town.

$25 for 8 back issues from PO Box 714, Philipsburg, MT 59858. (406) 859-3365.

Do Fence Me in

Ouch! It's been said that barbed wire played a role more important than the six-shooter in the development of Texas.

As the Plains states got settled in the 1860s, barbed wire started bitter wars between cowboys and farmers, but met a real need: it defined property lines and kept cattle in and intruders out. Hundreds of designs were invented, each more elaborate than the other, and are now valued by the thousands of collectors.

• **The Barbed Wire Collector.** Here's a publication to fill you in on how to get started collecting, where the barbed wire museums are — several of them are battling it out for the biggest and best — and how to join a collectors' group.

$12 year, 6 issues. 1322 Lark, Lewisville, TX 75067. (214) 436-6762.

• *Barbs, Prongs, Point, Prickers & Stickers* by Robert Clifton. A great field guide of what cowboys used to call "the Devil's rope." Lots of illustrations help identify year and manufacturer.

$17.95 + 1.50 shipping. University of Oklahoma Press, PO Box 787, Norman, OK 73070-0787. (800) 627-7377.

Black in the Saddle Again

The Black Cowboy Association. According to some historians, as many as 25% of all cowboys were African-Americans, many of whom headed west after the all-Black cavalry units disbanded after the Civil War (many other cowboys were Hispanic). Well-known Black cowboys included "One Horse Charley," Nat Love, Ben Hodges, and

Isom Dart, possibly the best horseman in the West. The BCA commemorates that heritage and teaches city kids about horses, starting with a shovel and working their way up. To join, you needn't be a cowboy, or even Black.

$15 year. 4207 Whittle Avenue, Oakland, CA 94602. (510) 531-7583.

Western Civilization

• **Gene Autry Western Heritage Museum.** A new, $54 million museum designed to convey the spirit of the West. Disney Studios assisted in staging the displays like Buffalo Bill's firearms, posters, costumes, and saddle and Annie Oakley's rifle and hat. Don't miss the Heritage Theater's imaginative films and special effects.

4700 Zoo Dr., Griffith Park, Los Angeles, CA 90027. (213) 667-2000.

• **National Cowboy Hall of Fame & Western Heritage Center.** There's lots to see in this museum sponsored by 17 western states like a gold mine, a stage coach, a chuck wagon from Texas, and a sheepherder's wagon.

Check out the Rodeo Hall of Fame, the Western art display, and the Western Performers Hall of Fame featuring John Wayne, Walter Brennan, Slim Pickens, and many others.

Or if you can't make it in person, subscribe to Persimmon Hill, the museum's official publication. $20 for four lavish issues.

1700 Northeast 63rd St., Oklahoma City, OK 73111. (405) 478-2250.

Bad Guys

Encyclopedia of Western Gunfighters by Bill O'Neal. The facts on 255 gunmen: dates and places of births, their aliases and nicknames, brief biographies, and — what makes for some especially fascinating reading — detailed accounts of each of their gunfights and their deaths. What's interesting is the number of famous gunmen — Wyatt Earp and Wild Bill Hickok for two — who easily jumped from being outlaws to lawmen and back again at the drop of a 10-gallon hat.

$16.95 plus 1.50 shipping from University of Oklahoma Press, PO Box 787, Norman, OK 73070-0787. (800) 627-7377.

Shirt-Kickin' Cow Gals

Full-colored photo silk-screen of 1940s rodeo queens on 100% pre-shrunk white cotton t-shirt. M, L, or XL.

$20.95 + 6.00 shipping from Ruby Montana's Pinto Pony Catalog, 603 Second Avenue, Seattle, WA 98104. (206) 621-PONY.

In the classic 1956 Western *Gunfight at the O.K. Corral* the shootout lasted 6 minutes on the screen but took 44 hours to film.

Selections from the Back Corral

Lonesome cowboys sang mournful tunes to pass time on the open range. Not only did they make the cowboy feel better, they soothed the cattle and made them easier to handle.

These are two of our favorite collections of cowboy music from the 1930s and '40s. Either or both are great samplers of Patsy Montana, Roy Rogers, Sons of the Pioneers, Tex Ritter, Bob Wills and more.

• *Legendary Songs of the Old West.* 4 records (only), 40 songs.

#M5548X, $23.95 + 4.50 shipping from Publishers Central Bureau, 1 Champion Avenue, Avenel, NJ 07131. (800) 752-3396.

• *Back in the Saddle Again.* 2 CDs (only), 28 songs, plus 24-page documentation.

#R1019, $35.00 + 5.50 shipping from the Country Music Hall of Fame, Mail Order Dept., 4 Music Square, Nashville, TN 37203 (800) 255-2357.

Dance Like a Cowboy

Be a cowpoke, not a slowpoke. These instructional videotapes will get you dancing two-steps, line dances, swings, waltzes and polkas in no time. While you can buy the whole set of 11 tapes, why not take it slow an' easy-like with tape #1?

#TDP001, Tape #1: *Two-Step Dancin' Beginner*— Cotton-Eyed Joe & more. $39.95 + 4.95 shipping. #TDP301, 11 videos. $399.45 + 6.95 shipping. Special Interest Video, 100 Enterprise Place, Box 7022, Dover, DE 19903. (800) 522-0502.

Talk Like a Cowboy

Cowboy Slang by Edgar "Frosty" Potter. Those cowpokes shore had a way with words — heck, I guess they had plenty of time to think up new expressions when the dogies weren't acting up.

Even if the closest you've got to a cow is a milk carton, you can spice up your conversation by dropping in a little cowboy now and then. We shore find it knocks the snakes outta the trees at cocktail parties. Try a coupla these out, and don't forget the twang:

• "Buckshot shore leaves a mean an' oozy corpse."

• "Hot 'nough to sunburn a horned toad."

• "As pleased as a little dog with two tails."

• "When the Lord poured in his brains, someone musta jaggled his arm."

• "He had a nose yuh could store a small dog in."

   • "Whatever jackass yuh got yore likker from shore musta had kidney trouble."

     • "He's so cautious, he'd ride a mile to spit."

$5.00 + 1.50 shipping from Golden West Publishers, 4113 No. Longview, Phoenix, AZ 85014. (602) 265-4392.

No Strings Attached

Sterling Guitar Earrings, #G0259, $32.50 + 5.50. Pin, #G0260, $19.50 + 4.50. The Country Music Hall of Fame, 4 Music Sq., Nashville, TN 37203 (800) 255-2357.

The Reel West

"*More six-shooters have been fired, more cattle rustled, more banks and stagecoaches held up, more cowboys have brawled in saloons, more wagons have rumbled westward, more Indians have been shot from their ponies and more cavalry have ridden to the rescue in the movies than the real West ever knew.*"

—Tony Thomas, The West That Never Was

Cowboy Commandments

1. He must not take unfair advantage of an enemy.
2. He must never go back on his word.
3. He must always tell the truth.
4. He must be gentle with children, elderly people and animals.
5. He must not possess racially or religiously intolerant ideas.
6. He must help people in distress.
7. He must be a good worker.
8. He must respect women, parents and his nation's laws.
9. He must neither drink nor smoke.
10. He must be a patriot.

—Attributed to Gene Autry

A Cowboy Needs a Hat...

The stetson, the traditional felt cowboy hat with a high crown and a wide brim, was named for its designer, John Batterson Stetson. He had gone west during the Civil War and discovered that cowboys didn't have the headgear they needed. He began to manufacture the new hats in 1865 in Philadelphia—popular with cowboys, who also called them a "John B."

I SEE BY YOUR OUTFIT...

The "Dark Brown Cattleman" felt hat has a faux reptile band, 5-1/2" crown, and 3-1/2" brim. Shepler's carries all manner of Western apparel—boots, moccasins, jeans, shirts, bolo ties, leather belts, handcrafted jewelry, and more. Call 'em for a catalog.

#L1-096-518D, $19.99 + 4.50 shipping from Shepler's, P.O. Box 7702, Wichita, KS 67277-7702. (800) 833-7007.

Head Lights, Trail Lights

Blazing Trails. Strings of cowboy-motif lights shaped like boots, cow skulls and covered wagons.

$20.95 + 6.00 shipping. Ruby Montana's Pinto Pony Catalog, 603 Second Avenue, Seattle, WA 98104. (206) 621-PONY.

Buffaloed by PR

The creation of the Western myth had much to do with "Buffalo Bill" Cody. He became the hero of the newsstands when author Ned Buntline wrote about him (Cody's resume: Pony Express rider at age 14, pal of Wild Bill Hickok, stagecoach driver, buffalo hunter, scout, and Indian fighter).

In 1883 Cody formed a wild west show which traveled for 30 years with a cast of 600 people and 500 animals.

On your way to Yellowstone? Visit the Buffalo Bill Historical Center displaying everything from his boyhood home to his guns, coach, career highlights and much more.

Contact the Center at PO Box 100, Cody, WY 82414. (307) 587-4771.

Deep in the Heart

The Homesick Texan. Though life has been cruel to those unfortunate folks who have had to leave Texas (or even worse, those who've never even been), there is solace available in the form of "the quarterly publication for Texans outside of Texas."

It's full of state news—politics, business, sports, "Texana" and more—and acts as a lifeline for poor souls damned to the hell of foreign states, even countries. Miss Texan eats? Check out the ads for mail-order goodies: barbecue beef (overnight on dry ice), hot sauce, tortilla chips, and cans of jalapeno peppers. **Weee-Haaa!**

$15 per year for 4 issues from: 4436 Amherst Dallas, TX 75225 (800) 733-TEXAN

"INJUNS!!!"

Ugh! Most Westerns portrayed Native Americans in a stereotyped way, either as stoic noble savages or more often as ferocious red devils. They usually spoke "indianlect," a form of broken English.

Some Western films attempted to show Indians more realistically, especially after the 1950s. But that was rare and white actors more often played Indians than true Native Americans. Still, there were some notable Indian actors long before *Dances With Wolves*:

• **Jay Silverheels.** Born with the name of Harold J. Smith, this Native Canadian (son of a Mohawk chief) played Tonto on the *Lone Ranger* TV series. Comedian Joe E. Brown had met professional lacrosse player Smith after a game and had urged him to try his hand at acting.

• **Chief Thundercloud.** Native American (Cherokee) Victor Daniels, while not strictly a chief, played dozens of roles in Westerns from the 1930s into the '50s. A former radio actor, singer, and rodeo performer, Chief

Thundercloud became a hero in his own serials in the 1940s.

• **Chief Dan George.** Actually Chief Nawanath of British Columbia's Burrard tribe, George (who started his acting career late in life) had an imposing demeanor that captured attention. He would only play positive native roles, including the humorous Old Lodge Skins in *Little Big Man*.

• **Will Sampson.** A Creek Indian who achieved notable success as Chief Bromden in *One Flew Over the Cuckoo's Nest*, Sampson played in a number of Westerns including *The Outlaw Josey Wales* and *Buffalo Bill and the Indians*.

• **Iron Eyes Cody.** Born in 1907, Cody's Cherokee parents took him to Hollywood at an early age (his father was a film consultant). He first played Indian children and grew into adult roles during a long career that ranged from a 1912 Western by D.W. Griffith to TV's *How the West Was Won* in 1982.

Custer Stand

The Custer Album: A Pictorial Biography of General George A. Custer by Lawrence A. Frost. Author Frost is a nationally recognized authority on the famously hapless general. He tells Custer's story from his boyhood through West Point, the Civil War (in a few short years he rose from lieutenant to the youngest general in the Union Army), and all the way to the Last Stand. Lots of photographs. Hero or fool? You decide.

$14.95 plus 1.50 shipping. University of Oklahoma Press, PO Box 787, Norman, OK 73070-0787. (800) 627-7377.

Custer's Army In Pieces

Over 100 artists have painted Custer's last stand, usually filled with gross inaccuracies (Custer with long hair, a sword, pistols, etc.). Edgar Paxson did 20 years of research before painting this 6 x 10' canvas in 1899. Put it all together again with this 500 piece puzzle.

#470001, $14.50 + 4.50 shipping from the Buffalo Bill Historical Center, PO Box 2630, Cody, WY 82414. (800) 533-3838.

Hip Hopi Music

Sounds of Indian America—Plains & Southwest. If you're interested in traditional Native American music, Indian House is a good source. For 25 years they've been recording songs of war, peace, love, and even peyote. For an overview, we like this one, recorded live at the 48th Inter-Tribal Indian Ceremony in Gallup, NM, which includes a Hopi Buffalo Dance, Zuni Rain Songs, a Crow Sun Dance, a Laguna Turkey Dance and a Kiowa Attack Dance.

#IH 9501 cassette, $10.00 + 1.00 handling. Indian House, P.O. Box 472, Taos, NM 87571. (505) 776-2953. Send SASE for free catalog.

Hollywood Cowboys

★ Tom Mix

Maybe the greatest cowboy star of them all, this former rodeo performer had a daredevil personality that came across "great guns" on the screen. He made hundreds of films from 1909 to 1935, earning over $10,000 a week before his death in a car crash.

• Mix was once night marshal in the one-room jail house of Dewey, OK, so the town built the **Tom Mix Museum,** with the most Mixabilia anywhere.
721 North Delaware, Dewey, OK 74029. (918) 534-1555.

• See the **Tom Mix Monument** (below) on Route 89 southeast of Phoenix, at the spot where Mix's 1937 Cord roadster missed a zig-zag.

• *The Tom Mix Book* by M.G. Norris tells his life story.
$24.95 ppd. World of Yesterday, Rte 3, Box 263, Waynesville, NC 28786. (704) 648-5647.

★ Gene Autry

The screen's first successful singing cowboy was the top money-making Western star from 1937 to 1942, when he went into the army. He later bought a number of television and radio stations and became owner of the California Angels baseball team.

★ William Boyd

The screen's Hopalong Cassidy was a good guy in a black hat. He got his Hollywood name playing a character in a 1935 film who limped as a result of a bullet wound. Boyd made 66 features for the movies; in 1948 the features started to be shown on television.

★ Duncan Renaldo

"The Cisco Kid" was a versatile actor who had played for almost every studio in Hollywood. Born in Spain, he was an assistant Captain in the Brazilian Merchant Marine, and was a portrait painter in New York.

★ "Lash" LaRue

The use of a 15' bullwhip was a publicist's brainstorm, but it created "Lash" LaRue's on-screen identity in his successful movie career in the '40s and '50s. In spite of an all-black outfit, he stood on the side of the law.

Sidekick Phenomena

Those Great Cowboy Sidekicks by David Rothel. Lots of the Western movie sidekicks were just about as popular with audiences as the stars themselves. In this book, 39 sidekicks are examined in depth with over 200 photos and annotated filmographies. Great comic character actors like:

• **George "Gabby" Hayes.** "Yore darn tootin'!" First played "Windy Halliday," Hoppy's sidekick in a 1935 film, then "Gabby" with Roy Rogers.

• **Leo Carrillo.** "Ceesco!" He played Pancho, the Cisco Kid's sidekick, on the long-running television series (1951-56). Started as a newspaper cartoonist and vaudevillian.

• **Andy Devine.** "Hey, Wild Bill, wait for me!" Devine, described as "a great barrel of a man with the scratchy, high-pitched voice of a child," played Jingles, on *Wild Bill Hickok* from 1951 to 1958.

$14.95 ppd. The World of Yesterday, Route 3, Box 263-H, Waynesville, NC 28786. (704) 648-5647.

High Browse

The British Film Institute Companion to the Western. A fine compendium of Western films. Includes summaries of films and TV shows and career roundups of directors and actors. Fun to browse.
$50.00 + 4.50 shipping. Macmillan Publishing, 100 Front St., Riverside, NJ 08075. (800) 257-5755.

Our Favorite Westerns

Stagecoach (1939). John Wayne became a star in this John Ford Western.

High Noon (1952). Gary Cooper in a classic showdown. Do not forsake me, oh my darling.

How the West Was Won (1962). Designed to show off Cinerama. Loose story line, but everybody was in it: Henry Fonda, Debbie Reynolds, Karl Malden, Gregory Peck, James Stewart, Walter Brennan, John Wayne, Spencer Tracy...

Butch Cassidy and the Sundance Kid (1969). Paul Newman and Robert Redford were two likeable outlaws in this "buddy film" that was a nostalgic look at the last days of the West.

Blazing Saddles (1974). Mel Brooks directed and played a double role in this romp into the world of Western cliches. It became, by 1983, the all-time top-grossing Western.

Roy Rogers's real name was Leonard Slye. John Wayne's was Marion Morrison.

DUKE'S UP

★ John Wayne

This legend of the screen holds the record for the longest career as a cowboy star. Wayne appeared in his first picture in 1930, and didn't say goodbye to the cameras until 1976 *The Shootist*. Born Marion Michael Morrison in Westerset, Iowa, Wayne embodied the American western spirit, and gave Jimmy Stewart competition for having the voice most imitated by stand-up impressionists. He put in an Oscar-winning performance as *Rooster Cogburn* in Paramount's **True Grit** in 1969.

6 Feet of Wayne

An ambitious, 21 volume, 72 movie collection of John Wayne videos that will take up over 6 feet of shelf space.

For information on this collection to end all collections, contact Zadoc Marketing, PO Box 9238, Kansas City, MO 64168. (816) 587-4400.

Join the Club

The John Wayne Fan Club, c/o Tim Lilley, 540 Stanton Avenue, Akron, OH 44301. Membership includes subscription to "the Big Trail." Send SASE for more information.

PILGRIMAGE

Travelers take photos and sometimes giggle. Guarding the John Wayne Airport in Orange County, CA against bad guys and communists, this bigger-than-life bronze statue of the Duke (left) sports weapons that would never get past the security gates.

Dukin' It Out

The John Wayne Scrapbook by Lee Pfeiffer. Surprising facts and trivia about John Wayne's acting career, including his salary for his top films, the products he endorsed (from mobile homes to tuna fish) and the stories behind his best and worst films. Written by a fan, this book provides an affectionate close-up look at a Western star who had what it took to stay on top for decades.

$15.95 + 3.00 shipping from Carol Publishing, 120 Enterprise Avenue, Secaucus, NJ 07094. (800) 447-BOOK.

Looks Like Wayne

Ceramic, full-color wall mask of John Wayne in his prime.

#H1120, $50.00 + 7.50 shipping from Clay Art, 1320 Potrero Avenue, San Francisco, CA 94110. (800) 252-9555.

Puzzle this Out, Pilgrim

You'll need true grit to take on this 1000 piece John Wayne picture puzzle (right).

#02-J2846, $14.95 + 3.95 shipping from Bits & Pieces, 1 Puzzle Place, Stevens Point, WI 54481-7199. (800) JIGSAWS.

Our Favorite Western TV Shows

• *The Adventures of Rin Tin Tin.* This dog showed the bad guys what was what as he teamed up with a young boy and the U.S. Cavalry at Fort Apache during the 1880s. 1954-59.

• *Annie Oakley.* Historically, she was a Wild West show performer, but in this TV series Annie, played by Gail Davis, was a law enforcer. 1953-58.

• *Bat Masterson.* Gene Barry played the dapper William Bartley Masterson, who took on the bad guys without a gun. 1959-61.

• *Bonanza.* An American favorite for 14 years, the saga of the tight-knit family on the Ponderosa.

• *Gunsmoke.* This show won the prize for longevity—it ran for 20 long years (1955-75). John Wayne originally turned down the role of U.S. Marshal Matt Dillon, but suggested James Arness, who took it.

• *Have Gun Will Travel.* Dark adult western starring Richard Boone.

• *The Life and Legend of Wyatt Earp.* Hugh O'Brian played the man who kept the peace first in Ellsworth, Kansas, then in Dodge City, and finally in Tombstone, Arizona. 1955-61.

• *The Lone Ranger.* Who was that masked man? An instant hit in 1949, opening with the *William Tell Overture* and "Hi-yo, Silver!" Star Clayton Moore was a former trapeze artist who was adept at both riding a horse and twirling a six-gun.

• *Maverick.* James Garner

played a cowardly but charming gambler in this classic series. 1957-62.

• *Rawhide.* The setting was the great cattle drives from Texas to Kansas in the 1860s, and the big winner in this long-running series turned out to be the new face who played cowboy Rowdy Yates: Clint Eastwood. 1959-66.

• *The Rifleman.* In 1958, 7 of the top 10 shows were westerns, and the Rifleman was the top new show. Chuck Connors played a peace-loving rancher forced to shoot for peace every week.

• *The Roy Rogers Show.* Rogers and Dale Evans combined adventure and music to make this a kids' favorite in the early 1950s.

HAPPY TRAILS TO YOU

There's a cult around America's favorite Western couple (no, not Ron & Nancy). You can join, too.

• **The Roy Rogers - Dale Evans Collectors Association.** These folks have conventions featuring western heroes like Lash LaRue, Iron Eyes Cody and (of course) Roy & Dale.

P.O. Box 1166, Portsmouth, OH 45662. (614) 353-4002.

• **Roy Rogers-Dale Evans Museum.** In a 30,000 square foot replica of a frontier fort, you'll find souvenirs of their personal and professional lives. And who would pass up seeing their

taxidermied faithful animals: Trigger, Buttermilk, and dog Bullet?

15650 Seneca Road, Victorville, CA 92392. (619) 243-4547.

• *Roy Rogers Western Hit Parade Video.* 59 minutes of Roy Rogers, Dale Evans, the Sons of the Pioneers, Cliff Arquette, and Dale Robertson as they appeared on ABC in 1962, with original commercials.

$19.95 + 4.00 shipping from Encore Entertainment, P.O. Box 25, Frankenmuth, MI 48734. (517) 652-9699.

Other High Caliber Videos

• *Annie Oakley,* 2 episodes. **$19.95 + $4.00 shipping. Encore Entertainment, P.O. Box 25, Frankenmuth, MI 48734. (517) 652-9699.**

• *Bonanza.* 4 tape set. **#17830, $59.95 + 6.60 shipping. Wireless, P.O. Box 64422, St. Paul, MN 55164-0422. (800) 669-9999.**

• *The Lone Ranger.* 20 episodes, boxed. **#949474, $199.95 + 4.95 shipping from Postings, P.O. Box 8001, Hilliard, OH 43026. (800) 262-6604.**

• *Terror of Tiny Town.* An all midget cast. **#105, $29.95 + 3.25 shipping. Video Yesteryear, Box C, Sandy Hook, CT 06482. (800) 243-0987.**

The Singing TV Cowboy

• Roy Rogers: Born Leonard Slye in Cincinnati, Ohio, in 1912, this clean-cut cowboy (who was part Choctaw Indian) was considered the #1 money-making Western star from 1943-1954. He and his wife Dale Evans produced 101 television adventure shows that appeared from 1952 through 1956, cheerfully wishing viewers Happy Trails to You in song.

The Wizard of AN?

• Oz appeared on the map when author Lyman Frank Baum was weaving a tale of fantastical creatures for some neighborhood kids. When asked where they lived, Baum glanced around. His eyes landed on the labels of his file cabinet. The top was labeled A-N and the bottom, O-Z.

• He didn't write the story down for some time after. But suddenly it took over and demanded to be written: "I was sitting," he wrote later, "in the hall telling the kids a [different] story and suddenly this one moved right in and took possession. I shooed the children away and grabbed a piece of paper and began to write. It really seemed to write itself. Then I couldn't find any regular paper, so I took anything at all, even a bunch of old envelopes." His pencil-written longhand manuscript

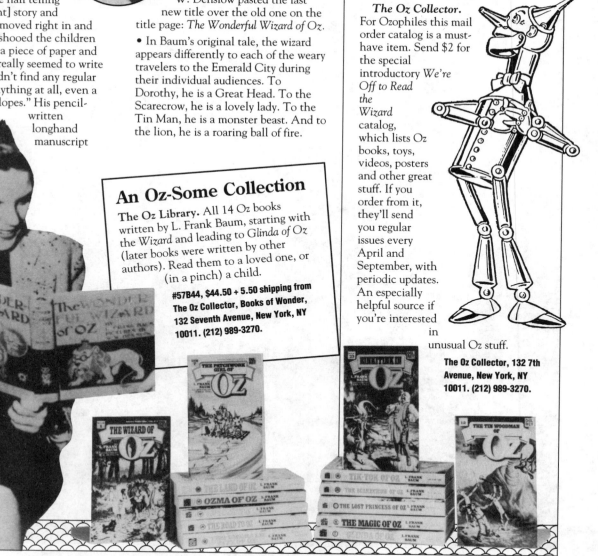

went right to the typesetter.

• He first called his story *The Emerald City*. But his publisher wouldn't release it under that title, citing a long-standing publishers' superstition that any book with a jewel named in its title was doomed to failure.

• Next it was to be called *From Kansas to Fairyland*, then *The Fairyland of Oz*, then *The Land of Oz*. They filed for a copyright under this last name, but Baum was still looking for something more colorful and eye-catching. Right before the book was to go to press, his long-suffering illustrator W. W. Denslow pasted the last new title over the old one on the title page: *The Wonderful Wizard of Oz*.

• In Baum's original tale, the wizard appears differently to each of the weary travelers to the Emerald City during their individual audiences. To Dorothy, he is a Great Head. To the Scarecrow, he is a lovely lady. To the Tin Man, he is a monster beast. And to the lion, he is a roaring ball of fire.

Facsimile First Addition

The Wonderful Wizard of Oz. A facsimile of the first edition, with all 154 color plates by W. W. Denslow.

#042649, $19.95 + 4.95 shipping from Conde Nast's Portfolio, PO Box 8002, Hilliard, OH 43026-8002. (800) 323-5265.

Get This Catalog!

The Oz Collector. For Ozophiles this mail order catalog is a must-have item. Send $2 for the special introductory *We're Off to Read the Wizard* catalog, which lists Oz books, toys, videos, posters and other great stuff. If you order from it, they'll send you regular issues every April and September, with periodic updates. An especially helpful source if you're interested in unusual Oz stuff.

The Oz Collector, 132 7th Avenue, New York, NY 10011. (212) 989-3270.

An Oz-Some Collection

The Oz Library. All 14 Oz books written by L. Frank Baum, starting with the *Wizard* and leading to *Glinda of Oz* (later books were written by other authors). Read them to a loved one, or (in a pinch) a child.

#57B44, $44.50 + 5.50 shipping from The Oz Collector, Books of Wonder, 132 Seventh Avenue, New York, NY 10011. (212) 989-3270.

ABC's OF MGM'S OZ

• The *Wizard of Oz* movie took 18 months to make and the total production and promotion costs were $3,777,000. The picture grossed only three million upon its initial release.

• Those Depression era wages let them afford 9,200 low-paid actors and actresses, including moving trees, flying monkeys, and 124 midgets as munchkins. Ray Bolger and Jack Haley were paid $3000 a week; Judy Garland, only $500 a week.

• *Oz* was nominated for five Academy Awards. But the competition was fierce and *Gone With the Wind* dominated the event, winning an unprecedented eight awards.

• Oz did win a few Oscars: for Original Score and Best Song—*Over the Rainbow,* written in a car parked outside Schwab's drugstore. Ironically, *Rainbow* was the song studio execs wanted to cut out—too slow, they said, and sung in a barnyard to boot.

• Judy Garland also walked away with an Oscar, albeit a miniature version, in the quasi-category of Best Performance by a Juvenile.

Words & Pictures

Multimedia set of *Wizard of Oz* video and script book so you can read along while you watch, even sing along with E. Y. Harburg's great lyrics.

Required Reading

The Wizard of Oz, The Official 50th Anniversary Pictorial History by John Fricke, Jay Scarfone, William Stillman. Devoted Ozophiles, the authors are all members of the International Wizard of Oz Club and each has published previous articles or illustrations in Oz fan magazines. Together, they have produced a comprehensive history with more than 400 photos, half in color and many never before published.

Have a Heart!

Save yourself a trip down the yellow brick road.

•**Brain.** Squishy rubber, grey, 6 inches long.

• **Heart.** Squishy rubber, vivid red with purple arteries.

• **Courage.** Replica of the Bronze Star.

The Little Girl With The Big Voice

When MGM was first planning OZ, Dorothy's ruby slippers were meant to go on the tap-dancing twinkle toes of Shirley Temple. That didn't work out. (Likewise, Frank Morgan was not first choice for Wizard. The lines were written for W.C. Fields who said no; so did Ed Wynn.)

While searching for another Dorothy, studio honcho L.B. Mayer viewed a short called *Every Sunday* and was taken by its star, Deanna Durbin. He told his assistant: "Sign up that singer— the flat one." (**Some** claim the musically untrained Mayer was referring to Durbin's vocal pitch).

What the assistant heard was, "Sign up the **fat** one." He thought Mayer was talking about baby fat, so he called Francis Gumm (quickly renamed "Judy Garland"). But don't cry for Deanna Durbin—she went on to Universal where her movies made $100 million in the next 10 years.

MGM's constant attempts at keeping Garland thin with pills may have led to her addiction and overdose death in 1969.

Join the Oz-sociation

International Wizard of Oz Club, Box 95, Kinderhook, Illinois 62345 .

Founded in 1957 by Justin Schiller, a teenager from Brooklyn, this organization began with 16 members. Since then, the IWOC has grown to a worldwide membership of 2,500. Publishes the *Baum Bugle*. Send SASE for membership information.

Short Shrift

The Munchkins Remember: The Wizard of Oz and Beyond by Stephen Cox. You want to hear how it was to be a Munchkin? Stephen Cox interviewed 31 surviving midgets and children who appeared in the movie for this book. Many found it a less than magical experience.

For one thing, they were paid $100 a week, of which their manager, Leo Singer, pocketed half. In comparison, Dorothy's dog Toto was paid $125 a week. Clearly the Lollipop Guild and Lullaby League were ineffective unions — having a Dunkin' Donut named after you is no substitute for decent pay and health benefits.

Still, many treasure the experience and their stories liven up the book. Alas, though, they refute that juicy and persistent rumor of drunken midget orgies (recently portrayed in the movie *Under the Rainbow*.)

$12.95 + 2.50 shipping from E.P. Dutton, 2 Park Ave., New York, NY 10016. (201) 387-0600.

The Wonderful Wizard of Oz

I'LL GET YOU, MY PRETTY!

• Buddy Ebsen, the original tin man, had an extreme allergic reaction when his lungs were coated by the aluminum powder dusted onto his tin makeup. He spent several weeks in the hospital and finally was replaced by Jack Haley.

• The Wicked Witch, Margaret Hamilton, was badly burned on her face and hands during her dramatic exit from Munchkinland when the fire effect went off before she was safely below the trap door. Ironically, a little water thrown her way might have helped. She was off the set for a month.

• Hamilton's double, Betty Danko, was injured when her broom exploded during a stunt shot.

• Two winged monkeys crashed to the stage floor when their support wires snapped. And Toto too? Yes—out of action for a week after being stepped on by one of the witch's huge O-EE-O-chanting Winkie guards.

Shoe Fetish

After 50 years, at least four pairs of Dorothy's ruby slippers have survived. They continue to bring out-of-sight auction prices (top price so far—$165,000). One pair is on exhibit at the Smithsonian, another at Walt Disney World-MGM Studios. The rest are in private hands…or feet, in this case.

One "foot" note: In the book, the slippers were silver. MGM changed them to ruby because they were paying good money for color film and they wanted **color**, dammit!

If I Only Had a Card

• Greeting Cards. Fold-out, pop-up birthday cards.

> #C9001 "Happy Birthday" or #C9002 "Surprise!" $4.95 each + 3.00 shipping per order (no matter how many) from: The Oz Collector, Books of Wonder, 132 Seventh Avenue, New York, NY 10011. (212) 989-3270.

• Trading Cards. Complete set of 110 Wizard of Oz cards in full color, with script excerpts telling the whole story on backs.

> $9.95 + 3.00 shipping from Pacific Trading Cards, 18424 Highway 99, Lynnwood, WA 98037. (800) 551-2002.

Seasoning of the Witch

Oz salt & pepper shakers. Your choice: the cosmic duality of the good/bad witches (#1251), or all four protagonists, paired (#1252).

> Either set $18.95 + 3.95 from:
> The Music Stand
> Rockdale Plaza
> Lebanon, NH 03766-1585
> (802) 295-7044

Off to See the Wizard

Until the twister picks up your house and drops you on a witch, here are some places you can experience a State of Ozness while still on this planet.

• *The Yellow Brick Road Gift Shop, Chesterson, IN. (219) 926-7048.*

Open all year, this boutique features a Wall of Fame with autographed photos of the cast, a replica of the witch's castle on the mountain and an annual Oz festival around Labor Day.

• *Dorothy's House, Liberal, KS (316) 624-7624.*

A replica of the MGM farm, this dwelling was built in honor of Dorothy and it has an extensive museum with the original miniature house used in the movie for the twister scene. *The Wizard of Oz* is shown daily.

• *Smithsonian Oz Exhibit, Washington, D.C.*

Every year, five million people visit this display which includes a pair of ruby slippers anonymously donated in 1979, a draft of one of Noel Langley's early Oz scripts and a Scarecrow costume, donated by Ray Bolger himself.

• *The Hotel Del Coronado, Coronado, CA. (619) 435-6611.*

This magnificent Victorian resort, built in 1888 across the bay from downtown San Diego, is and was magical by day and especially at night (Thomas Edison personally installed the lighting, at the time one of the largest electrical systems in the world). L. Frank Baum used to hang out here when he lived in San Diego, and he admitted using "The Del" as his inspiration for the Emerald City.

WRESTLING & the Junk Sports

Baseball, football, basketball and even hockey are all fine, but for some folks, they're just, well, a little bit too genteel. Not enough action. Not enough noise and uproar. No souped-up heavy equipment involved. Not enough threat of serious injury.

That's why there are the "junk sports" like pro wrestling, roller derby and monster truck rallies. Few can deny the primitive thrill of seeing two beefy behemoths in facepaint pummel each other senseless or watching a wrecking machine shaped like Godzilla chow down on an unwanted Buick.

What these games lack in subtlety, they make up for in sheer spectacle and noise. The players will never win any Olympic gold medals, but they sure know how to put on a damned good show.

The History of Pro Wrestling

The exact date of the invention of wrestling is lost in the mists of prehistory. The oldest known record of the sport, however, is a bronze figurine of a wrestler found in a 5,000-year-old Sumerian tomb.

In America, pro wrestling got its start soon after the Civil War. William "The Solid Man of Sport" Muldoon became the first national champion.

Although always a popular part of circuses and county fairs across the land, wrestling really came into its own following the introduction of television. The sport first aired on TV in 1948, as part of a Tuesday night lineup that included *The Milton Berle Show* and *Kukla, Fran and Ollie*.

One of the biggest wrestling stars of the 1950s was George "Gorgeous George" Wagner. Trained in psychiatry, George was the first wrestler to bring a sense of showmanship to the sport, sporting bleached-blond, marcelled curls and an orchid velvet robe. Before each match, his personal valet sprayed the ring with perfume and rolled out a red carpet for George to walk and prance upon. (For a brief-yet-hilarious parody of George's style, check out *Bunny Hugged*, a

Warner Brothers animation short.)

The 1960s and '70s were not kind to pro wrestling, but thanks to cable television's voracious programming needs, it made a huge comeback in the mid-1980s. Today's biggest stars command salaries well into the six figures and beyond, besides proceeds from the merchandising tie-ins—games, cassettes, clothing, sports equipment, toys.

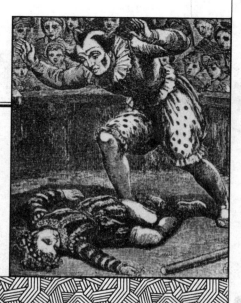

> *"The more violent the body contact of the sports you watch, the lower your class."*
>
> **—Paul Fussell**

Then there was Gentleman Jim Haney, who was very polite, even saying "I'm sorry" to the guys he clobbered and helping them up.

ROLLER DERBY

Roller derby got its start in 1935, the invention of Leo Seltzer, a Chicago promoter. As with wrestling, television gave the sport a huge boost in the 1950s and '60s, but the derby's popularity seriously declined in the fickle 1970s. (For some incredible reason, NBC-TV's *Rollergirls* series lasted only four episodes in 1978.)

In the 1980s, however, cable networks brought the sport to a new audience, and the six-team International Roller Derby League was resurrected.

Roller derby teams consist of two squads of five men and five women. Men and women are never on the track at the same time, but their scores are combined. The teams skate around the rink in a pack. The "jammer," gets a point every time he or she can lap an opposing skater and is the only player allowed to wear a helmet. But the rules are almost irrelevent—what's fun are the feuds, collisions and the times when a skater loses control and careens head first into the audience, arms windmilling wildly.

A variant known as *RollerGames* appeared briefly as a syndicated series in 1989 with a souped-up, figure-eight track and obstacles like an alligator pit and the Wall of Death.

Magazines That'll Bodyslam You

• **WWF** *Magazine*. From the World Wrestling Federation, this is the slickest of the bunch. The color photos are plentiful and of professional quality, the layout's easy on the eye and the articles are readable.

$20 for 12 issues. P.O. Box 420174, Palm Coast, FL 32142-0174.

• *TV Sports Pro Wrestling Illustrated*. Newsprint, 16 pages of slick paper, but includes coverage of ratings and arena reports.

$19.95 for 12 issues, includes the 100-page, year-end spectacular. Box 48, Rockville Centre, NY 11571.

• *Wrestling Confidential*. Allegedly "the wrestling magazine that dares to tell all." Consists mostly of full-page, badly posed photos interspersed with articles with titles like, "The Sad World of the Wrestling Groupie" and "The New Sex Appeal in Wrestling." Best feature is the section devoted to wrestling-related artwork submitted by fans. Appears to be available only on newsstands, so it's up to you to find it.

$2.95. Published bi-monthly by Dojo Publishing, Inc., 300 West 43rd Street, New York, NY 10036.

Roller Derby Double Feature

Regrettably, roller games haven't played a huge part in the history of American cinema, but there are a couple of movies we like.

• *Kansas City Bomber* (1972). Raquel Welch stars as a good-hearted roller derby queen contending with jealous colleagues and lecherous employers. Look for Jodie Foster in a supporting role.

• *Rollerball* (1975). The derby as it ought to be played, with motorcycles and spiked gloves. James Caan fights to stay alive in a futuristic sport where there are no rules.

Trucks of the Trade

Monster Madness. Turn it up loud! This roaring, smoking video features tractor pulls, monster trucks and mud-bog racing.

#SM024, $14.95 + 4.95 shipping from Special Interest Video, 100 Enterprise Place, P.O. Box 7022, Dover, DE 19903-7022. (800) 522-0502.

" Most sorts of diversion in men, children, and other animals are an imitation of fighting." —Jonathan Swift

600

Are You Game?

Challenge your friends in this "light-hearted" wrestling board game that has you taking on all types of people, no holds barred!

#6569, $16.98 + 3.50 shipping, The Lighter Side, 4514 19th St. Court East, P.O. Box 25600, Bradenton, FL 34206-5600. (813) 747-2356 / FAX (813) 746-2356.

KEEP ON TRUCKIN'

4 X 4 Remote Control Truck. Perfect for monster truck madness in your living room. This 1/10 scale giant pickup has a forceful 360 Mabuchi motor, balloon tires ideal for 45-degree climbs.

#R3657-5959, $69 00 + 6.50 shipping from C.O.M.B., 720 Anderson Avenue, St. Cloud, MN 56372-0030. (800) 328-0609.

Play With Dolls

All your WWF favorites are represented: Macho King Randy Savage, Million Dollar Man Ted DiBiase, Ultimate Warrior and, of course, the Hulkster. But where's Gorgeous George?

#16-00149, Hulk Hogan, $19.95 + 3.95 shipping from WWF Merchandise Department, P.O. Box 6789, Stamford, CT 06904-6789. (203) 353-2800.

Salt and Battery

If the yellow wrestler bodyslams the red one, you'll have to toss the spilled salt over your shoulder to prevent bad luck! Earthenware salt and pepper shaker wrestlers...an evenly matched set.

#8575, $12.98 + 3.99 shipping from Taylor Gifts, 355 E. Conestoga Road, P.O. Box 206, Wayne, PA 19087-0206. (215) 789-7007.

Save 'Em, Trade 'Em

Monster Truck Trading Cards. Includes all the greats: Bigfoot, Taurus, Grave Digger and more.

Foil case of 6,480 cards, $129.50 from The Scoreboard, Inc., 100 Dobbs Lane, Suite 207, Cherry Hill, NJ 08034. (800) 327-4145.

*P*rototypical Good Guys

Hulk Hogan—A music major in college, the young Hulk dreamed of being a singing sensation before starting a career in the ring. The most famous wrestler of his generation, the Hulkster got his big break by tossing Sly Stallone around in *Rocky III*. He also put comedian Richard Belzer in the hospital following an on-camera tiff (Belzer asked something along the lines of "Hey, isn't this wrestling stuff fake?")—this back before he mysteriously transformed from being a bad guy wrestler to a good guy.

Andre the Giant—Billed as "the eighth wonder of the world," this French-born star (France's repayment to America for giving the world Jerry Lewis) stands 7'4" and weighs nearly 500 pounds. Andre's forte is the "battle royal," in which a whole bunch of wrestlers duke it out to the finish.

Who's Slammin' Who?

"*Modern professional wrestling holds a very Manichean view of the universe. There are good guys, and there are bad. No gray areas allowed.*"

—Michael Berry

Invariably, yet understandably, Andre is the one standing.

Jimmy "Superfly" Snuka. From the Fiji Islands, Snuka takes his nickname not from the 1970s blaxploitation film but from his finishing maneuver, a flying body press, in which he climbs onto the top rope and jumps halfway across the ring to land on his opponent.

"Hulk Hogan" like Spiderman and so many other superhumans, is a trademark owned by the Marvel Comics Group.

Mayhem Majors, Summa Cum Loud

• **The Monster Factory.** Want to learn how to be the next Ultimate Warrior? Enroll in this wrestling school in rural Paulsville, NJ. "Pretty Boy" Larry Sharpe has trained hundreds of aspiring wrestlemaniacs since 1984. You must be at least 5' 10" and weigh over 200 pounds.

For information, call (609) 423-8255.

• **Nikita Koloff's School of Wrestling.** Another place to grapple with the rigors of higher learning.

P.O. Box 3151, Concord, North Carolina 28025. (704) 786-6800.

Don't Step On My Blue Suede Wrestling Shoes

Rock 'N' Roll Wrestling Music Television: The Special Edition. "Bobbin' bloodbath highlights with red-hot wrestling and right-on rock 'n' roll." Approx. 30 min.

#RNVD 904, $9.95 + 2.00 shipping from Rhino Video, 2225 Colorado Avenue, Santa Monica, CA 90404-3598 (800) 432-3670 / (213) 828-1980.

Prototypical Bad Guys

"Rowdy" Roddy Piper—This kilt-wearing Glasgow-born star is known more for his big mouth than for his fighting prowess. As host of his own wrestling interview show, *Piper's Pit,* Roddy never misses an opportunity to harass a guest. It was he who encouraged Captain Lou Albano to insult singer Cyndi Lauper and denigrate rock and roll. When the Captain and Cyndi later attempted to kiss and make up at Madison Square Garden, Piper smashed Lauper's platinum record over Albano's head. Classy guy.

Sergeant Slaughter—Once a super-patriotic good guy, Slaughter shocked his fans in November 1990 by swearing allegiance to the Iraqi flag and hiring an alleged Iraqi as his manager.

The Iron Sheik—Supposedly a member of the late Shah of Iran's elite bodyguard, the Iron Sheik sports a shaved head, a wicked mustache and curly-toed boots. Likes spitting

"America— hack pfui!"

Would You Like A Belt?

Record any past victory — or fantasy — on this hand-crafted, leather wrestling championship belt. Features include bright gold, all metal trim medallion; engravers brass; heavy-duty buckle. Seven colors to choose from. Adjustable up to size 45.

#W1, $120.00 postpaid from Clemmer Belt Co., 10318 Lorain Ave., Cleveland, OH 44111. (216) 252-2301.

WRESTLING ON YOUR SOFA

Whether your preferred wrestling is amateur, professional or female mud, you'll find plenty of films worth your attention at the local video store or by mail order:

• For tapes of official WWF matches, interviews and behind-the-scenes footage, check out the wares of Coliseum Video.

Free catalog. 430 W. 54th Street, New York, NY 10019. (800) 288-8130.

• The best in World Championship Wrestling action is available on tape from the WCW Fan Club.

P.O. Box 7283, Marietta, GA 30065. (800) 727-3267.

• *Golden Age of Wrestling* two-volume set, annual "Summerslam" contests, and more.

$39.95 + 3.00 shipping. TV Sports Video, Box 1672, Greenwich, CT 06836. (800) 729-0360.

The Whole Pop Wrestling Film Festival

• *The One and Only* (1978). Henry Winkler does his Gorgeous George impersonation in this comedy directed by Carl Reiner.

• *All the Marbles* (1981). Peter Falk manages two beautiful women wrestlers. According to Leonard Maltin, the climactic championship bout is "a real audience-rouser."

• *Vision Quest* (1985). Matthew Modine is a high school wrestler who falls for a tough-talking older woman. Madonna sings "Crazy for You."

• *Body Slam* (1987). Stars Dirk Benedict and Tanya Roberts but features performances by Roddy Piper, Captain Lou Albano, Ric Flair and the Wild Samoans. Barely released in theaters but available on tape.

• *No Holds Barred* (1989). Stretching his thespian talents, Hulk Hogan plays a TV wrestling star.

WRESTLING TO Rasslin'

ANCIENT SPORT TO AMERICAN SPECTACLE

Gerald W. **Morton** & George M. **O'Brien**

Blood Red, Bruise Purple

Jake "The Snake" Roberts Coloring Doll. This soft fiber-filled doll comes with a set of 10 markers.

$9.95 + 3.95 for shipping. WWF Merchandise Department, P.O. Box 6789, Stamford, CT 06904-6789. (203) 353-2800.

Bodyslams From the Ph.D.s

"And if nothing else of value can be found in professional wrestling, it does give us hope, hope that we can be greater than Russia, that Iran cannot push us too far, that the energy crisis can be licked, that America can survive whatever tests she faces— we know because we see it happen every Saturday night in some local high school gym, a National Guard Armory, or run-down old civic center where we come together to witness what we know to be true and hope for what we know to be possible."

— Gerald W. Morton and George M. O'Brien. From *Wrestling to Rasslin': Ancient Sport to American Spectacle*, Bowling Green State University Popular Press.

YESTERDAY'S VILLAINS

Wrestling's Greatest Villains. Remember Killer Kowalski, Yukon Eric, The Crusher, Dick the Bruiser, the Graham and, of course, Gorgeous George? They're all here with more wrestling greats of the '50s and '60s.

VHS #1002, $19.95 + 1.50 shipping from Combat Sports, P.O. Box 651, Gracie Station, New York, NY 10028-0011.

Hot New Sports for the '90s

Given enough boredom and/or alcohol, the human mind is capable of dreaming up all manner of bizarre pastimes. To wit:

• **Stock Enduro.** The poor man's auto race, open to amateurs of all stripes. Just about any car off the street is eligible, as long as you put a roll cage on it.

• **Swamp Buggy Races.** Every November, drivers gather in Naples, Florida, haul out their home-made swamp buggies and race each other across the bog. The event culminates in the dunking of the tiara-bedecked race-queen in a mud hole.

• **Bathtub Racing.** Each spring, the department of Mechanical Engineering at Southern Technical Institute in Marietta, Georgia, sponsors a contest in which cast-iron bathtubs are outfitted with engines, wheels, roll bars and seat belts. The tubbers race along a one-mile course, achieving speeds of up to 85 mph.

• **Destruction Football.** At Saugus Speedway on the outskirts of Los Angeles, teams of cars attempt to punt a 900-pound steel buoy between goal posts made of stacked tires.

• **Pig Races.** Compared to some of these other sports, the spectacle of swift-footed swine galloping down a track has charm to spare. The winner gets a cookie.

Kids, Try This At Home!

Little Hulkster T-shirt, diaper cover and socks.

$17.95 + 3.95 shipping. WWF Merchandise Dept., P.O. Box 6789, Stamford, CT 06904-6789. (203) 353-2800.

LITTLE HULKSTER

Despite popular image, most wrestling fans realize that it's faked.

Playing With Trucks

The amount of mayhem that can be done with a high-powered, 4-wheeled vehicle is virtually endless. Some of the more popular and inventive truck "sports" include:

• **Mud Racing.** Also known as "boggin'." Four-wheel-drive vehicles with names like Mud Monster, Hell Fire and Blue Bitch slog their way through a 100-foot-long pit filled four feet deep with viscous mud. Very popular with children. Some truck shows also feature a "Dash for Cash," in which members of the audience race on foot through the muck.

• **Car Crushing.** The undisputed star of this sport is Bigfoot, a 12-foot truck built in 1974 by Bob

Chandler to promote his four-wheel-drive shop. Packing the power of 650 horses and able to crush four cars at a whack, Bigfoot has appeared in a number of *Police Academy* comedies, as well as in *Take This Job and Shove It.*

Should you ever invoke the ire of a Bigfoot enthusiast, pray that you don't own a foreign car, which fall apart fairly easily. According to Bigfoot driver Ken Koelling, "Chryslers are the toughest to crush, especially the old ones." Except, of course, wood- and concrete-reinforced Volvos.

• **Pull-A-Car-Apart.** Exactly what it sounds like. Chain two monster trucks to opposite ends of some old clunker and let the drivers press the pedals to the floor. Make a wish!

• **Tractor Pulls.** The object of this sport is to pull a 50,000-pound sled, weighted with 1,000-pound lead blocks, as far down a dirt track as you possibly can. But don't think you can just fire up your Uncle Hiram's John Deere and expect to compete with the big boys. It takes a specially built vehicle with up to seven 2000 hp engines to do the job. (Pullers favor World War II V-12 bomber engines.)

A good puller can pocket up to three grand during a weekend competition. This apparently was incentive enough for Wayne Rausch, Ph.D., of Ohio State University to ditch his professorship and take up the sport full-time. Still, to get ahead in this field you need plenty of pull.

• **Transformers.** Vehicles that start out as one thing and wind up as something else. For example, "The World's Largest Transformer" appears on the scene as a box-like vehicle on tank treads but soon undergoes a metamorphosis that turns it into a fire-snorting mechanical dinosaur that lifts junked cars to its jaws and chews them to bits.

Truckin' Once a Month

Monster Truck Spectacular. This quarterly magazine features awesome color foldouts of some of the most amazing vehicles on four wheels or tank treads.

$3.95 on newsstands. Published by Starlog Communications International, Inc., 475 Park Avenue South, New York, NY 10016.

YO·YOS

Spinning Thru Time

Throw the yo-yo away from you and it comes back. When you're a kid, your yo-yoing enthusiasm fades, then comes back. National yo-yo crazes die out, then come back. The name "yo-yo" is from the Philippines, and guess what it means? "Come back," of course.

How far back does the yo-yo go? Archaeologists have found vases depicting Grecians playing with them.

The yo-yo was popular in 18th century France, where it was called *l'emigrette*. During the French Revolution, unfortunates on the way to the guillotine played with their emigrettes to reduce tension.

Yo-yos spread from France to England, where what they called "the quiz" became all the rage. In 1824, however, one writer decreed that the yo-yo was dead, a faded fad, a "bygone toy."

People in the United States started playing with the "bandalore" in the 1860s, but it was in the 1920s that Pedro Flores, a Philippine immigrant, began manufacturing a small number of yo-yos in Los Angeles. (It was a common toy in the Philippines, where it was thought to have descended from a jungle hunting weapon used to klonk animals on the head or trip up their legs, fates still known to novices to this day).

Yo-Yo Facts

• To prepare for the "Toys in Space" experiments in 1984, Space Shuttle astronaut David Griggs took a crash course in yo-yo tricks from expert Tom Kuhn. He subsequently discovered that some of his best tricks wouldn't work in zero-gravity. For instance, yo-yos won't "sleep" in outer space. Instead, they reach the end of the string and just bounce right back up.

• Some of the people who have had their pictures taken with yo-yos are Jack Dempsey, Bing Crosby, Richard Nixon, Abbie Hoffman, and the Our Gang Kids.

• **Oy Oy!** The world's largest working yo-yo, "Big-YO," stands 50 inches tall and weighs 256 pounds. The "string" is a 3/4 inch diameter braided Dacron rope. Once off Pier 39 in San Francisco, the string got wet ahead of launch time. As the cameras rolled for the *You Asked For It* television show, the slippery Big-YO kept spinning in a "sleeper" position and wouldn't return. Its axle overheated and the string burned through, plunging the oversized toy into San Francisco Bay. A frogman had to keep it from drifting away until it could be towed to shore.

• On November 23, 1977, John Winslow of Gloucester, Virginia, began to yo-yo and didn't stop for five full days—120 hours, a new world's record.

• "Yo-Yo Ma" is the name of a famous cellist. Despite what you may have heard, the phrase is *never* used as an insult during yo-yo competitions.

Donald Duncan, one of America's great sales wizards, saw the toy in 1927 and bought the rights to it from Flores.

Duncan's contribution to yo-yo technology was the "slip-string," consisting of a sliding loop around the axle instead of a knot. This was a revolutionary improvement—the yo-yo "slept" for the first time.

The first Duncan yo-yo was the "O-Boy Yo-Yo Top. The Toy with a Big Kick for All Ages." The yo-yo catapulted into prominence.

Luck, Wisconsin became "the Yo-Yo Capital of the World. " Duncan's massive factory could turn out 3,600 of the toys every hour, and for a while, even that was not fast enough for the demand.

Yo-Yo Marketing Has Its Ups and Downs

Donald Duncan, the marketing genius who was responsible for the first great yo-yo fad in the US also invented the Eskimo Pie, originated the Good Humor ice cream truck and successfully marketed the first parking meter. Duncan also co-patented a 4-wheel hydraulic automobile brake and developed the first premium incentive ("Kids! Send in two boxtops and receive a fantastic...").

He teamed up with newspaper magnate William Randolph Hearst and held yo-yo contests with prizes like bicycles, baseballs, and gloves. To be eligible, kids had to sell newspaper subscriptions.

Duncan also sent yo-yo experts across the country where they did tricks and staged contests. In Philadelphia alone, they sold three million yo-yos during a month-long blitz in 1931.

Duncan was bedeviled by the unpredictable demand, hot one week, cold another. Internationally, the yo-yo market fluctuated just as wildly. During an unexpected market lull in the 1930s the Lego company was stuck with warehouses full of unsold yo-yos. They solved the problem by sawing each in half and using them as wheels on toy trucks and cars.

World War II killed sales for a while, but the yo-yo climbed back up into massive popularity in the 1950s and reached its highest peak in 1962, when Duncan sold 45 million.

Unfortunately, this unprecedented popularity led to the Duncan Company's demise. The company eagerly spent money to fuel the craze, heavily invested in TV ads and yo-yo

demonstrators. It threw money into increased production to meet consumer demand. Unfortunately, in spite of enormous sales revenues, the company's costs outpaced sales.

> Johnny's got a yo-yo
> He got it from his dad
> He always let me play with it
> It's the best toy I ever had.
> He never lends it out to any other kids in town
> 'Cause I'm the only one who knows
> How to get it up and down—
> I'm older than the other kids and I've been around!"
>
> —**Ruth Wallis,** *Johnny's Yo-Yo*

Adding to the burden was a lawsuit over the "Yo-Yo" name. The court ruled against Duncan, making the term generic. The company that had been stringing along on success after success lost its spin. Duncan declared bankruptcy in 1965. The Flambeau Plastics Company of Baraboo, Wisconsin, bought the remnants and decided to continue operating the Duncan Company, where its fortunes rise and fall regularly with the vagaries of consumer demand.

Yo-Yos vs. Nintendo

"We are, as a society, into instant gratification. I can sit at my Atari and be immediately bombarded by pretty sounds and colors. A yo-yo requires time and effort. You have to put in at least an hour before you can make the thing spin. I don't think too many kids are interested in putting in that kind of effort."

—**Yo-yoist Michael Caffrey**

"Yo-yos are a tradition in this country. It breaks my heart to see American children in front of cold, impersonal computer terminals, while warm, friendly yo-yos are allowed to die. Maybe people would be willing to carry yo-yos as concealed weapons. If they find themselves confronted by a criminal, they could use the 'forward pass' trick and hit the criminal in the head. Do you think a video game could ever save your life?"

—**Terri Klein, New York publicist**

Yoda of Yo-Yoga

Yo-yo lovers have described a blissful feeling of oneness with the yo-yo as "The State of Yo." According to dentist and yo-yo manufacturer Dr. Tom Kuhn ("Dr. Yo"), it is "a charmed state of being where distinctions between the player, the yo-yo and the trick disappear." He believes it's more than a way of unwinding— "Yo-yos soothe the nerves, calm the mind and entertain the spirit." His "Yo" For It! T-shirt is de rigueur among the yo-yo meditative set.

100% cotton T-shirt, six colors. Sizes: Adult S, M, L, XL, $12. Child S, M, L, $10. Add 2.50 shipping. Tom Kuhn Custom Yo-Yos, 2283 California Street, San Francisco, CA 94115. (415) 921-8138.

Yo-Yos on Video

The Know Yo, Yo-Yo Video. This one-hour video by expert yo-yo performer Dennis McBride (*1958 California State Yo-Yo Champion*) will show you how to perform beginning and advanced yo-yo tricks.

The tricks are shot from different angles, so you can zero in on the exact moves required. Other volumes available for the same price: *Gallery of Two-Handed Tricks, String Tricks, Volume 1* and *String Tricks, Volume 2.*

Each tape, $25.00 postpaid. Includes free yo-yo. Dennis McBride, 27746 Santa Clarita Rd., Santa Clarita, CA 91350. (805) 297-5713.

Yo-Yos By Yo-S Mail

• **3 in 1 No Jive Yo-Yo.** Possibly the world's best wooden yo-yo, the 3 in 1 is made of kiln-dried, Eastern hard rock maple. Can be unscrewed for knot removal, and assembled in three different configurations for versatility in feel and performance.

$17.00 + 3.00 shipping from Klutz, 2121 Staunton Ct., Palo Alto, CA 94306. (415) 424-0739.

• **Yomega, The Yo-Yo with a Brain.** This yo-yo has a clutch! Throw the yo-yo down—the rotational force activates the clutch, and the yo-yo sleeps freely. When it slows down, the clutch engages and the yo-yo races back up the string. Makes it easy for even beginners to do tricks.

Colors: raspberry, blue, yellow, and lime. $10.95 + 2.00 shipping from Yomega Company, 1641 North Main Street, Fall River, MA 02720. (800) 338-8796 or (508) 672-7399.

TIPS FROM YO-YO EXPERTS

• Want to avoid that sore finger caused by hours of yo-yoing? Apply a band-aid before the fact. Or gut it out, if you want to be like the pros: in time, you'll develop calluses on your yo-yoing finger.

• Be careful cutting the knots that occur when your string gets tangled around the yo-yo's axle. Hacking away at the axle with a knife is a leading cause of yo-yo death, because the axle has to be smooth for proper functioning.

• To do a "sleeper" or "spinner," that essential step on your way to yo-yoing magnificence, throw the yo-yo down backhanded and try to "ease up" just before the yo-yo reaches the end of the string. The yo-yo should keep spinning loosely at the bottom of the string. Now you're ready to do all sorts of tricks like "Rock the Baby" and "Skin the Cat."

• Can't get your yo-yo to sleep? If it doesn't spin at all down there, the string is looped too tightly around the axle; if it keeps spinning and won't come back up, it's looped too loosely.

• A sharp tug with your finger will propel your sleeping yo-yo back up to your hand.

Join the Club

American Yo-Yo Association. This is a new organization, formed to educate the public about the benefits of yo-yoing, promote it as a sport, coordinate tournament activities, and provide guidelines for yo-yo tricks.

For information, send SASE to: Bob Malowney, Director 847 West 5th Street Chico, CA 95928

In the early 1900s, Hubert Meyer of Toledo, Ohio, patented an edible yo-yo.

It's the Yo-Yo Man!

Tommy Smothers is the definitive "Yo-Yo Man," yo-yoing on TV and in shows for millions. Subscribe to the Smothers Brothers Fan Club, and in addition to a photo of Tom and Dick, a biography of the brothers, and other stuff, you get a full-color poster of the Yo-Yo Man in action and a "Just Say YO!" bumper sticker. $8 first-year membership.

**The Smothers Brothers Fan Club
P.O. Box 74130
Los Angeles, CA 90004**

SMO-BRO YO-YO

Tommy "Yo-Yo Man" Smothers won't use anything but a Tom Kuhn yo-yo. This model is exactly like the one he used on his show and has Tommy's signature laser-carved into the side.

$25.00 + 3.00 shipping from Klutz, 2121 Staunton Ct., Palo Alto, CA 94306. (415) 424-0739.

World on a String

Round the world! Now you make the world spin on its axis powers with this colorful globe yo-yo.

#G1111, $4.95 + 2.00 shipping from What On Earth, 25801 Richmond Road, Cleveland, OH 44146. (216) 831-5588.

TO YO 'EM IS TO LOVE 'EM

In times past, the Duncan Yo-Yo Company sent dozens of demonstrators across the country to strut their stuff. Who are their contemporary equivalents? Three contenders for the Yo-Yo Hall of Fame:

• One of yo-yoing's master showmen is **Dale Myrberg**, a power company employee in Salt Lake City who won his first contest before he was 11, and worked for Duncan while still in his early teens. Myrberg has entertained thousands at corporate events, parks, fairs, tournaments, Las Vegas, and the *Smothers Brothers* TV show.

• In October, 1990, at age 16, **Mark Sitton** won the California Yo-Yo Championships (the first state contest held since 1963). The young Chico, California resident performed tricks like "Man on the Trapeze" (with two

somersaults), "Reach for the Moon," and "Two Handed Milking the Cow."

• **"Fast Eddy" MacDonald** of Toronto is the holder of a number of yo-yoing records. One of them is for the most yo-yo tricks in one minute: 32.

Yo the Book at 'Em

• *The Klutz Yo-Yo Book* by John Cassidy. This highly readable how-to guide will get you started performing basic yo-yo tricks in no time. Also includes sections on yo-yo history and yo-yo science (weight distribution is important: A couple of bicycle wheels make a fabulous yo-yo).

$9.95 + 2.00 shipping. Klutz Press, 2121 Staunton Court, Palo Alto, CA 94306. (415) 424-0739.

• *World on a String* by Helane Zeiger. This former Duncan pro shows tricks with great names: the Creeper, Sleeping Beauty, Guillotine, Pickpocket, Sky-rocket and Brain Twister.

$12.00 + 2.50 shipping from Tom Kuhn Custom Yo-Yos, 2283 California Street, San Francisco, CA 94115. (415) 921-8138.

STRINGING FOR A MAGAZINE

• *Yo-Yo Times*. This newsletter, edited by Stuart "Professor Yo-Yo" Crump, is full of tips and techniques, product information and conventions and competition.

$12 per year (6 issues). Send 1st class stamp for free sample copy. Creative Communications, P.O. Box 1519-WPC, Herndon, VA 23070. (703) 742-9696.

• *Spin-Offs*. A playful publication about tops, yo-yos, and other rotating toys, from the Spinning Top Museum in Burlington, Wisconsin.

$18 per year from Spin-Offs, 380 N. Pine, Burlington, WI 53105. (414) 763-3946.

Cheap Yo-Yos —No Choice

You get a set of three yo-yos, whatever they decide to send you. No choices in color or design, but the price ain't bad.

#M743, $8.50 + 4.00 shipping from Archie McPhee, P.O. Box 30852, Seattle, WA 98103-0852. (206) 547-2467.

Your Assignment, Should You Choose to Accept It

Our decisions about what to include in the *Whole Pop Catalog* were not influenced by bribes, social pressure, threats against our loved ones, guilt, or personal involvement. We strove mightily to make sure that the information in the *Whole Pop Catalog* is accurate. Still, nobody's perfect. Also, time makes mountains crumble, continents fall into the sea, companies go out of business and prices change, so we can't guarantee that everything here is available at the prices listed, or at all. We have tried to find good and reliable sellers, but we can't absolutely vouch 100% for anybody, so please take appropriate precautions when dealing with phone and mail order sources.

We've probably included a few products and sources you think we shouldn't have, and left out some that you know are superior. Great! This is your chance to have an effect on sequels and future editions of the *Whole Pop Catalog.*

- Send us your recommendations about anything you think we should've included.
- Let us know your experiences with any source, book or product we've listed here.
- If you run across any whopper mistakes we should've caught, tell us.
- Finally, if you're a club, a seller of products, books, videos, a chamber of commerce, whatever, and there's something you think we should know about, no matter how self-serving, we're happy to get information, products and review copies of whatever you've got.
- Contributors at the very least will get our undying gratitude. Who knows, maybe something more concrete as well.

Write to us: *the Berkeley Popular Culture Project*
PO Box 4020, Alameda, CA 94501